1987

Mass Co

W9-ADS-611

Introduction to
Mass Communication

Jay Black
Utah State University

Frederick C. Whitney
San Diego State University, Emeritus

ωcb
Wm. C. Brown Company Publishers
Dubuque, Iowa

Book Team

Kevin Kane
Assistant Developmental Editor

Gloria G. Schiesl
Senior Production Editor

Barbara J. Grantham
Designer

Shirley M. Charley
Visual Assistant

Mavis M. Oeth
Permissions Editor

wcb group

Wm. C. Brown
Chairman of the Board

Mark C. Falb
Executive Vice-President

wcb

Wm. C. Brown Company Publishers, College Division

Lawrence E. Cremer
President

David Wm. Smith
Vice-President, Marketing

E. F. Jogerst
Vice-President, Cost Analyst

David A. Corona
Assistant Vice-President, Production Development and Design

James L. Romig
Executive Editor

Marcia H. Stout
Marketing Manager

Janis Machala
Director of Marketing Research

William A. Moss
Production Editorial Manager

Marilyn A. Phelps
Manager of Design

Mary M. Heller
Visual Research Manager

Copyright © 1983 by Wm. C. Brown Company Publishers

Library of Congress Catalog Card Number: 82–072111

ISBN 0–697–04355–X

2–04355–01

Printed in the United States of America

Contents

Preface

In writing *Introduction to Mass Communication,* we have attempted to analyze the mass communication empires on their own terms, to recognize them for what they are—large, sometimes monolithic industries established to earn a profit as well as to serve the interests of their customers. The media are studied here within the broad contexts in which they operate. Technological, economic, political, philosophical, and sociological factors are considered throughout. We try to ask and then carefully answer such questions as:

How do each of the media operate; what technological, economic, and human factors are involved in the production of newspapers, magazines, books, recordings, radio, television, and film?

What is the nature of media auxiliaries—the indirect but enormously influential advertising, public relations, news, and feature services?

Why have the media developed as they have—into pervasive, profit-oriented concerns, often in conflict with both the government and the governed?

What might the alternatives be to the present mass communications network? Is the future likely to bring more of the same, or are major changes at hand?

What forces in government, society, and within the media themselves serve to put a check on media excesses? Left to their own devices, would profit-oriented media be responsible to society?

Answers to these and many other questions are sought through a balanced study of the overall mass communication system. They cannot be found without some attention to detail, but our approach is not encyclopedic; names, dates, and other details are cited, but not at the expense of the broader picture.

Mass communication is approached in this text as the central nervous system of society—a concept that suggests a deep, complex interrelationship between society and its means of communication. This approach, we feel, is consistent with "audience" reactions to the media, as well as with the inherent structures of the media themselves.

The media are often damned on the one hand as pollutants, filling heads with specious trivia, beclouding perception, and feeding confusion in the ranks through rising decibels of noise. On the other hand, media are often heralded as catalysts of the social organism—offering ever-changing, ever-multiplying views of both fantasy and reality—that enrich our lives and bring us to the brink of truth, or self-understanding. The mass media are regarded as both guardians of the status quo and radical vehicles of change.

This paradox emanates, in part, from the composition of the individual media. Because of their diverse, often corporate natures, the media cannot be appropriately perceived from within any one academic pigeonhole. They cut across journalism with their information content and media forms. Sociology and social psychology come into play insofar as the media's involvements with large and small audiences. Psychology encompasses the media's effects upon the individual. Political science and economics are involved because advertising provides a commercial base. This, combined with public relations, motivates discussion of the crucial issues of persuasion—dollars and votes. Economics plays an additional role in the relative affluence upon which mass communications is so dependent, and in the expanding technology responsible for this development. Most recently, mathematics and engineering have influenced media and communications, not only because of computerization but also because of instantaneous transmission and feedback of individualized, localized, and global information.

Thus, what we offer here is an integrated approach to mass communications that distills pertinent contributions from many disciplines. *Introduction to Mass Communication* examines each of the mass media in light of its historical development, its relationship to other media, its effects on audiences, and its probable future. The media are also discussed in terms of their broad social functions and their individual characteristics, which are surprisingly complementary.

Helping students understand media has been our foremost consideration as well as that of the book team. For this reason, attention to pedagogical techniques should be evident to even the casual reader. Several hundred pages of carefully researched and written text have been divided into five major parts according to function or theme. Each part is introduced by a short overview aimed at helping students understand that part's place within the broader context of the "social organism." Each chapter begins with an outline of the headings within the chapter to alert students to the topics covered therein. In addition, capsule commentary statements along the margins of the text highlight events, concepts, and concerns in the ever-evolving media scene. A glossary of terms is included at the end of the book to define and clarify terms used in this introductory study of mass communication. And for those students who desire additional reading resources, the bibliography will be a useful tool, for it is from many of these sources that we have gleaned much of our information when writing this text.

As practice of what we preach concerning service to clients, we request any feedback you care to give, so that, like other mass media producers, we can adjust our messages to suit our audience and to make ourselves heard. Comments may be sent in care of: Mass Communications Editor, Wm. C. Brown Company Publishers, 2460 Kerper Boulevard, Dubuque, IA 52001.

Lastly we would like to thank the following reviewers for their help with the manuscript: ElDean Bennett at Arizona State University; Carol Burnett at California State University in Sacramento; Raymond Carroll at the University of Alabama; Michael Emery at California State University in Northridge; David Gordon at the University of Miami in Coral Gables; James Hoyt at the University of Wisconsin in Madison; Val Limburg at Washington State University; Gerald Stone at Memphis State University; and also, Robert Carrell at the University of Oklahoma; Mary Cassata at the University of Buffalo; Barnard K. Leiter at the University of Tennessee; James T. Lull at the University of California in Santa Barbara; John Merrill at Louisiana State University; Sharon Murphy at Southern Illinois University in Carbondale; William Porter at the University of Michigan; and Keith Sanders at the University of Missouri.

Jay Black
Frederick C. Whitney

Mass Communication

Part 1 Overview

The mass media (newspapers, magazines, books, radio, recordings, television, and film) and their auxiliaries (advertising, public relations, and news and feature services) are significant institutions in today's world. They can be looked at in terms of how they perform in society. Why do they do what they do; how do they reflect and mold the priorities and values of society; what have they achieved in the past; and what will they be capable of achieving in the future?

The main purpose of our introductory chapter is to come to grips with the basic nature of the mass media and their audiences.

We begin by considering the fundamental character of communication. Without an appreciation of how meaning and information are exchanged among individuals, we cannot fully appreciate the more complex process of mass communication, or communication through complex media to large, anonymous, and heterogeneous audiences.

Our focus is on the four primary functions of communication: (1) information; (2) entertainment; (3) persuasion (which in contemporary society has acquired important commercial overtones); and (4) transmission of the culture. These functions are seldom performed singly; rather, they are performed in varying combinations. Their interplay with individual characteristics of the various media is examined. Even though no single medium serves all purposes to all people, somehow out of this pervasity and diversity of functions and characteristics emerges a wondrous battleground for our attention. Within this matrix of media and society exists a built-in system of checks and balances. Media both reflect and trigger society's needs and impulses. But as commercial institutions, the media are reliant upon consumer acceptance for their own existence. The balance is curiously and sometimes cumbersomely self-correcting.

In considering mass media as social institutions, we must talk about people, living entities, for it is this aspect of mass communications that has been too often overlooked. The reasons are unimportant, but evidence seems to point toward the fact that the mass media are easier to isolate and to treat; they are tangible, audible, and visible. This media emphasis does a disservice to communications by treating only a part of the process and, more significantly, by discounting people as an integral part of the process.

Mass media audiences must be looked at as individuals, not as merely the *lowest common denominator* into which media fare is divided. As individuals, we attend to the media, reacting as individuals seeking to gratify our own special interests and needs. If hundreds, thousands, or even millions of us choose to react similarly, it is still basically an individual decision, although it appears in the form of mass behavior. Media have come to appreciate this, catering to our particular habits. We respond according to certain predictable behaviors based upon demographic and psychographic characteristics. Demographically, our age, sex, income, education, and life-style traits are important to the media, as are our psychographic needs, values, and beliefs. Our affiliations with the broader mass or the more specialized publics, groups, or associations should be looked at as merely manifestations of our individualistic drives. When mass media are successful, it is because they recognize our distinct differences and our commonalities. Mass media, such as network television, remain to serve our most common interests. But they are being supplanted by the more specialized media, about which so much of this book is devoted.

Communication and Audiences 1

Introduction

The mass media are newspapers, magazines, books, radio, film, and television and its related technologies. They are generally divided into print media and electronic media. The print media are older media, having developed over the last 500 years, while the electronic media are products of the twentieth century.

What do the mass media do in society? They give us baseball scores and tell us about the Middle East; they explain inflation and they interpret current events. The media sell goods and services and candidates and opinions. They make us laugh, they create drama, and they bring music into our lives. In short, they communicate.

In order to understand *mass* media and *mass* communication, we need an elementary understanding of the communication process—the events that define communication. That is the subject of the first part of this chapter. The model we will use (fig. 1.1) is later expanded to account for the elements of mass communication. In the final sections we will look at the functions of mass communications and the nature of audiences.

The Elements of Communication

No single definition of communication is agreed upon by all scholars interested in the subject; diversity abounds. Sociologists, psychologists, anthropologists, linguists, and speech communication specialists all offer definitions, some of which follow. Communication:

Communication has a variety of definitions.

is the process of transmitting meaning between individuals;

is the process by which an individual (the communicator) transmits stimuli (usually verbal symbols) to modify the behavior of other individuals (communicatees);

occurs whenever information is passed from one place to another;

is not simply the verbal, explicit, and intentional transmission of messages; it includes all those processes by which people influence one another;

occurs when person *A* communicates message *B* through channel *C* to person *D* with effect *E*. Each of these letters is an unknown to some extent, and the process can be solved for any one of them or any combination.

For our purposes we will define communication in simple terms as s–r for the stimulus-response process. Although this may be an over-simplification, it is a reasonable beginning. Communication takes at least two entities: an event outside the individual (the stimulus) and the individual reacting (the response). Thunder and lightning striking fear in a young child constitutes communication. The thunder and lightning are outside the child and fear is the child's reaction. From this simplest example, another factor in the communication process can be inferred. The child is changed.

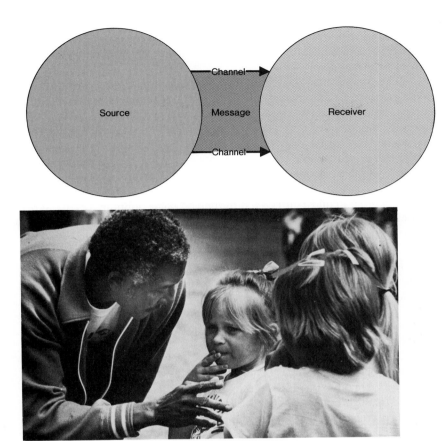

Figure 1.1
The basic communication model.

Communication—a human stimulus-response process by which we *inform, persuade,* and *entertain.*
Jill Cannefax/EKM-Nepenthe (top); Richard Kalvar/Magnum Photos, Inc. (bottom left); Robert V. Eckert, Jr./EKM-Nepenthe (bottom right)

The thunder and lightning have been programmed into his or her mental computer and will remain there as a part of his or her experience. This is the effect of communication, and all communication has some effect, if only that of total boredom.

The two principal factors in the communication process are a *source* and a *receiver*. Communication requires both. A thunderstorm in the wilderness out of sight and earshot constitutes no communication (there is no receiver, no human effect), and communication is a uniquely human phenomenon.

Further, this simple s–r model points up that all communication is an individual, even a personal process. Thunder and lightning over a city strike fear into many hearts, but into each one separately, without reference to any other. Each child will react differently—some sobbing, crying, cowering, or even curiously watching out the window—according to his or her bent. In this sense, the thunderstorm becomes a form of mass communication.

Different persons react differently to different stimuli. The fire alarm means different things to the firefighter and the theatergoer. Feminism evokes different reactions from Gloria Steinem and Phyllis Schlafly. Human communication involves a *message*—fire or feminism—that is carried over a *channel,* whether alarm bell or magazine article. Human communication has a purpose; it does not rise out of thin air. In these instances the purpose is to call attention to a fire (information) or to voice an opinion on a controversial topic (persuasion). That these messages were received differently is the crux of communication. Reception and, consequently, reaction and effect differ according to each individual's orientation. Orientation, in turn, depends on many factors, which can be reduced to the individual's experience—that is, the sum total of all that has gone before. Since a good deal of that experience has been communication, the complexities of the process and its circularity become apparent.

The Communication Model

Emerging from all this is a model of the communication process, which consists of a *source* or *encoder* sending a *message* over a *channel* to a *receiver* or *decoder*. Communication shorthand for this is shown in figure 1.1.

The source has a purpose in trying to communicate: to inform, to persuade, to entertain. In order for communication to occur, there must be some kind of effect on the receiver: a change in cognitive (thinking), affective (feeling), or behavioral (acting) processes. This response or reaction is seen as *feedback* and constitutes another element in the basic communication model. To indicate that this *feedback* is basically another phase in the same process of transferring messages between sources and receivers, we see in figure 1.2 that the roles of sender and receiver have been reversed and a communication cycle begun.

Overview

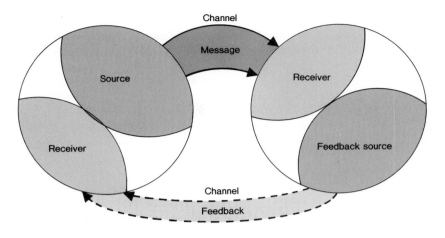

Figure 1.2
The interactive model of
communication.

The simplest illustration, of course, is an ordinary conversation. A woman says, "Good morning." She is the source; her purpose is to establish contact. The message is "Good morning," the channel is speech, and the man to whom the message is sent is the receiver. This may seem a bit complicated for such a simple transaction, but if the sequence and ingredients of this simple interpersonal communication are understood at the outset, it will enormously simplify the investigation of the much more complicated mass communication process.

Once the man has heard the greeting and responds, communication has taken place. The effect is one of warmth and reciprocity, and he responds, smiling and saying, "How are you?" This is his reaction; it constitutes feedback to the woman and completes the simple communication process.

Feedback

Note, however, that both the smile and response of the man were a part of the feedback. Note further that in replying the man became a secondary sender and the woman a receiver; thus, the model reverses itself with his reply. Note finally that the man's answer partially determines what the woman will say next. "How are you?" demands an answer: "Fine, thank you," or "Terrible." The principle here is that feedback conditions the course of future communication between the two by limiting the options available to them.

Feedback completes the
communication cycle.

Interference

There remains one more element in the basic communication process—interference. The technical term for interference is *noise,* and it consists of two types: channel noise and semantic noise. *Channel noise* is interference within, or exterior to, the channel or medium. If, for instance, the woman was seized with a fit of coughing when she said "Good morning," the man would have difficulty understanding her. The woman might have to repeat her greeting; in any event, there was channel interference in her speech. Alternately, if she said "Good morning" in a New York subway during rush hour, it is doubtful that anyone could hear her.

Channel noise can be corrected in two ways. First, the woman may try not to cough or sneeze, to use clear enunciation, and to speak loudly enough for the man to hear; in short, she may perfect the channel—speech. The other means is by repetition; if the man didn't hear her the first time, he may the second or third time.

Semantic noise, on the other hand, is more complex; it is interference within the communication process itself. If the woman greeted the man in a Chinese dialect, the man probably would not understand her if he spoke only English. This language barrier is the simplest example of semantic noise, but there are more prevalent and subtle forms indicated by differences in education, socioeconomic status, residency, occupation, age, experience, and interest.

Channel noise and semantic noise impede communication.

Communication is frequently ineffective due to both *channel* and *semantic noise.*
Frank Siteman/EKM-Nepenthe (left); Robert V. Eckert, Jr./EKM-Nepenthe (right)

Often one hears another say "I simply can't talk to him." This is an example of semantic noise. These two individuals may be poles apart in their orientation, interests, backgrounds, and habits. "The generation gap" is a glib description of semantic noise provoked by age differences.

The solutions to semantic noise, as in the case of channel noise, are incumbent upon the sender. After all, her original purpose was to communicate. One solution is to try to communicate on the level of the receiver. Kindergarten teachers use simple words, short sentences, and brief lessons because they know their students' vocabularies are as small as they are, and their spans of attention are short. These teachers are trying to eliminate semantic noise. In briefest summary, the solution to semantic noise is to appeal in terms of the receivers' interests.

Recognizing the semantic problems that can arise in one-to-one encounters, and the degree of interference that surrounds the simplest conversation, the scope of interference that is inevitable becomes apparent when such situations are multiplied by many in mass communications.

Mass Communication

For our purposes a simple definition will suffice: Mass communications is a means whereby mass produced messages are transmitted to large, anonymous, and heterogeneous masses of receivers. Basically, differences between one-to-one and mass communications are quantitative, but the discrepancy is so vast between the single one-to-one situation and contemporary mass communications, often involving tens of millions of receivers, that the numerical differences become differences in kind. Further, these differences stretch across the entire model, showing various changes in the source, channel, receiver, and feedback, as well as in noise.

> Mass communication occurs when mass communicated messages are transmitted to large, anonymous, and heterogenous masses of receivers.

The basic model of communication applies also to mass communication. A sender uses a channel to reach receivers, which prompts feedback to the sender. The main difference between mass communications and the interpersonal model is, of course, the matter of multiple receivers. Sometimes they receive simultaneously, immediately, as in network television; other times they receive individually over longer periods as with a movie, or even over centuries, as with some books, such as the Bible.

To make this distinction in the communication model, the sender is called the *source,* and the multiple receivers are called the *audience.* The channels, whether they be television, radio, newspapers, magazines, books, or movies, are known as *media.*

The Elements of Mass Communication

It should be obvious that audiences come in different sizes, from the 40 million or so of a network television program, to the several thousands of an average book, to the few hundreds of a scholarly journal. Regardless of size, it is crucial to remember that each audience is composed of that many

Audiences

> Audiences consist of individuals, not automatons.

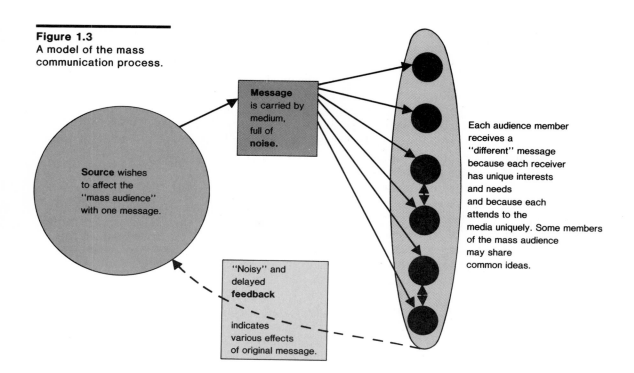

Figure 1.3
A model of the mass communication process.

Source wishes to affect the "mass audience" with one message.

Message is carried by medium, full of **noise.**

"Noisy" and delayed **feedback** indicates various effects of original message.

Each audience member receives a "different" message because each receiver has unique interests and needs and because each attends to the media uniquely. Some members of the mass audience may share common ideas.

individual persons, each one a separate thinking machine reacting to the medium's message in a different fashion, viewing the message through his or her own separate lens ground from his or her own experience and orientation. This individuality of audiences belies the concept of a single mass reacting as so many automatons.

Multiple receivers of a mass medium will also react with one another. The members of a family make comments to one another about a television show. Scholars discuss articles from academic journals. Did you see. . .? Have you read. . .? The papers said. . . . Have you heard. . .? They say. . . . The contents of mass media constantly become topics of conversation in daily life, and thus media influence is extended; indirect or secondary audiences may, in many cases, be far larger than the original receivers.

Thus, it appears that the effect of mass media reaches far beyond the initial audience. This is a significant point, for it illustrates the catalytic nature of mass communication in triggering individual reactions. However, for now it is enough to adapt the basic communication model to accommodate these additional factors, as can be seen in figure 1.3.

The new model indicates some subtle changes. First, feedback in mass communication is rarely instantaneous and direct, as it is in face-to-face conversation. Rather, feedback becomes an aggregate ingredient reflected to the source after a considerable lag in time, often from great distance, and frequently in a different nature. Feedback from the issues and rhetoric of a political campaign will be reflected, often many weeks later, at the ballot box on election day. The appeal of a television commercial or a magazine advertisement will be known at the sponsor's cash register. The popularity of a movie can only be measured in dollars at the box office, and the success of a book generally by over-the-counter sales, both of which may involve a wait of more than a year. Delayed feedback is indigenous to mass communication.

As a result of technological advances in computerization over the last couple of decades, this delay has been shortened by cultivating some new forms of feedback. In a political campaign, often costing millions of dollars, it is tactically unwise to await the verdict at the polls, by which time strategies cannot be corrected. Public opinion polling has proven able to offer an indication of election day results to perceptive candidates as a guide in their campaigns.

Similarly, when advertisers spend hundreds of thousands of dollars for prime-time television commercials, they need to know far in advance whether this kind of investment will pay off at the cash register. This need has led to television and radio ratings. There is an empirical correlation between audience size and the subsequent sales of consumer products. Consequently, the audience size of television shows, as reflected in ratings, gives a reasonable clue to the relative success of programs and commercials.

Public opinion polling as a feedback device has another use, too. By indicating what is acceptable and unacceptable to different audiences, polls tend to condition the kind of campaign or the kinds of programs that will be offered in the future. The candidate who finds his or her corruption-at-city-hall issue falling flat will abandon it. The advertiser who finds a science fiction TV series less appealing than a dramatic program will try to switch to a "Dallas" or "Hill Street Blues."

Noise in mass communication is a mammoth aggravation. Within the media, channel noise consists of such things as typographical errors, misspellings, scrambled words, or omitted paragraphs in the newspaper. It is the fuzzy picture on the tube, static on the radio, or missing pages in a magazine. It is also a broken television set, a dead battery in the transistor radio, the Sunday paper in a mud puddle outside the door, or the magazine subscription that doesn't arrive. Obviously, the more technologically complex society becomes, the greater the opportunity is for this kind of channel noise. As the numbers, varieties, and complexities of media increase, the greater the likelihood is that one will be exposed to mounting noise.

Delayed Feedback

Delayed feedback is indigenous to mass communications.

Channel Noise

Mass communication inevitably involves channel noise, or outside interference.

Since channel noise also includes outside interference, it encompasses such things as kids fighting during a television program, or visitors interrupting one's reading. Other such interferences may be the persistent ringing of the telephone as one watches television, a teenager's stereo at full volume while his or her parents are trying to read, or even competing programs scheduled in the same time slot, or a variety of magazines and media from which to choose. These examples show evidence that in many cases the media interfere with one another and constitute a considerable part of their own noise. As more media develop and become available, the problem will get worse.

One of the solutions for channel noise is repetition, and it is in use constantly in mass communications, especially in advertising. Disc jockeys repeat phone numbers; television commercials reappear during a program; and department stores advertise daily with multiple pages in both morning and evening papers. Repetition employs the law of averages. If the message was interrupted the first time—by the doorbell or by conversation—chances are it won't be the second or third time. Repetition in broadcast media offers an opportunity to reach those who tune in late. However, repetition operates on a law of diminishing return. There comes a point in repetition when the receiver, as an individual, will tune the message out. When multiplied by many individuals, the message is lost. Repetition must be used with discretion.

Channel noise is lessened by repetition of messages, and attention to mechanics.

Another cure for channel noise is perfecting the channel performance. This includes avoiding static on the radio, prolonging the life of transistor batteries, proofing the typos and scrambled paragraphs in the newspaper, and cleaning up the fuzzy picture on the tube. These are rather obvious solutions, but accomplishing them leads in several directions.

Removing static on the radio, for instance, may require increasing the wattage of the station, which calls for approval by the Federal Communications Commission (FCC) and demands considerable capital investment. The long-life transistor battery stems directly from improved technology—a constant probing of new frontiers. Such technology already has developed transistors (in lieu of bulky vacuum tubes), printed circuits, and miniaturization, making the radio a personal, portable mass communications tool.

A fuzzy picture may demand a new picture tube at the owner's expense, but it also may require new cameras at the studio or a new control console or better engineers. Perfecting the channel on television can run all the way from improving the transmitter's output via intricate engineering through the quality of engineers, the talent of directors, and the diction of the announcer.

The typos and misspellings in the newspaper demand better copy editors and proofreaders, of course, but they may also demand better computer operators, updated typesetting machines, or better-trained printing personnel. In the distribution system employed by newspapers, a part of channel noise will depend on the working condition of the newscarrier's bicycle.

Gatekeeping has generally been associated with the news, specifically with newspapers. The editors are the gatekeepers of the newspaper. They determine what the public reads, or at least what is available for them to read. The events they bypass are events that never happened as far as the public is concerned. Society's exposure to the day's reality and fantasy is in the gatekeepers' hands. Theirs is a prime responsibility.

Editors constantly have an eye on the audience as they sort through the day's events. They tend to place emphasis on the unusual, the sensational, and the spectacular, as well as on the criminal and the deviant. These types of stories historically make good reading; subscribers like them. Within the severe space limitation in which editors operate, they sometimes find they must forego a story on zoning controls in favor of a gory three-car accident, or pass up a scientific breakthrough for an axe murder. This is because the number of pages available for news is determined by the amount of advertising that has been sold. Typically, only 40 percent of the paper can be devoted to news.

Gatekeepers

Gatekeepers determine what audiences will read, see, or hear.

Gatekeepers sift and sort through the day's news.
Jill Cannefax/EKM-Nepenthe

Before an editor gets a story, the reporter has already exercised a form of gatekeeping in the selection and presentation of facts. No matter how objective the reporter has tried to be, something of that individual and his or her orientation has crept into the story. No two reporters will write the same story; more broadly, no two observers will see the same thing. Thus, the public's view of an event will be colored to a degree by the kind of fact-finding glasses the reporter wore.

Editorial policy is also a form of gatekeeping. Different newspapers have different values. Two examples that come readily to mind are the *New York Times* and the *New York Daily News.* The *New York Times* prides itself on completeness and detail in its substantive reporting. It plays down the sensational and deviant in the interest of propriety and taste. On the other hand, the *New York Daily News,* as a matter of policy, emphasizes the sensational, the odd, the different. Both approaches constitute forms of gatekeeping. While each newspaper deprives its audience of something, together they achieve a kind of imperfect balance for the residents of New York.

These examples illustrate how media tend to specialize in order to reach selective audiences. Gatekeeping activities reflect this specialization. Magazines and radio stations further emphasize this principle. Each has developed a format of appeal to a specific audience, and audiences differ. Some stations play rock 'n' roll, some classical music, some "oldies but goodies." These stations are not free to depart from their format, except at the risk of losing their established audiences.

Magazines also have equally well-defined formats to appeal to specific audiences: *Vogue* for the fashion-conscious, *Field and Stream* for the outdoor buff, *Cosmopolitan* for the unmarried working woman. Such audiences have grown to expect a certain point of view from these periodicals, and editors screen and prune all the available material to come up with the exact contents their readerships expect. There are no articles on fly-fishing in *Mademoiselle,* no economic forecasts in *Popular Mechanics.* Magazines and radio are as selective in what they present as the selective audiences they serve, and this is a form of gatekeeping.

Among the three major networks, programmers of prime-time television wrestle with what to air and what kind of a balance to strive for. From hundreds of potential shows—serials, specials, drama, situation comedies, police shows, mysteries, and news magazine shows—they must each screen out a dozen or so for evening viewing.

In television news, producers are affected by the limitations on time in the same way newspaper editors are affected by space. The result is highly fragmentary. Newscasters have little time for headline news representing perhaps no more than 2 or 3 percent of the total news of the day.

Even book publishers and movie producers who cater to a self-selective, numerically unpredictable audience have their gatekeeping problems. From hundreds of manuscripts, screenplays, and scenarios that come to their attention from authors and agents, solicited and unsolicited, they must select those to be published or produced. The public will never know of the remaining hundreds, the thousands in a year, that failed to be approved. For audiences they never existed, dying before birth.

From all this two things become apparent concerning the gatekeeping function. First, it is limiting in that it restricts what the public is exposed to as an audience, whether in news, television programs, movies, books, or radio. Due to the marvelous diversity of the media, however, a certain balance of exposure is achieved in the aggregate from so many media catering to so many different audiences. Second, the gatekeeping function is subjective, personal. It is the judgment of a surrogate substituted for that of the audience, and is basically a professionally educated guess as to what the public will like or react to.

The mass media can be described as having four functions: (1) information, (2) entertainment, (3) persuasion, and (4) transmission of the culture. In individual communication functional gears can be shifted at will: One pleads, asserts, instructs, jokes, questions—moving rapidly from one mode to another as situation and inclination demand. In mass communication altering the basic functional thrust of a medium is more difficult, if not impossible. This is because the highly organized, institutionalized nature of the mass media creates a ponderous inertia resistant to change. Like living organisms, the systems making up the media are in delicate balance, and even slight adjustments can have quite an impact.

Audiences have grown to expect one format or a certain combination of formats from each medium, and a departure deceives audience expectations and threatens profit. The thrust of the *New York Daily News* is basically entertainment, providing sensation, spice, and violence. The concern of the *New York Times* is information, to be "the newspaper of record."

For example, the *New York Daily News* could not one day be issued in the format of the *New York Times,* giving an analysis of international monetary policy. The tabloid presses could not possibly accommodate the full-page format used by the *New York Times,* and more significantly, the readership would be appalled. Nor could the *New York Times* issue sensational headlines of sex and disaster, because readers would desert and advertisers would cancel. When staid newspapers such as the *New York Times* wished to modify their format and physical appearance during the mid-1970s, they did so in slow, barely perceptible stages so readers would scarcely recognize the changes to larger type, wider columns, and more white space.

Functions of Mass Communications

Media inform, entertain, persuade, and transmit culture.

Information

When one thinks of the various functions of the mass media, the information function frequently comes to mind first. Information is the easiest of the functions to identify, since it comprises a part of each, and the most prominent form for information is news.

Print media have a strong informational thrust.

The emphasis on news has camouflaged the fact that 60 percent of the average newspaper is advertising and that a considerable portion of what is left over after the ads have been inserted is entertainment of one sort or another, starting with the comics and ranging from selected features, editorials and columnists to a variety of sensational and human-interest stories. However, the basic thrust of the newspaper remains informational. That is what its audience expects of it. The *New York Daily News* satisfies its information function, for example, by finding a high quotient of sensational material, such as violence and sex, and presenting it with proper news leads, written in a punchy style. Whether or not this constitutes the responsible exercise of the information function will be discussed more fully in chapter 12 when we consider the Hutchins Commission's report on press responsibility, and the four theories of the press.

As adjuncts to mass media, the wire services (particularly the Associated Press [AP] and United Press International [UPI]) have the highest information content. Their business is selling information, specifically news of current events gathered worldwide. Further, their customers or clients—the newspapers, television networks, and individual television and radio stations across the nation—represent such a broad spectrum of approaches, interests, formats, and editorial policies that the wire services tend to rely on straight news, an objective, unadulterated informational approach that avoids all attempts to color the news. The wire services leave it to their clients to choose specific items from those offered and to season those items as they see fit.

Textbooks, making up about half of the book publishing industry, are expected by their publishers and readers to consist primarily of information. Their voluntary readership is slight, and they are generally read at the direction of an instructor. For this reason publishers frequently attempt to interject humor (entertainment) as a relief from the heavy dose of information. Not incidentally, publishers also hope to sell a lot of books in order to make a profit. The other branches of book publishing—trade books, fiction, and nonfiction—are freer to depart from pure information as their thrust, but their information function is still relatively high, covering a wide variety of topics from which readers select and choose at their own discretion.

Taken in the aggregate, the print media as a whole have a basic informational thrust. Not only are they affordable; they also allow individualized and detached involvement. Readers can selectively attend to and perceive print content when and where they choose, thus gaining the satisfaction they seek.

Although television is primarily entertainment in function, it does include some information. There are regularly scheduled newscasts that tend to take on entertainment overtones. News commentators are not so much in competition with each other as they are with other prime-time personalities. Their formats are doctored to move quickly and dramatically regardless of the significance of the information they are presenting.

There are also the self-conscious documentaries. Here, again, they take on a dramatic quality and sometimes, but not always, develop a point of view that: (1) is designed to appeal to the presumed taste of their massive audience, and (2) is not necessarily objective in its analysis. Award-winning and top-rated "60 Minutes" is probably the most obvious example. The CBS team uses such dubious techniques as that of accosting unsuspecting news sources in the street with cameras rolling and choosing controversial story topics that are intended to raise ratings.

Television cannot be entirely blamed for this cursory treatment of serious topics. Profit is the motivating force. Television's ratings indicate massive regular departures of audience whenever a documentary appears. For instance, would you be more interested in watching an hour-long program on industrial waste or a network showing of *Star Wars?*

Entertainment

The broadcast media—radio, television, and film—have a basic although by no means exclusive entertainment thrust. Film is included in this category because, although there are differences, film is such a large part of contemporary television that one cannot realistically be considered without the other.

That the broadcast media are intensely, purposefully, and enthusiastically entertainment oriented is obvious to any observer. Also apparent is the persuasive, commercial aspect of television. Anyone who has had the misfortune of being hospitalized for a week or so can testify to the unremitting and highly imaginative diet of entertainment and persuasive fare that TV offers. Daytime television with its fantasies of soap operas, game shows, old movies, and reruns is simply the beginning. Prime time, during the evening, is a wonderland of scheduled police situations, private eyes, hospitals, situation comedies, personalities, serials, and premiere movies that move inexorably in the direction of sex, violence, and deviance.

The Public Broadcasting Service (PBS) is confirmation of broadcast's need to entertain. PBS—supported by government funding, private donations, and corporate underwriting—has no commercial requirements to make money or show a profit. Devoid of these commercial pressures, it is also free to offer programs of consequence (culture, education, documentaries), and it presents these to almost always smaller audiences than the commercial networks would tolerate. There is a serious question about how much incentive exists either to produce or to watch a public medium in a commercial society.

Broadcast media tend to be entertainment oriented.

The largest portion of radio is the same mixture of entertainment and commercials that television offers. Lacking television's video quality, radio must concentrate on what it does best, appeal to the ear, and this generally means music. The spectrum of music offered by radio is impressive. Station by station, radio has selectively carved out a segment of the audience to which it appeals, and station by station, it continues to move goods to these audiences: components to hi-fi enthusiasts, blemish ointments to teenagers, and annuities to the affluent. Radio's audiences are far more diversified than television's, and its costs of production are far less. This permits it to specialize toward selective audiences, and such specialization may take a form other than music.

Some radio stations have found their niche in broadcasting a series of constantly updated news bulletins, emphasizing information in a largely entertainment medium.

Film has shown a gradual metamorphosis in recent years. In its heyday during the 1930s and early 1940s, it was essentially a mass entertainment medium, playing in baroque palaces to large audiences. Now it has moved under television's competitive pressure to be a more expressive medium, freed from the tyranny of appealing to the tastes of the lowest common denominator (the number of people who share a characteristic or interest to which the media can appeal). In general, a less challenging interest has a larger potential audience, a larger common base. Further changes are starting to occur with the growth of the home video market.

Although most of film still has a basic entertainment thrust, particularly that portion serving the television industry, two other facets of filmmaking are becoming evident: (1) a distinctly persuasive-informative orientation in industrial or commercial films, and (2) a self-conscious role as social critic in the so-called popular movies, which typically play to smaller, more selective audiences.

While the broadcast media and film have been identified as the basic purveyors of entertainment, this function is always intermixed with others. A high degree of entertainment pervades all mass media, often serving as the vehicle for more serious functions.

The entertainment function of the media requires an extraordinarily affluent society to support the level inherent in American mass communication. When considering that mass communication is time-consuming, and that a substantial portion of it is pure entertainment, as evidenced by television, one becomes aware of the leisure and prerequisite affluence of our society, which enables us to spend so much of our time unproductively. But this makes a certain amount of sense in our democratic society when you figure the average consumer of mass media is consciously seeking to fulfill personal needs and interests.

The persuasive function of the media in contemporary society is as significant as the information and entertainment functions. Advertising, of course, is its most apparent form, but there are other more subtle manifestations of persuasion that are likely to have lasting effects on the future of mass communication. The more than $60 billion spent annually on advertising is only a portion of the amount spent on American mass media persuasion. Public-relations activities, special promotional events, and blatant as well as subtle efforts at image manipulation and public-opinion formation pervade the media environment.

Much of the persuasion in mass communications is concealed. Any public-relations practitioner can testify to the fact that a considerable portion of what passes for news in the media has a persuasive origin and an ulterior purpose. Much of what the public reads, hears, or watches in all the media is designed to influence in one way or another.

Political campaigns, which periodically command vast attention in the mass media, are almost pure persuasion. Much of governmental news at all levels has a propaganda base as government seeks to declare or justify its actions in a democratic society. A good part of business and financial news is advocacy. In today's environmental and consumer-conscious society, business is increasingly under attack and seeks to utilize the mass media in defense.

Persuasion

Persuasion, overt or concealed, is integral to mass media.

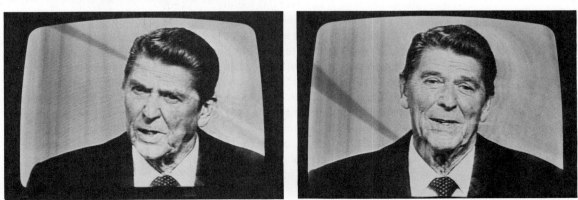

TV, basically an entertainment medium, serves also for persuasion, information, and transmission of the culture.
Barbara Alper / Stock, Boston

The doses of persuasion masquerading as information in mass communication are huge, and inevitably the functions have tended to merge, obliterating distinctions. This in turn leads to a credibility gap, since what appears to be bona fide news repeatedly turns out to be political or commercial advocacy, or is flavored by newspaper bias or television distortion.

Most of American mass media are supported by advertising in one way or another; commercial radio and television are 100 percent so. Newspapers and magazines in varying degrees rely heavily upon advertising revenues. The price of a newspaper does little more than cover distribution costs, leaving all editorial costs, all production costs, and all profit to be borne by paid advertising. Magazines vary widely in their use of advertising, but generally at least half their revenue, and hence, all their profit, comes from advertising.

It is obvious that television is not all entertainment. The schedule is regularly interspersed during daytime and evening hours with a mosaic of commercials touting used cars, beers, cosmetics, household sprays, fast-food restaurants, intimate hygiene products, major appliances, and ball-point pens. Some of the commercials, one might note subjectively, appear better than the surrounding programming. That advertising should conform to or even surpass the format of the medium is not at all surprising.

In fact, a good case can be made that the role of advertising agencies in mass communication industries is to inject entertainment into commercial persuasion, lest the public's attention, subjected to unrelenting exposure to so many sales pitches, begins to pall and thus defeat the advertiser's purpose. In any event, it becomes apparent that the purpose of television programming is to provide a vehicle for the commercials, to deliver customers to the advertisers.

It is also significant that although only 10 percent or less of the information or news that is available to media reporters and editors eventually appears in the news medium or newscast, nearly all of the available advertising is published or broadcast (with only minor exceptions, as for example ads that are obscene, for illegal or overly controversial products, or that simply cannot be squeezed into the available time and space). This may offer a commentary on the relative values placed on advertising and information in a commercial society.

We generally think of entertaining feature movies when we consider films, but of the 16,000 films produced each year in the United States, fewer than 200 are for theater distribution. A highly profitable aspect of film-making is concerned with persuasion and information. Commercials are an obvious example. In addition, there is the area of training, educational, and institutional films: travelogues, and driver-training, how-to-do-it, and sales-orientation films. Like textbooks, these films have limited appeal and are shown for specific reasons before captive audiences. They constitute a large portion of filmmaking, easily the greatest number of new films each year. But they lack the public exposure of either paid-admission films or television's "nights at the movies."

Film today shows considerable persuasive and informational content. It begins to lay serious claim as a prime medium of cultural transmission, recording and playing for inspection the triumphs, failures, and foibles of society. A good deal of social concern has proven profitable, and movies appear to have capitalized on this.

All mass media are inescapably transmitters of the culture. Media record current events and how the public reacts to them in the aggregate. This is as true for social customs as it is for items considered newsworthy. An analysis of media content will pinpoint interests and concerns of media producers and consumers, which becomes a record for future generations. Television, for instance, is a mirror of the times. Further, as television programs and original movies move increasingly to show previously taboo themes, such as nudity and sex, they reflect a change in the social structure.

> Some records are conscious and intentional; others seem incidental but are nonetheless important. The market ads, for example, and white goods sales in daily newspapers are good indicators of contemporary living standards and of the tastes and values of society. Anthropologists of the twenty-second century, in searching for a full record of twentieth-century culture, would do well to study the cultural records transmitted in the catalogs issued by Sears, J. C. Penney's, and Montgomery Wards. Although some may question the accuracy of television's portrayals of everyday life, in the aggregate this medium transmits today's cultural values. It has to, because it is a commercial medium.

> Another indicator of our culture is the sheer massiveness of the communications industry. The availability of all the different media indicates our living standards. The multiplicity of media catering to different audiences of varying sizes reflects the diversity inherent in the larger society. Never before has any nation had so clear and comprehensive a record written and recorded on film and tape of its growth, structure, and movement.

In many discussions of mass communication, as John Merrill and Ralph Lowenstein point out in *Media, Messages and Men,* scant attention is paid to the audiences of the mass media except to acknowledge their presence.[1] The mass media are tangible, audible, visible, and treatable—the institutionalized product of a corporate society. Consequently, it has been far easier to examine them in operational terms than it has been to probe audiences in terms of reaction and effect. Audiences are vague will-o'-the-wisp conglomerates composed of different individuals at different times.

> Though hard to define, audiences do exist in the plural. The best way to describe the range of possible audiences is to visualize a giant funnel with the largest audience at one end of it. This huge audience is served best,

Transmission of the Culture

Media reflect cultural values, consciously or unconsciously.

Understanding Audiences

Audiences are complex masses of individuals, difficult to understand.

although not completely, by national network television. The funnel narrows as it includes various publics and groups and associations until it culminates at the individual. This "single" audience is, of course, served by telephone and the mails and, most importantly, by face-to-face encounters with other individuals.

It is the individual, with all his or her differences (in different arrangements, for different periods of time), who composes different audiences. It is this single individual, not a crowd or a group, who casts a ballot in the sanctity of the polling place, who passes dollars across the counter, who buys an admission to the stadium or the theater, and who holds opinions and attitudes that, in an aggregate with others, will be translated into some sort of temporary and incomplete consensus called public opinion. Further, it is the individual who subscribes to a newspaper, buys a magazine, reads a book, laughs at a TV comic, or listens to the news on his or her way to work. In this technological age and with a social emphasis on size and quantitative measurement, attention has perhaps been too preoccupied with mass audiences.

Audiences Defined

Audiences include the masses, publics, groups, associations, and individuals. There are media for everyone.

Audiences, seen in the aggregate rather than solely in terms of individual components at a given point in time, move from the mass to publics, to groups, to associations, and, finally, to the individual. The totality of the mass is easy to recognize; so is the individual. Between, in the intermediate divisions, the distinctions are blurred.

Publics

Publics are vague, general entities; they are conglomerates of individuals who generally share a single trait. Membership in publics is scarcely voluntary, although this is not absolute. Members are characterized by what they are or what they do or where they live. Broadly, publics can be defined as geographic or functional bodies. The geographic breakdown is easiest to understand. There are southerners, New Englanders, and midwesterners; there are also New Yorkers, Georgians, Hoosiers, and Texans; and there are San Franciscans and Bostonians. There are also urban dwellers, rural dwellers, and inhabitants of suburbia. Regardless of the size of the geographic audience, some medium is available to serve it: state and regional radio and television networks, huge metropolitan daily newspapers, rural weeklies, and suburban dailies.

From a functional standpoint, there are even greater possibilities of diversification. There are men and women, Protestants, Catholics, Jews, agnostics, and atheists; there are Democrats, Republicans, and Independents; there are blacks, whites, yellows, reds, and browns; there are young

Publics have geographic, functional, or demographic characteristics.

25

and old; there are blue-collar workers and white-collar workers—and so on, ad infinitum. At least one medium, perhaps several, is generally available to serve each. Women are catered to by such magazines as *Redbook* and *Ms.;* Los Angeles and other cities offer Spanish television; the *New Republic* appeals to liberals; and Saturday morning television is directed at children.

A newer variation of these functional publics is that of demographic publics, identifiable with the help of the computer. In these contrived publics, more than one characteristic is identified in a sort of communications "twenty questions" game. For instance, in California, a given geographical public is given the limitation "male," which cuts the population in half; "college graduate" cuts the remainder by two-thirds; "lawyer" further reduces this number; and "Catholic," "golfer," "father of two," and "over fifty" will continuously refine the number of individuals meeting the specific requirements of this public until an extremely small segment of the overall population is defined. Applying these demographic factors across the board with the speed and efficiency of the computer permits one to identify an almost infinite number of small, discrete publics. Demography isolates people so that they can be found and persuaded.

One thing that should be noted about demographics is that the publics isolated may not even exist. The *New York Times,* in conducting a readership survey, found that it could isolate the number of "divorced young women with two children between the ages of two and five living in garden apartments in suburban New York who visited mid-Manhattan at least once a month to shop for paper clothing with an American Express card." While such an esoteric public might not be a public at all, a single individual may be artificially identified, even though he or she does not even exist.

Groups

Groups share more specific interests than do publics. "Membership" is voluntary.

Groups are generally smaller than publics and share a more specific interest than publics—interests such as bowling, dry-fly fishing, tennis, or antiques, for example. Groups are not necessarily subdivisions of publics, as neurosurgeons are of the medical profession, although they may be. Groups can be formed and identified without having a relationship to any larger public. An interest in astrology, for instance, to which several media cater, does not suggest a larger entity. In general, groups are voluntary in nature; people belong because they want to or because they have an interest in the group's purposes and activities. People belong to such groups because of a shared commonality. The members of a group may never meet and get to know one another, but if there is a common interest, a medium will be available to serve it. Those interested in dry-fly fishing, for example, are a scattered audience, spread in tiny numbers across the length and breadth of the nation, united only by their subscription to *Fly Fisherman.*

Associations

Associations are formalized groups. Their activities are regulated by codes; they are identifiable; and they keep rosters. Associations are formal audiences, reflections of the corporate structure of society. So defined, associations include the entire spectrum of American business and social life.

Across the entire spread, large and small, there are media to serve those audiences identified on the organizational or association rosters. Such media include employee newsletters, stockholder reports, trade association magazines, house organs, and professional and scholarly journals. Whatever the form and the purpose, these media are directed to a specific audience in terms of that audience's interests or livelihood, which frequently coincide.

As with publics and groups, it is the composition of these associations and their purpose that determines specific media content, and this content changes as the interests and orientation of that membership changes. Indeed, content analyses of association media frequently reflect subtle changes in the membership, philosophy, and objectives of the association.

Audience size, as we have seen, has a pronounced effect on the content of the media. The medium with the largest audience, network television, tends to program for the largest common denominator, while professional journals can publish abstruse articles that will be understood by only a few thousand people. In addition to size, there are other characteristics of audiences that affect media. Among them are longevity, specialization, and audience expectations.

Associations are formalized groups with regulated activities.

Audience Factors That Affect Media

Audience size, longevity, specialization, and expectations affect media content.

Longevity

Audiences come and go, and media effects vary accordingly.

Television's prime-time audience on any given evening will come and go over a three-hour period, while the audience for any given program will last only an hour or so. On the other hand, a popular movie may take a year to reach its audience in the thousands of theaters spread throughout the land, and a best-seller may take a couple of years or more to sell its quota. In effect, the more durable the audience, the more concrete the effect of the medium. While the impact of a book or film can be substantial and sustained, the specific effect of radio and television programs is usually short-lived.

Specialization

For a person to say that he or she is a Republican is no longer descriptive enough. There is an Eastern liberal wing and a conservative wing, there are moderates, and there are members of the John Birch Society. What used to be considered a cohesive women's audience is now broken into at least four subgroups: the young working woman, the traditional housewife, the professional, and the feminist. Large, monolithic audiences are becoming more fragmented for several reasons, one of which is an increase in knowledge.

Increased knowledge, leisure time, and mobility have brought about specialized media.

Increased knowledge has made general practitioners of medicine almost a thing of the past. Their place has been taken by specialists unheard of a generation or so ago: neurosurgeons, radiologists, ophthalmologists, and so on. In profession after profession, increasing specialization to meet the demands of society has evolved. As these professions specialize, they tend to develop their own languages, techniques, and body of knowledge, which not only demands their attention but requires media to feed it.

A second reason for specialization is increased leisure time. Shorter work weeks give Americans the opportunity to explore new interests and hobbies from cabinetmaking to boating. Others find satisfaction in matters of the mind that may be satisfied by a magazine such as *Psychology Today,* which caters to an audience of educated young liberals who have discovered fascination in the world of human behavior.

Personal mobility is a third reason. The growth of suburbs following World War II focused interest in suburban affairs and led to suburban newspapers and even some suburban FM radio stations. The huge metropolitan dailies lacked the physical resources, personnel, and space to adequately cover the civic, social, and governmental activities of the communities on their periphery. Nor could local merchants afford the space and time rates for the larger metropolitan media; these rates were based on wide-area audiences, only a fraction of which a local merchant could ever hope to serve. The answer from both an information and advertising standpoint was smaller, localized media serving a specialized audience.

Audience Expectations

Audiences, regardless of size, are not simply passive receivers of media; rather, they are active participants in the dynamic process of mass communication. Each audience determines within certain limits exactly what kind of material it will consume. Media gatekeepers attend to audience expectations by devising their programs' content mix, or specific titles that, in their professional judgment, will best appeal to the largest numbers of the particular audience they are trying to reach.

Audiences are active participants in the mass communication process.

This occurs in mass communications in the same way that it does in merchandising. The variety of clothes, furniture, housewares, and sporting goods available in the local shopping center is prescribed by the people who shop there. The mass media are like the stores on the mall, from the enormous chain stores to the tiny boutiques. Each store caters to certain customers in groups of various size and is available to customers who wander in and out more or less as the mood strikes them. Like mass media, shopping centers are social institutions whose gatekeepers, called buyers, are guided by management policy as to what public they will cater to, and by that public as to what they will buy. Sometimes the gatekeepers are successful and sometimes they aren't, but if they are to stay in business, they have to be responsive to the interests, needs, and expectations of their customers.

In most cases, the audiences for mass media are fairly large; network television, for example, counts the audience for each program by the million. When dealing with numbers of that magnitude, it is easy to overlook the fact that all audiences are made up of individuals.

The Importance of the Individual

Audiences are not necessarily permanent. Ordinarily they ebb and flow, changing as individuals move in and out of them. Audiences are comprised of individuals, each a unique member of society. Membership is voluntary for the most part, and an individual joins these different media audiences to satisfy his or her own needs for information, entertainment, professional advancement, diversion, and so forth. It is the individual who makes the choice and the media know it.

The Search for More Specific Audiences

During the 1930s and 1940s, a prevalent view of mass communications held that every media message was a direct and powerful stimulus that would elicit an immediate response. No interference was seen between the messages and the receivers, so a clear-cut, simplistic message would have a clear-cut, simplistic response. Public panic following Orson Welles' 1938 radio broadcast, "War of the Worlds," reinforced the theory. However, this hypodermic theory or bullet theory (both terms were used) proved to be inadequate.

Massive media efforts failed to sell the Edsel or former President Gerald Ford's "Whip Inflation Now" campaign. For former presidential candidates like George McGovern and Barry Goldwater, the media could not win the presidency. Disappointment with the failure of the mass media to deliver the goods—or the votes—has forced a reappraisal of the traditionally presumed homogeneous effects of the mass media on mass audiences.

By seeking smaller and more specific audiences, media have survived. Some media have specialized in toto—an entire magazine or broadcast station gearing itself to reach a singularly homogeneous audience. Others have recognized the value of partial or internal specialization—sections of a magazine or newspaper, or specific programs on the broadcast station—attempting to reach an audience that is homogeneous on both demographic (age, sex, income, education, etc.) and psychographic (values, needs, beliefs, interests, etc.) levels.

For example, radio, which could have died when television was born, not only survived, but prospered. Today it is far healthier and wealthier in the aggregate than it ever was when it was America's preeminent mass medium during the depression and World War II.

Television took radio's evening prime time and usurped radio's national advertisers and network operation. Like radio, television was enjoyed in the home, but it had the visual dimension of pictures and motion. On the basis of its ability to command the involvement of more senses for a more comprehensive communication experience, television should have killed off radio.

But radio found a new home and a new prime time, which television couldn't match—in the automobile when American goes to and from work each day. It also found new local markets, and it found music and teenagers and fed one to the other. Under technological pressure radio became portable, and under economic pressure it became local. It created the disc jockey as a personality. It diversified, with each station picking a segment of the total audience for its own. It fragmented, concentrated, specialized, and in so doing built up new audiences with transistors to their ears.

In instance after instance, specialization under pressure has restored obsolescent media, as they concentrate on that unique combination of media functions they are best able to perform. In the gestalt of American society each media form finds its own place where its particular formula of characteristics ideally makes it suitable to a particular grouping of people—its audience.

Media and audiences seek out, support, and affect each other.

Summary

Communication requires a source and a receiver. The source may be human or it may be inanimate but the receiver must be human, and if communication takes place, the receiver will be changed in some way. This can be described as stimulus–response. The response of the receiver is called feedback, which will affect the course of communication.

Interference, known as noise, will be either channel noise or semantic noise. Channel noise is interference within or external to the medium, such as the screeching sounds of the subway that prevent conversation. Semantic noise occurs when the meaning of the sender is unclear to the receiver.

Communication can occur within an individual (intrapersonal), between two individuals (interpersonal), or between a source and a large group of people (mass). Mass communications can be defined as a means whereby mass produced messages are transmitted to large, anonymous, and heterogeneous masses of receivers.

The model used for mass communication is similar to the model for basic communication, except that the receivers are plural and the feedback is delayed. Channel noise is a serious problem in mass communication that is likely to get worse as more media develop. Although gatekeepers are not illustrated on the model (fig. 1.3), they serve an important role in mass communication. Gatekeepers are the people who determine what will be printed, broadcast, or produced and consumed. Editors, reporters, television programmers, and movie producers are examples of gatekeepers.

The functions of the mass media are four: (1) information, (2) entertainment, (3) persuasion, and (4) transmission of the culture. The format of each medium is resistant to change. The print media tend to emphasize information, although other functions are evident in almost all of them. The broadcast media, including film, have a basic entertainment thrust. Advertising is the most blatant form of persuasion, but much of the persuasion in mass media is concealed and some is passed off as news. Finally, the mass media transmit the culture by preserving a record of events and by noting changes in the social structure. Less obvious examples of the latter are advertisements in newspapers. They reflect the products of society and even the availability of a multiplicity of media, both of which are indicative of a high standard of living.

Audiences for media are not monolithic. They are comprised of publics, groups, and associations. Audiences change and affect media by their longevity, their tendency to become specialized, and their collective expectations. Although media measure audiences in terms of size, all audiences are made up of individuals. Media have survived by specializing and by seeking more specific audiences.

Note

1. John C. Merrill and Ralph Lowenstein, *Media, Messages and Men: New Perspectives in Communication,* 2d ed. (New York: Longman, 1979).

Part 2 Print Media

The print media are the oldest forms of mass communications. They began essentially with movable type on Gutenberg's printing press in the fifteenth century. Gutenberg initiated a spiralling process as the availability of books prompted increased literacy, which created a demand for more books and more education. But the book was too slow to produce and to consume, which led to the development of other print forms: From the occasional tract evolved newspapers published on a regular basis and, later, magazines.

Society to date has been basically print oriented, and until very recently, the mass communications network in the United States was exclusively print. All of that has changed since the electronic revolution, however. Newspapers infrequently publish "extras," and national general-interest magazines have come upon hard times. The book-publishing industry has turned toward paperbacks as a quicker and more inexpensive mode.

The print media are presently in flux. But as we will see in case after case, new media do not crowd out the old. Instead they stimulate innovation and a search for new markets. Paperbacks are, in effect, a marriage of the book and magazine. Specialty magazines have become common in recent years. Newspapers have added Sunday and weekday supplements, or small special-interest magazines. These and other innovations represent the strivings of the print media to seek their own level following the tremendous impact of the electronic media.

In chapter 2 we will look at newspapers, exploring the development of the medium during the second half of the nineteenth century and into the twentieth century, the control and distribution of newspapers, and the structure of this form of periodical.

Chapter 3 is devoted to magazines, a hybrid print medium that allows for more in-depth analyses than is usually true of newspapers and is quicker to produce and disseminate than books.

The subject of chapter 4 is books, the medium that not only opened the world to mass communications but has remained the most durable.

Finally, in chapter 5, we consider the news and feature services, which feed information to newspapers, magazines, and radio and television news departments.

Newspapers 2

Introduction

The newspaper, as Emery and Emery point out, is a uniquely American phenomenon representing the highest achievement of the print medium.[1] Created in Europe, it was brought to North America where it was peculiarly suited to the rushed American temperament. The newspaper matured and flourished here, proving itself remarkably adaptable to changing times. Even though it has been superseded in some respects by the broadcast media, it nonetheless has provided the framework within which the broadcast media have grown. Local emphasis, advertising support, and audience appeal were all lessons that broadcast learned from the press. Further, the fundamental concept of press freedom was a newspaper doctrine disseminated by the founding fathers and subsequently applied to all media. The American newspaper is the traditional base of a growing mass communications network.

This chapter on the newspaper in American society begins with consideration of the peculiarly local nature of the medium. It is followed by a brief history of the newspaper in both European and American settings. Of particular importance is the rise of press freedoms. During the twentieth century the newspaper has had to compete with radio and, more recently, with television, which has prompted newspaper people to reconsider their medium's essential purposes and audience appeal. Contemporary newspapers are big business, typical of many industries in their mergers, consolidations, and potential for monopoly. The decade of the 1970s was one of technological revolution and economic retrenchment. We will discuss these changes, describe the basic characteristics of newspaper operations, the people who report and consume the news, and the types of newspapers currently available. Finally, we will consider the potential for this venerable medium to compete in an increasingly electronic communications environment.

The Medium Defined

Newspapers vary widely, but they tend to mirror their own locales.

A newspaper is generally considered to be a regularly issued, geographically limited print medium, which serves the general interests of a specific community. Printed on unbound newsprint, it commonly contains news, comment, features, photographs, and advertising. This definition has nothing whatever to do with frequency of publication, size, or format. Newspapers can vary as widely as the multiple editions of the economically plagued *New York Daily News,* whose 1.5 million copies per day have been read by some 4 million people, to economically secure monthly newspapers serving only a few hundred residents of small American communities. There are also weekly newspapers and suburban dailies. Some of these carry extensive regional, national, and international news, but most do not. With rare exceptions, all newspapers share a common preoccupation with their own locales.

By our definition, *Women's Wear Daily* and the *Wall Street Journal* are not newspapers, strictly speaking. They are more like daily magazines

Print Media

Robert V. Eckert, Jr./EKM-Nepenthe

serving specific national-interest groups, the fashion and financial worlds, respectively. On the other hand, the *Christian Science Monitor,* the *New York Times,* and the Gannett company's experimental *USA Today* would have to be classified as newspapers even though they are distributed to national rather than local audiences.

By and large, the American newspaper is a local medium whose allegiance is exclusively to the geographic area it serves. A geographically fragmented medium, each newspaper acts as a mirror of its community. This local emphasis is a twentieth-century heritage derived from an early nation of isolated and widely separated communities along the Atlantic seaboard, each self-reliant and each served by a self-reliant press. If and when a regional or national newspaper survives, it is only because it has managed to transcend local issues and to report, comment upon, and advertise more broadly-based items.

When movable type was invented in the 1450s, it was first used to print books. It wasn't until 150 years later that printers in England began distributing *tracts,* or pamphlets, containing topical news. By 1621 *corantos,* single-sheet tracts dealing with current foreign affairs, were common. Corantos were followed in 1641 by *diurnals,* four-page bulletins of local news.

Historical Development

Newspapers emerged from books, but they had predictable publication and circulation.

Print was becoming available to wider audiences. Being produced in days and sometimes in hours for only a few pennies, the scope of the medium was expanding, bringing print to whole new audiences in terms of cost and interest. Tracts encouraged literacy and accelerated the dissemination of news.

These new print media offered a more immediate, although cursory, overview of contemporary events at a much cheaper cost than a book, though admittedly sacrificing the elegance, permanence, and depth of a book.

Each of these forerunners to the modern newspaper grew in popularity. Early printers began to publish them regularly, discovering that they could count on roughly the same number of customers for each issue. Thus, the concept of circulation was born—the formal, quantitative expression of audience numbers. Such a profitable concept, in turn, encouraged schemes to increase sales. One method was to step up the frequency of publication from monthly to fortnightly to weekly and eventually to daily issues as technology improved, doubling and quadrupling circulation.

The *Oxford Gazette* (later the *London Gazette*) became the first regularly published English newspaper in 1665; in 1702 the *Daily Courant* became the first daily in England. In America Benjamin Harris tried to publish the first newspaper in 1690. But his *Publick Occurrences, Both Forreign and Domestic,* lasted exactly one issue. Apparently, Harris's version of the truth differed from that of the governing Massachusetts Bay Colony. He allegedly ran afoul of a 1662 ordinance that prohibited printing without governmental approval and consequently was shut down. The *Boston News-Letter,* a weekly started by John Campbell in 1704, became the first continuing American newspaper. Unlike Harris's *Publick Occurrences,* it had the full support of the governor and at one point was even subsidized by the state. During the next fifty years, some thirty other newspapers appeared in the larger American towns.

Although many of the first settlers supported education (establishing Harvard College in 1638, and at least a dozen other colleges before 1776), the majority of the population in pre-Revolutionary America was more concerned with farming or running small shops. Fewer than 200,000 of the colonies' 3 million people could read—hardly constituting the masses necessary for true mass media.[2] Still, the primary focus of media was political, economic, and literary, because that was what the small, sophisticated audience expected.

Early newspapers catered to literate, sophisticated audiences.

An illuminating study by William Ames and Dwight Teeter found that while small circulation newspapers in pre-Revolutionary days may have had high pass-on readership (or listenership, because many of the illiterates who gathered at coffeehouses and inns had newspapers read aloud to them), the primary subscribers were a kind of "Who's Who" of Colonial America.

In mid-1775 William Bradford's *Pennsylvania Journal* had only 220 subscribers in Philadelphia, the largest city on the North American continent, with a population of 35,000 residents. Those subscribers were the

rich and powerful leaders of the city; they were the heads of the political factions and, on the whole, were closely tied by business and religious connections, and sometimes by family bonds. In Philadelphia and in outlying areas, the *Journal*'s readers were important political leaders, or important *information disseminators,* such as postmasters, tavern keepers, or newspaper publishers who tended to reprint significant news and opinions in their own local newspapers.[3]

By the time of the American Revolution, an unencumbered press actively participated in the dissemination of information and opinion. One might easily conclude that the press had always been able to print at will, but such was not the case. For more than 200 years the governments of England and later the colonies had imposed restrictions on the press, and much of the early history of newspapers involved a struggle for the freedom to print.

Control and Press Freedoms

From earliest times, authoritarian leaders have seen all too clearly the threat that the mass production of ideas imposes on established order, and most authoritarian leaders, at one time or another, have undertaken steps to control such threat. In the 1530s, the English monarch Henry VIII, recognizing the danger posed by the new medium of print, began requiring printers to be licensed. Only those individuals fortunate enough to obtain a license were allowed to print, and they retained the license only with the continued approval of the king. Needless to say, few printers were willing to challenge the crown by publishing material offensive to Henry. Because the strategy of licensing effectively prevented dangerous ideas from being printed, it came to be known as *prior restraint*. The practice continued in England in one form or another for the next 300 years.

Freedom of the press is a relatively recent notion.

English monarchs who followed Henry devised other means to control the press. Elizabeth I made use of the Star Chamber, a governmental body willing and able to punish severely those printers who offended the state. Selectively enforced taxation, another favored method, could put a printer out of business. And laws against seditious libel (criticism of the state) intimidated many printers.

The sixteenth and seventeenth centuries were years of restriction for printers in England. The medium that promised enrichment and promoted literacy was made to serve the interests of the state. No dissent would be tolerated, but on occasion there could be heard a voice arguing for change. In the late seventeenth and early eighteenth centuries those voices became louder and more insistent.

Press freedoms came slowly and were granted grudgingly. English poet John Milton, among others, spoke out for freedom of the press when he wrote *Areopagitica* in 1644, an impassioned appeal for the government to trust the people to be able to discern the truth. His eloquence had little immediate impact; press restrictions continued in England. But support for licensing of printers was eroding, and by the end of the century, the statute had been abolished.

In the colonies the practice of licensing continued until the 1720s when James Franklin, the older brother of Benjamin Franklin, started the *New England Courant*.

Franklin defied the Massachusetts Bay Colony by publishing his paper without a license. Trouble arose when he began printing articles that criticized both the colonial government and the established church. He angered the two dominant institutions in the colony, prompting a jail sentence on contempt charges. After his release, Franklin resumed his activities to the chagrin of the government, which promptly forbade him from ever again printing the *Courant* without a license. Franklin's continued efforts eventually resulted in the grand jury refusing to endorse the charges of the government. Although the law proscribing unlicensed printers remained, it was no longer enforced.

James Franklin's heroics gave printers freedom from prior restraint, but the colonial goverment still exerted control by using the laws against seditious libel. That block to press freedom began to break down in the case of John Peter Zenger, an immigrant New York printer. Zenger had been hired to publish the *New York Weekly Journal,* a newspaper started by James Alexander and other opponents of the incoming colonial governor, William Cosby. When the *Journal* challenged the governor's behavior, which was viewed by many of the local citizenry as greedy, self-serving, and tyrannical, Zenger was arrested for seditious libel.

Franklin and Zenger fought against authoritarian controls.

According to the law, the task of the jury was to determine if the accused had, in fact, printed the offensive document; the judges were to determine if the material was criminally libelous. In the case of Zenger, the judges, appointed by Governor Cosby, were certain to uphold the charge. Imagine the impact on the audience in the courtroom that August day in 1735 when Peter Zenger's counsel, Andrew Hamilton, openly acknowledged that Zenger had printed the issues of the *New York Journal* on which the case was based. Hamilton, almost eighty years of age, was at the twilight of his career. Perhaps he felt he had nothing to lose, because before the attorney general could direct the jury to return a verdict of guilty, Hamilton launched Zenger's defense. He focused on the charge in the indictment that the newspaper contained "false, scandalous, and seditious libel." *False* was the key word, for as Hamilton admitted, if the words had been untruthful then "I'll own to them to be scandalous, seditious and a libel."[4] Hamilton's brilliant oratory, addressed to the jurors, strongly urged them to claim the right to determine if the printer's statements were true or false. When, at last, the jury retired to deliberate, they took less than ten minutes to reach a verdict of acquittal.

In retrospect, the Zenger case is perceived as important more as an indicator of a changing mood of the people than as a guarantor of press freedoms. At the time, the verdict was little noticed outside of New York and it set no legal precedent; seditious libel continued to be against the law. But it did serve notice on the colonial governors that the people were becoming less docile.

Forty years later the colonists rebelled. The press, which had been increasingly outspoken, was highly partisan in its support for the Revolution. The patriots used the press to instigate and sustain the fight. Samuel Adams agitated for rebellion in the *Boston Gazette.* John Dickinson, a supporter of business interests, presented logical arguments denouncing British restrictions on commercial activities. Isaiah Thomas of the *Massachusetts Spy,* James Otis, Thomas Paine, and others took up the cause. For the moment at least, freedom of the press was a fact used in the fight to secure other freedoms.

Within five years after the Revolutionary War, the Constitution was
ratified. Three years later, in 1791, the Bill of Rights was approved. The
First Amendment to the Constitution and the first of the Bill of Rights
states in part, "Congress shall make no law . . . abridging the freedom
of speech or of the press. . . ."

The statement is clear and direct, but as we will see in chapter 12, it
is not absolute. Regulations exist for all the mass media, including the press.
Many of the restrictions have been enacted by Congress and other governmental bodies; others are a result of controls imposed by the media themselves. The abundance of regulations notwithstanding, few would argue with
the assertion that the press in the United States is among the freest in all
the world.

The American Press

America's first regularly published newspaper, the *Boston News-Letter,*
came in 1704, published by the postmaster, John Campbell. The first daily
papers came eighty years later in America. The history of newspapers on
American shores can be split into eight eras of varying lengths, each making its own contribution to the press. They are: (1) the colonial press; (2) the
Revolutionary press; (3) the political press; (4) the penny press; (5) the
personal editors; (6) yellow journalism; (7) jazz journalism; and (8) the
present age of consolidation. The first three periods occurred prior to 1833.
From then until the early twentieth century we experienced the penny press,
the era of personal editors, and the flamboyance of yellow journalism. Since
1920 we have seen the last two periods.

Before 1833

During the 130 years from the establishment of the *Boston News-
Letter* in 1704 until the 1830s the press had limited circulation and tended
to be written for the educated, if not the elite. Opinion and viewpoints were
prevalent in published articles, especially after the 1740s when disenchantment with British rule began to spread.

The colonial press wasn't very impressive by present standards, but
it served a need. From the rumor mills of the coffeehouses and taverns that
had provided the original communications network in the colonies, the colonial press became established as a machine for institutionalizing gossip,
a role that the newspaper still maintains. Its publishers were often under-
educated printers. They dealt in rumor and in shipping news that was crucial to the mercantile concerns of the seaboard colonies.

Gradually, under pressures brought on by the rising mercantile class,
specialization took effect, and by the Revolution, more educated and ideological editors were in charge. The Revolutionary press established a role
of advocacy and reflected the political stirrings of a restless country. Thomas
Paine's *Crisis Papers* and later Alexander Hamilton's *Federalist Papers*
reflected the heavy doses of persuasion, propaganda, and public relations
that from time to time have been important adjuncts to the press. Paine
was an immigrant Englishman who arrived in Philadelphia two years be-

fore the colonies declared their independence. During the bitter winter of 1776–1777, he published a series of pamphlets entitled *The American Crisis,* designed to stiffen the resolve of the rebellious colonists. Ten years later the *Federalist Papers* were published. They consisted of a series of eighty-five essays written by Alexander Hamilton, James Madison, and John Jay, and they appeared in newspapers in 1787 and 1788 in support of the Constitution, which was then being ratified by the individual states.

After independence, the press quite naturally evolved into its role as political advocate. The successful part that the press had played in keeping the fires of revolution fanned led to extreme factionalism as it divided itself in vociferous support of the two warring political parties—the Federalists and the Anti-Federalists, or Republicans. Not only did the press support political parties, but political parties supported the press. The political press lasted until well into the nineteenth century, with subsidies paid newspapers by political factions to act as their mouthpieces. Since this was also an era of expansion, new publishers moving westward tended to take their political allegiances with them. Many were appointed postmasters, a kind of sinecure or political plum that permitted them to use the franking privilege and so distribute their papers through the mails at no cost. The official position further gave them unique access to news and gossip. From this era stemmed the American press's traditional political interest.

Throughout these colonial, revolutionary, and political press periods, the newspaper suffered from the same technological, geographic, and transportation barriers that hindered all communications at the time. From the dawn of mass communications until well into the nineteenth century, messages traveled no faster than people or horses could run, pigeons could fly, or boats could sail. There were a few exceptions—semaphors (*signaling with flags*), smoke signals, drums, or horns—but substantive messages entrusted to print media were limited by the terrain, weather, and durability of animals.

Carrier pigeons, used extensively in the early nineteenth century, could travel sixty miles an hour in good weather, and each pigeon could learn one basic route, not exceeding 200 miles. Horses, the standard message bearers until the end of the nineteenth century, could average fifteen miles per hour on short runs. The much-heralded Pony Express of the mid-nineteenth century, for example, required 190 stations, 500 horses, and 80 riders to average five miles per hour from Missouri to California.

The difficulties of travel had particular impact on communications in America, where continental distances are great. Geography has shaped the social structure of America and has played a significant role in the development of the mass media. The hardships of wilderness life, the settling and subduing of a vast continent whose boundaries were unknown at the outset, left little time for recreational reading. Pragmatic settlers and villagers of the young nation sought information they could use as tools, much as they used other tools in coping with their geographic and technological limitations.

Technological, geographic, and transportation barriers impeded the press prior to the 1830s.

Early American settlements were isolated, with few interconnections and only a tenuous sea link to the Old World. Transportation systems grew slowly. This factor placed a premium on self-reliance, which complemented the independent spirit of the settlers. Circumstances, as well as temperament, fostered devotion to the concept of local autonomy, which became one of the guiding principles of the growing nation. Home rule, states' rights, parochial education, and the local emphasis of the press were to be manifestations of this focus.

Through the late eighteenth century printing technology changed as slowly as did the methods of transportation. Printers of the fifteenth century would have been comfortable using the presses of America in the early years of the Republic, for the equipment was almost the same. It still took an experienced printer nearly an hour to produce 200 copies of a single page. The pages, made of parchment or rags, had to be hung up to dry, for the ink was still somewhat primitive and paper had to be wetted in a trough to take a good impression. After handsetting each individual letter for the opposite side of each page, the printer cranked down on the sturdy handpress, at the rate of 200 impressions per hour. Each impression, or "token," required thirteen distinct operations.

Many colonial printers were true craftsmen, despite their crude equipment. But 1800 spelled the beginning of the end of individual printers' intense involvement with their newspapers' entire production, and in many

Colonial and pioneer printers operated presses that had changed little in 300 years.
The Bettman Archives, Inc.

ways the beginning of the end of craftsmanship. The first year of the nineteenth century was the year Eli Whitney began mass producing muskets for the U.S. Army, introducing the concept of interchangeable parts, which encouraged other industries to innovate.

Technological developments during the century helped the press emerge as a mass medium. From 1811 to 1813, Saxon journeyman printer Frederick Koenig applied steam power and developed a printing press with an impression cylinder, relegating to museums the converted wine presses that had been the staple of the industry for centuries. The cylinder process was improved, and by 1830 the New York firm of R. Hoe and Company produced a flat bed and cylinder press that, within two years of its invention, was capable of printing 4,000 impressions an hour—compared with the 200 an hour of a few years past. Other improvements in printing presses followed, and by the end of the century presses were capable of printing 72,000 thirty-two-page newspapers in an hour.

All the speed in the world wouldn't have resulted in faster production of print media if there were no paper to feed the presses. Due to the limited supply of linen and cotton rags and parchment made from animal skins, substitutes had to be found. In 1799, N. L. Robert patented a paper-making machine (the Fourdrinier) utilizing principles still central to paper production. In the 1840s (at a time when northern printing presses felt the threat of southern curtailment of cotton) technology was developed whereby wood pulp could be made into paper, and within two decades paper making was big business.

1833–1920

As we learned earlier in this chapter, the newspapers and journals of the eighteenth century had not been distributed in mass numbers. Geography and the limitations of technology had something to do with it. Literacy, or lack of it, also had an effect; people who could not read bought few newspapers. Another deterrent to mass circulation was the content of newspapers, which tended to stress opinion, shipping news, and literature.

When Benjamin Day started his penny press, the *New York Sun,* on 3 September 1833, the first true mass circulation newspaper was born. The cost per unit for newspapers had decreased with improved technology, and growing literacy and urbanization meant that primary circulation impediments—illiteracy, geography, and technology—had been overcome. The price of one penny was achieved because Day had shifted the costs of producing the paper to advertisers. This reasonable price contrasted with the five or six cents a copy for other papers and appealed to the public, which quickly made the *Sun* the most successful newspaper in the country.

Other papers copied Day's model. Like the *Sun,* they included the use of sensational stories about crime, violence, and mayhem, and their circulation also improved. This must have been an exciting time to be in the newspaper business. Almost overnight the form and format of newspapers began to change. In 1835 James Gordon Bennett established the

The penny press arrives: Ben Day's *Sun* ushers in the lively, mass-circulation newspaper.

New York Herald, challenging the *Sun* with a combination of lively stories and news about the affairs of government and the financial community. Like Day, Bennett emphasized the reporting of events rather than the analysis of ideas. He reached beyond the local community for news, setting up couriers to speed the news from distant points. When the telegraph proved viable, Bennett and other editors promptly tied into the system, all for the purpose of getting more news to the public as quickly as possible to sell more papers and, not coincidentally, to attract more advertisers whose contributions kept the price per unit within the ordinary citizen's pocketbook.

Bennett, Greeley, and Raymond ("personal editors") advance journalism.

Bennett, the first of the great personal editors, was followed by Horace Greeley (*New York Tribune,* 1841) and Henry J. Raymond (*New York Times,* 1851). These men established some of the basic tenets of journalism as a discipline. They improved upon the strategy of emphasizing stories about events and in the process created reporters who sought out news. In their newspapers they provided the first evidence of social concern. They established the newspaper in its role as public watchdog; in keeping a constant check on government, they brought about the adversary relationship between the press and government that has continued until today. They created new techniques for improving circulation, including the use of newspaper crusades—campaigns to comfort the afflicted (appealing for social welfare, reforms in big business, and changes in many other institutions) and campaigns to afflict the comfortable (exposing corruption and venality wherever they could find it). They opted for specialized coverage of finance, religion, society, and the arts, thus beginning the departmentalization of newspapers that is known today. And most significantly, they discovered the potential of advertising. Each contributed to a golden age for newspapers, an era in which it all came together for the ink-stained journalists.

It was during this period, too, that newspapers seriously began to expand their coverage beyond the purely local and topical. Raymond, for example, organized relays of couriers stretching north to Newfoundland to meet incoming vessels from Europe so that his *New York Times* would be first with international news. He visited Europe to hire what were the first foreign correspondents to sniff out significant information exclusively for the *Times.* He personally accompanied presidential candidates on their campaign tours to give the *Times* firsthand political dispatches. His competitors soon followed suit, and news gathering became a specialized and, incidentally, an increasingly expensive function.

Samuel Morse's telegraph was prophetic in its first message—"What hath God wrought . . ."—as it ushered in the electric age and the communications revolution in 1844, connecting Baltimore and Washington. Newspapers adopted the telegraph immediately, and it brought about significant changes in them. With its many short, concise messages (longer messages were expensive, and correspondents feared mechanical failure and therefore wrote tighter stories, jamming the most important facts in the opening paragraphs) and its speed, the telegraph began to strengthen the connections between American cities and towns. Where the railroads went, there went the telegraph lines, and newspapers quickly followed, spreading into the outlying regions. From 1845 to 1856 in Illinois alone, some thirty daily newspapers sprang up with the appearance of the telegraph.[5]

By 1866 Cyrus Field had completed laying the transatlantic telegraph cable, bringing daily news from Europe; and ten years later Alexander Graham Bell invented the telephone, which greatly facilitated the gathering and dispatching of news. The diffusion of telephones was rapid. There were 54,000 telephones in 1880 and more than 7.5 million in 1910.

In 1848 the New York newspapers banded together to form the Associated Press, the first of the wire services, making it economical to gather news in Boston and other cities tied to New York by the newly invented telegraph. As a result, the *inverted pyramid form of reporting* developed. This form of reporting stated the basic information in the opening paragraph, and the following paragraphs elaborated basic data in decreasing order of significance. It was a drastic change from the long-winded expository style previously used to convey news, but a logical change when realizing that the telegraph was neither inexpensive nor fully reliable. When filing stories written in the inverted pyramid form, correspondents (Civil War correspondents in particular) could at least be assured that the most important points would be communicated before the wires were cut or usurped for more essential military or governmental purposes.

The telegraph prompted one other major change in journalism. Because the stories generated by the Associated Press were wired to newspapers who supported widely differing views, wire-service reporting became more objective and less biased toward one viewpoint or another.

The era of the personal editors, which lasted from about 1840 until 1870, was a bridge between the old press and the new. The personal editors who elaborated upon the principle of popular appeal also began a methodical organization of the press into a major social institution. Interlocking demands of expensive technology, advertising support, and popular appeal created a cause-and-effect relationship that characterized mass media from that time on. The press found it necessary to develop maximum circulation through sensational treatment of news events to attract advertisers who provided them revenue to competitively offer more popular appeal.

Inevitably, this process, which involved technological, sociological, and commercial factors, led to circulation wars in which the major newspaper publishers sometimes engaged in ruinous competition for audiences. The goal was to capture the growing volume of national advertising from businesses and industries prepared to sell material and services on a regional or national scale. This was the age of the great newspaper empires of Joseph Pulitzer, William Randolph Hearst, and Edward W. Scripps, who each owned several newspapers across the continent. Both Scripps and Hearst formed their own wire services—United Press (UP) in 1907 and International News Service (INS) in 1909—to consolidate this control. The great

westward push following the Civil War opened new territory and new population centers; a growing urbanization was born of the Industrial Revolution; and an influx of foreign immigrants further concentrated populations in the cities where the newspapers could reach them. The telegraph also assisted in dispensing national advertising, which was attracted by the population concentrations and by the press empires to serve many different geographical areas.

Pulitzer had moved from the *St. Louis Post-Dispatch* in 1883 to take over the ailing *New York World.* Within four short years he increased the circulation to an astonishing 250,000 a day. Hearst, Pulitzer's arch competitor, came to New York from the West Coast where he had been the editor of his father's *San Francisco Examiner.* During Hearst's years at the *Examiner* he had increased its circulation by applying the principles of sensationalism devised by the penny press fifty years earlier. In 1895 he bought the *New York Journal,* ready to take on Pulitzer and the *World.*

In his drive to add to the circulation of the *Journal,* Hearst hired a number of Pulitzer's best people, and Pulitzer, in turn, hired people away from Hearst. One of Hearst's catches was the artist who had created the cartoon strip called "The Yellow Kid," which featured a simplistic, folksy philosopher in a yellow nightshirt. The Kid became associated with the times and gave rise to the label *yellow journalism,* depicting the excessive sensationalism of that era.

This was flamboyant journalism in its most extreme form; an uninhibited time when editors invented incidents and headlines to go with them, and facts played a relatively small role in journalism. Indeed, Hearst was even accused of having started the Spanish-American War as a circulation device. It wasn't true; even Hearst wouldn't go that far. But inflammatory headlines proclaiming the sinking of the Maine to be the work of an enemy and an offer of $50,000 reward "for the detection of the perpetrator of the Maine outrage" could hardly be described as having a calming influence on the people who read the *Journal*.

The efforts of Hearst and Pulitzer paid off handsomely as circulation at both the *Journal* and the *World* increased to over 400,000 a day, making newspapers big business in a society that was becoming accustomed to big business. Remember that this was the age of industrial giants in steel, oil, and railroads, who made things happen just by flexing their muscles. The major publishers were simply the newspaper counterparts to those massive machines.

Advertising had become so significantly a part of the newspaper in this era that some realistic measure of circulation was required for the protection of both newspapers and advertisers. Advertisers in New York, buying space in dozens of newspapers across the country, had to be sure they were getting the paid circulation they thought they were buying. Paid circulation is a valid measure of a newspaper's readership. It demonstrates community interest in that the community is willing to purchase the news product. The Audit Bureau of Circulations (ABC) was founded in 1914 to give advertisers certified circulation figures for the nation's newspapers. The existence of this outside audit, in turn, led to numerous circulation devices—contests, prizes, and discount sales—all of which were sponsored by the newspaper and were contingent upon buying or subscribing to the newspaper.

The 1890s and early 1900s also saw an explosion of feature and nonnews content in the newspapers. Comic strips and advice to the lovelorn, games and puzzles, and features and columnists made their entrance. Basically, yellow journalism was an appeal to the semi-educated urban populations swelled by foreign immigration who demanded a substantial measure of entertainment in their press.

A relatively high ratio of nonnews had been a part of newspapers for some time. Throughout the nineteenth century nearly a third of the content of major newspapers had been devoted to literary fare: Nathaniel Hawthorne, James Fenimore Cooper, Mark Twain, and the like. In the 1880s the Bok and McClure syndicates furnished syndicated literary material to the press. But the period of yellow journalism redirected the material of appeal to the common citizen, and the comics, preprinted features, and popular columnists replaced serious authors as feature entries.

Yellow journalism emerges from the Pulitzer, Hearst, and Scripps newspaper empires.

Gradually, readers reacted negatively to the press's excesses as they did to other flagrancies in society. By 1910 a notable decline in yellow journalism was evident. Even Joseph Pulitzer had come to shun sensationalism in favor of more serious and socially responsible coverage of national and international events. Taking a cue from the increasingly popular *New York Times,* with its accurate, documentary, and clean news for an increasingly literate readership, Pulitzer's *World* began to follow suit. Some readers, it seemed, were growing tired of the emphasis on crime, sex, and faked stories.

Muckrakers react to institutional excesses.

In a wave of social reform, the times were characterized by crusading writers—the *muckrakers,* who focused their pens and typewriters upon major problems caused by rapid industrialization and urbanization. Investigations of business, political, and social ills were conducted with regularity. Although the majority of muckraking efforts were undertaken by magazine journalists, as we will discuss in chapter 3, the metropolitan daily newspaper devoted column after column to fulfilling its important watchdog function. Like their counterparts of the 1960s and today, the muckrakers sought to interpret important new trends in society and effect change by arousing public opinion. One muckraker, Upton Sinclair, attacked the newspaper industry in a book he published privately entitled *The Brass Check.*

It is also interesting to note that it was during this period that the P.M. or afternoon paper made its appearance. Some say it was a direct result of the electric light; electricity extended the day and made it feasible to read an evening newspaper in the twilight hours. Perhaps more important, afternoon newspapers were better able to keep up with a day's activities that included news from Europe distributed by the newly-formed wire services, while new press technology permitted more rapid dissemination of spot or breaking news. Rapidly, P.M. papers captured a substantial portion of the market, and many of the newspaper barons rushed after the afternoon circulation, often issuing both A.M. and P.M. newspapers within the same city.

Since 1920

The last two eras of press history, jazz journalism and the age of consolidation, bring us to the present. The early years of this century saw a more temperate press, epitomized by the resurrection of the *New York Times* by Adolph Ochs starting in 1896. Ochs set out to produce the "newspaper of record" and for many readers he succeeded in achieving his goal of providing the most complete and accurate coverage of local, national, and international news.

Jazz journalism reflects the Roaring 20s.

Although the *Times* became a powerful voice, Ochs did not speak for everyone. During the roaring 20s and into the depression of the 1930s, jazz journalism emerged, representing the renewed appeal of sensationalism. The *New York Daily News* was founded in 1919. Utilizing the smaller tabloid format (providing easier handling by subway riders) and extensive use of photographs, the *Daily News* quickly grew to be the newspaper with the largest circulation in America. Its audience was the working class and others in New York who were looking for excitement and entertainment in a newspaper rather than an in-depth analysis of current events.

These were the glamour years of journalism, with *Front Page* and a rash of other movies about the newspaper business during the 1930s that stereotyped the reporter as a tough, hard-drinking, fearless, sentimental man (seldom a woman), who spoke with a cigarette hanging from the corner of his mouth and never took off his hat with the press pass in it—a man who solved crimes, cleaned up city hall, and defeated dishonest politicians single-handedly, all in time to meet the everpresent deadline. This was a glorious age for reporters, arriving just before network radio began to usurp the market for both advertisers and audience.

The Great Depression of the 1930s took its toll of marginally profitable newspapers, as it did of other businesses. Newspapers also found it difficult to adapt to the threats posed by radio, which had come into its own as a form of cheap mass entertainment as well as a viable news medium. Given its ability to bring instantaneous news to America, radio did much to eliminate the "Extra" editions of newspapers, which until the 1930s were issued whenever major news stories broke. It was only later that newspapers and radio reached a separate peace, each doing what it was physically suited to do: Radio provided the up-to-date headline news, and newspapers gave the longer background stories.

Newspapers cope with threats posed by radio and television.

Bette Davis in *Front Page Woman*, one of many films of journalism's swashbuckling, sensationalistic times. The Bettman Archives, Inc.

World War II forced the nation's press into a more responsible role than it had during its jazz days. Newspapers were joined by radio in bringing America the sounds and feelings of global conflict. Some 200 U.S. correspondents were abroad in 1941, before Pearl Harbor. By the end of the war their ranks had been swelled to more than 1,600 accredited journalists. Perhaps the most famous were Scripps-Howard's Ernie Pyle and cartoonist Bill Mauldin.

The years following World War II saw newspapers having to adjust to the newest information, entertainment, and advertising medium: television. By the early 1950s newspapers feared television as they had feared radio before it. In part, their fears were legitimate: TV was a far more attractive medium. So paranoid was the press about television that in this period many newspapers refused to mention television in their columns or even publish a television log. This was a far cry from today's pattern of special television editors on major metropolitan newspapers and the publishing of elaborate magazine-type television supplements in the Sunday papers to rival the *TV Guide*.

In a sense television helped the printed press, just as radio had done a generation earlier. Because television could report the highlights of major events more quickly and graphically, newspapers were able to expand their interpretative content and provide a rational framework for understanding those events. Television's treatment of the news, typically incomplete fragments, stimulated the public appetite for more. In a familiar pattern, the electronic audience returned to print for explanation and elaboration.

Another change prompted by television was a move by newspapers to include more feature material, which national television has not learned to handle: food and fashion, travel, criticism, recreation and leisure, youth, and so on. Today, many newspapers rival magazines in the range and variety of coverage. In fact, many of the Sunday supplements to newspapers are weekly magazines, aimed at the same audiences as magazines and fully competitive with them.

Not all newspapers have thrived, of course. Those appealing to the lowest common denominator suffered the greatest circulation losses, which prompted many to go out of business. Generally, the more reflective newspapers have survived the competition from television, but even they have had to adjust. One of the most frequent forms of adjustment has been the consolidation of newspapers into chains. The costs of big business have forced this change and will be the subject discussed next.

The Structure of Contemporary Newspapers

At one time the local newspaper was a family-run operation. Many of them still are, of course, but more and more newspapers are now owned by chains and conglomerates. In this section we will look at the ownership patterns of American newspapers and then explore the operations of papers, including the roles of the reporter and other news people.

In the late 1960s, press critic Ben Bagdikian wryly commented that the newspaper business is a great, clanking industry that buys paper at seven cents a pound and sells it at thirty-six.[6] He was speaking at a time when newsprint sold for $143 a ton and the typical newspaper sold for 9.5 cents a copy on weekdays and 18.1 cents on Sundays.

A dozen years later, publishers were paying far higher wages to writers and printers utilizing incredibly more expensive equipment to implant ever more costly ink on a lighter weight newsprint that cost more than $500 a ton. The product was an average 60-page daily costing 22 cents and a 210-page Sunday edition costing 47 cents that reached a smaller proportion of the reading public. The newspaper business remained a great, clanking industry; with a workforce of 432,000, it ranked first in the government's listing of the nation's largest manufacturing employers.[7]

As newspaper production costs have skyrocketed, economic pressures have forced all newspapers to change. The most noticeable trend has been toward consolidation and group ownership. Consolidation finds separate newspapers signing *joint operating agreements,* typically sharing printing plants and sometimes sharing advertising departments and even editorial offices. More common is the movement toward *groups* or *chains,* in which two or more newspapers in different markets have common ownership.

Daily newspapers are published in 1,559 different American cities, but only about one out of twelve of those cities has two or more dailies. What's more, in the overwhelming majority of cases, the same firm owns or controls the operations of both papers, meaning that only a very small percentage of locales (perhaps 2.5 percent) are served by separate daily newspaper voices. Head-to-head competition is practically a thing of the past, as is separate ownership of morning and afternoon dailies.

The current picture, so drastically different from those earlier phases of newspaper history during which a few dollars and a small printing press meant one could become a publisher, is a reflection of economic reality. Communities today don't have competing newspapers, because the community and its individual entrepreneurs can't afford them. The *Cleveland Plain Dealer* was sold for $53.4 million in 1967 to Newhouse Newspapers. The same chain later paid $305 million for a relatively small chain of eight Michigan newspapers and *Parade* magazine. That represents $592.88 per reader for the Michigan papers, a price no individual capitalist could readily dig up. Just twenty-five years ago, the general formula used to place a value on a newspaper enterprise was established by multiplying its circulation by $100. Today, it is at least $500 and moving toward $1,000. Gannett's recent purchase of a 9,000-circulation daily in western Pennsylvania for $10 million is dramatic proof of the rising costs of newspapers.

Ownership and Consolidation

Increased operating costs help explain the move toward consolidation.

Individual, family-owned newspapers are becoming a dying breed for several reasons. Despite the expense of operation, they still tend to show a decent return on their investment, and are therefore attractive to chains whose larger capital base can better afford to update the plants and maintain operating standards. In addition, current tax laws encourage chains and conglomerates to reinvest pretax profits into the purchase of new papers. Because of the competition for their purchase, they have become increasingly expensive, and only chains and conglomerates can afford that escalated price. Some owners are happy to sell out while remaining aboard as local publishers, still reflecting the community, but now with certain inherent management economies and securities. The newspaper gets the benefit of group administrative expertise and the advantage of some centralized functions, such as bulk newsprint purchase. Also, a more appealing package can be made available to national advertisers; syndicates, columns, and features are more or less standardized where appropriate.

Sometimes this arrangement appears to work without disturbing the local orientation of individual newspapers. Some can continue to provide the same kind of service both to their communities and their local advertisers. But if chains are interested primarily in profits and not editorial content, there may be more disadvantages than advantages to the move. Lord Roy Thomson, who owned seventy-seven American papers as part of his international empire, bought newspapers to make the money to buy more newspapers in order to make more money. To him, the editorial content served only to separate the ads. This same philosophy is found in concerns dealing with oil, automobiles, shoes, and deodorants. But in the case of newspapers, we are talking about the only institution specifically singled out by the Constitution, one that day in and day out helps shape and reflect the national consciousness. Little wonder, then, that media observers are concerned.

At the turn of the century, there were only eight chains in the United States. They controlled twenty-seven daily newspapers, which accounted for 10 percent of the nation's circulation. The average chain, frequently a family concern that developed as children acquired newspapers in towns adjacent to the family stronghold, owned 3.4 newspapers. However, by 1982, 155 chains controlled some two-thirds of the nation's daily newspapers—a fact that cannot go unnoticed—and only 52 U.S. cities had two or more separately owned, competing newspapers.[8] (See table 2.1.)

The case for decreased newspaper competition can be argued both ways. The absence of competition removes a balance of viewpoints, but actually the diversity of other media compensates. It also removes pressure for timeliness, the scoop, and in theory allows for more in-depth reflection. A single newspaper is generally healthier financially, more stable, and less prone to either advertiser or political pressure. Nevertheless, although there are advantages to reduced competition, the tendency is always to view this situation with alarm.

Print Media

Table 2.1 America's largest newspaper chains, as of March 1982

Company	Daily circulation	Number of dailies	Sunday circulation	Number of Sunday editions
1. Gannett Co. Inc.	3,621,800	85	3,523,800	55
2. Knight-Ridder Newspapers Inc.	3,458,400	33	4,049,200	21
3. Newhouse Newspapers	3,133,500	29	3,768,100	21
4. Tribune Co.	2,806,600	8	3,552,800	6
5. Dow Jones & Co., Inc.	2,433,400	21	346,000	9
6. Times Mirror Co.	2,315,500	8	2,867,600	8
7. Scripps-Howard Newspapers	1,518,800	16	1,559,300	7
8. Hearst Newspapers	1,362,300	15	2,098,200	9
9. Thomson Newspapers Inc. (U.S.)	1,219,600	77	713,500	34
10. Cox Enterprises Inc.	1,165,100	18	1,245,600	13
11. The New York Times Co.	1,137,000	12	1,677,700	7
12. Cowles Newspapers	953,900	10	1,141,600	7
13. News America Publishing Inc.	917,600	3	187,479	1
14. Capital Cities Communications Inc.	900,500	7	774,100	4
15. Freedom Newspapers Inc.	798,400	31	740,000	20
16. Central Newspapers Inc.	774,600	7	792,174	4
17. The Washington Post Co.	696,200	2	926,700	2
18. Evening News Association	678,900	5	823,500	1
19. The Copley Press Inc.	635,000	9	626,000	6
20. Harte-Hanks Communications Inc.	584,200	28	582,300	21

Source: Morton Research, Lynch, Jones & Ryan, from "Facts About Newspapers '82" American Newspaper Publishers Association.

Much has been made of the decline in the number of newspapers, but as in most things statistical, figures can sometimes be misleading. Metropolitan newspapers have declined both in number and in overall circulation over the past couple of decades. However, this loss has been more than compensated by the growth of community or peripheral dailies, reflecting the overall social movement away from the central cities to suburbia. Let us not forget, however, that overall newspaper circulation, which has hovered between 60 and 62 million per day since 1965, has not kept pace with population growth. This means, of course, a net decline in readership and the effect of this medium.

To put the situation in perspective, these figures may merely reflect the addition of other media—radio, television, and the proliferation of magazines—wherein all are simply achieving their respective shares of the changing market in a competitive situation. The addition of a still newer medium will undoubtedly dilute the total media market even further.

Newspaper Operations

The circularity of a newspaper's basic operation has already been noted: how it must attract readers as an inducement for the advertisers who pay the bills. The organizational structure of a major metropolitan newspaper reflects this by being divided into five major divisions: (1) editorial—to produce the copy and handle the news; (2) advertising—to solicit and coordinate the basic revenue-producing activities; (3) production—to physically

Metropolitan papers have five divisions: editorial, advertising, production, circulation, and administration.

print the newspaper, converting copy into editions; (4) circulation—to sell and distribute the finished product; and (5) administration (purchasing, promotion, accounting, and the like)—to coordinate the activities of the other four.

A newspaper's deadlines for various editions are functions of several departments, but ultimately they depend upon circulation schedules, based upon the farthest home on the farthest route of the newspaper's distribution area. To meet those delivery schedules, production or printing schedules must be strictly followed. This places a burden on the editorial department to meet its news deadlines—the last second that new copy can be accepted. But the editorial department cannot begin filling its *news hole* (all the space devoted to non-advertising matter) until the advertising department has determined the number of ads sold and therefore the size of the paper to be printed on any one day.

At the top of the ladder in a major metropolitan newspaper is the publisher, who has overall control. Answering directly to the publisher are generally two people: a general manager in charge of administration, circulation, advertising, and production, and an editor in command of the paper's editorial content, who considers the significance of news.

Answering to the business manager are persons such as the comptroller, purchasing agent, advertising director, circulation director, production manager, promotion director, and industrial-relations manager, who is in charge of highly specialized negotiations with a half-dozen trade unions.

The news hole is determined by the advertising department.

All newspaper deadlines are determined by the ultimate deadline: When are the papers ready to be purchased and read?
Ken Robert Buck / The Picture Cube

Under the editor is the managing editor, who is responsible for the day-to-day content of the newspaper. Under the managing editor are principally the city editor, charged with local news; and the wire editor or news editor, who is charged with other-than-local news—the regional, national, and international stories that come in from correspondents and the wire services. The photo editor runs a staff of local photographers and screens wire photos for suitability. The copy editor checks raw copy for accuracy and style, writes headlines, and sets approved stories into a *page dummy* provided by the advertising department on which the advertisements for the day have already been indicated.

The major departments outside the city room are more or less autonomous. Sports, society, business and financial, and entertainment sections often have their own editors and staffs and are generally allocated a certain number of pages daily to be filled with their specialties. The Sunday department has charge of special Sunday sections (real estate, travel, television, home and garden, books, opinion, and the like) and generally special editors are employed for these various sections. It is in these special sections that the majority of feature stories occur. The editorial pages have their own staff who answer to the editor or publisher or both.

Within these departments are specialists, sometimes called editors, on such topics as science, medicine, youth, education, religion, environment, military, farming, senior citizens, and politics. Generally, they are not allocated specific space but are required through their expertise to keep up with the developments in their fields and present timely articles.

At the lower level of the hierarchy are the reporters and correspondents who actually unearth and write the news, who have most of the personal, on-the-scene contact. Some are general assignment reporters, delegated to stories at the direction of the city editor. They cover fires, murders, accidents, and Rotary Club luncheons, often taking a photographer with them. Special-assignment people stay on location at city hall; at state, federal, and county beats; at the courthouse; or at police headquarters. They, too, are specialists, assigned to the principal sources of the news, those locales where news is being made.

The News People

There are hundreds of reporters and correspondents and specialists on a metropolitan newspaper; they are supervised by dozens of editors. There are batteries of two or three dozen teletypes spewing out reams of copy daily, and all of this must be condensed by personnel into relatively few pages. In addition, there are scores of features on all conceivable topics, mail and phone calls from bureaus overseas and from Washington, New York, and the state capital. There are stringers and correspondents in outlying communities, and there are scores of press agents advocating their clients' causes in numerous fields.

All of these personnel funnel their output into the newsroom, where a half-dozen or so harassed senior editors sift through it to decide what to print. They are the gatekeepers of a newspaper; on their judgments rest what visions of reality the public shall see—what events, in essence, take place. A rule of thumb is that only about one tenth of the available news gets into print, leaving about 90 percent (an overpowering figure) in the gatekeepers' wastebaskets or on the floor beneath the teletype machines.

Fortunately, because of the variety and pervasity of competing media all along the spectrum, the chances of running into a news item, if it is significant at all, are pretty good. But this does not detract in any way from the responsibility and, in a sense, the power of the gatekeepers or editors or, for that matter, the reporters who write according to their own perceptions and views of the world.

For years reporters were told that the average reader had at best an eighth grade education, and to write accordingly. Naturally, such reporters and editors thought of themselves as members of that amorphous middle class—or even lower middle class—based on journalists' relatively low incomes prior to the 1970s. The popular myth was that journalism was peopled by "everyman" producing a product for "everyman," inherently distrusting both authority and establishment figures.

Investigations of readers and reporters have disproven both stereotypes. Sociologist John Johnstone and his colleagues demonstrated very clearly in the 1970s that American journalists had higher levels of income, education, and social status than the average American citizen. The typical journalists were white, Anglo-Saxon, Protestant (although not highly active churchgoers) males, younger than the majority of the work force, and moderate to liberal in their political beliefs. In short, they were not representative of middle America; instead they were members of the same elite classes over which they thought themselves to be watchdogs and for whom they were unknowingly producing their daily products.[9]

The myth of the journalist as a normal citizen was further shattered in a 1981 study of some 240 journalists and broadcasters working for the most influential media outlets in America. Residing primarily in northern industrial states, 86 percent considered themselves capitalists. This is not surprising considering that nearly half of them earned more than $50,000 a year. Half rejected any religious affiliation; only 8 percent attended church or synagogue weekly and 86 percent seldom or never attended religious services. On political matters, 54 percent considered themselves left of center, while only 19 percent described themselves as being on the right. In presidential elections between 1964 and 1976 no more than 19 percent of those interviewed had ever voted for a Republican candidate. Nine out of ten supported abortion on demand, three-quarters supported gay rights, and nearly all supported sexual expression and the rights of women, environmentalists, consumerists, and journalists. When asked which group would be best suited to direct and remake American society, the media elite tended to choose themselves rather than government or business groups.[10]

Gatekeepers can use only about 10 percent of available material.

The challenge for reporters and editors is to understand that there may be more distance between themselves and their readers than they realize and therefore they must take the necessary steps to become attuned to reader interests. It's never easy. Deciding what is important to readers and monitoring public preferences will continue to be vexing. In their recent book, Dennis and Ismach devote several chapters to the importance of journalists' understanding their own values and recognizing community needs. The authors conclude that journalists should stop thinking they can stay in touch with audiences through some mysterious process of osmosis. Rather, they should systematically utilize personal and recorded sources to track community trends and plan on never-ending professional development to intensify their own sensitivity.[11]

In the final analysis, news people and their newspapers mirror the community far more than they influence it. They must reflect the community in that the newspaper is a measure of public taste. It serves a basic economic purpose. If a paper does not ideologically pattern itself after the general mores of its community, readership will drop; this is the beginning of the end. Other media and other newspapers are anxious to steal readers and the additional revenue they represent, not only in subscriptions but, much more significantly, in added advertising volume and higher advertising rates.

Research reveals that neither journalists nor regular readers are "typical" Americans.

The Nature of News

Definitions of news abound; nowadays it means information that is useful or gratifying to audiences.

Although we have talked about the structure of newspapers and the people who gather the news, we have not described what it is that constitutes news. Perhaps that is because *news* is an elusive term to define. Walter Lippmann noted long ago that "something definite must occur that has unmistakable form" for it to be news. This is what happens at city hall and the courthouse and elsewhere when form and a tangible frame are given to human interactions that permit them to be isolated and written about. These are the events that comprise the news. Thus, while news is certainly the clearest expression of the information function, it is an artificially contrived form of information, leaving much unsaid, unreported, and unprinted.

Lippmann's definition of news reflects a concern with objectivity—the neutral, transmission-belt role of journalists. Dozens of observers have offered their own definitions of news that differ significantly from Lippmann's, some of which take into consideration contemporary thrusts for investigative and interpretive journalism. Typical definitions place value not only on the unusual and abnormal but, more recently, on materials deemed useful or gratifying to audiences. Additionally, cynics suggest that news is whatever editors and reporters (gatekeepers) allow to pass through institutional channels. Lack of consensus over what meets those gatekeepers' criteria may not necessarily be a flaw of the industry. That similar stories frequently appear from paper to paper is probably due to the influence of the wire services, whose daily news budgets suggest which stories "deserve" emphasis. Also, group norms within and among individual newspapers frequently result in the appearance of collective news judgments. But the pattern is more often (or more likely) a case of normal institutional behavior rather than one of conspiracy, as some critics suppose.

Contemporary editors sensitive to their audiences have been influenced strongly by pressures brought on by investigative and interpretative reporters in the past decade or so. In-depth and specialized journalism is not a new phenomenon, as our discussion of newspaper history has indicated. During several periods, the American newspaper stressed interpretation and opinion over straight news. During most of the twentieth century, however, news has become a value in itself. Only recently, during television's reign, has the journalist as interpreter returned to the fold. The return has not come about without a series of battles within and outside the newsroom.

"Purists" have objected to the recent tendency of newspapers to fill their columns with "soft" rather than "hard" news. By traditional definition, hard news is news that justifies its existence on the basis of: (1) immediacy, (2) impact on the greatest number of readers (minor impact on a great number is equated to major impact on a lesser number), (3) physical or psychological proximity to the newspapers' readers, (4) events surrounding prominent personalities, (5) uniqueness (first, last, biggest, smallest, oldest, youngest, etc.), and (6) conflict. Such news coverage relates to tangible events. Soft news (humor, offbeat incidents, personal "life-style," experiences, and so forth), by contrast, may be of interest to people but may lack significance. In the past several years, newspapers have responded to critics' suggestions that news should not be defined strictly in terms of events, but rather in terms of trends or changes in subtle ways of thinking about and dealing with environments. As a result, more and more editors are finding space for soft news stories calculated to help individuals cope with their circumstances.

The Types of Newspapers

There are no set categories for classifying newspapers, but we can easily see that differences between newspapers do exist. The *Los Angeles Times* and the *River Press* in Fort Benton, Montana, differ in more ways than in size. And yet, size is a logical category. So, too, is frequency of publication. For our purposes we will look at big-city newspapers, community newspapers, and the minority press.

Big-City Dailies

Most of our discussions of the development and structure of newspapers have emphasized big-city newspapers and those papers that are, on occasion, in the news. Most of these newspapers still stress local interests, although the definition of *local* varies from community to community as does the population being served. The *New York Times,* for example, has an immediate market of 15 million people living in the states of New York, New Jersey, and Connecticut; and the market for the *Chicago Tribune* stretches from the Wisconsin border to Northwest Indiana.

Most metropolitan daily papers concentrate on the news of their own cities.

Allen H. Neuharth, chairman and president of the Gannett newspaper group (right), and John J. Curley (left), editor-in-chief, look over prototype of *USA Today,* America's first national, satellite-delivered, general-interest newspaper.
United Press International

Table 2.2 America's largest daily newspapers, as of 30 September 1981

Rank	Newspaper	Daily circulation
1.	*The Wall Street Journal*	1,927,963
2.	*New York Daily News*	1,483,333
3.	*Los Angeles Times*	1,011,798
4.	*New York Times*	887,211
5.	*New York Post*	764,387
6.	*Chicago Tribune*	754,043
7.	*Chicago Sun-Times*	649,040
8.	*Washington Post*	635,439
9.	*Detroit News*	625,730
10.	*Detroit Free Press*	622,122
11.	*San Francisco Chronicle*	510,955
12.	*Newsday*	507,350
13.	*Boston Globe*	504,492
14.	*Philadelphia Inquirer*	423,746
15.	*Newark Star-Ledger*	409,278
16.	*Cleveland Plain Dealer*	401,210
17.	*Miami Herald*	399,690
18.	*Philadelphia Bulletin*	397,397 *
19.	*Houston Chronicle*	384,305
20.	*Houston Post*	348,571

Source: *Editor & Publisher,* Audit Bureau of Circulations, ANPA from "Facts About Newspapers '82," American Newspaper Publishers Association.

* Ceased publication 29 January 1982

In order to maintain a local focus, the *Chicago Tribune* publishes eight different suburban inserts several days each week that carry news and advertising for each suburban area. Other metropolitan dailies utilize a similar strategy.

The *New York Times* is a newspaper of national prominence, distributing by mail to any location and shipping to many cities for newsstand sales. But both methods are relatively slow and neither method provides for local advertising. In 1980 the *Times* changed that by inaugurating satellite transmission to Chicago. The paper is then printed locally each day, including local advertising. In 1981 the *Times* added Lakeland, Florida, for distribution in the South. Other cities are sure to follow.

Even the big-city dailies depend on the wire services for much of their national and international news, but their resources allow some to maintain bureaus in other cities, both within the United States and abroad. The larger newspapers (see table 2.2) also have the resources to support investigative teams that may work on an involved story for several months before their efforts appear in print. The daily papers in smaller towns rarely can afford to assign reporters to do investigative work.

Community Newspapers

Community newspapers, generally small nondaily operations serving the provincial interests of isolated communities or discrete suburbs, have assumed unique roles in American media history. A look at their statistics throughout this century tells us much about their place in the media mix.

In 1910, there were 16,227 weekly and 672 semiweekly and triweekly newspapers published in the United States, most of them in small towns. Since that time the number of weeklies has been drastically reduced to some 7,666, or about half the peak figure. The decline has been steady, particularly in rural areas, but appears to have leveled off and perhaps even to have reversed itself slightly since 1970. In the meantime, the number of semiweeklies and triweeklies bottomed out at 300 in 1944, reflecting the wartime economy and the move into the cities. Since then, however, their numbers have more than doubled, nearly reaching the 1910 peak. More often than not, those semiweekly and triweekly papers are published in suburban communities, serving clientele who have many of the same needs for local news and advertising as their parents and grandparents had when they lived on farms or in small towns.

The biggest growth area in newspapers is in suburban or community journalism.

By 1982, total circulation (45 million) and average circulation (5,875) of weekly newspapers reached all-time highs. (These papers are the real gossip sheets, concentrating on local news that is easy to acquire.) Many have printing operations for independent jobs on the side and may be run by husband-and-wife teams. More typical, however, is the utilization of centralized printing plants that turn out perhaps a dozen or more nondailies in the same region. The practice has saved numerous existing weeklies and allowed for the births of many others, papers that otherwise could ill afford purchase and upkeep of printing equipment they would use only a few hours a week. Rather than losing their autonomy, as some feared, the elimination of printing worries has allowed small operators greater amounts of time to devote to other concerns, such as newsgathering, advertising, and distribution.

The rationale for the increase in these smaller community newspapers in the outlying areas is directly related to American affluence. The major metropolitan press provides depth: national and international news, features of all kinds, the comics and entertainment, broad fare. Historical tradition, however, emphasizes the local community; the suburbs are where many people live, where they identify, where they belong. It is the local city councils and civic organizations that most directly touch residents' lives and it is the local school districts that educate their children. Further, it is generally in the regional shopping centers and from the local merchants that community members buy most of their goods. Suburban dwellers need information about their own communities, and local merchants need a vehicle in which to advertise their products and sales. These two needs meet in the community newspaper because the gross national product is large enough to provide sufficient disposable income to support the whole broad spectrum of media.

Community newspapers fill a void left by the major metropolitan dailies. No matter how large and wealthy, metros lack the resources—time, money, and personnel—to adequately cover all the news of each community. There may be dozens of separate communities within their circulation area. They are not necessarily in competition with community newspapers, as each fulfills essentially different roles. Even in their metropolitan editions, major newspapers cannot cover all the news of a dozen city councils and a half-dozen school boards, and the speakers and activities of several hundred civic, women's, veterans', labor, cultural, or charitable organizations. Yet it is these very activities that are meaningful to suburban dwellers.

Similarly, local advertisers cannot afford the advertising rates of the metropolitan newspapers, which are based on overall circulations of several hundred thousand or more. They do not need all that exposure; they need simply to reach the 10 or 20 percent of that number who live in their trading area. The community newspaper provides local merchants an advertising showcase pinpointed toward the community they serve at prices proportionate to exposure.

There has been a trend toward the establishment of minigroups of several suburban newspapers under the same management, attempting to serve several adjacent communities. The major portion of the content of these newspapers is the same, little more than editorial filler to carry advertising. However, as a gesture to locality, they prepare a new front page, filling it with specific information about each separate community. Often they publish under different *flags* (the name bar at the top of the front page) to further the locality illusion. With rare exception, these minichains abdicate their basic responsibility to provide a full quota of local news and gossip and become little more than *shoppers,* advertising throwaways.

Where there are audiences and advertisers, newspapers are bound to appear.

The typical newspaper maintains an average of 40 percent editorial content to 60 percent advertising, which means that if there are 60 pages of advertising sold, the newspaper will have 100 total pages. Since the customer pays only the cost of the newsprint, advertising covers the balance: equipment, salaries, overhead, and profit, for example. By contrast, shoppers or throwaways carry 25 percent or less editorial content (everything other than advertising, which does not necessarily mean news). These newspapers are often supported entirely by advertisers and are distributed free throughout the communities. Almost everyone is happy with the arrangement: Consumers get a free newspaper filled with advertising information and some trivial fluff; advertisers are guaranteed marketplace saturation because of free distribution; and publishers, with less effort than newspapers traditionally demand, profitably serve the consumers and advertisers.

Sometimes shoppers discover that their readers have more in common than spending their money at the same shopping mall, and the shoppers may evolve into "real" newspapers, with a bit of news, a television viewing guide, some wedding announcements, school lunch menus, and words of wisdom from a local philosopher, and *voilà!,* the publisher finds it possible to charge a token subscription price and produces a real newspaper, even though it has a lopsided advertising–news ratio. But it is not all that different from the mercantile press of colonial days, if we stretch our imaginations a bit. As these new newspapers become profitable, they will doubtless undergo the same cycle of economics seen in their larger brethren: small, shoestring operations bought out by chains, which are in turn bought out by larger chains and conglomerates.

Minority Newspapers

The audiences for some newspapers are determined by characteristics other than geographic proximity. Foreign-language newspapers and newspapers published for specific ethnic groups have a history that stems from colonial days. From the mid-nineteenth century until well into the twentieth century (during the years when immigration was highest), newspapers written in German, Polish, Swedish, Yiddish, and other languages were common in the cities where the immigrants settled. As each immigrant group became assimilated, the number of readers dwindled until the audience was no longer large enough to support publication. Some foreign-language papers did survive, of course, especially in close-knit communities such as the Chinese settlements in New York and San Francisco. In recent years the number of Spanish-language papers has increased due to the wave of immigration from Puerto Rico, Mexico, Cuba, and other lands where Spanish is spoken.

Foreign-language and ethnic newspapers have a long, but not always successful, heritage.

Freedom's Journal, the first black newspaper in the United States, was started in New York on 16 March 1827. In the initial issue the editors, Samuel Cornish and John Russwurm, expressed the desire to speak up for their own cause and not rely upon others to do it for them. Slavery still existed in both the North and the South, and even free blacks in the North were being attacked by some newspapers. Said the editors of *Freedom's Journal,* "Too long has the publick been deceived by misrepresentation, in things which concern us dearly, though in the estimation of some mere trifles." The quest for freedom, dignity, and moral improvement filled the pages of the journal during the three years of its existence.

In 1847 Frederick Douglass, the freed son of a slave, founded *The North Star* in Rochester, New York, for the purpose of promoting the abolitionist cause. Douglass was a brilliant orator and a talented writer who used the podium and the pen to argue against slavery, helping to build public sentiment for abolition.

Numerous other black journals appeared prior to the Civil War, most intended for intellectuals, regardless of color. By 1905, when Robert S. Abbott started the *Chicago Defender,* the black community was hungry for a general-interest newspaper. Abbott's plan to include sensational news for a mass audience paid off. The *Defender* was a success, prompting other black newspapers to pursue the general reader.

Several of the black newspapers started at that time are still published today. Among them are the *Afro-American,* a Baltimore paper founded in 1892 by John H. Murphy, Sr.; the *Amsterdam News* in New York started in 1909; and Robert L. Vann's *Pittsburgh Courier,* which began publishing the next year.

The circulation of black newspapers reached an apex during the 1940s and has dropped since then. Only two survive as daily papers, one of which is the *Chicago Defender.* It has a circulation of about 30,000 and is part of a chain that includes the *Pittsburgh Courier* and eight other newspapers.

The Changing Newspaper Business

There are fewer daily newspapers now than at any other period in this century.

Economic and other pressures have caused significant patterns of change in the newspaper industry throughout this century (see table 2.3). Fewer daily newspapers are published today than at the turn of the century; the number at first increased, peaking out at about 2,400 during World War I. Then there was a steady decline until World War II when the total was 1,750, a figure that has held relatively constant since. By the early 1980s, there appeared to be a slight decrease in the totals: a drop to 1,730 total daily papers. However, because thirty newspapers were being published "all-day," in several editions, another way of looking at the figures reveals 1,760 "different" newspapers on the streets of America each day. Even so, the apparent constancy is deceiving. Large metropolitan cities and small cities with less than 25,000 population have suffered losses in the overall number of papers published, while mid-sized cities and metropolitan suburbs have shown contrasting growth.

Table 2.3   Number and circulation of U.S. newspapers, 1950 to 1981

Year	Number of A.M.'s	A.M.'s circulation	Number of P.M.'s	P.M.'s circulation	Total A.M. & P.M.*	Total circulation
1950	322	21,266,126	1,450	32,562,946	1,772	53,829,072
1955	316	22,183,408	1,454	33,963,951	1,760	56,147,359
1960	312	24,028,788	1,459	34,852,958	1,763	58,881,746
1965	320	24,106,776	1,444	36,250,787	1,751	60,357,563
1970	334	25,933,783	1,429	36,173,744	1,748	62,107,527
1975	339	25,490,186	1,436	35,165,245	1,756	60,655,431
1980	387	29,414,036	1,388	32,787,804	1,745	62,201,840
1981†	407	30,541,252	1,353	30,891,182	1,730	61,432,434

Source: *Editor & Publisher,* from "Facts About Newspapers '82," American Newspaper Publishers Association.

*Totals may differ from A.M. and P.M. numbers combined because of some "all-day" publications.
†Preliminary figures

The figures reflect more than a shifting of American population; they reflect changes in newspaper readership patterns. Since 1955, the number of morning newspapers has increased substantially in all but the smallest cities, while the number of evening papers has declined in both major metropolitan areas and smaller cities. Between 1960 and 1981 the number of evening papers decreased by 106, and circulation dropped by nearly 4 million. Over the same period, the number of morning papers increased by 95, and circulation by 6.5 million. The shift from evening to morning publication was due not just to deaths of some P.M.s and births of A.M.s, but to a shift in publication schedule within many American dailies. Between 1979 and 1981 alone, at least 45 existing daily papers rotated their publishing times from an evening to a morning cycle (four times the number during the entire preceding decade). The flurry of conversions, according to the American Newspaper Publishers Association, was motivated by several factors: (1) to provide more timely information (including late-breaking news), final sports reports, and complete stock market tables; (2) to compete more effectively with television and other demands on readers' time; (3) to extend the publications' circulation areas; (4) to avoid traffic congestion during delivery; (5) to provide same-day mail delivery; (6) to save energy by distributing at night and in the mails and by not running printing presses during peak energy usage hours; (7) to provide all-day exposure and same-day response for advertisers; and (8) to increase advertising revenues.[12]

There has been a noticeable shift from P.M. to A.M. newspapers.

Publishers are reacting to perceived demographic changes when they shift their production from evening to morning. Typical newspaper readers are middle-aged with some college education. They can be described as middle-income, earning $15,000 or more per year, and employed in professional or managerial positions. Frequently their jobs are in the suburbs, where they and their families are also likely to live, shop, pay their taxes, attend

Demographic Changes

school, and engage in leisure-time activities. The growth of white-collar occupations means that a larger percentage of workers have more reading time in the morning and use their evening hours in other pursuits, particularly television viewing.[13]

Are typical newspaper readers representative of the larger population? Do most people still learn about the news by reading newspapers? The answer, it appears, depends on who you believe. When asked where they get most of their news about what's going on in the world today, Roper Organization survey respondents since 1963 have listed television more frequently than newspapers, with the spread growing more pronounced in recent years. But the American Newspaper Publishers Association has found that every day more people get news from newspapers than from any other medium (about 70 percent, compared to about 60 percent for television and 50 percent for radio). Other surveys indicate that somewhere between 73 and 80 percent of America's adults claim they read a newspaper regularly.

Circulation

Another way to answer the question is to look at circulation. Overall, newspaper circulation has not kept pace with population growth in recent years. Indeed, daily circulation peaked in 1973 at 63.1 million, then dropped off because of the energy crisis, years of newsprint shortages, and spiralling production costs. This trend contrasts with the early years of the century, when newspaper readership increased steadily. Between 1900 and 1930 circulation expanded from 15.1 million per day to 39.6 million. The depression slowed growth for a decade, but between 1940 and 1950 newspapers added 12.7 million readers, bringing the total to 53.8 million. Since then, large segments of the population have found other sources of information and entertainment. Circulation in 1980 was virtually the same as in 1970.

The lack of growth in circulation during the 1970s does not mean that all newspapers are suffering financially. In spite of the impact of television, the press still generates very substantial revenues from advertising.

Advertising

Advertising takes up nearly two-thirds of the space in the average American daily newspaper (62.6 percent, at last count). Not only is it the principal content of most newspapers, but in many instances it is their entire reason for existence. Advertising volume in the nation's daily papers was up to $17.4 billion in 1981. That figure, 28.4 percent of America's $61.3 billion expended on advertising for the year, was more than the combined totals for television ($12.7 billion or 20.6 percent of the total) and radio ($4.2 billion or 6.9 percent of the total).[14] By any yardstick, newspaper advertising is a significant function to both newspapers and the economy as a whole.

Newspaper advertising can be separated into two broad categories: *display* and *classified*. Displays are showcase advertisements occupying considerable space and distributed throughout the paper; they are generally measured and sold on a column inch or lineage basis. They sell goods and services, and sometimes ideas. Classifieds are notices—sometimes of sales, sometimes purely informational. They are concentrated in the classified sections of the newspaper, which generally carry no illustrations, and are often read as news. Whereas display seeks the buyer, the buyer seeks the classifieds.

Display advertising can be broken down further into two less concrete subdivisions: retail and national. Retail advertising is local advertising. It sells at a lower rate than national advertising and is aimed as a service to the local merchant. National advertising tends to be reinforcing or persuasive in nature. Retail advertising is a point-of-sale display. It is designed to promptly move goods and services, often being read as news—pure information as in the case of the market ads, theater and entertainment announcements, and notices of sales and weekend specials. The audience is presold by necessity or disposition and the retail advertisements give advice concerning where, when, and how much.

Newspaper advertising is sold by contract over the course of the year or off a rate card, a published schedule of prices for space and position in the paper. The rates are based on circulation, with larger circulation naturally demanding a higher rate. Recognizing the advantage that community newspapers have in soliciting advertisements of purely local merchants, metropolitan papers have gone increasingly to zone advertising in an attempt to appeal to the merchants of local communities. Breaking their press runs down by different geographical areas of a metropolis, they sell advertising in the editions going to these areas alone at a far cheaper rate than the general metropolitan run. This technique has not proved too successful because metropolitan newspapers lack the other elements of community appeal—local news, gossip, and civic information.

Newspaper reporters and editors joined broadcasters in the 1960s in paying diminished attention to governmental news and intensified attention to social issues. It was a decade of social awareness: women's movements, minority concerns, youth cultures, antiwar and antiestablishment movements, and the like. Quite obviously the public increasingly was interested in such issues. The following decade, dubbed the "Me-Decade" by journalist Tom Wolfe, found media catering to and creating increased self-awareness issues. "How-to" pieces on entertainment, finance, health, sex, and similar ego-centered concerns filled the news columns. This stress on news of personal utility (news to meet individuals' personal goals of self-fulfillment, self-gratification, and self-expression) continued into the 1980s. The American Newspaper Publishers Association's Newspaper Readership Council,

> Display and classified ads serve different purposes.

Reader Interests

> Today's newspapers emphasize "how to" pieces catering to the "Me Decade."

in more than two dozen reports, joined other researchers in telling news gatekeepers how to fulfill these audience needs. Without such studies, journalists would continue to rely on their often flawed instincts and news values for clues to reader interests. With the studies, they at least had indications of what would be read, whether or not they followed the guidelines.

A particularly revealing study conducted by pollster Louis Harris in 1978 showed that journalists really have not understood their readers' tastes in news. The survey was conducted among a national cross section of 1,533 adults, 86 top editors and news directors, and 76 major reporters and writers in the country. On topic after topic, the survey revealed that journalists either seriously underestimated or overestimated reader interest in news and editorial topics.

For example, while 34 percent of the media personnel believed the public was "very interested" in national news, a much higher 60 percent of the public indicated such an interest. Only 27 percent of the journalists polled thought the public had high interest in state news, but 62 percent of the public reported being very interested in events at the state level. Similar discrepancies occurred on other questions. When asked what percentage of the public would be greatly interested in international news, news personnel said 5 percent, while in reality 41 percent of the public expressed such interest. Reporters similarly underestimated reader interest in science and business news, while seriously overestimating the number of readers interested in sports news. Journalists guessed that three-quarters of American newspaper readers were enthralled with sports news, but only 35 percent of the readers indicated such an interest.[15]

Editors have become wary of studies such as these, however. They argue with some justification that there is a great difference between what the public tells pollsters it wants to read and what in actuality it spends its time reading.

Given the disturbing possibility that surveys may generate distorted data, several unmistakable patterns have emerged in recent years. Study after study (some by newspapers themselves and others by academic and external agencies with no vested interest in the outcome) demonstrated through the 1970s and into the 1980s that many different kinds of newspaper audiences in America are interested in and give different responses to various kinds of news items.

Those readers with strong community affiliation use the newspaper for hard news, while others with weaker local ties use it principally for entertainment. Young readers in the age group from twenty-one to thirty-four who are regular readers are more attuned to the aforementioned self-awareness stories than are older readers. The largest percentage of readers rely on the newspaper for its current events and other hard information; a second group uses it especially for sports; a third, for personal entertainment; and a fourth, for a guide to daily life in their community and from role models.

Print Media

The studies also revealed some disturbing trends to editors. A clear majority of readers indicated they feel the news is biased and distorted by the newspaper reporters and editors, and that newspapers ignore good, prosocial news in favor of bad news. One 1980 study receiving wide circulation indicated that 37 percent of Americans thought curbs placed on the press were not strict enough; that total was up from 21 percent in 1958. Further, the poll indicated a sharp decline in the public's perception of newspaper accuracy. Most disturbing of all, according to pollster George Gallup, was the finding that 76 percent of the respondents could not answer the question, "Do you happen to know what the First Amendment to the U.S. Constitution is, or what it deals with?" Gallup concluded that the American press is operating in an environment of public opinion that is increasingly indifferent, and to some extent hostile, to the cause of a free press in America.[16]

The above bad news to editors followed several years of hard statistical evidence that they were losing ground in the battle for circulation among the young, the minorities, the elderly, the poor, those who lived in rural areas or apartments, transients, and those weaned on or subsequently addicted to television. Attempting to reverse this trend has posed a challenge to the American Newspaper Publishers Association. It has suggested that journalists create the newspaper that today's readers want, by letting the editor and reporter be more personal, by mixing good news with the bad, by telling people the news in terms of people they know, and by making the paper more attractive by giving it personality.

The young, poor, elderly, rural or apartment dwellers, and TV addicts tend to be nonreaders of newspapers.

Although not all journalists agree with the conclusions, many newspapers are making some changes to attract new readers. Some newspapers have attempted *demographic breakouts*—specialized sections delivered to different parts of the community. Others have experimented with magazine style formats, "supermarketing" the newspaper with different themes or interest areas spotlighted on different days of the week. The addition of color on the front page and colored flags for special sections is giving newspapers a brighter appearance. Spanish language editions of papers in cities with large Spanish populations, such as the *Miami Herald,* are broadening the appeal of some newspapers. Most editors, however, have recognized that a newspaper and its audiences and advertisers exist in a delicate ecosystem, and that drastic adjustments to cater to one group probably means disaffection of another. For instance, hard-core loyal readers who utilize the newspaper for serious social, political, and economic matters are readily offended when editors water down the intellectual level of their newspapers. Such pandering to the nonreader, especially in terms of increased soft-core and self-awareness news, is best done inconspicuously.

In sum, newspapers and their readers exist in a delicate ecosystem.

Newspapers Today and Tomorrow

New electronic technology
and segmented marketing
techniques typify the
newspaper of the 1980s.

The massive newspaper industry, with its workforce of 432,000, has not been highly regarded for its innovativeness. Contemporary metropolitan papers in particular have been cursed with an inertia born of ponderous organization and bureaucracy, so change has frequently come from the smaller community dailies, which are more flexible than their metropolitan cousins and generally operate on a closer profit margin. They were among the first to move forward toward *offset printing,* a cleaner operation that drastically cuts makeup time for the newspaper and reduces the amount of highly skilled, unioned *shop time* that is a part of production. Relatively unskilled personnel can *paste up* full pages, which are then photographically transferred to thin metal or plastic plates for the presses. Likewise the smaller papers were quick to employ the *electronic newsroom,* creatively marrying computers and *video display terminals* (VDTs) for writing and editing. This system cut down the size of the work force in the backshop and put editorial employees closer to a more rapidly produced finished product.

The larger metropolitan papers were shaken out of their lethargy by such innovations. For nearly a century they had plodded along, using archaic techniques that had served them well in the days before electronic media. But the offset press and VDTs offered economies they could not ignore, despite the enormous capital investment required to transform huge plants and retrain hundreds of people. The *Sacramento Union,* a former Copley newspaper in the medium-metropolitan range, was the first in the nation to go fully offset in 1967. By 1980, 75 percent of the nation's dailies had followed suit, and the same percentage had initiated VDTs and electronic newsrooms.

Still in their infancy are portable VDTs, which allow reporters on assignment to enter stories directly into the system. Another technological innovation will be inkjet printing coupled with the use of lasers, allowing editors to update news items and advertisers to modify ads while presses continue to roll at top speed. These changes and others are aimed at decreasing the time lag between a news event and its delivery to readers. But what about the problem of a decreasing market penetration which we discussed?

To reach readers some publishers have experimented with the aforementioned segmented marketing by geographically zoning their papers, by redefining separate editions of the same paper to appeal to different groups within the same zones, or by publishing special types of papers on one or two days of the week. In the mid-1970s, the *New York Times* began publishing "Weekend," a leisure/entertainment guide, in its Friday editions. The *Los Angeles Times* put out "YOU," a consumer/leisure guide, on Tuesdays. The *Boston Globe* offered "Calendar," a cultural guide for families and youth, on Thursdays. And the *Louisville Times* came out with "Scene," a full-color Saturday magazine filled with advice on dating and astrology, tips on auto repair, how to spend the weekend, and how to shop; and even a children's pullout section called "Jelly Bean Journal."[17]

To some this change from newspaper to "use-paper" is troublesome—a professional cop-out. To others the trend is a natural and necessary one, particularly to market researchers who argue that traditional editors have been producing newspapers for other journalists rather than for readers. "I think everybody is going to win on this. It will help us find a niche as an industry and give readers a better choice of product," asserts Robert G. Marbut, president of the innovative Harte-Hanks chain.[18]

Segmented marketing of newspapers became popular once it was realized that technology and audience desires had melded. Faced with soaring postal costs, many advertisers turned to newspapers for distributing preprinted ads in *tabloid* or brochure form. Newspapers, they reasoned, had already established efficient distribution patterns, allowing them to reach the audiences most likely to be interested in the advertising. The *New York Times,* for instance, brags that it can guarantee an advertiser that a particular ad supplement will go only to readers on specified blocks of New York City, and smaller newspapers can insert or remove ads for separately zoned editions.

How far will this trend go? Theoretically, segmented marketing is limitless, with each individual receiving an individualized newspaper, unique to his or her own tastes, reading levels, interest levels, and purchasing behavior. How far in the future that theoretical day lies is anybody's guess, but it will never come about so long as present distribution patterns prevail. Marketers are stymied by the realization that the final link in the distribution channel is usually a twelve-year-old delivery boy or girl on a bicycle.

They will admit that these youthful entrepreneurs are on their endangered-species list, once they figure out how to tie the newspaper to an in-home electronic delivery system.

Many signs point to the electronic newspaper. Astronomical price increases for and shortages of paper have already resulted in streamlined newspapers with smaller-sized pages. Despite apparently successful experiments with *kenaf,* a fast-growing plant from which newsprint is being made, society recognizes the benefits of finding alternatives to the problems of ravaging forests for wood pulp and polluting the atmosphere with the residue of waste paper.

It is only a matter of time before the newspaper industry, cognizant of readers' tendencies to read only what appeals to them, ceases distributing the same mass-oriented product to everyone. Futurists looking toward tomorrow's newspaper see homes equipped with receiving units (modified teletype machines similar to today's VDT's) that offer electronic scans of the news and hard-copy printouts. Users will exercise almost limitless control over content. By checking the daily news index, they will call up, in as much detail as it takes to satisfy them, those stories of greatest interest to them. In the process they will be free to overlook whatever disinterests them, thereby voluntarily missing out on entire chunks of important daily events and ideas. This disturbs many socially responsible editors who know that readers in pursuing their self-interests will find it easier to overlook substantial information and in the process become less responsible citizens. We could, as Merrill and Lowenstein suggest, build political, social, and educational cocoons around ourselves, and our society could become divided into highly polarized, and probably unempathic, segments.[19] Considering how far Knight-Ridder and Dow Jones have already come in their experimental electronic newspapers, that future may already be upon us.

George Bernard Shaw used to refer to the daily newspaper as "the poor man's university."[20] When, not if, the electronic newspaper becomes fully operational, its first subscribers will be those customers who are wealthy enough to own the sophisticated electronic receivers. Families low in income and in educational and occupational achievement, who are already on the nonreader lists, will be even less likely to become readers.

It seems ironic, but the parent medium, the "poor man's university," may be at a turning point in its efforts to remain viable to serve the citizenry. As technological and economic factors coalesce, the newspaper is becoming more specialized. It has the option of either moving toward internal specialization, with each issue a potpourri of features, some of which will appeal to many groups, or moving toward unit specialization, in which each issue is tailored for each subscriber. It is uncertain which track the industry will follow, but from what we see, it appears likely the newspaper may opt for unit specialization, because of economic realities. If it does, the newspaper will change its primary historical function and cause still another shifting in the delicately balanced media–society ecosystem.

The newspaper of tomorrow may cause some social upheaval.

A newspaper is a geographically limited, regularly published print medium, serving the general interests of a specific community. Predecessors of newspapers, called corantos, appeared in England early in the seventeenth century, but the first daily paper did not appear until 1702.

The history of the press in America can be divided into eight eras: (1) the colonial press, (2) the Revolutionary press, (3) the political press, (4) the penny press, (5) the personal editors, (6) yellow journalism, (7) jazz journalism, and (8) the present age of consolidation.

During the eighteenth century newspapers were essentially journals of opinion written for the elite. Benjamin Day changed that in 1833 with his penny press, the *New York Sun,* which appealed to the masses. Mid-century was the era of the personal editors who created many of the features that exist in newspapers today. Late in the century, circulation wars among New York papers led to excesses that have become known as yellow journalism.

Many newspapers today are owned by one of 155 chains, which account for two-thirds of the daily circulation in the country. Regardless of whether the paper is part of a chain or is independent, the person who runs the paper is the publisher. Most newspapers are divided into five departments: editorial, advertising, production, circulation, and administration. The news people—reporters and editors, wire services, stringers, and correspondents—feed material to newsrooms that print only about 10 percent of what is available.

In addition to big-city daily newspapers, the medium includes smaller dailies, community papers, and minority papers. Each type of newspaper fills a need; but when needs change, some papers lose their audience and go out of business.

Newspapers are changing. Recently dozens of daily papers have changed from P.M. to A.M. editions in order to reach middle-income suburbanites. But that change alone has not yet increased circulation, which has been flat the last ten years. Fortunately, advertising has remained strong in spite of competition from other media.

Recent studies have shown that reporters and editors have not been very good at assessing what readers claim they want from a newspaper. Other studies reveal that what readers say they want and what they read are not always the same thing.

In the final section we discussed some of the efforts of newspapers to rekindle reader interest, and we proposed some changes (not all of them positive) that are likely for the newspaper of the future.

Summary

Notes

1. Edwin Emery and Michael Emery, *The Press and America: An Interpretive History of the Mass Media,* 4th ed. (Englewood Cliffs, N.J.: Prentice-Hall, 1978).
2. Ben H. Bagdikian, *The Information Machines: Their Impact on Men and the Media* (New York: Harper & Row, 1971).

3. William E. Ames and Dwight L. Teeter, "Politics, Economics, and the Mass Media," in *Mass Media and the National Experience,* ed. Ronald T. Farrar and John D. Stevens (New York: Harper & Row, 1971), p. 46.

4. S. N. Katz, ed., *A Brief Narrative of the Case and Trial of John Peter Zenger* (Cambridge, Mass: Harvard University Press, 1963).

5. Donald L. Shaw, "Technology: Freedom for What?" in *Mass Media and the National Experience,* ed. Farrar and Stevens, p. 70.

6. Ben Bagdikian, "The Press and Its Crisis of Identity," in *Mass Media in a Free Society,* ed. Warren K. Agee (Lawrence, Kansas: University Press of Kansas, 1969), p. 7.

7. American Newspaper Publishers Association, "Facts About Newspapers, '82," (Washington, D.C.: ANPA, April 1982).

8. *Ibid;* and "Independent Dailies Growing Fewer, All Sources Agree," *Presstime,* May 1982, p. 59.

9. John W. C. Johnstone et al., *The News People: A Sociological Portrait of Journalists and Their Work* (Urbana, Ill.: University of Illinois Press, 1976).

10. S. Robert Lichter and Stanley Rothman, "The Media Elite," *Public Opinion,* October/November 1981.

11. Everette E. Dennis and Arnold Ismach, *Reporting Processes and Practices* (Belmont, Calif.: Wadsworth Publishing Co., 1981).

12. Kathleen Hunt Baird, "P.M. to A.M.: Is a Trend Building?" *Presstime,* December 1979, pp. 6–9; and Clark Newsom, "The Beat Goes on for P.M.s to A.M.s," *Presstime,* December 1980, pp. 48–49.

13. Christopher H. Sterling and Timothy R. Haight, "Characteristics of Newspaper Readers," in *The Mass Media: Aspen Institute Guide to Communication Industry Trends* (New York: Praeger Publishers, 1978), pp. 338–39.

14. American Newspaper Publishers Association, *Facts About Newspapers '82;* and McCann-Erickson Inc.

15. Louis Harris, "Public Prefers News to Pablum," *Deseret News,* 1 January 1978.

16. Reported at the First Amendment Congress, Philadelphia, 16–17 January 1980.

17. David Shaw, "Newspapers Challenged As Never Before," *Los Angeles Times,* 26 November 1976.

18. Michael T. Malloy, "Newspapers May Some Day Let You Pick the News You Want," *National Observer,* 21 February 1976.

19. John C. Merrill and Ralph L. Lowenstein, *Media, Messages, and Men: New Perspectives in Communication,* 2d ed. (New York: Longman, 1979), p. 235.

20. David Shaw, "Newspapers Challenged As Never Before."

Magazines 3

Introduction

The ability of a medium to survive and to thrive after having been superseded by a faster, more efficient form is nowhere better illustrated than in a magazine. Nor is the remarkable diversity of American life better demonstrated than through the extraordinary variety of magazines. There are almost 20,000 magazines published in the United States today. Some look like newspapers and others look like books. Magazines are sold by subscription or on racks in over a hundred thousand retail outlets, and some are given away to preselected groups, and are called controlled circulation.

Magazines are published by magazine groups, by individual publishers, by newspapers, by small esoteric societies, by giant corporations, by trade associations and churches, by varying levels of government, and by all political parties. The roster of publishers is almost as varied as the titles themselves. Magazines are issued daily, weekly, semimonthly, and monthly for the most part; some are published bimonthly or quarterly, and a few come out once a year. They can be as general as the *Reader's Digest* or as specific as the *Flue Cured Tobacco Farmer*. As varied as the medium is, all magazines do share two characteristics: They are published regularly, and each appeals to the interests of some specific segment of society.

Our discussion begins with a general review of the historical development of magazines as a hybrid medium. As in our discussion of newspapers, we will concentrate on the medium's adaptations to twentieth century pressures, particularly those brought on by television and by rapid increases in the costs of materials and postal rates. The rise and decline of some mass circulation magazines will be considered, and we will look more closely at a couple of attractive magazines that have succeeded in recent years. Marketing techniques, and trends in ownership and audiences, will be surveyed. We will conclude our discussion with speculations about the future of the magazine.

Historical Development

Historically, magazines filled the gap between books and newspapers.

Historically, magazines developed as a hybrid form of print and appealed to audiences in the gap between newspapers and intellectually pinpointed books. They provided some entertainment and some culture in discrete doses, reaching neither populistic nor philosophical extremes that seemed to characterize the press and book-publishing businesses prior to and during most of the nineteenth century. For a period of time and to a limited extent, magazines seemed to provide the only national medium.

Magazines discovered early on publics other than geographical ones and began to appeal to these specific groups: farmers, women, professional people. They also discovered advertising and began to develop a specialized form of advertising geared to their specific publics, as was their content.

The history of magazines is somewhat obscure because print technology and accompanying literacy had to become fairly well developed before clear lines of demarcation could be drawn between newspapers and magazines. Generally, the first publications classified as magazines are the *Tatler* and the *Spectator,* published in England during the first quarter of the eighteenth century. Joseph Addison and Richard Steele contributed much to these periodicals by way of topical essays, satirical material, international news, and local gossip. Their formats included more opinion and entertainment than news.

The first magazines on American shores clearly defined as such were the *General Magazine and Historical Chronicle, for All the British Plantations in America* and the *American Magazine, or a Monthly View of the Political State of the British Colonies,* both originating in Philadelphia in 1741. In 1740 Benjamin Franklin announced his proposed *General Magazine,* but a competitor, Andrew Bradford, got his *American Magazine* off

**From European Roots
to the American Civil
War**

America's first magazines
were short-lived; the
colonies were not ready for
them.

the press three days ahead of Franklin. Both magazines quickly folded—Bradford's after three issues and Franklin's after six issues. America wasn't quite ready for magazines. Despite imitators, no American magazine during the eighteenth century lasted for more than fourteen months. Some of the nation's outstanding writers and politicians, including George Washington, Alexander Hamilton, John Jay, John Hancock, Philip Freneau, and Thomas Paine, were involved either as editors or contributors, but lack of advertising and limited circulation spelled doom for most of their efforts.

By the turn of the century the situation had changed; *Port Folio* was followed by *North American Review* in 1815 and the venerable *Saturday Evening Post* in 1821 (which, contrary to popular legend, Benjamin Franklin did not found). The *Post's* format of fiction, poems, and essays was typical during most of that period. By 1830, a hundred or so magazines were being published in the United States, which proved the need for the new medium. Also, 1830 marked the founding of *Godey's Lady's Book*—the first magazine to cater specifically to women and, more significantly, the first medium to attempt to identify an audience of its own.

Additional entries into the field were made by mid-century, with literature, graphics, science, and travel being added to the bill of fare. *Harper's New Monthly Magazine,* the *Atlantic Monthly, Gleason's Pictorial,* and *Harper's Weekly* were typical of the titles that filled this newly created interest vacuum between newspapers and books. Some of the new magazines were commercially successful; however, many were not. The little *Nation,* which made its appearance at the close of the Civil War in 1865, is significant because in over 100 years of continuous publication, it consistently lost money—every year.

The Golden Age: 1865–1900

The Golden Age evolved with improvements in distribution, printing, education, and urbanization.

The last part of the nineteenth century, from the end of the Civil War until 1900, has been called the Golden Age of the magazine industry, and for good reason. Several significant factors came together during that period. Channels of distribution were greatly facilitated when the transcontinental railroad network was completed in 1869. Then in 1879, Congress passed the Postal Act, allowing magazines to be distributed at less expensive second-class rates. Pulp paper made from cheaper wood and improved printing presses, coupled with the invention of the linotype (automatic typesetting) machine by Ottmar Mergenthaler and photographic reproduction techniques, meant the average magazine could be produced less expensively, more rapidly, and more attractively than ever before. Also significant were the growth in secondary education and national urbanization, which created broader and more literate audiences for magazines.

Between 1865 and 1885 the number of American magazines increased from 700 to 3,300. Their circulations were larger than those of prewar days, but a magazine with a circulation of 100,000 copies was still considered a giant in the industry. Then, in 1893, publisher Frank A. Munsey reduced the annual subscription price of *Munsey's Magazine* from three dollars to one dollar, while dropping the price of a single issue from twenty-five cents to only a dime. His philosophy—not a new one, since it had been successfully applied by the newspaper industry sixty years earlier—was to sell the magazine for less than the cost to produce it, with advertisers carrying the financial burden. Sure enough, as circulation grew—from 40,000 in 1893 to 500,000 in 1895—magazines became increasingly attractive to advertisers, who recognized the value of a national marketplace.

Other magazines followed suit, particularly those magazines aimed primarily at women: *Ladies' Home Journal, Women's Home Companion,* and *McCall's.* Of these three, the *Journal* may be the most significant. Founded in 1883 by Cyrus H. K. Curtis and his wife, the magazine became a reflection of Edward Bok's editorial philosophy after he joined the staff in 1889. At that time the circulation was 400,000 per month, although the magazine was considered typically mundane in editorial content. Bok broadened the appeal of the *Journal* by including advice columns and articles about health, fashion, home decorating, cooking, and child rearing. National advertising expanded as the circulation grew; soon the magazine was reaching over one million readers each month.

Among the other magazines seeking to compete for the increasing amount of advertising by national manufacturers were *McClure's, Cosmopolitan, Collier's,* and *American,* to name a few. *Cosmopolitan,* for example, was published by William Randolph Hearst as an "insurance publication" during his efforts to establish a newspaper empire. Those older magazines that refused to lower their newsstand prices below twenty-five or thirty-five cents, and counted on subscriptions or street sales to give them the finances needed to continue running expensive literature, suffered in the increasingly competitive marketplace.

As the twentieth century began, the features of the "modern magazine" had begun to take shape: low cost, large circulation, advertising supported, and service to diverse audiences. Over the next several decades, magazines offered numerous contributions to American culture. Historian Theodore Peterson credits the industry with providing social reform, putting issues in national perspective, fostering a sense of national community, providing low cost entertainment, serving as an inexpensive "instructor" in daily living, providing a cultural heritage for Americans, and offering a variety of entertainment, education, and ideas representing a wide range of tastes and interests.[1]

The Twentieth Century

Modern magazines have low cost, large circulation, advertising support, and diverse audiences.

The Muckrakers

Given their nationwide audience, low cost, and timeliness, it was perhaps inevitable that magazines became an instrument of social reform. In the first dozen years of this century many of them became "people's champions," investigating and attempting to correct political, social, and business ills. Theodore Roosevelt branded them muckrakers, after a famous painting of the *Man with the Muckrake*, in *Pilgrim's Progress*, who missed seeing the celestial crown because he was so busy raking the barnyard filth. Rather than accepting the derogatory term as intended, various writers and editors in the early 1900s took the title as a mark of distinction.

Leaders among the muckraking magazines were *McClure's, Cosmopolitan, Munsey's, Ladies' Home Journal, Collier's, Everybody's,* and the *Saturday Evening Post.* Outstanding writers such as Ida Tarbell, Lincoln Steffens, Ray Stannard Baker, Finley Peter Dunne, and David Graham Phillips, fired by missionary zeal, attacked and sought changes from oil companies, meat-packing firms, patent medicine manufacturers and distributors, city governments, labor organizations, abusers of child labor, and even the U.S. Senate.

Spurred by the muckrakers' efforts, businesses and legislators enacted numerous remedies to the exposed inequities. The Pure Food and Drug Act of 1906 and legislation regarding finance and fair trade followed the public outcry. In 1911 the magazine *Printer's Ink* prepared the Printer's Ink model advertising statute that urged states to make fraudulent and misleading advertising a crime. Many states passed bills in support of the model statute. But the movement tapered off after Theodore Roosevelt's third party candidacy, Woodrow Wilson's election to the presidency in 1912, and America's entrance into World War I several years later. After that period, criticisms of American institutions were somehow less substantial and seemed more sensational and frivolous, and the muckraking era drew to a close—for the time being, anyhow. Even though the majority of Americans during the early years of the century were reading escapist literature rather than social commentary, enough of them were aroused by magazine (and newspaper and book) writers to spark changes in the business community and to ensure social progress.[2]

Magazine Growth from the 1920s to the 1950s

During the decade or so following World War I, several giants were established, including *Reader's Digest* (1922), Henry Luce's *Time* (1923), and the *New Yorker* (1925), as well as H. L. Mencken's spirited *American Mercury* and the recently departed *Saturday Review of Literature.* Improved production processes made possible the reproduction of photographs, which required a higher quality paper. Magazines were becoming more attractive, using bolder graphics to complement the articles and fiction. The mid-1930s saw the great photojournalism efforts of *Life* and *Look,* and the first of the slick men's magazines, *Esquire.*

The battle for increases in circulation first experienced by newspapers also afflicted magazines. This trend continued as radio came into its prime. The mass media, it seems, were committed to a "numbers game."

Some of the more familiar characteristics of magazines are an outgrowth of this trend. The cover girl is probably the best known of these phenomena. Brilliant color photography of slim, suggestive, young, and beautiful models adorned the front covers of American magazines in an

Print Media

effort to dress up the magazines' competitive appearance on the racks of a 100,000 public outlets. This was the genesis of the "cheesecake syndrome," the attempt to use sometimes scantily clad but always alluring young females as bait for both male and female readers.

With scores of national magazines competing for attention on the newsracks of the nation, cover girls became big business indeed. At least two major modeling agencies (Powers and Conover) thrived on the aspirations of thousands of girls from every state who yearned for the recognition and prestige that being a cover girl or a Powers' model would bring. The depression years of the mid-1930s was a strange time, a time of dance marathons, crooners and swooners, gangster movies, cover girls, and magazine fiction.

Magazine marketing also became a reality as distributors fought for preferential position on the retail racks, making concessions and deals to outlets to place their magazines at top center on display racks and to bury their competitors' magazines. Magazines also outdid one another in seeking surefire material for public appeal. This generally took the form of the memoirs of famous people. Intense bidding among the national general-interest magazines in the post-World War II period resulted in magazine rights for Admiral William Halsey's memoirs going for $60,000, while

General Eisenhower's, long before he became president, sold for an amount unheard of at that time, $175,000. Later the *New York Times,* a consortium of *Life* magazine, and a book publisher paid Winston Churchill $1,000,000 for his story, while *Life* ventured $600,000 for the magazine rights to Harry Truman's autobiography.

For twenty years, until the mid-1950s, magazine publishing flourished in the United States, and national circulations grew as the magazines provided a specialized visual quality that national network radio lacked. Then, beginning in 1956 under the impact of network television (which provided its own pictures), the days of reckoning came. *Collier's* was the first to go under in that year, followed in time by *Coronet, American, Look, Saturday Evening Post,* and *Life.* Some have reappeared in modified form, but they are unlikely to seek or achieve the mass-circulation status of their heydays.

Television and Advertising

The magazine, more than any other medium, was drastically affected by television.

Many observers assert that no other medium has been so drastically and permanently affected by television as the magazine. Most of the major national magazines were essentially entertainment oriented, and television performs this function unsurpassingly better. However, the arrival of television does not explain completely the troubles encountered by magazines during the 1950s and 1960s. Although television has played a role, the basic reasons for magazine failures are economic. Examples are the two graphic giants, *Look* and *Life.* Both folded with extremely healthy circulations, each numbering more than six million copies, even while they were losing money. You may ask then, why did they fail economically? The reason, of course, is because of advertising. With huge national circulations of 6, 8, or 10 million at their peak, the big magazines had grown fat off national advertising revenues. Remember that, as with newspapers, only a fraction of the cost of a magazine is borne by its subscription rate or sales price. The largest portion of its cost and all of its profit is carried by advertising.

TV reached more people more effectively, and advertisers abandoned magazines.

When television appeared, it gradually acquired huge national audiences in previously unimagined numbers. The circulations of 6 million or so of the national magazines began to pall alongside the 20 million homes—or 35 million individuals, more or less—that a television network was able to reach on any weekday evening during prime time. Moreover, the advertising costs of television were comparable with those of magazines. A full-page advertisement in *Life* sold for around $60,000, color and production costs excluded. A network prime-time minute generally went for the same figure, production costs again excluded. In addition to having larger audiences, the presentation on television was dynamic, with action and complete control of sound, and, by the 1960s, color. Television advertising had real impact while a magazine display offered only a static presentation. Television was, all things considered, a more effective sales tool for many nationally advertised products. As national manufacturers and their agencies increased their use of television to advertise products and services, the sales results supported their choice.

Magazines found that they could not reduce the costs of their advertising. Production costs and postal rates were up, squeezing printing and paper and editorial budgets. They were caught in a vise of rising costs and declining revenues that even 6 million subscribers could not offset, and the effects of this dilemma were spiralling. As advertising fell off, gradually at first, magazines sought to economize. They spent less on production and research. Consequently, the quality of the product suffered and this, in turn, had an effect on circulation as subscribers, disappointed in the "new look," began to cancel subscriptions. Further, since the size of a general-circulation magazine, like that of a newspaper, is based on the volume of advertising committed (generally, at least in the days before television, on a 60 to 40 percent basis of advertising to editorial content), the magazines grew thinner as advertising fell off. Customers began to feel that they were not getting as much for their money. Thus, as circulation dwindled, national advertisers began to see that they were getting even less for their advertising dollar in the medium, which prompted a more rapid shift of advertising to television.

When the impact of television was first noticed, many of the nation's most popular magazines were engaged in a ruinous subscription war, which lasted from the early 1950s to the late 1960s. Caught up in a competitive struggle, they agreed to deliver eighteen, twenty-four, thirty, and even thirty-six monthly issues to new subscribers for a fraction of the listed cost, often offering thirty-six months for less than the original subscription price for a single year. At one point, *Life* was receiving only twelve cents per subscriber for a magazine that cost forty-one cents to edit and print.

The Circulation Wars

Magazines engaged in suicidal circulation wars.

While not apparent at the time, the cheap contracts would return later to haunt the magazines, often making it more expensive for them to go out of business than to continue publishing at a loss. Hundreds of thousands of three-year subscriptions representing little initial revenue were to become prohibitively expensive to buy up if a magazine wished to suspend publication. Since these subscriptions were indeed contracts to deliver, they were enforceable in court; hundreds of thousands of lawsuits would have been a ruinous undertaking.

The purpose of both the street sales and the subscription promotions was to build circulation, and no matter how that circulation was achieved, it represented solid figures in the Audit Bureau of Circulations' annual measurement. These audited figures served advertising agencies in making their selection of magazines. Furthermore, advertising rates were directly pegged to circulation size. The insanity of this particular course—sacrificing sales revenue in an era of rapidly mounting costs to try to attract additional advertisers in a declining market—became apparent after the fact. It is little wonder that so many of the giants folded willingly after such a long, hard struggle.

Finally, in desperation, the
falling giants tried to prune
circulation and seek new
audiences.

The next step undertaken by the large, general-interest magazines in their struggle for survival was exactly the reverse of the circulation war. They made an effort to curtail circulation: first, as a cost-saving device, and second, as an attempt to more specifically identify audiences in terms of their interests. To accomplish the latter goal, publishers turned to the computer to break down audiences or subscribers in terms of where they lived and their relative affluence, age, sex, and the like. These demographics of their audiences, the magazines reasoned with some cause, could categorize those persons to which an advertiser could beam a specific sales pitch, something television, by its massive generality, could not do. An additional reason for trying to curtail magazines' audiences was to remove a lot of the deadwood, those subscribers having only a marginal interest in the magazines who had bought long-term subscriptions at a fraction of the cost. If such subscribers would voluntarily remove themselves from circulation rolls, it would greatly assist in any subsequent cessation of publication.

Across America in the late 1950s and early 1960s, the public was confronted with the unexpected circumstance of magazines writing to subscribers, who only a year or so earlier had been actively solicited, telling them that they fell outside the parameters of the kind of people desired as subscribers. This was a technique scarcely calculated to win friends at a time when the magazine industry needed them so desperately.

This pruning technique was not successful to any great degree. At best it was a desperate measure. It did not sufficiently pinpoint audiences demographically for it to have been of any major appeal to specific advertisers, although it did reduce publication costs to the degree that it curtailed circulation and, to that extent, made subsequent liquidation less costly.

Regional Editions

There were other attempts to use demographics to forestall the inevitable. Computer technology, for a while, seemed to be coming to the assistance of the national magazines. Computers permitted magazines to break down their circulation geographically, a lesson learned from the *Wall Street Journal,* which had, since the early 1950s, been published in four regional editions as well as a national edition. The news and comment— the editorial content—was identical in each edition, but it did permit regional advertisers an opportunity to reach their spheres of interest at much less cost than if they were forced to buy for the entire national circulation of the *Wall Street Journal.* This was an advertising technique specifically designed for utilities, banks, and other financial institutions that were basically organized on a regional basis and comprised the natural interest market of the *Wall Street Journal.*

When this technique was adopted by *Life* it permitted the magazine to substitute purely local advertising for some of the national advertising that had been lost to television. Further, it permitted a Chattanooga utility or a Seattle bank the prestige of advertising in *Life.* At the peak of this experiment *Look* was running seventy-five regional editions at fantastic cost. *Life,* more conservative, published in seven regions and eleven metropolitan areas.

Cost differentials are apparent. To buy *Life's* full-run peak of 8 million or so would have cost an advertiser $65,000, but *Life's* 150,000 subscribers in Minnesota could be bought for a mere $2,500, and the advertiser could still have *Life's* prestige. The theory behind publishing regional editions was that through an active sales effort the volume of advertising in each of the magazine's regions or districts would balance out. By and large it did, but meanwhile sales costs had increased considerably, constituting an additional drain on already dwindling reserves. At best, the use of multiple editions was a stopgap for the general-interest magazines.

Regional, demographic editions met with mixed success.

However, such regional breakdowns in more specifically oriented journals, such as the *Wall Street Journal* with its financial emphasis and *Time* and *Newsweek* with their high news orientation, proved eminently successful. Regional editions in such instances permitted advertisers and manufacturers to reach financially-oriented potential customers or others whose demonstrated interest in news also indicated an interest in the world, a relatively high educational level, and a degree of presumed affluence. These qualities are considered valuable to many advertisers.

The computers assisted briefly in yet another way. They were also capable of breaking down magazine subscribers by their relative affluence. Such affluence was established by the census tract on the theory that those who lived in wealthier neighborhoods were wealthier and those who lived in middle-income areas were less so. Thus, reasoned the magazines in their death throes, they could approach such national manufacturers as the Ford Motor Company with the suggestion that the company could reach the most affluent circulation of *Life,* for example, with advertisements for Lincoln Continentals; they could advertise Pintos in the less affluent areas, and Fairlane models and the like filling in the middle ground. This was ingenious thinking, offering an element of product differentiation that television could not, but it did not work at the time.

As desperate as the situation appeared to be, not all magazines went out of business. By 1969 the *New York Times* said that magazines were thriving despite a few dramatic failures. Obviously, not all the effects of television were negative. Some magazines were born because of television, and others changed significantly—and successfully—due to the television environment.

The most significant change has been the move away from the national magazine of general interest, as represented by *Life* and *Look,* to more specialized magazines, many of which still have very broad appeal.

Television has also been largely responsible for a change in the editorial mix of many magazines. For instance, of those magazines that continue to publish fiction, the present ratio of nonfiction to fiction, about three to one, is almost exactly the reverse of what it was a half century ago.

The Types of Magazines

Magazines may be categorized by audience appeal or function.

Magazines may be categorized in several ways. Traditionally, they were broken down into consumer- or general-interest magazines, business magazines, and farm and company magazines. The Audit Bureau of Circulations has a more specific breakdown: automotive, brides/bridal, business/finance, entertainment guides, epicurean, fishing/hunting, general editorial, home service/home, mechanics/science, men's, music, news weeklies, news biweeklies/news semimonthlies, science, sports, travel, women's, women's fashions, and youth.

A third way of breaking magazines down is functionally, into three categories corresponding closely to the functions of communication. These are: (1) entertainment/escape; (2) news/information; and (3) advocacy/opinion. Within these categories fall some rather obvious examples. For instance, comic books, confessions, and science fiction all fall within entertainment/escape. The news/information category includes the well-known news weeklies of *Time, Newsweek,* and *U.S. News and World Report,* as well as a host of trade, professional, and scholarly publications, each specializing in some facet of the culture. Magazines with the category of advocacy/opinion that are oriented toward persuasion include not only those of the underground press but also most of the vast array of organizational or corporate publications, plus such watchdog publications as *The Progressive,* a periodical devoted to investigative reporting of governmental affairs. Most magazines represent some combination of these communication functions, with specific appeal being determined by the magazine's basic thrust or orientation.

Looking at magazines from another perspective, we can categorize them by the relationship between their content and their audience. The general-interest magazines of the 1950s had broad coverage of issues of importance in American society, and all of America was considered the audience. The adjustments made by many magazines during the 1960s and 1970s redefined the content and the audience in more selective ways.

Today the majority of magazines are narrow in both subject and audience. An example of this is *The American West,* a magazine devoted to the history, geography, and arts of the West, having a circulation of 75,000 readers each month. Few magazines today can be described as being broad in subject and in audience. The *Reader's Digest* is one of the few, although it is narrowing somewhat as its audience becomes older and more conservative. The magazine prints about 30 million copies each month, 11.7 million of which are published in fourteen different languages and sent overseas. Originally supported by its subscription price alone, it began to take advertising in limited quantities late in its history. While this advertising is important to the magazine today, it is far from its principal means of support. The *Reader's Digest* also goes to some pains to keep current with popular taste, running a random monthly sample of its readers to determine their continuing interests. Thus, to a degree, it has borrowed television's rating technique to ascertain the relative popularity of its offerings and to assess its gatekeepers' judgment.

Another atypical magazine is the *TV Guide,* which is narrow in subject but very broad in audience. The *TV Guide* and magazines representing other categories deserve a closer look.

TV Guide, with its circulation of over 19 million, is the largest circulating domestic magazine. It is the direct result of television's effect on the magazine field and is a classic example of one medium catering to another in terms of both interest and complementary functions. Television's ubiquitous popularity demands a ready reference in more tangible form than its passing self-promotions can offer. This weekly magazine gathers together in one handy place all programming data for the week and adds a few articles and commentaries about the medium. The magazine's basic function as an index illustrates a curious admixture of communication functions: information on entertainment. Apart from its huge circulation and reference function, *TV Guide* is noteworthy from a technical standpoint: It is forced to publish in a large number of geographical editions to accommodate the various FCC (Federal Communications Commission) channel allocations on the band. In so doing, it also allows the same number of options for local advertisers to ply their wares.

Another combination of characteristics is represented by the weekly newsmagazines, of which *Time*—with its circulation of 4.5 million—is the largest. It is interesting that *Time*'s circulation, despite the magazine's popularity, is only about half that of some of the major magazines that have gone under in the past dozen years, including its stablemate, the original *Life.* This is fairly conclusive evidence that circulation alone is not the answer to a magazine's success or failure; the homogeneity of that circulation is the prime operant.

From its inception in 1923 by Henry Luce and Briton Hadden, two young Yale graduates who scraped together $86,000, *Time* magazine has attempted to couple entertainment with information and, according to many observers, has overlaid the entire package with a dose of persuasion. *Time* uses a "group journalism" concept of gatekeeping. This means that few articles in the magazine are the work of only one person. Editors assign stories to correspondents who gather data and prepare a file that is sent to New York where the material is rewritten for style and restrictions of space. The result is a weekly package of facts put in *Time*'s perspective, a perspective that for most of its existence was Henry Luce's peculiar set of economic, philosophic, and political values.[3]

For all their influence, newsmagazines represent only a tiny fraction of magazine publishing in terms of both number and audience. Often overlooked is the fact that newsmagazines publish weekly, or four times more often than most magazines, a factor that both provides additional exposure and establishes firm habit patterns in their readers.

TV Guide

TV Guide is a classic example of media functional mix.

The Newsmagazines

Henry Luce, founder of the Time-Life Magazine group.
Wide World Photos

Weekly newsmagazines are
crosses between
newspapers and monthly
magazines.

Weekly publication also makes newsmagazines a cross between monthly magazines and daily newspapers, filling an information void by providing a limited perspective on current events. Newsmagazines are afforded a little more time than newspapers to digest the significance of contemporary developments. Also, their space limitations are acute in proportion to the scope of events demanding interpretation, and they must be highly selective in what they present. Another of their problems involves that of writing to make the quasi-historical appear contemporary—last week's news must seem current. This is a technique at which their team-writing staff has become particularly adept.

More than any other magazine *Time* has profitably perfected geographical zone distribution, both for printing facility and as an additional source of advertising revenue. In the spring of 1980 it bragged that it had made the jet age obsolete by its utilization of RCA's SATCOM II and the COMSAT Intelsat IV, communications satellites some 20,000 miles above earth. The system allowed *Time* to be the first publisher equipped to beam four-color finished pages as well as black-and-white photos and text by satellite, almost instantaneously connecting New York and Hong Kong. Satellite technology was combined with other printing and distributing innovations: full page, press-ready pagination via computer, and use of the telephone to relay completed pages between computers in the United States and Europe.

City and Regional Magazines

A relatively new phenomenon in the magazine field is the so-called city and regional magazine, such as the *San Diego Magazine, Washingtonian, Texas Monthly, Philadelphia,* and dozens more.

Interestingly, the famous *New Yorker*—first published in 1923—was the first and for decades the only example of this kind of magazine. However, as the *New Yorker* progressively became a national magazine catering to the sophisticated across the nation, it left a void in New York City, which in the late 1960s began to be filled by *New York,* published by the staff of the defunct *New York Herald-Tribune. New York* concentrates on life in the city and the problems of New Yorkers, but ironically because these subjects are of such magnitude they are capturing a certain national audience, and *New York* is well on its way toward becoming another *New Yorker.*

The original city magazines served major metropolitan areas. Some developed as the offspring of restaurant guides, television guides, chamber of commerce promotional pieces, and the like. Today, with circulations ranging from several thousand (*Desert Silhouette's Tucson*) to more than 150,000 (*Texas Monthly,* serving metropolitan areas of Texas), they have become significant media in their own right. They vary widely in appearance and editorial substance. While some still bear chamber-of-commerce overtones, others increasingly assume a watchdog role, probing local issues too delicate or complex for established media. Such magazines serve as a

Originally local boosters,
city and regional magazines
have become substantial
media, despite heavy doses
of commercialism.

Table 3.1 Audience composition of selected city magazines

	Percent college graduates	Percent professional managerial	Median income	Percent owning home
Circulation 5,000–14,999				
1. *Houston*	69	78	$46,300	83
2. *Louisville*	89	70	$29,300	85
Circulation 15,000–24,999				
1. *MPLS*	43	78	$25,000(est)	74
2. *Sandpaper*	84	78	$15,000(est)	91
Circulation 25,000–34,999				
1. *Fairfield County*	96	98	$40,000(est)	95
2. *Honolulu*	54	63	$27,700	92
Circulation 35,000–44,999				
1. *Cleveland*	72	76	$22,778	68
2. *D., The Magazine of Dallas*	64	67	$25,000(est)	79
Circulation 45,000-plus				
1. *Los Angeles*	66	63	$29,060	65
2. *Philadelphia*	30	32	$14,308	—

Source: Alan D. Fletcher, "City Magazines Find a Niche in the Media Marketplace." Used by permission from the Winter 1977 issue of *Journalism Quarterly*, p. 743.

showcase for local authors, poets, critics, photographers, and sometimes frustrated newspaper journalists seeking a less constrained writing outlet than their hometown newspaper allows.

As we might expect, however, the real viability of this magazine form is in its commercial nature. The city and regional magazines are geographically and demographically selective—the merchandisers' dream. Audiences on the whole are decidedly "upscale," or well-heeled and well-educated, discriminating in taste and culture. The epitome of such self-selection may be *Chicago's Elite.* Its publishers, who wanted to call the magazine *Chicago's Ruling Elite* but whose common sense prevailed, bragged in 1976 (the year of the *Elite's* inception) of a readership whose median annual income was $86,000—98 percent of whom had current passports, 40 percent of whom owned two homes, and 36 percent of whom had given a son or daughter an automobile costing in excess of $8,000. These demographics have been known to make some Chicago advertisers drool. Most city and regional magazines appeal to somewhat broader audiences. For samples see table 3.1.

In his national survey of city magazine publishers, Alan Fletcher found the medium to be flourishing. But he uncovered several problem areas that needed to be resolved if the business intended to become significant:

1. For city magazines to survive, they must establish strong local identities, taking advantage of voids that exist in other local and national media;
2. Circulations must be increased because of problems associated with ad revenue and production costs;
3. A continual supply of good editorial matter must be found;
4. Paper, printing, personnel, and distribution costs must be dealt with;
5. Advertisers must be convinced it is worth their while to sell via the high quality graphics and upscale audiences available.[4]

Magazines Without Advertisements

A few magazines survive with no ads but their subscription costs are high.

Magazines continue to cast about for survival formulae. One branch of the business avoids advertising completely, basing its entire financial operation on sales price alone. The best known is probably *Consumer Reports*. This type of magazine copies the formula under which the *Reader's Digest* was originally founded. Magazines that do not use advertisements come close to the book-publishing business; some are even in hardcover, such as *American Heritage*. They seek to combine the security of a subscription list with the relative freedom from advertising pressure that a book enjoys. The resurrected *Saturday Evening Post* was an experiment along these lines, which sought to capitalize on America's nostalgia as well as the 6 million subscribers it had owned before it went bankrupt. At a cost of $1.50 per copy, it served as an index of increasing American affluence.

Information without persuasion: *Consumer Reports* is probably the best-known advertising-free magazine.
Tom Ballard/EKM-Nepenthe

Print Media

Some magazines may pass along all the costs to the consumer. Others have been attracted to a new phenomenon in magazine publishing—the *controlled circulation* magazine. Controlled circulation generally is a euphemism for a free or marketing-directed magazine aimed at certain classes of people in terms of their presumed interests. Credit-card companies were the first in this field. They used magazines as vehicles for advertisers of luxury goods who were interested in the established credit ratings that cardholders had demonstrated. The facility of purchase was also appealing to the advertisers—who urged readers to "put it on your credit card."

Controlled Circulation Magazines

Controlled circulation magazines are delivered for free to predetermined target audiences.

Advertising and other pertinent data concerning America's magazines are contained in *Consumer Magazine* and *Farm Publication* editions of Standard Rate and Data Service (SRDS), published monthly. The SRDS lists nearly 10,000 magazines of general circulation in the United States, including their circulation size, areas of influence, general subject matter, and advertising rates. Not covered are at least an additional 9,000 magazines that are regularly issued publications of organizations and corporations and are aimed at their membership, employees, or stockholders. These rarely include advertising since they are basically informative or persuasive in content, and their cost is borne as a business expense by the organization or corporation involved. Yet they comprise an integral part of mass communications, providing members, employees, or stockholders with data pertinent to their interests, jobs, or investments, which are obtainable in no other way. These organizational publications comprise a sort of media subnetwork serving even smaller groups. Further, they often provide grist for the mills of the larger general media. For example, a corporate financial report may lead to extended articles in the financial press; or a technological development reported in an employee bulletin may spark an expanded piece in one of the trade magazines.

Organizational Publications

SRDS lists 10,000 general circulation and 9,000 organizational magazines.

It has been said that in the magazine world, more than in any other industry, the success or failure of a general-interest magazine can be traced to a specific individual, one having a unique personality and singular vision. Indeed, magazines so frequently take on the idiosyncracies of their founders that when the founding editors move on or die, the magazines are guaranteed to change. Clay Felker has observed that American magazines follow the human life cycle: "a clamorous youth eager to be noticed; a vigorous, productive middle-age marked by an easy-to-define editorial line; and a long, slow decline, in which efforts at revival are sporadic and tragically doomed."[5]

Perhaps because magazines historically have been the brainchildren of visionary individuals, today's chains, groups, and conglomerates still seem willing to let individuals experiment, but are happy to buy them out once the magazines appear to be making it. High prices are paid by companies

Life Cycle of Magazines

Magazines may be founded by individualists, but they tend to become institutionalized.

recognizing the potential of a small magazine, so entrepreneurs are increasingly willing to sell out. As Benjamin Compaine has noted, there is a good reason why most magazines are published by multi-magazine groups: A single title, especially one of limited audience circulation, must carry too great a burden of overhead to make economic sense. Periodicals reach a saturation point, ad revenue becomes limited, and the natural advantages of group ownership come to the fore: bulk acquisition of paper, better printing contracts, more attractive subscription packages, utilization of corporate research, management, and circulation expertise, and a greater possibility of gaining favorable deals with national distributors.[6]

On the other hand, since the various magazines owned by a group will differ so greatly editorially, each group finds itself hiring a separate editorial staff and frequently a separate advertising staff. Of course the objective of the group is profit, which the magazine industry has realized by its steady profit margins, but on a small scale. Because group ownership is interested in the steadiness of its profits, it can tolerate the percentage. As a whole, the industry reports 3 to 6 percent pretax earnings, even though many profitable magazines make 15 percent pretax earnings.[7]

Starting a New Magazine

We remember the success stories, but they are the exceptions.

We still hear of the occasional magazine that was begun on a shoestring. Hugh Hefner's *Playboy* was started with $7,000, and the first issue was laid out on a card table in his apartment. Bob Anderson's *Runner's World* got underway for a measly $100 in the mid-1960s when Anderson was a seventeen-year-old high school cross-country runner. That $100, coupled with Anderson's production and distribution work, and his success in persuading other runners to contribute free articles to what was at first called *Distant Running News,* eventually mushroomed into an impressive empire. Anderson went on to develop a complex of profitable publishing enterprises comprised of biking, soccer, canoeing, and cross-country skiing magazines, and he started a sporting goods mail order operation that by the late 1970s employed 115 persons and earned $4.7 million annually.[8]

But for every *Playboy* and *Runner's World,* there are probably a dozen—or perhaps even a hundred—failures; nobody knows for certain. Few individuals can sustain a struggling magazine through the decade-long, $30-million-in-losses gestation period that Time, Inc., tolerated for *Sports Illustrated* before the magazine became profitable, or the $13 million Bob Guccione poured into *Viva* before it took on life. The leading causes for failure include underfinancing, inexpert management, insufficient advertising, and public indifference. Sometimes even the old pros—including Hugh Hefner—have failed miserably when trying to imitate their own successes. Hefner made it with *Oui,* but lost a bundle on *Trump, Show Business Illustrated,* and *VIP.*[9]

Each magazine seeks its own successful mix of subscription or retail sales.

Magazine sales—for new and established publications alike—occur either through subscriptions or on a retail basis. Often the emphasis on one or the other is intentional; the publisher may want the security of the annual payments made in advance by subscribers or it may want to avoid

postage costs. In some cases the subject matter dictates whether the sales will be by subscription or at newsstands. For example, over 90 percent of the sales of *Modern Bride* occur at newsstands. All copies of *Woman's Day* and *Family Circle* are sold at newsstands and checkout counters, according to ABC Magazine's *Trend Report*. Sex-oriented magazines also tend to be sold at newsstands: 91.1 percent in the case of *Oui*, and 94.6 percent in the case of *Penthouse*. At the other end of the spectrum, 99.9 percent of the sales of *National Geographic* and *Smithsonian Magazine* are by subscription, and subscription accounts for 92.7 percent of the circulation of *Reader's Digest*.[10]

Subscription sales provide considerable security once a magazine is established, but that takes time. Nicholas Charney, who started *Psychology Today*, folded a second magazine venture, *Careers Today*, because buying subscription lists proved too expensive—this despite the fact that his new venture was already showing more than $100,000 worth of advertising per issue. Other magazines have chosen the newsstand for launching publications, hoping to develop sufficient interest and to acquire subscribers. The difficulty with this approach is the unassuredness of being allotted space for display at supermarkets and newsstands. Even the larger newsstands make room for only 100 to 200 different magazine titles, and, of course, give preference to the big sellers. Since magazines are frequently considered to be impulse purchases, chances for survival under such conditions are minimal for new magazines. Careful field testing in metropolitan newsstand markets is often in order. *People* was tested in eleven markets prior to its regular weekly publication in 1974. At thirty-five cents per copy, it sold an amazing 86 percent of available copies. That figure is especially significant because approximately half of all copies of nationally distributed magazines remain unsold on the shelf; they are then returned—at the publishers' expense—to the respective companies. Considering that each copy of a magazine like *Us* costs the publisher twenty-five cents in paper, printing, and delivery, such inefficiency in distribution makes it prohibitive for all but the wealthiest publishers to gamble on attracting customers at the nation's newsstands.[11]

In addition to the field testing and mass mailing of promotional materials to identified target audiences, marketing of new magazines is sometimes handled by buying space in existing magazines, such as by inserting a sampler of the proposed magazine's editorial content. This technique gives the existing magazine some additional editorial content assumed to be of interest to its readers, along with a few dollars in profit, while providing the new magazine exposure to potential readers and advertisers.

Contemporary Successes

In the United States today three magazines have a circulation greater than 10,000,000 copies per issue. These three—*TV Guide, Reader's Digest,* and *National Geographic*—represent the pinnacle of the medium in terms of number of copies printed and sold. All three magazines reach a much larger percentage of the population than did *McClure's* when it was selling 1,000,000 copies each month at the turn of the century. Table 3.2 reveals that at present two dozen magazines have circulations larger than 2,000,000 copies, and the top fifty magazines all sell more than 1,000,000 copies per issue.

How have each of these magazines become so successful? As we have seen, for the most part, a key element has been the ability of the publisher to identify a market segment and then tailor editorial content to attract that market. *Cosmopolitan* and *Psychology Today* illustrate this point.

Cosmopolitan

Cosmopolitan effectively serves a market—the unmarried working woman—designed to replenish itself. Advertisers love it.

In the early 1960s *Cosmopolitan,* one of the fourteen magazines published by the Hearst group, found itself a poor competitor in the national general-interest field, suffering from dwindling advertising revenues and a dwindling readership as public taste departed from the essentially fiction format so successfully utilized by the magazine.

Cosmopolitan felt the winds of change and decided to leave the general-interest magazine business and to seek a specific audience, chosen by interest rather than by demographics. Casting about for an audience not efficiently served by any medium, it hit upon that of the unmarried working woman. This was a happy choice in that it was a market designed to replenish itself. In addition, there was no other magazine catering to the interests of this group—to their tastes, habits, and life-style. To accomplish its purpose, *Cosmopolitan* hired Helen Gurley Brown (author of *Sex and the Single Girl*) as editor and began to offer a titillating choice of articles

Table 3.2 Circulation averages of top twenty-five U.S. magazines, for six months ending 30 June 1981

Ranking	Title	Total average paid circulation
1.	TV Guide	18,084,966
2.	Reader's Digest	17,876,545
3.	National Geographic Magazine	10,732,973
4.	Better Homes and Gardens	8,034,009
5.	Family Circle	7,437,863
6.	Woman's Day	6,896,819
7.	McCall's Magazine	6,206,424
8.	Ladies' Home Journal	5,516,511
9.	Good Housekeeping	5,305,545
10.	Playboy	5,200,936
11.	Penthouse	4,608,700*
12.	Time	4,476,504
13.	Redbook Magazine	4,304,125
14.	The Star	3,424,516
15.	Newsweek	2,955,099
16.	Cosmopolitan	2,750,516
17.	American Legion Magazine	2,594,397
18.	Senior Scholastic	2,548,748
19.	People	2,419,755
20.	Prevention	2,388,246
21.	Sports Illustrated	2,286,238
22.	U.S. News & World Report	2,103,024
23.	Field & Stream	2,017,729
24.	Glamour	2,003,882
25.	Southern Living	1,912,982

Source: Audit Bureau of Circulations FAS-FAX Report, 30 June 1981.

*1980 figures; data for 1981 not filed by FAS-FAX press time.

designed to help the reader become sexy and alluring, to snare a mate or shed a date. In some ways the magazine resembles soft-core pornography, especially in its daring covers, which are primarily responsible for 95 percent of its overall circulation occurring at newsstands and grocery checkouts.

When *Cosmopolitan* did these things, it did something else too. It attracted the advertising of manufacturers of perfumes, uplift brassieres, cosmetics, and other glamour products. Although circulation became far smaller, advertising revenues were assured and they grew as the magazine continually expanded its reach. By 1981 it ranked sixteenth on the list of America's circulation leaders, with an average monthly paid circulation of 2.75 million. *Cosmopolitan* made a successful adjustment during difficult years and is now financially healthy. Most likely the change could not have been made without the close correlation of the three factors we have mentioned: (1) the interest level of the magazine's editorial content; (2) the makeup of its audience; and (3) the kinds of products it advertises.

Table 3.3 *Psychology Today's* readers differ from the national work force*

Occupation	PT sample		National work force	
	Executive or manager	15.9%	Manager and administrator	10.7%
	Professional	43.4%	Professional and technical	15.1%
	Salesman	4.3%	Sales worker	6.3%
	Foreman or skilled worker	9.2%	Skilled worker	13.1%
	Clerical worker	13.7%	Clerical worker	17.8%
	Semiskilled or unskilled	5.7%	Nonfarm labor	5.0%
	Other	7.9%	Operatives (of equipment and transportation)	15.2%
			Service workers	13.7%
			Farm workers	3.0%
	Full time	92.7%	Full time	85.6%
	Part time	7.3%	Part time	14.4%
	Self-employed	6.3%	Self-employed	8.4%
	Wage and salaried	93.7%	Wage and salaried	90.7%
			Family business	.9%
Sex	Female	51.5%	Female	40.5%
	Male	48.5%	Male	59.5%
Age	Under 18	1.2%	16–17	3.4%
	18–24	19.3%	18–24	19.2%
	25–34	43.5%	25–34	25.6%
	35–44	21.8%	35–44	18.8%
	45–54	11.5%	45–54	17.9%
	55+	2.7%	55+	15.2%

Source: Reprinted from *Psychology Today* Magazine. Copyright © 1978 Ziff-Davis Publishing Company.

*Because of the sheer volume of response to *PT's* survey, *PT* took a sample of questionnaires for analysis. By a random-selection process, *PT* assured that the sample would be statistically representative of the whole. *PT* included every 10th survey form they received, in the order that they came in, for a total of 2,300 questionnaires. The table shows the characteristics of the *PT* readers participating in the survey, compared with 1977 figures for the nation provided by the Bureau of Labor Statistics.

Psychology Today

Psychology Today's success formula has been to give young, affluent, and educated readers insights into themselves.

A magazine success story of a different sort is that of *Psychology Today. PT* was the $10,000 brainchild of Nicholas Charney, who reasoned that sufficient interest in human behavior existed to justify a popular magazine, rather than a scholarly journal, on the subject. He was right. Five years after starting *PT* in 1966, Charney sold the magazine to Boise-Cascade for $20 million.

Psychology Today was born at a time when the postwar emphasis on education, stimulated by the GI Bill, and an accelerating public affluence had begun to merge. With less time required to produce the necessities of life, Americans turned inward, in a sort of mass introspection that manifested itself in curiosity about behavior and what motivates us to think as we think, act as we act. *PT* was an instant success. It attained a circulation of 600,000 within four years, with advertising revenues to match. From the

	PT sample		National work force	
Marital status	Single	30.4%	Never married†	22.1%
	Married	48.3%	Married, spouse present	65.6%
	Living together	7.7%	Married, spouse absent	3.1%
	Separated	2.3%	Divorced†	6.2%
	Divorced	10.6%	Widowed†	3.0%
	Widowed	.7%		
Income	*Annual income (before taxes)*		*Total money earning of persons employed (1975 figures)*	
	Less than $5,000	6.5%		
	$5,000-$9,999	23.4%	Less than $5,000	40.9%
	$10,000-$14,999	28.6%	$5,000-$9,999	26.1%
	$15,000-$19,999	19.2%	$10,000-$14,999	17.9%
	$20,000-$29,999	13.9%	$15,000-$19,999	8.6%
	$30,000-$49,999	6.0%	$20,000-$24,999	3.2%
	$50,000+	2.4%	$25,000+	3.2%
Last year of education completed	Grade school or less	.3%	Grade school or less	10.0%
	Some high school	2.3%	Some high school	13.7%
	High school diploma or equivalent	9.6%	High school diploma or equivalent	40.8%
	Some college	25.5%	Some college	17.2%
	College degree	20.1%	College degree	10.8%
	Some graduate or professional school	14.8%	Some graduate or professional school, or graduate or professional	
	Graduate or professional degree	27.5%	school degree	7.5%

†Includes persons who are living together. The Census Bureau estimates that 2 percent of the nation's 48 million "couple households" are living together.

end of the 1970s to the early 1980s it was forty-fifth in circulation, with over 1.165 million in paid circulation. Advertisers were secure in the knowledge that 85.8 percent of that circulation was being mailed to the homes of subscribers, a stark contrast to the nineteen out of twenty *Cosmopolitan* issues picked up at newsstands.

Consider the profile of *PT*'s subscribers, as given in table 3.3. A readership study conducted by *PT* in 1978 revealed subscribers to be relatively young, well educated, nearly equally divided between males and females, and affluent. What kind of advertiser seeks this sort of "new generation" marketing mix? It is not the manufacturer of esoteric psychological paraphernalia. Rather, it is the manufacturer of sports cars, modern clothing, modern furniture, liquor, and other amenities of fine living. Thus, *PT* differs from the *Cosmopolitan* approach in that its interest focus is not specific to its advertisers' products, but rather productive of a real demographic mix. It is important to note that this demographic mix is achieved naturally through self-selection on the subscribers' part and not artificially by the computer. There is a certain arrogance to demographically predetermining

readership affluence by census tract and then arbitrarily directing advertisements for sleek or sleazy product lines. However, an audience may preselect itself along these same lines, and in the end the magazine and the advertisers may be justifiably self-satisfied.

Filling the Gaps

Twenty years ago *Cosmopolitan* perceived a need and acted to fill it. For an example of a magazine that has filled a different need, consider Meridian Publishing Company, Inc., of Ogden, Utah. With only three editors and a dozen artists, it puts out 6.5 million copies of 1,500 different titles each month. Incredible? Not really, when you consider that Meridian actually produces the basic ingredients of only five magazines, each of which is sent to hundreds of different companies, airlines, travel agents, resorts, hospitals, credit unions, sports manufacturers, and so forth. In each case, the company, town, or institution buys the entire issue, 80 percent of which is preprinted for all customers. It contracts to have its own logo, local advertising, and editorial comments to fill the remaining 20 percent.

The oldest of Meridian's four basic magazines is *Your Home,* founded in 1947. It is used as the house organ of 600 different firms: home improvement outlets, decorators, realtors, and builders. *Accent* is a travel-oriented magazine, bought by resorts, airlines, and travel agents interested in the magazine's articles on how and where to travel, and how to save money when traveling, for example. *People on Parade* is an upbeat magazine filled with personality profiles, success stories, and light entertainment. It counts hospitals, business developers, and credit unions among its outlets. *Sports Parade* is used by many different sports producers eager to get their name before the public, and *Inflight,* the newest member of the Meridian family, services numerous regional and commuter airlines in the United States and Canada.

Why a <u>used</u> Mercedes-Benz is often more valuable than a <u>new</u> anything else.

For the automobile industry, retained value is the ultimate test of a car's true quality. Based on the average official used car prices over the past five years, Mercedes-Benz holds its value better than any other make of luxury car sold in America — any make. And even when used, a Mercedes-Benz is often more valuable than a brand-new anything else.

The reasons become obvious when you examine a Mercedes-Benz. Advanced engineering. Superb craftsmanship. Luxurious accommodations. The timeless qualities of every Mercedes-Benz ever made.

Come in and arrange a drive. Our Used Car Manager will be glad to help you discover the special pleasures and values of a Mercedes-Benz.

**European Motors, Ltd.
2915 Broadway
Oakland, CA 94611
Phone 832-6030**

**Where Mercedes Owners Go To
Be Treated Like Mercedes Owners . . .**

Printed Monthly by Meridian Publishing Company in the U. S. A. — August, '79   Cover: Fred Kaplan

PEOPLE ON PARADE

HOUSEWIFE'S
BEST
FRIEND

**Where Mercedes Owners Go To
Be Treated Like Mercedes Owners . . .**

Meridian Publishing Company makes it possible for hundreds of small companies or institutions to have their own "personalized" magazines.
Meridian Publishing Co., Inc.

TAKE YOUR CHOICE . . .

PONTIAC   *Cadillac*   GMC TRUCKS

. . . Then Come To The Right Place.

THE PLACE.

LARRY LANGE PONTIAC/CADILLAC is *the* place to save on the new models for 1979. Drive a little further north, to McKinney, and discover the deal that's waiting for you. See all the new '79's, plus a fine selection of pre-owned cars. Sales department open 8 a.m. to 8 p.m. weekdays and til 6 p.m. Saturdays.

LARRY LANGE
Pontiac   Cadillac
800 N. Central Expressway • McKinney

Printed Monthly by Meridian Publishing Company in the U. S. A. — August, '79   Cover: Fred Kaplan

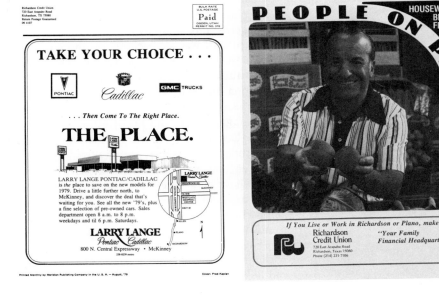

PEOPLE ON PARADE

HOUSEWIFE'S
BEST
FRIEND

If You Live or Work in Richardson or Plano, make
**Richardson
Credit Union**
720 East Arapaho Road
Richardson, Texas 75080
Phone (214) 231-7106
*"Your Family
Financial Headquarters"*

Free-lance writers contribute 90 percent of the editorial material in Meridian's magazines; over 5,000 different writers submit articles annually for the publishing house's editors to pick over. About forty articles are used each month in the four outlets. Fifteen artists are needed to localize the ad copy for the 1,500 different purchasers who expect each magazine to look uniquely its own. In short, it's a perfect business arrangement, with the publisher, writers, institutions, and readers all happily mass producing and consuming the "personalized" media.

The Editorial Task

From a production standpoint magazines fall somewhere between their print cousins, books and newspapers. They are not on the relentless daily schedule of a newspaper, nor do they experience the painstaking leisure of book publishing. Most magazines work further ahead of schedule than one might be led to believe. The average monthly general-interest magazine is prepared four to six months in advance of publication. That is, the staff will start "dummying up," or composing, a July issue in January, committing some articles and commissioning others with the thought that, for all intents and purposes, the issue will be closed by April except for some minor loose ends of material.

Newspapers are almost entirely written by staff members, and books are almost entirely written by outside authors. Magazines fall between these two poles. While some are completely staff written and others are completely contracted, most employ some balance of the two techniques, with an edge toward staff writing because, by and large, it is less expensive and more reliable than the work of outside authors. Good authors are hard to come by, and authors who have successfully published and have established some reputation generally command considerable fees for their material. The names of some of these authors also constitute an additional drawing card for the magazine. All this notwithstanding, there are surprisingly few full-time free-lance authors in the United States; probably fewer than 300 free-lancers support themselves entirely from their writing, and only a portion of them earn as much as $10,000 a year. Because of this, it is reasonable to ask where magazine articles come from. For the most part, they come from experts in a given field who hold jobs in the field and who write as a sideline. For example, *Psychology Today,* which is about half staff-written and half contract-written, commissions its outside articles from practicing psychologists, university professors, and the like. A considerable number of newspaper journalists augment their earnings with outside articles and feature material, as do book authors. The latter, of course, bring considerable "name attraction" to a magazine.

As in book publishing, magazine editors have either a stable of acceptable authors whose work and expertise they know, or they rely on literary agents whom they trust. Agents and authors also constantly suggest story ideas to the magazines in the form of queries or outlines in hope of a contract. Each magazine editor zealously tries to maintain a constant tone

Magazine articles are written by staff members or free-lancers; balancing content to meet reader interests demands sensitive gatekeeping.

or flavor to the publication—a proven format of exactly the right material mix, both written and graphic—that will continue to appeal to the magazine's specific readership. The editor's gatekeeping function is dictated less by the surplus of material than by the rigid requirements of the particular audience. The editor must ruthlessly prune everything, regardless of intrinsic merit, that does not exactly fit both the overall format of the magazine and the particular mix of a given issue. The task is, in part, a balancing act in which judgmental factors enter more sensitively than in the case of either newspaper editors, whose principle concern is the news, or book publishers, whose concern is with appeal in the singular sense.

As we have seen, advertising is of critical importance to the magazine industry. Without substantial advertising, most magazines would fold, as did *Collier's,* the original *Life, Look,* and *Saturday Evening Post* during the 1960s and early 1970s. In this section we will explore the relation between magazines and advertising—the use of reader surveys, the ways in which ads become part of the content of a magazine, and the potential for marketing directly to the readers of a magazine through the use of the subscription list.

Magazines and Advertising

Magazine circulation is deceptive. There is an exposure factor that is not reflected in raw circulation figures. In other words, the number of people who read or are at least exposed to magazines is far greater than the number who buy or subscribe to them (as happens, for example, in doctors' offices). This exposure factor will vary widely, of course, with the nature of the magazine, running as high as six times for the circulation of national general-interest magazines, to little more than single exposure for some of the smaller, more esoteric business or scholarly publications. In any event, this exposure factor is far higher for magazines than for either newspapers or books among the print media, or for all broadcast media.

Readership Surveys

Magazine readership is far wider than simple circulation figures indicate.

Readership surveys help to determine exposure. Most magazines subscribe to some rating service such as the Starch Report, which helps advertisers determine their true costs in reaching audiences. Magazine advertising, while sold on the basis of circulation, is calculated on estimated exposure. This is to say, a kind of double standard exists whereby advertisers purchase space off the rate card, which is a reflection of audited circulation, but calculate their *cost per thousand*—the cost to reach each one thousand members of the audience—on presumed exposure as indicated by the Starch Report.

Advertising as Content

The close ties between magazines and advertising frequently extend beyond the economic support provided by advertisers. In fact, advertising sometimes becomes a very real part of the editorial content itself, and may be one of the prime reasons for reading the magazine. Evidence of this fact stems from World War II when editions of national magazines with the advertising deleted were sent to troops overseas on the naïve theory that

Advertising is more than mere persuasion; it has an important informational component.

soldiers were interested only in the reading material and were in no position to purchase the goods advertised anyway. This brought immediate complaints from the troops, who felt that they were being shortchanged. They missed the ads and the memories of home evoked by the ads. A part of the pleasure experienced by the troops was their contemplation of the things to which they would return. This speaks much for the commercial base of American society, even for a serviceman lingering in a foxhole. It also demonstrates the integrated nature of mass communications, which acts as a carrier of culture, reflecting quite accurately the life-style of a society.

In fact, in many glossy-paged magazines, advertising has developed into an art form of colorful and aesthetic and sensuous appeal, which Roland Wolseley describes as "word, camera, and brush pictures of new products."[12] The smashing illustrations in *Vogue* and *Harper's Bazaar* come to mind immediately. In such magazines, the editorial content plays either a secondary or a supporting role. John Hohenberg, in *The News Media: A Journalist Looks at His Profession,* made the observation that in many of the specialized magazines dealing with fashion, travel, or the like the editorial matter serves purely as supportive material for the advertising, with substantial editorial preference and even "trade-out" material being awarded to major advertisers.[13] Trade-out material is that editorial matter promised to an advertiser in exchange for a substantial volume of advertising. Some magazines match advertising and editorial content for major advertisers on a page-for-page basis.

Marketing Audience Interest

Once identified, magazine subscribers become targets for all sorts of related goods, services, and persuasion efforts.

In *Psychology Today* and other such publications, the audience is far more than a source of subscriber revenue and a target for advertising. The audience is a self-identified market for a variety of goods and services made available by the publishers; in *PT's* case, this includes posters, games, videotapes, and a whole series of books. The magazine, in essence, provides the means for establishing a credible roster of potential customers for certain kinds of products. *PT* founder Nicholas Charney once said, "The magazine is simply a tool to identify an audience with a particular interest . . . and that special list of subscribers is a prime target for a whole range of other services."[14]

Other publications have followed *PT's* lead. *Family Health,* a relatively new magazine, had little over a million subscribers in 1971 and immediately moved into the business of marketing medical encyclopedia sets with resultant sales amounting to over 40,000 sets. *Southern Living* has used its subscribers for marketing quality Southern cookbooks, while *New York* envisages its readership as a base for selling a how-to-do-it series on survival in New York.

Magazines' complementary services reach beyond the magazines themselves. It did not take publishers long, for instance, to realize that a painstakingly developed, self-identified list of potential customers was in itself a valuable asset. Some magazines have taken to selling—or, rather, renting—all or portions of their subscription lists to other organizations as sales tools. If a test mailing is satisfactory, an organization or manufacturer may want to buy the entire list at so much per thousand names. Magazines also make a healthy profit selling their subscription lists to other magazines at three to five cents a name, and more than one entrepreneur has made a go of it by merely selling different sets of lists to interested buyers. A "good" mailing list is likely to bring as high a response as 15 percent, though 10 percent is considered very satisfactory.

In many respects, the future of the magazine industry is already here. The prevailing trend in media is the logical progression from elitism, to the pursuit of the largest possible audiences, and on into the age of specialization. The latter stage finds media seeking out, and catering to, individuals and groups identified by social, economic, educational, professional, cultural, recreational, religious, and many other interests. Surely the magazine industry has already gone that route; indeed, some of these interests were being catered to over a century ago, and we see no likelihood of a reversion to mass-circulation magazines that seek the broadest national common denominator.

Technologically and economically, the magazine of tomorrow will differ from that of today. As we have already seen in our forecasts about newspapers, the marriage of print to electronics will radically alter the production and distribution of print media. Magazines are no exception. In some ways, perhaps most significantly in terms of distribution techniques, where the bulky magazine has been hard hit by exponential increases in postal rates (nearly 500 percent in the 1970s alone), the magazine industry is ready for change. Smaller issues on lighter paper sent through the mail or distributed by individual carriers contracted by publishers have constituted one change. Experimentation with electronic, satellite, and laser technology for production, as seen in *Time* magazine, is another. Publishing houses of the future may find themselves contracting with electronic information-dispensing companies, or they will start up their own, to assure rapid and widespread dissemination of magazine matter that appeals to a few or to many consumers, each having his or her own in-home computer with page-printing capacity (see chap. 8).

As discussed in chapter 2, individual consumers will be given freedom of selection in the privacy of their own homes, using their home information systems—video-display terminals with printout capacities. Consumers will select news, information, entertainment, and advertising to suit their own purposes, much as they do now but with wider choices. More than in any other media form, tomorrow's magazine will be able to pander to the most individualistic characteristics delineated by demographic and psychographic research. This raises, of course, the specter of self-indulgent masses of heterogeneous individuals who lack a sense of community, a serious concern facing not only tomorrow's magazine publishers but all media producers.

The Future of Magazines

The magazine, more than any other medium, has seen the future: an age of specialization.

Summary

Magazines have developed historically to occupy a middle position between the time-consuming and self-selective book and the hurried, geographically circumscribed newspaper. All magazines share two characteristics: They are published regularly, and each appeals to some specific segment of society.

The first magazines were the *Tatler* and the *Spectator,* published in England in the first quarter of the eighteenth century. By the early nineteenth century magazines were available in the United States, the first market-specific magazine being *Godey's Lady's Book,* first published in 1830. The last third of the century is known as the Golden Age of magazines. The industry flourished because of technological developments, the existence of the transcontinental railroad, and the Postal Act which created less expensive second-class mail.

Muckrakers characterized the early part of this century, but their influence waned after the failure of Theodore Roosevelt's third party candidacy in 1912. By the 1950s, television began to usurp the national audience, and several general-interest magazines eventually ceased publication after costly circulation wars. The advertising had gone to television.

There are several ways to categorize magazines. One way is to categorize them functionally, for example, as entertainment/escape, news/information, or advocacy/opinion. We can also consider the relation between content and audience. Most magazines today are narrow in subject and narrow in audience. *TV Guide,* however, is narrow in subject but broad in audience. There are also newsmagazines and city magazines. Some magazines carry no advertisements and others, called controlled circulation, are given away free. Finally, there are organizational publications that number in excess of 9,000 in the United States.

Most magazines are owned by multi-magazine groups to share costs and expertise and to protect against the possible failure of one. While some magazines are started on a shoestring, the costs of publishing magazines today make that method rare.

Cosmopolitan and *Psychology Today* are two magazines that became very successful in the 1960s and 1970s, although they are quite different from one another. They attract different audiences and different advertisers; in addition, *PT* is sold primarily by subscription while *Cosmopolitan* is purchased at newsstands. Some magazines rely on staff writers for material while others buy the work of free-lancers; many use a mix of the two sources for their articles. Few writers make enough money to support themselves solely by free-lancing.

Advertising is crucial to most magazines. Reader surveys help to determine the pass-along readership, which is a measure of exposure for advertisers. In some cases, the advertising may be more important than the content to the reader, as is often the case with glossy fashion magazines.

In recent years subscription lists have provided advertisers with an additional channel to markets, and have provided additional revenue to their owners; magazines may use these lists to sell their own products or they may rent them to organizations and manufacturers.

Technology will soon make it possible for readers to select only that material they want to see. This is of concern to media producers who fear that it may isolate people, leading to a lack of a sense of community.

Notes

1. Theodore Peterson, *Magazines in the Twentieth Century* (Urbana, Ill.: University of Illinois Press, 1956).
2. Edwin Emery and Michael Emery, *The Press and America: An Interpretative History of the Mass Media*, 4th ed. (Englewood Cliffs, N.J.: Prentice-Hall, 1978), p. 274.
3. David Halberstam, *The Powers That Be* (New York: Alfred A. Knopf, 1979) and Herbert J. Gans, *Deciding What's News: A Study of CBS Evening News, NBC Nightly News, Newsweek and Time* (New York: Pantheon Books, 1979).
4. Alan D. Fletcher, "City Magazines Find a Niche in the Media Marketplace," *Journalism Quarterly,* Winter 1977, pp. 742–43, 749.
5. Benjamin M. Compaine, "Magazines," in *Who Owns the Media? Concentration of Ownership in the Mass Communications Industry,* ed. Benjamin M. Compaine (New York: Harmony Books, 1979), p. 155.
6. Ibid., pp. 156–57.
7. Ibid., p. 157.
8. Ibid.
9. Ibid.
10. *ABC Magazine Trend Report,* 1974–1978 (Chicago: Audit Bureau of Circulations, February 1980).
11. A. Kent MacDougall, "Magazines: Fighting for a Place in the Market," *Los Angeles Times,* 9 April 1978; reprinted in *Readings in Mass Communication: Concepts and Issues in the Mass Media,* 4th ed., ed. Michael Emery and Ted Curtis Smythe (Dubuque, Ia.: Wm. C. Brown Company Publishers, 1980), pp. 284–93.
12. Roland E. Wolseley, *The Changing Magazine: Trends in Readership and Management* (New York: Hastings House, 1973).
13. John Hohenberg, *The News Media: A Journalist Looks at His Profession* (New York: Holt, Rinehart and Winston, 1968).
14. Lynne Williams, *Medium or Message?* (Woodbury, N.Y.: Barron's Educational Series, 24 May 1971).

4 Books

Books serve a historical role in the development of mass communications and qualify as a mass medium on the basis of their aggregate audience, which is huge, rather than on the basis of the number of persons who might read any given title. Even blockbuster best-sellers rarely sell more than 2 million copies each year. Given pass-along readership, they still don't reach as many people as the *New York Daily News* reaches each day in New York City alone, or as many as *Time* or *Newsweek* reach in a week. But size is not the only measure of a medium. The hardback book is considered by many to be the most credible print form, followed by the paperback book, the magazine, and finally newspapers.[1] Books are credible because of their association with formal education, and because they are durable.

Books last; some books printed several hundred years ago are still in existence. And the ideas contained in some books last even longer, becoming transmitters of the culture from one generation to the next. They represent the consciences of times and people gone by, and they speak to each reader individually. They are private in a harassed and public time; according to Marshall McLuhan, they enhance individuality, orderliness, and logic.[2]

In our consideration of the book as a mass medium in society, we begin by taking an appropriate look into history and then concentrate on significant twentieth-century factors relevant to the publishing industry. Of special interest is the manner in which the oldest mass medium has adapted to contemporary media—with which it has come to coexist. We conclude the chapter with a discussion of the relative freedom in the content of books and the future of books in an increasingly electronic media world.

Books are durable and credible; they enhance individuality, orderliness, and logic.

The book transmits culture over generations.
Bob Adelman/Magnum Photos

Book publication and readership dates back about 5,500 years.

Books have a history that dates back nearly 5,500 years. The oldest known alphabet, on which the Phoenician alphabet is based, dates from about 1400 B.C. Using this alphabet, the Phoenicians created a writing system that they derived from speech rather than from unwieldy pictographs or abstract symbols, such as wedge-shaped cuneiforms. At the great library at Alexandria, in Egypt, scholars seeking to codify the knowledge of the ages accumulated more than half a million scrolls. Through the Greek and Roman periods writing became more standardized. Later during the Dark Ages, the Christian influence made itself felt as monks did their part in keeping literacy alive by transcribing ancient literary and religious works onto parchment.

As the writing process developed, materials used to write on became more portable. They progressed from clay tablets to animal skins to expensive but durable parchment, to linen and other ragstock, and finally—within the last two centuries—to wood-pulp paper, which arrived in time to accommodate the rotary printing press.

Comparative table of hieroglyphic and alphabetic characters.
The Bettman Archives, Inc.

Chaldaic Letters.	Conjectural Chaldaic Hieroglyphic Originals.	Phenician Letters.	Conjectural Phenician Hieroglyphic Originals.	Egyptian Letters.	Original Egyptian Hieroglyphics.	Literary Hieroglyphics	Hieratic Letters	Demotic	Coptic	Samaritan.	Phenician.	Syriac.	Arabic.	Ancient Greek	N'trus-tan.	
																A
																Bh or B
																Gh or G
																Dh or D
																H
																V or W
																Z or Ds
																CH or Hh
																T
																J or I
																CH or K
																L
																M
																N
																S
																Aa or Gn
																Ph or P
																Ts or Ss
																K or Q
																R
																Sh or S
																Th or T

The physical appearance of books, particularly their binding materials, also changed considerably. Papyrus or parchment scrolls, which were frustrating to handle, were replaced in the fourth century A.D. by the Roman invention of the codex, a system by which sheets of papyrus or parchment were tied by cords between wooden boards. This binding led to greater ease of reading and made possible the preparation of indexes, which enhanced the book as an information medium.

During the 1430s Johann Gutenberg, a little-known German printer, began experimenting with ways to improve the primitive methods of printing in use at that time. Although the Chinese had invented movable type several hundred years earlier, Europeans were unaware of this Asian achievement. Consequently, Gutenberg was credited with having invented it. In 1456 Gutenberg printed the Mazarin Bible, reputed to be the first book printed with movable type. And so began the era of mass communication.

Gutenberg's Bible and Movable Type

At that time most of the population was illiterate. With rare exceptions, priests and monks were the only ones who had access to hand-printed books and the advantages of some schooling. Nonetheless, only a few years passed before the practice of printing had spread across Europe. In 1476 William Caxton set up a press in England where he printed *Dictes or Sayengis of the Philosophes*. By 1500 some 30,000 different books had been produced, and several million volumes were in the hands of the clergy and the secular elite and had started to become available to the developing middle classes.

With the growth of the printer's craft the opportunity to become literate was enormously enhanced. It became possible for persons to sequester themselves with the Bible, read it, and develop their own interpretations of the Gospel—interpretations that were sometimes at variance with church dogma. As more people formulated new opinions, they won converts and then began writing their own interpretations of the Bible. Disputes occurred within the Roman Catholic church, which caused a fragmentation into different denominations, forming the social matrix of that period known as the Protestant Reformation.

Gutenberg's printing press ushered in the age of mass communications, with enormous social and political ramifications.

The first printing press in America was established at Harvard College in 1638, less than twenty years after the Pilgrims landed at Plymouth Rock. However, the orientation of the colonists and their successor Americans was less toward the book than toward shorter, more quickly digested forms of print. Little leisure time was available to the frontier settlers, and they took their information on the run.

Book Publishing in America

Different reading patterns existed among the affluent, who were the primary owners and readers of books. Aristocracy, even in colonial America, was frequently measured by the number of leather-bound books one possessed. Paperbacks of a sort didn't make their appearance until 1777, when Americans began buying some of the first 190 volumes of John Bell's "British Poets" series.

Colonial book publishers served an elite clientele.

Given a newly literate audience, textbooks and paperbacks were mass produced in the 1800s.

Technologically, the production of books did not vary much between 1450 and 1800. Hand-operated presses continued to crank out handset type a page at a time. Literacy rates were low and the cost of books was high, so there was no great pressure on printers to develop a more efficient process. It is estimated that only about 10 percent of Americans could read and write in 1800, and the average book cost about one dollar, or a week's wages for the typical worker. But when compulsory public education was instituted later in the nineteenth century, technology was also improved, which resulted in a lower per unit cost. Paper in a continuous roll and the durable iron press were two European inventions that improved the printing process. Steam-powered presses and ultimately mechanical typesetting machines coalesced during the nineteenth century, resulting in large-scale book production.

Despite the production of some 50,000 different titles (books, magazines, and newspapers) rolling off American presses between 1640 and 1820, most Americans were still relying on European printers to satisfy their literary appetites. Once mechanical, literary, and economic bases permitted it, however, home-grown publications flourished. By the 1840s, inexpensive editions of mass-produced books were available for ten cents a copy, spawning the age of books as a popular mass medium in America. E. F. Beadle, a New York publisher who started by publishing dime songbooks, discovered a ready market for entertaining prose as well. The first big era of the paperback was born with *Beadle's Dime Dialogues,* devoted to pioneer adventures.

Textbooks also got their start in the 1840s. William Holmes McGuffey, an educator in Ohio, may be called the father of the schoolbook for his work in compiling the McGuffey *Eclectic Readers.* Between 1836 and 1857, McGuffey wrote six primers (graded for difficulty) that became the standard reading textbooks for more than half a century. Total sales of the McGuffey *Readers* are estimated at over 122 million copies.

During the Civil War, soldiers seeking ready diversion constituted a market for escapist literature in inexpensive, portable packages. Horatio Alger, before his death in 1899, cranked out 120 different titles of such fiction, which sold to the tune of 30 million copies. America loved Alger's rags-to-riches sagas, which have helped to form America's social and cultural legacy.

Paperback publishing expanded for a time during the 1870s and 1880s. When the cost of newsprint dropped, the *New York Tribune* began publishing paperbacks in the form of newspaper extras, which sold for five to fifteen cents a copy. By 1877, fifteen different firms were competing for the paperback trade, and by 1885 about a third of the nearly 5,000 titles published annually were produced in paperback and distributed through established bookshops and by subscription.

The international copyright law of 1891 spelled the end of the second paperback generation in America, by granting royalties to overseas writers whose works had previously been pirated. By 1900 the paperback business went into a coma, after years of heavy competition, price-cutting among competing companies, soaring costs, large numbers of unsold books, and a dwindling supply of new writers.[3]

The hardback book business, on the other hand, had expanded steadily. Such authors as Henry James, Mark Twain, Edgar Allan Poe, and William Dean Howells contributed immeasurably to the growth of book publishing and distribution in the United States before the end of the nineteenth century. They were followed by the naturalists and the muckrakers at the turn of the century, who also found a ready market for their wares: gripping narratives and descriptions of institutional corruption and greed, the nature of power, the realities of life in an increasingly urban society. Social historians do not need to look any further than these books to recapture America.

Publishing houses before the turn of the century had developed into significant forces, and book publishing had gained a reputation as a gentleman's profession. Publishing houses that were family owned and operated respected each other's writers and products, and went so far as to acknowledge colleagues' rights to republish imported books on the basis of whoever gained first access to them. Decisions about what works would or would not be published rested as much on aesthetic as on economic grounds.[4]

By 1900 literacy rates had reached 90 percent, quite a jump from the 10 percent a mere century before. Free public libraries were giving even the penniless access to books. Works of history, fiction, science, and classical literature, as well as newspapers, magazines, and inexpensive dime novels, were being read by an increasingly literate population whose work status and economic conditions found them better able to utilize their time and finances.

The Twentieth Century

Most of the significant changes in the publishing industry during the twentieth century have occurred since World War II. The years prior to the war were characterized by the growth of major publishing houses catering to a mass demand for works of fiction, a decrease in the number of family-owned companies specializing in a single type of book, and cutthroat competition among literary agents that altered the gentlemanly understandings that formerly prevailed among publishers. The time might be characterized as the *commercialization of literature,* when printing and marketing practices became streamlined in conjunction with other big businesses. While some segments of the industry seemed to change very little—plodding along as usual with only marginal profits—the paperback industry was gearing up for a renaissance of unequaled proportions.

Literature has become commercialized: Book publishing is another big business.

In 1939 the scene was set. Taking a cue from Britain's Penguin Books, which were successfully sold through newsstands and chain stores, Robert F. deGraff introduced Pocket Books to the American consumer. Within two years they were sweeping the country. Their rapid popularity came about largely because of the twenty-five-cent price and because deGraff marketed them through independent magazine wholesalers, who could distribute them to newsstands in very busy train stations where Americans were passing to and from work each day. Avon Books followed in 1941, Popular Library in 1942, Dell Books in 1943, and Bantam Books in 1945. All of them published numerous war books—fiction and nonfiction—to qualify for paper allotments. This in turn made possible the publication of vast numbers of general-interest paperbacks, which were being consumed as rapidly as they could be produced and shelved.

The period since 1945 has been referred to by Charles Madison as the *publishing goes public* era. By the end of World War II publishing had become a risky business. Vast financial commitments for presses and production equipment forced some publishers to become timid about gambling on untried authors or untapped markets. Modernization was expensive, and many independent, family-owned companies realized the only way to survive was to go public, or to sell stock in themselves to individual investors. Many mergers occurred as publishing houses pooled resources for economic survival. Conglomerates also emerged as a result of the rapid growth during the 1950s and 1960s, realized by the sales in paperbacks and textbooks, which began when the large number of postwar babies reached school age and an equally large number of returning servicemen enrolled in college on the GI Bill. Ties between Hollywood and the book industry also strengthened after World War II, providing publishers with new opportunities for marketing books and, of course, with additional revenue. All of this painted a rosy picture for the large corporations. From 1952 to 1970, the industry as a whole grew at a rate of more than 10 percent annually, although it slowed down to around 7 percent shortly thereafter.

Given that growth rate, it was only natural for larger corporations to look at book publishing as a good investment. Instead of being controlled by family patriarchs, the finances of publishing houses are more likely to be in the hands of bookkeepers and financial experts of massive corporations. Electronics corporations such as Xerox, ITT, IBM, Litton, and others who entered the publishing marketplace recognize that the future of the book, and particularly the textbook, might well be closely aligned to electronic multimedia information storage and retrieval. Media conglomerates also became interested in publishing. Gulf & Western bought Simon & Schuster and Pocket Books; MCA now owns G. P. Putnam's Sons and Berkley/Jove. CBS, as another example, entered publishing in 1967 with the purchase of Holt, Rinehart & Winston. By 1981 it had added Popular Library, W. B. Saunders, and *Woman's Day* and several other magazines to the division, making CBS one of the largest publishing corporations, with annual revenues of $400 million.

Other print-oriented companies, such as Reader's Digest, Time Incorporated, McGraw-Hill, and the Times-Mirror Company of Los Angeles, have carved out places of their own in the book industry. In such organizational settings, book publishing contributes a certain prestige and small but steady profits—profits that are offset by the higher profits of the conglomerates' more mundane divisions.

Even though the entire mass communications network is becoming more interwoven, no more than a dozen major corporations seem to dominate the book industry. Given the worldwide trends toward consolidation and economic efficiency, any change in that overall picture seems unlikely during this decade. However, a significant new development has been uncovered in a recent census report: A sizable number of small new publishing ventures, many of them specialist houses, has had a substantial impact on industry sales. As John Dessauer, who regularly surveys the industry, noted in a *Publishers Weekly* article,

Even if the pace of expansion were now to slacken, even if some of the new imprints were ultimately to fail, a safe assumption is that the existence of so many small independent publishers is bound to affect the future of the book field profoundly and lastingly.[5]

The Types of Books

The book industry is made up of fairly distinct publishing divisions, which are determined primarily by the market the publisher wants to reach. To the layperson, the most familiar type of book is probably the *trade book,* the industry's term to describe books for the general consumer that are sold through bookstores. *Paperbacks* sold in bookstores and at newsstands form another category of books, although some paperbacks are considered as either trade books or textbooks. *Textbooks* are the third major category of books. They are published for elementary, high school (el-hi) and college-level students. Books published for post-college specialists are categorized as *professional* or *scholarly* publishing. Most university press books are for this market.

Books are categorized as *trade books* for general audiences, *paperbacks, textbooks* and *professional books.* It's a $7 billion-a-year business, with 50,000 different titles published each year.

By the early 1980s, Americans were spending some $7 billion annually to purchase books. Despite other claims on their time—especially the lure of television—they were devoting larger proportions of their available dollars and leisure time on a wider selection of increasingly expensive books. Although the number of titles published each year (including new books and new editions) increased from 38,000 in 1970 to nearly 50,000 by 1982, most of the increase in revenue book publishers enjoyed during that period can be attributed to rising prices. Reflecting the inflationary spiral, the *average* hardcover volume sold for $25.48 in 1981. Disregarding the special books in the over-$80 price range, the average volume cost $24.33, enough to put a dent in the book lover's budget. College students will not be surprised to learn that much of this expensive market was comprised of textbooks; science books, at an average of $33.97 per copy, led

Table 4.1 American book title production, 1981

Categories (using Dewey classifications)	Totals of all hardbound and paperbound books
Agriculture	391
Art	1,334
Biography	1,589
Business	1,156
Education	946
Fiction	5,107
General works	1,493
History	1,891
Home economics	816
Juveniles	2,780
Language	477
Law	1,113
Literature	1,426
Medicine	3,142
Music	338
Philosophy, psychology	1,250
Poetry, drama	996
Religion	1,913
Science	2,863
Sociology, economics	6,610
Sports, recreation	1,064
Technology	2,246
Travel	401
	41,538*

Source: Chandler B. Grannis, "1981 Title Output and Average Prices Preliminary Figures." Reprinted from the 12 March 1982 issue of *Publishers Weekly,* published by R. R. Bowker Company, a Xerox company. Copyright © 1982 by Xerox Corporation.

*Grannis notes that this preliminary total underrepresents mass market paperbacks, whose additional numbers, unavailable at press time, were expected to bring the grand total to somewhere between 45,000 and 50,000 titles.

the list, with the "bargains" found in the general literature, poetry, and drama categories, a mere $18.53 per volume. Some comfort could be found in the proliferation of paperback texts, but the prices in the paperback industry were inflating at more than 10 percent a year, to $9.70 per book, a figure that includes the millions of inexpensive "mass market paperbacks" that average around $2.65.[6]

Trade Books

Typically, trade books are hardcover editions, written for adults and children, that deal with subjects in a multitude of categories: fiction, current nonfiction, biography, literary classics, cookbooks, hobby books, popular science books, travel books, art books, and books on self-improvement, sports, music, poetry, and drama. They are distributed through approximately 12,000 retail outlets, 200 book clubs, and 30,000 libraries, primarily by a corps of *travelers,* the trade name for book salespeople.

Each year thousands of new trade titles are published. Fiction books account for only 2,000 titles, a number that has dropped in recent years because of the risks involved. Ten book publishers, led by Random House and Simon & Schuster, dominate the trade business with 68 percent of the market. Most publishing is concentrated on the East Coast, primarily in New York, Boston, and Philadelphia, its antecedents dating back to the Revolution, but many eastern publishers are branching out, with West Coast divisions becoming more common. Small trade publishers are located in all parts of the country. Some of them do a thriving business publishing books with a regional emphasis. Others focus on books that will appeal to special-interest groups.

Book publishing entails an enormous gamble, which probably accounts for its relatively small size in the sprawling communications field. For instance, fewer than 5 percent of the new trade titles published each year sell as many as 5,000 copies, and sales of at least that amount are necessary for publishers to break even on their investment. This figure is particularly significant because it demonstrates that only a tiny fraction of the books published will be money-makers; furthermore, the profits derived

Fewer than 5 percent of the trade book titles issued annually make a profit.

from this tiny fraction must compensate for 95 percent of the speculative titles that don't make it at all. This is one reason why books are so high priced and why the industry has had to economize somewhat and use a number of imaginative merchandising techniques.

Paperback Books

The postwar paperback boom was the publishing counterpart of a general communications explosion in the United States that was spawned by affluence, attendant leisure, and new technology. High-speed presses and offset printing from rubber mats made the printing process faster and more economical. The introduction of *perfect binding*—the practice of using adhesive to bind books instead of sewing them—produced additional savings. As the business grew, it gradually evolved along two lines: mass-market books and quality paperbacks. Mass-market books are compact volumes designed to fit paperback racks in bookstores and at newsstands. Quality paperbacks have a larger trim size and a higher price than the mass-market variety. They resemble other trade books except for their soft cover.

Paperbacks try to be all things to all people. Classics and trash abound.

There are about twenty major paperback publishers in the United States, although 85 percent of the mass-market business is controlled by ten publishers. Like their hardcover counterparts, most tend to specialize, some in entertainment, some in reprinting classics. Most try to achieve some sort of a balanced inventory of offerings, in an attempt to reach all segments of the potential market from several directions. Publishing is one of the few fields where an operator can be in competition with itself by bringing out a number of competitive and even contradictory titles. Its audience, more than in any other segment of publishing, is made up of individuals whose purchases need not be single and whose interests are not mutually exclusive.

When one thinks of paperbacks, the cheaper mass-market editions of former hardcover best-sellers generally come to mind. While this is certainly one practice, it does not tell the entire story. For example, there is a good deal of classical publishing in paperback for the simple reason that as copyrights expire, no royalties are required to be paid. Thus, with cheaper paperback publishing costs, profit can be shown on smaller sales. In this way paperback publishers seek to tap the college and university market in the same fashion as hardcover publishers who produce texts.

Few publishers attempt both hardcover and paperback work. While the profits from bringing out a paperback edition of a publisher's own best-seller are high, such occasions are limited. The temptation to build up a line of paperbacks from one's own hardcover inventory is great, but not necessarily profitable. Also, the hardback competitor may be leery of turning over valuable property to a company that publishes in both hardcover and paperback. The two forms of book publishing tend to remain separate primarily for economic reasons, with hardcover publishers selling the reprint rights to paperback publishers on an advance-and-royalty basis and paperback publishers making deals directly with authors for paperback originals.

When paperback companies find themselves bidding against each other for reprint rights, the auctions are frequently high drama. In the past decade at least a dozen million-dollar auctions have been held. Top money for bidding during the 1970s was $3.208 million which Bantam Books, Inc., shelled out to Judith Krantz for rights to *Princess Daisy*. This certainly eclipsed Mario Puzo's shortstanding record of $2.2 million for *Fools Die*. In Puzo's case, however, his hardback publisher, G. P. Putnam's Sons, accepted New American Library's offer to include an additional $350,000 for the right to reprint millions of additional copies of Puzo's *The Godfather*. Puzo was no loser; he garnered 60 percent of the $2.55 million package before giving his agent a mere $255,000 for her troubles. Generally, authors receive 50 percent of the reprint rights, but Puzo's track record put him in a better bargaining position and encouraged New American Library to print 10 million paperback copies of *Fools Die*. Puzo's publisher (and Krantz's publisher, who was well aware of her success with *Scruples*) knew the book would move quickly and become what the trade likes to call a sure-fire-box-office-hit.

There is also a substantial amount of original publishing in paperback. Authors' royalties per copy are generally less, hovering between 2 and 4 percent (contrasted with the 10 to 15 percent for hardcover editions), but the greater projected sales more than compensate. Generally, these originals are concentrated in the entertainment field where their lack of staying power is not significant. Occasionally, however, a paperback original of considerable merit appears. Western novels and romances are also published originally in paperback. In recent years these areas have become "hot," with some publishers producing ten or more titles every month. Harlequin romances is an example. The company has a stable of writers who follow a standard formula, cranking out books that often read alike and sound alike.

Harlequin romances have found a successful publishing and marketing formula.
Robert V. Eckert, Jr./EKM-Nepenthe

Table 4.2 Best-selling paperbacks in America, 1981

Rank	Title, author, publisher	Copies in print, 1981
1.	*The Simple Solution to Rubik's Cube,* Nourse, Bantam	6,640,000
2.	*The Complete Scarsdale Medical Diet,* Tarnower, Bantam	5,560,000
3.	*Princess Daisy,* Krantz, Bantam	4,000,000
4.	*If There Be Thorns,* Andrews, Pocket Books	3,382,704
5.	*The Americans,* Jakes, Jove	3,815,942
6.	*Petals on the Wind,* Andrews, Pocket Books	3,713,788
7.	*Rage of Angels,* Sheldon, Warner	3,519,000
8.	*The Stand,* King, NAL/Signet	2,893,000
9.	*The Dead Zone,* King, NAL/Signet	2,884,000
10.	*A Woman of Substance,* Bradford, Avon	2,867,478

Source: Sally A. Lodge, "1981 Paperback Top Sellers—Mass Market." Reprinted from the 12 March 1982 issue of *Publishers* Weekly, published by R. R. Bowker Company, a Xerox company. Copyright © 1982 by Xerox Corporation.

Sometimes paperback publishers will pay more for a reprint title or an original than they can hope to make in profit. They do this with the thought of enhancing their position with their distributors and their retail outlets, as well as gaining certain prestige in the upper echelons of the limited paperback business. If they were not to acquire the rights, a competitor would, and the monetary loss suffered is sometimes worth the less tangible advantages of having a best-seller.

Increasingly, as paperback publishing has developed in stature and status in the book world, some authors have found it advantageous to market their wares directly to paperback companies, who in turn sell reprint rights to the hardcover industry and perhaps even to Hollywood.

Textbooks

Textbook publishing is less of a gamble than trade book publishing.

In the publishing industry, textbooks are an appealing alternative to trade books. Instead of passing quickly from the scene, a successful text keeps on making money for both the author and the publisher, year after year, as new classes, and even new generations, of students enter schools and universities. Because a successful textbook becomes dated three to five years after publication, the author must update the material in light of new knowledge. The publisher can then bring out a new edition, profiting from the text's already established reputation. It is not unusual for a successful text to last for six to eight editions.

Textbooks differ from trade books in other ways. The number of potential authors is smaller, since texts are generally written by professors; and the market per title is smaller, since it is restricted to those persons enrolled in schools and colleges who are taking the pertinent subjects. However, the relative permanency of a long-term audience and the mandatory nature of sales more than compensate for these shortcomings.

It should be apparent that professors are not only a primary source of text material, but the means of its distribution. It is their responsibility to order the texts for the classes they teach; the bookstores merely stock

College students represent a steady and ready-made market for textbook publishers.
Daniel S. Brody/Stock, Boston

the books. *College travelers*—salespeople from the publishing houses—are familiar with academia and the professors within the respective institutions and disciplines. In addition to selling textbooks, they are manuscript scouts for their publishers, dealing with potential authors and distributors in one.

Somewhat different procedures are used in the development and sale of elementary and secondary school (el–hi) texts. For this market the text-books are typically written by teams of in-house editors. This is especially true of basal series for elementary programs in reading, mathematics, social studies, and science. The reasons for the team approach are to make manageable the task of putting together a complex package, which may include more than 200 pieces, and to give the publisher more control over the final product.

Control is necessary because of the substantial investment in development, which may exceed $5 million, and because the publisher has to tailor the series to appeal to the broadest possible market. The result is often a text that is criticized by educators as bland and inoffensive; but from the publisher's point of view, that may sound like praise. El-hi textbooks are frequently purchased by committees made up of parents and school-board members, so the series that is the least offensive often stands a better chance of being selected.

Elementary and high school texts are team efforts; like other mass media, the least offensive books sell the most copies.

Textbook sales obviously reflect the fluctuations in school populations. In 1945—at the end of World War II—textbooks accounted for one-fifth of the total gross sales of books in America. Once children from the postwar baby boom reached school age that total increased dramatically. Today the total exceeds 400 million books (hardbacks, paperbacks, assorted workbooks, reference books, manuals, etc.), which accounts for some 37 percent of all books sold. This shows a fairly steady increase in spite of a decline in the school-age population during the past ten years.

Professional Books

Professional books are by and for specialists, meaning high per unit costs.

Works written by specialists to be read by other specialists are generally referred to as professional or scholarly books. A monograph explaining the symbolism in James Joyce's novels qualifies; so too does a review of research on color perception in monkeys. For years publishers have been active in the fields of law and medicine because attorneys and physicians must keep informed about their fields. Other disciplines have not been as attractive, but in recent years growth in the behavioral sciences has prompted substantial interest by publishers.

Print runs on some books may be as low as 1,000 copies, resulting in an elevated per unit cost and a high list price. Consequently, a book of only 200 pages may be priced at more than thirty dollars.

Professional books in law and medicine are usually sold by salespeople who are assigned territories. This is possible because the price of each book is relatively high, often greater than fifty dollars per volume, and because the professionals may purchase several books at one time. Professional books in other disciplines are sold by direct mail to clinicians, practitioners, and college professors.

The Business of Book Publishing

The process of book publishing is basically the same for each type of book publisher. Editorial people are needed to acquire projects and to shape manuscripts; production people, including designers, produce the books; and the marketing and sales staff promotes the books. In addition, a company has an operations group that is responsible for processing orders and billings, and for keeping straight all financial matters for the company.

Editorial

The gatekeeping process in book publishing is often ruthless, because each product, or book, must try to make it on its own in the marketplace.

The overwhelming number of published manuscripts are solicited or commissioned. The idea for a book may arise from either an author or a publisher. When it originates with the author, he or she generally writes a relatively brief prospectus describing the idea—the approach, theme, and development. A couple of sample chapters generally accompany it to indicate style. It then goes through a successive and brutal screening process. In the trade industry the first screening is done by recent literature graduates, who can reject the manuscript, and often do. Most authors have impressive files of rejection slips, the number of which forms a sort of badge of professionalism.

Reprinted by permission of
Tribune Company
Syndicate, Inc.

If a manuscript passes the first screening, it goes to an editor for consideration. Should the editor like the idea, the manuscript will probably be sent out for evaluation by recognized authorities in the field. If the manuscript makes it this far, it may then go to an editorial board for a final decision. However, the manuscript may be rejected at any of these stages, or the author may be asked to further elaborate his or her idea. But it should be obvious that only a tiny percentage of the précis submitted survive to reach an editorial board decision. The competition for attention at the channel level is intense, and the gatekeeper's role in publishing is even more ruthless than at a newspaper. The numbers involved are frightening: Less than 2 percent of the prospecti submitted will ever see print, and less than 5 percent of that number will sell well enough to pay expenses.

The process can be exceedingly discouraging, but rejection is not necessarily a measure of the quality of an author's work. As an example, John Toole, author of *Confederacy of Dunces,* became so despondent by his inability to attract a publisher that he committed suicide. Toole's mother then took up the cause, approaching publisher after publisher until at last the Louisiana State University Press agreed to publish the book. Recognition followed. The book was praised by critics and in 1981 *Confederacy of Dunces* received the 1980 Pulitzer prize for literature.

The other route a manuscript may take occurs when an idea originates with the editor, whose business it is to keep in touch with the public pulse. The editor has to know what people are reading, what kinds of books are selling, and where the public interest lies. The process is somewhat simplified by the fact that publishers tend to specialize, first, in certain types of books—whether they be text or trade—and then in certain concentrations within these fields: fiction or nonfiction, mysteries or westerns, international affairs or politics, and the like. Consequently, most publishers only have to keep track of their specialized fragment within the market. If a publisher has an idea, the search begins for the right person to write it. The publisher does this from personal knowledge of an author's prior work or from gleanings from magazines and newspapers. Or the publisher may go to a literary agent to find the proper talent.

Manuscript ideas originate with either a writer or editor; the latter stands a better chance of being published.

Agents play a significant role in trade book publishing. Each has a stable of significant authors whose work is marketed. Agents maintain close contact with editors and publishers. They know their inventories and the kinds of material that editors and publishers are looking for and they know the market as well as the publishers do. Most successful agents have been in the business for years and have earned the confidence of the editors with whom they deal. Agents generally take 10 percent of a book, both advance and royalties, and generally earn it by winning more sales and more generous advances for their authors than the authors could win for themselves. In addition, agents have the time and contacts many authors lack.

Regardless of how a book gets started, the next step is the contract, which specifies the author's advance—a flexible figure depending on the author's reputation for dependability, performance, and popularity. An advance is a sum of money paid to an author for writing the book; it is chargeable, for the most part, against the royalties when and if they develop. Successful authors obviously can command larger advances than beginning ones. Generally, royalties are 15 percent of the list price of the book for every copy sold, less the author's advances. If the book does not sell enough copies to return its investment, the author keeps the advance anyway. Thus, the larger the advance, the better the author is protected regardless of subsequent sales. Successful authors gamble little; beginning authors gamble with their time and their publisher's investment of money.

Production

Several months before the final manuscript is ready for composition, the production team begins work. Production is the process of transforming a manuscript into a bound book.

Every book has to be designed. Someone has to determine the trim size of the book, the typeface to be used, the length of each line, how illustrations will be used, and whether footnotes will be placed at the bottom of the page or grouped as notes at the end of the chapter. These and a hundred other questions must be resolved, often at a meeting of the editor, the project editor who will shepherd the book through production, the production manager, the marketing manager, and the designer. Each person brings certain skills and experiences that will affect the appearance and quality of the book.

As we mentioned earlier, the risks involved in publishing increased dramatically following World War II. As a result, few book publishers today own the equipment for composing and printing books. Most will hire the services of a compositor to set the book according to the design specifications, and a printer to print and bind the book. Although a few compositors still use linotype machines—known as hot metal—the vast majority use computers, which are a faster and a cleaner method of type preparation. By making only a small change in the program a compositor can alter the design without having to reset large chunks of manuscript; likewise, editorial changes and proofreading corrections can be made with relative ease.

The liaison between the publisher and the compositor is handled by a production person. He or she hires the suppliers and arranges the schedule. When galley proof (the first printed version) is available, the project editor, proofreaders, and the author read for typos, dropped lines, and other problems. Galleys are usually printed on long sheets of paper without pagination or illustrations. Errors located at this stage can be corrected at less expense than later in the production process, when the book has been prepared in pages.

Page proof is also read by the author and project editor. Were the corrections made as requested? Do the pages look right? Is everything in place? When everyone is satisfied, the compositor prepares film for the printer, whose plant may even be in another state. The entire process from final manuscript to bound book may take as long as twelve months for a heavily illustrated technical book. That is why books in some rapidly changing fields will be dated even before they are published. For most trade books (especially fiction, biography, cookbooks, etc.) this does not present a problem.

As production nears completion, the marketing department gets more actively involved. The promotion of school and college textbooks will begin at least six months before the book is published, while trade promotion may occur a little closer to publication. All the work that went into developing and producing a book will mean very little if the book is inadequately or improperly promoted.

Marketing

Techniques of marketing and promotion have been refined over the years, but at base they still include complimentary copies of new titles to critics and book editors in the hope of gaining a review or a recommendation, plus a wide range of public relations activities that take advantage of the relationships among various media of information and entertainment.

The most desired review forum for books is the *New York Times Book Review* section, the bible of the publishing business. Here a review, even a bad one, is a treasured commodity, demonstrating credibility and assuring at least some sales. Competition for review by the *New York Times,* however, is intense, and publishers spend a lot of time and effort seeking it.

Making the *New York Times Book Review* section is nice, but not nearly as nice as making the *Times* best-seller list. That is nirvana, a lofty goal that publishers strain to reach.

In an intriguing article that takes book promotion to task, *Los Angeles Times* media critic David Shaw seriously questioned the legitimacy of most best-seller lists.[7] While sparing the *New York Times* list from some of his criticism, he described a variety of ploys used by publishers and authors to reach best-seller status. The compilation of newspaper and magazine best-seller lists was accused of being so haphazard, so slipshod, so imprecise, and, at times, so dishonest that most publishers would gladly do without it, were it not such a necessary evil. Most lists are compiled from

Book reviews and best-seller lists are keys to marketing books, but they aren't always what they appear to be.

weekly telephone calls to selected bookstores and to book departments of large department stores, and are based on weekly rather than cumulative sales. Bookstore personnel don't reveal their totals, but merely rank the top ten sellers in order, often off the top of their heads, by glancing around at their shelves or even by merely quoting the previous week's newspaper or magazine list of best-sellers.

Inertia is seen as a major factor in book sales. "Once you get on the list, the combination of inertia, self-generated momentum, and self-fulfilling prophecy keeps you on for months," one publisher told Shaw. For this reason authors and publishers stretch the limits of propriety to get on the lists. They use advertising and promotion, puffery and tricks, to get there. If it is possible to find out which bookstores will be called by newspapers and magazines, some authors will buy—or have their friends buy—their own books in quantity from those stores. The late Jacqueline Susann and her producer-husband Irving Mansfield had been known to introduce themselves to the bookstore clerks, then purchase and autograph a copy of their book for every employee in the store.[8]

Peddling books on TV and radio talk shows is a perfect example of media feeding off each other.

Such ploys are probably less frequent, and less useful, than the technique of promoting one's book on radio and television talk shows, where an author can reach millions of potential readers at a shot. Scientist Carl Sagan sold nearly a million copies of his book on evolution, *The Dragons of Eden,* largely because of his frequent appearances on the Johnny Carson *Tonight* show. An appearance on the *Today* show is said to generate 3,000 sales of a particular book on the day of the appearance, and a guest spot on the *Donahue* show can move 50,000 copies. Couple that with a mention in Ann Landers' advice column, and the author and publisher can smile all the way to the bank.[9]

Some writers balk at having to peddle their books, and themselves, since writing is, by nature, an individualistic and introverted profession. Novelist John Cheever says he fears the artificiality of promoting books. "Writing is a highly intimate exchange of communication, and merchandising puts it in a different light," he laments.[10] But purely from a marketing standpoint, charisma is more important than how well the author writes, according to a publicist for one publishing house. A case in point is the success of Erma Bombeck's *The Grass is Always Greener Over the Septic Tank,* which became a best-seller after the author's publicity tour on radio and TV shows. "People loved her as well as her book," her McGraw-Hill publicist said. "A wonderful human being comes across as a wonderful human being, and that can make people want to read the book."[11] Obviously, authors who are shy and who don't project well are likely to lose out on the broadcast circuit, which causes one to wonder whether Nathaniel Hawthorne would have scored with *The Scarlet Letter* had he bombed on the *Tonight* show.

Publishers have also been known to throw lavish promotional parties as part of their campaigns to make the best-seller lists. One such party was a $15,000 soirée in Beverly Hills promoting a first novel by Judith Krantz. Although the novel, *Scruples,* was seen by critics as "fun trash," or worse, it quickly climbed onto best-seller lists.

Utilizing demographics, book publishers have focused their promotions on seemingly appropriate audiences with great success. Joseph Wambaugh's *The Black Marble* deals with a dognapping, so promotion was aimed at California dog lovers. The author attended all the most important dog shows, presenting several of the best-in-show awards. The 2,800 dog-breed clubs with their own publications were sent news releases saying dogs were featured in an upcoming major novel. As a result, *The Black Marble* was a number one West-Coast best-seller *before* publication and quickly hit the national lists.[12]

How can a book be a best-seller before it is published? This disturbs media critic David Shaw, who pointed to several examples where there was so much advance publicity about a book that bookstores were reporting booming sales before copies of the book were even on the shelves.

In the meantime steady sellers—the Bible, Dr. Spock's books on child care, the *Weight Watchers Program Cookbook,* plus dictionaries and some others—don't appear on the weekly best-seller lists. Even cookbooks, which are staples in many publishing houses, rarely make the top ten. The capriciousness of booksellers can also keep other books off the lists. Even though *The Joy of Sex* sold 700,000 copies in hardback in 1973, several stores refused to list it in their weekly totals because they thought it was a dirty book. *Jonathan Livingston Seagull,* a thin, little book, sold 750,000 copies before finally making the *New York Times* list, while some "bigger" books made the list with only 30,000 sales. And *The Total Woman,* which sold 369,000 copies, never made any best-seller list.[13]

Book Clubs

Book clubs are a tempting marketing device. They offer, through membership rolls, an opportunity that publishers usually lack, the capability of predicting the approximate size of sales in the same way that magazines and newspapers can. A book club selection is a valuable publishing house asset, one that can be additionally merchandised in advertising and publicity. Publishers are eager to have their books chosen. However, there are certain shortcomings to this particular system. Recognizing their leverage on publishers, the book clubs often beat down the price on titles they accept, to the point where there is little profit to the publisher beyond the exposure that a book club selection offers. This, in turn, has led many publishers to organize their own book clubs, with varying results. The odds are against their success because of the temptation to restrict themselves to their own inventory, and the lack of broad selection that this implies.

Book clubs generate predictable sales for a given title, even though the "negative option" is a questionable marketing ploy.

An essential ingredient of the book club operation is the so-called *negative option.* Book club operators doubt that the system would work without it. Under negative option, club members receive their monthly selection unless they specifically decline it. Each month they are advised of what the selection will be. They receive it (and are charged for it) unless they immediately return a notice declining purchase. Since people have a tendency to be negligent in such matters, club operators rely upon their members' "laziness" not to decline the selection.

During the early 1970s, the negative option came under fire by consumer groups and was tested in the courts. The Federal Trade Commission, by a four-to-one vote, allowed the practice to continue despite complaints that consumers were being taken advantage of.

Book clubs have survived and proliferated. The original Book-of-the-Month Club (BOMC), founded in 1926, has attracted some 1,250,000 members, making it about one and a half times as large as its nearest competitors, the Literary Guild and Reader's Digest Condensed Books. As an indication of the specialization that is possible in print media, consider the Literary Guild's nearly two dozen subsidiary clubs, which deal with gardening, cooking, science fiction, mystery stories, and so forth. During the last decade the number of book clubs has tripled, and sales have kept pace with this growth. While earlier critics maintained that book clubs would hurt bookstore sales, it appears that the clubs have tapped new markets in areas where bookstores are scarce. They have provided opportunities for readers to fulfill their specialized interests, including such interests as pornography, without shopping for them openly in bookstores.

Serialization

Prepublication serialization in magazines and newspapers may help or hinder eventual book sales.

A technique that has been used sparingly but with considerable success is the prepublication serialization of a book in magazines or newspapers. Truman Capote's successful *In Cold Blood,* William Manchester's *The Death of a President,* and Richard Nixon's *Memoirs* are among the major works serialized in this fashion, having appeared, respectively, in *The New Yorker, Look,* and America's daily newspapers. The case for prepublication serializing can be argued both ways. While the additional revenue that comes to the publisher for the magazine and newspaper rights offsets a considerable amount of publication costs, serialization in a popular magazine or in many newspapers may detract from the eventual audience. For example, the sophisticated readers of *The New Yorker* had to be subtracted from the eventual sales of *In Cold Blood.* However, the massive exposure accorded a title by serialization can precondition a responsive public to buy the book when it does go on sale. The pros and cons of serialization have not been resolved; like everything else in book publishing, serialization is a bit of a gamble.

Paperback Marketing

Paperback distribution accounts for nearly all the basic differences between softcover and hardcover publishing, including the price differences between the two forms. Popular opinion has it that paperbacks are only a fraction of the price of hardbacks because of the less expensive binding, but such opinion is incorrect. In reality, differences in binding account for only a miniscule part of the price differential. More significant is the lower initial investment by publishers; if the book has already been printed in hardcover, it will need little if any additional editing. Also to be considered are the lower royalties generally paid to authors for paperbacks. Most significant, however, are the sheer numbers involved and the means of distribution utilized.

Paperbacks are likely to be printed in runs up to, and sometimes exceeding, a million at a time, drastically reducing the cost per unit. Given the quantities involved, efficient channels of distribution must be maintained. Taking their cues from England's Penguin books, American publishers quickly learned the value of saturating the shelves in the retail establishments where their smaller, pocket-sized books could compete for the premium spaces and be sold alongside incident merchandise.

Distribution of paperbooks is essentially magazine distribution. It utilizes basically the same distributors, some 800 wholesalers across the country, or the American News Company with its 350 distributors. Together, they serve around 100,000 retail outlets (drugstores, supermarkets, shopping centers, airports, and the like), always locations where the casual traffic is high. Like magazines, paperbacks are displayed in racks that generally have about 100 pockets holding three to five copies each. The racks occupy valuable floor space. However, there is a tremendous turnover in the paperbacks on display, with premium space going to the fast movers. Books that don't sell rapidly are either returned or destroyed, often after no more than a week. Paperbacks are fully returnable by the retailer for either cash or credit, and one of the biggest problems faced by the industry is to keep the percentage of returned books to a minimum. Through computerized merchandising, the most efficient companies are able to hold returns to 25 percent, but at some companies returns are more than 50 percent. This is one industry where a unique channel gatekeeper plays a role: The truckdriver faced with finding shelf space for a new delivery sometimes determines what books to remove from the channel.

On the retail floor, paperbacks are in competition with magazines for the customer's purchase, and the paperback proliferation has further hurt the magazine industry by cutting into its casual or street sales. But more often the book is the medium that is overlooked. People tend to associate a new issue of a magazine with previous issues. Even with highly visible authors, paperbacks are lacking such a conditioned acceptance and need a longer display period than do transient magazines. Since they are generally not permitted it under competitive conditions, only the best-selling titles remain on display.

The paperback is an omnibus medium—something for everyone.
Jay Black

While this system does not detract from paperback sales in the aggregate, it does tend to remove some of the "heavier" titles from circulation in favor of flamboyant fare represented by sex, western, mystery, romance, and science fiction offerings. Experience has shown that classical reprints will move well if given a long enough display time. As with hardcover marketing, a constant gamble is involved. Even if publishers do have to take back half of their books, a few fantastic successes can often balance the judgmental errors. As Clarence Peterson says, Fawcett's *Peanuts,* New American Library's *Fear of Flying,* or one blockbuster by Harold Robbins or James Michener could support "a kennelful of dogs."[14]

Stores specializing in paperbacks have become popular in recent years. Paperbacks have also found their way into traditional bookstores and the book areas of department stores where previously they were unacceptable. It was once believed their cheaper cost would detract from the more profitable hardcover book sales, but this has not proven to be the case. Rather, they have served as traffic builders for these outlets. Publishers who have released both hardcover and paper editions of the same title have found that less than 10 percent of their readerships overlap. Surprisingly, though their contents are the same, their audiences differ.

New Strategies in Book Publishing

The variety of books available should convince us not to stereotype books as a monolithic form among the media. Compared with the other mass media, however, books have always been bound more by tradition and have therefore experienced less innovation. Although innovation is not central to the world of books, neither is it unheard of. One fairly recent development is the growing relationship between Hollywood and the trade industry. Book publishers are finding it attractive to work with movie producers, selling film rights for very substantial sums of money and earning more money from increased book sales when the film is released. Another development is the appearance of *instant paperbacks*—an attempt to compete with the immediacy of newspapers and some magazines—which was made possible by the computer. The computer also allows publishers to produce *personalized books* for children. A final innovation we will discuss in this section is the *photonovel,* a book form that visually represents story lines with still photographs.

The "traditional" book business has begun to employ creative marketing techniques.

Cross-Media Ties

Lately, one sure way to make the best-seller lists is to produce a book in conjunction with a highly promoted movie. For years Hollywood has capitalized on best-selling novels as the basis for films, figuring the exposure already achieved would pay off at the box office. Recently, a reversal of this technique has shown some promise. Yale professor Eric Segal's *Love Story* was written first as a screenplay, then as a novel. However, the book appeared shortly before the film version, and the two media fed off each other's popularity. There was no way, of course, of predicting the fantastic popularity of *Love Story,* but at least the promotional costs were minimized; and by virtue of the dual reinforcement, both media probably got better promotion than either could have afforded individually.

Books used to become films, but today it's a chicken-or-the-egg situation.

This publicity and the accompanying advertising is aimed not only at the critics, but also at the general public in order to create a demand, or at least a little curiosity—enough to make people seek bookstores (which is not always easy) and spend their money (which is always hard). Once a fire is ignited, word of mouth does the rest.

Consider how those fires get started. For years, the television series *Star Trek* had a devoted following of Trekkies, who lamented its demise and retained enthusiasm during a zillion reruns. Fan clubs and national conventions kept interest alive. The *Star Wars* phenomenon demonstrated a broader based interest in science fiction than most film producers believed existed, and the owners of rights to *Star Trek* acted on this immediately, producing the multi-million-dollar Hollywood spectacular that was released during the Christmas season of 1979. Months before the film's release, trade journals, especially the influential *Publishers Weekly,* touted the simultaneous release of *Star Trek—The Motion Picture: A Novel,* based on the screen play. Pocket Books printed a million copies of the paperback picture book, a substantial run for a first printing. The $2.25 book was issued in the midst of an advertising and public relations campaign that included special floor displays inspired by the USS Enterprise, *Star Trek* bookmarks, rack cards, pocket pointers, acetate window streamers, and much much more. The proliferation of bookstores in shopping centers (which also house the theaters where the film was released en masse) became glutted with Christmas shoppers, allowing them to capitalize on this cross-media promotion. *Star Trek II: The Wrath of Kahn,* owed much of its success to a similar multimedia blitz in the summer of 1982.

Book and movie tie-ins saturate the media market.
Tom Ballard/EKM-Nepenthe

Such was the story of the *Jaws* phenomenon, in which author Peter Benchley and his publisher, Doubleday, auctioned off the paperback rights to *Jaws* for $575,000, picked up an additional $150,000 for the movie rights, and gained $85,000 more from book clubs. Doubleday spent $50,000 advertising the hardcover edition, and Benchley appeared on talk shows across the country as an expert on sharks. So much interest in the project was generated that a spin-off of the spin-off—*The Jaws Log,* a quickie describing the making of the book and the film—rested comfortably on the best-seller lists for some time while America enjoyed shark mania.

Instant Paperbacks

To fill the gap between books and magazines, "instant paperbacks" appear on a variety of nonfictional themes.

Emphasis on the information function has led to a minor revolution of sorts in the book publishing industry since 1964. On 28 September of that year Bantam Books put on shelves around the world more than a half-million paperback copies of its *Report of the Warren Commission on the Assassination of President Kennedy.* What was so unusual about the book was that eighty hours earlier no one at Bantam or at any other commercial medium had copies of the Warren Commission document or even knew how long or complicated it would be. As soon as it was officially released in Washington, D.C., the 385,000-word document with 158 illustrations was flown to Chicago, where it was edited, set into 800 pages of type, proofread, indexed, printed, bound, boxed, and shipped in a little over three days. Such a project under normal conditions would have taken at least six months, but the publishers accurately read the public interest in the Commission report and pulled out all the stops. Within a week Bantam had printed 1.65 million copies of the report, and the best-selling *instant book* was born.[15]

Spurred on by that success, Bantam published some fifty-six other "extras" over the next decade, including *The Pope's Visit to the United States, The Pentagon Papers, The President's Trip to China, The Watergate Hearings,* and several sports-related topics. Since most dealt with anticipated news events, they could be partially prepared in advance. *We Reach the Moon,* published seventy-six hours after Apollo 11 splashed down, had been in the making for a year and had awaited only the final news items and photos for completion. Others have combined background research and news coverage. *The Pope's Journey,* which earned a place in the *Guinness Book of World Records* under the heading "Fastest Publishing," came off the presses only sixty-six and one-half hours after Bantam received the first news articles produced by some fifty-one strike-bound *New York Times* writers and editors—journalists who found refuge in this new information medium. Like most instant books, the groundwork had been laid far in advance. The same is true of *444 Days* and other instant books that hit the marketplace within a week after the release of America's fifty-two hostages in Iran.

There are exceptions, however. *Strike Zion!*, the story of the 1967 Arab–Israeli war, was conceived, written, and published in twenty days. It sold 300,000 copies, garnered favorable reviews, and remained in print for several years. And, within two weeks of the obviously unanticipated major news story of 1978, the murders and mass suicide of some 900 cultists of the People's Temple in the jungle of Guyana, two different publishers had instant books at the world's retailers. Both of these books were written by news reporters who had been on the scene at the time of the tragedy, and the books combined their accounts with interpretive pieces and photos from other sources.

Given public curiosity, improved technology, smoother channels of distribution, and the credibility of the book medium, there seems little reason to expect a termination of this new journalistic format.

A mini-revolution of sorts in children's literature occurred during the mid-1970s when America's youngsters realized they could find their own names—and those of their family, friends, and pets—scattered across the pages of their own *personalized books*. Computers have entire book texts stored in them, awaiting insertion of personalized references to Johnny and Suzie Smith, or whoever, from Centerborough, or wherever, Midamerica. Not surprisingly, such books have raised children's level of interest in reading, which may offset the potential for exploiting naïve children who are delighted to see their names in print.

Personalized Books

Books are coupled to computers for highly personalized publications.

The late 1970s also saw the Americanization of a book form that had been popular in South America and Europe for nearly four decades: *photonovels,* which are paperbacks of movie scripts fully illustrated with frames taken directly from the movie. The idea is simple, yet brilliant, capitalizing on semi-literacy and movie fandom. Some 350 to 400 photographs from a particular movie fill the pages of each "Fotonovel," the name of the product and the American company that got its real start with the television show *Star Trek*. Fotonovels do not have a single page of printing, but the film's dialogue is superimposed over each photo or collage.

Photonovels

Photonovels cater to the semiliterate.

The first four *Star Trek* Fotonovels, based on the television series, sold 235,000 copies. *Grease,* which hit the bookstands two weeks after the film was released, sold 1.2 million copies. Successful sales have come from *The Champ, Invasion of the Body Snatchers, Hair, Ice Castles,* and dozens of additional titles that are cranked out annually. Producing a Fotonovel costs about $150,000, and each copy sells for $2.75. Since film studios are guaranteed an advance against a substantial percentage of the royalties, the young publishing company must sell 200,000 copies to break even. "The ultimate rerun," which Fotonovels have been called, serve as worldwide promotional aids for movies, but the relationship quite obviously works both ways.[16]

Book Publishing Today and Tomorrow

Traditionally, books have been characterized by a certain freedom of content, a freedom resulting from their smaller audiences. They are free to explore dimensions of radical politics or erotic interest that are not open to the broader-based family media. Further, books are free to experiment with new language and techniques, new expression. They are not tied to the "tried and true" because they can exist on much smaller audiences and they need not rely on the lowest common denominator of general appeal.

Charles Steinberg has made the point that the proportionately larger audiences that paperbacks attract show signs of eroding a part of this freedom. The paperback industry demands a certain level of proved acceptance to bring a title into existence. He notes that *Catcher in the Rye* aroused no criticism for its questionable content while it was in hardcover, but a rash of public indignation burst forth as soon as it appeared in the more widely distributed paperback edition.[17]

Merchandising techniques affect the freedoms and social roles of books.

A part of the traditional freedom of book publishers may be on unfirm ground as a result of what might be called vulgarization in paperbacks. As outlets multiply and press runs grow, there may be increasing pressure to emphasize formula writing, to avoid controversial themes, and to appeal to the largest possible audiences.

As the book becomes more a corporate product and less the handiwork of family-owned houses, the classic role of the book as a medium designed to enlighten is being altered. Under the impact of the communications explosion, book publishing is becoming a corporate activity promoted with techniques reminiscent of P. T. Barnum. Marketing becomes the dominant concern of publishers who sacrifice editorial considerations in their pursuit of profits. Book publishing still remains an essentially individualized mass medium, but that essential characteristic is gradually becoming eroded.

What can we expect in the future? Some change is almost inevitable due to the spread of electronic technology. No one knows for sure, of course, just what will happen in the years to come, but making predictions about an institution as diversified as book publishing is always interesting.

Like other media, books will change forms and roles in the new electronic environment.

Publishers Weekly, the authoritative trade journal of the publishing industry, asked several of the best-known futurists what they foresaw as the most important changes likely to occur by the turn of the century that would have a major impact upon books. Responses varied, but a pattern seemed to emerge.[18]

Alvin Toffler, author of *Future Shock* and *The Third Wave,* said that special-interest media, including diversity-producing cable and cassette television, will bring each of us more varied images through many more channels, and that less and less of the culture will be shared. Toffler's term for this process is *demassification.* Increasingly, Toffler said, we will live in a "blip culture" that bombards us with unrelated chips or blips of data. Forced individually to fabricate our own images of reality from these blips, we will cry out as a culture for synthesis. The answer to that cry, he maintained, is twofold: computers and "that powerful information technology called the 'book'."[19]

Edward T. Hall—author of many books, including *Beyond Culture*—told *Publishers Weekly* he expected the reading public of the year 2000 to be far more sophisticated and particular than today's readers, and less captivated by the cliché. Publishers will find additional demands to be both more discriminating and more venturesome, ultimately surviving only if they attract true talent and manage to distinguish between genius and hack writers. "The market will favor the real pro over those basing decisions simply on bottom-line considerations," Hall warned. "Good book design techniques will be increasingly important," he added.[20]

Ernest Callenbach, author of *Ecotopia* and editor of the University of California press, said that publishers should be able to make America the first culture to enjoy universally accessible books:

[They] could enter manuscripts [for a fee] on a centralized computer. The texts could then be printed upon demand by dispensing machines [rather like juke boxes] in libraries, bookstores, schools, supermarkets, post offices, banks, etc.— even in remote towns and in neighborhoods where books are virtually absent today. The would-be buyer could locate a title by punching Standard Book Numbers guided by a simplified title and author index, check reviews from an electronic *Book Review Digest,* and browse through sample pages electronically. The deposit of an indicated number of coins would produce carry-away copy. After such initial publication, some titles would then prove popular, and be bought up and printed by mass market publishers; illustrated books and fine printing would continue to be normally printed. In this Ecotopian future a bookstore's stock would consist of a few thousand popular titles, older publications not yet entered on the computer, imports and recycled copies of electronically produced titles.[21]

Summary

The industrial revolution, which was responsible for most of the techno-logical innovations of the mass media, was the direct result of technical knowledge recorded and transmitted through print. The industrial revo-lution could not have occurred without the technical knowledge made pos-sible by print, through its ability to record, transmit, and augment what went on before.

Book publishing in America has gone through several phases, the most recent of which has been the purchasing of independent publishing com-panies by conglomerates, larger shares of the market being devoted to pa-perback and textbook publishing, and the development of stronger ties between book publishers and the film industry.

The categories of books include trade books, paperback books, text-books, and professional books. Trade books are general-interest books sold in bookstores. They present a tremendous gamble; only 5 percent sell well enough to recover the investment made by the publisher. Paperbacks are primarily reprints of books that were originally published in hardcover, but as the paperback industry develops in stature, some authors have found it advantageous to sell directly to a paperback company.

Unlike most trade books, textbooks can sell for many years. The mar-kets are smaller but easier for the publisher to identify and reach. Revisions are published every three to five years, and some textbooks continue to sell for six to eight editions. The last category of books, called professional books, are written by specialists for other specialists to read.

Book publishing has three primary functions: editorial, production, and marketing. The marketing of books has been refined in recent years, but it still includes distribution of complimentary copies to reviewers and various other strategies for getting books on the best-seller lists. One of the best ways to insure substantial sales is for an author who has a lively per-sonality to be a guest on one of the popular network television shows. Book clubs and serialization are also utilized by publishers.

The major difference between mass-market paperbacks and hard-cover books is their distribution. Paperbacks are treated essentially as mag-azines and are distributed by wholesalers and the American News Company, while hardbacks are sold primarily through bookstores and book clubs.

In recent years publishers have become aware of the value of pro-ducing a book in conjunction with a movie. Other new strategies include instant paperbacks, which are original books written and published in a matter of days to explain a current event; personalized books, which are set on computers and include the name of the child who receives the book, the names of his or her friends, and the town where the child lives; and photonovels, which are paperbacks of movie scripts fully illustrated with frames taken directly from the film.

Books, traditionally the freest of the media, in terms of content, retain that freedom when published in hardcover and given limited distribution, but they face increasing public hostility when questionable content is widely circulated in paperback form. As book publishing becomes more and more market conscious, the essential libertarianism of the product may diminish.

Despite widespread arguments concerning whether the book is a dying medium in this age of electronics, we garner from expert testimony and current policies that the medium is adjusting to changes in technology and will continue, although in one of several modified forms, to serve the needs of consumers who will expect individualized information, consumable upon demand.

Notes

1. Edward Jay Whetmore, *Mediamerica: Form, Content, and Consequence of Mass Communication,* 2d ed. (Belmont, Calif.: Wadsworth Publishing Co. 1981), p. 16.
2. Marshall McLuhan, *Understanding Media: The Extensions of Man* (New York: McGraw-Hill, 1965); and *The Gutenberg Galaxy* (Toronto: The University of Toronto Press, 1967).
3. Clarence Peterson, *The Bantam Story: Thirty Years of Paperback Publishing,* 2d ed. (New York: Bantam Books, Inc., 1975), p. 5.
4. Charles A. Madison, *Book Publishing in America* (New York: McGraw-Hill, 1966).
5. John P. Dessauer, "The 1977 Census of Book Publishing Reveals Significant Industry Expansion," *Publishers Weekly,* 9 July 1979, p. 36.
6. Chandler B. Grannis, "1981 Title Output and Average Prices Preliminary Figures," *Publisher's Weekly,* 12 March 1982.
7. David Shaw, "Book Biz Best-sellers—Are They Really? Laziness and Chicanery Play Major Roles," *Los Angeles Times,* 24 October 1976.
8. Ibid.
9. Laurence Bergreen, "Just Don't Get Booked After the Animal Act," *TV Guide,* 17 March 1979, pp. 33–36.
10. Maria Lenhart, "The Author as Peddler," *Deseret News,* 4 August 1979.
11. Ibid.
12. Linda Deutsch, "Publishers Finance Lavish Book Promotions," *Salt Lake Tribune,* 28 April 1978.
13. Shaw, "Book Biz Best-Sellers—Are They Really?"
14. Peterson, *The Bantam Story,* p. 5.
15. Ibid. pp. 52–64.
16. United Press International, "Curl Up with a Good Movie," *Deseret News,* 30 July 1979.
17. Charles Steinberg, *The Communicative Arts* (New York: Hastings House, Publishers, 1970).
18. "Predictions: Changes to Conjure With," *Publishers Weekly,* 6 August 1979, pp. 26–28.
19. Ibid.
20. Ibid.
21. Ibid.

5 News Services

There is no way the average newspaper, radio, or television station could bring us the quantity of national and international news and specialized features we get every day if the local news staffs had to do it all themselves. On their limited budgets and with considerable time pressures, the local reporters and editors can scarcely generate enough material to keep us informed about our own communities, let alone the doings of Washington, New York, and overseas. In addition, we can hardly expect homegrown journalists to possess the myriad talents we look for every day in our media: the incisive understandings of federal budgets, major league sports, and international diplomacy; the ability to explain how to fix our autos, purchase a home, invest our dollars, tend to our health, and mend relationships; the artistry to create comic strips, crossword puzzles, and gourmet dinners, and so forth. Fortunately for the local media and for our eclectic tastes, the mass communications network has come to incorporate a wide variety of auxiliary news and feature services.

In this chapter we will consider some of the basic services found in our local media, with primary emphasis on the press associations, or wire services, as well as the feature syndicates. Such services have been with us in one form or another since the middle of the nineteenth century. They have a respectable history as packagers of information. Their existence came out of the costly business of news gathering that, as it became more competitive, also became prohibitively expensive for any single news operation to bear. Essentially, the news services are a pooling of costs and efforts—joint ventures.

Prior to the 1980s a discussion of news services would have been limited to the doings of the Associated Press and United Press International (the two primary wire services) and the various feature operations that mailed or wired their wares to subscribing news media. Things are no longer that simple; given the new communications technology of satellites, home computers, cable television, and the like, the means of distributing news and features have changed dramatically. Because of the complexity of the new electronic technology, we will have much to say about the latest distribution systems in chapter 8, "The New Electronics." An understanding of the new electronics follows logically from a discussion of how basic radio and television systems operate, so we will try to avoid confusing the issue at this early juncture. We will, however, attempt in this chapter to outline the services on which news media have to rely for such a large percentage of their content.

This chapter begins with an historical treatment of the major wire services, considers their current operations and problems and contributions to the news media, then continues with a discussion of the specialized feature services that contribute a generous dose of nonnews materials to the media. The effectiveness of the services cannot be underestimated. Some

Introduction

Auxiliary services provide news and features that the local media are incapable of providing on their own.

have calculated that the wire news and photos constitute 15 percent of the average daily newspaper. When you consider that 60 percent of a newspaper is advertising, the wire service contribution is greater than any other single source. Ten percent then goes to various syndicated features and another 10 percent to specialized departments—such as society, business and finance, sports, and the like—leaving only about 5 percent for local news. These percentages indicate how much of the average paper is "canned," or prewritten and delivered—at a cost—to the newspaper.[1] That being the case, the news services deserve a closer look.

Historical Development

From the beginning, the press in America served a dual purpose. It was isolated and local; it was also the principal public communications link to the old world. Even in colonial times, newspapers in the scattered population centers were eager to receive news from England and France as rapidly as possible, and through transatlantic shipping they had far better and more regular contact with Europe than they did with their sister colonies.

Telegraph operators helped shrink the globe in the mid-1800s.
The Bettman Archives, Inc.

It became common for publishers to send sloops out to meet incoming vessels and to return with the news from abroad, sometimes days before the slower oceangoing ships could beat their way into harbor and dock. Curiosity and economic advantage put a premium on such news. In due course, as the populations increased and newspapers became more competitive, relays of horse couriers sped foreign notices, the news of the world, first from the tip of Long Island and later from as far away as Nova Scotia, to the waiting presses in New York. The costs of riders, horses, boatmen, and relay stations were great, and rivalry between the competing couriers was intense.

In 1844 Samuel Morse invented the telegraph, the dim beginning of the electric age and the communications revolution. Newspapers were quick to see the advantages of telegraph, which meant that they could import distant national news from Washington and elsewhere. However, telegraph costs were high (involving stringing lines and hiring operators), and it soon became apparent that having six operators telegraph six stories about the same presidential message to six editors at more or less the same time was senseless.

The Associated Press

The Associated Press was formed in 1848 as a cooperative endeavor among six New York newspapers. Costs were drastically reduced, and each of the papers was assured that it would receive the same news at the same time. The Associated Press was, and still is, a membership organization, governed by a board of directors elected from among its client-members. It expanded gradually, acquiring new members in different geographical areas on an exclusive basis. Thus, AP membership was an extremely valuable asset to publishers, for it meant that they alone in their territory had access to outside news. Journalism history is replete with examples of faltering newspapers selling for high prices solely because of their AP membership.

Founded in 1848, the AP has always been a cooperative news service, with members.

However, as other newspapers were added to the AP membership roster, they reflected a wide variety of differing political and social viewpoints. Prior to the Civil War, Northern newspapers tended to be abolitionist; Southern newspapers were proslavery. Partisan differences at that time were even stronger than they are today, and the politically-oriented press often conveyed this partisanship in the news as well as in editorial columns. The AP quickly discovered the necessity of reporting the news objectively—that is, reporting the facts alone, without color or opinion. If AP member newspapers wished to inject subjectivity into the news accounts, they were free to add whatever insights (or biases) they wished to the fundamentally neutral wire-service accounts of political and social events. As a considerable portion of the news content of each newspaper gradually became wire-service copy, newspapers began to adhere to the cult of objectivity on which journalism was founded.

Service to diverse members via telegraph brought about objective reporting and "journalese"—the inverted pyramid.

By the Civil War, the wire services were fairly well established, and the eastern portion of the nation at least, where most of the action took place, was "wired." Apart from being the first modern war in the sense of its use of long-range weapons and massive firepower that de-emphasized individual combat, the Civil War acutely demonstrated the attraction of war as a news source. The major newspapers across the nation sent correspondents to the battlefields. Most of this news flowed to the nation's editors, in the North and South, over the wires. However, telegraphic performance in the din of battle was uncertain. Lines could be cut by artillery barrages or sappers could snip them purposely; therefore, correspondents developed the technique of sending the most significant news first in bulletin form and following up later with the details. Thus *journalese* was born in the heat of battle, whereby the lead to a story (who, what, when, where, why, and how) was sent first and the balance of the story followed in order of decreasing significance until the story was told or the wires went out, whichever came first. The journalistic principles of objectivity and the *inverted pyramid* style of writing were the historical contributions of the wire services, forms to which the wire services adhered almost slavishly for more than a century, long after many newspapers adapted newer (or reverted to older) narrative and interpretative forms of writing many stories.

During the years following the Civil War, the years of laissez-faire and "survival of the fittest," America's efforts went to rebuilding and to expansion—the winning of the West. Technological innovations mounted one upon the other, and the field of communications was no exception. The

The transatlantic cable
was laid in 1866.
The Bettman Archives, Inc.

older cities grew, and more and more people flocked to new cities that sprang up along the railheads across the continent. All demanded newspapers to serve them. The railroad and the Industrial Revolution, serving one another cooperatively, made national distribution possible, which led to both advertising and national magazines. The transatlantic cable, which sped world news to the waiting presses, was completed in 1866, and international coverage became a part of the budget allowance of the Associated Press.

The growth of telegraph led to the formation of the great newspaper empires of Edward W. Scripps, William Randolph Hearst, and Joseph Pulitzer. It permitted them a centralized control over basic editorial policy; it assured that the treatment of international and national news would be similar in all their papers; and it made possible national advertising on a local basis.

AP Shares the Wires

Scripps was the first to break loose from the AP's domination of the news industry, because several of his papers were denied world news by the AP's exclusive agreements. He founded the United Press (UP) in 1907 primarily to serve his own newspapers, but he sold the service to other papers that wished to use it, thus defraying a part of its cost. Such a system was logical because a part of the copy generated by the UP was local copy for Scripps' own newspapers and fed onto the wires when appropriate. Hearst followed suit in 1909 with the International News Service (INS), characterized from the beginning by the sensational Hearst style. Neither the UP nor the INS ever really rivaled the AP in coverage. They were stopgaps for major papers offering different viewpoints on world and national events. They made outside coverage accessible to many newspapers and communities locked out by the AP's exclusive franchises.

UP and INS differed from the AP in both policy and organization. While the AP was established as a nonprofit cooperative venture to serve its members, the services provided by Scripps and Hearst were private companies aiming to make a profit by selling information to clients. During its early years, the Associated Press had split into several factions, due to disagreements of its members over policies and organizational hassles. Until 1915, members were not allowed to use rival wire services, and established AP papers could veto membership requests filed by competing papers. Then, in 1945 the U.S. Supreme Court forbade the latter practice as an unfair restraint of trade, but by then the growing strength of UP and INS rendered the question moot.

Throughout most of the first half of the twentieth century, the AP was the largest wire service, UP was second, and INS was a distant third in number of bureaus and reporters. AP had established a reputation for objective, accurate, and factual writing. UP's forte was the human-interest, personalized journalism we associate with its founder, Mr. Scripps. INS, in the Hearst mold, became noted for its aggressive coverage of national and world news, and for high quality writing. In 1958, due to economic pressures, United Press and the International News Service merged, calling itself the United Press International (UPI). The new wire service was able to compete on a nearly equal basis of strength with the AP, and U.S. and world news media benefitted from having a choice between two large, aggressive services.

At last count AP had 10,000 customers worldwide, including 1,315 of America's 1,730 daily newspapers. With an annual budget of $151 million, it has 3,800 domestic radio and television stations as subscribers, plus some 400 cable TV systems that reach more than 3 million American households.

UPI, with its $100 million annual budget, serves 853 U.S. daily newspapers, 3,682 radio and television stations, and 525 cable TV systems reaching 3.5 million households. Although the number of newspaper clients has dropped slightly in the past decade, UPI's worldwide reach has been expanding (particularly via cable TV) and now services more than 7,000 clients.[2]

AP and UPI Today

Each wire service collects and distributes news in over 100 countries around the world. The AP has about 175 news bureaus, staffed by 2,500 people, of whom about 1,500 are involved in newsgathering and photography. The UPI has 177 bureaus and a total staff of some 2,000, of whom more than 1,200 serve in journalistic capacities.

Today AP and UPI cover the globe, serving thousands of media outlets. Competition is intense.

The two services are in intense competition. Probably nowhere else in the mass communications business, including the television networks, is competition so intense to be first with the news. Remembering that among the nation's 1,730 dailies and over 10,000 radio and television stations (and in the thousands of media outlets outside the United States) there is a deadline every minute, a minute's delay in flashing a wire service story may determine whether the AP or UPI version is printed or broadcast. In what must be some sort of record, for example, an AP reporter filed a story on the attempted assassination of President Reagan a mere 53 seconds after the shooting. The economics of the matter are simple. If an editor, looking back over a year's national and international coverage in the newspaper or on the station, discovers that one of the wire services has been used predominantly, the editor may easily decide to discard the other one. On a big newspaper, such as the *New York Times,* that's a $5,000 per week decision; on a small daily, it may be only a $100 or $150 per week decision.

Because the cost of news gathering increases with inflation and because the intense competition is driving the sales prices down, all is not well with the major wire services. UPI, supposedly a profit-making organization, has been losing money for two decades in a row. After being bailed out of its $5.5 million deficit in 1981 by the Scripps Company trust (which owned 95 percent of the stock), the Hearst Corporation (owner of the other 5 percent), and some subscribers who admittedly took the service just to keep it from collapsing, UPI was finally sold. In June 1982 Media News Corporation, a new company formed by a group of newspaper, cable, and television station owners, acquired the wire service, announcing its hopes that the UPI would become profitable once it moved fully onto the new electronic bandwagon. Old-time newspaper journalists must have winced upon hearing that the "wire service" they recently knew was about to stake its fortunes on cable television, direct broadcast satellite service, low-power TV, videodisc, videocassette, and computer data bases. (See chapter 8 for a fuller discussion of these media forms.) UPI's new owners were pleased to acquire a service whose previous owners had endowed with state-of-the-art equipment, including a $10 million computer, communications and technical center in Dallas, digital newspicture darkrooms in New York and Brussels, and some 500 video display terminals in its various bureaus around the world.[3]

Wire services turn to new electronic technology.

High distribution costs have plagued the wire services, and they are having to turn to the new electronic technology for survival. In the early 1980s UPI's annual phone bill was $13.5 million, and AP's was $16 million. That was the price of leasing telephone or land lines from ATT ("Ma Bell") for delivery of news and pictures to America's news media. There is little wonder that the wire services were anxious to transmit high speed verbal and pictorial data by means of communications satellites. Hundreds of subscribers (the newspapers and broadcast stations) were being equipped with satellite receiving dishes during 1981 and 1982, as AP and UPI anticipated saving some 70 to 80 percent of their telephone bills by bouncing signals heavenward.[4]

The Wire Service Operation

The wire services traditionally have operated a remarkably efficient two-way, dovetailed system of both news gathering and distribution. In the distribution link most wire service copy originated in New York for domestic consumption, then traveled over trunk lines to the wire services' major metropolitan subscribers. At various relay points across the country, its contents were scanned by *wire filers* who took appropriate items, major stories, and material of a particular regional or local interest and forwarded them onto the state and regional circuits for use by smaller clients. The system worked much like a transcontinental freight train being broken up in Kansas City, with some cars continuing on to the coast and others being sidetracked to Omaha or Dallas.

In days gone by, news gathering worked in reverse of its distribution. Many wire service bureaus, often one-person affairs located in local newspaper offices (AP bureaus) or independent shops (UPI bureaus), consisted of a bureau chief or a small group of gatekeepers who gathered stories from the local community and filed them on the wire. As the material moved in reverse, the wire filers had to decide whether to kill the item or pass it along to New York for national distribution. In the event of a major newsbreak in an out-of-the-way place, the wire services would send reporters to cover it from either New York or the regional bureaus. In smaller communities where there were no bureaus, the wire services hired stringers, generally reporters for the local papers who moonlighted for the wire services and were paid by the column inch or for each story used. In the smallest towns, services used housewives and high schoolers, paying them a flat rate for each story they submitted.

At the end of the pipeline, in the newspaper office, the wire service copy emerged on a battery of teletype machines, the number of which varied depending on how many of the services the newspaper subscribed to—whether a single national wire or a combination of national, regional, sports, business, and other wires. In the earliest days, the news was transmitted by a Morse code operator who, on a good day, could transcribe thirty-five words per minute. The teletype increased transcription to sixty-five words per minute, resulting in some savings to the newspaper, since it no longer had to pay a Morse code operator. Eventually, in the 1960s and 1970s, the teletype machines printed justified copy (copy with even margins, as in this text) ready to run, together with perforated tape on the typesetter (TTS) ready to be fed directly into the typesetting machines. The tape reduced composing room time considerably and permitted the services to operate a little closer to deadlines than previously, but still delivered news at only one word per second.

Thanks to computers and other new technology, all of this has changed in the past several years. Since the late 1970s, wire service gathering and distribution methods, and the speed with which they are carried out, have been altered almost beyond recognition.

Today, a system of nationwide distribution circuits is still in effect, with relevant stories being channeled to appropriate bureaus and media. However, due to the data storage capacity of large computers, an editor in South Succotash, for example, who desires to run a story about the eradication of hydatids in Tasmanian sheepdogs, no longer has to wait for the wire service to announce when the desired story will be released; instead, the editor merely calls up the wire service's central computer in New York or Dallas and requests the entire story. In other words, the local editor has more control of information. And when the information arrives, it doesn't dribble along at the sixty-five-word-a-minute limit necessitated by leased telephone lines and slow teletypesetters. The new high-speed teleprinters and satellite beams have brought about the computer-to-computer exchange of stories at the rate of 56,000 words per minute. Even though few

Since the late 1970s, wire service news gathering and distribution methods have been altered drastically.

readers in South Succotash will desire much information detailing the problems of Tasmanian sheepdogs, if they did and if the editor could process it and all the other data appearing on the VDT screen, the stories could be printed instantaneously whenever desired.

Editors connected to the UPI's "demand" service have the opportunity to order up on a given day those stories deemed of interest to the local community. A more typical pattern, however, is the wire services' traditional system of suggesting to their subscribers what they believe are the major stories of the day and the editors' traditional approach of allocating space for only those key stories designated.

Wire services provide news "budgets" during each daily cycle.

A day in the life of a wire service is divided up into cycles. Twice daily the wire services draw up a *budget* of news, choosing ten or twelve stories that, in their estimate, are the most important news events of the day. The services then wire or beam a summary of this budget to editors across the country, so they will know what to expect and can plan accordingly in making up their papers. The service then runs through the major stories, one by one, interrupting the cycle with bulletins of other major events and continual "updates" on the running budget stories. As updates and new leads are released, their written presentation is such that they can be fitted directly into what has been received previously with only minimal disturbance to material already set in type. After the cycle has been completed, it begins again. On a fast-moving story, there may be as many as a half-dozen updates and new leads within a cycle carried by the "A" or major news wire. Other news items are relegated to the "B" wire for secondary news and major features, or on the sports wire, business wire, or racing wire. Because of the two-way nature of the gathering–distribution system, a client is able to query the wire service for data of special local interest, such as how the local representative in Congress voted on a certain bill. In this example, the query would be relayed to the Washington bureau, where one of a hundred or so staffers would ask the Congressperson's office or their Capitol Hill reporter, and the private answer would be flashed back to the client.

The world headquarters of both AP and UPI are in New York City. UPI's central computer is in Dallas, as previously mentioned; AP has half a dozen or so regional computer centers, where much of the gatekeeping and wire filing take place. No longer does a story move from the small bureau to the "B" wire where it is judged worthy of "A" wire treatment or handled as second-class information. Now it goes from the small bureau to one of the AP's regional computerized centers or to UPI's central computer, where it is made available to clients.

Both AP and UPI operate separate radio and television wires. After 1935 UP began supplying radio stations with the same wires as newspapers. This required rewriting for the less formal, more immediate audio style of the air. When AP began serving broadcast in 1940, there was a competitive

Wire photos are
transmitted by UPI's
Unifax.
Ellis Herwig/Stock, Boston

incentive for both AP and UP to develop radio wires written in the audio style, so that newscasters could take the wire service copy directly from the teletype and read it on the air—*rip 'n' read,* the process is called. The radio/ television writing style is punchy, immediate, and pays less attention to spelling and punctuation than does newspaper style. In essence, it plays for the ear, not for the eye. In addition to the broadcast news stories, UPI maintains a daily radio pickup service for its clients whereby they can tune into UPI and carry a national news budget directly onto the air or tape it for future use. Both UPI Audio and AP Radio provide complete newscasts over leased telephone lines to their clients and members. In addition, both services offer television stations a steady diet of still and motion pictures for use in newscasts.

Most nonlocal photographs found in America's daily newspapers are courtesy of the wire services. Pictures are transmitted anywhere in the country via special circuits and satellite, and are reproduced instantaneously by facsimile machines in each newspaper. New techniques of electrostatic transmission electronically deliver glossy photos on dry paper, ready for printing.

Broadcast news and photographs are provided by the wire services.

Wire Service Beats

The wire services are no different in their news gathering operations than the typical newspaper, as we described in chapter 2. It's just that the wire services function on a larger scale. They, too, maintain beats with the presidency, on Capitol Hill, in the major executive departments, at the Pentagon, in the major state capitals, and on Wall Street. Internationally, they have major bureaus staffed in the leading capitals of the world—London, Paris, Rome, Berlin, Moscow, Tel Aviv, Cairo, Tokyo, and Buenos Aires—several of which have regional responsibility. For example, Tokyo carries most of the coverage for the Far East, and Buenos Aires is the focal point for Latin American news, as coverage of the British and Argentinian conflict in the Falkland Islands reminded us.

Wire services cover the world as a good newspaper would if it had the resources.

The press associations have their own versions of the *tickler file,* to remind themselves of regularly scheduled events that demand coverage: the World Series, the Super Bowl, the Indy 500, the national political conventions and elections, holidays, the winter and summer Olympics, and so forth. News of such significant events is in great demand by their clients and is awaited breathlessly by tens of millions of Americans. Gathering such news produces huge logistical problems of moving dozens of personnel around, shifting assignments, and temporarily leaving the more routine beats minimally covered to concentrate on the big event that, experience has shown, will often develop an unexpected turn or demand a continuing effort. For the unexpected, press associations also rely on their far-flung network of 175 or so bureaus apiece, the news gathering facilities of their thousands of clients, and their countless stringers.

The major areas in which the wire services concentrate correspond closely to the major departments of the daily newspapers. Concentration is on government and politics, on sports, and on feature or society news.

The Washington bureaus of press associations are staffed by more than one hundred people covering every aspect of government on a fairly regular basis. Even so, they are sadly understaffed considering the enormity of the federal bureaucracy and its hundreds of agencies. Consequently, a considerable portion of their time is devoted to watching the other media: the television networks, the bureaus of the big dailies, the press and broadcast groups, the major syndicated material, the national columnists, the foreign press associations, as well as the big lobbies and news magazines. These are all potential subsources of governmental material in addition to tips from the interested, both inside and outside of government. The approach is a good deal like that of the city editor of an afternoon paper who scans the A.M. coverage to be sure nothing is overlooked.

Politics is great copy because it represents the raw material of controversy. On the national level it becomes the epic struggle of two titans playing for real prizes—power, prestige, opportunity, and position. Political campaigns are gladiatorial in nature. Their ability to generate long-range emotion makes them indispensable to the American scene, and money in the bank for all the news packagers.

Sports shares with politics some of the elements of competition. Here again giants are seen struggling for supremacy. Everyone picks favorites and experiences a vicarious thrill in watching opponents vie. In a sedentary and white-collar nation increasingly removed from physical contact and from direct thrill and danger, athletes are surrogates, performing skills for contemporary society and doing its exercising.

The status of the participants in sports, government, and politics as news sources is yet another factor to be considered. In a nation of more than 200 million persons, only a tiny fraction of them can be in the news. Some of them rise to the surface at society's officially prescribed gathering points—the various news beats. Others (athletes, politicians, and officials) occupy positions that are, almost by definition, newsworthy. Society itself, in one way or another, has chosen such persons for preferred treatment, and in response to society's demand, the news packagers heavily treat their affairs, both public and private, because society's curiosity is ravenous. This formal and informal selection of individuals by society also constitutes a sort of self-screening device of news. In a circular process, news is what society says it is, and that is what the wire services will relay to the newspapers and broadcasters for replay to society.

The Nation's Gatekeepers

The widespread reach of only two major press associations occasions a similarity to the news that is striking. It is quite possible for a person to breakfast in New York while reading the *New York Times* and then fly to Los Angeles for lunch and find the same story verbatim in the *Los Angeles Times*. Anyone who has driven across the country has also been exposed to a progression of individual local stations airing the same radio wire material, differing only in the accents of the announcers. This sameness is heightened by the similarity of both the AP and UPI approach to the news and their objective style, which allows little leeway for individuality of treatment.

This situation places awesome responsibility and power in the hands of the relatively few editors and wire filers of the press associations who are, in fact, the gatekeepers of the nation's news. Since only a dozen or so major stories are included on the daily budget cycle, it is these stories, by and large, that will be carried on the country's front pages and over the daily radio and television news programs. Even editors who are not particularly enchanted with a story are under great pressure to carry it, if only because the wire service did. Radio news commentators are perhaps in an even more restricted position, having to use the radio wire material because there is no other news available. There's speculation that as the financial pressure becomes greater on the wire services they may be forced to curtail their coverage, thereby reducing their budgets and ultimately limiting the availability of information. Other auxiliary news and feature services may pick up part of the slack, but more likely in specialized rather than general news coverage.

AP and UPI could control the news agendas of the nation, but several forces limit the threat.

Four factors operate to balance the potential threat of wire services' power: (1) their historical dedication to news, their determination to uncover it, their long-term success in doing so, and their sharply honed news judgment; (2) the intense competition between associations, which involves constant watchdogging of each other, and consequently minimizes the opportunity for purposeful bias; (3) the increase in the number of correspondents and stringers employed by or representing the various newspaper and radio groups, the television networks, the several syndicates, and the larger metropolitan newspapers, which enhances competition and provides a greater variety of both news stories and treatment, and (4) the fact that more and more interpretative reporting is finding its way into the wire services, as a response to the demand of subscribers, who discovered that the old mode of total objectivity was no longer adequate for their better educated and more sophisticated audiences. The mainstay of the wire services is still objective reporting, but this is augmented now with an increasing number of interpretative, background, and even opinion pieces.

Gatekeepers for the World?

AP, UPI, Agence France-Presse, Reuters, and TASS dominate the world scene.

Lest we leave the erroneous impression that the Associated Press and United Press International are the eyes and ears of the world, we shall consider several other international wire services and the controversy surrounding the way the world's news is mustered.

At present five news agencies dominate the world scene. In addition to the American-based AP and UPI, the major watchdogs are the Agence France-Presse (AFP) in Paris, Reuters in London, and the Telegrafnoie Agentsvo Sovetskovo Soyuza (TASS) or Telegraph Agency of the Soviet Union.

AFP was organized at the end of World War II as an autonomous public body operating under the watchful eye of a board of directors comprised of French publishing representatives. With 100 foreign bureaus, it services thousands of newspapers and broadcast stations either directly or through joint agreements with national news agencies in individual countries. Like the AP, it is a nonprofit enterprise.

Press associations in the British Commonwealth own Reuters, but the old service, originating in the 1850s, is rapidly emerging as a respected and powerful agency worldwide. In 1980 it had revenues of some $172 million, compared with the AP's $137 million. Its income derived from its massive web of news reporting links plus its financial news and information–retrieval services, which were found to be especially attractive to banks and investment institutions around the world.[5] Reuters operates a half dozen bureaus in the United States and has around 1,000 correspondents scattered across 180 different countries and territories.

TASS is known as the official Soviet news agency. It serves not only as the voice of Moscow for the rest of the world to hear, but as the government's ears as well. Foreign correspondents in 100 nations gather local and international news, interpreting the world's affairs according to official policy.

If TASS is considered by the Western world to speak in the singular voice of Soviet policy, what can be said about the other four international agencies? Over the past decade or so, they have come under increasing attack from non-Western nations for their tendencies to see and report the world through Western, capitalistic lenses. All things considered, AP, UPI, AFP, and Reuters on a daily basis take the subtleties of world events and filter them through a gatekeeping system not compatible with much of the world's interests. Because of their enormous scope, these Western agencies gather up news from one Third World nation, process it in Paris, London, or New York, and then file it off to other Third World nations. In the meantime, Western knowledge of the outside world is coming almost exclusively from these wire services, and the rest of the world learns of the West's doings by the same means.

When you combine the influence of the wire-service gatekeepers with the fact that Western powers own and control most of the world's information delivery systems, it is little wonder Third World nations view the situation with alarm. Crying out against cultural imperialism or communications colonialism, they have raised in the United Nations calls for a *New World Communications Order*. They have requested independence and equity in access to global communication resources so that their own views, values, and developmental efforts will be reported more fully. They have sought the right to restrict the flow of information across national borders, and requested power to license journalists and impose an international code of journalistic ethics. When the United Nations Educational,

Nonwestern nations resent western news domination; they request a "New World Communications Order."

Western journalists tell the third world's stories, but some call it "media imperialism."
Susan Meiselas/Magnum Photos, Inc.

Scientific and Cultural Organization (UNESCO) issued its report on these problems in 1980, Western journalists were upset. The so-called MacBride Commission suggested that all news media, including the international news agencies, would be expected to promote governmentally established social, cultural, economic, and political goals. The commission's report was not adopted after some weeks of intense debate, but UNESCO supported a three-year study expected to lead to a document that would deal thoroughly with the questions of media imperialism.

Debates over media colonialism or imperialism, or what have you, will continue so long as the international news agencies monopolize the flow of information between and among the world's developed and developing nations. Given the tendency of any of us to see the world as we have grown accustomed to seeing it, there seems little hope for a quick or easy settlement to the issue. When we are in a position to open and close the world's information gates, we assume awesome responsibilities.[6]

Other Pooling Efforts

On a smaller scale, various news media pool their resources.

In the newspaper field, following the precedent established long ago by Scripps and Hearst, many groups are finding it advantageous to organize smaller wire and feature services principally to serve their own newspapers. Material written for one newspaper can, in some instances, be used by others in the group, thereby achieving some savings and lowering the unit cost. Alternately, some newspapers have syndicated their materials for mutual use, as, for example, the *Los Angeles Times–Washington Post* syndicate. Both papers profit from unparalleled coverage of the nation's capital and of southern California at no additional cost. Once this pooling occurs, whether on a group or independent syndicate basis, the next logical step is to offer the material for sale to other newspapers, defraying a portion of the original investment in the material.

Individual newspapers also get into the act. The *New York Times,* the nation's newspaper of record, offers outstanding comprehensive material and unsurpassed coverage of the nation's financial capital to its 500 or so clients worldwide. The *Chicago Tribune* and the *Chicago Sun-Times* offer material from, but not limited to, the nation's heartland; the *Toronto Telegram Services* covers Canada. In each instance, the service represents extra income from an investment already made. Using the same economic principle employed by the UPI, the suppliers put a teletype in the hands of their subscribers, billing them on a sliding scale according to each subscriber's circulation. Columnists and key sections (sports, business, politics, entertainment, and the like) from the host paper are made available on a same-day basis to whichever papers have subscribed. In this respect newspaper groups and private services have an advantage over the wire services in that they utilize pooled information directly and derive income through subscriptions besides, while the revenue of the wire services must come from media sales alone. Newsmagazines also have gotten into the packaging business, getting more revenue mileage out of their basic coverage. *Newsweek* is notable among these.

Many of these services also tend to specialize their coverage. The Women's News Service speaks for itself. Others in the list of a hundred or so specialized services include the National Black News Service; the Chinese Information Service; entertainment, sports, and religious services; and a plethora of others delivering their sometimes propagandistic messages wherever they will be paid for and used.

Related to the wire services are the various city and regional news services. These are local, private services that follow the press association principle. The city news services maintain reporters at the major beats within a city (city hall, courts, police stations, and the like), gathering news for the small dailies, the weeklies, and the radio stations within their area. They sell this data to local media, relieving them of the expense of maintaining reportorial staff, and yet enabling them to keep current on local happenings. The more enterprising city news services also operate a radio pickup wire for local stations, sometimes on a telephone "beeper," and a few shoot film for television.

These services in the larger cities are generally supplemented by the so-called *business wires*. Business wires are really public relations wires, and they operate in reverse of the other wires. Instead of charging the media, they maintain teletypes in the newspaper, radio, and television outlets, and they charge their sources for carrying the material. The service assures rapid and complete distribution of public relations material. The more enterprising public relations people reinforce their story with a phone call advising the editor that the copy is coming over the business wire.

Private businesses often subscribe to the Dow Jones Financial News Service.
Robert V. Eckert, Jr./EKM-Nepenthe

More legitimately deserving of the "business wire" title are the highly successful services provided by Dow Jones and the Commodity News Service. Dow Jones has for years provided newspapers and private offices with a financial wire, carrying the substance of *The Wall Street Journal*. Recently, in its efforts to stay in the thick of the information explosion, Dow Jones has begun offering its pool of financial data on an interactive or two-way basis to homeowners or anyone else who has access to a microcomputer and telephone. Its success stories include working with "electronic newspaper" delivery systems in Florida, Texas, and elsewhere; in academic institutions; and in the nation's boardrooms, large and small. (See chapter 8.)

Meanwhile, the Commodity News Service caters to a wide gamut of specialized market-analysis needs. From its Chicago and Kansas City headquarters, it distributes Farm Radio News and Grain Information News reports on crop reports and farm-market conditions; it distributes the Lumber Instant News for the lumber industry, providing information about wood prices, forest conditions, and national economic trends that would impinge upon the industry; and it distributes other specialized market reports to interested groups.

All in all, the diversity of opinions and information made available by the wide variety of auxiliary news services bodes well for the media. Not only do the participants receive a broader variety of information and opinion than they could generate on their own, but their readers, listeners, and viewers are spared the sometimes monotonous sameness of AP and UPI copy.

Feature Syndicates

In the 1880s Samuel McClure, who published *McClure's Magazine,* decided to capitalize on his investment in "nonnews." He recognized that the growing newspapers had a need for "untimely" material of a human-interest or feature nature. Material that made interesting reading, but did not have to make the next edition, could be held for a slow news day. McClure put out 50,000 words a week to newspaper subscribers on such topics as fashion, homemaking, manners, and literature. Thus, the *feature services,* or *syndicates,* were born, as packagers of the untimely. Newspaper publishers did not have the money to produce this kind of material themselves, but when it could be purchased at a fraction of its cost on an exclusive basis in their territory, it was a filler bargain; they could save some reportorial salaries while filling their newspapers with readable content.

A century old, feature syndicates fulfill media's vast appetites for nonnews.

As the wire services are basically packagers of the information content, the feature syndicates have become the packagers of entertainment content, both graphic and verbal, for the newspapers. Anywhere from 10 to 35 percent of the average editorial content of newspapers is composed of this prepackaged or "canned" entertainment. It includes the advice to the lovelorn columns, comics and cartoons, daily horoscopes, crossword

The Herald Journal –   Logan, Utah, Monday, September 13, 1982

The real world is beckoning Zonker Harris

It's finally time for a $20 haircut, and encounters with cocaine, herpes

FAIRWAY, Kan. (UPI) — Garry Trudeau is suspending his Pulitizer Prize-winning "Doonesbury" comic strip to rest and provide unreconstructed hippie Zonker Harris and the other residents of Walden Puddle Commune the chance to evolve into the "world of grown-up concerns."

Trudeau, who combines editorial-page gravity with funny-paper levity in "Doonesbury," announced Wednesday an unprecedented hiatus from cartooning — perhaps for as long as 20 months.

Universal Press Syndicate President John P. McMeel said "Doonesbury" would be suspended in more than 700 newspapers beginning Jan. 2, 1983. The specific length of Trudeau's leave was not announced but he told the syndicate he would likely resume the feature by the fall of 1984.

"This is simply a lull in the action," he said in a prepared statement. "It is not, repeat not, a mid-life crisis."

"I need a breather," said Trudeau, 34, a New York City resident and husband of NBC's "Today Show" host Jane Pauley. "Investigative cartooning is a young man's game. Since the industry frowns on vacations, I'll be claiming a medical leave."

Trudeau, who refuses to grant interviews, said he considered the time off a reprieve from the pressure of writing a daily topical comic strip. He often works only two weeks ahead of deadline while other cartoonists are as much as two months ahead.

A news conference "to amplify" Trudeau's decision was scheduled for today at the syndicate's offices.

Trudeau said it was time to reappraise his characters and review development of the strip, which he started while attending Yale. It went into syndication in 1970 with only 28 subscribers.

"There are a few problems that need to be ironed out," he said. "For almost 15 years, the main characters have been trapped in a time warp and so find themselves carrying the colors and scars of two separate generations. It was unfair to stretch their formative years to embrace both Vietnam and preppy.

"My characters are understandably confused and out of sorts. It's time to give them some $20 haircuts, graduate them and move them out into the larger world of grown-up concerns.

"The trip from draft beer and mixers to cocaine and herpes is a long one and it's time they got a start on it."

In "Doonesbury," the real and the fictive combine.

Former Secretary of State Alexander Haig, Interior secretary James Watt, President Reagan and even PLO leader Yassar Arafat are as likely to show up in one of Trudeau's strips as Michael J. Doonesbury, the perennial student and armchair liberal who often samples the world's lunacy from in front of a television set.

Joining him are Zonker, feisty feminist Joanie Caucus, right-wing quarterback B.D., dope-eating Uncle Duke, radical Mark Slackmeyer and the other iconoclastic members of the Walden Puddle Commune.

---

puzzles, word games, coin and stamp collecting columns, chess features, a wide range of how-to-do-it pieces, fashion, interior decorating, cooking, dressmaking, and nostalgia. Book, art, drama, and film criticism, and a variety of humor, gossip, financial, and political columns are also included.

Newspaper editors try to achieve some sort of balance of features depending on their evaluation of the mix of their particular readership. The larger newspapers try to achieve political balance in their national columnists, offering both liberal and conservative viewpoints. While ostensibly these are presented to permit readers to make up their own minds between two divergent viewpoints, they are actually a surefire audience formula in that readers will read the one because they agree with it and will read the other to get mad, which is a comparable "entertaining" emotional reaction.

There are some 400 different feature syndicates listed in the annual *Editor & Publisher Yearbook,* ranging from small, one-person outlets to giants like the Newspaper Enterprise Association and King Features Syndicate with their $100 million operations. Since all syndicates bill their clients on the basis of circulation promised, widely syndicated columnists like Dear Abby and Art Buchwald, or cartoonists like Garry Trudeau ("Doonesbury"), bring in hefty six-figure incomes annually. All told, more than 2,500 different features are available for purchase from syndicates. For fees ranging between $5 and $150 a week, newspapers are often offered exclusive local rights to publish individual features. The cost per newspaper isn't great, which explains why over the course of a year the average editor will have to cope with many dozens of syndicate salespersons, each claiming to offer exclusive rights to the Peanuts-type-sure-fire success feature. As in most commercial aspects of the media, competition is intense.

Feature syndicates invest as much as $100,000 in producing and launching a new feature; the average is said to be around $25,000. Syndicates themselves are besieged with thousands of would-be creators annually. From the 5,000 feature ideas it receives annually, the *Chicago Tribune–New York News* syndicate selects no more than a dozen for eventual syndication.[7] The normal split between the author–creator and the syndicate is fifty-fifty, which helps explain why those thousands of unsolicited comics, opinion pieces, special features, and what have you, keep crossing the desks of syndicate editors.

For a price, newspapers can try to be all things to all people.

Success breeds imitation, and once a newspaper has gambled and won circulation or interest by publishing a given feature, it is unwilling to see competing local or regional newspapers reap rewards without having to gamble. Thus exclusivity contracts are the norm in the features business. A newspaper signs a contract guaranteeing it exclusive rights to publish a given feature within a fifty-mile radius, or assuring itself that it will face no competition for the feature in any county where the paper circulates to 20 percent of the households. There may be other variations to these contracts, but the upshot of it all is frequently considered a form of censorship and restraint of trade by papers denied access to popular features.

If the wire services gained favor among the nation's newspapers during a period when objectivity was stressed, then feature syndicates are receiving patronage under differing circumstances. Last century an avoidance of opinion satisfied the relatively small range of opinion differences represented by wire service clients. Today, increasing affluence, a much higher educational level, and a diversity of interests and the proliferating media to serve them are requiring a higher degree of diversification than historically provided by the wire services. Objective news is not enough anymore; reflective news is demanded.

Into this breech come the feature services, which, in one form or another, have proliferated to serve a diversity of public tastes and the multiplying departments that the daily newspaper evidences. The features bring magazine content to the press. Society has again demanded fragmentation and specialization from even such monolithic enterprises as the two major wire services.

Print Media

Like the mass media that they serve, wire services have become ponderous corporate institutions, deeply ingrained and somewhat resistant to change. Only recently, in the face of a computerized technological revolution, have they had the flexibility to adjust to increasing demands for more diverse material. Thus, it appears that their very bigness has encouraged the development of smaller and more tractable services, some of which originated from the very newspapers served by wire services. Tomorrow, it may be that the wire services themselves fractionalize, offering individualized features to consumers upon demand; only time will tell.

Summary

The press associations, AP and UPI, are packagers of information in probably its purest form. They are the result of newspapers pooling their resources to offset the increasing costs of gathering news. The AP was founded in 1848, after the invention of the telegraph, by six New York newspapers to share wire costs. It was a membership organization, which soon admitted other newspapers on an exclusive basis in their respective areas. An AP membership became a very valuable asset. Early, AP developed the technique of reportorial objectivity in an attempt to answer the differing social and political viewpoints of its many members. Later, during the Civil War, the concepts of journalese and the "lead" were born to get the most important information out first in case of telegraph failure.

The telegraph also made possible the introduction of national advertising into newspapers and assisted in the centralized control necessary for the establishment of the great newspaper empires of Hearst, Scripps, and Pulitzer. Scripps ended the AP's nearly sixty-year monopoly on national and international news by founding the United Press in 1907. Two years later Hearst started the International News Service for the same purpose. Both organizations found it profitable to sell their services to other newspapers in order to defray costs. Neither was an effective competitor for AP until they merged in 1958. Today, AP has 10,000 members internationally, and UPI has 7,000. They are in constant, intense competition to be the first to bring the news to their clients. Somewhere out there, AP and UPI subscribers are fighting a deadline every minute of the day, and to run second means to be left out of the paper or off the air; to risk subsequent cancellation.

AP and UPI have turned to satellite transmission of data for more rapid and reliable and less expensive communication with subscribers. Modernization of the services includes reliance upon centralized computers and "on demand" access to news by editors scattered across the nation. The services continue to draw up daily news budgets, suggesting to editors the ten or twelve most important stories to be carried during the day. Both services cater to the special needs of their radio and television subscribers, offering satellite and wire transmission of photographs.

The wire services handle news beats in much the same way that metropolitan newspapers do, with general assignment and specialist reporters covering the news on beats when news is most likely to occur. Politics, sports, society, and business are the wire services' stock in trade. With their budgets, the wire services wield enormous influence as national agenda setters; the same versions of the same stories are repeated coast to coast, hour by hour, in the nation's subscribing media. Fortunately, the wire services' potential for abuse is limited by their own integrity and hunger for news, sense of competition, growth, and response to subscribers' demands for more interpretation and analysis.

AP and UPI share the world's newsgathering chores with a great many other agencies, the largest of which are AFP of France, Reuters of England, and TASS of Russia. The four Western services have been faulted for "communications colonialism," as they gather and report the world's news through capitalistic eyes. Calls for a New World Communications Order, with developing nations taking a larger role in their images around the world, are creating some difficulties for the Western agencies.

Today, an increasing number of smaller newspaper and broadcast groups have organized news services to serve their own papers in addition to making these services available to others. Also, some of the nation's major papers, alone or in concert, have made material available on a syndicated basis, which increases the diversity of news available in the marketplace. City news services condense municipal news for the smaller dailies and weeklies. The so-called business wires are used for public relations purposes where the source pays for inclusion and the newspaper receives it free. More significant are the financial and business services provided by Dow Jones and the Commodity News Service. Married to new technology, the business services are available to homes and small companies instead of to just large media subscribers.

Finally, there are the feature syndicates, the 400 or so organizations devoted to providing America's newspapers with nonnews, with the untimely content that fills so much space and attracts so many readers to the press. Comics, columns, crossword puzzles, games, and other self-indulgent fare have become big business. Successful features bring their individual creators six-figure incomes and keep syndicate sales personnel knocking on editors' doors with bargains they can't, but often should, refuse.

In a familiar pattern, media consumers are receiving the mix of hard and soft news, substance and fluff, news and entertainment, and even the persuasion they have requested.

Notes

1. Peter Sandman, David Rubin, and David Sachsman, *Media: An Introductory Analysis of American Mass Communications,* (Englewood Cliffs, N.J.: Prentice-Hall, 1972).
2. C. David Rambo, "In the Race for News, Technology Leads at the Wires," *Presstime,* August 1981, p. 21.
3. "UPI Is Sold to Media News Corp.," Logan (Utah) *Herald-Journal,* 3 June 1982.
4. Rambo, "In the Race for News," pp. 23–24.
5. Ibid., pp. 21–22.
6. Oliver Boyd-Barrett, *The International News Agencies* (Beverly Hills, Calif.: Sage Publications, 1980).
7. Drake Mabry, "Editors vs. Syndicates," *Presstime,* January 1982, pp. 20–21.

Part 3 Electronic Media

In the next four chapters we discuss the media that depend on electronics: radio, television, television's offspring, and film. Together they demonstrate the influence, potential, and problems inherent in instantaneous communication.

Electricity is significant for the speed with which it transports messages across distances, a quality that has had an inestimable impact on the slower print media. Instantaneous information transmission has radically altered our senses of time and space, and of knowing and being known, and has introduced a new factor into the information business. Whereas print media rely on the mass production of separate units of books, newspapers, or magazines for individual consumers, the electronic revolution has made it possible for a single electronically produced message to serve masses of individuals separated physically (and perhaps culturally, intellectually, and emotionally).

Film can be described as a kind of electric book. While it does not foist itself upon a specific audience and it must await its audiences, who visit it individually, being a member of its audience requires effort and money. Cinema is more permanent than radio and television, whose contents tend to disappear as quickly as they appear. Finally, like the book, film pays its own way without the advertising so dominant in radio and television programming.

Radio is no longer a national medium; it has fragmented to serve specific publics, often in terms of their special interests. In the process radio has applied electricity to the principle of specialization by which mass media have traditionally survived, making it a sort of electric magazine.

Radio provided television with a framework, a conditioned audience, the basis of programming, the networks and affiliate structure, and federal control. And of foremost importance, radio fought, won, and solidified the battle of commercial and advertising support. In other words, television inherited a ready-made game plan.

In terms of its massive audiences and its total effect, television is a medium more speculated about than understood. Politically, socially, and economically, its ramifications are enormous. More particularly, it has radically affected all other media—driving some magazines out of business, encouraging others, and altering the role of the newspaper. It has reduced radio to a supplemental medium closely aligned with the record industry. On the one hand, television has offered movies freedom from the tyranny of the masses; on the other hand, it has taken this freedom away as it offers movies vaster audiences in a single night than the average film could expect in its lifetime.

Significant competitors have arisen to threaten network television. The emerging media, still in their developmental phases, offer hundreds of channels, and hence service to special interests. In some cases (interactive cable television in its latest forms) the new electronics offer built-in, immediate feedback. Coupled to home computers and satellites, we have the world at our fingertips.

What we do with that new access to information remains uncertain. Computerized information delivered by media whose natures we scarcely understand has become available to us more rapidly than we can consume it. The producers of such information have responded to our requests by providing massive quantities of the same materials (movies, sports, music, and escapist programming) that Hollywood and the commercial networks have so effectively dished up for generations. But our new tools lend themselves to novel ways of dealing with our postindustrial, informational society; schooling, banking, shopping, interacting with our neighbors, and participating in the day-to-day running of our democracy lie within our electronically enhanced grasp.

Marshall McLuhan was fond of saying that we shape our tools, and then our tools shape us. A primary purpose of the next four chapters is to show how we have been shaping our contemporary communications tools and to improve our chances of being shaped in ways we, and not our tools, desire.

Radio and Recordings 6

Introduction

By 1982, there were 9,092 radio stations in the United States, including 4,630 commercial AM stations, 3,346 commercial FM stations, and 1,116 noncommercial FM stations. With over 457.5 million radio sets in operation, 99 percent of the nation's homes and 95 percent of its automobiles are equipped with radios. That means there are more than two radios for each man, woman, and child in the country. Nine out of every ten Americans over the age of twelve listen to radio each week, and three-fourths of the adults listen every day for 2.5 hours.

As a nation, we spend $2 billion each year to purchase another 50 million sets for our cars, purses, nightstands, family rooms, offices, and the like. Advertisers spend $3.2 billion annually to hawk their wares over radio, and station owners pocket more than $154 million of that as profits for their troubles.

Radio is bigger than ever before, but it has become a supplemental medium. It is a paradox.

Radio today is a bigger business than ever before in terms of programs, listeners, and dollars. However, radio has become a supplemental medium. Furthermore, it has become a necessary adjunct to the record industry.

It wasn't always this way. During the 1930s and 1940s the radio was America's prime mass medium; it was a time when most people got a good deal of their news and most of their entertainment from radio. Ironically, there were fewer stations, fewer sets, and fewer listeners then than there are now. Although fewer in number, they were all concentrated; radio was a national medium. Today, by and large, radio is a specialized or local medium, or both.

It is a medium of paradoxes. While larger in scope than ever before, it is the most readily overlooked mass medium. It ranks behind television and newspapers as a source of news and in terms of news credibility. Yet as the most portable and instantaneous medium, it is the one to which most people automatically turn in times of emergencies. At the same time, many listeners are using it as a background medium, and don't even realize they have heard a newscast during the hours the set has been within earshot!

Radio set the stage for television; it developed over-the-air advertising—the commercial base of broadcasting; it established major networks to serve local stations with a quality of programming that none could afford by itself; it prompted the creation of the Federal Communications Commission and the doctrines of fairness and public interest, convenience, and necessity; it pioneered ratings as a feedback device; it adopted the star system from the movies, developing its own personalities; it designed the formula of 90 percent entertainment and commercials, and 10 percent information, which has carried over into all of U.S. broadcasting; and it borrowed from print the idea of using content to deliver audiences—broadcasting's real "product"—to the advertisers.

On nearly every front, radio paved the way for television, and then in its moment of glory, radio turned broadcasting over to television and stepped back into the crowd. This was no noble gesture; it happened in spite of efforts of people in the industry. Radio was hard hit for a while under television's dynamic impact, but it recovered and went on to a healthier life in the aggregate than it had ever experienced, even when it was the nation's prime mass medium.

Radio developed new prime times during the driving hours; it became portable—a constant companion; and it served special interests. It developed a demography of its own and began to discover automation and cheaper ways of broadcasting, even as television grew more expensive. And then radio became the right arm of the record industry, the aural means of marketing aural products—records, then albums, and then tapes.

Samuel Morse's telegraph (1844), Alexander Graham Bell's telephone (1876), and Thomas Edison's light bulb (1879) constituted the first technology to escape the physical net of printing. The miracle of electricity grew apace, heralding a revolution in electronics that continues today.

During the 1890s, Guglielmo Marconi's incessant tinkering with electromagnets paid off. With financial help from his father he invented a way to transmit sound without using wires. Almost immediately Marconi's wireless became a functional way to communicate with ships at sea. Marconi, however, had more ambitious plans, including the creation of a communications link between Europe and North America. By 1901 he had succeeded, which spurred the growth of his wireless companies.

Other inventors, such as John Ambrose Fleming and Lee De Forest, were at work on other elements crucial to radio. In 1906, De Forest perfected the audion, which became the vacuum tube, and thus made voice transmission possible.

The earliest radio broadcasts were on the air before the second decade of the twentieth century. Charles Herrold dispensed a little music and a little chatter from San Jose, California, starting in 1909. In 1910 De Forest helped to broadcast an Enrico Caruso performance from the Metropolitan Opera House in New York. The equipment was crude and the reception poor, but it worked. Under the sponsorship of the New York *American* newspaper, De Forest reported the results of the tight Wilson–Hughes election in 1916. Ironically, radio's first newscast was in error: "Charles Evans Hughes will be the next president of the United States," it announced.

World War I intervened, postponing the development of commercial broadcasting for several years. It was not until 1919 that the government stepped back and private inventors, developers, and operators returned to the scene. In that year General Electric, Westinghouse, and American Telephone and Telegraph pooled their various patent rights for broadcasting equipment and receiving hardware, and they formed the Radio Corporation of America (RCA). The new company sought to control the

Historical Development

The Early Days

Marconi's wireless and De Forest's audion tube were key inventions.

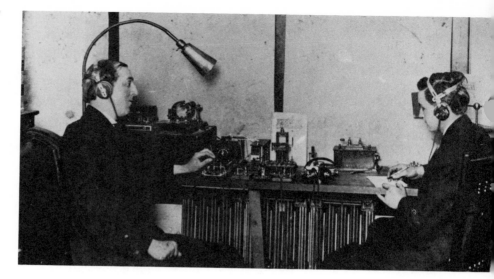

machinery of radio and prevent competition from entering the medium. They were especially concerned about protecting their rights to radio receivers, which RCA believed would be the primary source of profit to be gained from radio. The whole idea of wanting to capture as much of the business as possible through the exercise of patents was not unique to radio. It happened in the film industry just a few years earlier and then again when television came along. In each case, the effect was to retard development of the medium.

Entertainment, News, and Radio Advertising

Much credit for the development of radio as a national entertainment, news, and commercial medium must go to David Sarnoff. Sarnoff, a Russian immigrant who started as an office boy with the American Marconi Company, became a wireless telegraph operator when he was seventeen years old. Four years later, in 1912, he was on duty in New York City when he heard the faint signal "S. S. Titanic ran into iceberg. Sinking fast." For the next seventy-two hours, he was the key link between the Titanic disaster and the rest of the world. Due partly to his fame and partly to his ability and perseverance, he rose rapidly within the industry, becoming commercial manager at Marconi's American operations and then at RCA when it bought out Marconi in 1919. In 1921, he became general manager for RCA and was largely responsible for its formation of the National Broadcasting Company in 1926. In 1930 he became the president of RCA, and from 1947 until his retirement in 1969 he was chairman of the board. During his long association with RCA he fostered the emergence of monochrome (black and white) and color television from experimental stages to market saturation. He is generally credited with being the most influential person in the growth of American broadcasting.

Diligent and visionary David Sarnoff played a key role in broadcasting.

While Sarnoff was assistant traffic manager of the Marconi company in 1915 and 1916, he sensed that one of radiotelephony's major liabilities, its lack of privacy, could be turned into its major asset. In a memo to Edward J. Nally, vice-president and general manager of American Marconi, Sarnoff wrote:

I have in mind a plan of development which would make radio a "household utility" in the same sense as the piano or phonograph. The idea is to bring music into the home by wireless.

While this has been tried in the past by wires, it has been a failure because wires do not lend themselves to this scheme. With radio, however, it would be entirely feasible. . . . The receiver can be designed in the form of a simple "Radio Music Box" and arranged for several different wave lengths, which should be changeable with throwing of a single switch or pressing of a single button. . . .

The manufacture of the "Radio Music Box" including antenna, in large quantities, would make possible their sale at a moderate figure of perhaps $75.00 per outfit. The main revenue to be derived will be from the sale of "Radio Music Boxes" which if manufactured in quantities of one hundred thousand or so could yield a handsome profit when sold at the price mentioned above. . . .

Aside from the profit to be derived from this proposition the possibilities for advertising for the Company are tremendous; for its name would ultimately be brought into the household and wireless would receive national and universal attention.[1]

David Sarnoff's vision was incredibly accurate, except for his conviction that sales of receivers rather than ad sales would furnish the major revenue for the fledgling industry. Within a decade radio had become the household utility he had envisioned.

Westinghouse engineer Frank Conrad had been broadcasting phonograph music over a transmitter in his Pittsburgh garage in 1920 as part of his experiments in radiotelephony. Once Westinghouse realized that many area residents were tuning their homemade receivers to Conrad's signal and were even calling or writing him with special requests for music, Westinghouse stimulated a demand for its receivers by formalizing the programming over KDKA. Conrad's Westinghouse station was inaugurated on 2 November 1920 when it gave the results of the Harding–Cox presidential election, using telegraphed reports from its newspaper sources. The impact of the broadcast was so great that the public flocked to buy primitive crystal receivers from local department stores for as little as $10, not the $75 minimum Sarnoff had estimated.

There is some controversy as to whether KDKA in Pittsburgh, WWJ in Detroit, or WHA in Madison, Wisconsin, was the first true broadcasting station in the country; however, the first station to receive a regular broadcasting license was WBZ in Springfield, Massachusetts, on 15 September 1921. Those earliest commercial stations were owned by companies interested in promoting their primary business, such as the efforts of Westinghouse at KDKA. Several newspapers started radio stations in order to sell newspapers, the first being WWJ in Detroit. The *Detroit News* began broadcasting news in August 1920 and became a licensed commercial station the following year.

Prior to 1927 about sixty-nine different newspaper or other publishers built or bought radio stations. Some saw radio as a threat to their own newspapers and wished to keep control over local news dissemination; some saw it as a prestigious venture into new technology; and some, as a means of expanding their community service.[2] Other radio stations were owned by educational institutions, department stores, car and motorcycle dealers, music and jewelry stores, and hardware stores. According to Christopher Sterling, none of them were in the business of broadcasting for broadcasting's sake alone; they were selling their own image, their service, or their own name as a precursor to commercial advertising.[3]

Commercial advertising on radio probably began in 1922 when the American Telephone and Telegraph Company's New York station, WEAF, accepted $100 from a local real-estate firm for the broadcasting of a fifteen-minute message. The idea of such sponsors taking over the airwaves was not immediately accepted throughout the industry, however. Secretary of Commerce Herbert Hoover, for years in the thick of radio's struggles for identity and self-control, reacted to radio advertising with the statement, "It is inconceivable that we should allow so great a possibility for service, for news, for entertainment, and for vital commercial purposes to be drowned in advertising chatter."[4] But his voice, and the voices of other industry and civic leaders, was quickly drowned in the sea of chatter that was to become the lifeline of the industry. Quality programming cost money, prompting broadcasters to seek sources of capital provided by advertising. Audiences discovered early on that it was more convenient to put up with advertising in order to get good programming. The options, direct subsidies to each station or governmental funding of the medium, seemed less attractive and probably less realistic.

Electronic Media

Establishing the Networks

The networks and advertising are inseparable. In 1924 Eveready Batteries sponsored the "Eveready Hour" over a network of twelve stations that were linked together by telephone lines, which allowed for simultaneous broadcast in a dozen cities. This leasing of phone lines was the principal interest in ATT in the RCA consortium. By 1925 ATT had linked together twenty-six stations, stretching as far west as Kansas City, from its own master station, WEAF, in New York. The thought of reaching an evergrowing number of listeners in population centers across the nation proved irresistible to national advertisers, and the character of radio was no longer experimental; it had become highly organized. Catchy jingles were developed to promote product familiarity. Radio began to develop its own stars and its own drama; names and serials were guaranteed to attract listeners night after night, week after week.

Also in 1925 RCA (now including only Westinghouse and General Electric) set up its own flagship station, WJZ, in New York, and began to tie together stations to compete with ATT.

The network concept was perfected during the following year, 1926, when ATT sold WEAF to RCA for $1 million, an unheard of sum in the 1920s. Charges of antitrust by the Federal Trade Commission prompted ATT to get out of the broadcasting business and devote its energies to leasing lines to the broadcasters for network purposes. RCA created the National Broadcasting Company and suddenly had two fledgling networks to manage. WJZ became the flagship of NBC's Blue network, and the newly acquired WEAF operated as the key station in the Red network. Before the end of the year the NBC networks included about fifty stations operating coast to coast.

A year later, in 1927, the Columbia Broadcasting System (CBS) was established by the Columbia Phonograph Record Company, indicating even then the close relationship between radio, the music industry, and the record business. CBS was spearheaded by William S. Paley, who continued to dominate it throughout its formative years and into the 1980s.

A large number of stations became affiliated with networks, whereby they would carry network programming in return for a fee from the network. This financial arrangement surprises many people who think local stations should probably pay the networks, instead, for the privilege of receiving programming, stars, and newscasts that they could not possibly afford on their own. But the networks realize—as do the stations—that the programming assets attract large local audiences that add to the national audience. This permits the network to charge more for national advertising. The local stations, in turn, can charge higher rates for their purely local advertising. Network affiliation is a lucrative opportunity. By 1934 CBS had ninety-seven affiliates, NBC Red had sixty-five, and NBC Blue had sixty-two. About 40 percent of the stations broadcasting were network affiliates; the rest were independents.

Advertising and networks grew apace. NBC and CBS dominated the airwaves.

Local stations are paid to carry network programming and, of course, commercials.

The history of radio, and subsequently television and newer forms of electronic communication, has been a story of corporate struggles. The communications companies that had been so instrumental in establishing the medium squabbled among themselves, especially after they became aware of the commercial potential in radio. Other companies had entered the industry, starting stations across the country. There were more than 500 radio stations broadcasting by 1924 and more than 3 million receivers in operation. By 1927 the number of stations had increased to more than 700. Radio required no physical distribution and it crossed municipal boundaries and state lines indiscriminately, particularly on the crowded East Coast where it was born. But technological proliferation, unchecked by any systematic internal or external regulation, resulted in so many stations operating so close together on the band that none could be received clearly. Radio had become "a tower in Babel," according to Erik Barnouw.[5]

When the radio industry finally sought regulation, the federal government was the only logical agency to turn to, since cities and states could regulate only within their own jurisdictions, and radio signals carried across political boundaries.

Left to its own competitive devices, radio created a "Tower of Babel."

Governmental Regulation

Government's first direct involvement with radio came in 1912, when Congress passed the Radio Act. The law had modest provisions: Radio operators were expected to pass an exam before being allowed to transmit; and the Secretary of Commerce was responsible for assigning wavelengths or radio frequencies to whoever applied for a license. These regulations seemed reasonable enough, considering that so few stations or individuals were seeking to use the airwaves at that time.

But the 1920s saw a boom in radio growth, particularly in commercial stations. With the boom came chaos, since all commercial licensees were on the same frequency (remember, most of the earlier licensees were amateurs, hams, or naval operators) and had to work around each other's broadcast schedules if they hoped to be heard. In addition, the 1912 Radio Act gave government no authority to regulate the content of programming; consequently, the airwaves filled with commercial and noncommercial propaganda, and promotion of everything from snake oil to salvation.

A National Radio Conference, called to solve some of broadcasting's problems, began in 1922. The conference met again in 1923, 1924, and 1925. Secretary of Commerce Herbert Hoover, at the request of some broadcasters and other interest groups, began reinterpreting the 1912 Radio Act. He expanded the broadcast spectrum so that more broadcasters could be heard. He imposed schedules on stations and organization thus followed. Some station applicants were denied licenses—on technical grounds, generally because of limited frequencies. When broadcasters appealed what they said were Hoover's illegal actions, chaos returned to the airwaves and Congress again stepped in.

The federal government has been involved from radio's inception, and it happily stepped up regulating once invited to do so.

The Federal Radio Commission (FRC) came into being in 1927. It established a comprehensive set of regulations that affected every facet of the industry. Primary among its tasks was assigning frequencies to stations, but of broader significance was its coupling of broadcasting to the public welfare. There were those both inside and outside of government who felt that broadcasting had a public significance surmounting commercial considerations. They argued for public broadcasting such as England had with the governmentally controlled British Broadcasting Corporation (BBC). However, the commercial precedent for radio was already several years old and the battle for dominance of the mass media by commercial interests had already been fought and won in the newspapers. The clear statement of the First Amendment to the U.S. Constitution, that Congress shall make no law abridging freedom of the press, was difficult to circumvent, if radio was a form of the press.

As a partial salve to the proponents of public radio, the Federal Radio Commission made the requirement that the individual stations operate in the "public interest, convenience, and necessity" of their own communities. Congress was saying that the airwaves belonged to the public and could be leased to stations so long as they were behaving responsibly. That concept was retained by the successor to the Federal Radio Commission when the Communications Act of 1934 established the Federal Communications Commission (FCC) to oversee radio, telephone, and telegraph (i.e., all wire and radio communication). Defining the public interest, convenience, and necessity has constituted untold thousands of hours of bureaucratic time and energy in the meantime, as broadcasters attempt to meet the spirit of the law while turning a profit.

Radio as America's Prime Mass Medium

The Great Depression of the 1930s gave an unforeseen boost to radio. In a time of poverty, radio reception cost nothing more than the price of a receiver and a few pennies for electricity. Radio became America's home entertainment, establishing and solidifying a pattern that would be inherited intact by television. President Franklin D. Roosevelt also clearly saw that the broadcast media entered America's homes directly and without the interpretation and gatekeeping of the printed page. He made radio his own political instrument as he reached into America's living rooms to reassure the people through his fireside chats, a device that he parlayed into four terms of office and that set the pace for the political use of broadcast media in the future.

The Great Depression gave rise to radio's Golden Age. News, entertainment, and advertising flourished.

By the early 1930s the networks were in full competition with one another, vying for the attention of listeners. Recognizing the demography and differing sizes of audiences, time classifications developed: *AA* for prime time, 7:00–11:00 P.M.; *A* for the hours adjacent to prime time; *B* for most of the rest of the day; and *C* for the late, late hours that belong to stations broadcasting for insomniacs, students, night owls, and people with unusual work schedules.

FDR used radio to reassure an anxious nation during his fireside chats in the 1930s and 1940s.
Wide World Photos

Of course, *AA* time was the most costly for sponsorship and commercials, and *C* was the least expensive. These classifications, based on presumed audience size, helped to formulate a rate card for determining *costs per thousand* (cpm)—that is, cost to the advertiser per thousand listeners. A measuring device was needed to accurately determine, and prove, this presumed audience size, so an embryonic form of rating was developed, based largely on telephone polls. Public opinion polling was in its infancy and the yardstick was crude, but telephone polling was the first form of feedback, born of commercial necessity, which grew to the present-day ratings system.

Originally, advertising on radio had taken the form of sponsorships. National commercial advertisers would sponsor and often pay for a program that would carry their name ("The Eveready Hour," for example) and would permit them to insert commercials during the body of the program. As hour-long time slots became more expensive, half-hour sponsorships developed. Subsequently, some of the independent stations discovered that their survival lay in catering to the local community, and while few local merchants could afford a sponsorship, they could afford a minute or two, the price of which, when added up, netted the same amount of, if not more, advertising revenue. Network affiliates followed suit, selling advertising for their station breaks, or for the minute or so they were permitted to identify themselves each hour. Thus, the commercial came into being, which, by and large, has supplanted sponsorship.

Amos 'n' Andy
entertained a nation but
perpetuated racial
stereotypes.
The Bettman Archives, Inc.

Entertainment

A pattern of general prime-time entertainment catering to the largest possible audience developed in the 1930s with a packet of comedy shows, thrillers, westerns, and situation comedies. The 1930s was also a musical era, the time of the big bands: Benny Goodman, the Dorsey Brothers, and Guy Lombardo. These bands appeared periodically on radio specials and their records were daytime stock. One of the most popular prime-time programs of the 1930s was "Fred Waring and His Pennsylvanians," a weekly musical potpourri that even included baseball scores in season. "The Bell Telephone Hour" brought symphonic music into America's homes; the networks and some of the major stations even had their own house orchestras in which musicians of considerable stature played. Together, radio stations offered a spectrum of classical, pop, and "swing" for America.

"Amos 'n' Andy," starring a blackface comedy team, perpetuated the Negro stereotype in the early evening. The program was so popular, even in the late 1920s, that President Calvin Coolidge supposedly refused to miss an episode, and many theaters delayed their evening programs so people could listen to the radio show before coming to the theater.[6]

Jack Benny for Lucky Strike cigarettes and Fred Allen with "Allen's Alley" on Sunday evenings were comedy stars of the era. Benny was among

Comedy, thrillers, westerns, situation comedies, and music filled the airwaves.

the first to inject humor into advertising. Other comedians and entertainers of the 1930s continued their careers on television in later years, including George Burns and Gracie Allen, Edgar Bergen and Charlie McCarthy, Ed Wynn, and Kate Smith. Burns and Allen had the first continuing situation-comedy series.

"The Whistler" was the first of the Gothic thrillers to send chills up and down spines in darkened rooms each Sunday evening. Once each week "The Shadow" opened with a sinister voice asking, "Who knows what evil lurks in the hearts of men?" Mysteries, in particular, activated the imagination of the listener and broadcasters heightened the impact with sound effects—solitary steps in a lonely alley, creaking stairs, and a clap of thunder when least expected.

Then there were game shows, including the "64 Dollar Question," where the maximum a contestant could win was $64, arrived at in a geometric progression (a sign of depression values and subsequent inflation). There were westerns, of which "The Lone Ranger" was the model, with his super horse, Silver, and faithful Indian companion, Tonto—yet another racial stereotype. "Little Orphan Annie" and "Jack Armstrong" were for the children but were avidly followed by adults, too.

During the daytime hours, radio discovered that there was a demography present. The audiences were no longer mass and inclusive but were composed of different kinds of people at different hours. The late afternoon was kiddie time, served by a variety of breakfast food sponsors. The early mornings were news times for arising breadwinners, upstaging the morning newspaper. During the bulk of the day radio found itself appealing to a largely female audience of housewives, and the soap opera was born—so named because it was almost universally sponsored by soap manufacturers such as Lever Brothers, Procter and Gamble, Colgate, and Palmolive-Peet. Soap operas were depression-era escape, offering either poignant sorrow that listeners could sob over or a kind of saccharine wisdom of sweetness-and-light, or both. The soaps engendered incredible loyalty, with listeners sending gifts to the newborn babies, letters of sympathy to victims of series troubles, or letters of thanks to characters whose actions had helped listeners cope with their own lives. "One Man's Family," "The Romance of Helen Trent," "Our Gal Sunday," and "Portia Faces Life" were leaders of this genre.

The importance of radio during the depression cannot be underestimated. Sociologist and media theorist Melvin DeFleur has said that radio actually thrived on the depression. Advertising revenues and the number of sets in operation grew exponentially. Poverty-stricken families would scrape together enough money to repair their radio sets even if they had to let the furniture go back to the finance company or stall on rent payments. And on a summer night Americans could walk down a city street and hear their favorite program uninterrupted through the open windows of every house they passed.[7]

News

As early as 1922 the newspaper-dominated Associated Press refused to serve radio stations with news. Radio stations threatened to turn to the United Press (UP) and the International News Service (INS), an argument of some weight, since many of the station owners were newspapers that already subscribed to AP.

However, when the depression came, competition between radio stations and newspapers grew more intense. Newspaper advertising lineage was dwindling and radio was absorbing much of it. Furthermore, radio had gone heavily into the news business. For example, in 1930 KMPC, an independent in Los Angeles, had ten reporters on the newsbeat. Newspapers in duress just could not tolerate the direct competition with radio for both advertising and news.

> Newspapers sensed a threat to their news dominance, and years passed before the media learned to cooperate.

The battle reached a climax with the 1932 election results. The contest between incumbent Republican Herbert Hoover (the depression president) and Democrat Franklin Roosevelt attracted wide attention, and a good part of America learned of the results over the air. The American Newspaper Publishers Association (ANPA) had had enough, so in 1933 all news services stopped furnishing news to radio. Of course, this simply spurred the networks to organize their own news bureaus. The affiliated stations provided a natural national network of sources akin to the wire service bureaus and member papers, but abroad, where no such facility existed, they were more or less on their own. The irony of this is that the ban by the ANPA strengthened the position of the networks in a news-hungry America and probably would not have come about had it not been for the association's ill-advised pressure. Further, the loss of revenue to the wire services, particularly during the depression, was damaging.

An attempt to compromise resulted in the December 1933 "Biltmore Agreement" among publishers, networks, and press associations. Radio networks were to receive only enough news items from the press associations each day to present two five-minute news summaries. Morning news was not permitted until 9:30 A.M., and evening news not until 9 P.M., so as to avoid competition with the newspapers.

The Biltmore Agreement was short-lived, because Trans Radio Press, a new organization, started selling news to stations. The publishers then had to direct their guns at Trans Radio Press and they found they could whip the upstart by also selling news to the stations, just as in the good old days. By 1935 both UP and INS began selling full service to the radios again, while the more reactionary and press-controlled AP held out until 1940.

Throughout the 1930s and later, Walter Winchell bridged news and entertainment with a breezy, nightly report of gossip, opinion, and innuendo, plus a smattering of headlines, becoming the first radio columnist.

The forceful impact of dramatic international events on radio was demonstrated on 11 December 1936 by Edward VIII's poignant worldwide radio announcement that he was abdicating the throne of England for Wallis Simpson, a divorced American commoner. Meanwhile, the Spanish Civil War, which had begun six months earlier, provided a testing ground not only for Nazi weapons, but also for radio reporting techniques, which would be put to use in the inevitable, approaching holocaust of World War II. In 1937 CBS sent H. V. Kaltenborn and Edward R. Murrow overseas, where Kaltenborn broadcast live from battlefields in Spain.

The drama of Hitler's march into Austria and Czechoslovakia in 1938 mobilized CBS and its correspondents in Vienna, Berlin, London, Paris, and Rome to produce the first multiple remote broadcast in history. Later that year, during the three-week Munich Crisis, which culminated in Neville Chamberlain's misbegotten "peace in our time," as many as fourteen radio reporters aired reports live over CBS to anxious audiences in America, while H. V. Kaltenborn in New York sought to coordinate and interpret their reports, becoming history's first anchorman.

The impact of World War II on radio news was enormous. The war itself engendered interest far beyond usual human curiosity. Here real drama, written on an international stage with real actors and real stakes, was rendered the more piquant because survival was at stake. Radio brought the war home, and responding to public demand, it upped its coverage. For example, in 1937 NBC broadcast a bare half-hour or so of news each day; by the war's end in 1945, a quarter of its daily broadcast was news. For a twenty-day period during September 1938 (the anschluss, the forced political union of Austria to Germany) NBC's Red and Blue networks carried 443 separate news broadcasts, including "flash bulletins" of the war, taking up 58 hours and 13 minutes of airtime, while CBS was sending out 54.5 hours of broadcasts.[8]

Radio provided an international forum for the unmatched rhetoric of Winston Churchill, whose immortal speeches held a badly battered Britain together by the sheer power of words. He also consolidated the Allied cause in a time of doubt. With radio reporters, America witnessed the invasion of Poland and the surrender of France. Edward R. Murrow broadcast the battle of Britain from London rooftops amid falling bombs, which provided a dramatic backdrop for his remarks. Later he broadcast memorable reports about his flights in bombers over Germany, bringing the war ever closer to his audiences, as did front-line radio reporters who accompanied the troops. Most of the world learned of Pearl Harbor on 7 December 1941 by radio, and a day later a record audience listened soberly to Franklin Roosevelt's measured words to Congress for a declared war on the Axis powers. News developed its own star system, and the commentator, including the feisty Fulton Lewis, Jr., became a major figure, interpreting the events of the world into bite-size pieces for America to consume. At times, the commentators didn't allow the facts to interfere with their own perceptions of reality. Consider, for example, the words Fulton Lewis, Jr., zealously mouthed to an anxious America only five hours after the attack on Pearl Harbor:

The attack on the ships in Pearl Harbor [was] a very very foolish thing, as a matter of fact, suicidal fool-hardiness as a matter of fact, because the Japanese must know, as all the rest of the world knows, and all the rest of the navies and military men of the world know, that Pearl Harbor is the one invincible, absolutely invulnerable base in the world. It's stronger even than Gibraltar itself, and as far as an attack or siege of it is concerned, there could have been no possible sane intention on the part of the Japanese to such an end.[9]

Costs of Broadcasting

As radio grew, it became increasingly expensive. Studio staffs on major stations included news bureaus with up to a dozen reporters, a full orchestra with a musical director, program people, and a corps of engineers to balance sound and splice in both network programming and commercials, as well as people to tend the transmitters. Advertising sales forces, and continuity folk to develop the daily log, added to costs. Radio's hardware was far from cheap as transmitters became increasingly more powerful—reaching hundreds of miles—and remote facilities traveled to on-site broadcasts. Top announcers and star commentators drew huge salaries, and subscription to the radio wires added to costs. All this had to be paid for by commercials, and consequently split-second timing was the earmark of radio's peak when it was the preeminent mass communications network in America. As technology improved and radio reached larger audiences, its commercial rates went up and up until none but the wealthiest of advertisers could afford network exposure. This limited radio's potential to national advertisers of basic consumer goods, as they were the only ones who could use such large, undifferentiated audiences. More local advertisers found the newspaper their best buy, since it reached out into entire communities and metropolitan areas; and more specialized products sought advertising in the increasing number of specialized magazines on the market. Some, of course, found it possible to reach the desired local audience during network station breaks or on local radio programs.

The networks' costs began to prove prohibitive to many advertisers.

Eyeing the successes of CBS and NBC, two large independents, WOR in New York and the *Chicago Tribune*'s WGN (for World's Greatest Newspaper), organized the Mutual Broadcasting System in 1934, but they found themselves unable to compete on equal footing with the solidly entrenched networks. Subsequently, Mutual filed a complaint with the FCC against the networks for restraint of trade. Adjudication of the suit brought about the sale of NBC's Blue network in 1943, which became the American Broadcasting Company in 1945. The suit filed by Mutual did not particularly help that fourth-place network, a loose affiliation of weaker stations. In addition ABC, divorced from NBC's experience and in direct competition with its parent, also found the sledding rough.

Paramount Theaters later bought ABC in 1953 after the motion picture industry had been forced to divest itself of its theaters. It was a wise move to diversify interests while still remaining in the mass communications business, and to further exploit the threat of television, which, in 1953, was beginning to make serious inroads into the box office of the motion-picture industry. But Paramount's management was oriented toward motion pictures and Hollywood rather than toward broadcasting, and for nearly two decades ABC remained a distinctly third-place network, never really gaining on CBS and NBC, who were until the late 1970s the first and second place networks in television.

The Rivalry with Television

Just when it got it all together, radio lost it to television.

By the end of World War II, radio had set the stage for television, and America grew accustomed to listening. The principle of public interest had been established and its parameters defined. A strong national trade association (National Association of Broadcasters, NAB) had been established and a rating system had been pioneered. Advertiser and agency loyalties were developing, and the methods of doing business were understood.

It took television only a short while to catch up with radio, which was largely the result of network influence. The broadcast system was inherited ready-made: Major networks rapidly acquired wholly owned stations in major cities across the country, and they found it relatively simple to make affiliate agreements with other licensees. With their wealth and experience, the nets were able to develop national programming far superior to anything a local independent could afford, just as they had in radio. This expansion happened at the expense of their radio interests, despite the fact that radio income from the networks and local stations supported television for many of TV's years. However, radio gradually became supplemental and downgraded, and then was often supported by the increasing profits from television.

The radio industry was scared; it viewed television as radio with pictures, and the death of radio was predicted. Throughout most of the 1950s this was the prevailing attitude in the industry.

While radio lacked the visual appeal of television, it had certain inherent strengths: It demanded less attention than television, it could be perceived almost unconsciously while the listener went about doing other things, and it was also superior to television as a music medium; in general it offered less distraction. Finally, the air waves allowed for more channels in radio than in television, which permitted far greater diversification. This potential was never fully explored while radio was under domination of a limited number of networks and while the costs of radio production remained high.

As television gradually took over the evening prime-time hours, radio discovered that it had large audiences all to itself in the early morning when America arose and dressed. Radio was further assisted during the transitional decade of the 1950s by a number of technological improvements. Miniaturization of parts and certain technical innovations made car radios practical and cheap. Radio found it could extend its prime time to driving hours when America went to work and returned home again in the evening. Radio concentrated on a new split prime time from roughly 6:00 to 9:00 A.M. and again from 3:30 to 6:00 P.M. In fact, it increased its prime time from four to five and a half hours and changed its programming.

Radio had to find new techniques, new sponsors, and new audiences.

Instead of the costly dramas, comedies and such that had been staples of the 1930s and 1940s, radio experimented with music, and new formats presided over by disc jockeys. This strategy kept the medium profitable enough to keep it alive while it was trying to adjust to TV taking its advertising and audiences.

Miniaturization was helped by the development of the transistor, which did away with unwieldy and perishable vacuum tubes, and by printed circuits that reduced both the bulk and assembly expense of complicated wiring. The addition of miniature batteries freed radio from the necessity of an external power source and made it fully portable. Radio could take its instantaneousness anywhere that people could go. It became a constant companion, and as its parts became simpler and assembly less complex, it became cheap—almost disposable. It was possible for everyone to have a radio, perhaps several.

Such portability assured that there was an audience regardless of the time of day. Radio could be where people were; it no longer had to wait for them to gather around it. That was television's problem. Radio became a personal rather than a family medium, which naturally extended both its sales and reach.

Radio received another boost from the final development of FM, or frequency modulation. FM radio had two characteristics different from AM radio. Its signal, like that of television, was a line-of-sight signal, which meant it had a relatively short range because of the earth's curvature. It also had remarkable clarity of tone, which meant that it was ideal for broadcasting music. This characteristic was further enhanced by the fact that FM could be adapted to stereophonic sound, adding an orchestral dimension to the previously crude single-source sound of traditional radio.

Contemporary Radio

FM

The FM radio was originally developed in 1933 by a Columbia University professor, Edwin H. Armstrong, who successfully demonstrated its static-free, high-fidelity sound. Shortly before his death by suicide in 1954, Armstrong also patented multiplexing on the FM channel, which permitted stereo broadcasting. Experimental broadcasters in FM were held during 1939, and the FCC authorized regular FM broadcasting over thirty-five commercial, and five noncommercial, educational channels starting 1 January 1941.

Operation of FM had been delayed first by the depression and later by World War II. Then, in 1945, the FCC, seeking to encourage VHF television broadcasting, moved the FM frequencies from 88 to 108 megahertz, a higher and less vulnerable position on the radio spectrum. The FCC argued that the move on the dial was based on fear that sunspot activity would interfere with the lower frequencies, but Armstrong and other engineers charged that the FCC was trying to protect AM radio and VHF television by weakening the FM signals. This fight with the FCC, and later fights over royalties he felt were due him because of his original inventions, made Armstrong so despondent that he committed suicide. He never saw the proliferation of FM radio, nor the application of its multiplex capabilities.

Pressure prompted by competition from television encouraged rapid perfection of FM. Broadcasting hardware became miniaturized along with receivers, and magnetic tape came into use. Just as 78 RPM records yielded to the polyvinyl chloride 45s, and to the long-playing 33s, the record and radio industries discovered the values of magnetic tape. Cassettes and eight-track tapes provided greater clarity; there was no needle noise and there were no grooves to wear out. Used with automated equipment, tape greatly reduced the operating costs of broadcasting. Since large antennae and powerful wattage were not needed for local use, broadcasters discovered that they could build and operate FM stations for purely local consumption with minimal investment.

FM stations began to pop up in isolated or suburban communities by the early 1960s. Financially, FM stations had a rough time. Many of the FM stations that survived those years were operated by owners of more profitable AM stations. The FM stations served the same function in broadcast that the weekly or peripheral daily newspaper did in the press. They made it possible to carry a quotient of purely local news that the larger metropolitan stations had neither the time nor the resources to cover. Further, they permitted the local advertiser an outlet to a purely local audience at an affordable price.

By the 1970s FM demonstrated its audience-delivering potential with a vengeance. A fall 1979/spring 1980 national survey demonstrated that overall, FM's share of the listening audience averaged 55 percent, up from 52.4 percent a year earlier. In fact, the only time of day when AM listenership outstripped FM was during the morning drive time on weekdays, when AM had 54 percent of the audience. FM was strongest on Saturday nights (63.7 percent) and Sunday nights (63.5 percent).[10] FM's growth has been much faster than was predicted a few years ago. In 1973, when AM held 65 percent of the radio audience, industry forecasts held that by 1980 FM would take 43 percent to AM's 57 percent, and it would not reach the 55 to 45 lead disclosed by the 1980 survey until 1985.

FM was a key factor in the massive changes radio underwent after 1960. Portability, availability to audiences, developing musical clarity, and local emphasis began to develop a new kind of radio based on economical specialization in either music or local news, or both. In addition the FCC began to pay attention to FM. It authorized stations to broadcast stereo and required that FM stations originate their broadcasting at least half of the time rather than merely carry the AM programming where both AM and FM stations were under single ownership. FM grew apace; as table 6.1 shows, it has increased exponentially since 1960, and today it is almost equal to AM in the number of stations it airs.

FM became an ideal medium for radio's marriage to music.

Table 6.1 Growth of radio, 1922–1980

Year	Number of stations (commercial only)		FM non-commercial	Total	Industry revenues (millions)	Estimated % U.S. homes with radios
	AM	FM				
1922	30	0	0	30	N.A.	0.2
1925	571	0	0	571	N.A.	10
1930	612	0	0	612	N.A.	46
1935	616	0	0	616	$ 79.6	67
1940	765	50*	0	815	147.1	81
1945	933	3*	0	936	299.3	89
1950	2086	733	48	2867	444.5	95
1955	2669	552	122	3343	453.4	96
1960	3456	678	162	4296	597.7	96
1965	4012	1270	255	5537	776.8	97
1970	4319	2184	396	6899	1077.4	98
1975	4432	2636	711	7779	1479.7	99
1980	4559	3155	1038	8752	3200.0	99

Source: *Broadcasting/Cablecasting Yearbook*, with permission.

* Experimental stations

Specialization

Radio's ability to specialize makes it the equivalent of an electronic magazine.

Over the past three decades, radio has branched out. Prime-time radio of the 1930s and 1940s featured dramas, comedies, and soap operas, which disappeared in the 1950s. Music became dominant, but not all radio programming became musical. There have been purely local community news stations. Network news and major independents continued to serve the least populated areas of the country where newspapers were distributed only by mail, and where it was not economically feasible for television to call the audiences its own. Some radio operators found it profitable to broadcast pure news on a thirty- or forty-minute cycle. Others concentrated on sports. Radio offered diversity matched only by the variety of magazines. Just as with magazines, radio specialized because of the pressure of television, pursuing smaller, more loyal audiences and the advertisers who needed to reach those audiences. Local stations tended to be supported by local merchants. The regional stations carried a great deal of department-store and shopping-center advertisements; the classical stations advertised hi-fi components; pop stations sold vacation homes, travel tours, and annuities; country and western stations carried consumer products; and the various rock stations advertised musical paraphernalia and complexion-ointments, and announced rock concerts. Such still holds true today. In a very real sense, radio has become an electric magazine, just as film has emerged as an electric book.

ABC

Proof of this specialization can be illustrated by the successful experiment of ABC radio. In the 1960s ABC trailed the other two networks, NBC and CBS, always seeming to come in a poor third. While the two major networks could afford to operate their radio networks out of television profits, profits from television at ABC were not correspondingly high.

Consequently, ABC was forced to reconsider its entire radio network operation. Whereas previously it had affiliation agreements with a single radio station in most of the nation's major markets, it decided to scrap this arrangement in the mid-1960s and go to multiple affiliates. The truth was that ABC's affiliates, as well as those of NBC and CBS, were rated well behind the major independents in almost every market. The independents had found the new sound, or they had moved to the new format (time, news, and temperature), or to a variety of other highly specialized forms of programming.

Instead of offering a potpourri of national programming to a single station in a major market, ABC organized four subnetworks specializing only in the kinds of news, sports, or music that affiliates would seek: The American Contemporary Radio Network, The American Information Radio Network, The American Entertainment Radio Network, and The American FM Radio Network. It then made affiliation agreements with the principal independents for each of these specialties; in effect, there were four ABC affiliate opportunities instead of just one. This was a profitable plan all the way around. ABC had outlets for a wide range of national advertising on catering to specific audiences, which made it an easier and more economical package for advertisers of hi-fi equipment, for example, or aftershave. ABC managed to quadruple its advertising billings between 1968 and 1975 because of this arrangment. Such a system provided the affiliates with a broad range of services, concentrated programming, and access to national talent. It increased the size of their audiences and further reduced the costs of their own programming, as much of it—if not all—came from ABC. These were smaller audiences, but each was homogenous; each had a character of its own, a measurable demography. In 1980 ABC Contemporary had 407 affiliates, ABC Information had 611, ABC Entertainment had 505, and ABC FM had 203.

ABC's specialized subnetworks prove to be a successful formula.

New Formats

Radio's search for audiences in recent years has led to other innovations. One of these has been the talk show where a radio personality talks constantly to listeners over the telephone. From one perspective—probably an elitist one—there seems to be a bit of the "eavesdropper" in all this, as people expose their inner lives and opinions to listeners, who call in to the station to agree, disagree, or contradict. On another level, however, many find such programs a badly needed and sympathetic ear in an increasingly depersonalized world.

Talk shows, and all-news, ethnic, and dramatic programming, plus NPR are examples of successful formats.

There are parameters to this format that are forever being stretched. In New York City one radio station catered to homosexuals; in Long Beach, California, and elsewhere, other hosts developed a large following by discussing their intimate sex lives with their callers. However, the increasingly candid, risqué talk shows of the early 1970s were put to a stop by the combined efforts of the FCC and NAB. Such programming, when found today, is away from the mainstream stations, on peripheral FM outlets. The radio band seems broad enough to accommodate it in an era of increasing permissiveness.

In recent years about one in twenty listeners was tuned to an all-news radio station. Dropping teenagers from the sample, of the top ten radio markets in 1979 the all-news format attracted 17.3 percent of adult men, and 16.1 percent of adult women, during the 6–10 A.M. weekday slot. Those totals placed all-news radio as the most popular programming for men and the second most popular (behind "adult contemporary" formats by only three percentage points) for women. Such an audience cannot be ignored, especially since it is an increase of 50 percent men and 42 percent women over the popularity of news programming recorded for 1975.[11]

Recognizing the interest in news, NBC in 1975 enlisted twenty-seven stations in its round-the-clock News and Information Service (NIS). It broadcast approximately forty-five minutes of national and world news each hour, meaning the affiliated stations needed to provide only fifteen minutes of their own programming, including, of course, advertising. It meant the local stations could operate on a reduced personnel and concentrate on quality local programming. However, despite having seventy-two stations subscribing to it, NIS was terminated by NBC in May 1977. The reasoning was simple enough: NIS had lost more than $10 million in its short two-year existence, because advertisers could not be convinced that there was a large enough national market for them to reach. Other all-news efforts, primarily on the metropolitan level, have been successful, however, and the trend is expected to continue.

Segmentation of the market has enticed entrepreneurs to attempt such variegated formats as an all classified advertising station, which failed, and the National Black Network, founded in 1975 with seventy-five affiliates, which successfully provides ethnic news and entertainment programming. NBC, despite its failure with NIS, has been very successful recently with its second network entitled "The Source," which appeals to album-oriented rock stations. That station now has 101 affiliates.

Radio drama has made a comeback in recent years, partly due to the nostalgia trend sweeping America. CBS resurrected "Mystery Theater" in 1974, complete with name stars and high quality sound effects. Its success caused other networks—especially the National Public Radio web—and local stations to dig into their vaults for mysteries and soaps from the golden age of radio.

Radio's uniqueness was probably best explored by National Public Radio (NPR) during the late 1970s and early 1980s. NPR is the network made up of noncommercial stations by the Corporation for Public Broadcasting. These stations can secure grants for operating expenses and can broadcast according to the guidelines established by the CPB. NPR initiated a "space-age network" in 1979 by beginning to link its stations to a new satellite system that promised high quality sound distribution. By 1980 the linkups were completed to the stations, primarily at educational institutions or in metropolitan areas. Even so, only 20 percent of Americans said they had ever heard NPR, meaning four-fifths of us missed innovative programming such as "All Things Considered," its daily 90-minute afternoon news program; "The Morning Edition," another news-and-feature program; "Earplay," an original radio drama; "Jazz Alive" and other musical specialities; and two series produced by the British Broadcasting Corporation, "Shakespeare Festival" and "Masterpiece Radio Theatre."

The variety of programming formats available today provides radio listeners with numerous options, but we should not forget that for the last thirty years the most common format has been music. And there, too, variety has been the key. Radio broadcasters discovered a certain demography to musical taste: Youth wanted the new sounds of rock 'n' roll; parents provided a market for "pops"; and other segments of the population in varying numbers sought opera, classical, country, and folk sounds. Radio was ready to deliver, via the DJ.

The term *disc jockey* gained notoriety in the 1950s, but the concept of a broadcaster playing recorded music is as old as radio itself. To promote his audion tubes, Lee De Forest had broadcast music from the Eiffel Tower in 1908, and Frank Conrad had established his reputation around Pittsburgh in 1920 when audiences responded to his classical music selections.

Record playing did not dominate the airwaves during the 1920s and 1930s, however. Live music was the mainstay of radio programming during this period, partly because the playing of recorded music was fraught with difficulties. Until 1940 musicians, who feared that playing their records on radio would hurt sales of their records and violate their exclusive network contracts, intimidated stations into avoiding much recorded music. But a 1940 Court of Appeals ruling held that broadcasters could do what they wished with records, and the floodgates were opened wide.

Al Jarvis of KFWB in Los Angeles probably initiated the contemporary concept of the record spinning personality with his "World's Largest Make Believe Ballroom" back in 1932. Shortly thereafter Martin Block of New York's WNEW parlayed Jarvis's idea into a highly marketable package of music, advertising, and chatter. Block began by playing records during lulls in the famous broadcasts of the Bruno Hauptmann trial (the Lindbergh baby kidnapping trial) in 1935, and soon polished his routine so sponsors were waiting in line to reach the 4 million listeners Block was delivering.

After World War II, when drive time became prime time, the DJ's personality became a crucial ingredient in radio programming. As popular music fragmented into well-defined formats, DJs were needed who could program their own shows, choosing records in keeping with audience expectations.

The Disc Jockey and Music

Music has long been a programming staple, but the DJ emerged with a vengeance after World War II.

Records

DJs accepted payola to
make hits out of records.
The bottom-line ethic
prevailed.

It was at this point that radio started to become an extension of the recording industry. Record manufacturers found that the radio provided ready-made exposure for their wares, and that only after such exposure could they expect to sell records to the new generation of music-hungry individuals. They began providing the nation's DJs with records at no cost, which reduced the expenses of broadcasting. In many instances they paid popular disc jockeys to air their wares. *Payola* became a household word in the late 1950s because many disc jockeys earned more from their record payments than they did from their broadcasting salaries.

There was a pyramiding quality to all this as the record and radio industries grew closer. Weekly surveys revealed the "Top 40" records, which disc jockeys clamored to play because of their assured popularity, and the more these records were played, the more likely they were to make the "Top 40," since exposure led to sales. The "Top 40" in a real sense became the rating system for musical radio, and during the days of payola, DJs were frequently an unethical impetus in the gatekeeping process.

Today payola is no longer the key factor in the $4 billion recording industry. Indeed, one result of the payola scandal was the routinization of radio and a more sophisticated marriage of it to recorded music. Program directors, musical directors, or even entire radio staffs have taken over the musical gatekeeping decisions. The competitive market, particularly in the

"Top 40" or in "contemporary music" stations, has meant less likelihood of individuality and innovation. Playlists and charts from *Billboard* magazine tell stations what is working elsewhere and, by extension, what they should be playing.

"What works elsewhere" is most assuredly not accidental. Modern recording industry marketing techniques are incredibly sophisticated, and are largely responsible for increases in business, which zoomed from $511 million annually in 1958 to over $4 billion in records and tapes two decades later. Record companies utilize pervasive and systematically researched sales campaigns whose elements of "hype" include visits by artists and promoters to radio stations, discos, and record stores (accompanied, of course, by T-shirts, mugs, and very frequently under-the-counter trade-offs, such as lower wholesale prices to retailers who will offer larger window-display space). Promotions, including increasingly sophisticated and frequently stimulating jacket covers, are more and more tied to demographic and psychographic studies of potential audiences.

"Hype" is but one indicator of the incestuous relationship between radio and the $4 billion-a-year recording industry.

Hype has impact but it will not guarantee extensive air play. If the music doesn't attract the public, the record will not be played. In today's competitive radio marketplace, the search for audiences allows little room for marginal music. Payola still presents some problems; in the mid- and late-1970s, several recording executives were convicted of fraud for bribing radio station personnel with money and drugs, and the FCC conducted several hearings which pointed out that payola remained widespread. But the crucial factor in the radio–music alliance was audience ratings, since a drop in a metropolitan station's ratings of only one point (or about 15,000 listeners in a city the size of Washington, D.C.) would cost the station anywhere from half a million to a million dollars in ad revenues in a given year.[12]

Music Formats

To get its own piece of the pie, each station has settled into the routine of playing a particular brand or style of music. Formula or format radio has changed over the years as musical taste has changed, but there are numerous demographic and psychographic—and intuitive—musical profiles being satiated. We have seen musical taste change as Elvis Presley (who sold 300 million records before his death in 1977) began to share the stage with the Beatles and other rock performers. *Rock 'n' roll* ultimately segmented into *acid rock* with its hard driving sounds and frank lyrics; *chicken rock* or bubblegum music with its softer, non-controversial messages; *progressive rock,* primarily on FM stations playing albums and some Top 40 materials; and other splinter sounds such as *disco* and *punk rock.*

Middle-of-the-road, or *MOR,* attempted to serve diverse listener tastes, especially during drive time, and may well be a final remnant of radio's golden age of mass appeal. Soft rock, oldies and goldies, and DJ platter patter are mainstays of MOR, which in the late 1970s came to be called *Adult Contemporary.*

There's a format for any taste—rock, MOR, adult contemporary, country and western, easy listening, ethnic, and classical.

Alan Freed, whose life story was told in the 1978 film *American Hot Wax,* is the noted DJ who coined the term *rock and roll.*
Wide World Photos

The plaintive sounds of Nashville caught America by surprise as *country and western (CW)* music spread from rural to urban environs. By 1980 there were 2,000 CW stations on the air, rendering country music nearly as financially successful as the Top 40 format. With the infusion of rock and pop musicians in the CW market, it is difficult to distinguish the more mainstream sounds. Instead of such unforgettable down-home favorites as "Okie from Muskogee" or "Drop Kick Me, Jesus, Through the Goal Posts of Life" from a decade ago, we now find CW charts dominated by the likes of Australian Olivia Newton-John.

Easy Listening or *beautiful music* formats, which provide unobtrusive background sounds, rely upon few sponsors. Easy listening stations pride themselves on loyal listeners, who reject what they call the mindless noise of both Muzak and rock music.

In addition to the formats just mentioned are those of a smaller number of stations that specialize in *ethnic* or *soul* music (generally programmed for, but not frequently owned by blacks and other minorities) along with a few stations that play *classical* and *jazz* music. In each of the above formats, a specific market has been sought out and catered to with the primary expectation of making a profit and, perhaps, a secondary expectation of providing a needed community service.

Of all the media institutions we treat in this book, the broadcast media are the most risky to predict. In this chapter we have already noted that the history of radio has been one of randomness—random inventions coalescing with random social and economic trends, and seemingly random governmental regulations. You will learn that the same is true of television in our discussion in chapter 7. And given that background, it is especially difficult to forecast the results of new technologies, changing demographics, economics, and federal controls. Nevertheless, the past few years have shown us some trends that will no doubt affect the future of radio.

The obvious trend toward localization and service to specialized interests is reflected in both FCC actions and existing programmers. Recent congressional moves to deregulate radio, allowing it to reach its own level in the competitive marketplace, indicate some acceptance of the idea that radio is a localized medium. But such an idea must be questioned, if only because most local stations attempt to be clones of the most successful parent station of their genre, whether they are all-news, all-talk, Top 40, or what have you. So long as playlists are restricted to those sounds selling elsewhere, and so long as advertisers seek the largest audience with appropriate demographics, the tendency toward imitation and sameness will continue, no matter how much we claim to admire radio's sense of individuality and specialization.

The Future of Radio

Given its random history, radio's future is difficult to predict.

Is noncommercial radio the answer? Some feel that the answer to the problem is for radio to be supported by taxes or subsidized by its listeners or by an institution. They argue that by divorcing such stations from commercial interests, diverse audience needs will be met. As an example, they point to the National Public Radio and its variety of programs, but they ignore the surveys showing that only one-fifth of Americans have been exposed to NPR. NPR, of course, has no intention of being a mass mass medium. Appeal to the mass, it argues, means ignoring the needs of audience subgroups. So long as it relies upon its member stations for program materials, it will maintain its unique appeal. But recent moves toward satellite transmission of a fairly full programming day of network programs and news shows points toward a certain homogenization of appeal.

Thanks to satellites, there has been a resurgence of the networks. As *Broadcasting* magazine sees it, network radio has become an infant industry again, discovering a world founded on satellite technology's multichannel capacity.[13] Centrally located networks have begun to provide advertising, news, and special features to hundreds of affiliates and their well-defined demographic targets across the nation. The fact that the four ABC networks are the senior citizens in this resurgence may be viewed as an assurance of improved programming for even the small markets.

What lies ahead: deregulated, cloned, sponsored, or noncommercial satellite-delivered network, or individualized radio?

Technologically, the future of radio may lie not in the airwaves and their limited frequencies but in broad-band cable with its multifaceted capacity for two-way electronic transmission. We have already alluded to this in our consideration of print media's future. The place radio will have in such a system is open to some question, since the visual dimension of cable is the one most frequently considered. If anything, radio via cable and the Home Communications Center (HomeComCen) will probably offer higher fidelity sound than it does at present. Speculations are that it will come to us over several channels at once. Quadraphonic, or multiphonic, reproduction of sound will be linked to variable lighting, to change the "mood" of the room as the tempo of music changes.

While efforts to develop cable continue, satellite communications has developed so rapidly that direct satellite-to-home transmission is increasingly attractive. Since 1979 individual homeowners have been permitted to build their own receiving dishes in order to pick up all the programming they can, and it is only a matter of time before miniaturization of dishes makes it economically feasible—for the homeowner, that is. What such pirating of programs means to the producer and advertiser remains to be seen. Also at issue is the question, will the resultant development of several production centers beaming programs to the satellites spell doom for local stations? Obviously, moves in this direction will demand careful scrutiny from manufacturers, station owners, advertisers, the networks, and the FCC. If there is money to be made, we can expect existing media institutions to move quickly into the forefront.

Electronic Media

In the meantime, stereophonic broadcasting over the AM band has been refined, and AM broadcasters have found themselves competing for the musically sophisticated audiences that were taken from them over the past decade by FM. How this will change programming over the two bands is open to speculation.

On another level, it may be that citizens' band (CB) radio has already shown us the future of radio. In 1972 there were 850,000 CB users, serving truck drivers, police, and the like, but by the end of that decade there were 50 million CBers, mostly in American automobiles, filling the air with a babel reminiscent of the 1920s. Enthusiasts have become smitten with the direct involvement CB permits—it is a highly personalized medium and is one that we hesitate to include in our discussion of mass media.

Perhaps more significantly, CB is a medium that demands personal involvement; by its very nature it is a displacement of the highly commercialized institutions we all know network and metropolitan radio to be. It allows us to be our own programmers, and is probably preparing us for the inevitable interactive mass communications technology of tomorrow.

Summary

Radio had its start before the turn of the century, but public broadcasting did not begin until 1916. The pioneers in broadcasting expected the primary profit from radio to come from the sale of receivers. However, during the 1920s companies began buying air time and sponsoring programs. It was also during this period that the first of the major networks were created, when RCA bought WEAF from ATT and organized two NBC networks. Soon after, William Paley started CBS.

In the 1930s and 1940s radio was the prime mass medium in America. Network programming included comedies, mysteries, westerns, soap operas, live big-band music, and children's programs. After a protracted fight among broadcasters, publishers, and wire services, radio news became established and expanded dramatically during World War II.

During this last third of the century, television has become the preeminent mass medium, while radio has become a supplemental medium in league to a large degree with the record industry. In adapting to a changing environment, radio has grown to several times its previous size in the number of stations it airs and the number of sets it reaches. In the aggregate its profitability has been greatly increased.

In an attempt to appeal to audience interests, radio has become specialized; each station specializes in a "sound," in news or sports, in appeal to ethnic minorities, or in talk shows. The medium has also found new audiences for different kinds of music in highly fragmented sections of society. The growth of FM radio attests to this segmentation. Magnetic tape and automation have permitted FM stations to be operated at minimal cost, and overall, more Americans listen to FM stations than they do to AM stations. In a real sense, then, radio is an electric magazine, just as film is an electric book.

The future of radio depends upon the configuration of technological, economic, demographic, and regulatory variables, but it seems likely that satellite transmission, cable, increased fidelity, and interactive radio will bring about even further specialization. The recent growth of specialized networks augmenting the individualistic local stations is a case in point.

Notes

1. Frank J. Kahn, ed. *Documents of American Broadcasting,* 3d ed. (Englewood Cliffs, N.J.: Prentice-Hall, 1978), pp. 16–17.
2. Christopher Sterling, "Television and Radio Broadcasting," in *Who Owns the Media? Concentration of Ownership in the Mass Communications Industry,* ed. Benjamin M. Compaine (New York: Harmony Books, 1979), p. 63.
3. Ibid.
4. Alfred N. Goldsmith and Austin C. Lescarboura, *This Thing Called Broadcasting* (New York: Henry Holt, 1930), p. 279.
5. Erik Barnouw, *A Tower in Babel: A History of Broadcasting in the United States to 1933* (New York: Oxford University Press, 1966).
6. Eugene S. Foster, *Understanding Broadcasting* (Reading, Mass.: Addison-Wesley, 1978), p. 61.
7. Melvin L. De Fleur and Sandra Ball–Rokeach, *Theories of Mass Communication,* 4th ed. (New York: Longman, 1982), p. 90.
8. Sammy R. Danna, "The Press-Radio War." *Freedom of Information Center Report No. 213.* (Columbia, Mo.: University of Missouri School of Journalism, December 1968).
9. Ernest D. Rose, "How the U.S. Heard About Pearl Harbor," *Journal of Broadcasting,* vol. 5, no. 4 (Fall 1961).
10. "FM Growth Continues," *Broadcasting,* 16 June 1980, p. 84.
11. *Broadcasting,* 9 June 1980, pp. 44–46.
12. "Recording Industry: A 4-Billion-Dollar Hit," *U.S. News & World Report,* 30 April 1979, pp. 68–70.
13. "Up, Up and Away for Radio Networking," *Broadcasting,* 17 March 1980, pp. 38–44.

Television 7

Outline

Introduction

The adulation and patriotism that followed the return of the American hostages in 1981 after 444 days in Iran was not *caused* by television. But it most assuredly was aided and abetted by the networks. An enthusiastic demonstration of relief and thanksgiving, magnified by television, resulted in the hostages being elevated to hero status, and being showered with expensive gifts and extravagant ticker-tape and yellow-ribbon receptions in New York and Washington, D.C. The normal uninhibited exuberance of American public opinion was to be expected, but with infinite technical skill and outlays of millions of dollars, the practitioners of network television focused the eyes of America—and the world—on a single event with such adroitness that none of us were left untouched.

What manner of medium has such power?

By most statistical measures, television is an enormous, wealthy, and time-consuming enterprise.

The role television plays in American life during the early 1980s, about thirty years after its commercial birth, can be better understood by reviewing its statistical profile. There were 1,042 operating television stations in 1982, of which 524 were commercial VHFs (very high frequency channels 2 through 13), 248 commercial UHFs (ultrahigh frequency channels 14 through 83), 107 noncommercial VHFs, and 163 noncommercial UHFs.

More than 81 million American homes—98 percent of all residences—have television sets, and about 50 percent of them have more than one set. Of those about 71 million are in color. That reflects an increase since 1970 of 21.3 million homes with television, a 16 percent increase in the number of homes with multiple sets, and a doubling of color receivers.

The average individual—child, woman, man—is glued to the set four and a half hours daily. And according to A. C. Nielsen statistics, the American household now averages six hours and forty-five minutes a day in front of a set. Those statistics indicate that besides sleeping and working, television consumes the largest share of America's time, far more than any other leisure-time activity. One study showed that we spend 40 percent of our leisure time watching television, almost triple the time spent using *all* other mass media.[1]

The average child between the ages of two and five watches thirty-one hours and twenty-three minutes a week, much of that time unsupervised. The rate drops by a few hours for older children, but one-fifth of our children watch forty or more hours per week, the equivalent of holding down a fulltime job. By the age of twelve, the average child has already logged 12,000 hours of viewing time—the same number of hours he or she is expected to spend in the classroom between first grade and the completion of high school. Not incidentally, by high school graduation that same child has been exposed to 350,000 commercial messages—about 20,000 a year—and witnessed or vicariously participated in 18,000 televised murders.

Roper Organization surveys indicate that nearly two-thirds (64 percent) of the American public is now turning to television as its major source of news, and more than half (51 percent) rank television as the most believable news source. Television surpassed newspapers in credibility in 1961 and as the prime news source in 1963; and according to the Roper studies, television has improved its position steadily since then at the expense of all other news sources. When asked which medium they would most want to keep if they could have only one, Americans since the first Roper survey in 1959 have been saying "television," rather than newspapers, radio, or magazines. In fact, since 1967, television has held more than a two-to-one advantage over its nearest rival, the newspaper, as the medium to keep when we are limited to one.

The commercial stations in 1980 generated $8.8 billion in advertising revenues, of which they pocketed as profit some $1.8 billion. In 1981 the dollars were rolling in at the average rate of $100,000 per thirty-second prime-time network commercial; on top-rated programs, the cost was more like $175,000, while lower-rated spots cost $45,000. When advertisers are assured an enormous audience, they willingly pay more: Commercials for the final two-hour episode of M*A*S*H in February 1983 went for a record $450,000 per thirty-second spot.

Most television programming, including news and commercials, comes from the three major networks who directly or indirectly, through affiliates, dominate 90 percent of the commercial stations. Essentially, Americans have the choice of three programs at any given moment in the broadcasting day. But this choice is more illusionary than real, since the networks are in intense competition and they cater to the lowest common denominator as dictated by ratings. The higher rated shows tend to be initiated with regularity and that results in repetition of content, format, and style.

In this chapter we will focus primarily on network television. After a look at the history of the medium, we will discuss the way the ratings work and then explore programming, the strategies employed by the networks, and the cost of preparing shows. In recent years research has revealed interesting facts about audiences, and this information is of particular interest to advertisers. In the last two sections, we will look at television news and some of the criticism directed at the tube.

The Early History of Television

Television has been around a lot longer than most people would suspect. The electronic discoveries of the late nineteenth and early twentieth centuries that gave us radio, motion pictures, and the telephone were coupled with various mechanical scanning devices for the transfer of visual imagery. A Russian-born American physicist, Vladimir Zworykin, who worked in the Pittsburgh Westinghouse laboratories, patented an all-electronic television system in 1923. At its core was a camera tube he called the *iconoscope*. In 1926 he devised a receiving unit he called a *kinescope,* a cathode-ray tube that carried an image consisting of thirty horizontal lines—a very sketchy picture by today's 525-line standards. Practical demonstrations of the system were made in 1928. Meanwhile, Philo Farnsworth was devising his own system, independent of corporation laboratories. In 1927 he successfully transmitted his first picture—perhaps prophetically, since

Zworykin's iconoscope and Farnsworth's kinescope gave us TV during the 1920s.

it was a dollar sign! But years of squabbling over patent rights and financing meant there would be no commercial television for at least another decade, and by then the federal government had become inextricably involved.

In 1927 an experimental television program, in which Secretary of Commerce Herbert Hoover participated, was broadcast between New York and Washington D.C. Soon several other broadcast stations were experimenting with television: WGY of Schenectady, New York, broadcast television's first dramatic programming in 1927, and shortly thereafter, the Schenectady and Purdue University stations were sending television images thousands of miles over shortwave radio frequencies. In 1930 RCA, which had taken over the radio research projects of Westinghouse and General Electric, demonstrated large-screen television at a New York City theater.

By 1937 seventeen experimental stations were operating, and starting in April 1938, television sets were available in department stores for interested Americans. The least expensive were American Television Corporation's three-inch screens for $125, with General Electric and RCA

offering twelve-inch sets for up to $600. We should not forget that the dollar in 1938 went several times as far as it does today and that those depression-era dollars were being spent on experimental sets to receive experimental broadcasts. The FCC in 1937 had concluded that television was not yet ready for public service on a national scale, and that there should be no commercial sponsorship.

RCA negotiated patent purchases with the independent Farnsworth, in addition to the millions of dollars it had already spent in its own laboratories, so it could market a complete television system by the late 1930s. RCA was not alone; by July 1939, fourteen different manufacturers were in production, including Crosley, DuMont, Farnsworth, General Electric, Philco, and Zenith. The FCC was called in to systematize broadcasting equipment. In 1941, after several years of heated debate among the manufacturers, the FCC decided upon a 525-line, thirty-frames-per-second system, which is still in effect. It also authorized commercial television operations to begin, and by May 1942, ten stations went on the air. Television was off and running. Significantly, during the same year that the FCC authorized commercial television, it also assumed jurisdiction over program content, instead of merely regulating the technical aspects of broadcasting. Its 1941 "Mayflower Decision" held that a broadcaster could not be an advocate and outlawed broadcast editorials.

By 1942, the FCC had approved commercial TV, and equipment manufacturers were in heavy competition.

In 1942 a wartime freeze was placed on television, and only six of the original ten licensed stations continued broadcasting throughout the war. In 1945, following the war, the FCC allocated twelve VHF channels to commercial broadcasting, at the most favorable spots on the broadcast band. This move was a boon to NBC, which has been urging its radio affiliates to seek television licenses, and a setback for CBS, which had gambled on FM development.

Rapid growth followed; the rush for new licenses, three competing schemes for color television, reservation of channels for noncommercial educational and UHF use, engineering standards, and the need for a national assignment plan for all channels made it obvious that television was developing faster than the FCC could regulate. So, on 30 September 1948 the commission stopped granting new TV applications in order to study the situation. This freeze, which the FCC promised would be brief, lasted through the years of the Korean conflict and wasn't lifted until 14 April 1952.

Chaos after World War II resulted in an FCC freeze on TV licenses from 1948 to 1952.

Despite the freeze on new stations, television grew at a fantastic pace between 1948 and 1952. When the freeze began, only 172,000 U.S. homes, 4 percent of the country's residences, were equipped with television. Only four years later the figures had jumped to 15.3 million and 34.2 percent, respectively. (See table 7.1 for TV's growth between 1946 and 1980.) Viewers in 1948 saw Milton Berle, a radio performer who had turned to television, inaugurate the "Texaco Star Theater," and Ed Sullivan host the first "Toast of the Town" show, which restored vaudeville to the American scene for a full, incredible twenty-five years.

Borrowing the time-restricted format of radio—the training ground for most of the pioneers of television—programming was made to fit segments of fifteen minutes, half an hour, or more. Most shows were performed live, without the security of "retakes" or the profit generated by reruns, which film and videotape offered. Live shows were preserved by

Table 7.1 The growth of television, 1946–1980

Year	Number of stations * on the air	Television households	Percent of homes equipped with TV	Percent of homes with more than one set	Percent of homes with color sets	Industry revenues (millions)
1946	6	8,000	.02	—	—	N.A.
1950	107	3,875,000	9.00	1	—	170.8
1955	482	30,700,000	64.50	3	.02	1,035.3
1960	583	45,750,000	87.10	13	.70	1,627.3
1965	596	52,700,000	92.60	22	5.30	2,515.0
1970	892	59,700,000	95.20	34	39.20	3,596.0
1975	952	68,500,000	96.30	43	70.80	5,263.0
1980	1008	76,000,000	98.00	49	80.00**	8,800.0†

Sources: Adapted from *Stay Tuned: A Concise History of American Broadcasting* by Christopher H. Sterling and John M. Kittross, © 1978 by Wadsworth Publishing Company, Inc., Belmont, California 94002. Reprinted by permission of the publisher and *Broadcasting/Cablecasting Yearbook,* with permission.
* Includes VHF and UHF, commercial and noncommercial stations
† Estimated

making *kinescopes,* a film of the program taken directly from the screen. But these were of poor quality and were often unusable. Inadvertently, "I Love Lucy" helped to change that. When the show started in 1951, most television production emanated from New York. Lucille Ball and Desi Arnaz didn't want to move from their home in Los Angeles, so they convinced CBS to allow them to film the program in Hollywood. Because they wanted a live audience, the show was filmed with three cameras, which cut down on interruptions and retakes. As the show became a hit, the value of the filmed episodes increased. Eventually "I Love Lucy" was syndicated, and reruns of the show can still be seen today. Now, of course, live television is rare. Most programs are produced on film or tape, weeks or months before air time, always with an eye to the potential for additional revenue from reruns.

"I Love Lucy" was the top-rated show in the mid-1950s and stayed there for half a decade. Westerns, such as "Gunsmoke," also corralled large audiences. Quiz shows, typified by the "$64,000 Question," appealed to the viewers' dreams of instant wealth. Television had become the preeminent entertainment medium, consuming material at an incredible pace and spawning imitators of every new show that became a hit.

The quality of programming in television has been an issue since the first critic evaluated a show. But for many, the 1950s are looked upon as the golden age of television. Live dramatic theater attracted some of the best-known playwrights, such as Paddy Chayefsky and Rod Serling. "Studio One," "Playhouse 90," and "Kraft Television Theater," among others, added substance to programming.

Before 1955 some shows were being broadcast in color, and by the mid-1960s most network programs were in color. The transition was relatively swift once the FCC had made a final decision about the technology to be used. In the 1940s both RCA and CBS developed color equipment. Because the CBS machinery was more advanced, the FCC found it attractive. The problem, however, was in the television receivers; the sets designed by CBS would not carry black-and-white programs. After a complicated legal battle, the FCC approved the equipment developed by RCA, which could carry both black-and-white and color broadcasts.

The Networks

The three major networks—CBS, NBC, and ABC—dominate commercial television, as they have since 1948. Over the years the vast majority of America's commercial television stations have been affiliated with one or another of these webs. Prior to 1955, Allan B. DuMont, an independent producer of television equipment, competed against "the big three," but was forced out of business because he lacked the inherent advantages of the bigger networks. More recent competitors have specialized in sports, or news, or the like.

Coast-to-coast networks have dominated the TV scene from the beginning.

By 1937 New York and Philadelphia were linked by coaxial cable, which was required for long-distance hookups because television's line-of-sight signal rushes off into space as the earth curves (in the same way FM signals do, as we discussed in chap. 6) and because ordinary telephone lines are inadequate. Between 1946 and 1947 Boston and Washington were included in the linkage. Later, relatively inexpensive microwave relay systems were developed. By 1948 either cable or microwave linked the East Coast to the Midwest, and network programming became financially feasible. In 1951, before the freeze ended, coast-to-coast network linkage was ready.

With the technological apparatus lined up, all that was needed to make the system work was an audience. Prime-time programming—Milton Berle, Ed Sullivan, drama, sports, and the like—served as bait. Throughout the 1950s the costly quality drama of "Playhouse 90" served as loss leader. It cost more to produce than advertisers would pay, until larger audiences were in the fold. Once the audiences were hooked, however, television truly became a mass medium. According to some critics, the general quality of programming then began to slip.

The dominance of CBS, NBC, and ABC is based on their *owned-and-operated* as well as *affiliated* stations. The FCC permits a single owner to operate seven television stations, of which no more than five can be the generally profitable VHF variety. The networks during the 1940s and 1950s fought to establish their control of VHF stations—they still have not found it worthwhile to own UHFs—in the nation's major markets. CBS, for instance, owns stations in the first, second, third, fourth, and twelfth largest markets: New York City, Los Angeles, Chicago, Philadelphia, and St. Louis, respectively; ABC owns stations in New York, Los Angeles, Chicago, San Francisco (sixth), and Detroit (seventh); NBC, in New York, Los Angeles, Chicago, Cleveland (eighth), and Washington (ninth).

All three networks now have about two hundred affiliates, ABC having closed the gap from which it had suffered since the 1940s, as the new kid on the block. In the late 1970s more and more independent stations, as well as many that had been affiliated with CBS and NBC, saw the economic wisdom of aligning themselves with ABC. The reasoning was simple: Under the programming genius of Fred Silverman, who honed the situation comedy to a prime-time art, ABC's ratings improved so dramatically that stations in the hinterlands jumped onto the bandwagon with glee. Silverman, sometimes called "the man with the golden gut," was the programming whiz kid at CBS in the early 1970s. He then became a vice president for programming at ABC. Programs such as "Laverne and Shirley," "Happy Days," and "Three's Company" lifted ABC to number one in the ratings. Later Silverman was lured to NBC to attempt a rescue of that network. He left there in the summer of 1981 with NBC trailing the other two networks and has since gone into independent production of programs.

Affiliates

The affiliates, individually licensed by the FCC, carry the networks into less populated corners of America. An affiliation agreement between a station and a network is a franchise to that station to carry that network's programming in its licensed area. Individual stations are not required to carry the net, but generally do so because the programming is generally superior to and cheaper than anything they can produce on their own. The net is their guarantee of an audience.

Some stations carry more network programming than others. All have the right to preempt network programming to carry other material. As previously discussed in chapter 6, affiliated stations usually are reimbursed by the networks for carrying the web. The industry standard for payment to affiliates is around 20 percent of the networks' commercial rates for the time. To assure itself a greater number of affiliates, ABC began offering 30 percent on the rate card during the late 1970s, forcing NBC and CBS to raise the ante. In addition to this corporate windfall, affiliates have continued to sell local advertising for station breaks and *adjacencies,* or spot announcements before, during, and after network programming. That three-to-four minutes per half-hour can become highly profitable for local stations whose prime-time-network shows guarantee local advertisers a large captive audience. In fact, in some markets and for certain types of programming (the Super Bowl, major movies, and the like), enough local income is available that affiliates forego all network compensation.

Originally, the networks required their affiliates to carry a certain high percentage of network programming, and specified certain programs that could not be preempted. By doing this the networks could guarantee a certain audience size to their advertisers. The FCC, however, outlawed these requirements, and stations now may choose not to carry the net whenever they wish, although that seldom happens. They may also pick up a rival network's programming if its affiliate in that area does not choose to use it. Affiliation agreements are a lot looser now than they used to be, and the networks' respective positions are less secure, in light of competitive and regulatory forces.

While the networks and the individual affiliates need each other, their relationship is not an entirely happy one. The affiliates are concerned about the development of each year's schedule since what the network offers will affect audience size and, hence, profitability in their own areas. Regional differences can cause problems, because some kinds of programming that are acceptable in the more liberal Northeast are less so in the South and Midwest. These interests must somehow be balanced by the networks, for whenever an affiliate does not carry the net, network ratings are adversely affected.

Animosities also arise because affiliates sell against the network, in competition with the net. From a major advertiser's standpoint, it is much simpler to buy the net. However, it is sometimes more scientific and economical to purchase time from individual stations in specific markets in order to carry out a certain marketing plan. For example, a snow tire manufacturer may decide there is no market in the sun belt. Aware of this, the individual stations, through their national representatives (reps), are constantly trying to lure advertisers away from the networks to buy time from

Relationships between networks and affiliates are tenuous, with both sides keeping their eyes on the ledger sheet.

them individually, which would mean considerably more profit to the station and no additional cost to the advertiser. One of the problems with national advertisers buying local rather than network commercial time has been the difficulty of proving whether or not the spot was actually run.

The network situation is further complicated by the development of a number of station groups—that is, a number of stations (again, five VHF or seven total, by FCC ruling) under single ownership. Such powerful groups can exert considerable influence with the networks because they sometimes represent major outlets in large population centers (speaking in a single voice). For example, a large group, such as Group W (the Westinghouse organization of stations), can strike fear into network accountants' hearts by threatening to switch affiliations.

Educational Television

Always short of funds, ETV failed to live up to its potential.

All the complexity that plagues commercial broadcasting is multiplied in the noncommercial area. This area lacks the unifying theme of profit to keep it on course. Problems began during the FCC freeze between 1948 and 1952 when educators made strong presentations to the FCC concerning the potential of the new medium. As a result, the FCC initially set aside twenty-five channels for educational television (ETV), and the first of these stations went on the air in 1953 in Houston, Texas. ETV grew very gradually, and in due course, National Educational Television (NET) began to provide programming and distribution to the loose chain of educational stations.

Despite the enthusiasm of educators, ETV did not fulfill its promise. It was hampered principally by a lack of funds. Cut off from advertising revenues, it existed meagerly, receiving spasmodic contributions from municipalities, school districts, states, various agencies of the federal government, and from large foundations; but these contributions were never quite enough and never on an assured basis to permit anything more than a minimal subsistence. Furthermore, NET funds were lacking for either coaxial cable or microwave relay of programming, so ETV programs were delivered from one station to another by mail, which scarcely led to any degree of timeliness.

Public Broadcasting Service

Into this picture came the 1967 Carnegie Commmission Report to President Lyndon Johnson recommending the establishment of a public broadcasting system (PBS) distinct from ETV. One thing the Carnegie Commission Report would have provided was assured financing for PBS through a manufacturer's excise tax on television receivers sold. Although Congress implemented the report and established the Corporation for Public Broadcasting (CPB), it failed to provide the funding necessary to validate PBS as a television force capable of competing with the three major networks.

From the outset PBS operated on a shoestring. By the start of the 1980s, when the number of noncommercial stations had reached 267, public broadcasting was receiving slightly more than a half billion dollars per year from all sources, including the federal government, foundations, corporations, subscriptions, and auctions. While that may sound like a lot, it represents only about one-twentieth of what the three commercial networks spend on programming alone, and less than a quarter of the networks' total net profits. "On any scale of comparison," complained PBS President Lawrence Grossman, "public television in this country is subsisting on total revenues that make it the most desperately underfunded television system in the free world."[2]

During the decade from the late 1960s to the late 1970s, the federal government's level of support of PBS's income more than doubled, from 12 percent to 27 percent. During that same period, however, support from increasingly strapped local governments and schools was being cut in half. Foundation support, especially from the Ford Foundation, dropped similarly. To offset these decreases, support from individuals tripled, as a result of membership drives and auctions. Most recently, PBS has attempted to augment its income by selling advertising in its slick monthly program guide and feature magazine, *The Dial,* distributed to 650,000 PBS supporters in New York, Chicago, Los Angeles, and Washington, D.C., as an incentive to those who make a minimum contribution of $25. Meanwhile, poverty-stricken PBS stations have begun, tentatively, considering accepting direct sponsorship and commercials for programs.

Even though PBS was more ambitious than ETV, it has never had enough funding either.

Since their inception, PBS and local stations have also gone hat in hand to corporations, which now finance nearly the same percentage of original broadcast hours as the federal government. This is an especially sensitive issue, because four of the top five corporate contributors are Exxon, Mobil, Gulf, and Atlantic Richfield, prompting wags to label PBS the Petroleum Broadcasting System. Together they provide over half the corporate funding for PBS. PBS has adopted strict rules to bar underwriters from exercising any control over programming matters, including the selection of topics, but the potential for abuse exists nevertheless. The most inflammatory PBS program of 1980, for instance, was "Death of a Princess," a docu-drama depicting the execution of an adulterous Saudi Arabian princess and her lover. The show was sponsored in part by the Mobil Oil Corporation, which said it did not attempt to stop the program from being shown despite pressure from Congress and from Saudi Arabian lobbyists.

Corporation and government support may mean manipulation of programming. New means of funding PBS are being sought.

The fear of corporation influence is no less real than that of governmental influence. With the Carnegie Commission Report in 1967, the foundation was laid for taxpayer support and control of public broadcasting. A nonprofit corporation called the Corporation for Public Broadcasting (CPB) was established to develop educational broadcasting that would be objective and balanced when controversial, to facilitate distribution of the programs, and to assure maximum freedom of the broadcasters from interference with or control of program content or other activities. Unfortunately, CPB resulted in a bureaucratic maze which more often than not has been in conflict with PBS, its stepchild representing the individual noncommercial stations. Since the CPB members are appointed by the U.S.

president, politicizing became a factor, especially under Richard Nixon, whose appointees influenced budgeting to minimize controversial programming, such as "liberal" news, talk shows, and programs like "The American Dream Machine," which aired unflattering segments about Nixon.

A second Carnegie Commission report in 1979 reiterated the need for quality programming on television and suggested several new remedies to the financing and control problems of PBS. By the early 1980s, Congress was still evaluating the proposal.

PBS Programs and Audiences

Essentially, PBS provides only distribution, programming, and services formerly performed by the controversial NET to its ETV affiliates, who are under no obligation whatever to carry the network. Stations may use the material or disregard it, as they wish, or they may tape it for later use. Most stations augment the PBS feed with inexpensive local and filler material, and home classroom subjects.

To date, PBS's major accomplishments include the English-imported "Civilisation" series, which it acquired only after all three commercial networks had turned it down (it was a gift from the Xerox Corporation); "Sesame Street" and its offshoot, "Electric Company," produced by the Childrens' Television Workshop (CTW), originally foundation supported; the British "Masterpiece Theatre," in particular "Upstairs/Downstairs"; "Over Easy," geared to the elderly, a demographic group long since abandoned by the commercial webs; and science series such as "Nova," "Cosmos," "The Ascent of Man," "The Incredible Machine," and other National Geographic specials.

Electronic Media

Audiences for **PBS** remain minuscule, by network standards. Although PBS was supposed to be free of the tyranny of ratings in its operation, it has succumbed to an inevitable curiosity for evaluation. The results have not been encouraging. In the early 1970s, Nielsen gave it a rating of 0.4 percent of all viewing. Things have since improved, but not by much. Different studies in the late 1970s indicated that somewhere between twenty and forty million Americans were exposed to PBS in an average week. But on any given night, even today, some 90 percent of television homes will be tuned to network programming, 5 percent to independent commercial stations, and only about 5 percent to PBS.

In the final analysis the persistent problem for PBS is that it is broadcast over the same air at the same time as CBS, NBC, and ABC. For over a quarter century it has been the networks' business to find out what Americans want to watch and they have done this well; anything else simply cannot compete. A person can subscribe to *Reader's Digest* and *American Heritage* and read them both, but a person cannot watch CBS and PBS simultaneously.

Predictably, PBS provides quality programming for minuscule audiences.

The commercial cycle is comprised of a manufacturer with a product, a distributor, a consumer, and, generally, a financier. In television, the networks are the manufacturers, and programming is the product, which is distributed via affiliates to the audience-consumers, and advertising provides the financing. The manufacturer can judge the success of a product by the quantity purchased by consumers. But in television, the product is distributed without charge; there is no ring of the cash register. Instead, ratings are a form of feedback by which the networks and advertisers gauge the effectiveness of product consumption.

The Ratings

The ratings had their genesis in the days of early radio when the huge costs of production demanded an early warning system for measuring audience acceptance. Since the advent of television, technological improvements in computers and the refinement of public opinion polling techniques have developed the ratings into a near science.

Using a sample of about 2,000 households, the A. C. Nielsen Company measures the program tastes of over 200 million Americans in 81 million television homes. Numbers of that magnitude occasionally provoke criticism. Even Nielsen, the largest of the half-dozen major polling firms for national television (in some 200 independent firms conducting ratings for radio and television), is less than perfect; for example, the Rocky Mountain states have long been underrepresented. But, in general, the measurements are accepted as valid by the networks. Perhaps more important, advertisers consider the Nielsen ratings to be official, so they become official.

For all their shortcomings, ratings constitute the only valid feedback in the TV business.

Nielsen's

Nielsen uses the *audimeter* and *diary* to rate programs. Complex and immediate ratings are possible.

Each year the three networks spend about one million dollars for the Nielsen service, and receive some 90 percent of their audience feedback from that single source. Nielsen's ratings involve two feedback systems, the *audimeter* and the *diary*. Storage Instantaneous Audimeters (SIAs) are tuning meters with recording circuits inside which are hooked to carefully selected sets in some 1,160 to 1,170 American households. The SIA silently measures all TV set usage within each "Nielsen family" household, recording when each set is turned on, how long it stays on the channel to which it is tuned, and all channel switchings. It even captures this information on backyard or patio sets, via a transmitter mounted on the TV set and linked to the audimeter, which is installed out of the family's view, in a closet or in the basement. Each SIA is connected by special telephone lines to computers in Dunedin, Florida, where they are electronically read at least twice a day.

The audimeters indicate whether the sets are turned on, but Nielsen also tries to find out whether anyone is watching. Thus diaries are placed in another 2,300 households for thirty-four weeks each year. This sample of television homes, known as the National Audience Composition (NAC), is also equipped with a Recordimeter, logging the amount of time that each set is in use. The diarykeepers are then expected to record daily on their Audilogs the same information about set and channel usage picked up by the Recordimeters.

Until recently, audimeter tapes were mailed to Nielsen every two weeks, but computer sophistication and programming decision-making dictates have grown apace, and now instantaneous feedback is possible. Currently, Nielsen is able to provide networks with complete reports of prime-time audiences on the second weekday morning following the programs; the networks and major clients have data terminals in their own offices connecting them to the Dunedin computers. In addition to these daily national

The ratings have done a better job of counting the sets turned on than noting whether anyone is watching.
Patricia Hollander Gross/ Stock, Boston

ratings, Nielsen provides "weekly household ratings" on the second Monday following the end of each report week, and ratings in several other categories including ratings in top markets and ratings broken down by demographic characteristics.[3]

From the Nielsen family's perspective, the responsibility of each viewer representing the tastes of over 100,000 other Americans is sometimes overwhelming. One diary keeper told an ABC documentary team that he was so frustrated by the chore of recording all his selections that he started sending in marked-up copies of his *TV Guide,* and he felt such strain in representing 100,000 people he had never met that he soon quit altogether.[4] Others have admitted to upgrading their program taste while under Nielsen's surveillance out of concern that the rest of the viewers should be watching "better" programs than they naturally prefer. The Nielsen people claim they can compensate for these errors, however. For one thing, since Nielsen families are plugged into the system on five-year rotating schedules, there is little likelihood of systematically manipulating their inherent television preferences for the duration. For another, the diary and Recordimeter system is used to offset any systematic errors, such as sets left on while no one is at home, that crop up in audimeter homes.

Nielsen's nearest competitor in the ratings business is the Arbitron Company (ARB), which measures both radio and television audiences. Arbitron does not use audimeters (because audimeters are patented by Nielsen), but relies on weekly diaries kept by randomly selected households throughout the nation. Arbitron families receive one diary for each television set they have, since television is considered a family activity, and one diary for each person over the age of twelve for recording radio listenership. In addition, Arbitron employs a *telephone coincidental survey* in which viewers and listeners are queried on the spot, so to speak, about their current media

Arbitron

Arbitron limits itself to diaries and phone checks to rate TV and radio shows.

consumption. Periodically Arbitron also uses personal interviews to ascertain more specialized data or to check on its own sampling procedures. Perhaps the biggest difference between the two major rating services is that Nielsen's ratings concentrate on national or network programming and Arbitron's are concerned with more local audiences; numerous local stations subscribe to the Arbitron service, while Nielsen gets most of its income from the webs.

Of all the reports issued by the services, Nielsen's Television Index is probably the best known and most influential. Based on audimeters throughout the land, the NTI generates several types of data, the two most important being *ratings* and *shares*.

Ratings and Shares

Ratings show the percentage of TV homes tuned to a given show compared with *anything else* they might be doing.

The *rating* for each program reflects the number of sets tuned to that show in comparison to the other 81 million television households that conceivably could be viewing it. Nielsen gives "average audience ratings" or estimates of the number of households tuned to each network program during the average minute of the program, expressed as a percentage of all television households, and "total audience ratings" or estimates of households tuned to a particular program for six or more minutes. In addition, "persons ratings" offer such demographic data as sex, age, and family role of viewers of each program. In network television, a successful prime-time program has a rating of 17 or more, which means that 17 percent of American homes are tuned in at any given moment to the show in question. The rating, then, reflects how many have been captured by a particular show, not necessarily in contrast with other shows but in contrast with everything else there is to do—eat, sleep, make love, or what have you.

Shares show the percentage of TV homes tuned to a given show compared with *other shows* they might be watching.

The audience *share*, on the other hand, is a gauge of how a particular program stacks up against its other television competition. It is the percent of homes watching each program at any particular moment. This, according to network executives and advertisers, is a more crucial figure, and it is easy to see why. Broadcasters hope to capture at least one-third of all viewers, since—ideally, from the broadcasters' standpoint—the viewers will be watching one of the three networks at any given time. Such a situation, of course, is unreasonable, given the incursion of cable television, videotape playbacks, and other options that have become increasingly available. But networks are still fixated on the idea that a show must receive a 35 percent share to be considered a real success and they are quick to cancel shows whose shares drop below 25 percent. Even a lowly 25 percent share, we must remember, indicates that some 20 million sets may be tuned to a program—and this figure comprises an audience exponentially larger than any book, newspaper, film, or drama could be generating at a given time. Such is the tyranny of the television system.

For the last decade or so, it has not been enough to merely receive an audience totalling one-third of all viewers. Those viewers must be demographically suitable product purchasers. Nielsen now offers advertisers and programmers profiles of audiences, including their age, sex, education, socioeconomic status (ses) and so forth. Advertisers are enchanted with the young and relatively affluent, and with women, who comprise the majority of the viewing audience at all times during the day, drawing only approximately even to men during the late news. Networks charge the highest rates for shows appealing to young adults between the ages of eighteen and thirty-four, since that is the age group making the most use of kitchen, cosmetic, automotive, and drug products being advertised. The second most valuable audience, from an advertising perspective, includes viewers between the ages of eighteen and forty-nine. The assumption is that these groups are stocking up their households and garages with what *New York Times* television critic Les Brown calls the paraphernalia of middle-class life.[5] Probably no better evidence of this assumption is available than the data found in table 7.2, which indicates that the products promoted by the top twenty-five television advertisers most definitely reveal America's conspicuous consumption of nonessential goods and services.

Table 7.2   Top advertisers on television, 1981

Rank	Company	Total spent
1.	Procter & Gamble	$521,116,400
2.	General Foods	328,312,700
3.	American Home Products	171,765,500
4.	General Mills	169,324,700
5.	General Motors	160,808,100
6.	Pepsico	139,272,200
7.	Lever Brothers	137,992,100
8.	Ford	136,345,000
9.	AT&T	129,798,800
10.	McDonald's	129,379,300
11.	Bristol-Myers	121,450,000
12.	Philip Morris	119,547,300
13.	Coca-Cola	109,109,400
14.	Warner-Lambert	106,551,400
15.	Anheuser-Busch	105,145,800
16.	Johnson & Johnson	101,403,400
17.	Sears, Roebuck	99,519,500
18.	Dart & Kraft	97,392,100
19.	Pillsbury	91,698,500
20.	Gillette	84,984,800
21.	Ralston Purina	84,912,700
22.	Kellogg	84,440,600
23.	Richardson-Vicks	82,396,400
24.	Chrysler	73,855,900
25.	Consolidated Foods	72,013,800

Source: Television Bureau of Advertising; *Broadcasting,* 3 May 1982, pp. 82–83. By permission, Broadcasting Publications Inc.

Note: In 1981 almost $1.5 billion was spent on television advertising for food and food products. In second place were toiletries and toilet goods commercials, at a cost of $1.07 billion. Third was automotive advertising, with almost $785 million. The fastest-growing categories of products advertised on television were office equipment, up 48 percent over 1980 (total $105.6 million); records and tapes, up 44 percent (total $177.4 million), and gasoline and lubricants, up 35 percent (to $163.2 million).

One final observation about the ratings: Within the rating system there are *black weeks,* periods during the year when no ratings are conducted by network agreement. Recognizing their obligation to provide a certain amount of public-affairs programming under FCC dictum, and also that such cultural programming loses large chunks of the audience, the networks have used black weeks as a device to satisfy the public interest, convenience, and necessity requirements for their affiliates (and wholly owned stations) at one fell swoop. Black weeks are filled with documentaries and cultural and public affairs programming, which the networks can offer with impunity because there are no ratings with which to be concerned.

Programming

Television programming is a highly competitive and incredibly expensive gamble always conducted with one eye on ratings. Prime-time programming is not so much concerned with the thought of developing an enormously popular program, although this helps, as it is with providing an evening's continuity across the prime-time hours and slotting shows to compete with offerings on the other two networks. Historically, one of the most closely guarded secrets of the networks was their forthcoming season's schedules. Prior knowledge of one network's schedule would permit the others to slot competing attractions against its most appealing offerings. Over the past few seasons, with networks willingly jumbling their prime-time offerings around, sometimes at a moment's notice, this secrecy has been less a factor, however. The end result has been a running corporate chess game of sorts, with programs and viewers acting as the pawns.

The continuity of programming is significant. A weak show will lose an audience, which may not return to the network that evening. A weak show, therefore, can be presumed to lose an audience not only for that particular time slot, but for the entire evening. This is disastrous in ratings and, hence, in advertising revenue.

When a show fails in the ratings, it is often necessary to kill it outright. It is preferable to gamble with another program than to continue a proven loser, regardless of how devoted the supporters of the program may be. More often it is shifted to a different slot, in what is usually a sacrificial move. Certain viewing patterns are invariably destroyed by a move, which will further depress the ratings. In addition, the move is often to a slot against a highly rated competitor on another network. A few years ago, the critically acclaimed *Paper Chase* had a difficult time with the ratings. Instead of killing the show right away, CBS moved it several times. This allowed the network to recoup a portion of its investment in the program and to satisfy contracts it had with the performers. Eventually, however, failure was used as the excuse to drop the show. Complaints from loyal viewers may explain why star John Houseman and company later returned to the air in additional episodes filmed for cable TV.

A show's replacement, according to the theory of the *least objectionable program (lop),* does not have to be good, just less objectionable to most people than anything else on TV at that moment. Thus, it is possible for inferior shows to develop high ratings during prime time, provided the alternative offerings by competing networks are worse. In view of the costs of television production, this is a key point. There is no need for a network to spend exorbitant sums of money to develop an expensive program for competition against a weak program when a cheaper one will suffice.

The preoccupation with ratings, of course, means that each network must attract as much audience as it possibly can and if possible outdraw the other two networks proportionately. Appeal to the largest possible mass is an appeal to the lowest common denominator and dictates a broad-based (usually noncontroversial) type of programming. And the program is more likely to succeed if a star is associated with the show. There is also a good deal of formula programming and imitation. Whenever one network develops a successful format, be it police beat, hospital, situation comedy, quasi-musical, mini-series, or real people exhibiting their eccentricities, others are sure to follow. A case in point was the rash of handicapped detectives who came in wheelchairs, or were blind, obese, obsequious, or senile, but always got their man. Even in the daytime hours, networks copy one another's game and quiz shows. Such repetitive programming is bound to offer a striking sameness to network programs. See table 7.3 for a list of the top-rated shows since 1950.

Typically, as the program directors for each network arrange their season schedules, they decide which programs will be retained from the previous year and which will be discontinued. They are then faced with placing their shows in the most appropriately competitive time slots, shooting largely in the dark. They are also faced with the problem of deciding what new programs they should put into the schedule, relying on proven formats and star availabilities. They then entertain a number of suggestions for new programming, new serials, new approaches to old problems, new and old movies, specials, and so on.

In the case of new programming, the program directors generally commission pilot programs from independent production companies for several of the most promising ideas. Pilots are expensive to make, since they are actually full-length films or videotapes of one sequence of a new serial. They introduce the characters, the theme, and the treatment that will be followed through the entire schedule. Such was to be the case with "Love, Sidney," a pilot on NBC in the summer of 1981. Word spread before the pilot aired that the show's main character, played by veteran actor Tony Randall, was to be homosexual, which sparked a controversy. NBC changed

The theory of "lop" says that the "least objectionable programming," not the highest quality, will get the best ratings.

Next Season's Schedule

Planning a season's prime-time schedule is a corporate chess game.

Table 7.3 Top-rated television shows since 1950

1950–1951*	1. Texaco Star Theatre (NBC)	6.	Gilette Cavalcade of Sports (Boxing) (NBC)
	2. Fireside Theater (NBC)	7.	Arthur Godfrey's Talent Scouts (CBS)
	3. Your Show of Shows (NBC)	8.	Mama (CBS)
	4. Philco Television Playhouse (NBC)	9.	Robert Montgomery Presents (NBC)
	5. The Colgate Comedy Hour (NBC)	10.	Martin Kane, Private Eye (NBC)
1954–1955	1. I Love Lucy (CBS)	6.	Disneyland (ABC)
	2. The Jackie Gleason Show (CBS)	7.	The Bob Hope Show (NBC)
	3. Dragnet (NBC)	8.	The Jack Benny Show (CBS)
	4. You Bet Your Life (NBC)	9.	The Martha Raye Show (NBC)
	5. The Toast of the Town (CBS)	10.	The George Gobel Show (NBC)
1959–1960*	1. Gunsmoke (CBS)	6.	Father Knows Best (CBS)
	2. Wagon Train (NBC)	7.	77 Sunset Strip (ABC)
	3. Have Gun Will Travel (CBS)	8.	The Price is Right (NBC)
	4. The Danny Thomas Show (CBS)	9.	Wanted: Dead or Alive (CBS)
	5. The Red Skelton Show (CBS)	10.	Perry Mason (CBS)
1964–1965*	1. Bonanza (NBC)	6.	The Red Skelton Hour (CBS)
	2. Bewitched (ABC)	7.	The Dick Van Dyke Show (CBS)
	3. Gomer Pyle, U.S.M.C. (CBS)	8.	The Lucy Show (CBS)
	4. The Andy Griffith Show (CBS)	9.	Peyton Place (ABC)
	5. The Fugitive (ABC)	10.	Combat (ABC)
1969–1970*	1. Rowan & Martin's Laugh-In (NBC)	6.	Here's Lucy (CBS)
	2. Gunsmoke (CBS)	7.	The Red Skelton Hour (CBS)
	3. Bonanza (NBC)	8.	Marcus Welby, M.D. (ABC)
	4. Mayberry R.F.D. (CBS)	9.	Walt Disney's Wonderful World of Color (NBC)
	5. Family Affair (CBS)	10.	The Doris Day Show (CBS)
1974–1975†	1. All in the Family (CBS)	6.	Rhoda (CBS)
	2. Sanford and Son (NBC)	7.	Good Times (CBS)
	3. Chico and the Man (NBC)	8.	The Waltons (CBS)
	4. The Jeffersons (CBS)	9.	Maude (CBS)
	5. M*A*S*H (CBS)	10.	Hawaii Five-O (CBS)
1979–1980†	1. 60 Minutes (CBS)	6.	Dallas (CBS)
	2. Three's Company (ABC)	7.	Flo (CBS)
	3. That's Incredible (ABC)	8.	The Jeffersons (CBS)
	4. M*A*S*H (CBS)	9.	Dukes of Hazzard (CBS)
	5. Alice (CBS)	10.	One Day at a Time (CBS)

Sources: Craig T. and Peter G. Norback, eds., *TV Guide Almanac* (New York: Triangle Publications Inc., 1980), pp. 546–69; and *Broadcasting Magazine*, with permission.

*The television season from October to April
†The television season from September to April

its mind about Sidney's sexual orientation, and the pilot reassured network executives that the program had the potential for being successful. Because of their costs, many pilots will be shown several times as television movies and then sold to syndication companies for foreign showings on television and in theaters.

The majority of pilot films never become episodic series. Program directors and advertisers determine whether to contract with program suppliers for additional episodes on the basis of instincts, scientific pretests, and ratings of on-air pilots. Until recently a go-ahead meant production of a full year's—actually twenty-six—episodes. Nowadays, with competition and inflation taken into consideration, it is not unusual to order as few as four or six episodes. Usually the minimum order is twelve or thirteen, enough for half a season. If ratings hold up, additional scripts and films will be ordered. If not, it is unlikely that audiences will ever see the episodes again, and the networks will write off the expenses as gambling losses. And the production companies, facing the same gambles, inevitably respond by cranking out clones of their already successful series.

A network board shows every prime-time slot for all seven days of the week; the program director slots similar boards for the other two networks according to what hunches and commercial espionage reveal they are doing.

Other time slots are cheaper to fill and bring high returns.

Fred Silverman, the programming "whiz kid," validated the theory of *least objectionable programming* during his sojourns at all three major networks. Today he continues the effort as an independent producer.
Wide World Photos

Prime time, with its mass audience and lowest common denominator, is one situation in which television must find the way to appeal simultaneously to the sixteen-year-old Puerto Rican girl in New York City and the eighty-year-old North Dakota farmer and everybody between.

Non Prime Time

Weekdays

The daytime audience is overwhelmingly female: the homemakers of America—the purchasers of America. Daytime television is an incredible mixture of quiz shows, game shows, soap operas, old movies, and reruns. There is also a daytime audience of the elderly and the ailing, but they are scarcely considered by programmers, for they have little purchasing power. Daytime television also tends to be inexpensive programming, as the networks conserve their dollars for the competitive prime-time hours. Game shows cost only one-twentieth as much to produce per half hour as prime-time shows, but they generate proportionately higher advertising returns. Much of daytime programming consists of packages made by independent producers, and often as not are contributed to heavily by advertisers. Prizes are contributed by manufacturers in return for product mention. Since costs to the net are relatively small, and the drawing power of these programs is high, daytime programming is taken quite seriously in corporate offices.

Saturday Mornings

Saturday morning offers another specialty, kiddie cartoon time. Breakfast food manufacturers, toy makers, and others hawk their wares to tiny tots. The little people have no purchasing power themselves, but they have enormous influence over susceptible parents. According to Robert B. Choates, children are at a disadvantage when scriptwriters, actors, technicians, and psychological analysts combine to create a commercial directed at gullible eight-year-olds.[6] Others agree. In recent years, children's programming and advertising have come under intense scrutiny from the FTC, parent and citizens groups, and even the networks and program producers. (See chapter 10.)

Sunday Mornings

Sunday morning, a time of minimal viewing, is considered the "cultural ghetto" of television. Religious programs are quite naturally slotted into this period, as well as a considerable number of public affairs and quasi-cultural programs, to build up the public interest, convenience, and necessity portion of the weekly log. NBC's "Face the Nation" and "Meet the Press" have been stable public affairs programs for years. Now CBS is discovering an audience for news and feature stories during that same time period: By 1980 "CBS News Sunday Morning" had become an established part of Sunday morning programming.

Sporting Events

Sports is another facet of television programming that guarantees enormous audiences. Traditionally, these audiences have been male, and therefore advertising has been centered around "man" things, such as razor blades, shaving soaps, aftershaves, male deodorants, shampoos, and hair creams, with an occasional auto tire, gasoline, beer, or blue jeans commercial thrown in.

Television programming costs are enormous. During the 1979–1980 television season, the three major networks were spending more than $39 million for each week of prime-time programming. That came to more than one billion dollars for the twenty-six-week season, a 40 percent increase over the previous season. The going rate for a minute of network prime-time production was $10,000 at the most recent check. An average half-hour episode of a continuing series cost a quarter of a million dollars, and an hour episode cost more than twice that amount. Networks like prime-time news magazines because they come relatively cheap: $300,000 per hour for "60 Minutes." Spectaculars like "Buck Rogers in the 25th Century" chewed up more than $650,000 per hour because of elaborate sets and special effects. Saturday morning kiddie cartoons cost $150,000 per half hour, compared with $60,000 for a soap opera and a mere $12,000 for a game show.[7] NBC spent $20 million to produce the twelve-hour mini-series "Shōgun"; and an hour of the syndicated "Muppet Show," seen by some 250 million people worldwide each week, cost $260,000.

Where does all that money go? It is quickly spread to writers, directors, cast, crew, sets, wardrobes, transportation, special effects, and publicity. For example, Aaron Spelling Productions' ABC hit, "The Love Boat," costs $100,000 per show for five producers (a line producer and two pairs of creative producers), $125,000 for the cast (each celebrity guest receiving $5,000 for an appearance), $40,000 for extras (faces in the crowd and walk-ons), $40,000 for writers (three teams, each preparing one-third of every weekly script), and $35,000 for music (a thirty-piece orchestra for six hours). Once miscellaneous expenses are added in, the typical episode costs $350,000, not counting the $150,000 for the 80 to 100 people needed to produce and film the series, the $40,000 in fringe benefits, and another $50,000 in postproduction editing. If you add to this the fee Spelling Productions pays Twentieth Century Fox for studio space and the fees to compensate writers and performers for the network's second run of the episode later in the season, "The Love Boat" weighs anchor to the tune of $650,000 per episode.

ABC, by placing "The Love Boat" in the profitable 9 to 10 P.M. EST time slot on Saturday nights, is able to justify selling six minutes of commercial time to national advertisers at $90,000 per thirty-second spot. Thus the network receives as much as a million dollars for each episode for which it has paid Spelling Productions a mere $550,000 in "license fees." Has Spelling lost out on the deal? It would seem so, since its costs are $100,000

Costs of Programming

above its license fees. But Spelling and all other production companies know the real money is to be made when their successful series are rerun during the spring and summer, for second and third seasons, and in syndication or overseas; millions of dollars will be generated, and at no additional cost to the producers.[8] One television researcher maintains that it is very unlikely that a show will recover costs while in its first run before syndication, and that deficit financing has been a staple of the industry for many years.[9]

As television programming costs skyrocket, more and more attention has been given to reruns in an attempt to spread the cost over two or more time slots instead of one. As long as this has been done by all three networks, it has worked out well. However, reruns have scarcely been a service to the long-suffering television viewer accustomed to original productions night after night. As it stands now, original programming runs from mid-September through the new year or even sooner, depending upon the ratings. After that, the networks either begin repeats or air what they euphemistically call their "second seasons"—essentially these are series they didn't think good enough to air back in September. Reruns and second or even third season offerings—sometimes introduced with all the hype previously seen in September—are encountered more often than not in the prime-time slots until the end of the television year in June. Statistics and the lop seem to indicate that audiences will watch reruns in the same sort of stupor that they watched the originals, and that many people either missed the original or forgot it quickly. There is, however, reason to believe that the increasing use of reruns is driving away some of network television's audience to other media and activities.

Television Audiences

The network program directors are the principal gatekeepers of the television medium. Theirs is a different style of gatekeeping from that of newspaper or magazine editors, or even book publishers and film producers. Their style differs because they are concerned not only with audience appeal (specific or mass), as are the other media, but also with what their rivals are doing. They program as much against the other networks' offerings as they do for the audience. Thus, gatekeeping has a competitive, three-dimensional quality and a new sophistication that is peculiar to television.

The preponderance of appeal to the lowest common denominator is reflected in much of the blandness and sameness that appears on television: the high incidence of screeching auto chases, gun fights, fisticuffs, sickroom pathos, and young women in skimpy clothing. Theory holds that programming aimed at the so-called thirteen-year-old mentality will automatically reach everyone above that level: They will be capable of understanding it, and if the concept of the least objectionable program is correct, they will watch it. Those beneath this arbitrary level lack the competence and, more importantly, the purchasing power to be of concern.

Do viewership studies support these assumptions? Statistics cited at the outset of this chapter indicated that the average person in America watches television four and a half hours per day. The time committed to watching television has been increasing gradually over the past two decades and shows little sign of reversing itself. Significantly, though, only one third of the potential American audience partakes of two thirds of that daily viewing. That third is referred to by the television industry as the steady, habitual audience, who turn on the set whenever they're near it and demonstrate little discrimination in choosing fare. Another group of viewers, considered occasional watchers, view frequently but without addiction. Finally, selective watchers are those who seek out specific programs but on the whole can take or leave television. Programmers, naturally, concentrate on the habitual and occasional viewers while paying only token attention to the desires of the selective group.[10]

During peak periods of the prime-time season, about 70 million viewers will be tuned in at 7:30 P.M., and are joined by 20 to 30 million others by 9 P.M. Viewing levels gradually decline to 50 to 60 million at 11 P.M. As Les Brown puts it, there are two ways of looking at these statistics: either to recognize, perhaps with dismay, that about half the population is drawn to television each evening, or to take heart in the fact that the other half of the population does not feel compelled to watch without good reason.[11]

What do we know about the viewers—that half of our population who are likely to be watching television on any evening? We have already seen that women view more television than men. Also of interest is the fact that older men and women, those over 55, watch more than any other age group; that young children view more than older children and teenagers; and that the amount of viewing is greater for children who are black, who are from families of lower socioeconomic status, and who are lower in academic achievement and IQ.

Television is watched more in larger than in smaller families: Households with five or more members watch about fifty-seven hours a week, compared with fifty and one-half hours for households with three to four members, and thirty-seven and one-half hours for those with only one or two members. Television is watched seven hours more per week in households with color sets than in those with black-and-white sets.

Of those who describe themselves as super-fans of television, those with grade-school educations outnumber those with college educations nearly three to one. Overall viewership patterns, however, show that adult viewers with high-school educations watch more television than do those with grade-school educations, who in turn view more than those with one or more years of college. Similar patterns emerge when viewership is analyzed along income levels: The heaviest viewership is among middle-income groups, with upper middle income homes watching about an hour or two less per week. Those with the lowest income levels—who tend to live alone, to move frequently, and to make little use of any mass media—have the lowest level of television usage per household. At the other extreme, of course, lies another group of nonviewers. They are the individualistic intellectuals, frequently of high income, who consider television a waste of time.

TV gatekeeping is sophisticated and depends upon predictable audience behavior.

Two of the most exhaustive studies ever conducted about television, by Gary A. Steiner and Robert T. Bower, offer substantial insights into America's fascination with the tube.[12] Conducted a decade apart, in the early 1960s and early 1970s, respectively, the national surveys systematically demonstrated that most viewers are satisfied with television, but that the better educated are somewhat more selective in their viewing and feel guiltier than other viewers about engaging in the television habit. Steiner's respondents indicated that television, more than any other invention during the previous generation—including new cars, refrigerators, washers and dryers, cooking appliances, stereos, radios, or telephones—has made their lives pleasant and interesting. Most felt their children were better off with television than without it, although the Bower study found interesting skepticism among parents who were concerned about television's impact on their offspring.

America loves TV, but there are signs of disaffection.

The Steiner and Bower surveys indicate subtle shifts in America's attitudes toward its favorite invention. Other studies since the Bower survey, which is now a decade old, reinforce the trends. Essentially, those trends indicate a growing disenchantment with commercial television. A decreasing percentage of "super-fans" appear in all age and educational groupings; only females have remained faithful to the same extent they did during the early 1960s. Increased skepticism about advertising and television's disadvantages for children are evident. On the other hand, four-fifths of Bower's sample indicated that television plays an important educational role for their children, compared with fewer than two-thirds of the Steiner respondents. The increased number of viewers willing to pay for noncommercial television—30 percent in the Bower study, and 24 percent in the Steiner study—indicates growing support for pay television and alternatives to the long-standing attitude that "watching commercials is a fair price to pay for getting free TV."

The networks are aware of the diminishing stranglehold they once had on America and are seeking to compensate for it. They are diversifying their interests, getting into other kinds of business. Some have acquired publishing interests; others are buying into wholly different endeavors; and all have recognized the value of buying into or developing their own electronic media subsystems for that time ahead when the audience moves into control of its own media fare—videodiscs, videotape recorders, and the like.

The real question, of course, is, why are Americans becoming ever-so-slightly disenchanted with television? Part of the answer undoubtedly lies in the sameness of television. What was once enthralling has become a bore. Ironically, a part of the media specialization and fragmentation that television has forced upon books, newspapers, magazines, radio, and film is beginnng to take its toll of television. People are turning to other things more suited to their individual interests. In so doing, they forsake television. It may easily be that television's massiveness is bringing about its own demise.

In the United States advertising pays the media bills, more so in television than anywhere else. In recent years television has been taking slightly more than half of the advertising dollar spent on nationally promoted products. The biggest portion of this has gone to the three networks, which are uniquely equipped to offer national service, while individual stations in major markets have been receiving increasingly larger shares of those dollars.

Television Advertising

National advertising uses television primarily because of its massive "reach." Television saturation, however, is probably no greater than that achieved earlier by newspapers or radio. But television offers new dynamic dimensions to advertising: drama, humor, dramatic effects, motion, and color. The ability to create mood, excitement, and drama in connection with commercial products is a real asset; combined with vast audiences, it is overpowering. Advertising agencies have proven adept at conveying impressions, at probing the inner recesses of the mind, at developing ingenious appeals to the point where many of the commercials on network television are superior from production and entertainment standpoints to the supporting programming, and this may not be entirely without design.

TV is uniquely suited to carry national advertising.

The costs of making a network commercial are astronomical. The commercial, after all, is the reason for the entire medium. It is a painstaking and time-consuming endeavor, utilizing all of an agency's expertise and genius, and all the production talent of studio professionals. Just to stage and film a simple thirty-second commercial in which an announcer merely faces the camera and holds up a product will cost over $20,000 once labor, editing, and duplication expenses are included. A $20,000 to $40,000 price tag is typical for network spots, while local advertisers are spending from $500 to $4,000 to reach their more limited target groups. It is not entirely unusual for a half-minute network spot to cost more than $250,000 to get the message exactly right, to convey the perfect impression, to be "with it," and sell. At those costs—$8,333.33 per second—we're talking about the most expensively produced media fare in the world; a ninety-minute feature film would be in the $45 million range if similarly produced.[13] Advertisers expect to recoup a part of this investment by amortizing the cost over as long a period as possible. The more often a spot is run, the lower the unit cost on each run, even though actors are paid residuals for reruns.

Commercials cost more to produce per second than any other media fare.

So important is advertising to television that there was a time when the advertising agencies produced their own programs as well as commercials. The networks were little more than distribution channels for the agencies; they simply bought time for their clients and filled it as they wished. However, the quiz show scandals of 1959 brought an end to this practice, and the networks reassumed responsibility for programming. (See chapter 13 p. 420.)

Major advertisers can still sponsor an individual program or even a series but they have much less say about the content and scheduling of programs than they did in the 1950s. That doesn't mean that advertisers don't exercise influence on the programming. Rather, because of the enormous expenses and risks involved in national television programming, there is by necessity a close relationship between the networks and advertisers.

Since 1970, most network advertising dollars have been spent on the purchase of *participating spots:* isolated commercial messages inserted into the programming. Technically, these are known as *participating network TV spots* when the national advertiser buys on a nationally broadcast network program, and as *national spots* when purchased individually on stations in major markets. *Local spot TV,* a third category of television advertising, is that purchased by local advertisers peddling their goods and services to hometown audiences.

Whether they are network, national, or local, such spots are not necessarily identifiable with the program. That is, they will run side by side with other advertisements for other products, and the program will not carry the advertiser's name as it would a sponsor's name. Under a provision called product protection, similar products promoted by competing spot advertisers will be separated.

Rather than sinking all of their ad dollars into the sponsorship of a single show, participating advertisers will purchase spots according to a *scatter plan.* The same message will appear during many programs, at different times of the week, and on different networks according to advertisers' wishes and the availability of the programs. Advertisers consider the scatter plan to be cost effective, giving them both reach and frequency—a combination impossible in print media, and far less satisfactory in radio.

The factors that enter into an advertiser's program choice are not determined by ratings alone, although ratings always have a bearing. The kind of audience and personal predispositions are factors, as are public relations concerns, such as when the cigarette companies would not buy any time before 9:00 P.M. on the presumption that children would not be in bed until then, or Sears's proclamation that it would no longer buy time on violent programs.

All commercials are not sold at the same price. There may be as much as a 25 percent variation in the cost of spots across a ninety-minute prime-time program, depending on how far in advance the advertisers buy, how frequently they buy, or the sorts of packages or deals they have made. Television advertising, while based on a rate card which in turn is based on the ratings, is still negotiable. Networks, however, do their utmost to protect their *cpm,* or *cost-per-thousand,* rates, which is the amount they charge advertisers for exposure to a thousand homes (not viewers). At least one network has given public-service-announcement spots (PSAs) to the Boy Scouts rather than cut the price of commercial time for Sunday afternoon professional football.

Since the mid-1970s, more than four-fifths of television spots have been thirty seconds in length, in contrast with the minute-long commercials popular in the 1960s. This explains why more commercials are on the air today than there were some years back, even though the total amount of commercial time per hour has held relatively steady at about six minutes during prime time, a standard agreed upon by the voluntary National Association of Broadcasters but not imposed by the FCC.

Short commercials have nearly the impact of long ones, so we're bound to be seeing more of them.

Research indicated that a thirty-second commercial has almost two-thirds the impact of a sixty-second one, so advertisers refined the art of making a pitch with forty-five words jammed into twenty-eight and one-half seconds of audio. In that time span scenarios are set, problems faced, and solutions found. Recently, behavioral scientists have found that message retention remains high when speech and action are compressed even further. This can only mean a proliferation of ten-second spots in which flashes of images and slogans are hurled through America's ozone night after night. We are already seeing these "quickies" being used extensively for station identification and program promotions ("promos") between shows or nested amid blocks of half-minute commercials. Individually, such an appeal may be effective, but the sum total, of course, is cacophony. The airwaves are cluttered, as are the brains of viewers faced with making sense of the messages. As advertising expert Otto Kleppner says, "the kaleidoscope of clutter and commercials produces confusion among viewers and a high rate of misidentification of brands."[14] The clutter will probably continue, however, because each spokesperson has the right to spend his or her dollars as he or she sees fit, and no commercial television station is going to refuse the income.

Since it is the network affiliates that actually reach the audience and since there is some selling against the networks on the part of their affiliates and the independents, the prime concern of a television station is for it to be considered part of a major market. The advertising agencies of Madison Avenue define a major market as 100,000 homes. That is the magical breaking point below which a station will not ordinarily be included in a national advertising campaign. For this reason the tallest man-made structure on earth was built in North Dakota to rise 2,000 feet above the plains. It is a television broadcasting antenna designed to fan out over the northern flatlands to reach 100,000 homes before its signal disappears over the edge of the earth.[15]

Television News

Each weekday evening, some 32 million of America's 81 million television households watch network newscasts. Those 60 million viewers have made the news as popular as many other prime-time programs, and their legions are growing. During a one-year period, between 1979 and 1980, network news audiences grew by an amazing 13 percent. As Robert MacNeil, co-anchor of the PBS news program "The MacNeil-Lehrer Report" puts it, "TV has created a nation of news junkies who tune in every night to get their fix on the world."[16]

Now here's the news . . .

It is 10 A.M. on Thursday, Feb. 14, and 33 people are crowding into the scruffy conference room at ABC's Manhattan news center on West 66th Street. Some stand, some sit on boxes of supplies—ABC does not waste money on frills—while eleven others sit around a long conference table studded with microphones. The microphones connect this office with bureaus in Washington, Chicago, Atlanta, Miami, Dallas and Los Angeles, where other people are waiting.

Assistants read the day's assignments and other possible stories: there may be a breakthrough in the Iranian stalemate, there is trouble in Turkey and Lebanon, and Richard Nixon is arriving in Manhattan. Most of the stories have already been scheduled or discussed, and the reading goes swiftly, with only an occasional comment from Senior Producer Richard Kaplan or from his boss, Executive Producer Jeff Gralnick, who is calling in from Washington today. "We want to get into Turkey and Beirut," says Gralnick, "and we want to do it soon." Kaplan replies: "We'll get on to it, Jeff," At 10:20 the meeting disbands.

In ABC's eight domestic and eleven foreign bureaus, correspondents and camera crews go off on their assignments. On any one day there are approximately 20 three- to six-person crews at work around the world. ABC News employs more than 800 people; CBS and NBC are still slightly larger, with about 1,000 employees each.

In New York, Kaplan and Senior Producer Walter Porges take seats around a horseshoe-shaped command post that they call the bridge. Phones are everywhere, and there are two TV screens connected to computers. Without even having to whirl to one side, they can find out the latest on stories or watch footage coming in from the "birds"—otherwise known as satellites. The atmosphere is decidely informal.

At about 3 P.M. the satellite feeds begin to come in from overseas. Most of them are routed through London, where Peter Jennings, one of the show's three anchormen, is always stationed to read foreign news. London is five hours ahead of New York, and Jennings has already taped his segments, which are fed, along with everything else, into a warren of machines in the basement of 7 West 66th. There sound is meshed with video. The recent purchase of new equipment has greatly speeded up the complicated mixing process. Nonetheless, there is a frantic rush each afternoon; everything must be ready by 6. The other networks offer their affiliates a choice of only a 6:30 or 7 P.M. broadcast, but since the days when it had to try harder, ABC has always given its stations three choices.

As taped reports come in, each correspondent's words are transcribed and sent to the bridge, where Kaplan and Porges look at them. If they feel something is missing or needs to be changed, they ask the correspondent to do the report over again. In today's lead story about the hostages, for

Electronic Media

instance, U.N. Correspondent Lou Cioffi has begun his report with an interview with Irish Statesman Séan McBride, who has been acting as a mediator. Kaplan thinks that McBride should go at the end of the piece, and the change is made.

The only domestic reporter who is not edited beforehand is White House Correspondent Sam Donaldson, or "Sudden Sam," as he is sometimes called because his taped reports come in so close to deadline. Today, for instance, Donaldson is so busy tracking down news of a possible hostage settlement with Iran that he does not finish taping his stand-up report from the White House lawn until two minutes before air time. Still, Donaldson has discussed his reports and has gone through a kind of verbal editing earlier in the day.

At five minutes to 6, the captains on the bridge pick up their papers and rush down to the control room in the basement, where seven or eight technicians are already in place. There, facing a wall of TV screens, they orchestrate the broadcast. Porges makes sure that each segment adheres to its time schedule. Because of commercials there are only 22 minutes for news in the half-hour broadcast, not a second more. If something runs long or short, the two domestic anchormen—Tom Jarriel in Chicago and Frank Reynolds in Washington—have been given compensating sentences they can drop or add. Kaplan gives them directions through their earphones.

The 6 o'clock broadcast is like an out-of-town tryout, and changes are always made for the next show at 6:30. Tonight Kaplan does not like a head shot of John Connally. "He looks like hell," he says, and a young woman runs to find one that is more flattering. He is also unhappy with a Washington report by Tim O'Brien about an FBI crackdown on pornography. Says he: "O'Brien needs another eight seconds." As a result of the change, a bit about flooding in Los Angeles is discarded.

Speaking directly to Jarriel, who has been recapping the day's events at the Winter Olympics, Kaplan tells him that he has, through an error in the copy, reduced the 1,500-meter women's speed-skating race to 15 meters; he is told to add another 1,485 meters at 6:30. Later, Kaplan tells Jarriel how he himself knew the difference. "I got a call from a redheaded fellow who cares about these things." Translation: News Head Roone Arledge had been watching in Lake Placid.

The 6:30 show is taped in its entirety, and if nothing else goes wrong, the tape is simply replayed at 7. Tonight's broadcast was good, but Max Robinson, who is subbing for Reynolds in Washington tonight, says that he misread his opening. Though nobody else had noticed, he forgot to say the word "near," as in "the framework of a plan to free the hostages is in place or near at hand." The mistake is not very important, but Robinson nonetheless goes live for the first few seconds of the third show to rectify the error.

At 7:30 everyone scatters; still that is not the end of Thursday's nightly news. At 10:15 the chief producers hold a conference call from their homes to review the show just finished and plan the one to follow. Tonight, for example, there are some harsh words about the O'Brien piece on pornography— "it didn't tell much about what happened," Kaplan says—and there are questions about why there was no report on a $700 million settlement that American Oil Co. made with the Government to satisfy price-gouging charges. The answer, that it was too complicated to explain in a brief time slot, satisfies no one. Yet Kaplan is happy with what he and his colleagues have done. "I'm pretty pleased," he says. And 17.6 million people who watched with him probably agreed.

It has not always been that way. For over a generation, since the mid-1950s when the evening news was a 15-minute dose of headlines, network news shows had been looked upon as loss leaders. They were like those items in a grocery store that sell below cost to entice us into the shop where we'll spend much more on junk food and impulse items. Because news cost more to make than it generated in advertising dollars, networks looked upon their unprofitable news operations as public service gestures, and affiliated stations considered them paramount in meeting their public interest, convenience, and necessity requirements.

But no longer. With today's audiences, networks can now get prime-time rates for the commercial minutes available on the newscasts. Advertisers are happy to cough up $30,000 to be on the *CBS Evening News* for a half minute, even though that amount is triple what they were paying for the same time in 1970. And CBS sells ten such spots each half hour, meaning $300,000 income for a newscast that the network figures will cost only half as much to produce. The show "60 Minutes," which moved to the top of the ratings in the late 1970s, cost CBS between $275,000 and $300,000 each week to produce, which was about half the cost of filming an hour of CBS's popular fictional program about the news business, the "Lou Grant Show." But with commercial time going for $150,000 a half minute, "60 Minutes" was bringing in several times as much in revenues as it was costing to produce.

In 1980 CBS, NBC, and ABC each spent around $130 million to produce their evening, weekend, morning, midday, late-night, and prime-time news shows, double the 1975 outlay. But those same shows brought in far more dollars in advertising. In 1979, for instance, they generated $488 million from commercials. Some $138 million of that income went to the advertising agencies and to local affiliates to compensate them for carrying the programs. The $50 million left over was pure profit for the networks. Walter Cronkite's show, the "CBS Evening News," was the biggest money maker, netting $28 million in profits.[17]

Network news is big business indeed. CBS and NBC news divisions each employ about 1,000 people, and ABC has more than 800. The few members of those cadres seen by America each night, the anchorpersons, are stars in their own rights, demanding and receiving star salaries. When Walter Cronkite announced his retirement as CBS anchor, Dan Rather, the man with the inside track to the title of "America's most trusted man," was wooed by ABC and NBC as well. Each network recognized the dollar value of a noted anchor who could raise ratings, so each offered him an $8 million, five-year contract. He accepted the CBS offer, as all America knows. Surprisingly, there was less public outcry at the marketing of Rather than there was in 1976 when Barbara Walters was lured away from NBC by a million dollar a year offer from ABC to read the evening news and conduct interviews. Perhaps news critics finally recognized the influence of the anchorperson in attracting an audience. One *Journalism Monograph* study of network news viewing found that 41 percent of the viewers selected their news program on the basis of the anchorperson's personality and characteristics, 28 percent on the basis of channel, 9 percent on the basis of news quality or program format, and 22 percent on the basis of other or no particular reasons.[18] Other studies reveal similar, though not always as drastic, breakdowns.

Selecting an appealing anchor is only one of the commercial considerations made by network and local news operations. Some observers maintain that nearly all management and news gatekeeping decisions on television are made with an eye on the ratings. Consider the following:

TV News: Criticisms and Problems

Even in the news departments, ratings dictate gatekeeping behavior.

To attract the largest possible viewership, news presentation formulas are drawn up with firm clarity and adhered to rigidly. Style, form, shape, time of presentation, length of treatment, and sequence of presentation are all determined by pecuniary considerations. The multiplicity of possible news items accumulating throughout a day is whittled down and winnowed out by selection, editing, and inference designed to entertain rather than enlighten. To fit within the limited time frame left after the commercials are accommodated, most occurrences are reduced to mere headlines. Such processes distort perceptions of the world and its events for those who have come to rely on television as their primary source of news. And there is evidence that this proportion of the populace is increasing.[19]

We select the above indictment not necessarily because it is unusually severe and caustic, but because in a few words it summarizes many of the criticisms being leveled against TV news, although it may be overstated. Most television news reporters and editors publicly bristle at such comments, maintaining that news decisions are based on firm principles of journalism and a deep sense of obligation to the swelling ranks of television news viewers. Financial considerations are the concerns of network executives and station managers, and time and space and technological logistics are problems for the journalists, the gatekeepers maintain.[20] The truth, as in many such debates, probably lies somewhere between the extremes. Nonetheless, we can be certain that time, space, technology, and economics are the individual and collective tyrants in television news broadcasting.

Time, space, technology, and economics tyrannize TV news.

Television news has justifiably been called controlled pandemonium. This is because, from the viewers' perspective, television news is conveyed in palatable and readily digestible chunks by seemingly unflappable reporters and anchors. What the viewers don't see is the madness that goes on behind the scenes, where producers, editors, floor directors, camera operators, technicians, and other off-camera personnel rush frantically to package the events of the day.

Newscasts are tyrannized by the clock. In twenty-four or twenty-five minutes (once commercial time is excluded) the networks attempt to package the events that the reporters and camera personnel have recorded and the editors have judged newsworthy. This is a daily process that begins each morning when assignments are made to correspondents and reports are submitted from the various bureaus. Each network maintains offices in major American cities and in ten or more foreign cities, where on any one day the network will have approximately twenty three-to-six-person crews at work. Not all of the reports prepared during the day will be telecast and most will be edited to fit the exceedingly tight schedule.

Rare is the story that receives more than three minutes; more typical is the sixty-to-ninety-second report, which equates to between 200 and 300 words, or a couple of newspaper paragraphs. Therefore the visual messages have to carry a heavy burden of information. As many television news critics—including Walter Cronkite—have observed, the script from a typical network newscast will not even cover the front page of a newspaper, so viewers should not assume they have meaningfully absorbed current events. (Such awareness, however, never stopped Cronkite from ending his newscasts with a sonorous "And that's the way it is. . . .")

Another tyrant is the visual aspect of television. In the 1950s the camera tended to focus exclusively on the newscaster who reported the news to viewers. It is not difficult to understand how this drab style got the name "talking head." And it is not surprising that today newscasts succeed or fail on the basis of their film or videotape coverage. This makes the camera an arbiter of what is newsworthy. If a camera crew can get to an event, shoot it, and relay the film or tape to the station in time for the newscast, then the event is newsworthy. If not, it isn't.[21] Electronic newsgathering

Lightweight, portable TV cameras bring the viewer closer to the action.
Wide World Photos

equipment (ENG), including microwave and satellite transmission from camera to station, has made the process almost instantaneous in recent years. But the crews still must be at an event in order to record it. That truism means that events rather than underlying issues dominate television news, and that the predictable events—those to which reporters and cameras can be assigned in advance—stand the greatest chance of being covered. As sociologist Herbert Gans concluded in his study of national news coverage, anticipated stories provide a predictable supply of potentially suitable news, with access and availability made certain in advance.[22] The result is a variety of pseudoevents—political speeches, press conferences, and meetings—and other prescheduled activities of all kinds and shapes. Veteran politicians and lobbyists have long known how to play to television's attraction for the predictable and visual. Newcomers to the publicity business may initially object to such manipulation, but they either quickly adapt or are never heard from again. In their defense, it should be said that reporters and photographers have learned some lessons since the 1960s, when on more than one occasion they were bid to cover a demonstration and told it would be aired whenever they could get their cameras to the scene.

TV news occurs where cameras are. Pseudoevents abound.

Critics question whether TV allows a spontaneous, natural event to become news.
Wide World Photos

Part of the spatial tyranny is the location of camera crews. Since equipment and personnel are so expensive, networks and stations are limited in the number of crews they can support. Therefore the crews are placed where news is most likely to happen: Washington, D.C. for political news, New York City for economic news, Chicago for "heart of America" news (whatever that means), London for international news, and so on. News teams are assigned for practical, economic purposes to these major centers, despite the fact that the networks like to leave us with the impression they are covering the entire country and world.[23]

Location of camera crews and reporters is a temporal as well as a spatial tyranny. To appear on the early evening newscasts televised from the East Coast, "reportable" events on the West Coast must occur before noon and those on the East Coast no later than early afternoon. As with newspapers, networks have to plan early in the day for their news outputs, and the closer it gets to deadline, the less chance there is for events to be covered.

Although our discussion emphasizes network news, we cannot avoid mention of the significance of packaging in newscasting. At most stations the newscast is the most profitable locally produced show, which means the station is willing to invest in the maintenance and improvement of the program. Nowhere in recent years have media consultants been as evident to the casual media observer as in local television news. National consulting firms such as McHugh and Hoffman, Inc., of MacLean, Virginia, and Frank Magid Associates of Marion, Iowa, have significantly affected television news in America. For somewhere between $10,000 and $50,000, depending upon their market size, stations have been purchasing from the consultants insights into viewer preferences about anchorpersons, story types, tastes in weather and sports news, and even set design. The results of such studies, of course, are taken most seriously by lower-rated stations, who are quick to fire an anchor, hire a new and more psychographically and demographically appealing one, and rearrange the furniture. Formulas result: "Action News," "Eyewitness News," "News From the Newsroom," and the like, are packaged as neatly and uniformly as McDonald's and Kentucky Fried Chicken food chains. Entertainment, not information, becomes the overriding emphasis, because entertainment is inherent in the medium and because the consultants, whose backgrounds are in marketing, not in news, are hired by management, not by news editors.

In summarizing how temporal, spatial, technological, and judgmental factors affect television news, critics Mankiewicz and Swerdlow have written that some informal unacknowledged laws of television news have developed:

Unattractive faces are almost never on camera in "good guy" roles; a fire at night will almost always be shown though an equally serious daytime fire won't; every news story must be complete within one minute and fifteen seconds, unless the program is doing an "in-depth" treatment, in which case one minute and forty-five seconds may be permitted. All this has led to an overriding law—The

News consultants doctor up local news shows. Entertainment, not information, rules the day.

Salt Lake City's KSL-TV anchors Shelly Thomas and Dick Nourse face the cameras and begin their nightly newscast while weatherman Bob Welti, off camera, has a couple of minutes to put on his makeup and comb his hair (top). The TV news control booth, where most of the decisions about the show's pace and visual impact are made, is a scene of controlled pandemonium (bottom left). The TV newsroom, where dozens of reporters work on their assignments. Many of these journalists will rarely be seen by the audience (bottom right). Jay Black

Trivial Will Always Drive Out the Serious. There are other limitations and strictures. A story with film, for example, will almost always take precedence over one that must be read from the anchor desk or reported in a "stand-up" on the spot. If there is film, the action film will almost always replace the film that includes only a conversation or a discussion— "talking heads" are to be avoided if there's any possible way.[24]

What does this mean to the viewer? Does television's preference for the visual mean that broadcast news is geared to the emotional rather than the intellectual level? Does the emphasis on action rather than thought, happenings rather than concepts, protagonists rather than underlying issues, mean that television news is devoid of explanation and background and is therefore only comprehensible to the already well-informed members of the public? Is it possible, as Stanley and Ramsey insist, that most television news reporting does little, if anything, to develop audiences' potential to analyze, think independently, or learn from grasping overall social patterns in the unfolding of events?[25]

Critics of television news will receive little comfort from Dr. Jacob Jacoby of Purdue University or the American Association of Advertising Agencies. Dr. Jacoby's studies indicate that viewers routinely misinterpret between one-quarter and one-third of any broadcast, whether it is news, entertainment, or commercials. Facts as well as inferences become muddled by serious and casual viewers alike. And the AAAA study reveals that the vast majority of television viewers, more than 90 percent, misunderstand at least part of whatever kind of programming they watch.[26]

Questions raised by critics, and insights gained from empirical research, are provocative. In the meantime, many observers are accepting the conclusions of the Roper surveys at face value: that two-thirds of America's adults receive most of their world news from television; that half the population says television is its *sole* source of news; that most find television news more believable than any other source; and that a good percentage of them rely on television news because it is more convenient and requires less effort than any other media.

Show biz notwithstanding, TV news is the window to the world for most Americans.

Television Criticism

Television seems to have become the medium Americans love to hate. Criticism of television is as common as the many nicknames we have devised to describe it—the boob tube, the idiot box, and the one-eyed monster, for example. And yet we continue to watch television, even as we complain about it.

In 1938, E. B. White looked into the future and predicted that television would be the test of the modern world in which "we shall discover either a new and unbearable disturbance of the general peace or a saving radiance in the sky."[27] Perhaps television has brought us a little of each.

Other writers during the 1930s and 1940s were also willing to take a stand regarding television; many of them sided with Lee De Forest, who envisioned an enlightened populace dedicated to a strong home life: "Into such a picture ideally adapted to the benefits and physical limitations of television, this new magic will enter and become a vital element of the daily life."[28]

And it was magic to America recovering from the depression and World War II. People wanted to be entertained by the new medium and even the critics seemed optimistic. Television was often described in terms of its potential for good. In 1952 the National Association of Broadcasters revised the television code to encourage innovative programming that would deal with significant moral and social issues. This did happen, of course, but more often the viewer turned to "Queen for a Day," a shlocky show in which the contestant with the most pathetic hard-luck story won cash and prizes.

Edward R. Murrow described the paradox of television:

This instrument can teach, it can illuminate; yes, and it can even inspire. But it can do so only to the extent that humans are determined to use it to those ends. Otherwise it is merely wires and lights in a box. There is a great and perhaps decisive battle to be fought against ignorance, intolerance and indifference. This weapon of television could be useful.[29]

Earlier in his speech Murrow had commented on the "decadence and escapism" of television and how the medium provided "insulation from the realities of the world."[30] The potential of television, said the critics, had yet to be achieved.

Those who wanted television to become a medium for enlightenment became increasingly discouraged during the 1960s. FCC Chairman Newton Minnow acknowledged that "when television is good, nothing is better," and then added, "but when television is bad, nothing is worse."[31] And many were saying that much of what television offered was bad.

At one time television promised to be the saving radiance that even educators believed would improve the learning of children. But in the last two decades, writers and critics have faulted television, asserting that television perpetuates dependency in children and that, in the words of Dean George Gerbner, "it has profoundly affected what we call the process of socialization, the process by which members of our species become human."[32]

Recall the statistics cited in the introduction to this chapter, especially those that pertain to the number of hours children watch television. Consider the 350,000 commercial messages and the 18,000 televised murders. The evidence in support of Dean Gerbner's assertion is substantial.

The criticism has become sharper, sometimes shrill; and the defenders have become less vocal. Sander Vanocur has pointed out that "Television is in danger of becoming a whipping boy . . . a convenient scapegoat upon which we can . . . dump our frustrations."[33] Other defenders have expressed similar sentiments.

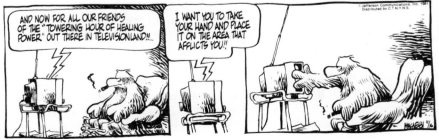

Peggy Charren, director of ACT: Action for Children's Television, the foremost TV watchdog group.
Martha Stewart/The Picture Cube

At a meeting of the Radio and Television Society in 1977, Fred Silverman, then president of ABC entertainment, denied that television should lift the public to a higher level of aesthetic appreciation. Said Mr. Silverman, "At ABC our primary programming objective is to entertain."[34]

Some critics in the early 1980s said television entertains in an inappropriate way and others said television does not entertain at all. Those who saw it as inappropriate, such as the Moral Majority and the National Federation for Decency, charged that the content of television, particularly sex and violence, was a destructive force in society. A 1981 threat to boycott manufacturers of products advertised on programs considered offensive seemed to have an impact as early as the fall of that year.

Evidence that television fails to entertain has been provided by two researchers in Massachusetts. They had thought that watching existing shows produced a high level of attention, but when they attached electrodes to the heads of children and adults who were viewing television, the researchers found the subjects' output of alpha or sleep waves increased. Instead of high stimulation the kids were almost in an "alpha trance."[35]

Is passivity the ultimate promise of television? To reach that conclusion one would have to overlook the variety and vitality that television now offers, and to ignore the continuing potential for television, especially now that it is being reformed by the impact of cable television and new technology.

Summary

Television has become part of the American way of life. More than any other medium it has infiltrated the lives of its audience. Television's almost instantaneous capacity and almost total saturation of nearly 98 percent of America's homes makes it enormously time-consuming, averaging daily nearly seven hours per household.

Ratings are important to television. They measure the total size of the audience and each network's share of that audience during any given time slot, both of which are important to advertisers. Recently ratings have also delved into demography as advertisers devote more attention to the young and affluent. Women, too, who control most purchasing and who comprise at least half of all audiences, are also important to advertisers.

Programming is dictated by ratings as programmers at major networks jockey for position in the various time slots across the prime-time board. Selections are made for the presumed lowest common denominator of taste. The least objectionable program (lop) concept contends that television is habit-forming and that people will watch regardless of what is presented, choosing only the least objectionable of what is on at any given time. Consequently, the gatekeepers of television have a complex task: They must second guess their publics and at the same time program against what they think the other networks are scheduling for the same time slots.

Television production costs are enormous. The networks spend more than $39 million per week for prime-time programming. Some hour-long shows cost $650,000 to produce, or about $10,000 per minute on the average. Costs keep rising, and the networks more and more frequently attempt to extend the lives of their investments by running repeats.

Research into the nature of the television viewing audience offers many intriguing insights. On any given evening, half the American public is likely to be found in front of the set. Networks understand the demographic profiles of addicts, occasional watchers, and selective watchers, and they program accordingly. While most viewers are satisfied with television, there has been increasing skepticism about the experience in recent years.

Advertising is the dominant factor in television. Advertisers deal in minutes and homes. Advertising minutes have far greater potential for both frequency and reach into homes than do sponsorships. Advertising is sold on the basis of cost per thousand (cpm), based on exposure to each one thousand homes. At today's rates, commercials are probably the most expensively produced media fare. Recently, the half-minute commercial has dominated, but indications are that shorter commercials, including ten-second spots, will be used more frequently, although at some cost in effectiveness and viewer satisfaction.

By the beginning of the 1980s, network news programs more than paid their own way, after a generation as showcase loss leaders. CBS, NBC, and ABC each spent some $130 million on news in 1980, and all three were willing to offer Dan Rather an $8 million, five-year package to anchor their evening newscasts. The offers were logical, since most viewers select their news stations on the basis of the anchor's appeal rather than on the quality of the news. Network news has been criticized for keeping one eye on the ratings, but it is equally plagued by the tyrannies of time, space, and technology. Because television has become an entertainment medium, television news has also maintained entertainment overtones.

The criticisms leveled at television are legion. It is accused of being bland, inoffensive, uninteresting, preoccupied with violence and sex, catering to the lowest common denominator while avoiding cultural uplift, and never realizing its full potential as a social instrument. It has been accused of almost everything currently wrong with the family, particularly children, and is said to be amoral and motivated solely by profit. Defenders suggest that we recognize the commercial nature of the beast and learn to use it wisely to serve our needs, not the medium's. Broadcast reform groups are proliferating, offering parents and communities vehicles to cope with the powerful medium.

Notes

1. George Comstock, *Television in America* (Beverly Hills, Calif.: SAGE Publications, 1980), pp. 33-34.
2. Tom Jory, "PBS and Corporate Underwriting," *Salt Lake Tribune,* 28 May 1978.
3. A. C. Nielsen Company, "Audience Research," ed. Craig T. Norback and Peter G. Norback, *TV Guide Almanac* (New York: Ballantine Books, 1980), pp. 70–74.
4. "ABC Evening News," November 7, 1977.
5. Les Brown, *Keeping Your Eye on Television* (New York: The Pilgrim Press, 1979), p. 12.
6. Robert B. Choate, *New York Times,* 17 September 1972.
7. Anthony Cook, "The Peculiar Economics of Television," *TV Guide,* 14 June 1980, p. 4.
8. Ibid., pp. 4–10.
9. Muriel G. Cantor, *Prime-Time Television: Content and Control* (Beverly Hills, Calif.: SAGE Publications, 1980, p. 73.
10. Brown, *Keeping Your Eye on Television,* p. 24.
11. Ibid.
12. Gary A. Steiner, *The People Look at Television* (New York: Knopf, 1963); and Robert T. Bower, *Television and the Public* (New York: Holt, Rinehart & Winston, 1973).
13. Jonathan Price, *The Best Thing on TV: Commercials* (New York: Penguin Books, 1978), p. 109.
14. Otto Kleppner, *Advertising Procedure,* 7th ed. (Englewood Cliffs, N.J.; Prentice-Hall, Inc., 1979), p. 118.
15. Martin Mayer, *About Television* (New York: Harper & Row, Publishers, 1972).
16. "The New Face of TV News," *Time,* 25 February 1980, p. 65.
17. Alan Pearce, "How the Networks Have Turned News Into Dollars," *TV Guide,* 23 August 1980, pp. 7–12.
18. Mark R. Levy, "The Audience Experience with Television News," *Journalism Monographs,* no. 55, April 1978, p. 7.
19. Robert H. Stanley and Ruth G. Ramsey, "Television News: Format as a Form of Censorship," *ETC,* Winter 1978, p. 433.
20. Herbert J. Gans, *Deciding What's News: A Study of CBS Evening News, NBC Nightly News, Newsweek and Time* (New York: Vintage Books, 1980).

21. Frank Mankiewicz and Joel Swerdlow, *Remote Control: Television and the Manipulation of American Life* (New York: Ballantine Books, 1978), p. 99.
22. Gans, *Deciding What's News,* pp. 87–88.
23. Edward Jay Epstein, *News From Nowhere* (New York: Random House, 1973).
24. Mankiewicz and Swerdlow, *Remote Control,* pp. 97–98.
25. Stanley and Ramsey, "Television News," pp. 433–34.
26. Ron Powers, "Where Have the News Analysts Gone?" *TV Guide,* 8 October 1980, pp. 5–6.
27. E. B. White, *The New Yorker,* 1938.
28. Lee De Forest, *Television: Today and Tomorrow* (New York: Dial Plan, 1942).
29. Edward R. Murrow, addressing the Radio Televison News Directors Association, 15 October 1958.
30. *Ibid.*
31. FCC Chairman Newton Minnow, addressing the National Association of Broadcasters, 9 May 1961.
32. Dr. George Gerbner, Dean of the Anneberg School of Communications at the University of Pennsylvania, testifying before the National Commission on the Causes and Prevention of Violence, 1969.
33. Sander Vanocur, *Washington Post,* 1975.
34. Jerry Kerporick, *Newhouse News Writer,* 14 November 1977.
35. "Learning to Live with TV," *Time,* 28 May 1979.

8 The New Electronics

The offspring of network television are many and varied, and are changing so rapidly that much of what we write about them will be subject to change before this book is off the press. But it is necessary to describe their development and modestly forecast their future impact, for they are bound to become as significant as film, radio, and television are among the mass media.

In this chapter we will consider community antenna television (CATV); subscription and pay TV; satellite communications; interactive two-way television; videodiscs and videocassette recorders; microcomputers and the home communications center; and teletext and videotex, the latest phase of what some observers call the era of neovideo. We have included mechanics as well as contents in our discussion, noting their impact upon established media, especially network and independent television services, and upon society.

Introduction

Significant offshoots of TV are cable, pay TV, videodiscs and videocassettes, satellite communications, microcomputers and the home communications center, and teletext and videotex.

Satellite (top). Viewers can now talk back to their TV sets (bottom). Robert V. Eckert, Jr./EKM-Nepenthe (top); Tom Ballard/EKM/Nepenthe (bottom)

Our discussion of these media is tempered by recognition of economic, technological, social, and regulatory realities. Technology exceeds adaptation, and new communications forms are constantly confronted before the old have been mastered. Economically, the investments required to install and perfect new systems are massive and may even lie beyond the grasp of our affluent society.

But the new electronics are already with us, and we do ourselves a disservice if we fail to come to grips with them.

Cable Television: The Wired Nation?

Cable TV's new role lies in programming, business data transfer, and interactive communication. Its recent growth rate is impressive.

When community antenna television (CATV, more commonly called cable) was first introduced in 1950, it was perceived as a way to bring clear reception to isolated regions. The television signal, which travels in a straight line, could not reach into the valleys of eastern Pennsylvania, where the first cable was installed. Now, however, cable has invaded the cities and suburbs in an altered form. Cable still provides sharp pictures but its appeal and its future are in the opportunities for programming, business data transfer, and interactive communication.

Over-the-air television is forever restricted to the available VHF and UHF frequencies, while many cable systems offer sixty-four clear channels (and some twice that), which increases the likelihood of more specialized programming, including all news stations, weather stations, sports stations, religious stations, and so on. In addition, some cable systems have the capacity to deliver specialized messages to individual viewers seeking business data, electronic mail delivery, banking, medical advice, and a wide variety of specialized information.

Television of the future, the wired nation, and other optimistic terms used to describe cable convey an almost science-fiction quality to the potential of the medium. Consider the following:

The *Time* magazine cover story for 7 May 1979 noted that cable TV was reaching about one-fifth of the national television audience, with the numbers growing so rapidly that Young & Rubicam (the advertising agency) was predicting that almost one of three TV households would be on cable by 1981.

Tom Wheeler, president of the National Cable Television Association, was quoted in late 1979 as saying that the number of homes connected to the cable was increasing about 2 percent annually, and that probably no more than 40 percent of American homes would ever be signed up. Less than a year later, in August 1980, he told the Cable Television Administration and Marketing Society that there would be 45 million subscribers by 1990 and that revenues by that time would be at the $14 billion mark, seven times the 1980 income.

Broadcasting, the trade weekly, said on 1 September 1980 that by 1990 cable would be connecting from 36 to 50 percent of American television homes. Others—including manufacturers, advertisers, program developers, and academics—have estimated that by 1990 nine out of ten American homes will be wired for cable, and one-fifth of the homes will be rigged for two-way interactive communications.

Still others are predicting that cable's day has already come and gone, that the cumbersome and expensive coaxial cable is going to be supplanted by direct satellite-to-home communication systems before the end of the decade.

What's the story? Is cable the medium of the 1980s? Predictions for cable's phenomenal growth have been occurring since 1971, when visions of "the wired nation" were commonly expressed by communications experts. Now, more than a decade later, many parts of the country are still without cable service, despite a phenomenal growth spurt in cable since the late 1970s. As this book goes to press, around 29 percent of American residences are being served by some 5,500 different cable systems; those 23 million subscribers represent a five-fold increase over the numbers served a decade earlier. Although a tad below *Time's* 1979 predictions, the numbers demonstrate a significant enough growth to justify the National Cable Television Association's claim that cable has come of age. See table 8.1, "Growth of cable television in the United States, 1952–1982."

The potentials of cable stem from the fact that it can both boost and import existing over-the-air broadcast as well as originate its own programming. Because it is wired like a telephone, it can be as individually selective as a telephone and yet utilize telephone's two-way capacity. These obvious assets, combined with the computer, impart a Buck Rogers aspect to the future of cable. Furthermore, because it is video, it holds the potential for facsimile reproduction, which means it can duplicate written materials in the home—including newspapers, specialized reports, and the like.

Cable imports, boosts, and originates programming.

Table 8.1 Growth of cable television in the United States, 1952–1982

Year	Number of systems	Number of subscribers (add 000)	Percent of TV homes with cable
1952	10	14	0.1
1955	400	150	0.5
1960	640	650	1.4
1965	1,325	1,275	2.4
1970	2,490	4,500	7.6
1975	3,506	9,800	14.3
1980	4,200	15,500	20.0
1982*	5,500	23,700	29.0

Sources: *Television Digest;* A. C. Nielsen; *TV Guide.*

*Preliminary figures

The computer capacity lends itself to information retrieval from memory banks that can either be flashed on the screen or reproduced in facsimile for the record.

Cable's growth has been stunted by costs, human nature, FCC rules, competition, and economics.

Does it sound exciting? Well, there are problems. Costs, human nature, FCC regulation, competition, and economics have deterred cable's progress. Ironically, one of its greatest strengths has proven to be its stumbling block: Cable is so versatile that it may easily be in competition with itself.

Consider, for example, that there are over 5,500 cable systems in the United States. Each of these is a little network that splinters the market to the point where none can develop an effective mass. When the audience numbers are not there, neither is the money for programming. Consider further that the majority of these new systems are not located in major population centers where the largest audiences are found. Rather, they are located in smaller cities and even rural communities where cable's ability to increase the fidelity of over-air broadcast is an asset. In these areas cable's primary use is to provide interconnection with one or more of the commercial networks.

Cable has only recently begun to prove profitable in the largest cities. Back in 1966, the FCC prohibited cable from operating in the largest markets until UHF reached its potential. In view of UHF's erratic performance and the considerable amount of pressure under which it operates, the FCC in 1971 decided to permit cable operators to wire the largest markets. In these markets, however, broadcast competition is intense. For instance, in the early 1970s, when cable was allowed back into the marketplace, New York City had eight channels, and Los Angeles had eleven. Although cable provides residents of some cities a clearer picture, there was little incentive to add cable unless it could offer vastly superior or unique programming. But at a cost of some $100,000 to lay underground cable in a metropolis, cash-short cable systems had little capability of producing anything that would have major appeal. They were forced into situations of bidding with the networks for first-run movies, talent, and the like, but they lacked the funds and audiences. To become viable, the metropolitan cable systems needed a gimmick or two. Toward the end of the 1970s, they began to discover those gimmicks in pay-cable feature films and sports events. And, as the 1980s got underway, large market systems started looking to their two-way capacity and appeal to special-interest groups as a way to carve out their place in the telecommunications environment.

Advertisers Take Note

Today, after several false starts, cable television appears ready to become a significant mass medium. Industry observers have long maintained that 30 percent of America's homes have to be connected to the cable before it can become a medium of any real importance. Thirty percent, they noted, was the magic number of television homes needed before national advertisers responded in 1949, and 30 percent was the number of color sets in use before advertisers began producing commercials in color. By that measurement, cable TV is just about where commercial network TV was in the 1950s.

Advertisers have begun to show fascination with cable's potential. Multimillion dollar ad packages have been put together for the largest cable networks: Bristol-Myers committed $25 million over a ten-year period to the Cable News Network; Budweiser has been spending the same amount in only a five-year period on the Entertainment and Sports Programming Network (ESPN); and Timex expects its $22 million ad package with ESPN to be a profitable venture. Nevertheless, when compared with commercial network advertising, these figures are small potatoes. Commercials carried over the largest cable networks in the first three months of 1982 brought in $498 per minute, compared with the $46,885 per minute that conventional networks charged.[1]

At current rates, advertisers find it attractive to sponsor entire programs, in ways reminiscent of network television in the 1950s. In so doing they can also experiment with commercial formats. Due to the nature of the medium, cable commercials need not be limited to the standard thirty- or sixty-second modes. Already there are experiments with commercial "mini-programs" of several minutes in length. They constitute fewer interruptions of the programs, on the premise that people paying for viewing CATV expect something different from the din of commercial networks. Of course, many cable systems have merely adopted the tried-and-true routines of the commercial nets, repeating the familiar pattern of new media being put to old uses.

Because cable audiences tend to be younger, better educated, and more affluent than noncable audiences, advertisers have something over which to drool. And the tastes of cable audiences, especially those on interactive cable systems, are easier to pinpoint, since much of cable's programming is specialized. This helps create an advertiser's dream, in which audiences' demographic and psychographic characteristics are available and somewhat predictable, and in which there are fewer wasted impressions or ad messages reaching unintended audiences. Finally, given that cable audiences are smaller in size than network ones, the costs per commercial minute are lower, and at this time remain within the reach of smaller advertisers.[2] Basically, cable has the same appeal to advertisers as do radio and magazines.

The Media React

One way of knowing when a new mass medium is to be taken seriously is to notice the reactions of the established media. In the case of cable television, its time must be at hand. The networks and television programmers, including cinema programmers, have begun to react, either by complaining about cable's incursion into their territory or more importantly by quietly going about grabbing a piece of the cable action.

As the federal government took steps to increase cable's access to programming, by granting cable operators the right to pick up as many signals as they want from distant cities and relay them to local subscribers, predictable reactions came from the National Association of Broadcasters (NAB), the Motion Picture Association of America (MPAA), and the Association of Independent Television Stations (AITS). The establishment argued that cable was getting something for nothing, that the infant industry hadn't had to pay its dues before starting to reap the heady profits possible in telecommunications.[3]

Meanwhile, back at corporate headquarters, several communications giants responded to the unfairness of it all by joining the cable bandwagon, buying into the bonanza.

Time Inc. owns the nation's largest pay-TV company, Home Box Office, as well as several regional franchises. American Express has bought into Warner Communications' cable operation, creating Warner Amex Cable. CBS Cable, the new unit of the Columbia Broadcasting System, was cancelled in late 1982 after a year and a half of financial losses, and ABC ARTS Cable Service have committed time, talent, and resources to bringing fine arts programming to affluent audiences. In the largest merger in the history of U.S. communications companies, the Westinghouse Electronic Corporation purchased the Teleprompter Corporation for $646 million in 1981. The Hearst corporation, known for its newspaper and magazine holdings, was reaching over 5 million homes each afternoon with "Hearst/ABC Daytime," aimed at a female audience. Walt Disney's company has been putting together a G-rated entertainment programming package to go on the air in 1983. Dow Jones, owner of the *Wall Street Journal* and other information services, has gone into the cable business via both land lines and satellite, bringing business news, stock quotes, and other information to customers upon demand. And American Telephone and Telegraph ("Ma Bell"), the largest corporation in the world, has been fighting a running battle with the government and existing communications systems over its rights to enter the cable market as either an information provider or merely a hardware and electronics service. Others, too numerous to mention and moving too rapidly to keep track of, have made cable television an industry worth following on the stock market. Keeping up with cable stocks is a dizzying proposition, but speculators are counting on the industry to continue its recent growth patterns.

Businesses eyeing cable are not limiting themselves to earning profits from entertainment alone. Market researchers expect cable revenues to be split equally among entertainment, business data, and other transaction services (mail, electronic newspapers, etc.) before the end of the 1980s. Local "loop market" revenues—including electronic mail, word processing, and teleconferencing—could become a $1.875 billion a year industry. Considering the fact that one in twenty-five office employees in 1982 had access to computer terminals (the ratio is expected to be one terminal for every 3.5 employees by 1990), the marriage of business and cable appears recession-proof.[4]

Electronic Media

Meanwhile, however, cable has tended to develop as a small duplicate of commercial television. Like most media that initially adapt older media contents to new media mechanics, cable has borrowed indiscriminately from commercial television's programming practices. A massive nationwide study, conducted in 1980, noted that 70 percent of U.S. cable systems were offering some form of local programming. This was an increase over earlier years, but before we conclude that it is a step in the right direction, we should look at the forms those local programs are taking. While 15 percent of the total available channels were devoted to locally originated programming, much of that number consisted of message-service channels, classified advertising channels, stock-market reports, sports news roundups, and television listings. Few systems were offering their own newscasts, and much of the local programming was being done by volunteers and students. One of the major areas of local programming was coverage of local high school, college, or community athletic events. The nationwide study also revealed a solid increase in the number of public-access channels (channels set aside for use by the public at a nominal charge), and additional political cablecasting on all levels.[5] Since the FCC forbids any program interference on the part of the cable operator with public-access programming, the result has been some very strange programming—pressing, in many instances, against the boundaries of both credibility and taste. This has done little for the cable's public image and scarcely constitutes a sales tool for potential subscribers.

In a familiar pattern, the new medium borrows its content from the old media—TV services cable.

Cable is the basic delivery system for which people pay an initial connection charge and a monthly fee. Pay TV is a different matter; generally, it is a part of the cable delivery system and involves additional charges for viewing selected programs. It has been a controversial issue since the FCC started considering it in 1955. Supporters claim it provides movies, sports, culture, travel, nostalgia, the esoteric, and self-improvement (all without commercial interruptions) that even mass-appeal, sponsor-supported free TV cannot bring. Opponents counter that pay TV, seeking maximum profits, woos the same mass audiences as free TV and buys off the same audience-pleasing attractions, leaving the wealthier public to pay for the same entertainment it has always gotten free, and the poorer public with nothing. While the old arguments continue, the pay-TV business has been burgeoning at exponential rates.

During the 1960s, pay television soaked up millions of dollars and shattered a lot of business hopes due to engineering, programming, and marketing difficulties. But having to endure rigorous regulation by the FCC and bitter opposition from broadcasters and motion picture operators who sensed in pay TV a serious threat to their livelihoods was only one of its problems. It wasn't until the late 1970s, about the same time satellite transmission became feasible, that the regulatory climate turned in favor of cable delivery and the pay-TV programmers. Once the FCC decided to allow

Subscription or Pay TV

Pay TV raises questions about a nation of cultural "haves" and "have nots."

Only recently has governmental policy favored pay TV.

cable companies to import distant programs merely by paying small royalties to the program owners and no payments to the stations or network airing the programs, cable TV and its stepchild, pay TV, were off and running.

In 1976 some 978,000 households received pay TV. The numbers increased to 13.5 million households within six years, and developers were maintaining that technology for further expansion was only beginning to be exploited. While pay-TV homes were still only a small percentage of the 81 million total television homes in America in 1982, most signs point toward continued growth. That is because pay TV is inexorably linked to the rapid development of cable, satellite, and in-home computerized communications, and to the federal government's spirit of broadcast deregulation.

Pay cable, subscription TV (STV), and Multipoint Distribution Service (MDS)—pay TV is off and running.

Three methods for providing pay TV to audiences are *pay cable*, over-the-air pay TV, known as *subscription television (STV)*, and *Multipoint Distribution Service (MDS)*.

Pay cable enables families who receive the regular cable services to pay an additional monthly charge to receive special channels of programs such as those from Home Box Office and Showtime. Most companies charge a flat monthly rate of $8 to $10 to their cable customers who wish to receive the films, sporting events, or other noncommercial specials offered. One study showed that only 40 percent of cable subscribers elect not to take the available pay-TV channel because of the added cost.[6]

Subscription television differs from pay cable in its use of over-the-air rather than cable transmission. STV systems use earth stations to pick up satellite-generated signals, then rebroadcast them to their subscribers. STV, which began in earnest in 1977, was available in eight major markets by the beginning of the 1980s, serving a half-million households and generating revenues in excess of $120 million annually. With another 100 or so STV applications on file with the FCC, forecasters predicted that by the end of 1983 STV would be reaching half the nation's TV households and generating a billion dollars a year in revenues. Rinaldo Brutoco, president of Universal Subscription Television and chairman of a newly formed association of subscription TV companies, said STV would soon incorporate such nonvideo services as electronic mail, newspapers, magazines, shopping and games, home security, and educational opportunities. It is the job of subscription television "to marry sophisticated technological intelligence to that humble cathode-ray tube to make true consumer choice possible," he maintained.[7]

The third form of pay TV, Multipoint Distribution Service (MDS), is a variation of over-the-air television, using a microwave signal to transmit pay programs, generally to a master antenna serving a motel or apartment building, and occasionally to an entire city (Sacramento, California, for example), but increasingly to single family dwellings. MDS operators can get into the business for about $250,000 to $500,000, the cost of a

Multipoint Distribution
Service (MDS) antenna
at a condominium
complex.
Robert V. Eckert/EKM-
Nepenthe

satellite earth station, allowing them to pick up pay-TV signals from else-where and relay them via microwave to rooftop receivers in a twenty-five to fifty-mile radius. Since rooftop receivers have dropped in cost from $1,500 to $85, such services are no longer limited to the wealthy. A study by the National Association of Broadcasters has concluded that MDS probably will not be a major factor in the long-term war for paying customers, both because cable television is growing more rapidly and because individual homes will soon be sprouting their own satellite receiving dishes for not much more than the cost they're now paying for an antenna that picks up the MDS microwave signal. In short, the MDS operators' primary function of receiving the satellite feeds and relaying them for a price to homeowners would become obsolete.

Regardless of the receiving system involved, pay-TV customers have shown a preference for paying a flat monthly fee rather than on a pay-as-you-view basis. Companies have found resistance on the part of customers billed via computer for each pay program they select. Some viewers consider it an invasion of privacy, knowing there is a decoding box hooked to their television set and telephone line, automatically recording and informing the pay-TV company of their viewing habits. From the pay-TV companies' point of view, an additional rationale against installing decoder boxes is the initial cost (an estimated $450 million to hook up two million homes in a large metropolitan area such as Los Angeles).

Of course, most customers probably would prefer not to pay at all for the privilege of watching pay TV. To the disappointment of pay-TV companies, the number of viewers who get away with pirating the signals, circumventing the cashier, has been exorbitantly high. Arguing that the airwaves are free and that anything passed over those airwaves and through

Pirates steal pay-TV signals.

their bodies can rightfully be intercepted, pay-TV pirates have made millions manufacturing and selling special antennas and decoder boxes that beat the system. The pay-TV industry has sought remedies from the courts, FCC, and Congress, and some states have responded by passing laws against the pirating of signals. Revision of the 1934 Communications Act and a federal privacy bill banning unauthorized reception of pay-TV signals have been initiated, as the pay-TV industry maintains it is illegal to intercept a private communication, just as it is illegal to eavesdrop on telephone calls relayed by microwave signals.

Sports and Movies

Sports and movies on pay TV please the customers but threaten the establishment.

Pay television has begun to be a force in some traditionally free-TV areas, particularly sporting events and movies. Networks sense in pay TV a serious threat to their lucrative arrangements with professional football. It would take only 400,000 television homes willing to pay one dollar a week (a low figure) over a twenty-week football season to more than cover the income a single National Football League franchise is currently getting from the commercial networks each year. As the number of homes having pay TV increases, the potential income to the NFL teams grows even larger, causing the commercial networks and their advertisers grave concern. One of their concerns, a socially responsible one, is that homeowners without access to pay TV will be denied their seemingly inherent birthright to spend their fall weekends ingesting pro football. Their other concern, less publicized, is that the loss of pro football and other major sporting events would be a devastating financial blow to the networks.[8] As stated by one observer, "Every sport at every level will be touched, lawsuits are inevitable, competition for contracts will become fierce, and team owners will continue to face a string of major decisions."[9]

The stakes are enormous. For professional football rights alone, the networks spent $400 million in 1982; the amount becomes staggering when compared with earlier contracts: $3.8 million in 1960, $46 million in 1970, and $162 million in 1978. The $400 million a year contract signed in 1982 was a binding, five-year agreement, which gave the networks some security against the program-hungry cable monster. But, perhaps as a sign of things to come, that contract allowed cable systems to broadcast any number of NFL games on Sundays within a thirty-five-mile radius of a stadium.

As cable technology improves, its potential for usurping the networks becomes more obvious. One pay-TV system, ON-TV, was outbid by only $35 million by ABC for the rights to show the 1984 Olympics. If the Los Angeles Olympic Organization Committee had been able to wait until 1983 to award the rights, a consortium of pay-TV interests might very well have come up with a billion-dollar package.[10] The deal would have ended all worries by the committee about making a profit on the games, but would have raised anew the question of the "haves" versus the "have-nots": Do all Americans have an inalienable right to view the Olympics, or does the right belong only to those connected to a cable or pay-TV system?

Meanwhile, similar battles rage in Hollywood. Film companies, which have a longer term affinity with telecommunications than professional sports have had, for quite some time have been in the business of providing movies for pay TV. Home Box Office (HBO) (a Time, Inc., subsidiary whose stock zoomed after it began transmitting across the nation via satellite in 1975) has claimed to be the largest movie buyer in the world, both in volume and amount of money spent annually. With such competitors as Showtime, Warner-Amex Satellite Entertainment's The Movie Channel, Home Theater Network, Spotlight, and others in the movies-at-home business, Hollywood would seem to have every reason to make its hits available to pay TV, and even to crank out special movies for the insatiable video. Given a market of 13.5 million pay subscribers, producers of hit films like *Kramer vs. Kramer, Stir Crazy, Nine to Five,* and *Ordinary People* are demanding $6 to $7 million for pay-TV rights, compared with a paltry $1 million from blockbusters shown to the 1.7 million pay subscribers in 1977. Since many of these films are shown on pay TV before being released to the commercial networks (which have been willing to pay as much, if not more, for the privilege) and are arriving at suburban and small-town theaters at about the same time, there have been many complaints about the encroachment.[11]

An indication of the market's complexity is seen in HBO's struggle for independence from Hollywood by investing in its own films prior to production, locking up the pay rights for itself by means of a "prebuy" arrangement similar to that used by some commercial networks. The practice is risky, because the films may bomb at the box office and therefore be worth little on pay TV. Paramount and Warner Brothers have released some films on videocassettes and videodiscs prior to releasing them to pay TV, because they can get more per customer and because it keeps viewers from taping their own copies off the air (a practice the courts and Congress are attempting to straighten out). Because a national survey of pay-TV subscribers indicated that the single most important reason for paying extra is to receive movies not shown on regular television, and because pay TV is burgeoning at a dizzying pace, competition among companies for films and audiences is bound to continue.

Pay TV's Future

Pay-TV growth seems inevitable, but at what cost to the status quo?

Most analysts see pay television as a growth industry despite current complications. Hollywood television producers, who have made their fortunes on syndicated reruns, are among those threatened by a system that should become an outlet for programming more adventurous than the familiar talk and game shows.

It might be said that the most enduring dream of pay TV remains unfulfilled: It has been unable to sell culture (such as opera, ballet, symphonic concerts, and Broadway plays) on a regular basis, despite the substantially increased presentations of such programs on public, noncommercial television.[12] This, of course, prompts the question: Why should we pay for such culture if the Public Broadcasting Service gives it to us free? The other key questions remain unanswered, however. First, the issue of two classes of society remains. Will those who are unable to pay for television programming, by reason of economic status or geographic quirk, be deprived of what is increasingly seen as an American necessity? (Not by accident, many welfare agencies consider the television set a necessity, not a luxury item.) Second, if we pay for the same programming we are now receiving free on commercial television, would we be subsidizing it by paying directly to the programmer, or would we be paying for it indirectly by buying advertised products? The ramifications are most assuredly not lost upon the networks and advertisers.[13]

Independent Network Services

Lost in the shadows of the giant networks, independent networks struggle to be seen.

When we speak of commercial network television, the big three come to mind: CBS, NBC, and ABC. Not to be overlooked, however, are the numerous attempts over the past third of a century by individual and corporate entrepreneurs who have recognized programming and advertising voids left by the three giants. As this book goes to press, new technology in cable and satellite communications is giving rise to innumerable efforts by independent organizations to serve both affiliated and nonaffiliated stations.

Allen B. DuMont, who contributed to the technology of early television, felt the urge to market his products by offering programming across the nation in the 1940s. By 1955 he had three times as many stations affiliated as did ABC, but he was never able to land the larger stations in major markets, and he folded up shop that same year.

Since DuMont's efforts, there has been periodic speculation about the development of a fourth major network. Indeed, one such network was in operation for a brief thirty-one days in 1967. Daniel J. Overmyer laid the groundwork and was taken over by a group of businesses in the western states who put the United Network on the air on 1 May 1967. The first program, a two-hour "Las Vegas Show," went out to 125 stations. But more could not be coaxed into the fold, and, unable to pay for line charges, United signed off on 31 May.

Special Function Networks

Sports, religion, news, movies, music, and ethnic programming are now available by satellite.

In one sense, there have been several successful "fourth networks." Programming to special interests, as indicated by their titles, the Spanish International Network (SIN), Christian Broadcasting Network (CBN), Praise The Lord Network (PTL) and others have been distributing programming via satellite to local television stations since the late 1970s. SIN programming originates in Central and South America. From headquarters in San Antonio, the network relays international news, sports (primarily live soccer and boxing), and variety shows to Spanish-speaking audiences in several states. The religious networks, CBN and PTL being only two of many, are among the most powerful currents of contemporary American broadcasting. PTL's drawing card is a daily two-hour program, "The PTL Club," which is syndicated to more than 200 television stations and claimed to be the most-viewed daily television program in the world. Unlike other independent networks, the religious ones are supported heavily by audience donations: PTL receives several thousand phone calls and 15,000 letters each day, most asking for help in solving personal problems, but a great many with donations.[14]

As previously noted, the Entertainment and Sports Programming Network (ESPN) is offering round-the-clock college football, slow-pitch softball, college soccer, tennis, curling, full-contact karate, bicycle racing, and the like to its 18 million subscribers. The network has capitalized on the enthusiasm of sports fans over events whose outcomes are unpredictable, regardless of the sport.

Other independent networks are entering the marketplace via cable and/or satellite. Black Entertainment Television, with black-oriented basic programming services, was reaching 9.2 million homes, expanding its service to forty-two hours a week in August 1982; a Cable Health network went on the air 30 June 1982, with 3 million subscribers, expecting to reach 8 million by 1983. The Disney Channel and Hearst/ABC's Daytime aim at special audiences, as does the Cable Jazz Network, a twenty-four-hour-a-day audio-only stereo service that is beamed to 15 million homes.[15] Spurred on the success of Nickelodeon, specializing in quality programming for children, Warner-Amex gambled and won with its Music Channel, consisting of audiovisual performances by recording artists appealing to the eighteen-to-twenty-four-year-old segment; within eight months of its inception, the Music Channel became the second best-known cable network on the air, behind HBO. Given that success, Warner-Amex laid additional plans for a Games channel allowing audience participation, as well as a shopping channel or "video department store." While such are not, strictly speaking, broadcast networks, the efforts consist of independent programming, which must be considered as alternatives to the big-three commercial nets. Recognizing the market potential, special networks have been developed by Hugh Hefner's Playboy empire and Bob Guccione's Penthouse organization. For those subscribers who are able to receive these and other networks but do not desire unlimited access to them by children, a special "Channel Blockout" went on the market in June 1982. For a mere $650 (for a nineteen-inch screen) or $1,400 (for a forty-inch wall screen), homeowners could use a four-digit code on their sets to block out or scramble any channel(s) for a period up to twelve hours.

The last several years have seen phenomenal growth in independent news and programming efforts. In June 1980, after two years of laying the groundwork, WPIX-TV of New York City offered its weeknight half-hour newscast in prime time via satellite to independent stations from coast to coast. The Independent Network News (INN) initially served thirty stations reaching 40 million homes, slightly more than half the television households in America. Independent stations are therefore receiving news,

Local unaffiliated stations benefit from independent news network efforts.

business, sports, and weather reports of higher quality than their limited local budgets permit. Most are using the concept of counterprogramming, airing the INN during prime time, between network early evening and late-night newscasts.

On the entertainment front, the initials MSN, OPT, and MPC have begun to intrude into prime-time programming. They are "ad hoc" networks: the Mobil Showcase Network, Operation Prime Time, and Metromedia Producers Corporation. Independents and network affiliates have banded together in rather loose confederations of stations to present new, made-for-TV movies, miniseries, dramatic specials, and other independently produced programming that competes head-to-head with the major networks. As many as 100 stations have opted for the alternative programs, meaning that affiliates preempt network feeds and make their own advertising arrangements. Most are happy to do so, since they get more income by taking all the revenue from spot sales than they would from taking a percentage of the network dollar. Entering the prime-time forays as MSN, MPC, and OPT have done means more lop (least objectionable programming) in the traditional network style. One observer points out that it would appear that ad hoc networks are establishing a firm beachhead in the prime-time combat zone, but that their weapons do not include especially innovative programming.[16]

Ad hoc networks provide competition during prime time.

All News

Tycoon Ted Turner shows the establishment how to satiate the public's news hunger. CNN is born.

Finally, although perhaps just the start of the real revolution against network television, the efforts of Atlanta businessman and sportsman Ted Turner must be recognized. In the late 1970s he turned his Atlanta station, WTBS-TV, into a "super-station" that relayed its programming via satellite to some 9 million cable subscribers in forty-eight states. By 1982 WTBS was reaching 22 million homes, over 4,300 cable systems, and was grabbing the lion's share of the cable advertising dollar.[17] Smitten by the success of that effort, Turner gambled by initiating the nation's first twenty-four-hour-a-day all-news television service. His Cable News Network (CNN) was launched in June 1980 with an operating budget of $25 million annually compared with more than $100 million for each of the news divisions of the big three. CNN was immediately available to 2.5 million homes hooked into cable systems that could receive the news and news features fed to the satellite from the Atlanta base. By mid-1982, CNN was being sent to 14.7 million households; however, viewers in only 5.8 million of those homes were tuning in the all-news programming in an average week. CNN's original staff of 300 (since doubled), many of them familiar faces such as chief Washington correspondent Daniel Schorr, formerly of CBS, operated out of bureaus in New York, Chicago, Los Angeles, Washington, Dallas, and San Francisco, and foreign bureaus in Rome, London, Tel Aviv, Cairo, and Tokyo. Their product was much like the formula established by all-news radio: cycles of regularly scheduled national and international hard and soft news, interviews and features, business, sports,

law, fashion, pet care, astrology, gardening, home repairs, gossip, and television criticism, using the latest in technological wizardry.

Prior to CNN's activation, news critics were hopeful Turner's team could offer a significant alternative to the big three, despite CNN's limited budget, which was one-quarter as many dollars to fill a twenty-four-hour news day as the networks were budgeting for in less than an hour of broadcasting each day. Initial reactions to CNN's on-air performance were not overly enthusiastic, however, as critics pointed to CNN's tendency to mirror the tried-and-true newscasting approaches already being offered by the webs, rather than opening up new vistas. Noting the frenetic demands posed by filling all twenty-four hours with news, CNN executives responded that they could not yet do true in-depth stories. Nevertheless, interest in the novel news service increased, fanned by *Newsweek* and *Time* cover stories and much attention in other, even competing, media. Turner signed up seventeen national advertisers at the outset, the largest being Bristol-Myers with a $25 million, ten-year commitment. And, given its early successes as a news network worth watching, CNN expanded in 1982 by offering a new package, CNN2 or CNN Headline News, to established TV stations anxious to boost their news offerings.

In the meantime, we can expect further encroachments into the major networks' domain, as technology and audience tastes allow and dictate independently originated programming.

Satellites

Satellite communication has been available since 1962. SYNCOM, COMSAT, and INTELSAT were the early birds.

Domestic satellites are being used for business and media communication at attractive rates.

We have already hinted at the importance of the communications satellite. The experimental 1962 SYNCOM (Synchronous Orbit Communication) established the optimum height of a communications satellite to be 22,300 miles orbiting over the earth. Originally, communications satellites had the shortcoming of passing out of television's range in relaying their signals back to earth. This was corrected by placing a number of satellites in geo-stationary orbit—that is, orbiting at the speed at which the earth revolves so that they might always be directly above a given point. Thus, at least one satellite is always within range of any point on earth for reception, and the signal can be relayed from satellite to satellite to reach any other point on earth. Satellite-fixed orbit coverage is total.

The Communications Satellite Corporation (COMSAT), a quasi-public corporation, was established by Congress in 1962, with ATT as the largest stockholder. Communications satellites, it should be noted, do a lot more than relay television signals. They transmit all kinds of other data, including computer information and telephone conversations.

Because satellites reach beyond national boundaries, it was inevitable that COMSAT would yield to the International Telecommunication Satellite Consortium (INTELSAT), a consortium of sixty-five nations engaged in international satellite communications. The INTELSAT efforts over the world's various oceans have resulted in transmission of a mind-boggling array of communications between and among nations.

In recent years, a large number of domestic communications satellites have been launched. Western Union's WESTAR and RCA's SAT-COM rent space to many cable systems and networks, and Satellite Business Systems (SBS)—a joint effort of IBM, COMSAT, and Aetna—has been sent up for newspapers and other business ventures. A year's lease for a satellite TV channel is about a million dollars. Since NBC, CBS, and ABC spend about $15 million annually to distribute their programs nationwide via land lines, the satellites offer an attractive savings. However, one reason the networks have been somewhat slow in exclusively using satellite is that if their affiliates have a receiving dish to get their network feed, they'll also be able to pick up all other satellite transmissions, including competitive network feeds. This means advertisers won't be assured of a constant audience, so the advertisers, affiliated stations, and webs are all concerned.

The cable systems have been the major benefactors of satellite communication. Earlier CATV companies could only pass along signals received by their super antennas, which were still limited due to TV's line of sight signals. But satellites vastly expand the number and quality of signals available. Home Box Office grew at an incredible pace after it went onto satellite in 1975. Satellite cable programming already available includes forty-four separate services, such as Nickelodeon, a children's program channel; ESPN (Entertainment and Sports Programming Network); Time-Life Films' BBC in America; SIN (Spanish International Network); live sports from Madison Square Garden; all-news channels from the Associated Press, United Press International, Reuters, and Cable News Network; C-SPAN (Cable Satellite Public Affairs Network), which broadcasts the floor sessions of the House of Representatives; at least three religious networks; and Satellite Business Systems' billion dollar gadgetry for beaming high-speed voice, data, and video services from the sky.

Satellites have been part of the newspaper, magazine, and wire service industries for years. Dow Jones & Co., Inc., has been using a satellite since 1975 to beam full-page facsimiles of *The Wall Street Journal* to remote printing plants across the United States. *The New York Times* in August 1980 began whisking pages from New York City via satellite to Chicago for its new Midwestern edition, and in 1982 to the West Coast. *Time* and other magazines have been doing likewise. United Press International said it expected to lop $8 million from its $13.5 million annual ATT land lines bill when UPI's 3,700-site satellite system became effective in 1983. The Associated Press expected smaller, but still significant, savings once its member newspapers and broadcast stations went to the sky. And the American Newspaper Publishers Association facsimile advertising project, SAT-FAX, has been testing the feasibility of distributing national advertising over satellite to newspapers. It has found the system advantageous because of speed, cost, and efficiency factors.[18]

Satellite communication received a major boost in late 1979 when the FCC decided to make licensing of receive-only antennas optional. That prompted newspapers, wire services, various businesses, and even private homeowners to investigate the potential of limited-usage receivers. Earth antennas for business use were made available in the $10,000 to $12,000 price range by the beginning of the 1980s, but the joint effort by COMSAT and Sears & Roebuck to develop a $200 home receiving dish had begun to excite the imaginations of communicators. Such dishes would not become viable until the FCC approved development of a direct-broadcasting satellite (DBS) with far more broadcasting power than the existing communications satellites; FCC approval came in 1981. After all the technical questions are answered, DBS should be alive and well by 1985. Despite the anticipated $700 to $800 million price tag for a direct broadcast satellite, several companies are convinced they will quickly fill the gap left by cable: the 20 million or so homes cable will not reach by the end of the 1980s.[19]

Not all reactions to the satellite boom have been positive. The networks, the National Association of Theater Owners, and others have fought and will continue to fight them, expressing a special brand of fear whenever DBS is mentioned. The federal government has proceeded slowly in setting up regulations; and regulatory uncertainty, we have seen, is a sure way of deterring a medium's development. Technically, since there is no ratings system to measure audience size, advertisers have not made any mass moves toward the superstations or cable TV interested in satellite transmission.

Direct-broadcasting satellites (DBS) may revolutionize the industry. Once again, the establishment fights back.

Also, satellites are costly enough (about $30 million, with some $80 million worth of equipment on the drawing boards) and have a short life expectancy (about eight or nine years) to be within the financial grasp of only the giant firms. Since NASA charges satellite owners $20 to $30 million to launch and track each satellite, the investments are substantial. (The Space Shuttle with its huge payload, which could include several giant, powerful DBS satellites, is expected to change some of this.) Finally, satellites have been known to malfunction or to even get lost, as happened to RCA's SAT-COM III late in 1979 when it disappeared somewhere in the ether.

Interactive TV: QUBE

What happens when we talk back to our TV? QUBE viewers know.

When public officials in the Columbus, Ohio, suburb of Upper Arlington want to know how taxpayers rate the police department, and whether residents think the city has enough parkland, they go on television and ask. The answers come back within seconds. When the producer and cohost of the popular talk show "Columbus Alive" wonders whether viewers think he should wear a toupee or what he should name the studio cat, he merely asks the viewers. They tell him, instantly. When the controversial PBS documentary "Choosing Suicide" raised questions about the propriety and ethics of suicide, the opinions of television viewers in Columbus were instantly broadcast to PBS viewers around the country. Would you label this: Electronic democracy? Participatory television? Instant market research? Or a Brave New World of demagogic video?

Children interact with the show "Pinwheel" on Warner Cable's QUBE system.
Wide World Photos

Since December 1977, audience interaction with television has been commonplace in the capital city of Ohio. Since 1980, the same has become true of Houston, Cincinnati, and Pittsburgh. If things follow Warner-Amex's master plan, viewers in cities all across the nation may soon have opportunities to talk back to their television sets. On the other hand, the entire experiment with interactive TV may find its place in history alongside the Edsel and other products that failed to capture the imagination of consumers.

The Warner-Amex system, called QUBE (no acronym—just someone's idea of a catchy title), has united two-way cable television with the computer. In each QUBE family home there is a small console that resembles a hand-held calculator. It is attached to the television set and allows viewers the ability to interact with the television programs by sending responses to the Warner-Amex central computer, called QUBE Central. The system provides thirty channels of programming. Ten are ordinary television channels, the local and distant signals pulled into the cable system. Ten are premium channels, for first-run movies, sporting events, and other specials. The rest are community channels, including children's programming, news, religion, and locally produced shows such as "Columbus Alive" and "Talent Search." There's nothing extraordinary about the ordinary channels. The premium channels are special in that it costs money each time one is tuned in (the pay subscription system). The real intrigue of QUBE is what viewers can do when the community channels are on, because that's the time they can talk back to their sets.

What distinguish QUBE from the other fancy cable systems are the five response buttons on the right-hand side of each QUBE control box. Not only does the control central computer keep track of what programs are being viewed, it also records and instantly tabulates which of the five special-response buttons are pushed by the viewer. "Talk back television," as Columbus residents call it, utilizes multiple-choice questions that are either flashed on the screen or asked by program hosts. It is used during interactive game shows with home audiences winning prizes; during auctions, town meetings, and market surveys; and even on a show specially designed for gauging audience response to the entire QUBE system in order to determine future programming possibilities ("QUBE At Your Service").

QUBE's central computer scans all QUBE residences every six seconds. It records what shows are being watched, automatically billing for the premium or pay programs, and it notes any feedback generated by the response buttons in each home. Without doubt, it is the most sophisticated and instantaneous ratings service in the mass media world. Of course, with each viewer having a choice of thirty programs at any given time, no single program tends to amass huge shares of the audience. In fact, QUBE programmers are not displeased when the "Home Book Club," a two-way discussion show about books, has only 100 households tuned in, with only fifty or sixty of these making use of the response buttons.

In addition to the instantaneous ratings and opinion feedback capacities, QUBE also offers a sophisticated home security and medical package, with its own emergency power and backup mechanisms. With delicate sensors in the TV room and around the home, the computer scans each household every six seconds and registers such things as smoke and fire in the home, and whether intruders have entered during times no one is supposed to be at home. Of course, when something is amiss, it is reported electronically to the fire department or police station. It even keeps track of the medical records of its subscribers, so that the computer can be alerted if medical attention is needed. The hospital and ambulance then receive a printout of a QUBE subscriber's medical history and needs.

Criticisms of QUBE

Is QUBE our "Brave New World?" Is it "1984" a bit early? Is it the end of our representative democracy? Or is it an expensive toy?

The latter capacities of QUBE, touted as the future of the electronic environment, have brought cries of despair from some social commentators. They see little difference between what QUBE does and what George Orwell and Aldous Huxley predicted for the totalitarian, mind-control societies of the future. To QUBE's developers, such complaints are totally unjustified, because the only way QUBE gets in the home is with the homeowner's permission and payment, and not by governmental mandate. Critics suggest that the sheer volume and sophistication of QUBE's audience profiles are so attractive to other marketing companies that such companies would probably be willing to lie, cheat, and steal to get their hands on them. QUBE insists that all its records (security, medical, program choice, and payment patterns) are kept absolutely secret, available to no outsiders. QUBE's critics are also concerned that when audiences respond to QUBE-generated questions, they are limited to five choices, all of which have been determined in advance by the programmers. That lack of generative choice, they insist, makes participation limited and passive; it comes only if and when QUBE Central poses a question and flashes "Touch Now" on the screen. Polling, they say, is not the same as democracy. QUBE's response is to broaden the base of participation, allowing more options more frequently, even to the extent of letting audiences suggest which plot alternatives should be followed during dramatic presentations.

To appreciate the kinds of audiences QUBE attracts, it may be revealing to note that 46 percent of the viewers participating in an interactive Arlington town meeting had advanced college degrees. Is that democracy at work? Even in upper-middle-class Arlington, that demographic profile is scarcely representative.

In his self-proclaimed guidebook to television for public-spirited citizens, Les Brown has reacted strongly to the realities and potentialities of QUBE. It is the implications for politics that worry Brown the most. He questions whether it is possible that the polls will be conducted prior to the public being fully informed of the issues. "Elected officials might endanger their careers if their votes on legislation did not follow the mandate of the QUBE poll, even though their own clear understanding of the issues might dictate a different vote." And what about the honest reporting of results? "Like a sighted person playing heads or tails with a blind person, the cable company is free to deceive by reporting a false tally on issues in which it has an interest and thus may influence legislation as it chooses."[20]

A final concern over QUBE is a financial one. To get started in Columbus, Warner Communications had to devote four years of research and development, and spend over $20 million. By 1982, QUBE had become a $40 million investment. That's no small outlay, even for a company that generated a billion dollars in revenues in 1977, the year QUBE came to town. Despite a massive public relations effort, only 37,000 of the potential 100,000 homes in QUBE's universe had signed up for the service by 1980. Many apparently feel the $10.95 a month in basic cable fees is not worth it. Others may be afraid of spending another $16 or so each month on premium movies and shows they don't necessarily need to watch. (The $16 is typical; at $1 to $3.50 for each premium offering, the total can go much higher.) Many don't have much interest in laying out $99 for fire alarms, anywhere from $190 to $300 for burglar alarms and other sensors, or an additional $12 a month to retain the emergency services. A 1982 survey of QUBE subscribers, however, indicated that most are happy with the two-way technology and the service it offers. Some 86 percent said they were "satisfied," and almost half were "very satisfied"; 92 percent said they believed QUBE would "continue to grow in importance and become the wave of the future."[21]

QUBE is not the only interactive system in operation, just the most appealing. In Reading, Pennsylvania, Berks Community Television has been offering "democratic television" for several years. A National Science Foundation grant was used to develop programming for the elderly, and the interactive service remained after the grant expired. Local citizens and the local government and businesses have continued funding for nineteen studios equipped with monitors and cameras where groups of people can interact. Reading residents get a true sense of community during town meetings, during live question-and-answer sessions with Social Security administrators, and on entertainment and consumer programs conveyed on split screen in black and white. It is a low-budget operation, replete with humor, pathos, and sincerity not found in the more slick QUBE offerings.

On the other side of the globe, a neighborhood in Osaka, Japan, is making interactive television history. Some 158 families were connected to a cable circuit and given video cameras, microphones, and computer keyboards linking them to a central studio. Programs produced for the local community, such as panel discussions for homemakers, allowed participants to experiment with electronic intimacy, each family being connected to every other family. Results of the experiment include an unexpected

Other Interactive Systems

Elsewhere, people talk back to their TV sets and to each other.

feeling of togetherness on the streets and in the stores, with former strangers smiling and saying hello to newfound electronic friends. Since it cost tens of millions of dollars to interconnect those 158 families, it is unrealistic to expect any massive, national adaptation of such a system. But futurists see in the experiment some tantalizing possibilities.[22]

In Seattle, Washington, some 200 homes are participating in a variation of QUBE. VOXBOX, a TV-ratings system that records how strongly an audience likes or dislikes what it is viewing, has overcome the Nielsen's inability to assess qualitative ratings to programs. On an eight-point scale, viewers rate programs and commercials as being anywhere from "excellent" to "dumb." As with QUBE, the ratings are instantly tabulated. Companies such as Coca-Cola, United Airlines, and Sears, Roebuck & Company are paying up to $10,000 a month for computerized reports on their commercials and the programs they sponsor. As *Newsweek* asks, what could hold more promise for upgrading the viewers' diet than a ratings system that respects their minds as well as their numbers?[23]

Additional interactive systems are popping up all across the globe. A few of them are briefly considered later in this chapter in our discussion of teletext and videotex.

Electronics for the Home

Consumer electronics have changed dramatically since the early 1970s. Citizens-band radio gave a voice to the traveler isolated in an automobile. And about the same time, video games (especially one called Pong) launched the home-video-entertainment era. Advances have been swift. Today the consumer can purchase videocassette recorders, videodiscs, an array of computer games, or a personal computer—the centerpiece of a home communications center.

Videocassette Recorders

VCRs overcome TV's control of the viewer's time, but only for a price.

The birth of alternative television came several years before Qube made its appearance in Columbus. The pivotal year was probably 1975, when Sony introduced its Betamax, a home videocassette recorder (VCR) that quickly became one of the hottest selling items in electronics shops across America. Competition from other manufacturers resulted in more sophistication and lower prices, and by 1980 more than a million VCRs had been sold in the United States. Many machines now offer remote controls enabling owners to edit out commercials; computer programmable timers that can be preset to record selected programs on any channel up to two weeks in advance; and fast forward, reverse, and pause controls.

Very soon after VCRs came on the scene, manufacturers and other entrepreneurs began offering prerecorded tapes for sale or rent. They included material not generally available over the air—including classic and first-run films, concerts, educational features, sports and recreational pieces, and, of course, pornography. And do-it-yourselfers were purchasing blank tapes, good for up to six hours of recording. The market received a boost

in 1979 when Universal Studios and Walt Disney Productions' $10 million lawsuit against Sony Betamax was settled in Sony's favor, permitting free use of copyrighted programs for noncommercial home use. But a 1981 Court of Appeals decision indicated greater protection for holders of copyrights, meaning the issue remained for the Supreme Court and Congress to settle.

Videotape may have a salutory effect on the increasingly expensive performing arts, such as Broadway and off-Broadway theater, ballet, opera, and symphony. Appeal of these arts has generally been restricted to around 4 percent of the population—an audience too small to justify network television coverage. Videocassettes offer a potential whereby performances can be recorded and the tapes sold to aficionados for home consumption with the producer receiving a royalty on sales. Even with fewer than 2 percent of U.S. homes being equipped with VCRs, as was true in 1980, the possibilities for stimulating the economy of the performing arts are quite obvious.

It is interesting to note how the first generation of VCRs was being used. A 1980 study of 250 VCR owners in sixteen cities revealed that on an average day the typical VCR household was viewing television for four hours, was watching playbacks of material it had recorded for an additional hour, and was recording programs for another nineteen minutes. A combination of these three activities, 323 minutes, was forty minutes less than the average viewing time of the typical American household without a VCR. Like the first owners of TV sets back in the 1940s, VCR users were typically young, affluent, educated professionals—unlikely to be heavy TV viewers to begin with. Nevertheless, over 90 percent of the material they recorded was regular TV series, movies, and specials, with soap operas and situation comedies in the fore. Almost all the broadcasts were recorded in their entirety, and nearly all recordings were given a complete replay. The major source of recorded programs was network affiliated stations. The typical VCR household spent one-half hour per week viewing prerecorded tapes, half of which were borrowed and half of which were purchased. If these 250 VCR households are typical, the commercial networks need not roll over and play dead quite yet. Mark Levy, a researcher, concluded that despite the relatively "upscale" demographics of VCR families, most VCR owners record programs with wide, mass audience appeal, and VCR use works to maintain current positions of strength among competing broadcast organizations.[24] Even in its infancy, then, the videocassette recorder appears to have melded into the electronic media mix without causing a drastic shakeup. The day may come, however, when we stop using this new technology to perform old tasks and begin to recognize its new possibilities.

The VCR—one more new medium being put to old uses. When will we learn?

Videodiscs

The latest and probably most exciting form of television's progeny has actually been around as long as television itself, since 1928. That year a London department store began selling a phonograph that played sound pictures in motion, with some in color. The "television gramophone" used standard wax disc records to project a coarse, low-resolution picture viewed through a perforated whirling disc. Although the novelty items were marketed for seven years, there's no record of how well they sold, and the fact that hardly anybody has heard of them today may be significant.

Videodisc—the omnibus medium or an electronic Edsel?

Their successor, however, the contemporary videodisc, is being called by many observers the "omnibus medium." It can reproduce and effectively combine the best qualities of virtually all the other communications media: books and other printed materials; stills—slides, transparencies, photos, etc.; motion pictures; videotapes of all formats; digitized computer data; audio; and stereophonic sound.[25] Former RCA President Edgar Griffiths said he expects the videodisc to start a new industry, "bigger than the broadcast industry, two-and-a-half times the record industry."[26] Since his corporation has invested more in its videodisc SelectaVision than it did in perfecting color television, Griffiths' videodisc may deserve our attention. If nothing else, we should take note of an invention that will either become the hottest new visual medium in history or electronics' most expensive flop.

Basically, a videodisc is merely a prerecorded disc the size of a 33 1/3 RPM audio record. The gold or platinum discs run up to an hour per side when played on a videodisc player and viewed on a home television set. Like commercial records, the videodiscs are for play only. Home units cannot be used for recording.

As described, it hardly sounds like a revolutionary piece of technology. But its advantages over other electronic media are numerous. In one form, sold under the name Magnavision, laser-beam technology is used to read pictures and sound from grooveless discs. Since no stylus ever touches the discs, they never wear out. Fidelity is as good on the millionth play as on the first. The Magnavision players include sophisticated features such as slow and fast motion, stop action, single-frame advance, and instant search and reviewability capacities. Newer systems for home usage designed by RCA utilize grooved discs, much like hi-fi records, and the less expensive playback units lack some of the sophisticated features of the Magnavision units.

Unlike videotape, the discs provide rock-steady still frames in playback. When used to its full potential, a single disc is capable of storing a complete library of 360 books, each with 300 pages, assuming that each page would occupy one of the disc's 108,000 frames. Or a disc could be used to record 108,000 separate photographs or slides, or 13 billion bits of digitized information. Extremely high fidelity stereophonic sound is possible on the discs; a single disc can hold fifty hours of prerecorded music. Since the sound is recorded separately on two channels, movies on videodiscs have been recorded in two languages. Viewers can switch from English to Japanese in the middle of a word if they wish.

Although to date the several systems of videodiscs are incompatible, many manufacturers are moving ahead with unique applications. Telefunken/Decca has designed a system using ten-minute discs for a Video Jukebox. Matsushita of Japan has been perfecting a combination video and color printing system called "Picture Paper," much like a television set with a color printing press spewing out sheets of hard copy upon viewer demand. MCA Incorporated (Universal Pictures and Decca Records) is producing thin flexible discs that may be inserted in periodicals, indicating hopes that the market will be ready for videodisc catalogues, magazines, or talking encyclopedias. The fact that the entire *Encyclopedia Britannica* could be stored on a single disc with room to spare has not been wasted on industrial visionaries. Libraries, concerned about the deterioration of their holdings, are contemplating transferring masses of documents to discs. Educators are starting to recognize the possibilities of combining text with audiovisual demonstrations.

One of the beauties of the videodisc system is its cost. Hollywood is especially intrigued by the fact that it costs only fifty cents to manufacture each duplicate of an original disc. Even at $5,000 for the master plate, the costs are far cheaper than videotape or film reproductions. To date, the

A videodisc can offer a bilingual, stereophonic, hifidelity encyclopedia, or a grade B movie. Educators and Hollywood are intrigued.

Coupled with the
microcomputer, the
videodisc holds great
promise for education and
business.

$5,000 initial cost has limited production to those commercial and educational establishments that expect mass production of their discs; more esoteric and limited-appeal programs are not yet economically feasible. CBS Inc. and MGM have initiated a joint marketing venture for both videodiscs and videocassettes, with MGM's 1,600 films the cornerstone of the library. Its major competitor, MCA, has the entire film supply of Universal Studios to put on disc. For the home user, the costs are in the neighborhood of $300 to $800 for the playback unit and between $15 and $20 for each feature-length movie. Old TV movies and sports and educational programs have been available for as little as $5.95.

With over a billion dollars invested in developing and marketing various systems, manufacturers expected 1981 to be the decisive year when the home videodisc units found their way into the electromedia marketplace. RCA alone, which spent $150 million developing its SelectaVision, invested an additional $20 million during 1981 on promoting the units. Given investments like this, it is little wonder the manufacturers are saying that the videodisc will emerge as the hottest new visual medium in history, having a bigger impact than the entire movie business or the audio record industry.

Sales of the videodisc players lagged behind industry expectations in the early 1980s, but in educational functions the videodiscs have already shown promise for such diverse purposes as language training, musical studies, and cognitive development of the mentally retarded. Students can select whichever language they choose to learn, and move back and forth at will between their native language and the one they're attempting to master. Music students can not only hear chosen works in stereo but can also watch the performers, conductors, or musical scores. When interfaced with microcomputers, the videodiscs provide individualized, self-paced instruction for slow learners and valedictorians alike.

Indeed, it is the videodisc's ties with the computer that have corporate and educational minds spinning. Philips Research Laboratories in The Netherlands has developed an experimental teaching system that combines the videodisc and the TV monitor to a home microcomputer with a built-in monitor screen. The microcomputer controls the videodisc and provides the graphics—such as the table of contents, questions, and so forth—on its own monitor screen. The student can follow instructions on the computer screen, respond to questions about the material, and request a repetition of any or all parts of each program. The student's progress can be made dependent on giving correct answers to the computer's questions. Another program, in experimental stages, allows teachers to design their own questions and instructions to go along with any prerecorded videodisc of their choosing.[27] At Utah State University, instructional media faculty members working on a Videodisc Innovations Project have developed a series of "videodisc vignettes" to supplement instruction in several academic areas. They are particularly excited about the industrial videodisc systems and microcomputers that allow students to physically interact with the program by merely touching the television screen in appropriate places. Doing so allows them to go from still-frame to lineal information in full color and motion almost instantaneously; to gain instant access to any frame on the disc; and to utilize the Matsushita "Picture Paper," giving them and their instructors hard copy printouts of any and all exercises attempted.

It may be significant that videodiscs have only been offered on the American market since 1978. The speed with which the industrial giants have proceeded to enter the competition is intriguing. Even though the four major systems (RCA's SelectaVision, Philips/MCA's Magnavision, Pioneer's LaserDisc, and Japan Victor's VHD) have not developed compatible units, each has staked a small fortune on the eventual success of this new generation of television.

Many problems must be solved before the videodisc establishes its place in history, including technological refinement and compatibility of systems; the cost to consumers; regulatory involvement over copyright and other issues; and a continuing supply of software (contents) to justify customer interest. When these questions are resolved, the fate of the videodisc will have been settled in a far shorter time span than it took for any other mass medium in history. The growth rate of videodiscs represents a phenomenon; the newer technology is emerging on the scene far more rapidly than did any of the older technology, and with more rapid effects on the established media.

Microcomputers: The HomeComCen

Miniaturization and lower costs bring the computer into the home. A new definition of literacy results.

The proliferation of home and office computers heralds the information revolution about which so much has been said. At its base is the refinement of miniaturized electronic components that reduced the cost of computer power by a factor of about fifty during the 1970s. Components that in 1950 took up an entire room have been reduced to the size of a cornflake, with no loss in productivity and with the promise of greater economic productivity and growth. In 1980 about 100,000 word-processing machines were installed throughout the country, giving homes and offices much greater efficiency in handling and storing written material than was ever before possible. Annual sales of the machines were expected to be double by 1983, after which the information revolution should be underway in full force.[28]

With the new information revolution will come revised definitions of literacy and illiteracy. Scientists and technicians are warning that within a few years it will be necessary to be able to program and operate microcomputers in order to get and hold a job, let alone enjoy the full potential of a new home communications system of entertainment and information processing. By 1990, 40 million persons will have to know how to use the computers already affordable for institutional, business, and personal use. With the prospect of 10 million computers of all sizes being in use as early as 1985, the task of training people to program, operate, and service them looks staggering. Obviously, one task of the computer industry and business is to develop a system of interactive self-teaching programs for the microcomputers and word processors. At least one college, St. Thomas in St.

Paul, Minnesota, has instituted a computer literacy requirement for graduation. Elementary and high schools will undoubtedly have to add computer science programs to their staple of reading, writing, and arithmetic.[29] The unpleasant alternative will be a new version of functional illiteracy, a national debility we can ill afford. "Why Johnny Can't Program" might well become the most popular theme of supermarket magazines in 1990.

For the homeowner, the information revolution will take the form of a complete home communications center, or HomeComCen. In its fullest form, as envisioned today, it will include a computer keyboard, a video-cassette recorder and videodisc, a television set (perhaps a wall-sized projection screen), an interactive cable, a home satellite receiving dish, a telephone interface, and a facsimile printer, perhaps with color capacity. Once the hardware became available in 1980, such a system cost over $5,000 for the basics (a regular-sized television and no home satellite receiving dish). But as technology progresses and mass marketing permits lower per unit costs, the same hardware should go for a more easily affordable $500 by 1990, according to some futurists.[30]

And what will we do with all this fancy hardware? Because of the economic nature of the beast, the HomeComCen will initially serve as an in-home adjunct to the financial world. Payment Systems Incorporated, a subsidiary of the American Express Company, is one of several corporations committed to making the HomeComCen a place where consumers can pay bills, transfer money from one account to another and conduct most of their banking business and other forms of money management.[31] Shopping over the HomeComCen becomes relatively easy. A consumer freezes the frame on an advertised (or video catalogued) item desired, examines it, requests fuller data over cable's two-way capacity, and presses the purchase switch, which automatically debits the consumer's bank balance, credits the store's account with the purchase price and the state with the sales tax, and starts the item on its way from the warehouse to the consumer's home. America's recent romance with plastic credit cards indicates a willingness to transact business without cash, so financial institutions expect little rebellion when the entire procedure is handled electronically. See page 270.

The marketing potential has been especially intriguing to such merchandising giants as Sears, which is gearing up to catalogue and market over cable and satellite. It is no accident that Sears has made arrangements to market an inexpensive rooftop satellite receiving dish for about $200, a move that will revolutionize media delivery systems. As soon as America's rooftops sprout a suitable number of these dishes, Sears will be joined by any number of merchandisers in sending up their own satellites or leasing transponder space on larger satellites, as networks and other information industries are already doing.

Several of the biggest names in American business have invested hundreds of millions of research and development dollars on the new television-computer-telecommunications hardware. ATT, IBM, RCA, and ITT are the best known of the breed. They are being joined by innovative electronics firms such as Scientific-Atlanta, Texas Instruments, Intel, Wang Laboratories, and Northern Telecom. All accept the statement of Representative Lionel Van Deerlin, former chairman of the House Subcommittee on Communications, that the new video options "will transform not only the face of broadcasting, but the lives of Americans as profoundly as the Industrial Revolution of the nineteenth century."[32] Even though there has been no national policy regarding the development and implementation of the hardware, it appears likely *neovideo,* as the systems are sometimes called, will have a dramatic impact on, and perhaps even abolish, over-the-air television broadcasting as we now know it; will hasten deployment of interactive information retrieval and utilization; and will bring about a decentralization of the office. It has been suggested that the resultant back-to-home movement will become the single most significant social trend of the 1980s, and that automobile usage will decrease dramatically. One program now in operation at Control Data in Minneapolis has employees ranging from secretaries to managers working at home with small computers. The response has been encouraging, but most companies are moving slowly into "telecommuting" with numerous pilot programs now being evaluated. Even if the new technology remains out of the reach of the average American household for some years to come, there will be enough neighborhood computer-TV centers and computerized branches of major corporations to allow millions of us to perform our jobs without going far from home. As Desmond Smith has said, it is the merging of the new technologies (fiber optics, satellites, pay TV, interactive TV, computer communications) that is going to change our lives drastically. As the United States enters the information age, it is the television set—not peanut shells or corn husks—that is the most promising candidate to lick the energy shortage.[33]

"Neovideo" could mean the death of over-the-air TV and change the meaning of "going to work."

Teletext and Videotex: The Information Explosion

All the gadgetry in the world will be wasted on potential users if it has no practical use. That is why the communications industry is as busy developing and packaging information software as it is promoting the neovideo hardware. The message may become the medium so rapidly that whatever we describe here is bound to be significantly altered and confronted by new forms of competition before this book (a product of the slower technology) is published and in your hands.

To appreciate recent developments in electronic information processing, it is necessary to be familiar with teletext and videotex. These generic terms refer to products called Cable Text, Prestel, Viewtron, Telidon, Teletel, Telset, Inteltext, Ceefax, Oracle, Antiope, and Captain. All offer owners of television sets a nearly infinite amount of up-to-date information upon viewer demand. They differ primarily in whether they deliver that information over the air encoded on an unused space on the ordinary TV signal (teletext) or by interactive cable or telephone lines connected to a central computer, thus permitting a greater array of selectivity (videotex).

Teletext and videotex offer information upon viewer demand. Videotex is interactive and allows more viewer discretion and greater services.

Teletext and videotex were first developed in Great Britain, where three separate systems of delivering electronic information have been operational since the late 1970s. Ceefax (see facts) and Oracle (Optional Reception of Announcements by Coded Line Electronics) are teletext systems owned by the British Broadcasting Company (BBC) and Independent Television Authority (ITA), respectively. They were broadcasting over the air to 42,000 specially equipped television homes by 1980. The only cost to the consumer was the purchase or rental price of the decoder. The prototype videotex system, Prestel (press tell), is owned by the British Post Office and transmits over telephone lines.

Ceefax and Oracle have offered their teletext viewers choices of about 100 different topics. They are indexed under broad categories, but most have numerous subtopics, including headlines, news, people in the news, and features. Instantaneous updates are included on breaking and sports stories, literally creating a deadline every minute for the BBC and ITA journalists. Weather and travel information includes maps and schedules; consumer information includes food prices, recipes, science news, police news, and special information on education, farming, and gardening; finance news includes headlines, the *Financial Times* index, industrial news, reports from stock markets, exchange rates, and national and international finance. In addition, the teletext systems provide "reveal" buttons for "hidden answers" in puzzles, games, or educational topics seen on the screen.[34]

If teletext offers a plethora of information, videotex goes it one better, because it provides for consumer control via interactive cable or telephone lines. Great Britain's Prestel has a theoretically unlimited supply of information available to any home with a specially equipped television set and a telephone. For a small charge (to cover the phone call and cost of however many pages appear on the TV screen) viewers can seek any information in the post office memory bank. Experimental runs included basic news and entertainment information; travel guides; education; jokes; quizzes and games; home and family help; advertising; information about cars and motoring, houses and insurance, jobs and careers; and assorted facts and figures. The 160 sources of Prestel information included Reuters news service, Westminster Press, the *Financial Times,* the British library, the British Medical Association, consumer organizations, the Tourist Board, Barclay's Bank, the Commodities Exchange, the *New York Times,* and Harte-Hanks Communications of San Antonio, Texas. All sources pay to have their services included in the data bank.

As an interactive system, videotex is particularly well equipped to generate and respond to a series of viewer questions, and for banking and other financial transactions. To use the service, viewers begin by choosing a general subject, then a division of the subject, then further subdivisions up to ten steps. It takes no more than ten seconds to take the steps necessary to choose among any of 25,000 subtopics.[35]

Teletext and videotex have moved across the Atlantic and elsewhere in the world. Best known in this country are the FCC-approved teletext experiments by CBS's KNXT-TV in Los Angeles, KSL-TV in Salt Lake City, and KMOX-TV in St. Louis, plus independent setups by Micro-TV in Philadelphia and Microband National System in Bethesda, Maryland. The Los Angeles, St. Louis, and Salt Lake City projects are receiving strong support from CBS, the first American network to become so involved. KNXT's "Extravision" considers itself to be a video magazine, including pages on local and national news, sports, weather reports, stock market and financial information, consumer tips, airline flight information, various forms of advertising, entertainment lists, traffic conditions, and captions for the hearing-impaired.[36] Texas Instruments has designed a relatively inexpensive decoder ($125 in 1979, perhaps only $20 by 1985) to attach to any television set receiving the KNXT, KSL, or KMOX teletext signals. Meanwhile, marketing plans are underway for equipment to generate paper printouts of any TV "page" (coupons, ads, news articles, etc.).

Videotex has become as appealing in America as it is in England, and perhaps moreso. Making the most of interactive communications hardware, videotex provides all of the information service available on teletext, while allowing consumers to stay at home and bank, shop, make theater and travel reservations, take computer-based educational courses, send and receive electronic messages, and conduct a wide variety of other transactional services. Given its linkage to telephone or other linkage systems, videotex provides a community bulletin board and a sort of "video mailbox" for persons on the system.[37]

Knight-Ridder newspapers have spearheaded the print media's involvement in testing interactive communications services in America. Following a successful test in Coral Gables, Florida, for fourteen months in 1980 and 1981, Knight-Ridder gathered information from fifteen separate sources and financial support from eighteen advertisers, and ATT provided

The British systems have been adaptive to American needs.

Knight-Ridder's experimental "Viewtron" project offered a multitude of informative, persuasive, and entertaining messages. VIEWTRON® a service of Viewdata Corporation of America, wholly owned subsidiary of Knight-Ridder Newspapers, Inc.

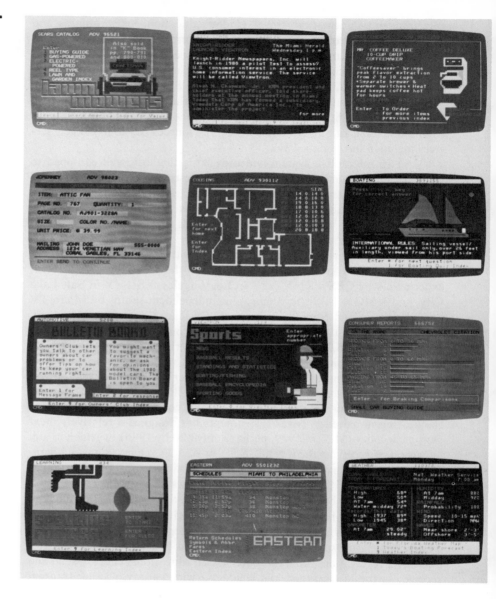

Electronic Media

the communications hardware for a larger experiment aimed at 5,000 Florida households starting in 1983. The scope of this Knight-Ridder "Viewtron" project is indicated by its sources of information: The *Miami Herald,* Consumers Union, the American Cancer Society, Macmillan Publishing, The *New York Times,* Dow Jones & Company, HP Books, Associated Press, *Congressional Quarterly,* Addison-Wesley, Universal Press Syndicate, Intercontinental Press Syndicate, CBS Publications, United Media Enterprises, and the United Press International. As mentioned in chapter 2, this may indeed be the newspaper of the 1990s.

New newspapers do without the youth on a bicycle.

When teletext and videotex were first demonstrated, some members of the newspaper and commercial broadcasting industries emitted death knells—their own. On first glance it appeared that the stage finally had been set for the birth of the electronic newspaper and the death of advertising-supported television. TV set manufacturers, on the other hand, were delighted at the prospects of a nation—and world—dissatisfied with outmoded sets and greedy for completely new models equipped to receive teletext and videotex. (This may explain the interest of RCA and General Telephone, both of whom are in the television set manufacturing business.) And the involvement of Knight-Ridder and Harte-Hanks newspapers, among others, can be interpreted as a farsighted sense of fiscal reality: When the electronic newspaper does come, who better than newspaper companies to be in the forefront?

The Impact of Teletext and Videotex

But old-fashioned newspapers are hiding their heads in the sand.

It is much too early to speak in precise terms about the impact of teletext and videotex. In general, however, they appear likely to cause the most disruption to newspapers and commercial broadcasters who fail to become a part of the action. Ignoring them won't make them go away, and wishing them ill won't keep them from capturing their share of the audience. Recognizing them as an inevitable part of the media mix, and planning accordingly, appears to be the safest bet for all concerned.

Already we have seen computer companies such as Texas Instruments looking upon teletext and videotex sets as the first logical step toward the microcomputerization of American households. Large information corporations, Dow Jones in particular, recognize in the new systems an ideal way to speed financial and other data to their anxious customers. Some newspaper corporations, appreciative that newsprint supplies and circulation problems have become enormous and that their electronic newsrooms are well on their way toward supplying the input, are embracing the new technology.

And perhaps of greatest interest to news audiences will be the recognition by newspapers and network television that news can and should transcend the time and space limitations now imposed upon them. Teletext and videotex may create new definitions of news: news based on the consumer as gatekeeper. Tomorrow's newspaper and television newscast may have to become more involving, more entertaining, offering greater depth and human interest to augment and offset the instantaneousness of teletext and viewdata.

Teletext and videotex transcend the time and space limitations so bothersome to TV and newspaper news.

Financial support for the new systems will come from two primary sources: the consumer and the supplier. Additional charges to the homeowner for the equivalent of pay TV will bear part of the burden. The remainder will be shared by the special-interest groups producing information, and by advertisers. Advertising, which has presented a vexing problem in teletext and videotex's earliest stages, may have to become more informative and less manipulative than the network television commercials of today. Because teletext and videotex offer information only when requested, advertising will have to be appealing and informative to compensate for the intrusiveness factor. Indeed, the classified ad and *Consumer's Report* are perhaps the parents of tomorrow's new technology commercial. But, since it will cost far less to produce ads on the new media than for commercial television and print, we may find a less elaborate marketing system evolving.

The risks must be borne by industry without governmental support.

Today, television and cable companies are in better positions than newspapers to get into the teletext and videotex businesses. That is simply because the FCC has prohibited newspaper owners from acquiring broadcast properties in their home markets. And it always has been somewhat difficult for outsiders to be granted broadcast licenses. This picture may be changed by recent FCC moves to licence hundreds of localized, low-power television (LPTV) or "drop in TV" stations, to award franchises to minority and special-interest groups, and to deregulate and thereby enhance new delivery systems. But the very expensive gamble must be initiated by industry; the U.S. government is not likely to take the risks that Great Britain has because it has less of a vested interest. Even when industry invests research and development monies into the projects, the FCC will have to adopt industry-wide specifications, a process that could take years.[38]

Fiber optics may lessen the risks. Is America ready to be rewired?

The enormous costs of wiring the nation with broad-band or interactive cable must also be considered. Only a few of America's existing cable systems employ two-way cable, but lately it has become a requirement for cable companies seeking franchises in metropolitan areas. One of the most exciting developments in this respect is that of *fiber optics,* tiny flexible strands of glass capable of carrying beams of light or electromagnetic energy around curves and corners. A single 0.005 inch strand can carry 167 television channels, and the potential for each home to be wired for hundreds, even thousands of channels is not beyond speculation.[39] Mass production of the inexpensive technology may mean the wired nation is closer to becoming a reality, depending in part on the success of the direct-to-home broadcast satellites, but it still will involve an expenditure of energy and a commitment equal to that of the two earlier wirings of America for electricity and telephones. The question, of course, is whether America is as committed to a wider range of news, entertainment, and advertising as it was to lights and conversation.

Television has been called the most profoundly democratic medium in history. Today some are saying that the new electronics spell the end of that democratization process. Others disagree. Similar differences of opinion dominate discussions of society's new means of receiving information and entertainment, of the impact on established telecommunications, and of government's role in neovideo's development. Arbitrary conclusions are premature, but we do ourselves a disservice if we fail to consider the problems.

Marshall McLuhan's global village was supposed to be a byproduct of commercial television. With its appeal to the largest (not necessarily the lowest) common denominator of society and with its instantaneousness, network television was to have given us a global sense of community. Whether it has is surely debatable. At the very least, it has given us some common social, economic, and political agenda items to consider. However, neovideo is very likely to eliminate even that superficial sense of community. NBC Vice-Chairman Richard Salant is among those who suggest that the greatest danger of new electronic technology is a destruction of the common data base demanded by democracy. He is joined by Robert Haiman, executive editor of the prize-winning and progressive St. Petersburg, Florida, *Times,* whose expressed fear is that the new technology promises too much diversity in news information for an increasingly disengaged citizenry.

If we realize that even the most primitive efforts of Ceefax could bring a 100-page newspaper or magazine to the home in an amazing twenty-four seconds, we have to ask who among us has the capacity to consume that much information? Who *cares* to absorb that quantity and diversity? Given as much choice as teletext, videotex, and other neovideo promise, are we likely to shortcircuit due to information overload? Will the bewildering array of choices induce in consumers what Swedish social scientists are predicting, a clinical catatonia triggered by neurotic indecision over what to consume?[40]

Forecasters like Salant and Haiman suggest that individuals will grow socially alienated once they obtain information in the home rather than through interpersonal interaction. There are, however, credible arguments to the contrary. Among them is the suggestion that the availability of sophisticated communications services might enhance social integration due to the increased lines of communication through public-access channels on cable and in teleconferences. One might also argue that neovideo will be more demanding than today's television and will result in more active involvement, more participation, and more family or group discussion of media contents than ever before. This is predicted because the content of neovideo is actively sought out and is inherently more involving than passive viewing of conventional network television. At the end of a typical neovideo "program," there will be either a blank screen or a series of video questions, with the expectation of answers. Microcomputers in particular are demanding, and should increase intellectual activity. School age children,

The Dangers of Neovideo: Some General Concerns

What's going to become of TV, the most democratic medium ever known?

Will neovideo eliminate our superficial sense of community?

How do we cope with information overload?

Could neovideo be more demanding—resulting in active citizen involvement—than regular TV?

Children are already comfortable with part of neovideo—the microcomputer games. But what is the ultimate cost to society?
Ellis Herwig/Stock, Boston

among the first to be introduced to microcomputers, have taken to them with enthusiasm, playing the games, challenging the programs, creating new and unique images, displays, and sequences on the video screens and adding special effects to the preprogrammed packages. Family togetherness might possibly become an unexpected byproduct of the new technology.

Included among society's questions about neovideo are the current and predicted changes the new technology will bring to traditional television. Television networks have prepared for the changes by increasing their production of nonfictional programming on the assumption that only they possess the resources to supply consumers' demands. Fred Silverman, when president of NBC, maintained that news will be the most important service the networks can provide in the 1980s: "We have something unique, something none of the new technologies will *ever* have—a professional staff of journalists with the ability to transmit world events into every living room in the country."[41] Ted Turner respectfully disagrees, as does CBS Broadcast Group President Gene Jankowski. Jankowski has predicted that by 1990 the big three networks' share of viewership in homes with cable will have dropped to 57 percent.[42]

Our own oft-repeated observation is that the twentieth century has yet to see any major new media displacing older forms that preceded them. Coexistence of neovideo and traditional television is forecast by CBS's Gene Jankowski and others. "As I see it," Jankowski assured television employees, "the winds of change are not the icy gales of death but the warm breath of continued life."[43]

A modest proposal: Neovideo, old TV, and newspapers will learn to adapt to each other.

Finally, there remains the question of society's priorities. We must consider whether this kind of investment in the future, requiring enormous risk capital, is where Americans wish to spend their money. Money, like time, is limited, and what is spent for this fantastic system of full-color, stereophonic, two-way, three-D, multiple-channel, computer-controlled, ultimately flexible, and completely selective information system must come from something else. In the long run, it is not merely an economic question, but an economic-educational-social-psychological-political one whose ramifications at present remain a mystery. Such systems are already here, and billions of dollars are being expended on their development. The kinds of judgments made this year and next, and the year after that, may prove irrevocable in terms of commitment to a path or a system.

Summary

The forms of television other than national network television are many and varied. The television field, however, is so dominated by the networks that few of the other forms, despite their potential, have had an opportunity to realize even a fraction of that potential. Nor has the situation been helped by confusing and often contradictory FCC policy and rulings.

Neovideo includes CATV and pay TV in its mind-boggling diversity. Independent services, including around-the-clock satellite-fed newscasts and low-power TV, serve special-interest groups such as the Spanish-speaking, the religious-oriented, sports fans, and the elderly. Interactive television, the prototype of which is the QUBE system, offers instant feedback, electronic democracy, instant market research, and a suggested solution to the energy crisis by resurrecting cottage industry. Coupled with videocassette recorders, videodiscs, video games, and microcomputers, the neovideo system now joins sophisticated teletext and videotex systems of information retrieval, some at the customer's request.

This chapter has uncautiously opened a Pandora's box. We have considered the current and potential natures of several forms of telecommunications. Serious questions have to be asked about their impact upon existing media and upon society as we know it. We speculate that the present and past hostility that established media have displayed toward television's progeny will ultimately succumb to a new state of integration, but not until there have been several more technological, regulatory, and economic battles fought. From today's perspective, we cannot predict with any certainty about society's ultimate response to these neovideo. We have suggested several alternatives, ranging from concern over America's loss of a sense of community to a newfound individualism that manifests itself in more caring, sharing family structures.

Notes

1. "Cable Advertising in First Quarter: WTBS Gets Half," *Broadcasting,* 10 May 1982, p. 106.
2. Jack Friedman, "Suddenly Cable is Sexy," *TV Guide,* 19 July 1980, pp. 28–32; and "Radio, Magazines Are Examples for Cable Advertising to Follow, Says Warner's Schneider," *Broadcasting,* 11 August 1980, p. 30.
3. "Cable Restraints Dropped," *NAB Radio/TV Highlights,* 28 July 1980, p. 1; and Jack Valenti, "The Politics of Cable," *Media Digest,* Spring 1980, pp. 9–18.
4. "Cable Opportunities Beyond the Horizon of Entertainment," *Broadcasting,* 10 May 1982, p. 71.
5. "NCTA Report on Local Cable Programming," *Broadcasting,* 1 September 1980, p. 42.
6. *Broadcasting,* 25 August 1980, p. 111.
7. *Broadcasting,* 21 July 1980, pp. 40–41.
8. William Barry Furlong, "The Monster Is Lurking Just Over The Hill," *Panorama,* March 1980, pp. 50–53.
9. Kent Baker, "Cable TV Reshapes Sports," *The Press,* June 1982, p. 41.
10. Ibid., p. 42.
11. Doug Hill, "Will the Latest in Home Video Empty the Movie Theaters?" *TV Guide,* 20 March 1982, pp. 21–22.
12. Leroy Pope, "Pay TV, After a Shaky Infancy, Is Off and Rolling," *Deseret News,* 1 August 1979.
13. F. Leslie Smith, *Perspectives on Radio and Television,* (New York: Harper & Row, 1979), p. 418.
14. Ibid., pp. 372–74; and "The 'Praise the Lord' Television Network," *BM/E* (Broadcasting Management/Engineering), March 1980, pp. 75–83.
15. "Cable Throws a Party in Las Vegas," *Broadcasting,* 10 May 1982, p. 42.
16. Tony Chiu, "MSN, MPC and OPT," *Panorama,* March 1980, pp. 57–59.
17. Neil Hickey, "The Birds Are Taking Off," *TV Guide,* 20 February 1982, p. 20; and "Cable Advertising in First Quarter: WTBS Gets Half," *Broadcasting,* 10 May 1982, p. 106; and "Shaking Up the Networks," *Time,* 9 August 1982, pp. 50–56.
18. Margaret Genovese, "Transmission by Satellite: Pages Today, Wire News Tomorrow, Ads in the Future," *Presstime,* October 1980, pp. 18–22.
19. Hickey, "The Birds Are Taking Off," p. 20.
20. Les Brown, *Keeping Your Eye on Television* (New York: The Pilgrim Press, 1979), p. 52.
21. "Qube Report Card," *Broadcasting,* 31 May 1982, p. 8.
22. "Turn on Your Neighbor," *Panorama,* April 1980, p. 21.
23. "Talking Back to the Tube," *Newsweek,* 25 February 1980.
24. "Public TV Study Says VCRs Don't Detract from Viewing Levels," *Broadcasting,* 21 July 1980, p. 46; and Mark R. Levy, "Home Video Recorders and TV Program Preference" (Paper presented to the Mass Communications and Society Division, Association for Education in Journalism Annual Conference, Boston, Mass., August 1980).
25. R. Kent Wood, "The Utah State University Videodisc Innovations Project," *Educational and Industrial Television,* May 1979, p. 31.
26. David Lachenbruch, "The Coming Videodisc Battle," *Panorama,* April 1980, p. 59.

27. "Videodisc," *Media Digest,* Spring 1980, p. 4.

28. David Salisbury, "The Third 'Industrial Revolution': Robot Factories and Electronic Offices," *Christian Science Monitor,* 8 October 1980, pp. 1, 9.

29. United Press International "Computers Make Many Functionally Illiterate," Logan (Utah) *Herald-Journal,* 24 September 1980, p. 15.

30. *Broadcasting,* "Perils and Prospects Over the Electronic Horizon," in *Readings in Mass Communication: Concepts and Issues in the Mass Media,* 4th ed., ed. Michael Emery and Ted Curtis Smythe (Dubuque, Iowa: Wm. C. Brown Company Publishers, 1980), pp. 223–24.

31. Ibid., p. 223.

32. Desmond Smith, "What Is America's Secret Weapon in the Energy Crisis? Your Television Set," *Panorama,* April 1980, p. 30.

33. Ibid., p. 32.

34. Kenneth Edwards, "Information Without Limit Electronically," in *Readings in Mass Communication,* by Emery and Smythe, pp. 205–6.

35. Ibid., pp. 206–8.

36. J. Roger Moody, "Television Tomorrow: An Eyeful of Opportunity" (Speech to Computer Dealers and Lessors Association, Puerto Rico, 30 April 1982).

37. Ibid., (Referring to an experimental CBS videotex system in New Jersey); and William Whiting (Presentation on Knight-Ridder's Viewdata Corporation, Association for Education in Journalism's Mass Communications and Society Division Spring Meeting, Atlanta, Georgia, 27 February 1982).

38. Kenneth Edwards, "Teletext Broadcasting in U.S. Endorsed by FCC," *Editor & Publisher,* 18 November 1978.

39. F. Leslie Smith, *Perspectives on Radio and Television,* pp. 433–34.

40. Hickey, "Goodbye '70s, Hello '80s," *TV Guide,* 5 January 1980, p. 12.

41. Ibid; and "Shaking Up the Networks," *Time,* 9 August 1982, p. 53.

42. Gene Jankowski (Speech to Academy of Television Arts & Sciences, Los Angeles, 29 November 1979).

43. Ibid.

9 Film

Film is based on an optical illusion, wherein the still frame of individual photographs are mechanically speeded up and synthetically projected until they blend into one another, creating the illusion of motion. Movies, motion pictures, film, and cinema all refer to essentially the same thing; but each has a slightly different connotation ranging from the commonplace to the aesthetic. This in itself gives a clue to the diversity of *film,* which is the term we will use.

Film is counted as a major mass medium because of the effect it has upon large masses of people over a relatively long period of time. In all its variations—the art film, the cartoon, the popular extravaganza, the industrial showcase, the educational teaching aid, the social documentary, and the new genre of the television "quickie"—it has unquestionably had a massive effect upon society. In this sense, as a carrier of the culture, a changing mirror of changing times, film is unexcelled.

However, in another sense it is scarcely a mass medium. Commercial films are not regularly issued and their specific audience sectors are not so clearly identifiable as they are with magazines and radio stations. While film does not foist itself upon its consumers daily, it has an advantage shared by no other medium. It commands attention, generally playing to captive audiences in a format over which the producer has complete control of emphasis, order of presentation, continuity, dramatic effect, and timing. These characteristics have made it over the years a superb medium for instruction and persuasion. A large portion of filmmaking is not commercial in the usual sense, but is devoted to sales, training, information, and other public relations purposes of corporations, governmental agencies, trade associations, and almost any other sector of society that has a message to communicate.

Introduction

Film is a common carrier of culture, and to think it is all based on an optical illusion!

With all the other mass media crying for our attention, why do we still go to the trouble of patronizing the movies? Donald Dietz/Stock, Boston

In chapter 4 we referred to film as an electric book, and rightfully so, because there are striking similarities between films, an electric medium, and books, a print medium. Principally, both are long-term undertakings; both are relatively expensive and hard to acquire; both embrace a certain unity and specificity of subject matter; and neither is supported by advertising. An additional parallel can be seen by comparing the commercial film and its desired box-office appeal with the trade book and its aspirations for making the best-seller list. The counterpart of this comparison is equating the noncommercial film, which is privately produced and contains a high degree of informational, educational, and persuasive content, with the textbook. The analogies are not exact but they do indicate a similarity of function between the two media. Also, the commercial film must excel at the box office within the first year or so, which is essentially the time frame for a best-seller, whereas the noncommercial film has a longer life dictated essentially by its purpose, just as a textbook does.

Another factor of comparison is that film, like the book, has a long and honorable history, stretching back into antiquity to drama. Film is, in effect, the mass production of drama and provides the same entertainment, and educational and persuasive purposes for which the dramas of ancient Greece were originally performed.

Most of this chapter will focus on commercial films. After a brief history of film, we will explore the business of filmmaking, especially production, distribution, and exhibition. We will also discuss the impact of film on audiences and the ways society has developed to modify those influences, non-theatrical films, the cross-cultural nature of commercial films, and the future of film as a mass medium.

Historical Development

"Persistence of vision" was discovered and exploited.

The psychological principle on which film as a medium is based is known as *persistence of vision*—that the eye retains an image fleetingly after it is gone. For centuries inventors and magicians made use of this principle. Leonardo da Vinci's *camera obscura,* a darkened chamber in which an image was captured and focused, and Athanasius Kircher's 1671 *magic lanterns,* which attempted to project moving pictures, were early developments in the field. In 1824 Peter Mark Roget, more famous for his *Thesaurus,* refined the theory of the persistence of vision with regard to moving objects. Roget maintained that a sequential series of still pictures, when viewed or projected in rapid succession, would give the illusion of motion. For the next several decades, while the science of still photography was being refined, inventors were marketing hand-cranked "toys" that employed the persistence of vision principle.

In 1877, two photographers synchronized twenty-four cameras to check a hunch of Leland Stanford, a railroad magnate. Stanford thought that at some point while his race horse was running, all four of its feet would leave the ground. The two dozen cameras proved him correct. Then

Thomas Edison, whose many inventions helped bring about film, radio, and recordings.
Wide World Photos

when the twenty-four pictures were projected in sequence on a machine with the unwieldy name of *Zoopraxinoscope,* photography and projection were united.

With Thomas Edison's 1879 invention of the electric light providing a better source of illumination, mass viewing became possible. Within a decade, three other essential technical ingredients of the film were developed: a motion picture camera, flexible film, and the sprocket wheel.

Thomas Edison gets much of the credit for creating the motion picture industry. Unfortunately for him, he forgot to get some patents.

Much of the credit for early film innovations goes to Edison and his gifted assistant, William Kennedy Laurie Dickson. They were intrigued with the possibilities of combining the newly devised phonograph with the flexible film being produced by George Eastman. In October 1889 Dickson managed to link the two in a demonstration on the *Kinetoscope* of a film in which Dickson's visage and voice were captured. As film historian Arthur Knight expresses it, what was in all probability the first actual presentation of a motion picture film also marked the debut of the talkies.[1]

Temporarily ignoring the sound dimension, Edison marketed the hand-cranked Kinetoscopes and their minute-long peep shows throughout the United States. Within five years they were also in Europe, competing—unfortunately for Edison, who hadn't bothered to secure an international copyright—against numerous imitations and separately invented systems in England, France, and Germany. By 1896 the Kinetoscope, Biograph, and others were refined to project the films onto a screen so an entire paying audience, instead of only one customer, could view them at one time. Film was on its way toward becoming a mass medium.

Turn of the Century

Novelty of the "flickers" soon wore off. New gimmicks for newly sophisticated masses were needed. Melies and Porter provided them.

Edison's Kinetoscope offered its penny-paying customers sensational but jerky pictures of locomotives rushing toward the cameras, fisticuffs, cockfights, Annie Oakley shooting down clay pigeons, hootchie-kootchie dancers, vaudeville acts, practical jokes, and sea waves. Not surprisingly, the novelty wore off quickly, even among the unsophisticated. When the "flickers" left the peep-show arcades and were projected before larger audiences in vaudeville palaces, the same cycle occurred. Initial wonderment at the technology was soon followed by boredom with the content. It was time for the fledgling industry to take a cue from the legitimate theater, and to do it one better.

Between 1896 and 1914, a French magician named Georges Melies "discovered" trick photography—stop motion, double exposure, superimposition, fadeout, fast-and-slow motion, and animation. He created over a thousand short films, including a twenty-minute version of Jules Verne's *A Trip to the Moon* in 1902 that made use of professional actors, animation, many varied costumes and sets, and a detailed scenario.[2]

Melies's theatric artistry was recognized and copied by many contemporaries. One in particular, Edwin S. Porter, an employee at Edison Company Studios, was especially impressed with the potential of film to tell stories. In 1902 he assembled and edited a collection of short films about firefighters into one longer dramatically narrative work, which he called *The Life of an American Fireman*. A year later, he improved upon his editing techniques in a production historians say revolutionized all moviemaking: *The Great Train Robbery*. In eight action-packed minutes, audiences were able to see a band of desperadoes hold up a mail train and get hunted down by a posse of cowboys. Tight editing and violations of normal time sequence characterize the film. At the film's conclusion, a gun was fired directly into the camera, horrifying many moviegoers who were adjusting to the new mode of storytelling.

The *Great Train Robbery*, 1903, was the first film to tell a story.

Porter's 1903 *Great Train Robbery* is frequently cited as the first film to tell a story. A similar claim could be made for several other films because the narrative film was developed almost simultaneously in America, Europe, and Australia. But Porter can be singled out for assuring film a future that would transcend novelty and trickery. No longer could movies be mere reenactments of stage plays. They had become an art form in their own right.

The United States took the lead in filmmaking at the turn of the century, largely as a result of the huge waves of immigrants who arrived from Europe. For those people, mostly illiterate and unfamiliar with English, the silent movies provided a rare escape from the drudgery of daily life. They flocked to see the one-reel thrillers, and their enthusiasm created a demand for more.

By 1908, the film industry's basic formula was set by the simple nickelodeon.

The earliest theaters were storefronts where half-hour showings ran continuously. In 1905 the first true theater was constructed in Pittsburgh and was named, appropriately, the *Nickelodeon,* because the price of admission was a nickel. Soon these specially designed pleasure houses spread

across the nation. The period from 1903 to 1908 was the time during which the basic foundations of the film industry were laid, and the principles of wide—or mass—appeal, audience turnover, formula production, and character stereotyping became firmly established. The period from 1908 to 1914 was a time of struggle for the economic control of the new medium.

Early studios centered in New Jersey and New York formed a trust called the Motion Picture Patents Company with a subsidiary called the General Film Company. Members of the trust had exclusive contracts to purchase film and equipment, guaranteeing them a virtual monopoly. In addition, they sought to control production and to tie exhibitors' film releases to contracts on their equipment rental at two dollars a week, with no purchase possible.

Independents found the going difficult. They bootlegged materials from Europe or from friendly associates in the trust and they produced longer and more innovative films than their trust counterparts; but the independents were constantly disrupted by goon squads and harassing litigation brought on by the Motion Picture Patents Company. If that weren't enough, the states of New Jersey and New York began taxing the studios.

The solution to the independents' problems was found in an isolated, small town in Southern California. Amid fruit orchards and attractive hills and valleys, which lent themselves to the filming of Westerns, the independents set up shop. For some of them, the move across country was one step ahead of the summonses being issued by New Jersey or New York sheriffs. Hollywood, the dream factory, offered inexpensive real estate, a seemingly endless supply of bright, sunny days ideal for the production of films, and a quick escape to Mexico if necessary.

Battles over production and distribution rights brought us to Hollywood.

The struggle with the Patents Company and the emergence of the feature length film gave shape to the industry and the three major elements that describe it: production, exhibition, and distribution.

The Feature Length Film

Longer films cost more to produce, but the public seemed willing to pay more to see them. This provided an incentive to producers. At the same time the longer films began to attract a more educated and sophisticated audience and to compete effectively with the theater as an evening of entertainment. Film, as it developed, radically altered the nature of the legitimate theater, effectively removing it from the national scene, more or less restricting it to a purely provincial New York medium and, incidentally, using it as a proving ground for film musicals.

Finally, the longer films reduced audience turnover and necessitated larger theaters; thus the ornate movie palaces of the 1920s and 1930s replaced the nickelodeons. The turning point in this chain of events can be marked by the 1915 production of *The Birth of a Nation,* a film as significant as the *Great Train Robbery* a dozen years earlier.

Griffith's *Birth of a Nation,* 1915, revolutionized the industry.

The Birth of a Nation was a three-hour historical epic produced at a cost of $110,000 by David Wark Griffith. Griffith, a Kentuckian and the son of a Confederate officer, selected the Civil War as the focal point around which he filmed his version of history—one in which the heroes were Ku Klux Klansmen. The eloquent and powerful film, a masterpiece of camera and editing techniques, was presented with full orchestration. The stereotypes it presented—particularly the "fallen" family of the south, carpetbaggers, and renegade blacks—caused race riots and mob behavior in many cities where the film was shown. Woodrow Wilson referred to the film as being "like history written in lightning." Indeed, Griffith proved in 1915 that film could have powerful emotional and propagandistic effects, at a time when the film industry was reaching wider and wider audiences who were coming to larger and more opulent theaters with greater expectations of entertainment and involvement.

The larger theaters had a voracious appetite. They had to be kept supplied with films, films of a certain kind. Since there was no demographic identification to the potential audience once films had become popular with the middle class, they had to appeal to everyone, young and old alike. They could not as a rule be controversial, but they had to be good entertainment—that is, exciting, spectacular, sensational—and they could not depart too far from a proven mode. For example, Griffith's 1916 *Intolerance,* a massive sociohistorical study of human imperfection presented in four separate stories bound together by the theme of intolerance, was a commercial failure primarily because it was too novel, too confusing. Indeed, it was years ahead of its time and caused Griffith and his peers (including Charles Chaplin and Mack Sennett) to direct creative efforts along more tried-and-true lines in the interest of making a dollar. Recognizing the need for profit, filmmakers tended to foreshadow television's later offerings in blandness, tentative sensationalism, and formula emphasis.

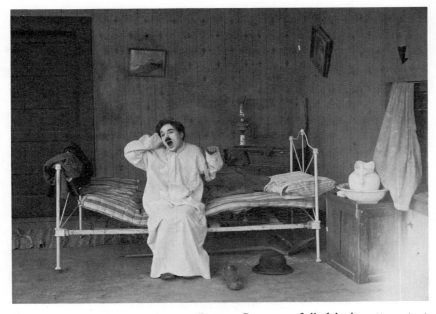

After the Motion Pictures Patent Company failed in its attempt at control, power shifted to the studios, which created the vertical film empires that ruled Hollywood for thirty years. Companies such as Metro-Goldwyn-Mayer (MGM) integrated production, distribution, and exhibition through their own movie houses. Distribution was the key to success, and *block booking* was the means used. Under block booking, exhibitors could not be selective; they were forced to contract for a number of pictures from a studio in order to get any major productions. If exhibitors refused, they got nothing and would go out of business. If they agreed, the exhibitors were assured a steady supply of films, many of which were second rate "B" pictures. At the time of booking, many of the films would be unproduced, and since they were being booked sight unseen, they were sold on the basis of proven factors, such as actors, actresses, plots or story lines, authors, directors, and sometimes even production costs.

Studios controlled distribution as well as production. "Block booking" kept the studios healthy.

As block booking became prevalent, the *star system* evolved into a type of insurance. The public became acquainted with the names and faces of performers by the 1920s and demanded to see more of their favorites. Among them were Douglas Fairbanks, Mary Pickford, and Rudolph Valentino. Cost controls became less important than the production budget, the size of which constituted another guarantee of success. There were numerous ways to spend money: on the stars who commanded fabulous salaries, on authors of best-selling novels for the film rights, on other proven writers to provide screenplays, on well-known directors, on an array of increasingly sophisticated technical innovations, and on promotion.

The Hollywood Method

The star system helped guarantee success, at some cost to quality.

Film, by its nature, demanded promotion to call attention to its wares in the marketplace. In the historical sense it qualified more as a consumer product than as a medium. A 1915 Supreme Court decision held that the exhibition of films was a business, pure and simple, originated and conducted for profit, much like circuses and theaters; as such, it deserved no protection from the First Amendment. This attitude, coupled with the unquestioned fact that numerous film producers were growing increasingly rich, led to Hollywood's demand for press agentry and star promotion, and at the same time gave the fledgling public relations profession a substantial boost.

As film became more and more organized as a major industry, it was inevitable that the artistic considerations of the medium would be subordinated to the practical. There was little room for experimentation, for art, and for departure from proven formulas. As production costs rose, Hollywood had to turn to Wall Street more frequently to finance its ventures. This move compounded the formula situation, for the bankers were far more apt to lend speculative money on a proven project than on an unknown quantity. In turn, there was an acceleration in the demand for best-selling authors, for expensive sets, for name stars, for proven formulas in the scripts, and for huge advertising and promotional budgets.

Sound and the Depression

Sound changed the nature of the industry, and made or broke many stars.

Popular mythology holds that sound came to films when Al Jolson turned to the audience in the middle of *The Jazz Singer* in 1927 and exclaimed, "Listen! You ain't heard nothin' yet." Like much folk history, this is erroneous. During the years after Edison's assistant William K. Dickson demonstrated talking pictures, experimental efforts were underway, including Warner Brothers' Vitaphone process and Dr. Lee De Forest's audion tube, which was modified for film. The achievement of *The Jazz Singer* was the synchronization of sound with the picture. Al Jolson's 1927 utterance was prophetic, as audience desires for the *talkies* spelled the end of the silent era and a revolution in film technology and artistry.

Sound disturbed Hollywood because many of the carefully built stars of the silent era couldn't make it in the talkies. Whether it was because of accents, vocal pitch and timber, or the new methods of acting dictated by the single but omnipotent microphone, stars like John Gilbert, Emil Jannings, Lillian Gish, and Clara Bow were quickly out of work. Just as quickly, new stars appeared, including Wallace Beery, Marie Dressler, William Powell, Myrna Loy, Gary Cooper, Clark Gable, James Cagney, Edward G. Robinson, Cary Grant, Spencer Tracy, Humphrey Bogart, Katherine Hepburn, John Wayne, and Bette Davis. The millions of dollars that had been spent promoting silent screen stars were lost assets, and the new, talking stars had to be created from scratch. Furthermore, the nature of sound changed the vehicles, and the story lines that had been appropriate during the silent era yielded to more dramatic scripts. New formulas were required, and the dimensions of sound required new and infinitely more expensive technology.

In 1927 some 20,000 movie houses were situated in America, but only a dozen were equipped for sound. Within two years nearly half the nation's theaters were wired, including almost all the metropolitan theaters, which generated the most income. At first Hollywood had counted on a dozen years or so for the changeover, but audiences stopped attending silent films—even though the average pre-1927 silent film was artistically superior to the first generation of talkies. By 1930, some 95 percent of Hollywood films were talkies, as the industry adjusted to the inevitable. Interestingly, not one major Hollywood studio folded during the changeover. They were more careful about the production and directing of the new films, which typically cost one and a half times as much to make as their silent counterparts. And the involvement of big banks to finance the projects meant less artistic freedom, particularly during the years of the depression.

According to a former production chief of Paramount studios, the new era of talking films resulted in "more craftsmen, less teamwork, more complex organization, less pioneering spirit, more expense, less inspiration, more talent, less glamour, more predatory competition, and less hospitality."[3]

Sound had barely come to the screen when the Great Depression began, injecting new social factors into moviemaking. Radio was a relatively new and "free" medium. It provided home entertainment in the lean depression years, when even the price of twenty-five cents to see a movie was often prohibitive. While the excitement of sound delayed the full economic effect in the movie business for several years, the depression years for Hollywood, like the rest of the nation, were thin. Color technology, which

Hollywood helped America escape from the Great Depression.

had been held back by Hollywood lest the industry would be disturbed again, made its appearance in 1935 (with *Becky Sharp,* starring Miriam Hopkins) as a counterdepression measure to offer something so vividly and dramatically new that America would spend money to see it.

For those who could afford the price of admission, the magical movies were a way to forget one's troubles. They provided escape to *The Wizard of Oz* and to war-torn Atlanta in *Gone With the Wind.* Busby Berkeley became famous for making tap-dancing musicals with long lines of high-kicking chorus girls.

While westerns, mysteries, and situation comedies were more or less stock fare, there was a certain faddishness to Hollywood productions in the 1930s and 1940s. A series of gangster movies in the early 1930s was followed by a rash of musical extravaganzas, of which Busby Berkeley's *Flying Down to Rio,* with a chorus line on the wings of an airliner, may have been the all-time high. These extravaganzas were followed by a religious revival, and finally a blaze of spy and war films. Once a plot achieved any kind of success at the box office, every other studio rushed variations of that theme into production to capitalize on the trend.

A companion trend developed as the syndicated Hollywood columnist lent gloss to the scene, filling the nation's newspapers with gossip, sex, and the doings and misdoings of the movie colony. Several dozen magazines vied to outdo one another in dramatizing the scandals of "tinsel town," both on and off screen; Hollywood provided a kind of vicarious romance for a nation in the throes of depression.

Table 9.1 Average weekly motion film attendance in the United States

Year	Average weekly attendance	Year	Average weekly attendance
1925	46,000,000	1955	46,000,000
1930	90,000,000	1960	40,000,000
1935	75,000,000*	1965	44,000,000
1940	80,000,000	1970	17,700,000
1945	90,000,000†	1975	19,900,000
1950	60,000,000	1980	19,644,000

(Sources: Christopher H. Sterling and Timothy R. Haight, *The Mass Media: Aspen Institute Guide to Communication Industry Trends* (New York: Praeger Publishers, 1978), p. 352; Cobbett Steinberg, *Reel Facts: The Movie Book of Records* (New York: Vintage Books, 1978), p. 371; and reprinted with permission of Variety, Inc.

*Sterling gives figure of 80,000,000 for 1935.
†Sterling gives figure of 85,000,000 for 1945.

During World War II, the film industry also provided an additional form of escape and even a form of patriotism as it reached its full impact in the late 1940s, immediately following the war. The industry reached its peak in the period from 1945 to 1948, when 90 million Americans attended movies each week. In 1949 the major studios—MGM, Twentieth Century Fox, Paramount, Columbia, RKO, and Warner Brothers—cranked out over four hundred celluloid fantasies. Thirty years later, fewer than half as many feature films were being turned out annually.

In World War II, Hollywood helped carry the colors.

The bubble of the film industry burst, primarily due to the *consent decree of 1946.* Sued by the Department of Justice for being in restraint of trade, the film industry reluctantly agreed to divest itself of its chains of movie houses. In essence, the empires were to be broken up, meaning the separation of exhibition from production and distribution. By the early 1950s the full impact of the consent decree was being felt; the studios lacked outlets for their potboilers, and the independent exhibitors demanded higher quality movies.

The Postwar Decline

When the federal government made studios sell their theaters, and TV came along, the celluloid bubble burst.

Other factors also entered into the decline of the studios, one of which was the formation of separate production companies by some artists. Actors, actresses, and directors banded together to produce films. Often they relied on the major studios for distribution of the final product, and sometimes for bankrolling. Increasing numbers of films were produced abroad, primarily as a result of tax advantages to the participating stars, and also because of cheaper foreign labor. Inevitably, some of the new independent producers came under the influence of the experimental and artistic techniques employed by foreign filmmakers.

Another blow to the film industry was dealt by a combination of national hysteria over communism and Hollywood's cowardice. During the years following World War II, right-wing groups scoured the countryside for Communist sympathizers or other "lefties." Scriptwriters and filmmakers who earlier had shown sympathy toward Russia, an American ally during the War, were hounded out of business—*blacklisted*. To protect their profits, studio chiefs turned against their former colleagues, and many of those named before congressional committees were unable to find work for more than a decade. The blacklisting is regarded as one of the film industry's low points.

Then there was television. Television took audiences out of the movie palaces and placed them back in their homes. Hollywood could not compete with television on its own terms by providing an evening's entertainment, which forced the film industry to offer radically different techniques that were unavailable to the home viewer. Wide screens, stereophonic sound, and three-dimensional films were a part of the answer; so were the super-spectaculars and the so-called first runs playing at premium prices in selected movie houses. Another approach was the exploration of previously taboo subject matter: drugs, sex, homosexuality, and nudity.

But the strategies were not successful. Attendance dropped from a high of 90 million weekly admissions in the late 1940s, as indicated in table 9.1, to less than half of that a decade later, and was again reduced by half by the 1970s. As the market declined, so did the need for the big movie palaces; they were the first casualties.

The Impact of Television

TV was not all bad news for Hollywood. Cooperation and independent efforts came about.

Television wasn't entirely bad for the film industry; there were some hidden benefits. First, television freed the film industry from a slavish devotion to the lowest common denominator. It also freed film from a reliance on the pseudoguarantees of success: the star system, formula plots, huge promotion budgets, and the like. The breakdown of these accoutrements within the industry further encouraged independent production as a new breed of artistic directors began to take control. Film was and is a corporate art form demanding the talents of writers, directors, and actors. Where previously the economics of filmmaking emphasized the stars, the newer trend placed emphasis on the director in whose production the actors were more or less incidental. This, too, was a carry-over from the influence of foreign films and the reputation of such impresarios (directors) as Federico Fellini.

The other big assist that television ironically offered the film industry was television itself. When television first began to make inroads on film's audiences, Hollywood fought television by prohibiting its productions from appearing on television. Beginning in 1955, however, the film industry discovered that television provided a brand-new market and source of revenue for old movies that were fully depreciated and had no other potential use for the future. Hollywood began selling old movies to television and in some recent cases has earned several million dollars a showing. The most noteworthy example is *Gone With the Wind*, for which CBS paid MGM $25 million for multiyear exclusive rights.

The next step in this particular chain was the use of studio facilities, first for making television serials and later for making television films. The major studios had the technical hardware, the personnel, and the know-how to crank out television programs. More complex, however, was the television movie. Not all the contemporary films, especially those exploring the more permissive themes of sex and violence, were appropriate to family viewers, especially since television's mores are audited by the FCC. A new type of film was required—one made for television—which would have its initial showing over the air, and then later would be exported for foreign exhibition in theaters, where profits were almost guaranteed. Not only did the television movie provide an opportunity to tailor the subject matter to the limits of family viewing, but it could also produce films to meet television's exact specifications as to running time and commercials, something that Hollywood film, which was produced for other purposes, could never do. It was possible to interrupt the action on television movies at the exact time that a commercial would run without disturbing continuity. Further, television films were designed to run ninety minutes, less commercials, and would not require the extensive editing that often removed significant action from the Hollywood product adapted to television.

Conversely, the smaller audiences of theater movies were younger, better educated, and more affluent than the audiences of television, and therefore they dictated different themes, like social justice, violence, and sexual freedom. (See tables 9.2 and 9.3.) They also demanded, and received, different techniques of pacing and camera work. By and large, the theater audience was also more sophisticated, and more aware and appreciative of graphic technique, being more educated and having grown up with video from childhood. But with the critical successes of such TV films as *Roots, Holocaust, Shōgun,* and *Masada,* the distinction between theater and TV films has blurred.

Table 9.2 Demographics of movie attendance, 1979. Ages of moviegoers.

Age	Percent of yearly movie attendance	Percent of resident civilian population
12–15	20	9
16–20	29	12
21–24	14	9
25–29	13	10
30–39	11	13
40–49	6	13
50–59	5	13
60 and over	2	19

Source: Opinion Research Corporation of Princeton, for the Motion Picture Association of America.

Table 9.3 Demographics of movie attendance, 1979.
Education of moviegoers.

Attendance	Some college	High school completed	Less than complete high school
Frequent	27	20	10
Occasional	37	28	16
Infrequent	13	17	11
Never	23	35	63

Source: Opinion Research Corporation of Princeton, for the Motion Picture Association of America.

The Business of Filmmaking

Conglomerates have replaced moguls of old, and filmmaking may never be the same again.

Today, perhaps moreso than ever before, filmmaking is a business. The Hollywood studio system of old, which succeeded or failed largely on the basis of the star system and the instincts for public taste of studio moguls and directors, has given way to conglomerate mentalities, where boards of directors and accountants as often as not make the final decisions. Independent producers, working alone or using studio properties, must convince the studios and parent corporations—often insurance and investment concerns, banks, or oil companies—to take the increasingly large risks involved in producing a major motion picture.

Production

The average film costs $10 million and must take in double that to be profitable. Little wonder an occasional blockbuster keeps a studio afloat.

And risks there are. Between 1972 and 1979 the cost of an average film released by the Motion Picture Association of America (MPAA) skyrocketed 338 percent, from $1,936,000 to $8,482,000. That was far higher than the Consumer Price Index rate of inflation, which was 74 percent during the same period. It also does not include newspaper, television, and radio advertising, which totalled between $600 and $650 million in 1979. In 1980, according to MPAA President Jack Valenti, the average cost for a negative of a film from an MPAA member company topped $10 million. After print and marketing costs were added the "typical" feature film had to recoup $20 million in theater rentals before showing any profit.[4]

According to *Variety* (the entertainment industry's trade magazine), only 100 or so films in history have earned over $20 million in domestic rentals, and slightly over 200 have earned $10 million. If we double those figures to include foreign rentals, reissuance at later dates, and sales to television (and doubling the totals is a generous guess), we're left with the startling realization that the overwhelming majority of films being released today will never make a profit. Since the mid-1970s the MPAA has issued fewer than 200 films per year, so it's obvious that a few (*Star Wars, Jaws, Superman, Raiders of the Lost Ark, E.T.*, and the like) are going to have to keep the industry afloat, paying the bills for the big budget films (*Heaven's Gate, Raise the Titanic*) that may never show a profit.

Distribution

All manner of hype and glory are needed to lure us into the theater.

Faced with rising inflation and an uncertain box-office attendance pattern, the MPAA has been running scared. Box-office take was showing a slight increase at the beginning of the 1980s, but it was somewhat artificial—the cost hikes in ticket prices barely offsetting a slight decline in the number of admissions. Since 1975, when moviegoers started standing in lines to watch the horrifying thriller *Jaws,* producers have increasingly recognized the value of media blitzes and marketing strategies to garner the needed return on investment. Paid advertising, press releases and publicity, exploitive gimmicks, stunts, and the like, and special promotions involving tie-ins between the movie and a product and/or personality have been successfully orchestrated for mass-appeal science fiction films (*Star Wars, The Empire Strikes Back, Star Trek, Close Encounters of the Third Kind, E.T.*) and the disaster (*Jaws, The Deep*) genre.

The most typical tie-in involves a movie and a book, which increases the attention given to a title being promoted in both forms. Tradition holds that a good book might become a successful film, but contemporary media practice often finds a reversal of this process, starting with screenplays and ending up with best-selling books—frequently mass-marketed paperbacks filled with photos from the film, of which the best example might be the paperback versions of *Star Wars* and *E.T.* Such tie-ins are forged with the hope that the popularity of one version will spur the other on to success. Not infrequently, television enters the picture, as the complexities of media marketing demonstrate which tie-in combination—film, television, book— will return the largest number of dollars on the investment.[5]

> Film-book-TV tie-ins help assure an audience.

Another aspect of a tie-in is the relationship between a film and magazines and newspapers. In the magazine world, there are dozens of publications devoted to film. And newspapers generally have entertainment sections that lean heavily toward the movies, quite naturally since a good deal of their revenue comes from theaters advertising current showings.

In addition to publicity and promotion schemes aimed at improving attendance and profits, the film industry has resorted to some questionable distribution practices. Selective contract adjustments, blind bidding, four-walling, and the older block booking methods are commonplace. Under *selective contract adjustments,* theater owners who cooperate with distributors in promoting and running their films are given preferential treatment. *Blind bidding,* which demands that exhibitors sign contracts for films before the films are released, has come under increasing fire on the state and federal levels and may be outlawed in the near future. *Four-walling* became popular in the early 1970s when distributors rented the theaters directly from the owners, and kept all the box-office receipts for the limited

> Questionable distribution practices also improve attendance.

engagements of their numerous low-budget films. Such films were frequently released or re-released simultaneously across the country in carefully selected markets. They were accompanied by heavy television advertising campaigns, which often exceeded the cost of producing the film. Four-walling by the major studios was ruled illegal but remained a viable way for smaller independent firms, such as Sunn Classic Pictures (*The Life and Times of Grizzly Adams, Beyond and Back, Chariots of the Gods,* and biblical docu-dramas), to compete in the marketplace. *Block-booking,* the practice of forcing exhibitors to accept a producer's mediocre films along with the money-makers, is illegal but continues to be practiced in modified forms.

At the beginning of 1983, when *Variety* (the entertainment industry's trade magazine) listed its annual "All-Time Film Rental Champs" in the U.S. and Canadian market, the value of promotional efforts made in recent years became increasingly obvious. Consider the mass appeal films listed in table 9.4 and note how many of them are of very recent vintage. It is important to note that the list does not include foreign theater income, which is quite substantial, and that the data included will undoubtedly change by the time this book is in your hands. Also, recall our previous observation that by 1980, a film had to earn $20 million to be considered a success.

Exhibition

Movies have come to the shopping centers in the form of modern-day storefront nickelodeons.

The smaller audiences of the 1950s rendered the big palaces obsolete. Monsters like Radio City Music Hall in New York City, with its 6,000-plus seats, couldn't be filled, and the cost of upkeep was too great. Consequently, many were torn down or were renovated and divided into two or more small theaters. The movie houses built during the 1950s were small, even tiny, and were located in shopping centers where parking and other services were available, or they were drive-ins where the customers brought their own seats.

Today, there are around 14,000 movie theaters in the United States, of which there are fewer than 4,000 drive-ins. On the average, an indoor theater has about 500 seats, compared to 750 in 1950. The newer movie houses reflect minimal construction costs and maintenance and often have multiple auditoriums. This allows a single operator to manage three or four minitheaters simultaneously from a central projection room, thus offering a range of movies to filmgoers. No longer is the audience limited to one selection; there may be three or four choices, and a moviegoer may be lured into attending three or four times during the same week. In their never-ending struggle to lure the TV audience back to the movies, film exhibitors in the early 1980s started reversing their practice of constructing "mini-cinemas," which had averaged 150 seats. Today, the move is back toward the 500-seat theaters, and even toward some luxurious theaters that take advantage of the latest in neovideo. In addition, as the economy has forced a slowdown in shopping center growth, film exhibitors are returning to more traditional sites or expanding their present facilities.[6]

Table 9.4 *Variety's* all-time film rental champs,
of U.S.–Canadian market, 1983

Rank	Film	Release year	Total rentals*
1.	*Star Wars*	1977	$193,500,000
2.	*E. T. The Extra-Terrestrial*	1982	187,000,000
3.	*The Empire Strikes Back*	1980	140,000,000
4.	*Jaws*	1975	133,435,000
5.	*Raiders of the Lost Ark*	1981	112,000,000
6.	*Grease*	1978	96,300,000
7.	*The Exorcist*	1973	88,600,000
8.	*The Godfather*	1972	86,275,000
9.	*Superman*	1978	82,700,000
10.	*The Sound of Music*	1965	79,748,000
11.	*The Sting*	1973	79,419,900
12.	*Close Encounters of the Third Kind*	1977	77,600,000
13.	*Gone With The Wind*	1939	76,700,000
14.	*Saturday Night Fever*	1977	74,100,000
15.	*National Lampoon's Animal House*	1978	74,000,000
16.	*Nine To Five*	1980	65,359,000
17.	*Superman II*	1981	64,500,000
18.	*Rocky III*	1982	63,450,045
19.	*On Golden Pond*	1981	63,000,000
20.	*Kramer vs. Kramer*	1979	61,734,000
21.	*Smokey and the Bandit*	1977	61,055,000
22.	*One Flew Over the Cuckoo's Nest*	1975	59,188,598
23.	*Stir Crazy*	1980	58,408,000
24.	*American Graffiti*	1973	56,662,000
25.	*Star Trek*	1979	56,000,000

Source: *Variety*, 12 January 1983. Reprinted by permission Variety, Inc.

*Rentals refers to dollars paid to the distributor, and is not the same as total box-office ticket sale grosses. Only the U.S. and Canadian markets are included here, which means the foreign market rentals, which sometimes equal or surpass the domestic rentals, are not considered. *Variety's* list appears annually the second week of January and is referred to by film buffs as the definitive account of the success of films.

Audiences and Their Guides

There is a psychology of moviegoing that has long been recognized and exploited by governmental and educational agencies as well as by commercial interests. The experience of seeing a film, as described by Jowett and Linton, emphasizes the vivid visual presentations in which images are already fully established, easily identified, and easily followed, even on the elementary levels. Viewers seem to attend films to enhance identification with film characters and to enjoy the aesthetics of the dramatic forms and vivid presentations. If these are the filmgoers' "needs," movies are historically meeting those needs through appeals to primary emotions and sentiments. The impact on audience members who attend films to be entertained is especially heightened: If they paid admission to laugh or cry, or to be frightened, angered, or sexually aroused, or merely to be removed from their everyday lives, their minds are particularly open to receive the

Film is a powerful medium because we are so willing to be manipulated.

producers' messages. Film is an unusually strong type of communication process, since the viewer is willing, even eager, to receive what the communicator has to offer.[7]

Whether for instructional, persuasive, or purely commercial purposes, film has unparalleled advantages as a mass medium. Complete control over emphasis, continuity, and effect—the use of special effects for dramatic purposes, the genius of editing, the ability to incorporate sound and music—are all designed for maximum purposeful impact on the audience. Film tells a special story vividly, commanding attention. Further, it plays to a captive audience, and generally under ideal conditions. Theaters are designed to minimize outside interference (channel noise) and to concentrate all attention on the screen. Films have a pleasurable connotation, and whether instructional or not, they are regarded as play, not (at least by the audience) as social control.[8] Add to this the element of suspension of disbelief, and audiences are likely to be responsive to whatever message the screen offers them.

The connection between the message and the content is not automatic; for one thing people are complex creatures who do not always act in predictable ways. Also, the message or the content has to be in the film in order for people to respond to it, and for many years filmmaking in America was governed by a restrictive code. Finally, in order for a film to have an effect people have to see it.

Film Controls

Early excesses brought on a variety of controls over the industry.

Film was probably the first mass medium to bring public attention to moral behavior. The lax lives of the major stars in Hollywood's heyday, heavily fanned by publicity, kept focusing attention on licentiousness, the disregard for correct moral behavior. During the 1930s Hollywood's constant pressing against the outer boundaries of nudity and sexual themes perturbed PTAs, clergy, and parents across the nation. Numerous state and municipal censor boards drafted restrictions on the content of films that were codified by the Motion Picture Producers and Distributors of America under the direction of Will H. Hays. By 1934 Hays' office had completed the Code of the Motion Picture Industry, for the purpose of helping studios anticipate the objections of local censor boards so as to avoid defacement of their films. The code, generally adequate for films of the 1930s and 1940s, broke down completely after smaller, independent producers began to explore new themes, and a considerable number of foreign films began to attract their own following.

Voluntary classifications— G, PG, R, X—place the burden of control on the theater manager, not the producer.

By the 1960s the code had lost its power and in 1968 it was abandoned entirely in favor of the voluntary classifications *G, PG, R,* and *X.* The new system, which places the censorship burden more on the theater owner than on the producer, and on the family most of all, has met with mixed success. (See chapter 13, "Movie Codes.")

The moral indignation that has recently been unleashed on television was at one time directed at the movies. Now that television has become the preeminent mass medium, less concern is expressed about the less omnipresent and more self-selective cinema. The smaller, younger, and more sophisticated audiences of this day do not generate the kind of moral concern that the filmgoers of yesterday did.

Critics

Critics attempt to keep up with film; by devoting their lives to it, they develop a familiarity with it and an expertise that audiences could never hope to achieve. The public's time is too limited; their interests are too diversified. The critics serve as a kind of intermedia gatekeeper who use their opinion in an attempt to separate the wheat from the chaff for others, and to save them from exposure to the useless and meaningless. Like other media experts, critics have different goals. Critics writing for the *New Yorker* and *New York* magazines, and the *New York Times,* the *Los Angeles Times,* and many other metropolitan newspapers make honest efforts to evaluate the social and artistic merits of the various films to which they are exposed. Too often, however, as John Hohenberg points out, film criticism becomes merely an adjunct to the entertainment pages and a boost to advertising.[9] Some critics on smaller papers write reviews in addition to performing their other reporting jobs, and are entirely too prone to accept the publicity handouts and photos flowing from theatrical press agents—along with the free tickets from the advertising theaters.

Film critics play an important, but sometimes questionable, role in the industry.

Do critics make the difference between the success and failure of a film? Some producers of films that have been panned are certain that reviewers are to blame for poor attendance. Others say that word-of-mouth endorsements from individuals who have seen a film is more important than what a critic says. This is one reason why sneak previews are so popular. They also help a producer determine if there is negative audience reaction before committing funds to an expensive advertising campaign.

Michael Cimino, director of the $36 million *Heaven's Gate,* did not pretest the film via sneak previews. Negative reviews from newspapers in New York City, where the film was shown in November 1980, claimed that "Watching the film is like taking a forced four-hour walking tour of one's own living room" *(New York Times)* and that "Frankly, had the movie been filmed entirely in Russian without English subtitles it might have made more sense than it does in its present state" *(New York Daily News).* On the basis of that reception, Director Cimino and United Artists withdrew the film from circulation to attempt a $10 million reediting. Apparently Cimino believed in the power of the critics. But the reception the second time around was not much better, and the film disappeared quickly.

Sneak previews help establish a film's place in the market.

The Oscars

One should not overlook the "Academy Awards" in a discussion of film evaluation and promotion. One night each year two hours or more of television prime time are devoted to one of the most universally watched and extravagantly produced spectaculars on TV. The cost of the cast of this extravaganza alone would be prohibitive (if they did not appear gratis) when one considers the name stars, directors, composers, authors, and artists who

The coveted Oscar—
a guaranteed boost to an
actor or actress's
career.
Wide World Photos

Hollywood's annual two-hour
commercial is a key
promotional technique.

are gathered by the hundreds to participate. While the "Academy Awards" may have begun as an effort to honor the artistic performances of the movie colony, some critics complain that with the advent of television it has become a promotional tool for old movies. They see it as an attempt to use television and the massive audiences it commands to publicize films that, by and large, have run their life course during the last year and to inject new life into them. There is no doubt that an Academy Award in a major category or even significant nominations for the award can start a film back on the circuits again at first-run prices, often playing to far larger audiences on the "academy circuit" than it did the first time around. An Academy Award is not a guarantee of second-time success, but exposure of the film industry to 50 or 60 million people is almost bound to have some salutary effect on its wares. Winning an award almost always provides a boost to the career of the honored talent. Timothy Hutton won the award for best supporting actor in 1981 for his first film, *Ordinary People*. Overnight he became a star, being offered large sums of money to appear in other films.

Attention thus far has been concentrated on commercial filmmaking, which is the entertaining and glamorous side of the medium. However, as in all media, film covers a wide range. There are cartoons—the ultimate in fantasy—which are often used as fillers but occasionally are developed into full-length movies, particularly by Walt Disney, who saw the childhood nostalgia of America's adults. There are also hard-core pornographic films, which are produced and marketed through an underground circuit. But these are the fringes of the film entertainment function.

Not to be forgotten are informational and persuasive films. Typically, these films play to smaller audiences than the entertainment films, but in the aggregate they outnumber commercial films by far. About 16,000 informational and persuasive films are produced each year for governmental, industrial, agricultural, educational, cultural, and community organizations, such as a chamber of commerce and a visitor's bureau; and the number has more than doubled since 1960. Together these films comprise well over a billion-dollar-a-year industry. In recent years many of these productions have used highly imaginative multi-media, wide-screen, and stereophonic effects to highlight their purpose and lend drama to the prosaic business of selling. Combining slides, film, and still photos in rapid flashes, using colored lights and multiple projectors, and most recently, adapting such neovideo as videocassettes and videodiscs, have almost created a new industrial art form. In the aggregate they offer widely expanded opportunities for employment, and absorb many of the university students who are training for film and video careers.

The information function of films started early with the filming of the inauguration of President William McKinley in 1897. As the film industry grew, newsreels became standard fare in the nation's movie houses. Produced weekly by such specialists as Pathe News, they were a sort of mini-magazine on celluloid, concentrating as much on features as on hard news. Along with animated cartoons and live organ music, they provided a varied bill of fare in the movie houses of the 1920s and early 1930s. Like the picture magazines, they added a visual ingredient to the oral world of radio, the nation's principal mass medium at that time. In many larger cities, minitheaters exclusively showing newsreels found a ready market. But television did away with newsreels; coverage was easier and better done on the evening and late news and could be presented daily instead of almost a week late.

Related to the newsreel is the documentary, a film feature exploring in depth some aspect of society or the natural world. One such documentary is *Nanook of the North,* a natural history of an Eskimo family, which was produced in 1920 during the silent film days. Since then documentaries have focused dramatic attention on some of the major areas of American life. But they, too, yielded to television, or rather were absorbed by it, and such classics as CBS's *The Selling of the Pentagon* and *Poverty in America* are the direct lineal descendants of the film documentary.

Other Film Types

Informational and persuasive films may have smaller audiences, but there are more of them.

Newsreels and Documentaries

Newsreels and documentaries exploit the medium's informational function.

Propaganda and Education

Recognizing the universal quality of film, the U.S. International Communication Agency (formerly the U.S. Information Agency) has made a number of films interpreting life and values of Americans for showing abroad. The efforts of the USICA have been hampered somewhat by the fact that these films run in competition with, and are far outnumbered by, Hollywood movies that show a different side of America. Thus, a credibility gap is established within the same medium. And the USICA films, no matter how well intentioned, do not operate in a vacuum. Other exposures—to American tourists and to U.S. advertising and products, such as Coca-Cola and McDonald's—create a confusion of American values difficult to understand.

The USICA is essentially a propaganda agency in the broadest sense of the term, and is restricted by Congress from domestic distribution of its materials, including film. One film, *Years of Lightning, Day of Drums,* a masterfully produced history of the thousand-day administration of John F. Kennedy to be shown to worldwide admirers, required an act of Congress to permit its exhibition in the United States.

The United States is not the only nation to have recognized the enormous propaganda function of film. The USSR has 154,000 theaters—about 58 percent of the world's total and more than ten times the number in operation within the United States. A prime reason for Soviet addiction to film has been that historically, especially before the advent of television, film was a key medium of propaganda and indoctrination in Russia. Today, it also serves as a prime social event, a break from routine.

An increasing number of educational films are being made for use in the classroom, and new educational techniques are being developed that make heavier use of video materials, including both film and television. This is an interesting innovation that may modify the educational system considerably but it is still too early to make any substantive judgments. The use of video materials may be one way to keep up with the acceleration of technological change, and with the visual orientation of the young. As this happens, of course, print will be de-emphasized and the entire structure of education will change.

Film as a Cross-Cultural Medium

One of the peculiarities of film, noticeable from the beginning, is that the language barrier is minimal. The immigrants who first populated the storefront theaters at the turn of the century were aware of this. Film has lent itself to cross-cultural transfer in a sense that no other medium has. Print demands language familiarity by its nature. The broadcast media, even television, are so heavily laden with verbal overtones that they hinder foreign comprehension. But film—like drama, its ancient ancestor—is universal. Dubbing and subtitling in native tongues can be done inexpensively, enhancing the universality. Film is also far more transportable than drama, and from its earliest history became an export product with significant international effects.

Film, whether we like it or not, is our unofficial ambassador around the world.
Peter Menzel/Stock, Boston

From the beginning of filmmaking, the United States has dominated the industry. American producers had the early incentive to make an ever-increasing number of films commercially because of superior technology and large audiences, which found sufficient leisure to support film even around the turn of the century. Inevitably, these films found their way overseas to fill foreign movie houses with a U.S. product in the absence of a sufficient quantity of local films. Thus, film became an early communications export of the United States. Americans were visible on the world's movie screens to a degree that no number of emissaries or even tourists could ever achieve. But theirs was an unrealistic presence composed of fantasy and dreams. Exposed to the nations of the world were societal stereotypes and quaint moralities, a love of violence, and a sort of synthetic history, both past and present. An incredible wealth ran through all the pictures as celluloid strived mightily to portray the good life—a wealth bound to contrast unfavorably with the surrounding facts of life in much of the world. An unbelievable technology spread itself across the screen, generating a sense of awe, and the nations of the world thought they were seeing America.

What's wrong with Hollywood's international diplomacy? Nothing, so long as we don't care how others see us.

Fantasy vs. Reality Abroad

Unaware of the American experience and lacking native perspective, other nations accepted American fantasies for fact. While American films were produced in America for the entertainment of Americans, as an escape from reality, there was no reason for other nations not to accept them as truth. This appears to be a pitfall of mass communications transfer, and it is quite possible that what originated in Hollywood as harmless entertainment, following a proven formula, emerged in Europe, in Asia, or in Latin America as a social document engendering awe, envy, and resentment.

It was not so much the treatment of American films—their improbable plots, their worship of sex symbols, and their cowboys and Indians—that caused this effect. It was the sheer overpowering volume of American export films, in the absence of other exposure, to a point where the films became America. Further, the more technically perfect the films became, the greater this delusion grew.

Moreover, it was the hundreds and thousands of "B" potboilers that offered this false view of America, rather than the big-budget extravaganzas. The very factors that characterized the old Hollywood—a large volume of production, the sacrifice of quality and technical perfection—were the same factors that betrayed the American image abroad. Rather than distorting the values of other lands, American films have distorted the foreign view of America, subtly and perhaps irreparably.

Foreign Influences Here

Foreign films taught us many lessons.

The transportability of film works two ways, and foreign films were not without influence in the United States. Playing small "art" houses, foreign films gained a currency of modishness in the 1950s and 1960s. Principal among the foreign influences on contemporary film in America was the neorealism of the postwar Italian producers, such as Roberto Rossellini and Vittorio DeSica. Their films dealt with the nitty-gritty and the hopelessness of life. French directors brought their "new wave" of films, which explored the actions and events of the lives of their characters—events that were often meaningless. France's contribution was also one of technique—freeing producers from studios and taking them into the open—which even at the sacrifice of technical perfection brought a greater realism to the screen. English producers, meanwhile, discovered England's lower classes and their accents. In a sense they set the stage for the English revolution, which eventually erupted in gangs of Teddy Boys and the clothing styles of Carnaby Street and the Beatles. Indeed, a good deal of the American youth cult had its origin in English cinema.

Swedish films were and still are dominated by the genius of Ingmar Bergman who, more successfully than anyone else, introduced metaphor in film, raising cinema to an art form and exploring in the ancient Greek traditions the timeless themes of life and death, truth, and the like.

From Japan came incredibly beautiful films, whose technical artistry and use of light, color, space, and misty camera techniques were entirely captivating. They brought the understated beauty of Japanese art to the screen. And, most recently, the history, geography, and cultural values of Australia have come into America's and the world's consciousness via film. All these forces found a refocus in the United States as its film industry underwent the throes of reorganization.

Foreign films, after a slow, almost "groupie" beginning, became increasingly popular as the volume of production in the United States slacked off and was diverted to television. And American films abroad frequently reflected the cultural influences of their host countries. American audiences began to look for more complex themes, encouraging American independent producers to pay greater attention to the integrity and artistic merit of their work. Many major films, bankrolled and produced by both studio chiefs and independents, experienced a renaissance.

The extravaganza did not die completely. There were still studios that focused on tried-and-true techniques and used lavish promotional budgets to sell their wares. However, in the 1970s they began to fade, and the film has become more and more like its lineal ancestor the book in its independence of production.

The Future of Film

There have been few serious attempts at systematic predictions about the film industry, perhaps because most writers about film are caught up in the here and now, or perhaps because film has shown a curious resiliency whenever it has been threatened in the past. Taking a cue from Jowett and Linton, who have devoted a complete chapter to the future of film in their thoughtful *Movies as Mass Communication,* we will look briefly at technological developments, demographic variables, and economic trends that may affect film in general and theatrical movies in particular.

Film's future is tied to technology, demographics, and economics.

As we have noticed in discussing the future of print media, and as we cannot help but notice when discussing electronic media, much of what happens to film is dependent upon the television industry. After their initial, mutual animosity, film and television appear to have struck a bargain, with Hollywood producing made-for-TV movies and emptying its vaults—for a price—to satisfy TV's enormous appetite for time fillers. But William Fadiman suggests that Hollywood may be cutting its own throat by counting so heavily on television, especially since old movies are a nonrenewable resource and production of feature films has declined recently.[10] Also, if television should increase its own film production, it will have little difficulty undercutting Hollywood.

Burgeoning systems of in-home entertainment facilities such as videocassettes and videodiscs, which eliminate the necessity of "going out" to be entertained, will no doubt affect film distribution and theater practices if not film manufacturing. Pay television, such as Home Box Office and Showtime, is already absorbing large quantities of Hollywood's new movies (movies that are six to eighteen months old), and the trend is expected to continue. Improved technology of in-home units, including "projection television" sets producing six-foot-tall images, is bound to make staying home for movies almost as exciting an experience as heading to the theaters downtown or in suburban shopping centers. To compete with these innovations, theatrical films are expected to mount technological campaigns to match those of the early television era, when three-dimensional and wide-screen extravaganzas were developed. In fact, 3-D was revived in 1981 with the distribution of *Comin' at Ya*. Bigger screens, 70-mm prints in lieu of the standard 35-mm size, and clearer images are among exhibitors' ploys to lure the neovideo stay-at-homes back to the movies.[11] Already, vastly improved sound systems have made their appearance. The Dolby noise-reduction stereo involves the rewiring of the theater at a cost of about $16,000. Another sound system, Sensurround, used low frequency sound to give *Earthquake* audiences heightened awareness of impending doom—but at a cost to the theater owners. Drive-ins are experimenting with Cine-Fi, a system by which the sound track of the film is transmitted through the car's radio. Meanwhile, experiments with screen size and shape continue, in further efforts to give paying customers something they cannot experience at home.

Film futurists take some comfort in recognizing that population trends indicate an increasing bulge in the young, educated, and affluent. By 1985 45 percent of the world's population will be between the ages of twelve and thirty-nine. In the past, persons within that age group have found films a satisfying way to spend their leisure, and with increased leisure time on the horizon, they may continue to do so. Should that be the case, Hollywood might be able to satisfy the social inclinations of the younger group while tapping a broader market (one that includes an older audience) by producing and distributing films for in-home use. Cumulatively, then, commercial films may reach broader audiences even if theaters have fewer patrons. To do so, however, more sophisticated marketing techniques, probably based on increased use of psychographic testing, may become more prevalent.

An example of the lengths to which Hollywood will go to milk its occasional blockbuster is the media tie-in blitz surrounding 1982's smash hit *E.T.—The Extraterrestial*. Books, posters, "reach out and touch someone" telephone commercials, and products from bicycles to dolls to underwear to video games make Steven Spielberg's *E.T.* a potential billion dollar baby.

Economically, film companies have already recognized the wisdom of participating in in-home as well as theatrical arenas. Some are already producing videocassette and videodisc systems, and are experimenting with other consumer-controlled technologies that will involve the book, newspaper, and magazine distribution systems described earlier.

One futurist, Wilton Holm, has suggested that neighborhood theaters, even within apartment house complexes, will continue, but will use

Filmmakers are realizing the wisdom of providing grist for newer media's mills.

different distribution systems. He sees movies being sent electronically by cable and microwave, or even satellite, which would expedite delivery and reduce theater personnel.[12]

Others suggest that theaters will become communication centers where prerecorded films will be sold on tape or videodisc and where audiences will be more sensually involved in multimedia presentations. Crowd psychology will be exploited, and audience involvement in the film experience will be enhanced through the use of interactive feedback systems. One such system, experimented with at the Czechoslovakian pavilion at Canada's Expo '67, allowed the audience to vote for different plot alternatives at various crisis points in the film. It necessitated seventy-eight different reels of film to accommodate the plot configurations the audience could conceivably choose.

Theatrical innovations, all efforts to more fully involve the audience in the moviegoing experience, are expensive and tentative. In addition, they are frequently employed at some cost to the film itself, since audiences have grown accustomed to basic narrative and cinemagraphic formulas. Such formulas cannot be changed without affecting audience perceptions and moods, as Edwin Porter found in 1903 when his *Great Train Robbery* broke so many theatrical rules. As Jowett and Linton observe, North American audiences are too accustomed to feature-length fictional, and narrative movies in which attention is consciously diverted from technique and focused on subject matter. Sophisticated technological innovations will be successful only if they can be incorporated adequately into existing storytelling techniques.[13]

Summary

Through its antecedents, graphics and the drama, film stretches back to prehistory. Following the technological development of the electric light, roll film, and sprocket feed, and the application of the psychological principle known as persistence of vision, the curtain rose for the first halting one-reelers around the turn of the century. The first theaters were storefronts in major East Coast cities, where droves of immigrants, uneducated and illiterate, flocked for their only available entertainment in an alien land. Storefronts yielded to nickelodeons, which in turn yielded to the big movie palaces of the 1920s and 1930s, as a steady supply of films arrived from Hollywood.

Film was treated as a mass medium, catering to the lowest common denominator of appeal and sacrificing artistic considerations for economic discipline. The star system, lavish promotion and publicity, and huge budgets for formula pictures were all attempts to minimize the risk inherent in filmmaking during the years before television. The coming of television helped burst Hollywood's bubble, but the movie city was already in trouble as a result of the 1946 consent decree wherein the industry agreed to divest itself of its theaters. Within a decade film's audiences dropped 50 percent, and within a generation, they dropped by half again.

In a pattern familiar to media historians, the new medium—television—was first viewed as a threat, and only later was it joined by the film industry, which sold old movies to TV at a considerable profit and eventually joined production forces. The two media found separate audiences. Film's audiences were smaller, younger, better educated, more sophisticated, and more demanding than before. TV's audiences were represented by a truer cross-section of America, the lowest common denominator.

Contemporary filmmaking, more than ever before, is a commercial business, controlled by economic decisions rather than artistic hunches. Three major elements constitute the business: production, distribution, and exhibition. The risks can be traumatic, even for the conglomerates who finance feature films, which today average over $10 million per feature. The industry has gone increasingly to publicity, advertising, marketing research, and gimmickry to gain a return on its investments.

Films generally play to captive audiences under ideal conditions in which the viewer is prompted to suspend disbelief. For these reasons, film is an ideal mass medium for instructional, persuasive, or commercial purposes. From the 1930s to the 1960s the content of American films was controlled by the Code of the Motion Picture Industry. Since then voluntary classifications have placed more responsibility on the theater owner. Critics help the viewer determine which films are worth seeing, while the Academy Awards are used by the industry to attract more patrons.

In addition to commercial films, the industry produces about 16,000 instructional and persuasive films each year. Other film types include newsreels, documentaries, propaganda films, and educational films. As a tangible consumer product, film became an early communications export. For better and for worse, it extended America's influence abroad; at the same time, foreign films with their unique production and artistic techniques influenced the American market and brought international understanding—and misunderstanding—back across the oceans.

To a large extent, the future of film is tied to the television industry, both in terms of product exchange and in consumer-controlled, at-home technology that is bound to affect theater attendance. Theatrical film is expected to become more sensory and more involving, particularly to retain its youthful, educated, and sophisticated adherents. Whether form or substance emerges victoriously is a key issue to be resolved, for new technology, like the 3-D and wide-screen innovations of the 1950s, may not suffice to demand loyalty.

1. Arthur Knight, *The Liveliest Art: A Panoramic History of the Movies,* rev. ed. (New York: New American Library, 1979), p. 7.
2. Steven C. Early, *An Introduction to American Movies* (New York: New American Library, 1979), p. 6.
3. Peter Andrews, "The Birth of the Talkies," *Saturday Review,* 12 November 1977, p. 43.
4. *Variety,* 18 June 1980, p. 3.
5. "Media Tie-ins," *Publishers Weekly,* 11 April 1980, pp. 33–43; and Richard Reeves, "Lucas and Spielberg Strike Back for America," *Logan* (Utah) *Herald-Journal,* 17 August 1982.
6. David Steritt, "Movies Try New Tactics in Battle With TV," *Christian Science Monitor,* 23 August 1982.
7. Garth Jowett and James M. Linton, *Movies as Mass Communications,* (Beverly Hills, Calif.: SAGE Publications, 1980), pp. 89–90.
8. William Stephenson, *The Play Theory of Mass Communications* (Chicago: University of Chicago Press, 1967).
9. John Hohenberg, *The News Media: A Journalist Looks at His Profession* (New York: Holt, Rinehart & Winston, 1968).
10. William Fadiman, *Hollywood Now* (London: Thames and Hudson, 1973).
11. Steritt, "Movies Try New Tactics in Battle with TV," p. 1.
12. Wilton R. Holm, "Management Looks at the Future," in *The Movie Business: American Film Industry Practice,* eds. A. W. Bleum and J. E. Squire (New York: Hastings House, 1972), pp. 253–57.
13. Jowett and Linton, *Movies as Mass Communications,* p. 131.

Notes

Part 4 Persuasive Media

Advertising and public relations are service media. They are highly organized products of a complex and corporate communications system, but they have no audiences of their own in the sense that the mass media do. They work with other corporate entities through which they filter to people only indirectly. In some cases the persuasive media provide information and commercial content to the mass media; more often their purpose is to persuade.

It is necessary to differentiate between the advertising and public relations industries. Advertising deals in paid time and space by identified sponsors; it provides the economic incentive for most of the mass media, so that in addition to persuasion it provides the grease that keeps the mass communications' wheels turning. Public relations, on the other hand, is charming and sometimes devious. Its persuasion offered free of cost to the mass media is often disguised as news, whereby it sometimes conceals its purpose and source. However, most worthwhile public relations jobs call for integrity and solid journalism skills, and it is also true that public relations is a necessary adjunct to the information business. The mass media rely on it far more than they like to admit to acquire legitimate news of events and organizations, for which they lack the necessary human and economic resources.

Thus, it seems that the functions of communication are intermixed in the persuasive media as much as they are in the mass media. Advertising deals in persuasion and information. Further, one of the basic jobs of advertising agencies is to inject entertainment into persuasion to make it palatable. By nature public relations is informational and persuasive, and possibly entertaining. It is ulterior communications. Both advertising and public relations reflect contemporary values of the society in which we live.

The pervasity of these indirect media, their influence upon the media they serve, and their indirect effect upon various audiences, publics, and each individual are the subjects of these two chapters.

Advertising 10

Outline

Introduction

A peculiarity of the American mass communications system is that advertising pays most of the bills. This has both advantages and disadvantages. On the plus side is the fact that the American people get an incredible variety of information, entertainment, and culture at minimal cost. A disadvantage is that nearly all of America's mass communications is heavily overladen with commercial or persuasive messages. The two go together. Commercial persuasion permeates American mass communications, as opposed to the political persuasion that is evident in most of the totalitarian countries. The private sector, seeking profits, has been able to come up with the massive investment necessary to develop America's diversified and sophisticated mass communications networks, while other nations that support mass communications by government financing have had to balance communications expenditures with many other kinds of national interests. Additionally, we should recall that government financing of the mass media inevitably brings with it governmental influence on the news and entertainment content. America has opted for "Laverne and Shirley" and "Mork and Mindy," just as Red China has saturated its media with propagandistic opera and drama. "He who pays the piper. . . ."

Advertising is a necessary adjunct to mass production and is, in fact, mass sales: It is an automated sales force, playing the law of averages that grows out of the correlation between degree of exposure and subsequent sales. It is on this correlation that ratings are based. The ratings measure

In today's commercial environment, one doesn't have to be a cynic to observe that information and entertainment lure audiences to the advertisers.
Richard Kalvar / Magnum Photos, Inc.

audience size, and subsequent sales confirm the relationship. However, most advertising people believe that exposure is not enough; an effective message is also needed. The principal role of the advertising agency today is to combine exposure (media buyers) with appeal (the creative group).

In some cases the purpose of the advertising message is to be informative, and in other cases, to be persuasive. For example, the classifieds in the daily newspaper provide commercial information, but information nonetheless. So do the movie ads. Both indicate the availability of a product at a place, and sometimes at a time and price. They differ little from the stock market quotations or television logs, which provide pure commercial information.

Most of this chapter will be directed at persuasive advertising. Following a discussion of the development of advertising, we will explore the role of advertising agencies and their functions, including media buyers and the creative group. The next two sections will emphasize several advertising strategies that have been influential during the last thirty years and some reasons why advertising works. Because advertising is so highly persuasive in nature, many people in the industry are concerned about deceptive practices. This concern has prompted efforts at governmental and self-regulation and attempts to make the business more professional. Nonetheless, advertising is still criticized frequently for its effects and costs, which will be the subject of the final section of this chapter.

Advertising is an ancient practice, but most of its early history is undistinguished. Following hundreds of years of usage, advertising began to grow very slowly only after the development of print technology, and it has matured only within the last century under the pressure of the industrial revolution.

Historical Development

During the illiterate times of bygone centuries, advertising was graphic and informational. The wineshopkeeper and the sandalmaker advertised their wares by hanging out a wineskin and a pair of sandals. To natives and travelers alike, these signs told where wine and sandals were sold. This was pure information, which indicated the availability of a product. However, human ingenuity never sleeps, and one day an enterprising wine seller hung out a larger wineskin. Not only was this bigger wineskin visible at a greater distance, thus automatically expanding its audience, but the size itself psychologically said that here was a bigger and better wineshop. In the course of events more people frequented the wineshop with the bigger wineskin. The sandalmakers followed suit. They made pairs of giant sandals and discovered that the sandals became conversation pieces and that folks came to their shops out of curiosity. Orders increased, and the correlation between exposure and sales became established.

From Wineskins to National Advertisers

Even to the illiterate in centuries past, advertising represented both information and persuasion.

The point is that the ordinary wineskin or pair of sandals provided pure information. However, once a bigger wineskin was built, an element of persuasion was injected: Bigger is better. Then, as now, advertising represented varying combinations of information and persuasion, plus an important extra: something to catch the audience's attention—the bigger wineskin and the enormous sandals were both a big plus in the competition for attention.

The invention of movable type, as we discussed in chapter 4, led to increasing literacy, and it was natural that advertising, while retaining its graphic elements, should also take advantage of the new medium. Most of the early printers were also booksellers, who took quite naturally to advertising available or forthcoming titles in tracts and flyers. Because literacy was required to read a book, only the literate could read a flyer and only the potential customer could decipher the advertisement. This early example of advertising selectivity is a form that has achieved extraordinary sophistication in the past several decades.

Early advertising was local and selective.

By the early nineteenth century newspapers carried some classified advertising. One of the more intriguing ads appeared in several St. Louis papers during February and March of 1822.

TO
Enterprising Young Men

The subscriber wishes to engage ONE HUNDRED MEN, to ascend the river Missouri to its source, there to be employed for one, two or three years. For particulars enquire of Major Andrew Henry, near the Lead Mines, in the County of Washington, (who will ascend with, and command the party) or to the subscriber at St. Louis.

Wm. H. Ashley

Some of those who responded to the small ad became the most famous names in Rocky Mountain history, for they were the free trappers of the Rocky Mountain Fur Company who spawned legends and opened the West.

Ashley's ad, and all early advertising, was local, serving local merchants and a local audience. But the industrial revolution changed this. It brought about the mass production of products, requiring mass purchases far in excess of what the local community could support. By the 1840s railroads were an effective method for wider distribution of goods, which encouraged national advertising. Further, in a competitive, free enterprise economy, the success of one new product prompted the development of almost identical products by competing manufacturers seeking their share of a proven market. The task of the advertiser became that of distinguishing between products that were more or less identical. More often than not, any distinction lay in the advertisements rather than in the products.

The new emphasis on advertising began to take hold before the middle of the century with the establishment of a number of advertising agencies. In actuality, these early agencies were little more than publishers' representatives or space brokers. Often they would contract with a publisher for a certain amount of space in a newspaper, and then sell this space to advertisers for whatever amount the traffic would bear. There were no published rate cards in those days and no certified circulation figures. National advertising was on a happenstance basis, removed from the local familiarity that exercised a certain degree of control between a publisher and a merchant operating in the same town or city.

Ad agencies were in operation before 1850, helping to promote sometimes identical products.

It was not until 1869 that some semblance of order came to the growing advertising scene. The publication of Rowell's *American Newspaper Directory* gave the approximate circulations of the nation's press, which led to the establishment of published rates based on circulation size. During the same year America's oldest advertising agency, N. W. Ayer & Son, was formed. This agency worked with the newspapers on behalf of the clients it represented. At about this time the *commission system* also originated, whereby accredited advertising agencies discounted their payments to the media by 15 percent in return for preparing and placing an advertisement. Publishers found the commission system an incentive to agencies to do part of the selling of space while still leaving the publisher free to sell other advertisements directly.

Order and Competition: 1869–1890

In the 1880s and 1890s, the competition for attention among almost identical and competing national products became intense. Department stores became the local warehouses for national products and they competed with each other in the largest markets. Advertisers discovered that informational advertisements were no longer sufficient and that considerable doses of persuasion in one form or another had to be injected if their products were to move in a competitive economy. This was the period, too,

Persuasion became an essential component in the industrial, competitive age.

when print and graphics began to merge, graphics illustrating a product or a situation and print glowingly describing it. Graphics served as an attention getter; even then a picture was worth a thousand words.

National advertising promoted the product's concept; local advertising said where, when, and how much it would cost to buy it.

The competitive market situation also led to the embryonic beginnings of different forms of cooperative advertising. In one form, which is still in existence, the national manufacturers maintained a national program, generally trying to establish the superior nature of their product, while the local dealers or distributors advertised locally, giving the where, when, and price. Newspapers recognized then, as they do today, the difference between these two essentially different forms of advertising; as a result, local advertising (sometimes called retail advertising) generally carries a lower rate than national advertising, as an incentive to local merchants. In broadcast, in most cases, national advertising is carried by the networks while local is sold by affiliates and independents. A variation on this theme is co-op advertising, wherein the national manufacturer shares a part of the cost of local advertising with the distributor or dealer.

Brand Names

By the 1890s, ads had to create any distinction among identical products. Brand names were established.

By the 1890s it was quite clear that most consumer products were nearly identical, and any distinction would have to be created by advertising. The first attempt to do this was through the establishment of a *brand name*. Using positive reinforcement on a more or less continual basis, an effort was made to establish the brand name as synonymous with the product or with quality. In England in the 1890s, Pears' soap was the subject of the first mammoth attempt to identify a name with a product. "Pears' Soap" appeared in English magazines and newspapers, on buses, light posts, board fences, and vacant walls until Pears' meant soap. The English did not ask for soap; they asked for Pears'. Coca-Cola, Kleenex, and Xerox are contemporary examples to the point that Kleenex means "facial tissue," and Xerox so describes "photo duplication" that the Xerox Corporation may have spent millions of dollars clarifying the distinction, while at the same time firmly planting the name Xerox in consumers' minds.

Slogans

Slogans were catchy capsule summaries of the product's merits.

While brand names were an effective advertising technique, something more was required to really overcome the competition for attention. From the realm of political campaigning, advertisers borrowed the *slogan,* a catchy capsule summary of the product; and as early as the 1890s Eastman Kodak came up with the first really distinctive slogan, "You Push the Button, We Do the Rest"—a masterpiece of simplicity, describing simplicity. Meanwhile, Pears' updated its campaign, introducing a slogan that became (to the utter delight of the Pears' Company) a standard British greeting for at least half a century, "Good Morning, Have You Used Pears' Soap Today?"

The use of brand names and their accompanying slogans has carried on into the present. As a mark of the technique of persuasion, slogans—like the various forms of the media—continue to be successfully used even after more sophisticated techniques have been developed. Often they are used in combination with other techniques, pyramided on each other for maximum effect.

In the philosophical climate of the early twentieth century, advertisers were facing attacks levelled by muckrakers and concerned citizens. The industry responded with self-protective calls for professionalism and high ethical standards. In 1911, for example, several thousand practitioners gathering for the national convention of the Associated Advertising Clubs of America heard one spokesperson exhort, "If you are to become a profession, you must here and now formulate a code. That code need spell but one word, 'truth', and all worthy things shall be added unto you."[1] Despite the lofty idealism, there was little change in advertising ethics from the turn of the century until after World War II.

The Early Twentieth Century

Under attack, advertisers tried to enhance their "professional" image.

Gradually, the industry expanded. Radio in the 1920s brought an aural emphasis superimposed upon the print techniques; it facilitated the use of jingles and set them to music for added impact. During the 1930s, public opinion polling was quickly adopted by advertising agencies as a device for measuring audience size and program popularity in radio, which, unlike newspapers and magazines, provided no circulation figures. The clearly observable fact that women listened to radio more during the daytime while men were at work and that entire families listened in the evening led to the concept of prime time and an early form of demographic appeal represented by the radio soap operas. The concept of the lowest common denominator was also born during this period. Sponsorships gave way to spot announcements as a more profitable means of selling radio advertising.

Advertising agencies grew and prospered. The advent of radio introduced a new element into mass persuasion, and increasing complexities demanded expertise that few product organizations possessed. Creativity and advertisement testing became part of the agencies' stock-in-trade. Techniques for measuring the readership of magazine advertisements were superimposed on magazine circulation figures. These still exist in the form of the *Starch Reports,* which gives a clue to the exposure and drawing power of a print advertisement, taking into consideration such things as appeal of the artwork, layout, copy readability, and the like.

The method of advertisement testing in the beginning was remarkably simple, and variations of it are still in use. Two different ads on the same subject were placed in a *split run* in a newspaper; that is, half of the edition carried one ad and the other half carried the other ad. The ads asked readers to return a coupon for a product at a reduced price, and the relative appeal of the two ads was gauged on the basis of how many people responded to each ad.

Despite growth and refinements in the advertising business, nothing really new was developed for almost a half century. Following World War II a new spirit invaded advertising. Interest in psychological warfare and propaganda had injected heavy doses of the social sciences, particularly psychology and sociology, into the persuasion field. Computers, which first had a practical application during the war, greatly facilitated public opinion measurement, polling, and testing, and gave birth to more accurate ratings. Further, the lapse in civilian production during the war years had created a demand for consumer goods, and as America's corporations turned their enormous capacity to peacetime manufacture, they generated gigantic pressure to move the goods. Advertising had a renaissance generated by new techniques, new products, and new audiences. Returning servicemen, reunited families, and a baby boom created an unparalleled demand for almost everything. Also, the genesis of television in 1948, only three years after the war, added new dimensions to advertising, as it did to most other phases of life.

Following World War II, advertising adopted heavy doses of social science.

Advertising was a $4 billion industry in 1947. In 1970 it reached $20 billion. By 1980 advertising passed the $50 billion mark, and it broke $60 billion in 1981 despite a slowdown in the American economy. Refer to table 10.1 for a listing of the top twenty-five American advertisers in 1981. The figures given, however, do not include the additional billions of dollars spent for packaging products, which is difficult if not impossible to separate from point-of-sale advertising. Over a half million people are employed in the various facets of advertising within the United States—in agencies, in the internal advertising departments of both industrial and retail establishments, and in the media.

Newspapers still take the greatest share of the national advertising dollar, between 28 and 30 percent since 1960. Television takes about 21 percent, up from 13 percent in 1960. However, it should be noted that the

Postwar Growth

Advertising has passed the $60 billion-a-year mark with all media involved.

Table 10.1. America's leading national advertisers, 1981

Rank	Company	Advertising $ (in millions)	Total sales $ (in millions)	Advertising % of sales	Type of business
1.	Procter & Gamble	671.8	11,944.0	5.6	Soaps, cleaners (and allied)
2.	Sears, Roebuck & Co.	544.1	27,360.0	2.0	Retail chain
3.	General Foods Corp.	456.8	8,351.1	5.5	Food
4.	Philip Morris Inc.	433.0	10,885.9	4.0	Tobacco
5.	General Motors Corp.	401.0	62,698.5	0.6	Automobiles
6.	K mart Corp.	349.6	16,527.0	2.1	Retail chain
7.	Nabisco Brands	341.0	5,819.2	5.9	Food
8.	R. J. Reynolds Industries	321.3	11,691.8	2.7	Tobacco
9.	American Telephone & Telegraph Co.	297.0	58,214.0	0.5	Telephone service, equipment
10.	Mobil Corp.	293.1	68,587.0	4.3	Miscellaneous
11.	Ford Motor Co.	286.7	38,247.1	0.7	Automobiles
12.	Warner-Lambert Co.	270.4	3,379.1	8.0	Toiletries, cosmetics
13.	Colgate-Palmolive Co.	260.0	5,261.4	4.9	Soaps, cleaners (and allied)
14.	PepsiCo Inc.	260.0	7,027.4	3.7	Soft drinks
15.	McDonald's Corp.	230.2	7,129.0	3.2	Food
16.	American Home Products Corp.	209.0	4,131.2	5.1	Toiletries, cosmetics
17.	RCA Corp.	208.8	8,004.8	2.6	Appliances, TV, radio
18.	J. C. Penney Co.	208.6	11,860.0	1.8	Retail chain
19.	General Mills Corp.	207.3	5,312.1	3.9	Food
20.	Bristol-Myers Corp.	200.0	3,496.7	5.7	Toiletries, cosmetics
21.	B.A.T. Industries PLC	199.3	4,592.2	4.3	Tobacco
22.	Coca-Cola Co.	197.9	5,889.0	3.4	Soft drinks
23.	Johnson & Johnson	195.0	3,025.9	6.4	Toiletries, cosmetics
24.	Chrysler Corp.	193.0	10,821.6	1.8	Automobiles
25.	Ralston Purina Co.	193.0	5,224.7	3.7	Food

Source: Reprinted with permission from the 9 September, 1982 issue of *Advertising Age.* Copyright 1982 by Crain Communications, Inc.

Note: These are only the national advertising dollars, and do not include local advertising. Careful examination of these figures reveals much about America's consumption habits and our corporations' advertising behaviors. Which products receive the largest percentage of their corporations' sales dollars on advertising? Why? What elements of risk are involved in such products? What techniques of advertising seem to work best for such products? How do unique selling propositions, positioning, brand names, slogans, and positioning apply in each case? Check *Advertising Age* each fall for the previous year's advertising totals.

newspapers' share is spread out among about 1,730 daily newspapers and 10,000 weeklies, while television's percentage is concentrated among 772 commercial stations and the three networks. Further, newspapers tend to serve both national and local advertisers in about equal numbers, while network television concentrates on national advertising. Magazines handle about 6 percent of the national advertising volume, down from 10 percent in 1960. Radio receives 7 percent, up from the 6 percent it garnered during 1955. The remaining 38 percent of national advertising goes for such things as direct mail, which gets a whopping 14 percent of the ad dollar, and billboards.

Direct mail advertisements are sent to individuals through the mail and are designed to stimulate responses by return mail. The full impact of direct mail is often difficult to gauge because the persuaded consumer often has the alternative of purchasing the products at retail stores. Attempts have been made to sell almost every type of product and service by direct mail—from insurance to antique autos. Some companies, such as the Spiegel mail-order house in Chicago, base their entire advertising plan on direct mail.

Agencies

There are 6,600 ad agencies in America, several of which do more than a billion dollars a year in business.

Around 100,000 people are employed in 6,600 U.S. advertising agencies. These agencies vary from local one-person shops employing a principal and a secretary in smaller communities, to the creative boutiques of Madison Avenue employing unique individuals specializing in unusual effects, to the largest, highly organized, and even institutionalized variety.

J. Walter Thompson is America's largest agency, placing over $1.5 billion worth of ads annually. It is the second largest worldwide, far behind Dentsu of Japan, which has billings of $2.2 billion and a gross income of nearly a third of a billion dollars. Close behind Thompson are McCann-Erickson and Young & Rubicam, with Ogilvy & Mather International also billing more than a billion dollars annually. Other familiar agencies are Batten, Barton, Durstine & Osborne, Inc. (BBDO); Grey Advertising; and Doyle, Dane and Bernbach.

The major agencies tend to concentrate where the money is—on national campaigns for the nation's major clients—leaving local advertising to the smaller local agencies or to the individual advertiser, who is often served creatively by the local newspaper or broadcaster. Both newspapers and broadcasters provide ancillary services, either at a minimal fee or free, to local advertisers to help lay out ads or produce commercials.

A persistent controversy in the advertising world concerns whether clients are better off with a small boutique where they can receive the creative attention of the firm's principals, or with the highly organized superagency whose wealth commands superior talent and whose depth of services and personnel provide across-the-board coverage.

The advertising agency is a mediator between the advertisers (manufacturers or distributors) and the mass media (print or broadcast). To be successful, the agency must serve both interests.

It should be noted that agencies have certain client preferences. Some deal in automotive accounts almost exclusively; others in food and beverages, electronics, clothing and fashion, travel, or proprietary drugs or cosmetics. Through this kind of specialization, agencies are able to become intimately acquainted with the particular facets of their clients' distinctive pricing, marketing, and manufacturing problems, all of which have a bearing on the creation and placement of ads. The specialty situation is reinforced because an agency's success with a campaign for one client is quite likely to lead product competitors to that agency. Some agencies tend to favor print as their basic medium, while others concentrate on television or radio. As communications technology grows more complex, this specialization breeds a certain expertise in the medium that advertisers are likely to find attractive. Thus, the trend toward specialization that has been noted in the media has its parallel quite naturally in advertising, which serves the media.

Despite the increasing trend toward specialization, either in client type or media, all of the very big agencies are broadly based, serving a variety of clients in many lines of endeavor and maintaining the kind of in-house expertise in both product classification and media usage needed to meet any campaign. Quite obviously, only the very largest agencies can afford this kind of diversification.

However, size and institutionalization lead to a certain inertia and resistance to change. The smaller boutiques are neither so wealthy nor so ponderous and are therefore a lot more flexible in their ability to keep up with rapidly changing approaches to organized persuasion.

Because agencies serve both the client and the media, all embrace certain functions: client liaison, creativity, production, placement, and housekeeping. In a very large agency the *account executives* (AEs), often working under account supervisors, maintain a constant liaison with clients. They interpret the clients' problems to the agency's creative people, and then in turn explain the developed campaign to the clients. Since large agencies generally deal with large clients, the AEs usually deal with the clients' advertising managers or advertising departments—experts dealing with experts, each interpreting the other to their respective organization. Account executives are personality people; they are organizers who know how to work with others; they are the gray-flannel suiters.

The creative group is composed of art directors and artists, copy supervisors and copywriters, and layout people and graphics experts. Using a team approach, they develop the print ads, write the copy, determine how to use illustrations or photographs, decide on black-and-white or color, and make up the *storyboards* for broadcast commercials, which are static graphic depictions of what eventually becomes a live, moving commercial.

Agencies as Mediators

Agencies must serve the interests of manufacturers, distributors, and media.

Agency Functions

Agency functions include client liaison, creativity, production, placement, and housekeeping.

Ad agency illustrators work from rough sketches to finished advertisements, taking special care to match colors and tones to give ads the desired effect.
Jay Black

Production turns the layouts or storyboards into actual commercials in the form of matrices or camera-ready proofs for the press, into sets of expensive colorplates for magazines, and into tape, videotape, or film for radio and television.

Meanwhile, the media people select the media to be used by taking the budget and the composition of the audience into consideration and by choosing between and among communications vehicles: which newspapers, magazines, and radio stations; how much television on which stations or networks; or whether to use billboards or direct mail. They consult Standard Rate and Data Service (SRDS) and talk to the various national "reps" of groups of magazines, radio stations, newspapers, or broadcasters, always keeping in mind the ratings and cost per thousand. One irony that Martin Mayer points out in *Madison Avenue, U.S.A.* is that the agency media buyer who spends millions of dollars of client money annually is generally a woman just out of college, and the people she deals with most are highly paid national reps with years of media experience behind them, backed by reams of statistical data as to why their particular group is best in cost per thousand, in exposure, in purchasing power, or a variety of other complex demographic factors. Someone once said that anything can be proven with statistics, and the national reps do it daily.[2]

The housekeeping function of major agencies includes such things as accounting (a key function), research to develop the facts to be used in planning a campaign, personnel to take care of employees (sometimes thousands), and administration.

Some agencies—attracted by the huge commissions generated by major national automotive, food and beverage, drug, or cosmetic accounts—have tended to throw in a variety of other services in an attempt to attract and hold clients. These include public relations, public opinion sampling, market research, and promotional activities. The results of these extra services have not been spectacular. Since they are generally thrown in as an extra service, the agency tends to spend as little on them as possible; thus the job done is not generally of the highest caliber. "You get what you pay for" in advertising as elsewhere. Further, the lack of performance has tended to give many of these specialties a bad reputation among clients, particularly with regard to public relations.

A large advertising agency is a complex operation. Some of the major agencies, for example, have review boards composed of major executives who play devil's advocate with any planned campaign before it goes to the client. At the review board's request the client liaison and creative teams are forced to defend their handiwork before a critical panel of peers. The rationale for having a review board is that it is better to find the weak points of a campaign before the client or public does, millions of dollars later.

Large, complex agencies carefully integrate various departmental efforts to conduct ad campaigns.

An integrated national campaign involves network television, which is supplemented by local television in certain markets. It involves major spreads in a dozen or so carefully chosen magazines. Also included are national newspaper coverage and supplementary radio, in both the major markets and the very minor ones that are reached effectively only by radio. Billboards on highways across the country and a direct mail campaign to certain selected demographic audiences are utilized. The problems of the traffic department are mind-boggling, especially those of coordination and scheduling, which involve tying the media presentation together into a single theme, determining presentation priorities, coordinating with point-of-sale displays, tying in with public relations and promotional activities, and harnessing the energies of distributors and dealers and subsidiary agencies in fifty states and in a number of foreign countries with language differences. However, the big three automobile makers—Ford, General Motors, and Chrysler—go through orchestrated national campaigns every year when they introduce their new models. Most of the other manufacturers of consumer products contract similar campaigns whenever they launch a new product, which is often.

It is important to remember that whether the agency is a one-person shop, a creative boutique, or a major international agency, it must deal with both client and media in performing creative, production, placement, liaison, and housekeeping functions. A one-person agency gathers all these functions together under one hat: The owner spends the day running from a meeting with a client to the drawing board to a conference with television sales reps, overseeing the shooting of a commercial on the side, hiring the models and photo crew, and keeping up with the bookkeeping at night. A big agency apportions these functions amongst a platoon of overlapping experts. In either case, all such activities are performed under intensely competitive conditions. Madison Avenue is a jungle—and an ulcerous jungle at that—as agencies seek to steal each other's accounts and to hire each other's personnel, and account supervisors leave to open their own boutiques, taking the agency's clients and creative people with them.

The Commission System

The simple 15 percent commission system has gotten very complex.

The commission system began back in the 1880s as a mutual protection device for the newspaper publisher, agency, and client, assuring that all got their fair share of the advertising dollar. As it has evolved, however, there seems to be ample evidence that the system has outlived its usefulness, despite the fact that about 75 percent of ad agencies' income is still from commission.

Recognized agencies are permitted by the media to discount their bills by 15 percent for advertising purchased on behalf of a client. For example, an agency buys a full-page ad costing $1,000 in a local newspaper for its client, the Gas Company. The agency bills the Gas Company for $1,000 and receives payment; in turn, the agency discounts the bill by 15 percent and pays $850 to the newspaper at the *open rate*. Theoretically, it was worth $150 to the newspaper to have the agency close the sale, and for this $150 the agency was expected to prepare and furnish the completed ad, minimizing the newspaper's work. However, a number of problems are associated with even this simplified example. If this were a new ad, the $150 probably would not cover the agency's costs for research, account representation, and liaison; for the time of the creative team; for the cost of new artwork; and for preparation of camera-ready proofs. Thus, the agency may bill the Gas Company for some of these services in addition to the $1,000, or operate at a loss. Further, since the Gas Company advertises in the local newspaper somewhat regularly, it probably buys its advertising on a *contract,* which means that it gets a progressively lower rate if it buys 1,000, 5,000, or 10,000 column inches of display advertising within a year. The contract rates can be commissionable or the agency may add its commission to the bill. The add-on rate would be 17.65 percent rather than 15 percent.

This arrangement has resulted in a pyramiding of charges by advertising agencies, which approaches the absurd. Some agencies charge a commission (discount or add-on) plus out-of-pocket expenses—that is, any costs for entertainment, mileage, long-distance phone calls, travel, and the like—incurred on a client's behalf, plus an hourly charge for agency personnel working on the client's account (AE, artists, writers, producers, researchers, and the like). In addition, an agency may add an overhead charge representing a client's share of the agency's continuing expenses (rent, utilities, insurance, secretarial, etc.). A bill can get pretty large and, even more confusing, can reach the point where it takes teams of accountants to both prepare and interpret it. This billing confusion is another of the factors that have contributed to advertising's poor reputation in recent years.

Furthermore, the commission system may work a hardship on the agency and/or client. In the example of the Gas Company it was noted that the agency probably did not recover its costs from the commission alone. The agency was, in effect, underpaid under the commission system. However, another agency may prepare a single ad that will run nationally several times in 100 major newspapers to the tune of $300,000, reaping a commission of $45,000. In this case it seems that the agency was overpaid when you consider that the work required for preparing this single ad was essentially the same as that of the Gas Company's agency.

The commission system also places a temptation on agencies to seek the highest costs possible or to urge needless advertising in order to increase their commission. On the other hand, clients are not without fault and have been known to demand commission rebates from their agencies (a sort of bribery) as a condition of keeping the account.

As a result, more and more attention is being paid to the negotiated fee as an alternative to the commission system. Under a negotiated fee, a representative of the agency and the client sit down to develop an approach or campaign. Once the dimensions of the approach are known, a mutually acceptable fee is agreed upon, which covers the agency's services for all advertising functions, allows for a profit, and reimburses the agency for its planning time. There are pitfalls to this system, too, and as in most things, little can be accomplished except in an atmosphere of integrity and mutual trust. It is fair to say that advertising, like the mass communications system it supports, is far from perfect.

Advertising Strategies

After World War II, advertising agencies moved into the public spotlight and became increasingly competitive. The 1950s were the years when Madison Avenue became a household street and advertising people became stereotyped as manipulators of public opinion.[3] A rash of books appeared on advertising, among them Vance Packard's *The Hidden Persuaders* and Martin Mayer's *Madison Avenue, U.S.A.*[4] Both were popularizations born of public fascination with the manipulative techniques of applied social psychology.

Unique Selling Proposition

Unique selling proposition (usp) dramatizes and exploits a product's basic characteristic.

The first manipulative technique to capture public attention was the *unique selling proposition* (usp) originated by the agency of Ted Bates & Company. The usp took as its starting point the fact that there was no real product differentiation among the various mass-produced products of competing manufacturers. In essence it said that, within a relatively narrow range, all soap is alike, all beer is alike, and all toothpaste is alike, and that advertising must establish whatever difference there is to make the public buy one product instead of another. The unique selling proposition was based upon a characteristic of the product that could be dramatized, exploited, and made synonymous with the product on behalf of the manufacturer, *even though all other products shared the same characteristic.* This non-existent difference was exploited by advertising and through the sheer power of public exposure was made to appear unique. For example, Bates originated the slogan "Cleans Your Breath While It Cleans Your Teeth" for Colgate toothpaste. This was usp, and Bates built an entire campaign out of it. The slogan was a natural selling device implying a better toothpaste. However, even a cursory examination of the proposition suggests that all toothpastes clean the breath while they clean the teeth. There was nothing unique about Colgate, except that Bates had hit upon the slogan, and by exploiting it he had effectively prevented any other toothpaste manufacturer from utilizing it. Even an attempt on the part of another manufacturer's agency to utilize a similar slogan would actually reinforce Bates's claim for Colgate. The usp is central to the advertisement.

Another Bates usp for Schlitz was that its bottles were "washed with live steam." This had a peculiar appeal in the 1950s when sanitary America was concerned about the hygiene of reusable glass beer bottles. Actually, the slogan was a redundancy (is there anything other than live steam?), because all brewers washed their bottles with steam, but Bates, by exploiting this point, had usurped it for Schlitz.

Brand Image

Brand image used snob appeal to promote a product.

Brand image and sexual connotations sell products.
Margaret Thompson/
Picture Cube

The next technique of pseudoscience applied to advertising was David Ogilvy's *brand image.* The brand image concept also recognized that there was no essential product differentiation. However, it sought to establish a distinction on the basis of snob appeal, to create an image for products that placed them a little above the average. The thought was that people would

Persuasive Media

transfer the brand image to themselves, and by using that product, they could consider themselves a little better than their neighbors who didn't use that brand. Ogilvy developed the brand image of Hathaway shirts by employing Baron George Wrangel, a Russian nobleman who wore a suggestively romantic eye patch and exuded "class." The Baron always wore a Hathaway shirt and other stylish clothes while fondling an exquisite antique ship model or a fantastically expensive, silver-chased, over-and-under shotgun. Brand image advertising reasoned that male America transferred this "class" to itself in hopes that if it wore Hathaways, it too would magically assume some of the Baron's breeding, taste, and distinction. The snobbery associated with brand image was a shortcut to the aristocracy. As Ogilvy himself said, "It pays to give your product a first-class ticket throughout life."[5] Commander Edward Whitehead's bearded British accent dripped culture as he extolled Schweppes' "schweppervescence" for "only pennies more." The Commander was also an Ogilvy creation.

Motivational Research

The most extreme form of advertising's romance with the social sciences was Ernest Dichter's *motivational research (mr)*. Highly Freudian in its approach, mr maintains that people buy things for hidden reasons unknown even to themselves, and that these hidden reasons are more often than not sexual in origin. Through depth interviews mr sought to explore people's hidden motivations as to why they buy and then, utilizing this data, to build an advertising campaign. Depth interviewing by psychologists and the administration of projective psychological tests, designed to induce interviewees to project their real feelings into their interpretations of pictures shown to them or into their completion of sentences, gave marketers valuable insights for designing and selling products.

Classic examples of Dichter's mr in action were campaigns for Chrysler Motor Company and Ronson lighters. When working with Chrysler, Dichter inferred through mr that the average American male, who at that time was the principal decisionmaker in automotive purchases, remained with his wife but secretly coveted a mistress. By equating a sedan with a wife, and a convertible with a mistress, Dichter concluded that a hardtop "convertible" would satisfy the inner needs of a man for glamour and romance, and at the same time, it would be safe and dependable like a wife. Once it was introduced, the hardtop convertible made history with its level of acceptance by an avid market.[6] Later, Dichter achieved similar success with Ronson lighters. He built his campaign on huge color reproductions in magazines and billboards of the lighter's flame, which in his view was an enormous phallic symbol appealing to both men and women alike: men through wishful thinking, women from lust. Dichter went on to construct a television campaign for Ajax cleanser that utilized a white knight carrying a great lance astride a white charger and galloping down the streets of Hometown, U.S.A., paying no attention to the traffic laws. The lance, representing a large phallic symbol, was designed to stimulate housewives in Hometown, America.

Motivational research probes our deeper selves; then advertisers play on our weaknesses.

Subliminal Advertising

Through subliminal stimulation, advertisers are said to trigger our responses.

The late 1950s was also a time of considerable public consternation about *subliminal advertising,* which was the development of Jim Vicary, an advertising researcher. He inserted a few single frames of "Coca-Cola" or "Eat Popcorn" into movies at different intervals. A single frame would pass so quickly as a movie was viewed that the viewers' eyes would not be aware of having seen it, although their brains would have picked it up and registered it subconsciously. Using a theater in New Jersey across the Hudson River from New York's Madison Avenue, Vicary discovered that when sublimated movies were shown to 45,000 spectators over a six-week period Coke sales shot up 57 percent and popcorn sales did nearly as well. At about the same time, San Francisco radio station KGO embellished its record programs with inaudible messages telling listeners that "someone is at the door." Many in the audience, some as young as ten years old, obediently checked their locks, according to researchers. Critics maintained that such techniques represented a threat to the integrity of the human mind. The FCC concluded that the use of subliminal perception is inconsistent with the obligations of a broadcast licensee, and broadcasts employing such techniques are contrary to public interest. The FCC continued with the statement that, whether effective or not, such broadcasts are clearly intended to be deceptive. Psychologists and advertisers are divided over whether such techniques are used and are effective, so regulators have tended to ignore them.

Despite the stir, research evidence seems to indicate that the power of mass media and advertising is far less than generally supposed. While Vicary did not believe that subliminal advertising was capable of altering attitudes, he did believe it triggered an existing predisposition toward Coca-Cola or popcorn among thirsty and hungry movie audiences, who were pretty well predisposed toward the concessionaires anyway.

Positioning

Through careful positioning, ads for nearly identical products carve out individual markets.

Since the late 1960s, a new concept of specialization has come to national advertising, called *positioning.* Earlier advertising was based on the concept of the *lcd,* appealing to the lowest (or largest) common denominator in the hope that differentiation in the advertising, regardless of product similarity, would attract a vague maximum response. This was really a sort of hit-or-miss approach. However, advertisers and their agencies watched as successful media specialization occurred—particularly in the radio and magazine fields where the various media pinpointed their appeal to specific audiences—and as a more sophisticated advertising concept evolved. It was possible, they reasoned, to appeal to specific audiences even within the broad mass that newspapers or, especially, television represented. Positioning recognized the inherent differences in people as individuals and the inherent impossibility of any product capturing the entire potential market. Advertisers were willing to settle for a share of the market, yielding a part of the pie to their competition and continually seeking to increase the size of their own slice.

Positioning is applied in advertising soap, for example. Some soap users are concerned with antiseptic cleanliness. Dial goes after this market,

Persuasive Media

stressing its fresh smell, its cleansing qualities, its ability to banish the curse of body odor. In so doing, it reaches out to the tens of millions of television viewers who are concerned, if not obsessed, with cleanliness and the fear of offending; it offers a haven to the insecure. Theoretically, it locks up this slice of the market. There are others in this vast audience, however, who are less concerned with hygiene than they are with their complexions. Dove emphasizes its one-quarter cleansing cream content, and gives hope to the consumers seeking to perpetuate the peaches-and-cream complexion of their youth. In effect positioning directs itself to the mass within the mass.

The same occurs in advertising beer. One beer directs its appeal to the swingers: It is always being poured in happy surroundings, with people laughing, dancing, and singing. To the party people in the audience, it is a natural; it is their beer. To the wallflowers sitting at home, this beer represents companionship and gaiety, and holds the promise of popularity by association. Another beer appeals to the manly; it is a robust beer consumed by active, energetic people. It is a he-man beer, and he-men should drink it; ninety-seven-pound weaklings buy it in the hope that some of this manliness will rub off on them.

Positioning applies the most practical, daily use of motivational research. It seeks to segregate audiences by their very personal interests and appeal to them alone, forsaking all others. In this, of course, it is an update of the brand image, without snob appeal.

Positioning has some weaknesses. For the woman who is interested in both personal hygiene and her complexion, positioning has offered little alternative: Does she choose between or use both soaps, or does she become confused and in her desperation buy another brand? What beer does the man who is both a would-be swinger and an erstwhile he-man drink, or does he turn to liquor in his desperation? Some of positioning's appeals are rather esoteric. Salem cigarettes appealed to romance recaptured with young lovers in a bucolic setting; smoking Salems promised to bring back those sunny years. Silva Thins went after the homosexual market, while Virginia Slims appealed to feminists— "You've come a long way, baby." Ban sought the naturalists, the environmentalists, with a wholesome, modly bespectacled young woman poignantly telling her tragedy: "I wouldn't use a deodorant if I didn't have to. . . ." On the other hand Secret is "strong enough for a man, but made for a woman."

Another of the problems with positioning is that of overkill. The more specifically directed the approach is to a market, the smaller the potential market and the greater the numbers of people reached and paid for who have no potential interest in the product approach. Positioning is a stride toward the future, but it is a dangerous game fraught with the perils of overkill, which is expensive, and stereotyping, which places the product in a cage from which it cannot escape. Yet, the rationale of sharing the market is hard to destroy, and the presumed cohesiveness of the mass audience on which the lowest common denominator is based is hard to maintain.

Institutional Advertising

Institutional advertising takes on the image-building task of public relations.

Recent environmental concern points up another facet of advertising termed *institutional advertising*—sometimes called *public relations advertising*—which has been in existence for some time but now enjoys considerable emphasis. Institutional advertising does not seek to sell a product; rather it seeks to sell an idea or an institution. Many of America's major corporations, faced recently with a loss of credibility and public trust, as well as attacks from both consumer groups and the environmentalists, have taken to blowing their own horns in the mass media. Print and broadcast are filled with their protestations of good citizenship—their environmental concern, their research for a rosier future, their emphasis on equal opportunity employment, and their stress on minority rights and in-house racial and sexual equality.

The nation's utilities, operating as controlled monopolies, have been in the forefront of institutional advertising for years. The "Bell Telephone Hour" of symphonic music, first on radio and later on television, was essentially public service, institutional advertising, designed to paint ATT as a patron of culture. Gas and electric companies today focus ironically on energy conservation, seeking to slow rather than promote growth. Their generating capacity is outdistanced by demand, resulting in shortages and brownouts with an accompanying acceleration in public dissatisfaction.

The question arises, of course, as to why a utility operating from a monopoly position needs to advertise at all. The answer is simple. Private utilities do business on public sufferance; they are reliant upon public goodwill to maintain their privileged position. There is a considerable body of sentiment, both social and legislative, that holds that utilities should be publicly owned and operated, as many municipal utilities already are. Consequently, the volume of institutional advertising from the nation's utilities has traditionally been considerable.

Two of the most innovative commercial uses of institutional advertising were developed during World War II by the Ford Motor Company and Lucky Strike cigarettes. Ford had no cars to sell; its entire productive capacity was devoted to the manufacture of tanks and airplane engines. However, it realized that at some unspecified future date the war would end, and the built-up public deprivation would result in an unprecedented demand for cars. It wanted the public to buy Fords. Throughout the war it maintained a campaign based on "There's a Ford in Your Future," always showing a crystal ball containing a Ford in a variety of imaginative settings. At the time the thought was not to sell cars; the intent was to sell the idea "Ford"—to keep it alive—and it did, getting nearly a two-year head start over General Motors when the war ended.

Lucky Strike used to have a dark green package, readily identifiable with its red bull's-eye in the center. When green dye was required by the armed forces during the war, Luckies switched to a white package with the same red centerspot, backed by an enormous campaign, "Lucky Strike Green Has Gone to War." This capitalized on the patriotic fervor of the time, put American tobacco in the van of patriotic companies and, incidentally, engendered enormous sales that were backed up by the weekly donation of thousands of cartons of Luckies to servicemen overseas. There are cynics who say that the armed forces didn't need Lucky's green dye at all, and that the entire idea was the brainchild of packager Raymond Loewy, who was paid a million dollars by American Tobacco to redesign the Lucky package to appeal to women.

It is necessary, as far as advertising is concerned, to separate inconsequentials from matters of substance. Inconsequential items include beer and toothpaste, even motor cars, and a whole range of consumer goods that the general public tends to recognize as being alike, and even though consumers realize that it makes no appreciable difference which product they choose, they may have preferences. Matters of consequence, however, involve beliefs and attitudes ingrained in the person. These do not readily change and advertising is relatively impotent against them.

Advertising, for example, has not proven particularly successful in political campaigning, which is perceived by the public as being a matter of substance affecting the welfare and future livelihood of each individual. While there have been some very well-financed political campaigns that have resulted in victory, one does not hear as much about the expensive campaigns that ended in failure. The results of political campaigns seem to hinge on factors other than advertising, and the best that can be said for political advertising is that it usually does no harm.

The Impact of Advertising

Advertising is great at focusing our attention on a new product or politician, but it has definite limitations when it comes to changing opinions on matters of substance.

On the political scene, advertising is unsurpassed at calling attention to issues and candidates, but is of questionable value in actually selling them to the public.
John R. Maher/EKM-Nepenthe

Martin Mayer has summed the case well: Advertising is of little use in combating a trend against a kind of product. Brewers have spent hundreds of millions of dollars to advertise their beer, backing the ads with a full panoply of motivational research, but per capita beer consumption has not increased, because advertising cannot add values great enough to overcome primary factors that lead consumers to find less and less satisfaction in using a product. Here, as on the political scene, advertising is the wind on the surface, sweeping all before it when it blows with the tide (of public opinion), but powerless to prevent a shifting of greater forces.[7]

Related to the consideration of inconsequentials and matters of substance in advertising is the fact that advertising is unsurpassed as a device for exposure—to call attention to, to introduce a product, concept, idea, or candidate. Once exposure is achieved, the purchase, acceptance, or election are in other undetermined hands hidden in the complexities of public opinion formation and change. Advertising is essential for product introduction or candidate introduction—for example during the primaries. Once introduced, some will buy and some will vote, out of curiosity, but success depends on the product or the candidate.

The Psychology of Advertising

In *Motivation and Personality,* psychologist Abraham Maslow defined a seven-stage hierarchy of needs. The needs progress from basic biological demands—such as hunger and thirst—to a complex psychological stage of self-actualization—a need to find self-fulfillment and realize one's potential. According to Maslow, needs low in the hierarchy, as shown in figure 10.1, must be at least partially satisfied before higher needs can become important sources of motivation.[8]

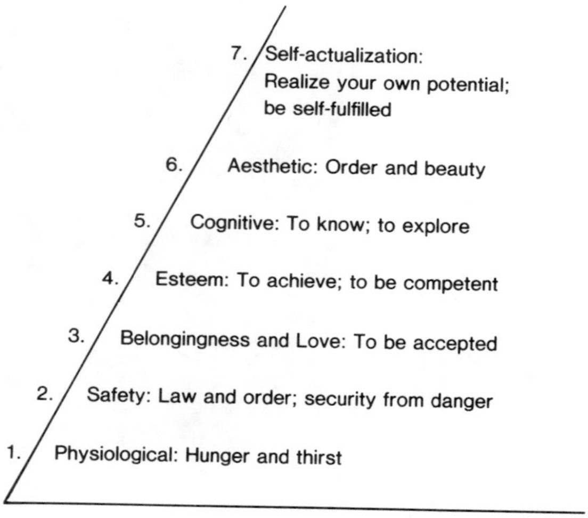

Figure 10.1
Abraham Maslow's hierarchy of needs.
Data for diagram based on Hierarchy of Needs in "A Theory of Human Motivation" in *Motivation and Personality,* Second Edition, by Abraham H. Maslow. Copyright © 1970 by Abraham H. Maslow. By permission of Harper & Row, Publishers, Inc.

7. Self-actualization: Realize your own potential; be self-fulfilled

6. Aesthetic: Order and beauty

5. Cognitive: To know; to explore

4. Esteem: To achieve; to be competent

3. Belongingness and Love: To be accepted

2. Safety: Law and order; security from danger

1. Physiological: Hunger and thirst

How does advertising relate to each stage on the hierarchy? While advertising seems capable of reinforcing basic awareness of, and stimulating us to satisfy, the lower order needs such as hunger, thirst, and safety, it is less capable of doing anything *significant* about our need for belongingness, love, self-esteem, and order and beauty in life. Those who have had what Maslow calls "peak experiences" or transient moments of self-actualization (nonstriving, non-self-centered states of perfection and goal attainment) are not likely to have achieved this fulfillment through advertising. Advertising does an excellent job of alluding to each level of need, reminding us that we share common desires. But in terms of triggering these responses in us, advertising is less successful at marketing self-actualization than it is at emptying grocery shelves of Hostess Twinkies.

Advertising can affect lower level needs more readily than higher level ones. You can't peddle self-worth.

Advertising executive Otto Kleppner, whose book *Advertising Procedure* has become a standard reference since its first edition was published in 1925, tells advertising practitioners they can trigger a multitude of significant motivations in consumers.[9] Some are physiological (like hunger, thirst, and mating—the satisfaction of which is essential to survival), while others are secondary or social (the desire to be accepted, to succeed). The motivations to which advertising can supposedly appeal include our tendencies to be acquisitive, to achieve, to be recognized, and to dominate. Kleppner doesn't maintain that advertising can actually fulfill all these motives and needs, but he argues that to be successful advertising must empathize with the goals, needs, desires, and problems of the people it is addressing. Even though we don't always understand our own motives for responding to advertising appeals, we tend to consume and display products that tell the world how we would like to have it think of us.

Social psychologist Milton Rokeach, who has spent decades studying the nature of human values and belief systems, has suggested that while advertisers try to empathize with different needs, they are unlikely to change important ones.[10] Rokeach has ranked human beliefs along a continuum ranging from important, centrally-held beliefs to inconsequential ones. He has depicted them as a group of concentric circles, with centrally-held beliefs at the core and inconsequential ones in outer rings.

Inconsequentials, not central beliefs, are advertisers' targets.

Important, primitive beliefs, which most people share, relate to the nature of physical reality, social reality, and the self. They are fundamental and highly resistant to change. The next three circles shown in figure 10.2—beliefs arising from deep personal experiences, authority beliefs, and beliefs derived from whatever authorities or spokespersons we have accepted—are also fairly stable. Finally there are the inconsequential beliefs that can be changed at will without causing disruption to any of our other beliefs. All five kinds of beliefs are organized into a belief system that has a definable content and a definable structure.

Advertisers spend billions of dollars each year tampering with America's inconsequential beliefs, playing on brand loyalty and using unique selling propositions and slogans to stress relatively meaningless differences among products. Rokeach says that when advertisers try to connect those

Figure 10.2
Milton Rokeach's
depiction of the human
belief system.

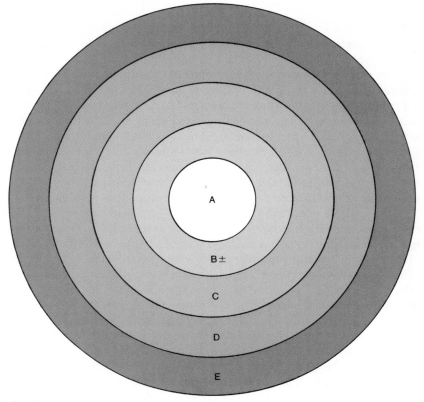

A = Central / primitive beliefs about one's physical world, self, and generalized other (100 percent consensus)

B = Central / primitive beliefs about one's social / physical world and self-identity arising from personal experience (B+ = positive beliefs; B− = negative beliefs)

C = Intermediate authority beliefs

D = Peripheral beliefs and opinions

E = Inconsequential beliefs and opinions

brand changes (inconsequential beliefs) to other beliefs, they more often than not pander to our reliance upon authority figures to help us choose. As a consequence, athletes, movie stars, and even old politicians expect us to transfer our positive images of them onto the products they tout. An appeal to change brands or try new products is based on playing with our negative self-concepts at the second level of beliefs: exploiting our primitive phobias and neurotic anxieties about self-worth. Rokeach has taken strong issue with advertisers who picture humanity as being fundamentally irrational, guilt-ridden, and neurotic. The resultant advertising is exploitive, debasing, and insulting to human dignity, Rokeach maintains.[11]

Conclusions about advertising's ability to influence people, to stimulate motivations and trigger responses, appear to rest on the model of humanity adhered to by whoever is drawing the conclusions. If one believes

Table 10.2 The 1981 TV advertisements that people remember most

Rank	Brand	1981 TV spending (millions)
1	Miller Lite	$33.9
2	Coca-Cola	36.3
3	Pepsi-Cola, Diet Pepsi, Pepsi Light	33.7
4	Dr Pepper	12.9
5	McDonald's	54.1
6	Bell System	28.1
7	Polaroid	31.5
8	French's Mustard	3.2
9	Seven-Up, Diet Seven-Up	27.6
10	Oscar Mayer	12.1

Note: Ask yourself and some friends why these particular product advertisements were memorable. How would Maslow, Kleppner, and Rokeach explain the success of such campaigns?

humanity is readily manipulated, subjected to whims and motivations over which it has little understanding and less control, all manner of mayhem may be laid at Madison Avenue's collective doorsteps. On the other hand, if one holds to a more democratic view, picturing humanity as rational and capable of making important decisions while being untroubled over inconsequential choices, a more forgiving picture of the advertising business emerges. (See table 10.2, "TV advertisements that people remember most.")

Recent Efforts at Self-Regulation

Self-regulation intensifies in an age of consumerism, but there are limits.

Since the muckraking years at the turn of the century, self-regulation of advertising has expanded almost as rapidly as the industry itself, resulting in a range of organizations covering all aspects of the business. In 1971 the three leading advertising groups—the American Association of Advertising Agencies (AAAA), the American Advertising Federation (AAF), and the Association of National Advertisers (ANA)—joined the most comprehensive self-regulating apparatus in advertising history, the National Advertising Review Council (NARC). Working with the Better Business Bureau (BBB), the advertising groups organized "to seek the voluntary elimination of national advertising which professionals would consider deceptive."

The BBB and NARC have no legal power; they rely upon "moral suasion" to terminate deceptive advertising. More than a third of the complaints brought by consumers, advertising competitors, or the BBB have been dismissed because the advertisers, when questioned, have substantiated their advertising claims. Another third have been resolved once advertisers modify or discontinue their claims. The remaining are dealt with administratively by the NARC or turned over to appropriate governmental agencies, such as the Federal Trade Commission.

As we consider the role of the various advertising associations in attempting self-regulation, we must remember that they are limited in their abilities in ways other than philosophy or differences of opinion over what constitutes professionalism. Should the associations attempt any actions that give the appearance of interfering with open competition in the economic marketplace, they will run afoul of federal antitrust laws.

Advertising Organizations' Codes

Codes of ad ethics try to protect the innocent.

In their own bailiwicks, large advertising organizations have established codes of ethics and attempts at professionalization. The Association of National Advertisers (ANA), whose members produce three-quarters of the commercials seen on national television, has established extensive guidelines for children's advertising.

ANA's guidelines try to guard against any presentation that capitalizes on a child's difficulty in distinguishing between the real and the fanciful. The objective is to produce ads that are accurate in their representation of products and the benefits perceived by the child. The commercial must not mislead the viewer, in the specifics of copy, sound, and visual presentation, or in the total impact. If parts are sold separately, the advertisement should so indicate. If assembly is required, that too should be indicated. Finally, the average child for whom the product is intended should be able to duplicate product performance as shown in the ad.

Likewise the American Association of Advertising Agencies (AAAA) has given itself Standards of Good Practice. It conducts an investigation of each advertising agency wishing membership in AAAA, reading the agencies' contracts with clients to determine whether the agencies are behaving honorably. If accepted into the association, agencies are expected to produce no advertising that appears to contain:

False or misleading statements or exaggerations, visual or verbal. Testimonials which do not reflect the real choice of competent witness. Price claims which are misleading. Comparisons which unfairly disparage a competitive product or service. Claims insufficiently supported, or which distort the true meaning or practicable application of statements made by professionals or scientific authority. Statements, suggestions, or pictures offensive to public decency.

Since 1916 local Better Business Bureaus, outgrowths of local vigilance committees of the Associated Advertising Clubs of America, have also been a controlling force in advertising, though not strictly an internal self-regulatory one. Currently, there are some 122 separate bureaus scattered across the United States. They are supported by more than 100,000 different companies and businesses, which spend $6.5 million annually to guard against improper business activities, including deceptive advertising. Each year the BBB deals with 2.5 million inquiries and complaints from businesses and the public, and checks out more than 40,000 advertisements annually for potential violations of truth and accuracy.[12]

Better Business Bureaus

Until joining forces with advertising groups in 1971, the BBBs were essentially locally oriented. Collectively, however, the bureaus have been influential in establishing an agenda for advertising across the land. In 1978 the BBB issued a Code of Advertising to augment its *Do's and Don't's of Advertising Copy,* which had been a standard reference work. The newer code is a highly specific set of guidelines covering such disparate ad practices as comparative price and savings claims, warranties and guarantees, layout and illustrations, comparisons and disparagement, superlative claims and puffery, and testimonials and endorsements.

Although the Better Business Bureau's code of advertising, much like the codes of many other trade organizations, lacks the power of enforcement, the BBB has become a bridge between governmental control and self-regulation. Its Printers' Ink model statute has been adopted, in one form or another, in forty-five states and therefore has become the law of the land, guiding local and state governments in their efforts to prosecute deceptive advertising practices. And BBB's involvement in the National Advertising Review Council attests to its ability to influence practitioners from within the industry.

The Better Business Bureaus' codes and Printers' Ink statutes have a long and influential history.

Media Efforts

Concerned that they may be in violation of federal, state, or local law, a great many newspapers, magazines, and radio and television stations have created their own standards that govern what advertising they will accept or reject. As legal scholars Nelson and Teeter point out:

The newspaper or broadcast station which permits dishonest or fraudulent advertising hurts its standing with both its readers and its advertisers. Publishers and broadcasters, who perceive psychological and economic advantages in refusing dishonest advertising, also appear to be becoming more cognizant that they have a moral duty to protect the public.[13]

Some of the resulting standards of advertising practice set up by individual media are highly complex and detailed. The *New York Times,* for instance, publishes a pamphlet, *Standards of Advertising Acceptability,* that includes generalized philosophical statements about credible advertising, and discusses the means it uses for self-checking and enforcing its standards. It also lists various kinds of unacceptable advertising and discusses "opinion advertising" of a political or philosophic nature, as well as the typography, format, and production of ads.

Louisville, Kentucky, newspapers have produced guidelines reflecting their strong concerns with sex discrimination. They list what they consider discriminatory terms frequently found in classified ads, along with their suggested substitutes. For example, *attractive, pretty,* and *handsome* are to be replaced by *well-groomed* and *presentable; barmaid* is to be replaced by *bar help* or the conjoined *bar waiter* or *waitress; foreman* to become *foreman*—male or female; *maid* to be *domestic help* or *housekeeping;* and so on.

Because nonlicensed news media are not legally considered to be common carriers, such as city or state owned utilities, they have enjoyed the right to carry on business activities with whomever they please. Despite recent thrusts by various interest groups and individuals seeking access to the advertising pages, the print media still retain the right to reject any or all ads they feel are inappropriate for their publications. Many, in the interest of carrying out public debates on controversial issues, have adapted their own concepts of the broadcasters' "fairness doctrine" (which will be discussed in chapter 12), sometimes running ads they personally and institutionally abhor. In the process they may be operating in their own best interests, as they adopt one more technique of social responsibility that will help curtail public and regulatory incursions into their freedom.

Advertising Regulation

Self-policing efforts notwithstanding, the government has become involved over the years in the regulation of advertising. Increasingly, as a result of the consumer movement, truth in advertising has become an issue of national importance. Several federal agencies, and numerous state and local ones, have gotten into the act. The most active and the most influential, insofar as most consumers are concerned, is the Federal Trade Commission (FTC). It is joined by the Federal Communications Commission, the Food and Drug Administration (FDA), the Post Office Department, the Securities and Exchange Commission (SEC), and the Alcohol and Tax Division of the Internal Revenue Service, among others. In all, there are over thirty federal statutes containing advertising regulations. In addition, nearly all states have enacted statutes making fraudulent and misleading advertising a misdemeanor. In some areas, at some levels, enforcement is quite vigorous. In others, it isn't.

Within the past fifteen years, the FTC, increasingly sensitive to consumer pressure, has moved with considerable success into the areas of *truth in lending* and *truth in packaging*. Fresh from its triumphs in these related fields, it has undertaken the more complex problems of *truth in advertising*.

The Federal Trade Commission

Truth in advertising presents a slightly different problem from earlier campaigns because another element is introduced. While campaigns in packaging and lending involved only the FTC and the individual offender, whether manufacturer or financial institution, truth in advertising involves both the offending source of the advertising and the mass media that carry it. Thus, truth in advertising by the FTC will affect all mass media, print and broadcast alike, and not merely the broadcast media falling under the jurisdiction of the FCC. Since advertising comprises the largest revenue portion of most of the mass media, a strengthened FTC cannot help but have significant repercussions on most of mass communications.

FTC oversees all media, using several means to control offenders.

As an example, the American Dairy Association ran a series of television commercials consisting of celebrity monologues on milk and winding up with the semipun, "Every*body* needs milk—even Pat Boone's." On complaint the FTC demanded that the commercial be changed, as doctors indicated that milk is indeed harmful to some people. The amended commercial said, "Milk has something for every*body*—even Pat Boone's." While milk may be bad for an individual, it has something. So, we turn to the abstract nature of truth, which haunts the truth-in-advertising plans of the FTC, concerned with what is unfair, what is misleading, and what is deceptive.

Long known as "the little gray lady of Pennsylvania Avenue" because of its reluctance to investigate and prosecute advertisers, the FTC has developed into one of the largest of the independent regulatory agencies. It has recently attacked advertising problems with five basic weapons:

1. *Letters of compliance,* in which advertisers promise informally to put a stop to questionable advertising practices;
2. *Stipulations,* in which advertisers agree to cease and desist ad practices the FTC has investigated and found misleading; the FTC still reserves the right to prosecute if it appears the ads in question have been damaging to segments of the public;
3. *Consent orders,* handed down after formal complaints have been issued; as in numbers 1 and 2 above, advertisers are not required to formally admit guilt, but merely to discontinue a certain practice;

4. *Cease and Desist Orders,* based on findings of advertiser guilt after formal hearings; such orders can be appealed in Federal Courts; if not appealed and if advertising practice in question continues, FTC can seek injunctions; and,
5. *Publicity,* in which the FTC issues news releases to the media publicizing the complaints and cease-and-desist orders it has acted upon.

In addition to such formal and informal actions, the FTC continually takes steps to inform advertisers and the public of its concerns over fair advertising. It holds *trade practice conferences* and emerges with proposed rules based on public hearings; it issues *industry guides* in which its rules are interpreted; it offers *advisory opinions* to advertisers curious about the legality of a proposed ad campaign; and it publishes *trade regulation rules* in their final form.[14]

Documentation

Advertisers should be able to prove their "factual" claims.

One of the most effective tactics taken by the FTC is to require advertisers to fully document the claims made in their advertising. This has taken the form of submitting huge dossiers of statistics and scientific tests to the commission. If the advertisers fail to convince the commission that the ad campaign is fully justified on the basis of the documentation submitted, the FTC will usually issue a consent order asking them to stop making certain claims. Entire industries were brought under the FTC's microscopes during the 1970s, specifically the makers of over-the-counter medicines, automobiles, and antiperspirants, for example. Some documentation was incredibly complex—such as a seventy-two-page packet of documents, some in French, to support Renault's gas mileage claims—which prompted the FTC to demand that advertisers supply a brief summary, in layperson's language.[15]

Corrective Advertising

The guilty go to confession.

Another tactic of the FTC has been an imaginative extension of the FCC's Fairness Doctrine, in the form of remedial or corrective advertising. In this scheme advertisers found guilty of employing false advertising over a long and apparently successful campaign are required to use a certain percentage of their future advertising to acknowledge the earlier misrepresentation—in other words, to confess their sins.

In April 1978, the U.S. Supreme Court upheld the FTC's authority to enforce corrective advertising, which was the first time the policy was fully tested in the courts. The case concerned Listerine mouthwash, which for 100 years had been advertising that it helped cure colds and sore throats. FTC finally proved, based on current medical research, that colds are not caused by mouth bacteria, but by viruses entering the body through the nose and the eyes, which refuted Listerine's longstanding contentions.

Warner-Lambert, which withdrew the advertising claims while the case was being adjudicated, was told to run language in $10.2 million worth of ads admitting that its product does not help prevent colds or sore throats, or lessen their severity.[16]

A controversy over the effect advertising has on children, which had been simmering for years, was brought to a full boil in February 1978 with the release of a massive *FTC Staff Report on Television and Advertising to Children.*[17] Contained in the 346-page report and its more than 100 pages of supporting documentation is evidence leading to the report's conclusion that it is both unfair and deceptive to address televised advertising for *any* product to children who are still too young to understand the selling purposes of, or otherwise comprehend or evaluate, the advertising. The report recommended that the FTC adopt the following regulations:

Commercials and Children

1. Ban all televised advertising for any product which is directed to, or seen by, audiences composed of a significant proportion of children (below the age of 8) who are too young to understand the selling purpose of, or otherwise comprehend or evaluate, the advertising;
2. Ban televised advertising directed to, or seen by, audiences composed of a significant number of older children (8 to 11 years old) for sugared products, the consumption of which poses the most serious dental health risks;
3. Require that televised advertising directed to, or seen by, audiences composed of a significant proportion of older children for sugared products not included in paragraph (2) be balanced by nutritional and/or health disclosures funded by advertisers.[18]

How fair is the tug-of-war between the multibillion dollar advertising empire and the young, impressionable mind?
J. R. Holland/Stock, Boston

Ensuing public hearings revealed, to no one's surprise, that the advertisers had point-by-point rebuttals to each of the FTC's criticisms.

Debates rage over whether the FTC or parents should protect children from manipulative advertising.

Advertisers argued that the FTC should not be concerned with the effects of advertising on children, because parents make the overwhelming majority of decisions about what to purchase for their children and because young children have little access to money. The FTC countered that children are highly influential in the marketing process, successfully nagging their parents to purchase advertised products, especially sugared foods. Should the FTC become involved in parent–child relationships? Columnist James Kilpatrick reacted as follows:

Something has gone woefully awry, or so it seems to me, when the whole might and majesty of the federal government is marshaled to smash the insidious cupcake.

In my old-fashioned view, it simply is no business of the federal government if children nag their parents, or parents capitulate to their howling brats. The federal authority has no writ to cure every imperfection in society. Some obligations ought to be left to individuals, for good or ill, if personal responsibility is not to be fatally undermined.[19]

Reactions from the FTC and supporters of the proposed ban were equally vociferous. Media critic Rose Goldsen, in an essay whose title "Why Television Advertising Is Deceptive and Unfair" offers a clue to her basic position, maintained that our contemporary media environment demands serious readjustments of our belief in "let the buyer beware" marketing. She contended that the basic intent of commercials, and the relationship between the corporation producing and marketing products and television viewers is so different from printed advertisements that it demands special legal consideration.[20]

Deregulation may signal a change in FTC power and consumerism.

Given this polarity, it is likely that the debate will rage for years to come, regardless of special legislation or FTC action. Personnel changes and budget cuts at the FTC have had some impact on the activities of the agency. Under the Reagan administration, the FTC dropped its efforts to tightly control children's advertising, perhaps forecasting a move toward deregulation of the entire advertising industry.

Criticisms and Defenses of Advertising

Omnipresent advertising is the most talked-about aspect of U.S. business. Most observations are negative, not based on economic principles.

Advertising is an essential element in our contemporary economic system and is therefore an integral part of American life. Even though only 5 percent of the world's population lives within its borders, the United States generates 60 percent of the world's total advertising expenditures. Because advertising is so omnipresent, it is perhaps the most talked-about aspect of the national business scene. Merely being exposed to the hundreds of ads that bombard us each day (some estimates run as high as 1,500 for the typical adult, although fewer than 100 are consciously noted) has made each of us somewhat of an advertising expert. As experts, we have no shortage of opinions about advertising; not surprisingly, most of our opinions are negative. As consumers rather than economists, we tend to react personally to the offensiveness of commercial messages, frequently overlooking the fundamental economic "nature of the beast."

But even the economists are sharply divided in their assessments of advertising's true values. Some take the extreme position of historian Arnold Toynbee, who said, "I cannot think of any circumstances in which advertising would not be an evil." At the other end of the spectrum, President Franklin D. Roosevelt once mused that were he to start life again, he would most likely go into the advertising business. Such is the range of opinions about advertising; but more observers do seem to view the business negatively. Satirist-turned-advertising executive Stan Freberg once explained:

In talking to college students, I have asked them why they thought I went into the commercials business, and invariably *they* assume it was for the money. Or because "there's a lot of opportunities for advancement in that field," or, "advertising is glamorous and exciting!" True, I have experienced tremendous stimulation, creating some rather unorthodox advertising campaigns, which in most cases were successful in making the sales curve jump, to say nothing of the client. I have also managed to successfully unnerve several hundred account executives along the way. In my day I have made gray flannel turn white overnight. That in itself is an exciting sport. But the thought that I might have been motivated to go into this business not as an advertising man but as a totally outraged *consumer* rarely, if ever, occurs to them. Indeed, the main thing that has held me in advertising is the thing that got me into it in the first place. That is the challenge of proving daily that advertising does not necessarily have to be dull, insipid, nauseating, or irritating in order to communicate and thus sell the product.[21]

Over the years the criticisms and defenses of advertising have remained fairly consistent. Most of the criticisms have been aimed at the supposed psychological effects—namely, that advertising creates needs and wants and, in so doing, encourages people to emphasize materialism and live beyond their means. To the extent that these wants are left unfulfilled, it also breeds frustration and encourages aggressiveness and perhaps crime. While some evidence may be available to support these claims, there is little doubt that advertising is the product of a commercial and competitive society. It is the natural partner of the free enterprise system and it provides the distribution extension of mass production. For dramatic evidence of this, look again at table 10.1 on page 319. Careful examination of the figures reveals much about the consumption habits of Americans and the advertising behaviors of corporations. Notice which products get the most advertising as a percent of sales. Consider how the money spent on selling these products relates to the psychology of advertising and the ideas of Maslow and Rokeach. Would you say that the advertising for these products creates wants and needs?

Critics maintain that advertising creates desires that cannot be fulfilled, that it clutters the media with insignificance.

The Cost of Advertising

Whether advertising makes products cheaper or more costly is open to debate.

One of the dominant criticisms levelled at advertising is its cost to the consumer. Such costs are considerable. Because advertising costs are passed on, consumers are placed in the position of paying for the privilege of being persuaded. For example, over $100 of the cost of the average American car represents advertising costs that the consumer pays when buying the vehicle. And the price of many cosmetics represents little more than the cost of the advertising that goes into them. Combined with the criticisms previously cited, this essentially means that members of the public are paying liberally to be urged to live beyond their means, to buy products they don't need, and—in the long run—to be spendthrifts.

At the beginning of the chapter we noted that advertising is an automated sales force, which is advertising's strongest defense. The existence of advertising has made possible a greater demand for goods and services. Translated into terms of mass production, this increased demand has led to economies and savings on the assembly lines and in purchasing, and may have rendered many products, including the automobile, far cheaper than they would otherwise have been—even with the extra advertising increment.

There are other assets. Advertising makes possible the most diversified mass communications system of any nation, providing unparalleled entertainment and considerable information and culture to the individual at a fraction of its true cost. Martin Mayer addresses himself to the psychological factors in advertising in his *value-added theory*.[22] He claims that advertising adds a vague dimension to a product: The woman who buys a particular soap with the belief that it will improve her complexion may be more satisfied in that belief—she may be a happier person—whether it does or does not; the assurance that comes from purchasing a product of believed quality—a Hathaway shirt, for example—provides a confidence to the individual that would have been unobtainable with a cheaper brand. According to Paul Samuelson, lipstick ingredients that cost pennies are transmuted by the alchemy of Madison Avenue into expensive cosmetics that essentially represent packaged hope, and what's the matter with hope?[23] In essence, Mayer and Samuelson are making a case for the psychological concept of confidence: We are what we believe and for some of us this is the added value of advertising.

Mayer's "value-added" theory says ads increase psychological value of a product.

CATHY   **by Cathy Guisewite**

There is little doubt that advertising increases the cost of some goods; that advertising encourages consumption, often at the expense of thrift; and that advertising often works upon the public's psyches in various ways. But there is also little doubt that advertising supports the largest and most diverse mass media network in the world and, without doubt, the mass media system freest of overt governmental manipulation and propaganda; that advertising is a major employer and contributor to the overall economy; and that advertising, through increased demand, reduces the overall cost of many products.

On the plus side, advertising maintains the world's most complex and diverse mass media system.

Advertising is, therefore, both a blessing and a menace, and both these roles must be recognized if the operation of mass communications in society is to be understood. As in almost everything that we have discussed pertaining to mass communications, there are trade-offs. The bad is accepted with the good. It is not a question of either/or. It is a question of both, because under the existing system, which has had a long evolution and tradition, we cannot have one without the other, or we shall have a different system entirely.

Summary

It is advertising, by and large, that supports the diverse mass communications system within the United States. This relationship evolved largely as the result of a competitive, free enterprise economy where the private sector has provided the investment needed to expand the mass media in return for their use in selling goods and services.

Although ancient in origin, most of the growth of advertising has occurred during the years following World War II. Rapid improvement in media technology, interest in the social sciences, and a backlog of consumer demand all contributed to its postwar impetus. Today advertising is a $60 billion a year business divided into national and local advertising. Newspapers still get more of the national advertising than any other medium.

Agencies can be one-person operations, creative boutiques, or large and institutional organizations, such as J. Walter Thompson. Regardless of size, all agencies perform five functions—client liaison, creativity, production, placement, and housekeeping—for which they are paid a commission or a negotiated fee.

Since World War II, strategies used by advertising have become more sophisticated. The first strategy developed was Ted Bates' unique selling proposition, followed by David Ogilvy's brand images, Ernest Dichter's motivational research, and Jim Vicary's subliminal advertising. Currently in favor is positioning, an advertising strategy that concedes part of the market to the competition. In positioning, the job of the advertiser is to identify and reach a segment of the larger market.

Advertising seems to be remarkably effective in selling consumer goods, inconsequentials that the public recognizes as trivia. It is much less effective in convincing the public in matters of substance, such as elections or higher level human needs or values. It is unequalled in calling attention to a new product or candidate. However, by its sheer pervasiveness, it has probably done as much as any other institution to propagate society's myths of progress and self-betterment: "A better world through advertising."

The industry itself, recognizing its questionable public image, has taken several steps toward effective self-regulation. From ludicrous turn-of-the-century efforts at mystifying their critics by calling themselves "doctors of felicity," advertisers have progressed to sophisticated internal checks and balances. Deceptive advertising has received most of the attention, primarily with an eye toward warding off formal governmental controls over the industry. Nonetheless, the government does exert substantial influence over advertisers, particularly through the Federal Trade Commission. The FTC now requires documentation for claims made in advertisements, and in some cases the agency requires corrective advertising.

There is no shortage of criticisms of advertising, nor a shortage of defenses. It is attacked and defended mainly on psychological and economic grounds. Social critics and economists remain divided on advertising's shortcomings and contributions, but all recognize its integral role in contemporary America.

Notes

1. Quentin Schultze, "Comments on the History of Ethical Codes in the Advertising Business" (Paper presented to Association for Education in Journalism, Mass Communications and Society Division, Logan, Utah, 30 March 1979).
2. Martin Mayer, *Madison Avenue U.S.A.* (New York: Harper & Brothers, 1958).
3. Sloan Wilson, *The Man in the Gray Flannel Suit* (New York: Pocket Books, 1967).
4. Vance Packard, *The Hidden Persuaders* (New York: Pocket Books, 1968); and Mayer, *Madison Avenue U.S.A.*
5. J. A. C. Brown, *Techniques of Persuasion* (Baltimore, Md.: Penguin Books, 1963).
6. W. Keith Hafer and Gordon E. White, *Advertising Writing* (St. Paul, Minn.: West Publishing Company, 1977), p. 244.
7. Mayer, *Madison Avenue, U.S.A.*
8. Abraham Maslow, *Motivation and Personality.* (New York: Harper & Row, 1970), pp. 80–92.
9. Otto Kleppner, *Advertising Procedures,* 7th ed. (Englewood Cliffs, N.J.: Prentice-Hall, 1979), pp. 301–2.
10. Milton Rokeach, *The Open and Closed Mind* (New York: Basic Books, 1960); *Beliefs, Attitudes, and Values* (San Francisco: Jossey-Bass, 1968), and *The Nature of Human Values* (New York: The Free Press, 1973).
11. Milton Rokeach, "Images of the Consumer's Mind On and Off Madison Avenue," *ETC., A Review of General Semantics,* September 1964, pp. 261–73.
12. Kleppner, *Advertising Procedures,* p. 556.
13. Harold L. Nelson and Dwight L. Teeter, *Law of Mass Communications,* 4th ed. (Mineola, N.Y.: The Foundation Press, 1982), p. 567.
14. Ibid., pp. 538–39.

15. Charlene J. Brown, Trevor R. Brown, and William L. Rivers, *The Media and the People* (New York: Holt, Rinehart & Winston, 1978), p. 400.
16. *FTC* v. *Warner-Lambert Co.,* 435 U.S. 950 (review denied).
17. Summary and recommendations found in *Advertising Age,* 27 February 1978, pp. 73–77.
18. Ibid.
19. James Kilpatrick, *Washington Star* (syndicated column), 16 May 1978.
20. Rose Goldsen, "Why Television Advertising Is Deceptive and Unfair," *ETC, A Review of General Semantics* Winter 1978, pp. 365–67.
21. Stan Freberg, "The Freberg Part-time Television Plan." In *Mass Media in a Free Society,* ed. Warren K. Agee (Lawrence, Kansas: The University Press of Kansas, 1969) p. 64.
22. Martin Mayer, *Madison Avenue, U.S.A.*
23. "American Issues Forum No. 8: Courses by Newspaper," February 1976.

11 Public Relations

Public relations is an enigma that defies simple definition. In its broadest sense it is an umbrella that includes publicity (with which it is too often equated), propaganda, promotion, press agentry, and even advertising, plus such subspecialties as political campaigning and lobbying. Perhaps the best definition is "ulterior communication." As such, public relations makes extensive use of the mass media, contributing considerable portions of media content in contemporary society.

Public relations and advertising are frequently confused in the public's mind. Part of the confusion can be lessened if we try to imagine our society without advertising and without public relations. You'll undoubtedly find it more difficult to imagine society without advertising—without the obvious, overt, paid-for, commercial persuasions—than without public relations—the frequently subtle, behind-the-scenes, covert, ulterior communications. Advertising uses paid time and space in the media, usually to deal directly with consumers, primarily to promote and sell goods and services, secondarily to promote and sell ideas. Public relations, on the other hand, uses free time and space in the media to promote institutions or ideas or candidates; it is more interested in reputation than in sales—more concerned about image than distribution of goods and services. However, if publishers were to leave blank that space in newspapers and magazines occupied by any story with a public relations origin, and if broadcasters were to omit from the air any program or item that had its genesis in public relations, the sheer volume of white space and silence would indicate impressively the extent to which the mass media are dependent upon public relations. More to the point, the experiment would reflect the extent to which society is perhaps unwittingly exposed to ulterior material.

Public relations is both a condition and an activity. We say a corporation has good PR; that generally means we have a particular image of that corporation's condition. On the other hand, when we say a corporation practices good PR, we are referring to a range of PR activities: writing news releases, giving speeches, arranging special events, and the like. The activities typically fall into one of eight major areas: (1) opinion research, (2) press agentry, (3) product promotion, (4) publicity, (5) lobbying, (6) public affairs, (7) fund raising and membership drives, and (8) special events management.

Practitioners of PR have made numerous attempts over the years to define their livelihood. *Public Relations News* holds that public relations is the management function that evaluates public attitudes, identifies the policies and procedures of an individual or an organization with the public interest, and plans and executes a program of action to earn public understanding and acceptance. The World Assembly of Public Relations Associations maintains that public relations practice is the art and social science of analyzing trends, predicting their consequences, counseling organization

Introduction

Although it defies simple definition, public relations appears as ulterior communication throughout the mass media.

PR differs from advertising in its stress on reputation or image, rather than on sales or distribution. It is not paid for in the same way that advertising is.

Public relations is a broad term, encompassing internal, organizational communications, community service, political campaigning, and public opinion research.
Ellis Herwig/Stock, Boston (top left); Tim Jewett/EKM-Nepenthe (bottom left); Martha Stewart/The Picture Cube (top right); John Maher/EKM-Nepenthe (bottom right).

Persuasive Media

leaders, and implementing planned programs of action that will serve the interests of organizations and the public. These and other definitions all point to a similar goal: All functions labelled public relations are for the purpose of influencing public opinion.[1]

In this chapter we will attempt to distinguish public relations from other forms of mass communications. We will consider the irony of PR—the bad image of an industry created to promote a good image for clients—and the industry's attempts to improve its image. The history of public relations in America and abroad will be considered, with attention paid to the movement toward social responsibility in business. Specialized roles of PR in contemporary society, and particularly within the political sphere, will be noted. And we will discuss propaganda and the inevitability of organized persuasion in today's world.

Historical Development

Efforts to change public opinion are as old as recorded history. Greeks and Romans mastered the art.

The antecedents of public relations can be traced to earliest recorded history, including ancient biblical times. In terms of publicity, lobbying, and even press agentry, we might look to ancient Greece, where the poets were the public relations people. Use of the poetic form in rhyme and meter facilitated memory, assuring that messages would be passed along in more or less the same form. Two poets, Simonides and Pindar, made a good living writing and selling odes of praise for those willing to pay. They were among the first press agents. The use of poetry to manipulate public opinion became so widespread in the Greek democracy that Plato in his *Republic* advocated the prohibition of all poetry—except that written for the government. Not only was this the first example of attempted governmental control of the mass media (such as they were), but it was the first advocacy of governmental public relations, which is, of course, a big business today.

In Rome, the same techniques of poetry and praise occurred with a number of Roman refinements. The Romans refined the poetic form, adding subtlety to public relations. Virgil's *Georgics* was, on the surface, a bucolic poem extolling the virtues of country living, the pastoral scene, clean air, fresh water, and a closeness to nature. Its purpose, however, was devious. Rome was overcrowded at the time, an early version of urban sprawl. There was not enough food to feed the population. The *Georgics,* commissioned by the government, was a public relations attempt to urge people to leave the city and take up rural residence, thus alleviating the population pressure and providing more farmers to feed city residents.

Gaius Julius Caesar was a master of public relations, who developed the first long-range public relations program. Early in his career his talent and ambition caused jealousies, and the Senate in effect banished him to Gaul to be in charge of an army, hoping that the people, with whom he was extraordinarily popular, would forget him.

Over the Roman roads that supplied the legions, Caesar sent back messengers regularly to Rome with his *Commentaries,* familiar to any beginning Latin student. The *Commentaries* were not reports to the Senate; they were reports to the people telling of his exploits. They were read and posted in the forum for all to see. They were written in the language of the people—punchy and alive. His famous "veni, vidi, vici" is a fine example—"I came, I saw, I conquered." The technique worked; over the long years of foreign battles—in Gaul, Spain, and Britain—he kept his legend alive until the day when he returned at the head of his victorious army. The people hailed him and made him emperor.

Throughout the Middle Ages and the Renaissance, public relations proceeded in a relatively informal way as troubadours spread messages from castle to castle and from town to town. By the time of the American Revolution, print had become an established medium. Mass communications helped make the world more complex and soon there emerged a need for new forms of public relations.

One of the two basic sources of American public relations as an organized practice can be found in political campaigns. When the founding fathers set up the electoral structure, they expected that natural leaders would emerge to be elected by the people. However, because political office meant preferment, it was not long before ambitious individuals began taking steps to assure that they would be counted among the natural leaders at election time.

Public Relations in America

In America, democracy made PR inevitable.

Some of the early political campaigns were masterpieces of excitement. Catchy slogans, torchlight parades, brass bands, and beer busts were used in the effort to win votes. It was Andrew Jackson who changed the ground rules. An Indian fighter of repute and victor at New Orleans in the War of 1812, he campaigned on a populist ticket with a slate of electors pledged to him. His election in 1828 proved the merit of populist appeal, and the business of national campaigning was born.

The other basis of public relations was theatrical press agentry, of which P. T. Barnum (1810–1891) was the great exponent. Barnum recognized that people enjoyed being conned (directed). He was the author of the statement, "There's a sucker born every minute," and he exploited this principle throughout his life as a showman. His buildup of General Tom Thumb, a midget masquerading as a Civil War general, was a masterpiece of promotion. Later, the production of General Tom Thumb's wedding to another midget, complete with a parade down Broadway in a tiny coach drawn by tiny horses, was another pinnacle of publicity. People knew that Tom Thumb was no Civil War officer, no hero of Antietam or Vicksburg, but the idea was so preposterous that they enjoyed it and were willing to pay money to hear his exploits and to see him strut in his little uniform and

P. T. Barnum's "There's a sucker born every minute" reflected his concept of public opinion.

cockaded hat. It is from this origin of public relations that much of its criticism stems. The theory was that anything was valid if it generated publicity. "I don't care what you say about me so long as you spell my name right" was a summary of the substance of press agentry. While political campaigning introduced specificity of appeal, press agentry introduced the outrageous as a device in the competition for attention. In the orchestra of public relations, Cutlip and Center remind us that press agentry represents the brass section; the aim of press agentry is more to attract attention than to gain understanding, since notoriety can be more useful than piety, thriving as it does in the box-office world.[2]

The years following the Civil War were the years of America's expansion, the winning of the West when much was suborned to the practical business of exploiting a continent. This was the time of the robber barons and the railroads, of "survival of the fittest" (widely misinterpreted from its biological origin in Darwin to a social doctrine), and of laissez-faire, its political and economic expression. The era had its public relations counterpart in William Henry Vanderbilt of the New York Central Railroad who, in 1882, expressed contempt for public opinion. When one of his advisers suggested that the public would not be particularly pleased with one of Vanderbilt's proposals, the magnate is said to have responded: "The public, why, sir, the public be damned."

The turn of the century brought reaction in the form of the muckrakers—authors and journalists—who saw business corruption and government collusion running rampant and set out to correct them, using the mass media of the time—books, magazines, and newspapers. Ida Tarbell's series "The History of Standard Oil," Lincoln Steffens' "The Shame of the Cities," and Upton Sinclair's novel *The Jungle*, an exposé of the meat-packing industry, are all examples of an unorganized campaign that ran a decade or so and resulted in some of the first social legislation. The muckrakers were the expression of a stirring social consciousness repulsed by the excesses of business and the timidity of government.

The Father of PR

Business did not take this lying down. It turned to press agents to whitewash its reputation, but the glaring discrepancies between business's whitewash and the all too visible inequities created an early example of a credibility gap. Business was in trouble. Into this picture in 1908 stepped Ivy Lee, the father of modern public relations. Lee, a press agent who dealt in truth, had an unprecedented idea. He published a declaration of principles and sent it to editors with whom he was associated. It said that he dealt in news and factual information, and that the editors were free to check any of his facts independently. Furthermore, if they felt his material would be better placed in their advertising columns, all they had to do was throw it away.

Ivy Lee had an enormous respect for the aggregate wisdom of the people. He felt that if they were given the facts they would make correct judgments. His basic tenet was that the public should be honestly informed of good news and bad. He proved this in the case of the Pennsylvania Railroad. The Pennsy had a wreck in which a number of lives were lost. Management's first reaction was to hush it up, but Lee pointed out that a wreck could not be hidden. With cars and engines strewn over the New Jersey landscape and bloodshed on the right-of-way, the public was certain to find out about it. Lee ran special trains for the press to the scene of the accident. He announced a system-wide survey of the company's roadbeds so that a similar wreck would not happen, the indemnification of the families of those who were killed, and hospitalization to the injured. In short, Lee converted a tragedy into a public relations triumph for the railroad, which was widely applauded by the press for the manner in which it handled the accident. Lee knew that it is far better to face bad news frontally than to let it linger and fester in secret until it destroys credibility.

The first decade of the twentieth century was a time of expanding mass media—proliferating newspapers, the development of the huge newspaper chains, stepped-up wire services, national magazines, and an embryonic movie industry—that breathed life into public relations. Its organized practice stemmed from this decade.

By World War I, public relations was sufficiently well established as a profession for President Wilson to call on it for assistance. He established the Creel Committee as an adjunct of government, so named because it was headed by George Creel, a newspaperman who was one of Wilson's friends. The committee was charged with censoring war information, helping to finance the war through the sale of Liberty Bonds, convincing the American people of the war's necessity, popularizing the draft, and encouraging sympathy for the Allies and hatred of the enemy—a mammoth assignment that it carried out with considerable success.

World War I to the Present

It took a massive public relations campaign to sell millions of dollars worth of Liberty Bonds during World War I.
Wide World Photos

The next milestone in the development of public relations as an organized practice was engendered by Edward Bernays. Bernays, who had been a member of the Creel Committee, set up practice in New York following World War I. He wrote the first book on public relations, *Crystallizing Public Opinion,* which was published in 1923.[3] He also taught the first course in public relations at NYU during that period. Bernays' philosophy of public opinion manipulation is summed up in his phrase, "the engineering of consent."

In 1930, with the beginning of the Great Depression, Paul Garrett became the first public relations director of the General Motors Corporation. When asked by GM how it was possible to make a billion-dollar corporation look small (wealth was suspect during the depression), Garrett replied that he hadn't the faintest idea. Alternately, he proposed a program in which GM could use a part of its resources to provide high school and college educations for youngsters who would otherwise go without, and in which GM could make significant contributions to schools and municipal improvements in those communities where its plants were located. These were all windfalls to public agencies during the constricted years of the depression. Garrett reasoned that GM would receive public relations credit as a benefactor, in addition to which it would be making its plant communities more efficient and would also be developing a backlog of educated executive talent against the future. Garrett referred to this as "enlightened self-interest," and his program was the first of the socially conscious programs of industry.

Public relations was hard pressed during the depression to serve business, which had been cast as a villain. Furthermore, because of its intangible nature, public relations was one of the first business services to be curtailed in a time of tight money. Labor unions and government, however, forged ahead in using public relations, and Franklin D. Roosevelt became one of the masters of its use.

FDR, JFK, and Beyond

FDR's fireside chats, employing radio in the depression years to reach into America's homes, were inspired. They reassured a frightened people and helped Roosevelt sell his then radical programs of monetary and social reform. It was a technique that softened the depression.

At a later time, John Fitzgerald Kennedy displayed the same inherent understanding of television that FDR did of radio. He used television to talk to the nation disarmingly, exploiting his personal charisma while prompting a sense of trust and optimism about the future. All presidential candidates and incumbents since have followed JFK's clues; the fortieth president, Ronald Reagan, himself a former film actor and television series host, is certainly no exception. These examples indicate the extent to which public relations has infiltrated government and show how adroit media usage constitutes the means of projecting an image. The public relations image is not necessarily a mirage; it can easily be a reality (as it was for FDR and JFK) that needs only the proper lens to project it where it can be seen by everyone. Choosing and using that lens is a part of public relations.

World War II provided additional impetus to public relations as techniques of propaganda and psychological warfare were perfected, and the term *war of nerves* became part of our vocabulary. President Roosevelt's Office of War Information (OWI) under Elmer Davis had charge of a full public relations and propaganda service, both domestic and international, focusing not only on American allies to strengthen and reassure them, but also on enemies to sow the seeds of doubt and despair.

In the years following World War II, public relations grew apace. These decades saw journalism and the social sciences form a loose union in organized practice. In spite of the growth, the field of public relations still lacks a concise definition. The problem is compounded by the image of public relations, whereby many people performing essentially public relations functions in government and industry and elsewhere are given different titles. The armed services lean heavily on the public information function as opposed to public relations. The terms *public affairs* and *vice-president of communications* are becoming increasingly popular, but these are actually euphemisms for *public relations* that, by seeking to avoid the stigma, merely emphasize it and create a crisis of credibility.

Social sciences are applied to PR following World War II.

The Business of Public Relations

Much of public relations counseling is conducted on a local basis, for two reasons. First, a considerable portion of public relations deals with the community and community relations as a specialty—painting the organization as a concerned corporate citizen. Even the largest corporations have diversified their community relations into the communities where their branches and plants are located, and it is a local public relations counselor who serves these individual plants. Second, and more significantly, public relations is still print oriented in our electronic age. Newspapers have remained the principal vehicles of public relations practice because material that appears in print provides a tangible record of the public relations person's efforts. It is, thus, the local counselor who can best contact the local newspaper in his or her community.

PR tends to be print oriented and local.

There are, of course, some major national public relations firms. At least thirty-three of them, at the start of the 1980s, did a million or more dollars worth of business annually. The top five are Hill and Knowlton (672 employees and $22,558,248 in 1978 income), Burson-Marsteller (670 employees, $22,190,900 income), Carl Byoir & Associates unit of Foote, Cone & Belding Advertising (408 employees and $12,457,000 income), Ruder & Finn (240 employees, $7,762,000 income), and Harshe-Rotman & Druck (165 employees, $4,855,000 income).[4] Many of these top firms operate internationally as general public relations counselors. In addition, many of the major advertising agencies have public relations divisions: J. Walter Thompson Company, Grey Advertising, and others.

There are at least 100,000 identifiable public relations practitioners in the United States, and the number is more likely two or three times that. There are at least 1,500 public relations counseling firms. All told, several billions of dollars are expended each year on public relations efforts. All PR practitioners work in one way or another for organizations: governmental agencies (whose public information officers probably outnumber public relations people in the private sector), business and industry, charitable and cultural organizations, educational institutions at all levels, hospitals, labor unions, churches, professional associations, and even the mass media. All organizations have public relations whether they want it or not, just as all individuals have personalities; some are good, some are bad, and some are indifferent. Like individual personality, organizational public relations is capable of being changed by dint of hard effort over a long period. Public relations is necessarily long-term and is, in fact, a corporate personality dealing with publics rather than other individuals.

Public relations may be either the "brushfire" or "fire prevention" type. Brushfire public relations moves from crisis to crisis seeking to put out the fires; it awaits imminent disaster before taking corrective action. It is not particularly efficient. It is also widespread. Fire prevention public relations seeks to foresee a crisis and avoid it. It is a continuing effort, constantly upgrading the organization, planning for the future, evaluating its own results, and utilizing this evaluation as updated research for future planning. There is a kind of "iceberg" analogy to all this. Like the iceberg, with only about 10 percent of it showing above the sea, only about 10 percent of public relations is apparent to the publics in the form of news releases and news stories, films and promotions, speeches and mailings, spot announcements and television programs, and so forth. The rest is meticulous, grinding research and planning, painstakingly accomplished: deliberate statistical analysis, interviews, and long hours of reading and writing. It is far from the glamorous vocation that has been depicted—a misplaced stereotype of three-martini luncheons in exclusive bistros, glamorous travel, and lavish expense accounts.

Public relations serves organizations either internally or externally. Internally, the public relations executives are on the organization's payroll; they are a part of the company. Externally, they are consultants retained by the company to review its public relations program, to undertake certain specific assignments, or to conduct its overall public relations program on a part-time basis; they are independent counselors.

Both the internal executives and the outside counselors have certain inherent assets and liabilities. The internal executives know the company intimately; in all probability they grew up with it. They know the channels necessary to get anything done; they are aware of the personality quirks of the other executives; they are always available, and they know where any skeletons are hidden. On the other hand, because of their availability their time is too often frittered away with trivia, allowing them little time to think or plan. They traditionally get all the problems that do not fit neatly into someone else's pigeonhole. Their familiarity means that they are often not given the proper deference for their ideas. Further, they tend to become ingrown; they lack broad exposure and become enmeshed in their own corporate world. They also may, regrettably, become deferential to management, "yes-people" too often unwilling to disagree. They cannot see the forest for the trees.

The counselors, on the other hand, bring an outside viewpoint, a degree of objectivity to the organization's course; they can see the forest. They also bring a wide range of contacts and outside experience to bear on the organization's problems, and perhaps some valuable expertise in a specific field. But even the largest organizations cannot afford to keep platoons of public relations specialists on the payroll to be on hand for the relatively few times their services will be needed. The disadvantages of employing counselors is that they are unfamiliar with the organization and they don't know where the skeletons are hidden. Nor are they always available. While their opinions are listened to with respect, because they are outsiders and because they are expensive, there is also a certain resentment attached to them because they are outsiders.

There is a pattern to public relations development as an organization grows. Initially in a small organization, one of the principals assumes the public relations responsibility in addition to other duties. Later, as the volume of this work increases, the organization hires a counselor on a part-time basis. As more and more of the counselor's time becomes involved with the growing organization's work, a full-time public relations person is employed at a fraction of the counselor's billing. The PR executive's scope then expands into a department, perhaps with branches in other cities, and finally a counselor is retained again for specific assignments, such as introducing a new product, lobbying the legislature, performing duties in connection with a proposed merger, or simply bringing a fresh and objective analysis of the ongoing public relations program—for example, an outside public relations audit.

Internal and External Public Relations

Organizations have their own PR divisions or they hire outside consultants. Each system has assets and liabilities.

Tools and Functions

Ideally, public relations is a two-way street. Not only must it use its expertise to identify the organization's various publics and interpret management policy to them, but equally important and too often overlooked, it must use this expertise to interpret public opinion and anticipated reaction to management as a guide to corporate policy. Unless it does the latter and unless management is both willing to listen and willing to provide the atmosphere in which this mutual exchange can take place, public relations is not doing its whole job and thus management is deprived of an invaluable tool in the decision-making process.

The tools used by public relations to reach its various publics are many. There are the mass media, of course, but there are also specialized media—public relations films, tapes, and publications, or house organs—that are used extensively to reach essentially captive audiences. Corporate annual reports are a form of public relations; so are addresses to groups, and seminars and conventions, which is why speakers bureaus, often supplemented by films and videotapes, are a stock-in-trade for major public relations operations. Public relations pays a good deal of attention to schools at all levels, providing educational films and tapes, and in some cases, course material. The idea is to condition the young with the thought that they can influence their parents and, then when they grow up, they too will become consumers and believers. The Bell System is particularly active in communications instruction of this type.

Too often public relations is confused with publicity; in fact it has been identified with it. While publicity is one of the important tools of public relations, it is far from the sum and substance of the profession. Publicity consists of obtaining free space or time for promotional material in the press or on the air, and although this material masquerades as news, its purpose is often hidden. One of the advantages of publicity is that in a quantitative society it can be measured; the number of column inches obtained in the press and the number of minutes on the air can be totalled. Therefore a tangible record of publicity can be kept, which has led to reliance on the *clipping book* as a measure of public relations effectiveness. Public relations practitioners proudly haul their clipping books to management on a regular basis, saying, "Here's what I've done for you lately; here's how I earned my pay." Further, the number of column inches or air minutes can be applied to media advertising rate cards and a dollar volume of publicity computed: "This coverage would have cost you $10,000 if you had not used my services," a PR practitioner might say. These are meaningful figures to cost-conscious management, but they do not measure the effect of the publicity. Nor do they tell who, if anyone, read it or heard it, nor how the audience reacted.

Like advertising, public relations includes two separate but related functions: information and persuasion. By far the easier to explain is the information aspect. This function also comes closest to public relations as a legitimate adjunct to the news, an auxiliary news source in its own right.

Information, whether offered through the press or before groups or in house organs, keeps the various publics advised. It describes, delineates, and explains goods, services, events, and ideas; it seeks to break down the barriers of confusion and misunderstanding. It is this aspect of public relations that has proven most effective.

Public relations professionals often assert that their most important responsibility is to communicate their employer's side of the story to the public, since it frequently is not known. The PR function is important because few staff people in organizations have the skills and understanding necessary to communicate such messages.

The manipulative aspect of public relations, which has been called news management in government circles, is far more difficult. Persuasive news management is heavily bound up in the phenomena of public opinion formation and change. One method is the use of reinforcement, repetition of a theme until the public becomes supportive. It can backfire easily, accomplishing the opposite of its purpose. So little is known about public opinion that manipulative public relations has to be treated with extreme caution, as politicians are increasingly aware. Manipulative public relations tends to ignore the collective wisdom of the people. Abraham Lincoln saw this and expressed it succinctly: "You may fool all of the people some of the time; you can even fool some of the people all of the time; but you can't fool all of the people all of the time." He was talking about *public relations,* although the term hadn't been coined yet.

Manipulative PR can readily backfire.

Successful public relations in an informational sense is dependent upon an atmosphere of mutual respect between the media gatekeepers and the public relations practitioners. The relationship is a bit flimsy, since each is wary of the other. Editors know that PR people represent special interests, and that the material prepared by them is often of inferior quality, requiring rewriting. PR people know that editors deal in the sensational, often, although not always, to the disadvantage of PR clients. Attracted by reasonable hours and good pay, many PR people have come from the media, generally from newspapers, which presents considerable advantages: They are familiar with newspaper style; they know what news is and how to write it; they are aware of media problems; and they have their own contacts in the city room. The most successful PR people are the ones who know that they are performing a useful information service in providing the media with news that could, in the ordinary course of events, be obtained in no other way. This is because none of the mass media have the physical or human resources, money, or time to fully cover all events. For some media, public relations people are needed to provide much of their news.

Although PR people do not go hat in hand a-begging, they are aware of the intense competition for attention. They know that they are in competition for newspaper space with a platoon of reporters, with the chattering teletype batteries from around the world and nation, with the reams of feature material, and with every other press agent in town. They have established a working rapport with the media; the good ones have proven their integrity. For these pragmatic reasons, most public relations material in the mass media has a legitimate claim on news. It may be self-serving, but frequently it is news.

Events and Pseudoevents

Public relations deals in events. Outside of special areas of public relations, it makes extensive use of the mass media, particularly the press. The press deals in news, and events become the peg on which public relations can hang its client's hat. Events provide the vehicle to carry a story to the press and, at the same time, the rationale for an editor or news director to use it. An event may range from a simple item such as the citizen-of-the-year award by the local Kiwanis Club to the dazzling production surrounding the dedication of London Bridge at Lake Havasu City, Arizona, in 1972. The London Bridge dedication imported the Lord Mayor of London; transported a catered banquet for 1,000 across the desert in a caravan from Beverly Hills; provided a name band for dancing on the bridge and fireworks that lit thirty square miles of sky with a full color portrait of Elizabeth II that dissolved into crossed English and American flags. The Lord Mayor was brought to the site by Indian war canoes (for which the Indians had to attend paddling school), and the event was climaxed by thirty skydivers descending into a circle a mile in diameter as 10,000 doves rose into the desert sky. All of this was for the purpose of announcing a new housing complex.

Events and pseudoevents are related and bespeak two separate techniques. Public relations people find the means to tie their interest into a legitimate event; southern California's nursery industry has capitalized on

The London Bridge dedication at Lake Havasu City—a masterpiece of hyping a pseudoevent.
United Press International

autumn forest fires by donating seedling pine trees to reforest the devastated lands, an act that generated much favorable publicity. Pseudoevents, on the other hand, are public relations fabrications whose exclusive purpose is to generate publicity.[5] The dedication of London Bridge is a classic example of a pseudoevent used to publicize Lake Havasu City for the purpose of selling real estate. It was fantastically successful, although it cost over one million dollars. It generated front-page wire-service coverage on nearly every major metropolitan newspaper in the land, including the conservative *Wall Street Journal.*[6] All three networks covered it live with follow-up. Radio and magazine coverage is uncounted. The dollar value of this publicity on television alone, at $85,000 a minute for just the single four-minute breaks on three networks, exceeded the million dollar outlay. Such an ostentatious pseudoevent, which by its very scope and outrageous nature demands media coverage, is known in the trade as *pizzazz.* It is a device to overcome the competition for attention that plagues an accelerating society.

Pseudoevents are PR fabrications whose exclusive purpose is to generate publicity. "Pizzazz" is the name of the game.

Publicity is far better achieved when the media cover an event than if the public relations person simply provides a release. If the media invest their own time and effort in covering an event, in shooting film or videotape, the material and footage are more likely to be used than if they are provided free by public relations. Thus, the most accomplished publicists spend little time writing releases; they put more effort into creating a situation that will demand the media's own coverage, from the standpoints of significance and interest. Increasingly, publicists become actual adjuncts to the press, in addition to becoming more subtle and sophisticated in their operations.

The Audiences for Public Relations

In order to secure attention, public relations must pinpoint interest. This requires a clear definition of *audience,* or *public relations publics.* These publics range from the consumer to the government. Several publics are related to a business or industry: employees, dealers, suppliers, and competitors, for example. Other publics are part of the larger environment: the community, educators, and financial interests, for example. To a major corporation, many of these publics are discrete but interlocking. Each has a different interest in the corporation: employees in wages and fringe benefits, stockholders in dividends and appreciation of investment. Yet they all share an interest in the corporation; it is their rallying point. But the matter is not all that simple; an employee may easily be a stockholder and a consumer. The public relations people of the corporation must communicate with employees in different terms than they use in materials presented to the stockholders if they are going to hold the interest of each group. Defining these audiences, determining how to reach them most efficiently with the least overkill, and framing what to say to them is the job of public relations. At the same time, PR must try to measure the separate and collective pulses and give the readings back to management as guidelines to policy.

PR has to link management to its many diverse publics. It is not an easy task.

How does public relations reach these publics: by utilizing all forms of communication, not just mass media. It will prepare policy bulletins for employees and financial statements for Wall Street. Each year the public relations arm of the corporation will produce glossy annual reports for shareholders. It relies heavily on word of mouth. Public relations makes use of conventions, seminars, group addresses, and individual contacts with opinion leaders. It also employs mass media, from network television to community newspapers. Public relations has developed audience identification to a fine art, and ingeniously devises some imaginative means of reaching particular, discrete publics. Extensive use is made of demographics and public opinion polling. It is fair to say that both public relations and advertising, the organized forms of persuasion, are devoted to generating word-of-mouth coverage between individuals, for it is only through this means that a message perpetuates itself once it is let loose.

Specialization in Public Relations

PR people are no longer generalists. Community relations, political campaigning, financial PR, lobbying, and fund raising are just a few of the specialized tasks.

Only a generation or so ago, the public relations practitioners were jacks-of-all-trades; they were generalists counseling management, developing product promotion, handling political campaigns, and writing publicity. Similar to the general practitioners in medicine, they are rapidly becoming a thing of the past; as in medicine, law, and other professions, public relations has become increasingly specialized.

Some of the major specializations that come under the public relations umbrella are community relations, political campaigning, financial public relations, lobbying, and fund raising. These are in addition to the broader fields of community, industrial, commercial, and organizational public relations, product and personality promotion, propaganda, press relations, and public affairs.

As television developed, it had a profound effect on political campaigning. Television's ability to reach huge masses of people simultaneously, in addition to the growth of computer-based demographics, put new and sometimes contradictory dimensions into politics. It became necessary to find an appeal to television's masses, even while constructing separate and noncontradictory appeals to smaller demographic breakdowns of the same mass. This is because politics is concerned with the entire spectrum of audiences, from the TV mass down to the single individual. Whitaker and Baxter, a campaign management house based in San Francisco, was the first to specialize politically in the late 1930s. Twenty years later Baus and Ross, a Los Angeles general public relations agency, gave up its roster of commercial clients to concentrate on politics in 1958.[7] Since that time, there has been a proliferation of campaign specialists across the nation as campaigning has become more sophisticated.

Political campaigning differs from organizational public relations in several important respects. From the practitioner's standpoint, it is seasonal. Political campaigns occur only at certain specified intervals. The campaign specialist, therefore, is faced with a feast or famine situation, which is one of the reasons for the high costs of campaigning. Second, political campaigning is a crisis situation wherein all activity is always concentrated into too short a time frame. Everyone knows about the harrowing schedule of a politician on the campaign trail: the twenty-four hour days, the jet travel, and speeches in Pittsburgh, St. Louis, and Los Angeles all in one day. The public relations people who arrange, schedule, and promote all this activity have equally appalling schedules. They worry about the press, the advertising, the crowds, the advance arrangements, the timetable, the speeches, the sources of money, the budget, the press kits, the infighting, the polls, and the candidate's blunders. Years of public relations activity are crowded into a couple of months.

Politics and Public Relations

Political campaigning demands special and intensive PR tools. Its results are clear-cut. The candidate or platform wins or loses on election day.

Political campaigns run the public relations gauntlet, from conventioneering for a state schoolboard post (top), to handling tough questions from journalists during a U.S. Senate race (bottom). Robert Eckert, Jr./EKM-Nepenthe (top); Eric A. Roth/The Picture Cube (bottom).

Political campaigning, too, is the one form of public relations that operates within a known time frame with a known cutoff date—election day. Campaigning is also the one form of public relations that is accurately measurable—at the ballot box on election day. The results are tangible, to be sure, but some method is needed to measure effectiveness during the process. Too much is at stake to leave campaigning to intuition alone. Public opinion polls became an extremely popular tool to judge the effectiveness of a campaign, uncover weaknesses to be minimized, and indicate strengths to be capitalized.

Finally, political campaigning differs from more traditional public relations in that there are usually only two candidates in a general election, and only two points of view in a ballot proposition or a bond issue: candidate *A* or candidate *B*, yes or no, for or against. Thus, the entire spectrum of public opinion must be compressed into only one of two choices. In society as a whole there is a wealth of personal opinions, interests, and tastes. But this is not so in politics, where general elections force a choice between two alternatives, neither of which may exactly meet anyone's criteria. As often as not this choice is made on the basis of the lesser of two evils rather than on genuine conviction. This being the case, the political campaigners must seek to enhance the stature of their own candidate while seeking to discredit the opponent. A vote taken away from an opponent counts as much as a vote attracted to the cause.

Political campaigning has, with its charges and countercharges, occasioned enormous criticism aimed at public relations, advertising, and the mass media. This is perhaps because of all the forms of public relations, political campaigning is the most visible, the most clearly identified, and the most concentrated. A national presidential campaign takes on the aspect of a Roman circus. There are those who claim it provides a catharsis, an emotional safety valve every four years that permits the public to keep on a more or less even keel the remainder of the time. In defense of political campaigning, however, we should note that it is a no-holds-barred activity in which truth and misrepresentation are intermingled on both sides, and from whose massive exposure the public can come to a reasonably well-informed conclusion.

Financial Public Relations

Financial PR is specialized and it avoids the general mass media network. Economists and accountants speak to other financial experts and investors.

Finance is a highly technical field devoted to corporate mergers: the issuance of new securities, stock splits, and acquisitions, and the enhancement of the market value of corporate securities. Financial public relations (FPR) is that specialty dealing in this sophisticated realm. It grew out of corporate abuses and subsequent regulation of corporate finance by the federal Securities and Exchange Commission (SEC) during the depression.

Financial public relations people are the liaison between their corporate clients and the financial analysts on whose recommendation large blocks of corporate securities will be bought and sold. Consequently, specialists in FPR require a talent in accounting, meticulous understanding of

all the complex regulations pertaining to corporate finance, plus a feel for public relations. They generally deal person-to-person with analysts and they make little use of the mass media except for the specialized financial press, such as the *Wall Street Journal*. These particular specialized talents acquired by FPR counselors fairly well preclude them from operating in any other field, just as electricians do not make good plumbers even though both are specialists in the construction trades.

It is the right of all citizens in this democracy to make their wishes known to their representatives. Unfortunately, is has been difficult for the individual to make his or her point of view known to those influential in government. As society became more and more institutionalized, individuals organized groups that could speak with enough force to attract the attention of those in the state house or congress.

Lobbying

Many of the labor unions and the major business and professional associations—for example, the National Association of Manufacturers (NAM), the American Medical Association (AMA), and, for that matter, the National Association of Broadcasters (NAB)—employ lobbyists. These trade and professional associations have found it expedient to watchdog legislation, to encourage passage of certain measures and to discourage others as they effect the goals of their respective memberships. There is a certain imperfect balance to this: The AFL/CIO rarely sees eye-to-eye with the NAM, and from their conflicting arguments, a certain broad exposure to all the factors involved in an issue will emerge for the legislature. From this tension among conflicting sets of information and persuasion, truth occasionally surfaces. Indeed, lobbying is an irreplaceable source of information for legislators in particular and government decision makers in general, who cannot be expected to know all the background and conflicting

Lobbying results in an imperfect balance of public opinion and legislation, but it gives people a voice.

Lobbying—an important
branch of PR.
Ellis Herwig/Stock, Boston

arguments of every piece of legislation they enact. Too often, unfortunately, legislators and policy makers ignore lobbyists altogether, missing the opportunities to gain information contained in lobbyists' otherwise persuasive campaigns.

The lobbyists are the representatives of society's institutions, just as mayors, city councils, assemblies, and members of Congress are representatives of the people. Like FPR people, lobbyists work person to person and make little use of the mass media except in specialized cases where a volume of publicity can be used to reinforce a case they have already made personally.

Lobbying is a highly specialized form of public relations. As most corporation PR people come from the press and most FPR people come from economics or accountancy, most lobbyists come from law. It takes years for lobbyists to establish beneficial contacts in the bureaucratic maze of Washington. Lobbyists are held in check by an unwritten law, an effective means of informal control. It is their duty to plead the cause of others, but not to misrepresent them. Once found lying or withholding pertinent information, the word is passed through the legislative halls and they become outcasts, pariahs. Years of apprenticeship are required to do the job effectively, and few professionals are willing to throw it away for a one-shot advantage.

Propaganda and Public Relations

The word *propaganda* stems from the establishment by the Catholic Church in 1622 of the "Sacra Congregation de Propagande Fide"—Sacred Congregation for the Propaganda of Faith—charged with spreading the faith through missionaries and the like. Since its inception, the word has taken on an unsavory connotation. Throughout the present century, propaganda has been considered as the manipulation of opinion toward political, religious, military, economic, or social ends. In both world wars, propaganda and brainwashing became interconnected in the public's mind, leaving Americans convinced that such techniques had no part to play in a democratic society unless that society was engaged in a war for survival.

Why is propaganda a dirty word? Does it belong in a democratic system?

The fear of propaganda has lessened since World War II, as social scientists have realized that mass media in and of themselves lack the absolute mind-molding powers once attributed to them. But the word *propaganda* has taken on broader connotations, being associated with a multitude of social and economic special pleaders. Our ideological enemies, we would say, employ propaganda agencies. We, on the other hand, make use of information, communications, and public relations agencies. Still, there is doubt concerning the appropriateness of propaganda in a society whose democratic myths are based on the belief that the public should remain curious, questioning, open-minded, and unwilling to accept simple, pat answers to complex questions. Pluralism and mental freedom are expected to operate hand in hand: They exist when people have the capacity, and exercise the capacity, to weigh numerous sides of controversies and to reach their own conclusions, free of outside constraints such as those created by high-powered persuasion agents.

Social psychologist Milton Rokeach, in his seminal work *The Open and Closed Mind,* concluded empirically that the degree to which a person's belief system is open or closed is the extent to which the person can receive, evaluate, and act on relevant information received from the outside on its own intrinsic merits, unencumbered by irrelevant factors.[8] To Rokeach, open-minded individuals seek out mass media that challenge them to think for themselves, rather than media that offer easy solutions to complex problems. However, the literature of media criticism in general and public relations more specifically demonstrates that much in the media mitigates against open-mindedness. Gilbert Seldes, for one, expressed fear that the mass media inculcate in their audiences a weakened sense of discrimination, a heightening of stereotypical thinking patterns, and a tendency toward conformity and dependence. In the long run, Seldes argued, the mass media may discourage people from forming independent judgments.[9] Even in their packaging of news, let alone its persuasive components, the media are said to have the power to establish our agendas and help shape our view of the world. Critics from all sides of the political spectrum, and supposedly even neutral social scientists, have made cases against patterns of bias, propaganda, and unchecked persuasion within the media.

Do modern media systems curtail open-mindedness and independent thinking?

There is, of course, an argument that people need these predigested views, since they can't experience all events firsthand. By definition, media come between realities and media consumers, so this is not an argument for the elimination of media. But the logic of Jacques Ellul is compelling in this regard. He argued that the individual in a technological society *needs* to be propagandized, to be "integrated into society" by means of the mass media. Propaganda offers explanations for all the news, classifying it into

Do we *need* propaganda and predigested opinions?

such readily identifiable categories as good and bad, right and wrong, and worth worrying about and not worth worrying about. Media propaganda in general and the efforts of special pleaders in particular furnish an explanation for all happenings—a key to understanding the whys and wherefores of economic and political events. "The great force of propaganda lies in giving man all-embracing, simple explanations and massive, doctrinal causes, without which he could not live with the news," Ellul argued, and added that we are doubly reassured by propaganda because it tells us the reasons behind developments and it promises a solution for all the problems that would otherwise seem insoluble. "Just as information is necessary for awareness, propaganda is necessary to prevent this awareness from being desperate," the French social scientist concluded.[10]

It is evident that a conflict exists between the principles of democracy—particularly its concept of the individual—and the processes of propaganda. The notion of rational man, capable of thinking and living according to reason, of controlling his passions and living according to scientific patterns, of choosing freely between good and evil—all this seems opposed to the secret influences, the mobilizations of myths, the swift appeals to the irrational, so characteristic of propaganda.[11]

Is the most effective propaganda in the news pages rather than in advertisements or on the editorial pages?

Propagandists and propaganda analysts have known for many years that the most effective means of manipulating public opinion via the news media is not through advertisements and editorials, but, in Nazi propaganda minister Joseph Goebbels' terms, in slanted news that appears to be straight. Terrence Qualter noted that, with the growing recognition of the extent to which opinion governs the selection and manner of presentation of news, any division between editorial opinion and straightforward presentation of facts on the news pages is an artificial division.[12] Thus, students hoping to better understand contemporary media propaganda need tools to discern the mind sets and techniques utilized by propagandists. This is easier said than done, however, since many forms of propaganda do not actually reflect the conscientious efforts of the special pleader. Even journalists who fancy themselves as objective—or at least fair—in their treatment of news can fall into propagandistic patterns. As John Hohenberg has said,

The temptation is great, under the pressures of daily journalism, to leap to conclusions, to act as an advocate, to make assumptions based on previous experience, to approach a story with preconceived notions of what is likely to happen. To give way to such tendencies is to invite error, slanted copy, and libelous publications for which there is little or no defense. An open mind is the mark of the journalist; the propagandist has made up his mind in advance.[13]

Techniques of Propaganda

John Merrill said journalists act as propagandists whenever they spread their own prejudices, biases, and opinions—whenever they attempt to affect the attitudes of their audiences. They, and others, are manipulative when they use stereotypes to simplify reality or when they present opinion disguised as fact. The process of information selection becomes a propaganda technique, according to Merrill, when a pattern of news selection or a viewpoint is exercised with some consistency.[14]

Numerous examples of propaganda are found in everyday news gatekeeping practices.

Merrill maintained that mass media practitioners generate their own propaganda and spread the propaganda of others to a far greater extent than most citizens believe. His list of techniques covers eleven major points, including fictionalizing (creatively filling the gaps in a story, making up direct quotations, and so forth). An example surfaced during the summer of 1981 when a *New York Post* reporter included a fictitious British officer in his story about the unrest in Northern Ireland. The reporter defended his action, saying that what he wrote was true but he made up the character to protect his sources.

Other propaganda techniques include those proposed by the Harvard Institute for Propaganda Analysis before and during World War II,[15] and a list developed by J. A. C. Brown.[16] Two techniques presented by Brown are *repetition* and *pinpointing the enemy*. "The propagandist," says Brown, "is confident that, if he repeats a statement often enough, it will in time come to be accepted by his audience." In the technique of pinpointing the enemy, the propagandist realizes the value of not only being *for* something, "but also being against some real or imagined enemy who is supposedly frustrating the will of his audience."[17]

Several analysts have commented that public relations handouts are highly propagandistic elements of news media. Nelson and Hulteng, for example, noted that public relations has characteristics of delayed propaganda if the readers of newspapers do not recognize that many of the stories they are reading originated from "interested sources."

Not that the PR man minds. He knows that the credibility of the information about his client is enhanced if the reader believes that a working journalist rather than a propagandist originated the story and wrote it. It is better to have a friend tell others how good you are than for you to do it yourself.[18]

While not all techniques of propaganda are applicable to the news pages of the mass media, most have been used at one time or another by the media and by public relations practitioners. The conclusion reached by Robert Cirino is that the great volume of news, the way it must be processed, and the public's need to make some kind of order out of the chaos of news events, makes bias, and therefore propaganda, inevitable.[19]

Propaganda Redefined

Over the years, authors have attempted to distinguish between propaganda and education, or between propaganda and any other means of inculcating values and changing beliefs and attitudes. Some authors have made a distinction between *pernicious propaganda* and *honest persuasion*. This seems speculative in that often the only distinction between pernicious propaganda and honest persuasion is whether *they* do it or *we* do it. Propaganda can be more usefully defined in terms of the methods used, the manifest content, and the motives of the user. In a politically competitive democracy and a commercially competitive free enterprise system mass communication functions by allowing a competitive arena in which the advocates of all can do battle. Propaganda therefore becomes part of that open marketplace of ideas; it is not only inevitable, but it is probably desirable that there are competing propagandas in a democratic society. In that regard, propaganda has all the trappings—and inherent problems—of public relations. Like PR, it demands definition while seemingly defying it.

Propaganda (and propagandistic behavior) describes particular types of mass communication messages, and involves certain traits of the mediators and certain expectations of those receiving propaganda. One of the goals of the propagandist is to convince the receiver to accept the propaganda without further investigation. How does propaganda work? It appears to rely on a half-dozen specific techniques:

1. A heavy or undue reliance on authority figures and spokespersons, rather than empirical validation, to establish its truths or conclusions.
2. The utilization of unverified and perhaps unverifiable abstract nouns, adjectives, adverbs, and physical representations, rather than empirical validation, to establish its truths, conclusions, or impressions.
3. A finalistic or fixed view of people, institutions, and situations, divided into broad, all-inclusive categories of in-groups (friends) and out-groups (enemies), situations to be accepted or rejected in whole.
4. A reduction of situations into readily identifiable cause and effect relationships, ignoring multiple reasons for events.
5. A time perspective characterized by an overemphasis or underemphasis on the past, present, or future as disconnected periods, rather than a demonstrated consciousness of time flow.
6. A greater emphasis on conflict than on cooperation among people, institutions, and situations.

This description allows both practitioners and observers of media and persuasion to investigate their own and their media's behavior. It applies to the news as well as to entertainment and persuasion functions in the media. Audiences willing to accept distorted pictures of reality, simple explanations for complex issues, and other propagandistic perspectives promulgated by mass communicators will find no shortage of these propaganda elements in their media.

It is possible to conduct public relations and persuasion without being propagandistic. As we have argued, a democratic society needs persuasion. But it needs pluralism in its persuasion, and not the narrow-minded, self-serving propaganda some communicators inject—wittingly or unwittingly—into their communications. Open-mindedness and public relations efforts need not be mutually exclusive.

One of the basic problems surrounding public relations as a practice is the difficulty of measuring its effect. Advertising can be measured at the cash register. But public relations is a necessarily long-term intangible, so completely interrelated with everything that an organization does that it is difficult to separate the effects of public relations alone. This, in turn, has contributed considerably to the questionable reputation that public relations has. It is ironic that a field that professes to mold public opinion, to change organizational images, and to accomplish corporate and political miracles should itself have such a poor public image. There are a number of incompetents in the field calling themselves public relations practitioners. As their substandard work multiplies, the reputation of the profession as a whole becomes damaged. There are neither standards (such as passing the bar for lawyers), nor a stipulated course of study (as for doctors), nor licensing (as for architects, engineers, and accountants) for the practice of public relations. Anyone can hang out a shingle.

Recognizing this, the Public Relations Society of America (PRSA) has embarked upon a program of accreditation for its members. Beginning in 1960 on a voluntary basis, accreditation became mandatory in 1969. Members must have a minimum of five years of public relations experience. In addition, they must pass an eight-hour examination in public relations principles and techniques, history and ethics, and they must also undergo an oral examination by a panel of three accredited peers. The exam is discriminating: Typically about 40 percent of those who take the test fail. By the end of the 1970s, of the 100,000 or so self-professed public relations practitioners in America, only 9,137 belonged to PRSA and only 2,905 were accredited. In a study of both accredited and nonaccredited practitioners, Donald Wright found some evidence of increased professionalism among the accredited. They attended more professional meetings, workshops, and refresher courses; they held office and served on committees in professional societies; they spent some time each week reading about the occupation; and for the most part, they performed more specialized public relations tasks than did the nonaccredited practitioners. Even Wright hesitated to call any of these practitioners true professionals. He noted that claims of professionalism among PR people continue to be more self-serving than realistic.[20]

The hope of PRSA is that gradually business and government and other organizations will come to recognize that PRSA membership and accreditation mean that the PR person has satisfied at least the minimal qualifications of experience and knowledge and can be expected to bring a certain amount of professionalism and expertise to any job. Such a person should be the best choice for an assignment; PRSA accreditation should mean that the individual is a competent practitioner who has satisfied professional requirements. The PRSA program has been slow to develop; there is much to overcome. More recently, particularly as a result of the political campaigning excesses for which public relations must share a part of the blame, there have been movements in several states toward public

Self-Regulation of Public Relations

One of PR's ironies is that the field has such a bad public image.

The Public Relations Society of America (PRSA) has worked to raise PR's public image, and with mixed results.

relations licensing. Some communities have instituted stringent regulations of the public relations practice as it affects lobbying before public agencies and political campaigning. It is quite possible that PRSA's movement toward professionalization, which is a form of self-regulation designed to forestall governmental control, may fail as being too little and too late. If widespread regulation and licensing of public relations does come about, it is inevitable that in the name of social responsibility it will be another form of communications control. Government regulation may not be entirely undesirable, but public relations is so interwoven with the entire fabric of mass communications that control cannot help but have side effects on the content, utilization, and future development of the mass communications complex.

Summary

Public relations, though relatively new as an organized practice, is as old as humanity. Its historical genesis can be seen in the poets of ancient Greece and Rome, through the Dark Ages, and in early American history. As a modern profession—though we use the word *profession* with some reservations—it is essentially an American product, having its origins in political campaigning, theatrical press agentry, and the Industrial Revolution.

Most public relations is conducted on a local basis, although there are national public relations firms. At least 100,000 practitioners are working in the United States. Some conduct "brush fire" public relations—meeting crises as they arise. Other forms—like "fire prevention"—utilize research, planning, and evaluation in an attempt to foresee and forestall potential trouble spots. The industry serves organizations either internally as a part of a company or externally—as independent counselors.

One of the major tools of public relations is publicity, but it is not the only tool. Its functions are informative and persuasive, dealing with events and pseudoevents. Ideally, PR is a two-way street in which the practitioners not only attempt to interpret organization and management policy for various publics, but they also attempt to monitor the public pulse in order to advise management of the probable results of a proposed policy.

Special areas of public relations have arisen. These include political campaigning, financial public relations, and lobbying.

The uniting of PR and the social sciences has resulted in a vast and unmeasurable volume of promotional activities; PR pervades all media with attempts to manipulate thoughts, votes, and dollars. As such, it is a form of propaganda. However, as we have seen, propaganda has taken on negative connotations of purposive manipulation that are not necessarily part of the public relations platform. If we consider instead that propaganda is any communication that attempts to diminish the options for thought by its receivers, then public relations, news, advertising, and all other aspects of the mass media can lend themselves quite readily to being propagandistic—although none of them need to.

Another irony of public relations is that the craft itself suffers from a poor public image. The PRSA, through a program of accreditation, is working toward increasing professionalization in an area where there are no legal standards.

As an organizational or corporate personality, public relations exists, whether good, bad, or indifferent, and through the application of appropriate techniques is capable of changing for better or worse.

Notes

1. Scott M. Cutlip and Allen H. Center, *Effective Public Relations,* 5th ed. (Englewood Cliffs, N.J.: Prentice-Hall, 1978), pp. 8–12.
2. Ibid., p. 9.
3. Edward Bernays, *Crystallizing Public Opinion* (New York: Liveright, 1961).
4. Raymond Simon, *Public Relations: Concepts and Practices,* 2d ed. (Columbus, Ohio: Grid Publishing, 1980), p. 102.
5. Daniel J. Boorstin, *The Image: A Guide to Pseudo-Events in America* (New York: Harper & Row, Harper Colophon Books, 1964).
6. Hal Lancaster, "Mr. McCullough Plans a Little Celebration for a Certain Bridge," *Wall Street Journal,* 5 October 1971.
7. Herbert M. Baus and William B. Ross, *Politics Battle Plan* (New York: Macmillan, 1968).
8. Milton Rokeach, *The Open and Closed Mind* (New York: Basic Books, 1960).
9. Gilbert Seldes, *The New Mass Media: Challenge to a Free Society* (Washington, D.C.: American Association of University Women, 1957).
10. Jacques Ellul, *Propaganda: The Formation of Men's Attitudes* (New York: Alfred A. Knopf, 1965).
11. Ibid.
12. Terrence H. Qualter, *Propaganda and Psychological Warfare* (New York: Random House, 1962), pp. 91–92.
13. John Hohenberg, *The Professional Journalist* (San Francisco: Rinehart Press, 1969), p. 330.
14. John C. Merrill and Ralph L. Lowenstein, *Media, Messages, and Men: New Perspectives in Communication,* 2d ed., (New York: Longman, 1979), pp. 188–201.
15. Institute for Propaganda Analysis, "How to Detect Propaganda," *Propaganda Analysis*, I, (November 1937), pp. 1–4.
16. J. A. C. Brown, *Techniques of Persuasion: From Propaganda to Brainwashing* (Harmondsworth, Middlesex, England: Penguin Books, 1963), pp. 26–28.
17. Ibid.
18. Roy Paul Nelson and John Hulteng, *The Fourth Estate: An Informal Appraisal of the News Information Media* (New York: Harper & Row, 1971), p. 278.
19. Robert Cirino, *Don't Blame the People: How the News Media Use Bias, Distortion, and Censorship to Manipulate Public Opinion* (Los Angeles: Diversity Press, 1971), pp. 134–79.
20. Donald K. Wright, "Premises for Professionalism: Testing the Contributions of PRSA Accreditation" (Paper presented to the Public Relations Division of the Association for Education in Journalism Annual Convention, Houston, Texas, August 1979).

Part 5 Controls

This final section of the text considers how the mass media are regulated, how they are permitted and encouraged to fulfill their functions of informing, educating, persuading, and entertaining society. In chapter 12 we treat the media's relationships to government; in chapter 13 we treat media's self-regulatory activities.

The divergent theories of press and government are considered in these two chapters. The logic of authoritarianism and its inequities, the hopes of libertarianism and its flaws, and the call for social responsibility and its ramifications must be analyzed, along with numerous other perspectives on the proper relationships between media systems and their constituent societies and governments. As we shall see, most of the history of controls over mass media is a history of compromises, sometimes more subtle than at other times. The path of these compromises is not always clear, but we are able to follow it to some logical conclusions.

Today's mass, diverse, and complex society cannot be kept in check by informal and unwritten codes, as in days gone by. Instruments of mass communications, as we have seen, are as massive and complex as the society in which they function. Media's efforts to earn a profit and serve society are not terribly dissimilar to other corporate enterprises. However, journalism is the only business to have been singled out in the U.S. Constitution for special privileges. Government was explicitly told to pass no laws abridging freedom of the press. Nonetheless, American history has demonstrated that such guarantees are not absolute. As government and media have grown more complex, in tune with the complexity of society, certain precautions have been necessary. Laws of libel, privacy, obscenity, and the whole of broadcast and advertising controls were instituted to protect society. Informal controls also went into effect: Codes of ethics, in particular, served to protect the media from bearing the burden of additional governmental regulation.

The greatest control of all may be that exerted by the body politic in the formation of that vague reality called public opinion. Media simply are not free to print or broadcast or produce anything that comes into their heads. They must conform to the expectations of their respective and often highly selective audiences. Ultimately, then, the imperfect balance between public taste, governmental sanction, and individual and corporate media behavior is reached, but not without sustained and severe differences along the way.

Regulation and the Law 12

Introduction

We have already sketched numerous explanations of how and why the media do what they do in society. Now let us take a look at how and why the media operate as they do within the political and regulatory environment. Panoramic views of media's appropriate roles in society must include details about who and what permit the media to exist, to inform, to make a profit, to entertain, to persuade, to challenge conventional wisdom, and even to be irresponsible.

In the first half of the chapter we will discuss several theories of the press and the regulations and controls that apply to the print media. The second half of the chapter is devoted to the unique regulations applicable to the broadcasting industries. Unlike the print media, especially the newspaper, they have had to operate under the watchful eye of governmental agencies created solely to keep them in check, to assure their responsible behavior. In addition, we will consider the adversarial relationship between journalists and government, and means used by vested interests to manipulate media personnel. To conclude we will investigate the difficulties arising from media coverage of court trials and other areas in which the First Amendment comes in direct conflict with other amendments.

Theories of the Press

All media reflect the political and social philosophies of the countries in which they operate.

The mass media, as leading scholars have pointed out, always take on the form and coloration of the social and political structures within which they operate, reflecting the system of social control in which relations between individuals and institutions are adjusted.[1] This means that what is acceptable journalism, entertainment, and persuasion in the American system could be highly irresponsible media performance under a different system. Tentative explanations of the different systems have been offered, but the treatise by Fredrick Siebert, Theodore Peterson, and Wilbur Schramm has remained one of the most durable. In general, they demonstrate that media operate under two general philosophic modes, *authoritarianism* and *libertarianism,* or their respective offshoots, *Soviet totalitarianism* and *social responsibility*. Scholars continue to quibble over the lack of precision in these designations, and over whether all presses are inherently socially responsible. However, the designations continue to provide a useful framework for discussing controls on media.

Authoritarianism

Authoritarians tend to exercise prior restraint by means of licensing, taxation, and seditious libel laws.

From the earliest times rulers attempted to control their domains. After the printing press came into use during the fifteenth and sixteenth centuries, English monarchs (especially Henry VIII and Elizabeth I) devised new strategies to exert their authority. You will recall from chapter 2 that the English government imposed restrictive controls on printers through the use of licensing, taxation, and seditious libel laws. *Licensing,* which was started by Henry VIII, was a form of direct censorship (prior restraint), since there could be no publication whatsoever without the permission of religious or secular authorities. Having paid an exorbitant fee or bond for the privilege of printing, few printers were willing to lose their investment by irritating the authorities. Besides, they quickly learned that those printers who cooperated with the authorities received numerous side benefits, such as exclusive and relatively lucrative rights to print authorized books, pamphlets, and posters.

Taxation was the second means of controlling the press. In 1712 Parliament passed the first Stamp Act, a tax on newspapers and pamphlets, on advertising, and on the print paper itself. This basically amounted to a tax on knowledge and was selectively enforced to punish scandalous and licentious publications, to force publications to register with the government, and to bolster the treasury. Such stamp acts lasted until 1855 in England.

Laws regarding *seditious libel* (criticism of the state) were a third form of control over the press. Seditious libel originated somewhere around the thirteenth century in England, when it became illegal to spread rumors about the crown and nobility. The crime was so serious that it was completely irrelevant whether the rumors were truthful or not. Until the eighteenth century, all a jury had to do was to ascertain whether the accused had indeed published the rumor or criticism. Since truthful criticism was more likely to stir up the angry crowds than readily-disproved untruthful criticism, the general principle for many years was that *the greater the truth, the greater the libel.*

The Fox Libel Act in 1792, which permitted juries to decide if in fact libel had occurred, and Lord Campbell's Act in 1843, which established truth as a defense in criminal libel cases, made it more difficult to obtain convictions of seditious libel in England. But this was only after several centuries of intimidation and self-censorship.

It would be wrong to discuss authoritarianism in the past only. Even today, most of the peoples of the world live under governmental systems that follow authoritarian principles rather than libertarian principles. Despite the fact that for the past thirty years the United Nations' Universal Declaration of Human Rights has demanded that its members guarantee freedom of speech, only two-fifths of the world's people actually receive this and other parallel freedoms: freedom of assembly, freedom of religion, and freedom to petition their governments. Annual analyses of worldwide trends in freedom and control demonstrate the fragility of such assurances. In the mid-1970s, for example, the world's largest democracy, India, summarily abolished its constitutional guarantees of free speech, press, and assembly. The beseiged Prime Minister, Indira Ghandi, called her action "The Emergency," and justified it on the basis of economic and political instability in her nation of a half billion people. Ghandi's rationale mirrored that of both revolutionaries and established dictators around the globe. All of them—from Albania to Zanzibar, and most certainly including Iran, Nicaragua, Greece, Venezuela, and Chile, among others—are merely following the well-established political theory that holds that the less stable or secure the governors are, the less they tolerate dissent from the governed.

> The majority of the world's nations still have authoritarian media systems.

Communist Application

Communist media are part of the state and reflect party decision making.

The Soviet–Communist theory of the press, logically, is an extension of authoritarianism, with one important exception. Authoritarian theory holds dear the need to control, but it still recognizes the press as an entity outside of government. In Communist theory as exemplified by the Soviet Union, the press is a part of the state; it does not exist outside the state. Consequently, all media reflect the national policy or the party line, and all media efforts are pointed toward furthering the state's aim. There can be no repression of the press, for the press is the state.

Since the communist press has the responsibility of perpetuating and expanding the socialist system, it spends its time transmitting policy, not searching for a nebulous truth that might emerge from a clash of ideas. As one might suspect, the content of the communist press is neither escapist nor entertainment oriented. Media are responsible for informing and indoctrinating society, and as such, media reflect what William Stephenson refers to as "social control" rather than "communication play."[2] Such is the nature of media functioning from the top down, operating as the voice of government.

Libertarianism

Milton, Jefferson, and Mill argued in favor of an unfettered, libertarian press, maintaining that people are inherently rational truth seekers.

Karl Marx, whose ideas are the basis of communist thinking, felt that we have to improve society in order to improve men and women. Marx's views are diametrically opposed to the arguments of libertarians, who believe that we improve society by improving the individual.

During the Age of Reason, beginning in the seventeenth century, a period of unparalleled medical and scientific discovery, a new view took hold in which people began to be seen as rational and capable of making decisions. Philosophers from John Milton to Thomas Jefferson to John Stuart Mill defended the rationality of people and the ability of truth to withstand discussion.

Poet John Milton, as far back as 1644, argued in ringing terms before the British Parliament many of the basic tenets of libertarianism. His speech, "Appeal for the Liberty of Unlicensed Printing" (later reprinted as the poem *Areopagitica*), called for the "open marketplace of ideas" and the "self-righting process." Let all with something to say be free to express themselves, Milton argued. The true and sound will survive. "Though all the winds of doctrine were let loose to play upon the earth, so truth be in the field, we do injuriously by licensing and prohibiting, to misdoubt her strength," the blind poet claimed.

Lest we be smitten by the ringing tones of *Areopagitica,* we should remember that Milton's motives were self-centered. He was expressing irritation over censorship of his own writings. He wanted serious-minded writers, such as himself, to be free to share their honest, although divergent, opinions. Interestingly, though ironic, he was serving as a censor for the British government several years after the speech. Milton's motives were somewhat narrow in that the freedom he was advocating was negative (freedom from licensing) rather than positive (freedom for certain ends).

He still maintained that government had the obligation of prohibiting certain types of publications, particularly those that were blasphemous or seditious. Despite the narrowness and selfishness of Milton's arguments, they were powerful statements made about one century ahead of their time.

Thomas Jefferson's views on a free press were soundly libertarian in nature. He felt that although individual citizens may err in exercising their reason, the majority as a group would inevitably make sound decisions, so long as society consisted of educated and informed citizens. The way to help people avoid making errors of judgment, wrote Jefferson to a friend in 1787,

is to give them full information of their affairs through the channel of the public papers, and to contrive that those papers should penetrate the whole mass of the people. The basis of our government being the opinion of the people, the very first object should be to keep that right; and were it left to me to decide whether we should have a government without newspapers, or newspapers without a government, I should not hesitate a moment to prefer the latter.[3]

Editors, reporters, and other defenders of press freedom have frequently quoted the last sentence of the quote just cited, forgetting that Jefferson went on to qualify the seemingly anarchistic statement: "But I should mean that every man should receive those papers, and be capable of reading them." The qualification is significant, for it recognizes that even the philosophy of libertarianism is meaningless if the people being promised liberties have no means of utilizing them.

A third major contributor to libertarian theory was English philosopher John Stuart Mill. Liberty, to Mill, was the right of mature individuals to think and act as they pleased so long as they harmed no one else in the process. Mill's 1859 treatise *On Liberty* states that all human action should aim at creating the greatest happiness for the greatest number of people. According to Mill, the good society is one in which the greatest possible number of persons enjoy the greatest possible amount of happiness. And, unless they have the right to think and act for themselves, they will never reach this point.

Mill's philosophy is attractive to many Americans, especially those who are interested in the media. Mass communications in America are anchored in libertarian ideas, and America has, for the most part, endorsed a libertarian point of view. Whether or not America, or any country, approaches, or ever could approach, the fullest form of libertarianism is open to debate.

New legislation, to control the effect of mass media and to protect their freedom, is constantly advocated under social pressure, which has prompted a new theory of *social responsibility*. The theory originated with the Commission on Freedom of the Press, a group that was led by Robert Hutchins and met in the 1940s to assess the state of the press in America.

Social Responsibility

Social responsibility theory attempts to strike a balance between freedom and responsibility.

Essentially, the theory of social responsibility is an extension of libertarianism in that it seeks to protect free expression. It requires the mass media to adequately represent all hues of the social spectrum. It seeks to make the mass media responsible for the quality of their offerings, print or broadcast. It seeks to inject truth in advertising and remove the concept of *caveat emptor* ("let the buyer beware"), which in the uncontrolled commercial world has seriously eroded a part of media credibility. Social responsibility charges the mass media with the development of, and enforcement of, ethics in the public interest. The theory is a formal recognition of the corporate organization, and institutionalized nature, of mass media. We will have more to say about the impact of social responsibility in chapter 13.

Limitations on the Media

Press freedom depends greatly on government's moods. Even a "free press" has limitations.

Although the predominant view of media in America has been libertarian, no medium can operate with unlimited freedom. Government imposes restrictions despite the apparently absolutist nature of the First Amendment to the Constitution.

A thoughtful analysis of such limitations has been offered by journalism historian John Stevens. In his essay on freedom of expression, Stevens added two propositions on freedom to the two suggested by Fredrick Siebert in his monumental study on freedom of the press in England. The four are:

1.   The extent of governmental control of the press depends on the nature of the relationship of the government to those subject to the government.

The First Amendment to the U.S. Constitution

Congress shall make no law respecting an establishment of religion, or prohibiting the free exercise thereof; or abridging the freedom of speech, or of the press; or the right of the people peaceably to assemble, and to petition the Government for a redress of grievances.

2. The area of freedom contracts and the enforcement of restraints increases as the stresses on the stability of the government and the structure of society increase.[4]
3. The more heterogeneous a society, the more freedom of expression it will tolerate.
4. The more developed a society, the more subtle will be the controls it exerts on expression.[5]

American history has already shown us the validity of Siebert's two propositions, and recent history appears to confirm Stevens's as well. As examples, we will look to our media's rights to print, to criticize, and to report about government and society.

The first newspapers printed in America had to be approved by colonial officials, but before the middle of the eighteenth century, journalists were arguing for freedom from censure and prior restraint. Their independence was seen in their total disregard of the Stamp Act of 1765, which the Crown imposed in an attempt to bolster its depleted treasury, not to impose absolute prior restraint as in earlier cases in Britain.

Limitations on Printing

American journalists have continued their opposition to any taxes that might be seen as discriminatory. Even in the twentieth century, when governments have attempted to place a tax on information, the press has successfully fought the taxes through the courts. In the most notable example, Governor Huey Long of Louisiana convinced the state legislature in 1934 to enact a 2 percent tax on the gross receipts of newspapers having circulations over 20,000 per week. Since Long was feuding with all but one of the thirteen largest newspapers in the state, the U.S. Supreme Court unanimously declared the tax an unconstitutional misuse of governmental authority.

Media's ability to fight this type of taxation does not mean the media are immune from all taxes. Historically, they have been subjected to those ordinary forms of taxation that are considered legitimate support of their government. For instance, the Associated Press wire service lost a 1937 court case over taxation because the Supreme Court said the taxes in question were not threats to freedom of the press or freedom of speech, but were merely equitable and nondiscriminatory taxes on business.

Limitations on Distribution

Government has several ways of controlling media distribution.

The right to print is meaningless if the right to distribute is impeded. From time to time throughout its history, American government in its several forms has subverted the provision of the First Amendment for a free flow of information. The majority of court cases attempting to reconcile the conflict have involved limitations imposed upon the distribution of leaflets or pamphlets, usually those that are political, religious, or commercial in tone, but other significant issues center on mailing permits.

The U.S. Supreme Court, in several cases during the 1930s, 1940s, and 1950s, concluded that cities and states have no right to prohibit distribution of handbills or pamphlets that propagate unpopular ideas. Neither can governmental bodies establish discriminatory licensing or distribution systems solely to inhibit religious or political tracts. On the other hand, if the distribution is likely to interfere with public safety, or if the material distributed is commercial rather than ideological in nature, the local authorities can exercise some controls, such as requiring the distributors to gain permission before soliciting or establishing hours and locations for such distribution.

Additional control has been available to the government through the use of second-class mailing permits, which have helped the print media—especially magazines and promotional material—reach their audiences. Such permits were created by the government to encourage and subsidize distribution of knowledge, and thus became a form of licensing. But the policy of granting permits for second-class mail was terminated in 1979.

Some control over distribution continues to exist. By their simple ability to determine the rates to be charged, the postal authorities intimidate publishers operating at slim profit margins. Some mass circulation magazines have cut down their size and weight to offset rising postal costs, and during the 1950s and on through the 1970s others went out of business because they were unable to cope with distribution costs, which rose 413 percent between 1971 and 1979 alone.

We need to look no further than the Nixon administration and a perplexing 1979 case to see evidence that government has other ways of dealing with unpopular or dissident news and views. Sometimes, as in the 1971 Pentagon Papers case and the 1979 *Progressive Magazine* controversy, the government will attempt to curtail potentially troublesome journalism before it is printed or aired. Before looking at these two fairly recent cases, some background is in order.

During the 1920s the state of Minnesota had a law that permitted a court to declare any obscene, lewd, lascivious, malicious, scandalous, or defamatory publications as public nuisances. Once a publication was declared a public nuisance it could be prohibited from further printing or distribution. When the publishers of *The Saturday Press* consistently and intemperately maintained that gangsters and racketeers controlled city and county officials in Minneapolis, they were hauled into court and the newspaper was prohibited from further publication under the state law.

Their 1931 appeal to the U.S. Supreme Court resulted in a narrow 5 to 4 vote, overturning the nuisance statute. Chief Justice Charles Evans Hughes, writing the majority opinion in *Near* v. *Minnesota,* maintained that the prior restraint of *The Saturday Press* was unconstitutional, but

that prior restraint might be constitutional under other conditions, including cases of obscenity or material inciting violence or endangering national security during wartime.[6] Hughes's observations about legitimate prior restraint continue to disturb media and tie up the courts.

The most famous test case was probably not the most significant. But because it involved the Vietnam War, the Nixon administration, and the media giants (particularly the *New York Times* and the *Washington Post*), the 1971 case of the Pentagon Papers is viewed as a highly significant struggle over prior restraint.

In June 1971 the *New York Times* culminated a three-month effort of rewriting and editing a purloined forty-seven-volume secret study of the origins of the Vietnam War entitled the "History of the U.S. Decision-Making Process on Vietnam Policy." It had been compiled by think-tank experts at RAND Corporation, one of whom was Daniel Ellsberg, who was convinced that the American public had a right to know how it had gotten involved in the long and unpopular war. Although the story told by the *New York Times* was basically historical and revealed nothing that could significantly affect current U.S. military strategy, it was politically and diplomatically embarrassing to the Kennedy, Johnson, and Nixon administrations. The *Times* was convinced that the public's right to know overshadowed governmental embarrassment and the ethical questions surrounding the printing of top secret information. The Nixon administration disagreed. When the newspaper refused to honor Attorney General John Mitchell's request to suspend publication, the government successfully obtained a temporary restraining order—in effect, creating prior restraint—assuring that the series would not be continued until the issue was decided in the courts.

The case went to the Supreme Court and two weeks later, after the justices had a relatively brief time to deliberate the particulars of the case, press attorneys gained a small victory when they convinced a six-member majority of the court that the government could not prove that anything in the Pentagon Papers actually endangered national security. Publication of the papers then continued, but the essential question about the right of government to impose absolute prior restraint went unanswered.[7]

In 1979, more of an answer was provided when the 40,000 circulation liberal magazine *The Progressive* found itself in a legal and ethical vortex after its editor assigned a freelancer to write a story on the hydrogen bomb. The story, to put it mildly, was explosive. Writer Howard Morland, who had majored in economics in college and had taken a smattering of physics courses, did an excellent job of researching textbooks, the *Congressional Record,* encyclopedias, and scientific articles, and taking guided tours of atomic power plants—all sources that were readily available to anyone inclined to use them. The magazine scheduled Morland's piece for publication in April 1979 under the title, "The H-Bomb Secret: How We Got It and Why We Are Telling It." *Progressive* Editor Erwin Knoll defended publication of the piece, claiming it did not disclose any new or classified information and that it served the important purpose of demonstrating laxity in governmental security over what is supposed to be one of government's best kept secrets.

But the article was such an accurate and definitive treatise on how to build a hydrogen bomb that when *The Progressive* voluntarily but reluctantly sent it to officials to review for accuracy before publication, the government reacted swiftly and severely. It asked the magazine to delete some details in the story, but editor Knoll refused. The Justice Department then filed suit in a federal court and obtained a temporary restraining order against publication of the article. The government's case, logically, was that public dissemination of the information would increase the proliferation of nuclear weapons and thereby severely undercut the arms control and disarmament policies of the United States.[8]

Federal District Judge Robert Warren in Wisconsin agreed with the government, saying, "If a nuclear holocaust should result, our right to life becomes extinguished, and the right to publish becomes moot."[9]

The *Progressive* appealed Judge Warren's injunction, and was preparing to carry the case all the way to the U.S. Supreme Court. Some critics, including journalists, hoped it wouldn't get that far, because it seemed likely the high court would rule against the magazine.[10] As it turned out, the Burger court never ruled on the case, because nearly identical information about the construction of an H-bomb was printed in the *Madison Press Connection.* In the face of mounting pressure from the press and the public, the federal government dropped its charges against *The Progressive,* which went ahead with its original story plus additional stories about its legal hassles over the bomb. As Jack Anderson commented before the final outcome of the case, "regardless of the outcome of the investigation and the entire *Progressive* case, journalists and their sources will become more and more timid in their efforts to inform the public of things it has a right to know. Governmental harassment," he said, "will result in self-censorship."[11]

Sedition

The 1735 trial of New York publisher John Peter Zenger saw the jury revolting against the obviously anti-libertarian tradition that truth was no defense against seditious libel charges. Zenger's acquittal helped establish the rights of journalists to criticize the government, but it did not settle the issue permanently. Such rights are tenuous. Proof came shortly after the new nation was established and the Constitution with its press freedoms was adopted. The Sedition Act of 1798–1801, instigated by President John Adams's Federalist party, was an effort to quell verbally abusive editorial criticism by newspapers under the control of rival anti-Federalists or Jeffersonians. The Sedition Act expressly outlawed false, scandalous, and malicious publications against the U.S. government, the president, and

Governments in stress impose sedition laws; the United States did so in 1798 and during more recent war times.

Congress. Fifteen people were prosecuted under the Sedition Act, some for offhanded witty remarks about President Adams. When Adams was replaced by Jefferson as president in 1800, the act expired, and Jefferson pardoned everyone who had been convicted under it.

Of the lessons learned from the Sedition Act of 1798, media law scholar Don Pember maintains that the most important one is the proposition that constitutional guarantees, in and of themselves, do nothing to assure freedom of expression; American citizens and their courts must support the First Amendment before it becomes workable.[12]

Further support of Siebert's proposition that press freedoms expand and contract in inverse relationship to the government's sense of security can be found by looking at the political repression during World War I. While most Americans were demonstrating solidarity in the effort to keep the world safe for democracy, those who questioned the will of the majority were regarded with suspicion. Given the socially and politically homogeneous, and therefore (by Stevens's definition) intolerant, climate of the times, it is not surprising to find that another Sedition Act was put on the books. The 1917 Espionage Act and the 1918 Sedition Act made it illegal to openly oppose the war effort and resulted in the prosecution of 2,000 offenders. As a result the Supreme Court had to resolve the issues of what was and was not protected by the First Amendment.

In a 1919 test case, *Schenck* v. *United States,* Justice Oliver Wendell Holmes maintained that sedition occurs only when the words used create a "clear and present danger" to society.[13] For four decades courts attempted to interpret Holmes's test until a 1957 case in which the court agreed that merely advocating the overthrow of government was not seditious; rather, there had to be a "clear and probable danger" that the government would actually be overthrown. Abstract arguments were not a crime, but incitements to immediate action were.

Due to the difficulty of proving what constitutes actual incitement, the government has brought few prosecutions for sedition since the 1950s. Criticism of American government is as robust as ever, but courts are spending relatively little energy in the attempt to balance the rights of government to remain secure and the rights of critics to complain. However, history's tendency to repeat itself has given us the political truism that an insecure government and a homogeneous populace might result once again in repression.

Libel

Libel laws give ordinary citizens a chance to hold their own against powerful media. The news media find libel cases an expensive and sometimes crippling form of intimidation.

Seditious libel may be fading into the background, but civil libel isn't. Civil libel is a dispute between two private parties (individuals, corporations, associations, etc.) in which the government, through the court system, acts as a referee.

Recently American news media have been hit with some 500 lawsuits a year, charging them with damaging the reputations of individuals or groups of people. Even when they win these civil libel suits, the media are likely to be spending tens of thousands of dollars in legal fees, plus suffering

Controls

the obvious disruption of daily reporting and editing that is entailed in being dragged into court. When they lose (which they do on occasion), not only do they pay out what are sometimes astronomical damage awards, ranging into millions of dollars, but they also find themselves a little more timid and a little less likely to engage in robust investigative journalism.

According to many Americans, it serves the press right. There are few ways for the celebrated and uncelebrated people in the street to hold their own against the powerful news media, so a libel suit—or even the threat of one—now and again may balance the power. As the laws of libel have developed, the common citizen gets a few considerations to offset the handicap of not being rich enough or politically powerful enough to go one-on-one against the press.

The best known libel cases involve investigative reporting and editorial writing, but the *Associated Press Stylebook and Libel Manual* warns journalists that in 95 percent of libel cases, ordinary citizens claim that their reputations were injured by reporters who carelessly reported charges of crime, immorality, incompetence, or inefficiency. When factual errors or inexact language crop up, people's reputations can be damaged. If the media report a drug arrest at 250 South Main Street and it actually occurred at 260 South Main Street, the upstanding citizens at the incorrect address are likely to be humiliated and embarrassed among their friends and acquaintances, and the media will have caused the problem.

Innocent-appearing stories damage more reputations than sensational, investigative ones.

In order for the plaintiffs to prove that libel has occurred, they have to show the presence of four things: *defamation, publication, identification,* and *negligence.* Different states have different definitions of defamation, but most include the idea that defamation is communication that exposes persons to hatred, contempt, or ridicule; lowers them in the esteem of their peers; causes them to be shunned; or injures them in their business, trade, or profession. Examples of words and expressions that juries have found to be defamatory are those that imply that someone has done something illegal or has engaged in questionable sexual behavior, for example, or that cause others to shun a person's business because of things said about the person's business practices.

Plaintiffs must demonstrate defamation, publication, identification, and negligence.

A defamation is considered to have been published if it appears in a form in which another person, besides the writer and the person being defamed, is likely to see it. Anyone handling the copy during the publishing process can be hauled into court, although only those who can afford to pay damages are likely to be named in a suit.

To collect for libel, plaintiffs have to prove that they were singled out, in some way that would leave no doubt in the minds of their associates that they were the subject of the attack, such as being shown in a picture or identified in context. When the media do name individuals, they have to be careful not to injure other people who have the same name. Full identification, including middle names, initials, ages, and addresses, is standard operating procedure in most newsrooms.

The fourth criterion, negligence, is fairly recent. Key Supreme Court cases of the 1960s made it difficult for public officials and public figures to win libel suits unless they were able to prove *actual malice* (i.e., the defendants had known that their articles were false or had recklessly disregarded whether they were true or false). In the 1970s and early 1980s, however, the tide began to turn somewhat against the media, as Supreme Court rulings made it easier for both private citizens and public officials to win libel suits; the issues have centered on whether the defendants have been negligent in their journalistic practices.

If plaintiffs are unable to convince juries that defamation, publication, identification, and negligence have all occurred, their case will probably be thrown out. Even if judge and jury agree with the plaintiffs that all four are present, victory for the aggrieved party is not yet assured. It is time for the defendants to build their cases, which they can do with any or a combination of complete or partial defenses.

The most common defenses are *truth, privilege,* and the defense known as *fair comment* and *criticism.* In some states, truth alone is not enough; the defendant must also prove lack of malice. Privilege is the right of the media to report activities of public officials acting in an official capacity. Impartial and fair abridgments of what transpires in legislative and judicial proceedings are considered privileged and protected from charges of libel.

Media frequently get away with defamations because of the well-established defense known as fair comment and criticism. Generally it holds that it is permissible to publish defamatory material consisting of comment and opinion, rather than fact, about issues of public interest or importance. The editorial, review, or criticism must focus upon the public aspects of the subject at hand: A drama critic can harshly judge an actress's performance with impunity, but not her home life. A sportswriter can criticize a quarterback's ability to pass a football, but not his morals. Additionally, the opinions expressed should be those of the journalist, not just those of somebody being quoted about the person being criticized. Finally, responsible journalists should include factual data in their commentaries, so audiences have the opportunity to understand the basis of criticism being made.

As long as the editorial, commentary, or report is based on the above, journalists can probably win a libel case unless the plaintiff is able to prove *actual malice.* Carol Burnett's successful $1.6 million suit in 1981 against *The National Enquirer,* which falsely implied that the actress known for her anti-drug abuse stance had been drunk in public, reminds us that fair comment has its bounds. Another in a recent spate of similar suits found *Penthouse* magazine appealing a $14 million libel judgment after it printed a humorous article about the sexual exploits of an allegedly fictional Miss Wyoming. The real Miss Wyoming didn't find the article amusing, and convinced a jury her reputation had been damaged. And retired General William Westmoreland, who commanded U.S. forces in Vietnam, sued CBS for $120 million in late 1982 over a CBS documentary that maintained Westmoreland suppressed and falsified figures on enemy troop strength to present a rosier picture of the war than he should have. These recent cases indicate the media are increasingly being held accountable for investigative reports, fictional accounts, and even minor news items that disparage either private or public citizens.

Invasion of Privacy

Courts and state legislatures have developed another means of checking media excesses as they have put teeth into the vague concept known as the *right of privacy,* or the *right of an individual to be left alone.* Because of our national concern over dossiers (files of detailed information) compiled by credit bureaus, Uncle Sam's "super information bank" containing an incredible amount of private information about each citizen, the omnipresent closed-circuit television camera where we bank, and so on, Americans have gained a new awareness of this so-called right to be left alone.

Privacy laws protect a person's right to be left alone or to have peace of mind, while libel laws protect a person's reputation.

The "law of privacy" is relatively new, tracing its ancestry to an 1890 *Harvard Law Review* article by two young lawyers, Samuel D. Warren and Louis D. Brandeis. Offended by the snoopy Boston press, they argued that citizens should have legal redress from the prying, gossiping media. Since then, six states have passed privacy laws, and courts in some thirty-four other states have demonstrated sympathy with the basic principles. Privacy lawsuits involve any of four different torts, or legal wrongs: *appropriation, intrusion,* publication of *private information,* and putting someone in a *false light* by fictionalizing.

Privacy laws apply to appropriation, intrusion, and publication of private or false information.

America's first invasion of privacy suit involved the utilization of a picture of a young girl on a flour sack without her permission. This is known as *appropriation.* After she lost the case in 1902, the New York State Legislature produced the first state statute protecting people in such cases. Recently, plaintiffs have won damages for the right to control their own publicity and to make their own profits from it.

When the name or likeness of well-known persons are used in news stories such persons cannot sue for appropriation, but when these persons are imitated or appropriated in commercials, they can. Since many advertisers use full names of people (Fred Whipple may become a classic), sponsors get a signed permission from one person having that name and then they are cleared. Thus the name, not the identity, is the key.

Intrusion into a person's solitude, including the use of microphones or cameras, is a second form of invasion of privacy. A classic case occurred in 1973 when a federal court enjoined freelance photographer Ron Galella from his continual and bothersome photographing of Jacqueline Kennedy Onassis. He was told to stay at least twenty-four feet from Mrs. Onassis, and thirty feet from her children. He was also prohibited from blocking their movements; from doing anything that might put them in danger or that might harass, alarm, or frighten them; and from entering the children's play area at school.[14] After repeatedly violating the judge's orders,

Galella in 1982 was permanently prohibited from filming the Onassis family. The original issue raised by Warren and Brandeis was the use of *private information,* which has involved the most controversy: To what degree does the press have the right to publish gossip, the substance of private conversations, and the details of private tragedies and illnesses, especially if the people in question do not want such information made public? Courts have generally agreed that if the public is interested in it, the press has the right to publish it. Only when good taste and good sense are totally abandoned will the press find itself in deep water.

The kinds of issues in question include the publishing of rape victims' names, digging up old information about a person and repeating it even though it may have questionable relevance today, reporting distressing details, or publishing articles or pictures that are in poor taste.

The fourth area of privacy to be considered is *false light,* which entails putting plaintiffs in a false position in the public eye. It has been a problem area for photographers misusing pictures, and "new journalists" and "docu-drama" writers who tend to stretch the truth to make their stories more interesting.

A photograph not taken in a public place or a caption to a picture that creates a false impression of someone, even if the impression is not unfavorable, should not be used unless the subject has granted permission. Examples from court records show that if a newspaper prints a picture of a couple kissing in public or of an accident scene because it is newsworthy, then there is no problem; but if a newspaper reprints the same photo later to illustrate an article on a slightly different subject, it is guilty of false light invasion of privacy.

Fictionalization is a growing problem for some contemporary journalists and for script writers who frequently embellish their true stories with some small touches, such as descriptions of people or dialogue that might not be entirely accurate. To avoid being charged with invasion of privacy, such writers resort to using composite characters (giving a fictitious name to a person who represents characteristics of several people) or changing the names of central figures. If real persons are so clearly described in the stories that they can convince a jury their peace of mind has been disturbed despite the writer's attempts to disguise the identity, they may win their suits.

Copyright

An understanding of copyright is important for mass media students for two basic reasons: (1) to know how to protect one's own efforts from theft, and (2) to know how to avoid illegally taking the work of someone else. These two reasons demonstrate that copyright law is both a protection for, and a limitation of, media efforts.

Copyright laws protect an author's property but impede the flow of information.

America's first major revision of its copyright laws since 1909 went into effect in 1978. Recognizing the rapid development of technology and the information industry, the revised copyright laws extend copyright protection to original works of authorship fixed in any tangible medium of expression, now known or later developed, from which they can be perceived, reproduced, or otherwise communicated, either directly or with the aid of a machine or device. Copyright holders can now secure rights for their lifetime plus another fifty years. Most of the civilized world has been on the life-plus-fifty system for quite some time, so the United States has just caught up with world practice.

Protected by the new copyright law are literary works; musical works and accompanying words; dramatic works and accompanying music; pantomimes and choreography; pictorial, graphic, and sculptural works; motion pictures and other audiovisual works; and sound recordings. The works must be original efforts of the author in order to be copyrighted; they cannot just be quotes from somebody else. Facts or ideas cannot be copyrighted. Copyright applies only to the literary style of an article, news story, or other intellectual creation—not to the theme, ideas, or facts contained therein. News cannot be copyrighted, but the unique treatment of a news event can be.

Facts or ideas cannot be copyrighted but most means of expressing them can be.

Copyright doesn't give you unlimited control of your material. Courts for years have been ruling that the idea of literary merit was to serve the time-binding purpose of allowing others to learn and benefit from published works without having to create each work anew every generation or so. Because of this, *fair use standards* have emerged, whereby a limited amount of copyrighted material may be used for the purpose of advancing science, the arts, criticism, and general knowledge without constituting an infringement. Decisions over the past few years indicate that courts will permit use of copyright material if such publication is done in the public interest, when

Fair-use standards allow general knowledge to benefit from copyrighted works. Common sense and ethics should eliminate violations of the copyright law.

the materials are newsworthy or otherwise of general interest. From this last principle, for instance, we have seen permission granted to photocopy scholarly articles if the articles are to be used for academic and not commercial purposes.

What does infringement of copyright entail? Courts have ruled that the plaintiffs have to prove that four separate acts have taken place: (1) that the material being copied was an original; (2) that the defendant had access to the copyrighted work; (3) that the original and the defendant's work are so similar that the defendant's version has been copied from the original; and (4) that there is substantive similarity between dramatic works or adaptations of dramatic works. As Pember says, "The simplest way to avoid an infringement suit is for authors to make certain that a substantial portion of their work is original, and that the borrowed portion is not the heart of their article or script."[15]

Obscenity and Pornography

Until the 1930s, extremely strict standards controlled obscenity.

For some fifty-five years, American courts relied upon a 1868 British court decision known as the Hicklin Rule, which stated that something is obscene when its tendency is to deprave and corrupt those whose minds are open to such immoral influences and into whose hands a publication of this sort might fall. American courts added a *partial obscenity* qualifier, meaning that if some passages of a book or one picture in an entire book of pictures tends to offend or sexually stimulate the most vulnerable and neurotic person into whose hands the work might fall, the entire book would have to be considered obscene.

In 1933, the James Joyce novel *Ulysses* was denied importation into the United States because of the Hicklin rule. The judge hearing the importer's case overruled the decision of the customs office, however, stating that the original Hicklin rule and the American qualifier (partial obscenity) were improper, and that the book should be judged as a whole. The book was admitted to the country because the judge found that when considered as a whole the book did not lead to sexually impure and lustful thoughts in a person having average sexual instincts.

The 1973 Miller case checked the trend toward more liberal standards brought on by the 1957 Roth decision.

In the U.S. Supreme Court's 1957 Roth decision, the majority opinion, written by Justice William Brennan, made it clear that the court had always assumed that obscenity was not protected by the First Amendment. Implicit in the history of the First Amendment is the rejection of obscenity as being utterly void of redeeming social importance, Brennan noted. In that case the court held that the test for obscenity should be "whether to the *average* person, applying *contemporary community* standards, the *dominant* theme of the material *taken as a whole* appeals to prurient interest" (italics added).[16] The definition, as one can see, is loaded with qualification.

Since then the Court has taken a somewhat more restrictive stance. In the controversial *Miller* v. *California* case in 1973, which involved the mailing of sexually explicit brochures, Chief Justice Warren E. Burger criticized the "redeeming social value" test. He argued that states are not constrained to judge obscenity in terms of a particular national standard. Instead, juries should use their own ideas of what their own dominant community standards are in deciding what appeals to prurient interests and what is patently offensive.[17]

Communities can now determine their own standards of obscenity.

The Miller decision threw an immediate scare into many people in the media, particularly film producers and book and magazine publishers. Their concern was what was apparently acceptable to communities in such areas as New York or Los Angeles, where much of their production was done, would be found completely illegal in America's hinterlands, where community values differed. Numerous test cases went through the lower courts, some arriving for final determination at the U.S. Supreme Court, over the ensuing years.

Hustler Magazine, October 1978, p. 5. Reprinted by permission

PUBLISHER'S STATEMENT

Glad to Be Back!

From the beginning HUSTLER was meant to be your magazine—created by the reader for the reader. For the most part I think we have succeeded in this goal; I believe that all of you out there who supported us and stuck by us through all the controversy and hardship of our development have made HUSTLER the success it is.

Any doubts I might have had about this were more than dispelled by the overwhelmingly generous outpouring of letters I received while recuperating from the almost-fatal shots fired at me last March. Because of these letters, I realized (more than ever before) that you, the readers, have shared the battles with me—enjoying the same victories and suffering the same defeats. In that sense it wasn't just me who was gunned down on the streets of Lawrenceville, Georgia; it was every American who holds dear the values that have made this country great.

I feel no regrets about my fight for free expression. Even though I have been crippled, I am not intimidated by the people who shot me, nor will I be intimidated by standing trial in Georgia again. I will continue to fight for what I believe in, even if I have to stop another assassin's bullet as a result.

I don't know who shot me and I don't want to know. The important thing is the knowledge that a particular element living in America feels so threatened by our ideas that they will subvert justice and one of God's commandments ("Thou shalt not kill") to stop us.

These people are the real victims of society. They have been victimized by sexual, religious and political repression; by the lack of love inherent in sexual repression; by the fear of honesty intrinsic to organized religion in order to maintain its control; and by the hypocrisy of politicians who are not only lying to the American taxpayers but also lining their own pockets with *our* hard-earned money.

This is HUSTLER's message. It is not a very different message from the one we started with; it is only more mature and more responsive to the needs of the people. HUSTLER will remain essentially what it has always been. The only difference is that I have a new set of values for myself, among them the desire to help eliminate discrimination against women.

HUSTLER will continue to be honest, sexually candid, outrageous and iconoclastic. We will continue to explore social and sexual taboos in the belief that an ongoing dialogue is the best hope for solving the problems that afflict our society. And it is you, our readers, who will still dictate our direction.

No single personality or ideology formed HUSTLER. It is a magazine for the average American, and it's put out by average citizens like you and me. I'm glad to be back.

Larry Flynt

Publisher & Chairman of the Board

Harry Reams, who earned $100 by "starring" in the hard-core film *Deep Throat,* was tried and found guilty in Memphis where the film was shown, not where it was made. The sentence was later overturned on a technicality.

New York publisher Al Goldstein was found guilty on eleven counts of conspiracy and for using the mails to distribute his magazines *Smut* and *Screw* to Wichita, Kansas, even though New York postal inspectors were primarily responsible for requesting the mailings.

And the publisher of *Hustler* magazine, Larry Flynt, whose offices were in Columbus, Ohio, was tried and convicted in Cincinnati, 100 miles away. He was found guilty of pandering obscenity—specifically advertising that his magazine would appeal to lewd interests.

Film Censorship

Recently, films have been protected by the First Amendment, but that has not always been the case. A 1915 Supreme Court decision ruled that exhibition of films was a business rather than a form of literary expression deserving constitutional protection. Since 1952, however, films, even if considered obscene or sacrilegious by some elements of the community, have received at least limited benefits of First Amendment protection and usually get their day in court before arbitrary censorship and prior restraint can be applied.

Films receive First Amendment protection, but censorship and prior restraint remain.

That is not to say that censorship and prior restraint of films no longer occur. Indeed, even the Supreme Court has ruled that individual city ordinances that provide for prescreening and licensing of motion pictures prior to public viewing are constitutional. In Chicago this ordinance was upheld in 1961 by a 5–4 majority: "It shall be unlawful for any person to show or exhibit in a public place—any . . . motion picture . . . without first having secured a permit therefore from the superintendent of police."[18] In the ordinance's defense, Justice Tom Clark said, "It has never been held that liberty of speech is absolute. Nor has it been suggested that all previous restraints on speech are invalid."[19] Four years later, a similar law in Maryland was overruled because it didn't assure theater owners of procedural safeguards if they wanted to question its prior restraint, and a Dallas ordinance was overturned for its vague references to guaranteeing suitability of films to children. Thus city and state censorship boards have been found acceptable to the Supreme Court, so long as they operate under clear, precise guidelines that do not undermine constitutional guarantees of due process.

Since Supreme Court decisions are the law of the land, they have generally been successful in preempting state and local regulations of obscenity in most mass media, leaving only self-regulation and social control to the state and local levels. This means that audience acceptance becomes the principal restraint upon obscenity and pornography in the media. Such social controls, while a form of restriction, generally work fairly well in removing unsavory material from the mainstream while permitting its availability to the smaller audiences who actively seek it.

We have shown how the First Amendment is supposed to protect media from government involvement, but the government has made an impressive argument that without external regulation, there would be no freedom of broadcast communication and, ultimately, no broadcasting industry. Its argument, simply, is that because the broadcast spectrum is finite, access to airwaves is limited; should private interests prevail, they could readily monopolize the marketplace of ideas. Additionally, because broadcast media enter the home directly, with little opportunity for preview by consumers, and since a massive percentage of the audience consists of children, broadcasting is said to need supervision lest it behave irresponsibly. Finally, the government reminds us, the infant broadcast industry of the 1920s took the unusual step of specifically requesting governmental regulation when it found it was unable to control itself.

The 1927 Federal Radio Commission and the 1934 Federal Communications Commission, which we discussed in chapter 6, maintained that broadcasters had to operate in the "public interest, convenience, and necessity" if they expected to earn and retain their licenses. Thus, for half a century, Congress has maintained that the airwaves are public, not private, property; their use is contingent upon "responsible" performance. Interest, convenience, and necessity—an admittedly vague generalization—served the purpose of screening the worthy from the unworthy.

Broadcasters have long been expected by the FRC and FCC to operate in the "public interest, convenience, and necessity."

When Congress wrote the 1927 and 1934 acts, it specifically precluded the commissions from exerting control over programming. The acts concentrated on technological and economic concerns: How much power was to be used; what areas were to be served on what frequencies and at what times; and what were their call letters and locations to be? A clause in the 1927 Radio Act, followed by a nearly identical statement in the 1934 Act, went so far as to state,

Nothing in this Act shall be understood or construed to give the licensing authority the power of censorship . . . and no regulation or condition shall be promulgated or fixed by the licensing authority which shall interfere with the right of free speech by means of radio communications.

However, whatever Congress can giveth, Congress can taketh away. Not only did these two acts permit the commissions the most severe form of subsequent punishment that a broadcaster could face—removal of its license and therefore the termination of its business—they even spelled out a few areas in which the commissions are granted specific censorship rights: obscenity, indecency, profanity, fraud, and lottery information. These criteria to broadcast in the "public interest, convenience and necessity" do, in fact, constitute a form of program control because they describe the boundaries within which a station may program if it expects its license to be renewed. The airwaves, broadcasters are reminded again and again, belong to the people, and a broadcast license is merely a temporary lease of the facilities, implying no rights of ownership.

On the other hand, the regulatory agencies have made it clear that broadcast stations are not common carriers like telephone and telegraph companies, who, as monopolies, are obligated to accept business from anyone who wishes to use their services. Broadcasters have the right to refuse access to their facilities to various members of the public, should they so desire. And when they do make their facilities available, they can charge whatever prices traffic will allow. In that sense, at least, broadcasting is founded on the basis of free competition among licensees.[20]

In the following discussions pertaining to television, keep in mind that the FCC historically has had no direct jurisdiction or control over network operations. Networks do not actually broadcast; they simply feed programming to their owned or affiliated stations. The FCC, of course, does exert considerable control over the owned and affiliated stations.

Licensing Procedures

According to Congress, the FCC's primary task is to grant and renew licenses.

Congress established the broadcast regulatory agencies and continues to legislate the industry's behavior. The Federal Communications Commission's primary responsibility is to grant and renew licenses. Its combined executive, legislative, and judiciary roles are handled by seven members, each of whom is appointed for a seven-year term by the U.S. President with the approval of the Senate, and a support staff of some 2,500. Under authority granted by Congress, it writes, administers, and interprets a vast array of rules and regulations. Most of them deal with technological questions, but those covering the license application and renewal process fill a good-sized book.

For applicants, the licensing process is an administrative jungle. Potential licensees find their first major hurdle to be getting the station's construction permit. In addition they must demonstrate to the FCC that they are American citizens who have the financial resources and technical expertise to construct and operate the station for at least one year before taking in revenue.

Applicants must also disclose to the FCC any other broadcast interests they are involved in, since the commission vigorously enforces its standards concerning multiple ownership: No one can own more than seven television stations, of which no more than five can be very high frequency stations (VHF—channels 2 through 13), seven AM radio stations, and seven FM stations.

License applicants and existing licensees have had to demonstrate their intentions of operating in the public interest by conducting a *community ascertainment*. Basically this entails an assessment of the pressing social, political, and economic needs of their respective communities, and an explanation of how their programming will meet those needs. Each year the station must report how, through programming, it has responded to those needs. Recent FCC rulings have reduced the significance of ascertainment as it applies to radio, in recognition of the fact that so many radio stations are on the air; the public's needs and interests will probably be met from one or another of the competing broadcasters.

Since most of the desirable frequencies have long been occupied, the government spends most of its time concerned with relicensing practices. Despite the constant recordkeeping for station operators and the concern over how well they are meeting their license expectations, most existing licensees have overwhelming odds of being relicensed, even if they are challenged by another party wishing to take over the license. In its first forty years of license renewal practices, the FCC revoked or failed to renew only 100 of the 50,000 or so licenses that came up for review.

The greatest abridgment of broadcast freedom has resulted from the application of two interrelated and sometimes confusing doctrines: those of *equal opportunities* (usually called *equal time*) and *fairness*.

Equal Opportunities

Section 315 of the Communications Act of 1934 establishes the principle of opportunities. Note that the principle does not apply to print media, which are not required to give equal time. This concept applies only to candidates for political office and provides that all bona fide candidates for a given office must be accorded the same amount of air time on the same terms or at the same cost. Thus, if one mayoral candidate in a race is given an opportunity to appear on the air and make a political appeal, all twelve or fifteen other qualified candidates must be given the same amount of comparable time, and if the time was purchased by the first candidate, none of the other candidates can be charged a higher rate. In no case can broadcasters charge more than their minimum or lowest unit rates to any of the candidates. Also, they cannot censor what the candidates say on the air, which at least protects the licensee from any subsequent libel suits. The original law said broadcasters were under no obligation to allow the use of their stations by *any* candidates, but a more recent Act of Congress requires that stations accept advertising by federal political candidates.

FCC's Section 315 says broadcasters must afford "equal opportunities" for air time to bona fide political candidates.

Section 315 has been modified to exempt certain types of programming from adhering to the above provisions: bona fide newscasts, news interviews like "Meet the Press," news documentaries, on-the-spot news events, and, since 1975, press conferences. Coverage of face-to-face debates between two candidates has been a difficult issue. In 1960 it took an act of Congress to suspend the equal-time requirement in order to permit the famous Kennedy–Nixon debates to be aired. The 1976 Carter–Ford debates and the 1980 Carter–Reagan debate occurred only because they were sponsored by an outside agency, the League of Women Voters, which is not controlled by the candidates or the broadcasters and is therefore exempt from the requirements. Otherwise, nearly a half-dozen minor presidential candidates would have had to participate in the debates or at least been granted comparable prime time; and because few viewers would have watched, such an arrangement would have cost the network millions of dollars in lost revenue.

Fairness Doctrine

Unlike Section 315, which as part of the 1934 Communications Act has been passed by Congress, the fairness doctrine is the creature of the FCC, gradually evolving over the years in answer to specific problems. The fairness doctrine applies not to people or politicians but to items of controversy. In 1929 the Federal Radio Commission revoked a license because the station had not presented both sides of a controversial issue. That a station may not be an advocate became the theme of the FRC. The effect, of course, of such a doctrine was that radio stations across the land avoided controversy in any form; not only did they not advocate anything, but they refused to editorialize on significant community issues, and they avoided any programming that might bestir differences of opinion. This was the source of broadcast's blandness and was scarcely a fulfillment of the charge to operate in the public interest, convenience, and necessity.

In 1949 the FCC had second thoughts on this issue and encouraged the airing of divergent viewpoints. The fairness doctrine as it now stands states that stations must devote a reasonable amount of time to controversial public issues, and in so doing, they must actively encourage the presentation of all perspectives. They are similarly encouraged to editorialize on community issues, to make their station position known, provided they accord a balance of views. If during the course of editorializing individuals or organizations are attacked, they must be offered comparable free time in which to reply. News is exempt from all the foregoing.

Although the ground rules are now a little clearer, fairness is still a complex doctrine, subject to many strange innovations. The net result, far from encouraging broadcasters, still tends to discourage them from active participation in controversy.

The fairness doctrine was extended in 1967 to include broadcast advertising. For example, cigarette smoking was held to be a controversial issue, and stations were required by the FCC to give free time to smoking opponents to answer the barrage of cigarette commercials on the air. Such remedial advertising can be an expensive burden on a station. Although Congress subsequently resolved part of the problem by banning cigarette commercials entirely, the question of fairness in advertising remained.

In its 1969 Red Lion Broadcasting decision, concerning a Pennsylvania radio station that preached religion and right-wing politics and excluded opposing views, the U.S. Supreme Court reaffirmed that because broadcasting is a limited facility, the rights of the public, not the broadcaster, are paramount. Consequently, the court ruled that Congress and the FCC are not violating the First Amendment when they require a radio or television station to give reply time to answer personal attacks and political editorials.[21]

Confusion still exists concerning who determines what is a controversial issue of public interest, and even whether the Fairness Doctrine is constitutional. Pember says that one needs a clear mind and a pure heart to wade through the hundreds of FCC rulings that interpret one or another

Controls

aspect of this infamous doctrine.[22] Recent FCC maneuvers to replace the Fairness Doctrine with something to be called "The Equity Provision" have not cleared up the confusion.

In our earlier discussion of mass media obscenity, we concluded that currently the biggest thicket is determining what are or are not appropriate reflections of community standards. In broadcasting, the issue is somewhat different, and for apparently logical reasons: the pervasive and intrusive nature of broadcasting, and the omnipresence of children in the broadcast audience. In a 1977 FCC hearing concerning a George Carlin monolog ironically entitled "Seven Words You Can't Say On Radio," the commission noted that radio—and by extension, television—requires special treatment because of four important considerations: (1) children have access to radios and in many cases are unsupervised by adults; (2) radio receivers are in the home, a place where people's privacy interest is entitled to extra defense; (3) unconsenting adults may tune in a station without any warning that offensive language is being or will be broadcast; and (4) there is a scarcity of spectrum space, the use of which the government must license in the best public interest.[23] Despite the 1934 Communications Act's prohibition against censorship of programming, Congress granted the FCC authority to outlaw obscene or indecent speech over the air. In 1948, after the Communications Act was modified to remove the obscenity clause, punishment for broadcast obscenity reappeared in the United States Criminal Code, with violators subjected to $10,000 fines and two years of imprisonment.

Two of the best-known incidents, both occurring in the 1970s, were the "Femme Forum" talk show and the George Carlin monolog. In the former, an Oak Park, Illinois, FM station carried a five-hour daily risqué radio format that included, among other controversial topics, a detailed discussion of oral sex. The FCC fined the station $2,000, citing the federal obscenity statute, and warned talk show hosts to be more careful in their moderation of program topics.[24]

In the Carlin case the U.S. Supreme Court split 5–4, the majority agreeing that the FCC had the right to ban broadcasting of indecent speech from the airwaves during hours when children may be in the audience. In suggesting that Carlin's monolog was not essential to the exposition of an idea, the court rejected arguments presented in other cases that speech must be legally pornographic to be regulated.

Part of the controversy over this case, which took five years to reach the Supreme Court, was the validity of the concept of "channeling" programming to periods when children would be unlikely to overhear it. One study cited showed that large numbers of children are in the broadcast audience until 1:30 A.M. and that the number of children does not fall below one million until 1 A.M. If true, how would it be possible for broadcasters to air legally permissible adult fare and reach only the audience they seek?[25] The FCC and the Supreme Court have not answered this question.

Broadcast Obscenity

Broadcasting receives special consideration in obscenity cases because it's a unique medium.

Comedian George Carlin learned that there really are seven dirty words you can't use on the air. Wide World Photos

The presence of children in the audience of intrusive broadcast media presents legal difficulties.

Control of Cable

Since 1966 the FCC has regulated cable and Community Antenna Television. Originally, the FCC held that since CATV did not operate on an interstate basis, it had no jurisdiction. By the mid-1960s it recognized the simple reality that cable indeed does deal in interstate signals.

The rules governing cable are complex and confusing, perhaps in part because of the rapid and recent growth of the industry. By 1972 the FCC had prepared a 500-page book of regulations designed to guide cable development without doing significant harm to existing broadcasters. There has been no peace since.

In practical terms, the rules maintained that cable systems had to carry the signals of all stations within a thirty-five-mile radius, but they couldn't duplicate commercial programming within a specified period of time. All systems had to carry educational stations and they had to grant local governments and interested citizens *public access* to a channel. The number of channels available for immediate or potential use depended on the size of the market or the size of the system. These variables also were considered in many of the other rules contained in the document.

Some of the rules have changed in recent years. The 1978 revision of the copyright laws at long last made cable operators responsible for paying royalties to program owners for the distant nonnetwork programs they carry. To date the amount has averaged about one percent of each system's gross revenues, which are considered by some in the more established media to be an inappropriately low figure. Restrictions on the use of distant signals were eased in 1979 when the FCC voted 6–1 to allow cable operators access to as many distant broadcast stations as they wished without having to obtain consent from the broadcasters whose signals they picked up. The only obligation of the cable operators is to pay royalties to program owners. Also in 1979 the Supreme Court struck down the FCC's *public-access rule* on a federal level. Because many groups had been partially violating the intent of the public-access proviso by filling the cable with dull and frequently obscene amateur programming, cable operators had protested. Local authorities can still require cable systems to make public-access time available, but it is no longer part of the federal law. (Remember, authority over cable exists at federal, state, and local levels.)

These and other changes indicate that the FCC is interested in the gradual deregulation of cable on the federal level. As such it appears to represent a return to a laissez-faire philosophy of allowing natural marketplace forces to determine economic survival.

There has been a gradual trend toward deregulation of cable TV on the federal level. State and local regulations continue.

Broadcast Deregulation

In keeping with its efforts to deregulate the trucking and airline industries, the Carter administration sought to minimize federal involvement in the broadcast arena. Between 1978 and 1980 several efforts were made in both the House of Representatives and the Senate to rewrite the 1934 Communications Act, and despite the inability of the Ninety-fifth and Ninety-sixth Congresses to implement the massive changes, the efforts have continued under the Reagan administration.

One reason for movement toward deregulation is a new recognition of the difficulties broadcast station licensees have with the maze of FCC rules. If broadcasters can be freed from some paperwork, they will be able to devote more time to serving their audiences.

Another reason can be traced to the economic philosophy of the Reagan administration, which is eager to encourage the growth of American business by allowing marketplace forces to prevail wherever possible. In order for stations to survive economically, they must give people what they want. Those that succeed will prosper; those that do not will go out of business.

Many of the bills brought before Congress support the movement to deregulate. Some have tried to adjust the troublesome concept of stations operating in the "public interest, convenience, and necessity." Other bills would either eliminate or modify the equal-time provision and fairness doctrine, giving radio more freedom than television. The FCC itself in 1981 extended the licensing period to seven years for radio and five years for television, eliminated the ascertainment requirements for radio, and dropped news and public affairs programming rules along with suggested limits on advertising time for radio.

At this writing the exact scope of deregulation efforts under the Reagan administration cannot be judged. By the time this book is in your hands, much of the earlier discussion of broadcast controls may be outdated, so it behooves the reader to keep abreast of current events.

The Adversary Relationship

We have already investigated some of the formal means that government employs to minimize media excesses. But there are numerous other external controls over journalism, some of them dealing with the news reporting functions, others relating to the economic functions.

In today's sophisticated climate, instead of overt and obvious attempts to control the press, government generally tries manipulating or outmaneuvering it. This is Stevens's fourth proposition. Most frequently at the federal level this takes the form of *classification.*

Certain kinds of information deemed in the national interest are labelled as secret or top secret and withheld from the press. Dissemination of such material is punishable by law. No one reasonably questions the right or wisdom of government to withhold certain information from the public view that would seriously jeopardize the nation's position in its sensitive and sometimes perilous international dealings. However, in reality, this practice works differently. Classification is an invitation to government authorities to hide their shortcomings, errors, duplicity, and poor judgment in the guise of national security.

But the mass media are nearly as institutionalized as government itself. They are not without power to obtain some classified materials. Washington provides ample opportunities for the press to get information. Ambitious or disgruntled government insiders who are anxious to serve their own devious ends make it almost impossible to keep a secret or even a top secret for very long without the voluntary cooperation of the press. Using sources and other methods, the media probe and seek to uncover sensational and scandalous stories. They frequently cloak their investigations with references such as "it is the public's right to know how tax dollars are being spent," but media critics correctly argue that the media are looking for the kind of spicy news that will attract audiences in droves.

Regardless of the motives of the media, the adversary relationship heightens the competition with government for information. The greater the competition, the better the balance. If government were more forthright, the press would be less diligent; if the press were less alert, the government would be more secretive.

News Management

Because the government cannot classify everything in Washington, those in power have devised other methods for controlling the dissemination of information. Such techniques come under the general heading of *news management*.

One technique favored by government is that of *backgrounders*. The theory of backgrounding is commendable; it provides reporters a depth of perspective in sensitive situations with which they can better interpret the events they report. As some of the background data may be classified, reporters are asked not to reveal them.

News management is maintained by "off the record" and "not for attribution" backgrounders.

In practice, however, this technique has frequently acted as either a kind of gag on journalists or as a perversion of its purposes. Backgrounders are of two types: Some are *off the record* and others are *not for attribution*. In an off-the-record statement or interview, an official talks quite candidly about a whole range of highly classified material. The press is free to listen but not to report. There is an informal honor system to this, for if off-the-record statements are reported, the journalists' sources of information may dry up. No one will talk to them again, not even to say good morning. Nor are reporters free to use the material from an off-the-record statement even if they get it from another source; they are effectively muzzled on that topic.

One needs little imagination to see how a backgrounder can be used to gag the press. If officials suspect that an embarrassing matter may be made public from another source, they have merely to call a press conference and discuss the matter openly, off the record; this effectively silences the press. This technique has been used often enough that some reporters and media have refused to participate in backgrounders lest they cut themselves off from future news sources.

A second type of backgrounder involves not-for-attribution statements, whereby the press is quite free to use the background material as it sees fit, but it may not quote the sources nor specifically acknowledge where the information came from. Not-for-attribution backgrounds are responsible for those phrases so often encountered in the news: "a generally reliable administration source disclosed today. . . ." or "a high Pentagon official has announced. . . ."

The not-for-attribution backgrounder is often used as a *trial balloon.* A projected government policy is released not-for-attribution, and public reaction to it is assessed. If public reaction is favorable, an appropriate spokesperson confirms the policy on record and takes the credit. If public reaction is unfavorable, there is no one to blame.

These practices are tolerated because backgrounders often do what they set out to do: They provide a realistic framework for interpretation. Furthermore, out of the entire operation some scraps of significant information do come to the experienced player—information that is probably not obtainable in any other way.

The First Amendment guarantees press freedom—the public's right to know. As applied by the courts it upholds the common-law principle of a public trial in which the press is the representative of the people. The Sixth Amendment guarantees an individual a speedy and public trial by an impartial jury. A conflict arises when the press's preoccupation with the sensational, and its diligence in seeking it, results in a trial by press wherein defendants are often found guilty in public opinion before their judicial trial has commenced. For example, in the 1954 trial of Dr. Samuel Sheppard, who was accused of killing his wife, the Cleveland press found Sheppard guilty even before the jury went out to deliberate. Not surprisingly, Sheppard was convicted. Also not surprising was the 1966 Supreme Court decision that overturned Sheppard's conviction due to publicity. It is apparent that such instances make it increasingly difficult to form panels of objective jurors, particularly in sensational cases. This was an issue in choosing a jury for the trial of Jack Ruby after Ruby shot Lee Harvey Oswald on national television, when John Hinckley, Jr., shot President Reagan in full view of millions, and in other cases that have attracted national attention before and during the actual trial.

It says something about the nature of the controversy that journalists refer to it as a free-press–fair-trial issue, while members of the bar call it the fair-trial–free-press issue. Attempts to balance the constitutional provisions have had lengthy and sometimes nasty histories in this country, and there are signs that it may become worse before it becomes better.

Is there a way to find a middle ground between the public's right to know and the defendants' rights to fair trials? Supreme Court Judge Felix Frankfurter expressed the need for such a balance:

A free press is not to be preferred to an independent judiciary, nor an independent judiciary to a free press. Neither has primacy over the other; both are indispensable to a free society. The freedom of the press in itself presupposes an independent judiciary through which that freedom may, if necessary, be vindicated. And one of the potent means for assuring judges their independence is a free press.[26]

To date some twenty-six states have developed voluntary press–bar guidelines with the purpose of balancing the needs of the news media, the judiciary, and the public. While they differ from locale to locale, in scope

Conflict: The First and Sixth Amendments

Media's guarantee of access to information often clashes with defendant's rights to a fair trial. The search for a balance has been arduous.

and application, such guidelines generally tell media they should not print: (1) confessions or stories about confessions; (2) results of lie detector tests or whether the defendant would or, in fact, did take such a test; (3) stories about a defendant's past criminal record; (4) stories that question credibility of witnesses or personal feelings of the judiciary; (5) stories about a defendant's character; and (6) stories that inflame the public mood against the defendant. A frustrating 1982 case clouds the issue of whether such guidelines are legally binding; often they appear to work if only because they allow well-meaning journalists and members of the bar a framework for mutual understanding.

At times, the formal procedures allowed by law and the informal guidelines accepted by the press and the bar aren't enough. In extreme cases, courts have resorted to closing some court proceedings to the public, sealing some court records, and issuing *restrictive orders,* whereby trial judges lay out whatever rules they think necessary, and can get away with, to protect the sanctity of their courts.

Gag Orders

Courts use gag orders to stifle inquisitive reporters.

Restrictive orders place limits on what attorneys and court officials can say to the news media and even what the media can share with their audiences. The latter constitute *gag orders,* which are legally binding dictates that reporters are forced to follow regardless of their constitutionality. When reporters violate gag orders, relying upon First Amendment guarantees, judges utilize their authority to hold the reporters in contempt of court. Reporters can be, and have been, sentenced to prison until the case is terminated or until they agree to comply with the judges' orders. Since most reporters find such contempt authority a repugnant violation of their constitutional rights, many have become media celebrities by serving out their sentences.

A key gag order case occurred in 1976, in *Nebraska Press Association* v. *Stuart,* after a judge ordered the Nebraska media to refrain from publishing the existence and scope of a confession or other material implicating an accused mass murderer, including materials presented in open court. Media protested the gag, and a unanimous Supreme Court agreed that gag orders against the press are in most cases unconstitutional. Chief Justice Warren Burger ruled that prior restraints on speech and publication are the most serious and the least tolerable infringement on First Amendment rights.[27] Whether the Nebraska case was truly a victory for the public's right to know remains to be seen. Some observers have noted that the ruling protected media in their printing of what occurs in open court, but increasingly more and more courts are making important decisions behind closed doors, plea bargaining, sealing court records, and restricting trial participants from communicating with the press and the public. If the trend continues, and everyone, including defendants, is restricted from talking to the press, media may find themselves having to cope with something reminiscent of the Star Chamber procedings of Elizabethan England. The issue, obviously, is far from resolved.

One side note to the issue is the interesting history of attempts to open courts to film, video, and still photography. Since the popping flashbulbs and unwieldy cameras made a mockery of justice during the 1935 trial of Bruno Hauptmann, accused of kidnapping and murdering the infant son of national hero Charles Lindbergh, cameras in the courtroom have created discord between the press and the bar. Two years after Hauptmann was found guilty, the American Bar Association adopted Canon 35, calling for a complete ban on courtroom photography. As amended in 1952 and 1963, the ban also extended to television and radio broadcasting.

As photographic and broadcasting equipment have become more miniaturized and less conspicuous during ensuing decades, journalists have fought for equal rights with their pencil-and-pen brethren. Experiments have met with varying results. Some of the least satisfactory resulted in Supreme Court intervention.

Recent attempts in the thirty-nine states experimenting with televised trials have proven to the satisfaction of some that televising court proceedings, if done inconspicuously, need not be detrimental to jurisprudence. The most famous televised trial to date was the murder trial of teenager Ronald Zamora, whose defense argument drew as much attention as the fact that the case was being televised in a Florida experiment. His lawyers maintained that Zamora's mind had been programmed from watching so much television violence that he was temporarily insane at the time of the murder, but the jury disagreed.

Cameras in the Courtroom

The U.S. Supreme Court has agreed that cameras and electronic equipment do not necessarily jeopardize a fair trial.

Ronny Zamora was found guilty of murder in a noted 1977 televised trial. Zamora's lawyer had argued that the boy was driven to murder by television-induced insanity.
Wide World Photos

Such experiments have now been condoned by the U.S. Supreme Court. In a January 1981 decision, the Court ruled that an absolute constitutional ban on broadcast coverage of trials cannot be justified. Its opinion was a rejection of an appeal by two Miami Beach policemen who argued that their burglary conviction should be repealed because the presence of cameras in the courtroom denied them a fair trial.

Shield Laws

One other point of contention between the law and the news has come to the fore: the question of *confidentiality,* or reporters' *shield laws.* It involves whether or not reporters can be forced by a grand jury, a court, or Congress to reveal their sources of information. There are those who hold that such confidentiality of sources is essential to press freedom. How else, they ask, can a reporter acquire privileged and sometimes dangerous information?

State and federal statutes protect journalists' sources of information, but the laws are not absolute.

Journalistic investigations of the social, economic, and political environment have need for sources such as the government insider, called Deep Throat, who provided Bob Woodward with information about Watergate. Since many sources are willing to talk with reporters but fear being dragged into court, this kind of journalism has served as an investigative agency, which many see as having a highly significant role in the judicial process. Such investigations, media insist, must remain absolutely above and beyond official governmental investigations, or else the press will be seen as merely another branch of government.

On the other hand, confidentiality of sources is subject to abuse by journalists themselves. Witness the infamous Janet Cooke case, in which the young *Washington Post* reporter refused to divulge to her editor—the same Bob Woodward of Deep Throat fame—the identity of an eight-year-old heroin addict about whom Ms. Cooke wrote a gut-wrenching story. Eventually, it became obvious that a prime reason for not identifying the boy was because he was a figment of Ms. Cooke's fertile imagination. America's journalists may take years to recover the public confidence lost in that episode.

Meanwhile, the First Amendment argument is countered by a clause within the Sixth Amendment that states, "In all criminal prosecutions, the accused shall enjoy the right to be confronted with the witnesses against him; and have compulsory process for obtaining witnesses in his favor."

In one of its final moves of the last decade, the high court indicated it had little sympathy for reporter confidentiality. *New York Times* investigative reporter Myron Farber found that the New Jersey shield law had a loophole large enough for the courts to reach through and send him to jail for forty days and fine his newspaper $285,000. In 1976 the *Times* published a series by Farber implicating a New Jersey doctor, Mario Jascalevich, in the deaths of a number of hospital patients. As the criminal trial proceeded in 1978, Farber was asked for all his notes and anything that would help the court determine the innocence or guilt of Dr. Jascalevich. Farber at first refused the subpoena, citing the state shield law and

basic First Amendment rights. The trial judge held Farber and his newspaper in contempt of court, even after Farber submitted a large body of
material to the court. The New Jersey Supreme Court upheld the contempt
decision, and the U.S. Supreme Court refused to review the celebrated case,
indicating that in this incident the Sixth Amendment took precedence over
the First Amendment.

In the aftermath of several similar cases, as reporters started shred-
ding their notebooks and taking out safety deposit boxes for their photo
negatives and important papers, then-President Jimmy Carter got into the
act, calling for special legislation that would effectively overturn the Supreme Court and limit the courts to subpoena power in dealing with media
sources of information. The bill was signed into law in late 1980, sharply
restricting police seizure of material belonging to reporters, authors, filmmakers, photographers, academics, and free-lance writers, so long as they
are not suspected of a crime or if the material in question cannot be otherwise obtained.

Summary

The press operates according to four generally recognized theories: authoritarian, communist, libertarian, and social responsibility. The American system is best described as libertarian, but even under this theory controls are imposed on the mass media. The amount of control exerted by a government, according to propositions made by Siebert and Stevens, depends on the relationship between a government and the governed, the stability of the government, the heterogeneity of society, and the degree to which the society is developed.

Although many restrictions on print media have only modest application to American society today, American citizens and the courts must support the First Amendment in order to make it work. Because the airwaves are finite and because of the intrusive nature of radio and television, the government has long been active in controlling the broadcast media, primarily through the FCC. Most broadcasters who comply with FCC rules can expect to get their licenses renewed, although some challenges to existing licenses have succeeded in the courts. Equal Opportunity is a federal law dealing with access to airwaves by office seekers. The Fairness Doctrine is a complex set of rules created by the FCC that pertains to issues of controversy.

An adversarial relationship between government and the press exists in the United States. This provides government with opportunities to try to manipulate the news, and occasionally results in a conflict between the First Amendment and the Sixth Amendment. Backgrounders are a common type of news management by government. Some are off-the-record statements and others are not-for-attribution statements. To balance the rights of the press and of defendants, courts have resorted to issuing restrictive orders, which sometimes include "gagging" the press. Shield laws are supposed to protect the confidentiality of press sources, but the case of Myron Farber indicates that the Supreme Court is not currently very sympathetic with reporter confidentiality.

Student journalists are reminded of their freedoms and responsibilities.
Jay Black

THE FUNCTION OF THE PRESS IS VERY HIGH. IT IS ALMOST HOLY. IT OUGHT TO SERVE AS A FORUM FOR THE PEOPLE THROUGH WHICH THE PEOPLE MAY KNOW FREELY WHAT IS GOING ON. TO MISSTATE OR SUPPRESS THE NEWS IS A BREACH OF TRUST. Supreme Court Justice Louis Brandeis

1. Fredrick S. Siebert, Theodore Peterson, and Wilbur Schramm, *Four Theories of the Press* (Urbana, Ill.: University of Illinois Press, 1963), pp. 1–2.

2. William Stephenson, *The Play Theory of Mass Communications* (Chicago: University of Illinois Press, 1967).

3. Edwin Emery and Michael Emery, *The Press and America: An Interpretative History of the Mass Media,* 4th ed. (Englewood Cliffs, N.J.: Prentice-Hall, 1978) p. 94.

4. Frederick S. Siebert, *Freedom of the Press in England 1476–1776* (Urbana, Ill.: University of Illinois Press, 1952).

5. John D. Stevens, "Freedom of Expression: New Dimensions," in *Mass Media and the National Experience,* ed. Ronald T. Farrar and John D. Stevens (New York: Harper & Row, 1971), pp. 14–37.

6. *Near* v. *Minnesota,* 383 U.S. 697 (1931).

7. *New York Times Co.* v. *United States,* 713 U.S. 403 (1971).

8. "Could the Progressive Help Make Possible a Nuclear Holocaust?" *Quill,* April 1979, p. 6.

9. Ibid.

10. James J. Kilpatrick, "Time to Announce, 'We've won'," syndicated column, *Deseret News,* 9 April 1979.

11. Jack Anderson, "FBI Pursues Author of H-bomb Story," syndicated column, *Logan* (Utah) *Herald-Journal,* 29 May 1979.

12. Don R. Pember, *Mass Media Law,* 2d ed. (Dubuque, Ia.: Wm. C. Brown Company Publishers, 1981), p. 57.

13. *Schenck,* v. *United States,* 249 U.S. 39 S. Ct. 247 (1919).

14. *Galella* v. *Onassis,* 487 F. 2d 986, cited in Pember, *Mass Media Law,* 2d ed. pp. 212–13, 238.

15. Don R. Pember, *Mass Media Law* (Dubuque, Ia.: Wm. C. Brown Company Publishers, 1977), p. 233.

16. *Roth* v. *United States,* 354 U.S. 476, 77 S. Ct. 1304 (1957).

17. Harold L. Nelson and Dwight L. Teeter, Jr., *Law of Mass Communications: Freedom and Control of Print and Broadcast Media,* 4th ed. (Mineola, N.Y.: The Foundation Press, 1982), pp. 313–18.

18. Ibid. p. 328.

19. Ibid.

20. Pember, *Mass Media Law,* 2d ed., p. 430.

21. *Red Lion Broadcasting Co.* v. *FCC,* 395 U.S. 367 (1969).

22. Pember, *Mass Media Law,* 2d ed., p. 458.

23. *Pacifica Foundation* v. *FCC,* 556 F. 2d 9 (D.C. Cir. 1977).

24. Sonderling Broadcasting Corporation, Station WGLD-FM, 27 R. R. 2d 285 (11 April 1973).

25. Nelson and Teeter, *Law of Mass Communications,* p. 337.

26. *Pennekanp* v. *Florida,* 328 U.S. 331 (1946).

27. *Nebraska Press Association* v. *Stuart,* 96 S. Ct. 2791.

Notes

13 Media Ethics and Social Responsibility

The previous chapter demonstrated that within the libertarian framework, there has come a shift in emphasis from freedoms to responsibilities. We have seen that early in their history mass media fought for the right to gather and report news, to express opinions, and to operate in the market-place of ideas and goods. Once those beachheads had been established, no matter how tentatively, the shift away from ideal libertarianism toward social responsibility followed quite naturally. Even the most eloquent spokespersons for a free press, Thomas Jefferson included, came to maintain that there was a need for some checks on extremely irresponsible media. The question is, which groups or organizations will prevent the media from issuing biased propaganda, misleading advertising, antisocial entertainment and programming, and the like? Social responsibility theorists maintain that the government should guide the media along the proper path. Strict libertarians would rely upon public opinion and consumer response to do the job. Self-control on the media's part is another possible check. Sometimes self-control springs naturally from individuals attempting to serve society. More often, perhaps, it emerges as a defensive reaction when faced with real and perceived control from government or an outraged public.

How media practitioners have responded to ethical questions is the subject of this chapter. Throughout, we will use the terms *social responsibility* and *ethics* almost interchangeably, because it is our belief that members of institutions do have certain obligations to function in a socially responsible fashion and that, at base, ethics are manifestations of that social consciousness.

In April 1981 the Pulitzer Prize for feature writing was awarded to Janet Cooke, a reporter for the *Washington Post*. Shortly after the prize was announced, Cooke revealed that she had fabricated parts of her story about an eight-year-old drug addict. The child did not exist, the writer admitted before the *Post* returned the Pulitzer and asked her to resign. Why did she do it? "In my case, the temptation didn't derive from ambition," Cooke said. "I simply wanted to write a story that I had been working on so that I wouldn't have to go back and say, 'I cannot do it.' I did not want to fail."[1]

Ethics are moral guidelines for the resolution of difficult dilemmas. Indeed, there would probably be no need for ethics if there were no dilemmas, no choices to make. However, as can be seen in the Janet Cooke example, journalists do have to make choices. Frequently the decisions involve ethics, complicated by conflicting guidelines—economic and political ones, and tyrannies of deadlines and media mechanics, for example. Put to a pragmatic test, journalistic ethical standards fall back too often in a fanfare of rationalization.

Introduction

Who, or what institutions, should keep the media ethically and socially responsible?

Ethical Dilemmas

Ethical choices are complicated by conflicting guidelines and everyday forces.

THE MIRAGE

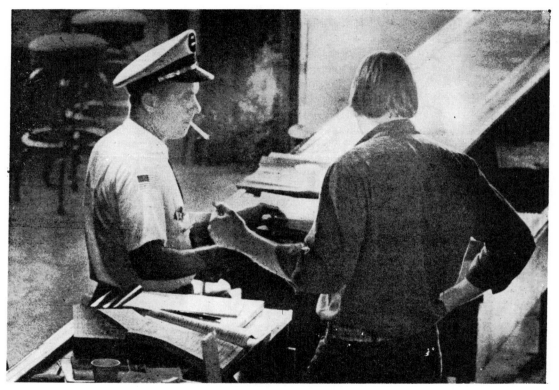

A report on the 'fix' in Chicago

That man wearing a uniform is a Chicago Fire Department lieutenant. He has just taken a payoff for overlooking code violations in the Mirage, a small Chicago tavern. We know. The Mirage was our tavern. We had to make the payoff. It was a not-so-hidden cost of doing business. With a civic watchdog group, the Better Government Assn., The Sun-Times owned and operated the Mirage to uncover and document firsthand public and private corruption in the city that works—if you know how to work it. Inside is the full Sun-Times series, reports on the reaction and comment from the editors and readers.

Behaviors institutionalized in news reporters, particularly investigative journalists, frequently involve questionable moral acts, and sometimes even prize-winning reporters have to make—or *do* make—decisions offensive to many.

The 1978 Distinguished Service Award winner of the Society of Professional Journalists—Sigma Delta Chi (SPJ/SDX)—for general reporting in newspapers was a *Chicago Sun-Times'* investigative team that exposed shakedowns from city and state inspectors. In June 1977 the *Sun-Times* purchased a bar, named it "The Mirage," trained a couple of reporters as bartenders, and went into business. A pair of photographers was concealed in a loft above the bar, photographing the action below through a ventilation duct. Throughout the summer and fall the reporters dealt with a variety of city and state inspectors who disregarded fire, health, and construction violations by the dozen in exchange for payoffs ranging from $10 to $100.[2]

In accepting their national SPJ/SDX award, *Sun-Times* reporters said they were concerned over the ethical questions involved in the investigation, but they insisted that they remained perfectly legal in every one of their activities: They engaged in no illegal entrapment, they used no hidden microphones, and they reported all bribes. Finally, they argued, the good they did for the city of Chicago and the state of Illinois more than justified any questionable behaviors on their part.

The ingenuity demonstrated by the *Sun-Times* so impressed the nominating jury for the Pulitzer prizes that it submitted the Chicago paper's entry to the Pulitzer prize board, which makes the final selections. But no Pulitzer prize for local reporting went to the Windy City newspaper, because a majority of prize-board members expressed serious reservations about the *Sun-Times'* undercover methods of reporting.

Earlier Pulitzer prizes have been awarded to journalists posing as workers in non-journalistic occupations. As ambulance drivers they exposed collusion between police and private ambulance companies, and as social workers they investigated social problems. But by 1978 the profession of journalism was growing leery of stepping across that narrow line separating "pretense" and "deception." Prize-board member James Reston of the *New York Times* said he had no problem with pretense, a passive act in which reporters allow someone to draw the wrong conclusions about a reporter's identity and level of information. But he was bothered by deception, in which reporters actively intend to mislead.

Is undercover reporting ethical if it results in benefits to society? The jury is split.

The issue was further heightened when another board member, Ben Bradlee, the editor of the *Washington Post* who had coordinated the *Post*'s Pulitzer prize-winning investigations of Watergate, asked:

How can newspapers fight for honesty and integrity when they themselves are less than honest in getting a story? Would you want a cop to pose as a newspaperman?[3]

(Bradlee, of course, had a bitter pill to swallow three years later when his young staffer, Janet Cooke, proved herself less than honest.)

Other board members said they weren't convinced the *Sun-Times* had not engaged in entrapment, and still others criticized the newspaper for having taken the easy, theatrical approach to solving a civic problem. Some pointed out that the reporters were engaging in illegal activities whenever they paid bribes to inspectors, regardless of the fact that each bribe was promptly reported to the Illinois Department of Law Enforcement.

In short, these professionals are divided over what constitutes honorable service and what constitutes unethical behavior.

On a different level, some years ago protesters of the Viet Nam War were picketing the Oakland Induction Station. A peaceable eight hours of orderly sign-carrying passed, except for an approximate two-minute interlude in the early afternoon when one of the pickets slugged a cop, was slugged back with a billy club, and was then hustled off in the paddy wagon. On national network news that evening, that single two-minute incident was shown in its entirety, to the total exclusion of seven hours and fifty-eight minutes of peaceable demonstration. This reporting created an unrealistic impression across the nation; but it was visual, it did happen, and it fully met television's criterion for action in the news. Photos of the incident appeared in the nation's newspapers. Since the mass media are in intense competition, the newspapers could not afford to ignore a dramatic incident already aired on television.

Research studies help to shed light on why journalists react to ethical dilemmas as they do. The studies indicate confusion over values, recognition of the need for formalized codes of ethics, and belief that some journalists are more ethical than others.

When asked, journalists cannot agree over values, codes of ethics, or their own "profession's" standards.

A mid-1970s study of 203 Chicago print and broadcast journalists suggests agreement among journalists as to what should or should not be done in practice but disagreement over whether such practices are indeed ethically based. Over one-fifth of the respondents admitted that ethical principles did not play a very large role in their professional lives. Most indicated their superiors were more supportive of ethical behavior than were their co-workers. Print journalists thought their media behaved far more ethically than did the electronic media, but broadcast journalists thought both print and electronic media behaved about the same. Two-thirds of the respondents agreed that a need existed for formal principles of journalism ethics, with print journalists more positive than their electronic counterparts about the need for such formalized codes.

One Chicago journalist adequately summed up journalistic concerns over ethical principles in light of the realities of reporting, editing, and gatekeeping under daily pressure:

I believe all journalists with any talent and sense want to be ethical (fair, accurate, truthful) reporters but when you're faced with standing firm on a bunch of abstract principles you learned in college, or losing your job because you won't allow your publisher to review a story before it's printed, the decision becomes a very economic one. Sure it's unethical, but you can't get hired by presenting a resume filled with short-term jobs you left because of "ethical principles."[4]

Journalists, particularly editors and reporters engaged in the gatekeeping function, are frequently offered *junkets* (expense-paid trips) in the hope that they will write glowing articles. To a lesser degree, theater critics, entertainment editors, and sportswriters get their share of *freebies* (free tickets and press invitations, passes to special events, copies of books, records, and even art). This is done, from the hosts' points of view, to gain favorable attention of the media personnel who may find it difficult to be dispassionate in writing about their hosts.

There is a balance to this, however; many newspapers and smaller media cannot afford to buy all the tickets involved, so the alternatives are either freebies or no coverage at all. The solution to this problem is not easy.

There are at least two primary issues involved with freebies: (1) Acceptance of a freebie may consciously or unconsciously influence the journalist's objectivity; and (2) the acceptance of a freebie, when known, may give the public reason to distrust the news medium, even though the journalists may not be (or think they aren't) affected. Consequently, many major media pay their own way to everything, even insisting that their reporters pay the government for travel on governmental aircraft or convoys during political campaigns or junkets. Recently enacted codes of ethics in many media clearly state that nothing of value is to be accepted by journalists. Other guidelines indicate that journalists can accept food or drink as long as it can be eaten or drunk in ten minutes.

In response to a national survey of newspaper journalists, slightly more than a third of those queried indicated that their newspaper had a stated policy concerning the acceptance of freebies; a quarter said their newspaper had no policy; and 35 percent said there was no written policy but that a general understanding existed among staff members as to what was acceptable. Individual respondents showed a very low regard of their colleagues' ability to remain objective when offered freebies and junkets, even though only 15 percent of those queried admitted to having been so influenced themselves. The lower the dollar value of the freebie, the less likely the journalists were to feel compromised. In other words, there's a parallel between ethical practices and monetary enticements.[5]

In sum, the national study on freebies indicated a strong regard for individual professionalism, a general distaste for freebies, a rejection of freebies as essential, and a general support for codes of ethics, particularly the code of the Society of Professional Journalists, Sigma Delta Chi, which is the nation's largest professional journalism group.[6]

Bribes

Commercial influences have frequently been seen as primary tests of media ethics. In the late 1950s there was a great network scandal about "The $64,000 Question." Glued to their television chairs, Americans rooted week after week for the young father with the fantastic memory. Would he win the $64,000? Then, disillusionment came. The public learned that he had been coached by the network. Producers of "The $64,000 Question" and other prime-time network quiz programs had been seeking to maintain audience interest for the commercial sponsors by making sure that some attractive contestants did not make mistakes that would eliminate them from competition. When challenged in this unethical practice, producers justified their behavior with the argument that they were producing entertainment programs, not genuine intellectual contests. Few people supported them in this argument, and big-money quiz shows disappeared from the schedule for several years. After the Federal Communications Commission added a Section 509 clause, making it illegal to assist any contestant in a quiz program with the intent of deceiving the listening public, and after networks made a great deal of publicity out of their claims that henceforth they, and not the commercial sponsors, would determine rules and procedures of quiz and game shows, such programming returned to the air.[7]

Quiz show scandals, plugola, and payola are examples of commercial influences over TV and radio programming.

While quiz show scandals were going on in the 1950s, the practice of *plugola* was in full operation. Publicity agents representing manufacturers of certain products would pay a program's writers and director for giving on-camera exposure to their products. Many people in the broadcast industry were on the take, including performers, whenever they slipped in the free boosts or ads, called *plugs*.

The most widespread and publicized use of plugola was found in the recording industry in the form of *payola* to disc jockeys. Record companies quite openly put disc jockeys on the payroll to play their records on the air, because such exposure from a popular personality often guaranteed sales. Many DJs were making more from payola than they were from their salaries, and some refused to play anything without payola. Payola was essentially advertising for which the stations received no income and which, since it was not labelled as advertising, deceived the public. Despite congressional hearings and attempts by the FCC and broadcasters to terminate the practice, reports of payola continue to surface within the industry.[8] Obviously the law is circumvented, and the issue remains a legal as well as ethical one.

Magazine and newspaper editors, particularly in the fields of fashion, travel, and real estate, often trade a certain amount of editorial coverage in return for significant volumes of advertising. An advertiser can, in effect, double or sometimes triple the product's exposure in a single issue at the same cost.[9] Frequently the editorial content of these sections of newspapers is simply an excuse for the advertising volume-filler material to meet the sixty-forty advertising-editorial ratio. More often than not, this filler material is supplied by publicists for advertisers, as can be seen by even casual readers of newspaper "progress editions" or boat show, home show, county fair and other sections.

Commercial Influences

Print media sometimes exchange editorial coverage for advertising. The price to be paid: credibility.

There seems to be a kind of double damage here. Not only are the magazine's subscribers reading puffery, and assuming it is fact, but preferential treatment is being shown to certain advertisers who are acquiring greater space at lesser cost. Other advertisers, ignorant of or unable to take advantage of such arrangements, have legitimate cause for complaint. Ultimately, of course, the greatest damage is probably to an unmeasurable commodity: credibility. It is only natural for credibility to suffer when audiences expect media to be serving the information function while in fact they are serving the advertising and persuasion function.

A good many columnists supplement their incomes by taking advantage of their unique positions as influential gatekeepers. We might call these advantages perquisites (meaning privileges) or *perks*. Some go so far as to include favorable (or unfavorable) mention of individuals or companies for pay. Others, especially syndicated columnists, have joined the lecture circuit, where they receive tidy sums per visit to college assemblies or other groups. Jack Anderson, for one, makes so much from his lectures that he takes no income from his widely syndicated column. Charging an average of $6,000 per speech, he has done quite well.

Perquisites

On another front, financial editors of newspapers and magazines are often in a position to glean inside knowledge of proposed transactions. These financial editors have a double-barreled opportunity. They can enhance a financial situation (or detract from it) through mention in their pages, and

they are in a position to personally profit from privy information by speculation. Because of the sensitivity of financial transactions, distorted news read as fact can adversely affect readers where it hurts, in their pocketbooks.

Consider, for instance, the plight of Stephen L. Castner, a *Milwaukee Journal* reporter who was fired by his newspaper in 1975 because he had invested in a company about which he had written. His editor maintained that Castner did nothing illegal, nor did he take advantage of any inside information, nor were his reports inaccurate or biased. The editor maintained, however, that the newspaper's standards of objective reporting demand that reporters avoid any situation that might lead the public to believe they have a conflict of interest. Castner, who had made the only bid on 6,060 shares of American Bankshares Corporation stock, argued that his purchase was ethical because it was an investment based on knowledge available to anyone who read the newspaper, that the stock was openly advertised, and the bidding was open to anyone.[10]

Owners and Advertisers

There are many who, looking at the enormous corporate power of the mass media and their commercial advertisers, fear misuse. A case might well be made, however, that there are some practical reasons why these fears may be overemphasized.

Two thirds of the nation's 1,730 daily newspapers are chain owned and are generally controlled financially by corporations that are far removed from the daily news-reporting and editorial activities. Although the primary commitments of chain owners are to net profits, occasionally abuse of ownership becomes blatant. In 1977 Panax Corporation told its eight daily newspapers and forty weeklies to publish a pair of front page articles critical of President Carter. Two editors refused and were subsequently dismissed. The furor that followed became national news in trade journals and on network television, and assuredly warned other chains that such meddling would not go unnoticed.

Editorial abuse by media owners and advertisers is possible, but several factors tend to limit manipulation.

In principle, of course, the trend to corporate ownership could spell the end of local autonomy and diversity of opinions. Conglomerates have the power to control the content of media, and when they do, editors and reporters have few defenses. It is an issue that many media observers take very seriously, if only in the abstract.

By the same token, the relationship between advertisers and media decision making is a concern. At one time in its history, the American news industry was heavily influenced by advertisers who assumed that because they paid two-thirds the cost of print media and nearly all the cost of electronic media, they could call all the shots. Advertiser ideology was omnipresent, creeping into news and editorial functions.

Today it has become more and more obvious that the mass media in larger markets are greater and more powerful than their advertisers. They do not need to jeopardize their audience position to satisfy advertisers anymore. Whereas advertisers once enforced their will by threatening to withhold or cancel their advertising, in general they can no longer do so. The truth is that they need the media to market their goods as much as the media need them for financial support. To cancel advertising is self-defeating in the long run. Institutionalized media demonstrate time and time again that neither party can long exploit the other without destroying the delicate relationship.

Codes of Conduct

Mass media ethics are pretty much a product of the twentieth century. During the early years of the Republic, the press was dominated by political interests that subsidized many newspapers. But political control of the press diminished with the success of the penny press in the 1830s and the growth of advertising. Throughout the rest of the century the press reflected the spirit of the time—freewheeling days of national expansion, the winning of the West, and social Darwinistic ideas of the survival of the fittest.

This climate lasted until the turn of the century when the muckrakers, individual journalists, discovered their considerable influence and touched a public nerve with their crusade against business corruption and government collusion. For a decade, they attacked social injustice through

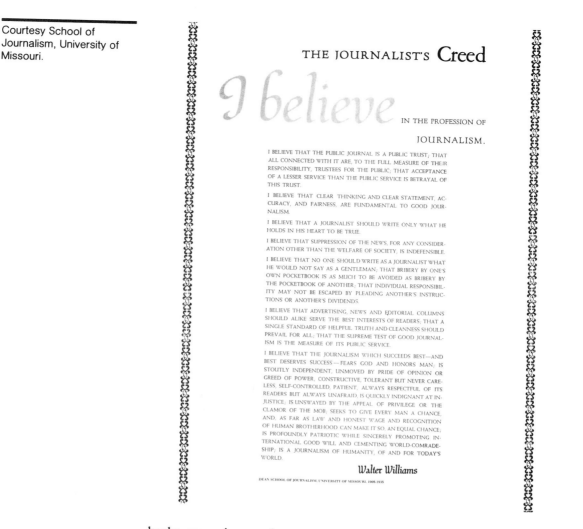

THE JOURNALIST'S Creed

I believe IN THE PROFESSION OF
JOURNALISM.

I BELIEVE THAT THE PUBLIC JOURNAL IS A PUBLIC TRUST; THAT
ALL CONNECTED WITH IT ARE, TO THE FULL MEASURE OF THEIR
RESPONSIBILITY, TRUSTEES FOR THE PUBLIC; THAT ACCEPTANCE
OF A LESSER SERVICE THAN THE PUBLIC SERVICE IS BETRAYAL OF
THIS TRUST.

I BELIEVE THAT CLEAR THINKING AND CLEAR STATEMENT, AC-
CURACY, AND FAIRNESS, ARE FUNDAMENTAL TO GOOD JOUR-
NALISM.

I BELIEVE THAT A JOURNALIST SHOULD WRITE ONLY WHAT HE
HOLDS IN HIS HEART TO BE TRUE.

I BELIEVE THAT SUPPRESSION OF THE NEWS, FOR ANY CONSIDER-
ATION OTHER THAN THE WELFARE OF SOCIETY, IS INDEFENSIBLE.

I BELIEVE THAT NO ONE SHOULD WRITE AS A JOURNALIST WHAT
HE WOULD NOT SAY AS A GENTLEMAN; THAT BRIBERY BY ONE'S
OWN POCKETBOOK IS AS MUCH TO BE AVOIDED AS BRIBERY BY
THE POCKETBOOK OF ANOTHER; THAT INDIVIDUAL RESPONSIBIL-
ITY MAY NOT BE ESCAPED BY PLEADING ANOTHER'S INSTRUC-
TIONS OR ANOTHER'S DIVIDENDS.

I BELIEVE THAT ADVERTISING, NEWS AND EDITORIAL COLUMNS
SHOULD ALIKE SERVE THE BEST INTERESTS OF READERS; THAT A
SINGLE STANDARD OF HELPFUL TRUTH AND CLEANNESS SHOULD
PREVAIL FOR ALL; THAT THE SUPREME TEST OF GOOD JOURNAL-
ISM IS THE MEASURE OF ITS PUBLIC SERVICE.

I BELIEVE THAT THE JOURNALISM WHICH SUCCEEDS BEST—AND
BEST DESERVES SUCCESS—FEARS GOD AND HONORS MAN; IS
STOUTLY INDEPENDENT, UNMOVED BY PRIDE OF OPINION OR
GREED OF POWER, CONSTRUCTIVE, TOLERANT BUT NEVER CARE-
LESS, SELF-CONTROLLED, PATIENT, ALWAYS RESPECTFUL OF ITS
READERS BUT ALWAYS UNAFRAID, IS QUICKLY INDIGNANT AT IN-
JUSTICE; IS UNSWAYED BY THE APPEAL OF PRIVILEGE OR THE
CLAMOR OF THE MOB; SEEKS TO GIVE EVERY MAN A CHANCE,
AND, AS FAR AS LAW AND HONEST WAGE AND RECOGNITION
OF HUMAN BROTHERHOOD CAN MAKE IT SO, AN EQUAL CHANCE;
IS PROFOUNDLY PATRIOTIC WHILE SINCERELY PROMOTING IN-
TERNATIONAL GOOD WILL AND CEMENTING WORLD-COMRADE-
SHIP; IS A JOURNALISM OF HUMANITY, OF AND FOR TODAY'S
WORLD.

Walter Williams

DEAN SCHOOL OF JOURNALISM, UNIVERSITY OF MISSOURI, 1908-1935

books, magazines, and newspapers. This period may have been the high-
water mark of journalistic ethics, paralleled perhaps only by post-Water-
gate self-analysis.

A study by University of Illinois researcher Clifford Christians found
a great deal of media self-criticism in the 1920s, as thoughtful journalists
recognized public disaffection with media excesses, and called for commitments to journalism's professional status.[11] Schools of journalism, most
offering courses in journalism ethics, attempted to place journalism in an
academic framework. The ethics literature of the period demonstrated a
strong moral responsibility to one's professional community, ethics being
construed as right action toward one's fellows.

Codes of ethics and courses in media ethics emerging from this period displayed a concern for common values of a shared culture. One of the earliest was the journalist's creed, written in 1908 by Walter Williams, the first dean of the University of Missouri's School of Journalism. Williams emphasized honor amid the search for truth. "I believe that no one should write as a journalist what he would not say as a gentleman," he wrote in the creed. This concept of journalism ethics as "moral responsibility to my fellows" faded from view after the beginning of the 1930s. Into the vacuum moved a new understanding of what constituted ethical journalism, the *cult of objectivity,* which went unchallenged for the next several decades. Ethically responsible journalism was seen as achievable only through factual accuracy and verification of details, devoid of analysis or interpretation. Readers were left to draw their own conclusions, which oftentimes was an impossible task especially when they were not provided the framework within which an event took place.

Early codes of ethics were supplanted by the cult of objectivity.

An example of this occurred during the tyranny that surrounded the late Senator Joseph McCarthy in the early 1950s when McCarthy labelled prominent State Department officials as Communists and homosexuals. The press duly reported this factually—the fact of his utterance. They did not report that this was a familiar tactic used by McCarthy, nor that many of his past allegations had proven erroneous. They did not report this because it would have been an expression of editorial opinion contrary to the accepted tenets of objective reporting.

The environment that gave rise to objectivity led to debates about media morality. Starting in the 1920s, first journalists and then broadcasters formulated codes, attempts to define acceptable and unacceptable professional behavior.

In the last sixty years the press has developed numerous codes of ethics, some prepared by editors and others by reporters. The codes share many elements, differing primarily in the perspectives of the two groups.

Newspaper Codes

American Society of Newspaper Editors Code

Social responsibility as a press theory probably goes back to the Canons of Journalism adopted by the American Society of Newspaper Editors (ASNE) in 1923. It should be observed that members of the society were the working editors, not the publishers, and that their doctrine of press responsibility was adopted in the heyday of jazz journalism. In essence, they reflected their own individual repugnancies and consciences.

The ASNE Code stresses
social ethics, but it lacks
the power of enforcement.

As originally written, the 1923 Canons of Journalism (amended in 1975) reflected the social concerns, the group ethics typical of the times. In their preamble, ASNE members maintained that:

The primary function of newspapers is to communicate to the human race what its members do, feel, and think. Journalism, therefore, demands of its practitioners the widest range of intelligence, of knowledge, and of experience, as well as natural and trained powers of observation and reasoning. To its opportunities as a chronicle are indissolubly linked its obligations as teacher and interpreter.

Many saw the Canons as an interesting but toothless collection of lofty thoughts suitable for framing on the newsroom wall. Indeed, early in its history the ASNE tried to expel one of its members, *Denver Post* editor Fred G. Bonfils, who was accused of blackmailing oil millionaire Harry Sinclair in connection with the Teapot Dome Scandal, the Watergate of its day.[12] It could not agree to exercise its self-policing powers, however, so the ASNE appeared to many as a less than adequate means of guaranteeing media responsibility.

It was no coincidence that the ASNE Canons were created three years after author Upton Sinclair had turned his muckraking attention toward the press, equating it to a house of prostitution. In a book he had published by himself, because he was unable to find an established publishing house willing to take the chance, Sinclair said journalists constantly violated the public trust by taking the "brass check," the medium of exchange in brothels.

The Brass Check is found in your pay-envelopes each week—you who write and print and distribute our newspapers and magazines. The Brass Check is the price of your shame—you who take the fair body of truth and sell it in the market-place, who betray the virgin hopes of mankind into the loathsome brothel of Big Business.[13]

Society of Professional Journalists/Sigma Delta Chi Code

The SPJ/SDX code
stresses social
responsibility for the largest
group of working reporters
in America.

Quite similar to the ASNE Canons, both in justification for existence and tone, is the code of ethics adopted by Sigma Delta Chi (SDX) in 1926. SDX consisted of reporters and journalism students, as distinct from ASNE's management and editorial constituency. As such, SDX reflected the concerns of the bulk of working reporters, gathered together into an organization dedicated to their freedoms and professionalism. In the 1970s SDX, the largest group of journalists in America, renamed itself the Society of Professional Journalists, Sigma Delta Chi, and revised its code of ethics to reflect contemporary issues.

The SPJ/SDX code maintains that the duty of journalists is to serve the truth, that public enlightenment is the forerunner of justice, and that the Constitutional role to seek the truth is part of the public's right to know the truth. "We believe those responsibilities carry obligations that require journalists to perform with intelligence, objectivity, accuracy, and fairness," the code says; it then goes on to list a bill of ethical particulars. Like the ASNE code, it has been subject to considerable debate. Detractors insist that it artificially relegates journalism to a false sense of professionalism. Adherents say it helps remind journalists of their responsibilities.

There's a major distinction between the earliest codes drawn up by the newspaper industry and those drawn up by broadcasters. In a phrase, it's the difference between positive and negative liberties. Newspapers, with their tradition of centuries of fighting for freedoms, expressed in their codes a belief in the self-righting process and the general rationality of audiences, and, secondarily, a commitment to garner and maintain the public's trust.

The codes of the radio industry (1937) and its successor, television (1952), along with the Motion Picture Production Code (1930), differ markedly in intent and scope. All are patent efforts to forestall new governmental regulation or to deal with existing regulation, and as such primarily view responsibility in negative terms—"Thou shalt not"—rather than in positive terms stating the scope of responsibility to the various publics that support them. The codes reflect the electronic media's emphasis on entertainment, although they do give some attention to educational functions. Displaying a shift from rationalism prevalent under libertarian philosophy, the codes appear to depict audiences as readily corruptible: Page after page of the codes tell practitioners how to treat issues of sex, religion, manners, and morals so as to operate in the public interest, in entertainment, advertising, and news.

Broadcast codes stress negative liberties, as though to forestall governmental intervention.

The Radio Code

Since 1937 the Radio Code has gone through some twenty revisions, now filling a thirty-page pamphlet. Its index alone lists nearly 100 different topics, ranging from *adult themes* to *vulgarity*.

The Radio Code also contains several pages devoted to regulations and procedures, outlining the functions of the Code Authority of the National Association of Broadcasters (NAB), the organization to which broadcasting stations belong if they wish to carry the prestigious "seal of good practice." Revoking a station's subscription to the code is the most serious direct impact the Code Authority can have on a violator. Obviously, if a station wishes to violate the standards of the code and cares not whether its membership in the NAB means anything to its audiences and advertisers, there's nothing to stop it from doing so. Significantly, only one-third of the nation's radio stations are code subscribers. In hard times or in highly competitive markets where a couple of extra minutes of advertising per hour or some questionable programming practices can bring solvency, the owners can opt for profits and forego the public relations.

Radio code adherents receive the NAB's "seal of good practice," but adherence is voluntary.

The Television Code

Essentially similar to the Radio Code is the Television Code, which has also gone through some twenty revisions since its inception in 1952. It is even longer and more specific than the Radio Code, due in part to the pervasiveness of the medium and the controversial nature of much of its programming, especially its programming to children. Modifications in the TV code have come on the heels of public and political outcry against violence, deceptive advertising on programs for children, and news practices. In 1975 the code was amended in light of Senate hearings on nutrition and human needs and public outcry against television advertising's exploitation of children; its utilization of real and cartoon characters from the regular programs to sell products; its reliance upon peer pressure and fear appeals to foster buying habits; and its appeal to violent, dangerous, or otherwise antisocial behavior.

Many of television's "Special Program Standards" codes are nearly identical to those in the radio code. Some of the areas treated are narcotics, gambling, betting, the handicapped, sex, quiz programs, payola, lotteries, fictionalization of the news, and advertising. In almost every case the standards are expressed negatively—shall not, should avoid, should be de-emphasized, is prohibited, and so forth. Likewise the television code's statements on the treatment of news and public events, controversial public issues, political telecasts, and religious programs read much like those in the radio code, differing mainly in statements regarding visual impact.

At this writing, serious questions have arisen over the NAB Code's viability. Following a 1982 federal appeals court decision that a portion of the code was in violation of antitrust laws, NAB's Board of Directors cancelled the code's advertising provisions. Shortly thereafter, a furor arose when numerous radio stations began carrying commercials for hard liquor, a product the code had long maintained should not be advertised over the airwaves. Litigation continues, and the weaknesses of voluntary codes have again become apparent.

Family viewing time is one area that has been troublesome for the NAB's Television Code, especially in its relationship to external, governmental regulation. The code calls for the elimination of entertainment shows that are inappropriate for the entire family during the first hour of prime time each evening. The policy originated when then CBS President Arthur Taylor and NAB officials met with the FCC in 1974 after a wave of public criticism of television violence. Intimations of government regulation by the FCC chairman prompted the networks and NAB stations to incorporate the principle of family viewing time into the NAB Code during the following year. Children were expected to be shielded from violent or sexually oriented programming for the hour prior to the onset of prime time and during prime time's first hour (i.e., from 7 P.M. to 9 P.M. Eastern Standard Time), and advisory warnings were created when those hours included potentially offensive shows.

Controls

The policy suited many television critics and parents, but greatly offended many producers, directors, and writers of programs, who sued the networks for conspiring to damage them financially. They claimed the FCC had meddled in programming and that some lucrative shows, especially "All in the Family," had suffered because of their forced shift to later time slots. When the case went to Federal District Court, Judge Warren Ferguson ruled that the FCC had indeed meddled with the broadcasters' rights for self-determination and that FCC pressure to adopt the family viewing time was illegal, but what had become a "self-regulation" by the networks and broadcasters could stand.

Historically, movies have not received the same freedoms or restraints as other media. Early in their history they were not even considered media of information, and were granted no First Amendment protection. That may have something to do with their strange history of self-regulation, which has ranged from an incredibly strict and controversial 1930 code to more realistic attempts at variable self-restraint beginning in the 1960s.

Movie Codes

At the turn of the century and into the 1920s, the accepted theory was that mass media had great potential for manipulation and mobilization of society. Given this prevailing view, it is no wonder that strict controls were placed on the film industry after Hollywood established its reputation as a sin and scandal center during the swinging 20s. Again, in the familiar pattern, real and imagined external threats for control brought about efforts at internal house cleaning. The first was the 1922 creation of the Motion Picture Producers and Distributors of America (MPPDA), chaired by Will Hays, former Postmaster General and Chairman of the Republican National Committee.

On 30 March 1930 the MPPDA adopted its Motion Picture Production Code. The Code's stipulations caused difficulties for filmmakers who were forced to submit their films to the MPPDA authorities before being permitted to hold public showings. That policy, including the practice of insisting that any code violations were removed from the films before they would be released, came about several years after the code had been written. At first, it was intended to be a voluntary set of guidelines. But when film attendance dropped off somewhat at the outset of the depression in the 1930s, filmmakers began taking liberties with the code in order to boost attendance. Public outcries that brought about the code in the first place were heard and felt again. This time it was the Catholic Legion of Decency and its pledge by 11 million Catholics to boycott offensive films. After 1934, the Hays Office (as the MPPDA was known) started issuing its seal of approval to acceptable films. Within a couple of years it was reviewing and approving almost all films exhibited in America (97 percent in 1937), sanctifying the "family film."[14]

In its formative years, the film business was subjected to very strict censorship. The MPPDA Code prevailed from 1930 to 1966.

Although undergoing minor changes, the code continued in effect well into the 1960s. For three and a half decades, critics blasted its attempts to create what they considered to be a highly untrue and misleading picture of life and the code's jellolike platitudes. It may have served its basic purpose, however, as it apparently played a role in reducing the scope and influence of state and local censorship boards and perhaps even warding off a federal motion picture censorship organization.[15]

In 1966, the Motion Picture Association of America (MPAA), which served the same purposes as the MPPDA it had replaced in 1945, developed its Motion Picture Code of Self-Regulation. The new code applied to production, to advertising, and to titles of motion pictures. It differed most significantly from the earlier code in its vigorous encouragement of responsible artistic freedom, and it attempted to establish a framework within which films deemed to be unsuitable for viewing by children could be so labelled.

MPAA set up the current rating system in 1966 so films could present more realistic portrayals of a changing time.

Movie Ratings

Almost immediately, it became obvious to the MPAA that the revised code would not suffice. In the words of MPAA President Jack Valenti:

The national scene [in 1966] was marked by insurrection on the campus, riots in the streets, rise in women's liberation, protest of the young, questioning of church, doubts about the institution of marriage, abandonment of old guiding slogans, and the crumbling of social traditions. It would have been foolish to believe that movies, the most creative of art-forms, could have remained unaffected by the change and torment in our society. . . .

The result of all this was the emergence of a "new kind" of American movie—frank and open, and made by filmmakers subject to very few self-imposed restraints.[16]

By 1968 the U.S. Supreme Court granted states the power to prevent children from being exposed to books and films suitable only for adults, and Hollywood immediately jumped on the "variable obscenity" and variable availability bandwagon. Instead of attempting to control the content of individual films, the MPAA decided to allow filmmakers to voluntarily submit their films to a rating board, where they would be rated on a four-point scale according to their suitability for viewing by children.

Presently, the system includes the categories: G for general audiences—all ages admitted; PG for parental guidance suggested—some material may not be suitable for preteens; R for restricted—children under age 17 must be accompanied by a parent or guardian; and X, no one under 17 admitted. (At first the MPAA had an "M" category for "suggested for mature audiences," but it caused some confusion and was replaced by the "PG" classification.)

G, PG, R, and X ratings are supposedly based on a film's theme, language, nudity and sex, and violence. Theater managers do the enforcing.

Films are rated by a full-time, seven-member board located in Hollywood. Many observers have felt that overly explicit sexually-oriented films were the only ones to get the X rating, while graphic murder and mayhem

Leonard Freed/Magnum
Photos

were supposedly suitable for children. But Valenti insists that, despite popular opinion, all films are judged on four basic criteria: (1) theme, (2) language, (3) nudity and sex, and (4) violence.[17]

It is important to point out that producers do not have to submit their films to the MPAA for ratings; those who produce or import films are free to assign an X rating to their films, but they cannot assign other ratings. However, most films released commercially are submitted for rating, and nearly 98 percent of the American filmgoers at any given date are likely to be viewing rated films.[18] Of course, it is up to the individual theater managers to enforce the code provisions at the box office.

Codes: A Conclusion

Good and honorable people, disturbed by the appearance or practice of social irresponsibility, have labored long hours to develop equitable means of improving both the image and reality of their businesses. In recent years a growing proportion of journalists and other media personnel have joined professional organizations (one list consisting primarily of working news reporters and editors includes 119 such groups[19]) that have devoted more and more of their meeting time and publications content to ethical dilemmas and questions about heightening levels of performance and status.

A general summary of media industry codes has led us to the present conclusion that overall the codes seem to have certain elements in common: They have few if any teeth; they are both unenforced and unenforceable. They are incumbent upon members only, and the only sanction that can be applied against a member is expulsion from membership, sometimes a small penalty. The codes tend to be bland statements drawn up in response to public disenchantment with media operations. At best, they are a stopgap of semiserious self-regulation in the hope that somehow their platitudes will satisfy both public critics and government's temptation to regulate.

By their existence, they are an attempt to organize, to standardize, and to codify ethics. This is a large order and, in the complexity of institutionalized mass media, comprises really only a halfway measure toward the regulation that media are trying to avoid. Codes arise in response to public demand, but they are framed to cause the least commotion.

Commission on Freedom of the Press

We have already seen that calls for social responsibility in all the mass media have been in existence from almost the beginning. Various codes of ethics, whether created spontaneously or as a defensive response to external pressures, have been common in mass media for half a century. Insofar as the news media were concerned, the codes probably had minimal effect on the daily performance of journalists. It may be that hanging a code of ethics on the newsroom wall was sufficient; when challenged on their daily performance, media practitioners could point to their code and say, "We're trying."

But when an influential external group comes along and seriously questions a craft's basic operating premises, something more than a feeble "We're trying" seems in order. Such was the case in 1947 when the Commission on the Freedom of the Press, a sort of blue-ribbon public conscience, issued its broad-ranging report.[20] The commission had been created in the middle of World War II (1942) with University of Chicago Chancellor Robert M. Hutchins as chairman. It was funded in part by *Time* magazine's Henry Luce and the *Encyclopedia Britannica*.

As seen by the commission, freedom of the press is a moral and not a natural right. Therefore, the right can be lost or forfeited when abused. Underlying the basic social responsibility theory postulated by the commission are two very fundamental propositions:

1. *Whoever enjoys freedom has certain obligations to society,* and since the media enjoy a libertarian heritage, they have the concomitant responsibility to use those freedoms to serve the welfare of society as a whole.
2. *Society's welfare becomes the most overriding concern.* Essentially, this demonstrates a shift in the theoretical foundation of press freedom from the individual to society. Individual rights to speak

out are balanced by group rights to be free from invasion of privacy, or libel; personal rights to free expression are described in terms of public access to the media, or the "public's right to know."

Based largely on testimony from journalists and from the literature of journalism organizations, the Hutchins Commission settled on a list of five basic requirements, or expectations, society believes the press should fulfill. Those requirements have been the subject of a great deal of debate since the time they were outlined, and serve as a valid framework for contemporary press criticism.

The first requirement was that the media provide "a truthful, comprehensive, and intelligent account of the day's events, in a context which gives them meaning." It is a call for accuracy in news, but beyond that, it is a call for the clear separation of fact from opinion. Recognizing the value of objective, value-free journalistic reporting, the commission also said the media fail society if they fail to place the news in perspective. "It is no longer enough to report the *fact* truthfully. It is now necessary to report *the truth about the fact,*" the commission concluded. In an ever more complex society, people need to know more than the basic "who said what to whom, when and where." They also need to know the "how" and "why" of news. False objectivity, as in merely reporting that Senator McCarthy has announced existence of communists in the state department, is socially harmful, even though it may be true that the senator did say so. What is

Meaningful News

Media were told to provide a "truthful, comprehensive, and intelligent account of the day's events, in a context that gives them meaning." Objectivity was not enough.

Journalists were objective in the 1950s when they quoted Senator Joseph McCarthy, who said there were homosexuals and communists in the U.S. State Department. But were journalists reporting the truth? Wide World Photos

needed, the commission said, is to report the greater truth, which is the question of whether, and just how many, communists there really are in the state department, what are the motives and special interests of the senator, and what was the overall political climate in which the statement was made. Many people may not recognize or appreciate the attempts to add socially responsible interpretation to the news, especially since much interpretative news becomes somewhat hard to swallow. But despite short-run problems with credibility, more and more news media have begun to recognize the values of making the effort, spending the extra dollars on news staff trained in complex political, economic, and social issues that will enable them to give that truthful, comprehensive account of the news.

Access for Comment and Criticism

Media should serve as "a forum for the exchange of comment and criticism," especially since media were falling into the hands of fewer and fewer owners.

Second on the Hutchins Commission's list of requirements was that the media should serve as "a forum for the exchange of comment and criticism." Because ownership and control of the news media were falling into fewer and fewer hands, the commission said there was a need for those media to serve as "common carriers" of controversial ideas and views that individual and corporate gatekeepers may not otherwise allow into the news flow. While the media should not be seen as common carriers in the sense that railroads have legal obligations to carry diverse freight, and they need not give space and time to everyone's ideas, they should as a matter of policy carry views contrary to their own, according to the commission.

Within the past two decades this question of public access to the media has grown in intensity, and many attempts to resolve the question have emerged. Most newspapers have put into practice their own voluntary fairness doctrines, opening up their editorial pages for divergent political views. *Op-ed* pages (opposite the editorial pages) have become commonplace, serving as cafeterias of opinions written by a broad spectrum of society. This valuable newspaper space emerged as a logical outgrowth of the socioeconomic turmoil of the 1960s, when disenfranchised minorities, disgruntled youth, and others realized they could not be heard by the general public by merely grabbing a bullhorn or cranking out a few hundred copies of their underground newspapers.

A Representative Picture of Society

The third requirement of the press laid down by the commission was that the media project "a representative picture of the constituent groups in society." Media were asked to take into consideration the values and aspirations, and the weaknesses and vices, of different social groups, and to avoid stereotyping the different groups in news coverage and entertainment shows.

Media have no reason to disagree with this request. Indeed, through their various codes of ethics they had already placed the same responsibility on themselves. But whether they have met that responsibility is entirely another matter.

Of all the complaints against the media that surfaced during the 1960s and 1970s, those by minorities were perhaps the most vehement. Tired of being depicted as shiftless, rhythmic, happy-go-luckies in films, or as newsworthy only in newspaper sports and crime stories, black Americans began asserting their own identities in media. Likewise women, long seen as either sex symbols or domestics, fought for and began to win greater representation in gatekeeper roles. Other groups, including Chicanos, the elderly, religious minorities, and others long overlooked, have slowly cut away at culturally chauvinistic media organizations. Although there has been substantial progress, by no means have the battles over stereotyping in news, entertainment, and persuasive media been won.

Media were asked to project "a representative picture of the constituent groups in society." Some progress has been seen in news, entertainment, and advertising of minorities.

Fourth on the list of requirements is that the press be responsible for "the presentation and clarification of the goals and values of the society." Here the media's educational function is called for, with the Hutchins Commission telling media to assume a responsibility like that of educators in stating and clarifying the ideals toward which the community should strive. Rather than appealing to the lowest common denominator of taste and value, media were asked to elevate public interests.

Clarifying Goals and Values

While agreeing in principle with this dictate, the press has found it difficult to fulfill. Different subgroups within society have widely divergent goals and values, and to carry all of those goals and values to the satisfaction of every group is impossible, especially since so many of them are contradictory.

The press was also asked to improve its "presentation and clarification of the goals and values of the society." Being the national educator is difficult.

Fifth on the Hutchins Commission's list of requirements for the press is that the media should provide "full access to the day's intelligence." Recognizing the exponential nature of our information explosion, coupled with what appears to be an exponential increase in the individuals' need to know how to cope, this becomes an awesome requirement.

The Right to Know

Federally mandated freedom of information laws have followed vigorous efforts by the Society of Professional Journalists and other news organizations to eliminate or at least curtail governmental secrecy, the classification system, closed meetings, and inaccessible records. As we saw in chapter 12, this social responsibility mandate flies in the face of government's natural inclinations, and the issue is far from being resolved. Recent court decisions have held that the media do not have rights of access to news events exceeding those of the general public, and some seriously question whether the public really needs to know all that the press says it does.

Finally, Hutchins asked the press to provide the public with "full access to the day's intelligence." Serious questions arise over the public's "right to know."

Ultimately, one might argue that the burden for being fully informed falls back squarely on the shoulders of the individual citizen, as it theoretically did under libertarianism. Such a burden is just what the Hutchins Commission was attempting to avoid, since it pictured the citizenry as being far more lethargic than did the promulgators of libertarian theory.

The Responsibility of Freedom

Perhaps what bothered the media the most about the Hutchins group was the shift in liberty being suggested. For two centuries American journalists had operated on the basis of negative liberty, or freedom from external restraints. Suddenly, however, the thrust was on positive freedom, a freedom for pursuit of some predetermined goals. According to Theodore Peterson, the new social responsibility theory is grounded on a school of thought that sees negative liberty as insufficient and ineffective, somewhat like telling people they are free to walk without first making sure they are not crippled.

To be real, freedom must be effective. It is not enough to tell a man that he is free to achieve his goals; one must provide him with the appropriate means of attaining those goals.[21]

Social responsibility stresses positive freedom—freedom to pursue predetermined goals; while libertarianism stresses negative freedom—freedom from restraints. The shift in freedoms is vexing to many; they call it authoritarianism.

Who better than government is able to provide humanity with the "appropriate means"? Government, even a democratic government, is seen by social responsibility adherents as the only force strong enough to guarantee effective operation of freedom.

This doesn't set well with observers who find social responsibility to be only a slightly disguised version of authoritarianism. John Merrill has been one of the most outspoken critics of the theory. To him the proposition that pluralism of ideas should be governmentally mandated is ludicrous. Journalists, he says, must retain their freedom to make their own news and editorial judgments. Even well-intentioned attempts by outside groups seeking media improvement are self-serving, and inevitably lessen the autonomy of journalists, Merrill maintains. As long as journalism voluntarily gives up its capacity to think for itself—its editorial self-determinism—it is in "grave danger of becoming one vast, gray, bland, monotonous, conformist spokesman for some collectivity of society."[22] Merrill's views seem to be in the minority, however, as moves increase toward social responsibility in all public areas—press, business, government, and so forth.

Improving the Media

Self-criticism and academic analysis of the press were suggested by Hutchins. Since 1947 much has been done in this arena.

When the Commission on Freedom of the Press suggested that the media engage in vigorous mutual criticism and that an independent agency for evaluating the media be established, it was calling for new vehicles for media improvement. Also novel were its recommendations that academic–professional centers of advanced study, research, and publication in communications be established and that journalism schools guarantee their students broader liberal training. Since that 1947 report, activities have taken place on all these fronts. Whether such activities are entirely beneficial to the media and society may be debatable. Let us look at evidence of change in each of the areas posed by the Hutchins Commission.

Journalism Reviews

Criticism of the mass media, most notably that of self-criticism by practitioners seeking improvement in their product, has taken on new dimensions since the Hutchins Commission report. Only in the last two decades have practitioners collected their observations and published journalism or media reviews on a regularly scheduled basis.

One of the earliest of the *j-reviews* is the *Columbia Journalism Review,* the professionally written and edited, almost staid journal we have cited several times in this text. *CJR* appeared first in the fall of 1961 and was published quarterly until the 1970s, at which time it was issued bimonthly from Columbia University. Underwritten by private donors, foundations, subscriptions, and, belatedly, advertisers, *CJR*'s policy, as stated in its first editorial and repeated in each subsequent issue, is "To assess the performance of journalism in all its forms, to call attention to its shortcomings and strengths, and to help define—or redefine—standards of honest, responsible service . . . to help stimulate continuing improvement in the profession and to speak out for what is right, fair, and decent."

In *CJR*'s pages can be found ongoing debates over media behavior. "Darts" and "laurels" are handed out to media seen deserving of criticism or praise. Editorials, book and article reviews, original research on media performance and scholarly articles (some of them perhaps overly stuffy and sometimes establishmentarian in tone) about ethics, economics, and press–government relations are there for *CJR*'s steadily growing readership.

Among the best-known j-reviews put out by reporters was the *Chicago Journalism Review* (1968–1975), a feisty journal established "to fight news management, news manipulation and assaults on the integrity of the working press." The review emerged to criticize the media coverage of the 1968 Democratic National Convention in Chicago. Many reporters had felt as though they had been manipulated by their editors, and their editors by local officials—especially Mayor Richard Daley—in covering the confrontations between Chicago police and demonstrators during that convention. Demonstrators in full view of network cameras had chanted "The whole world is watching," and a sufficient number of Chicago journalists became so disillusioned at the distorted pictures conveyed of police–demonstrator

Columbia Journalism Review, Chicago Journalism Review, and two dozen others have actively criticized the press.

Columbia Journalism Review, Edward Sorel, artist; *Washington Journalism Review,* Donal Holway, photographer; Mother Jones, *Presstime,* the journal of the American Newspaper Publishers Association. Reprinted by permission (left to right)

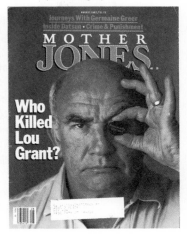

Presstime, the journal of the American Newspaper Publishers Association. *The Bulletin* of the American Society of Newspaper Editors/David Lawrence, photographer (left to right)

Management courses complete the puzzle for J-school students

The Bulletin

How We Cover TV

The Oliver Sipple Story:

You probably won't remember his name, but there's a lesson here for us →Page 1

confrontations that they risked their jobs to tell what they said was the whole story. That whole story included police brutality—unprovoked clubbings of reporters—condoned by the mayor's office and covered up by editors, according to many reporters.

Over the next several years the *Chicago Journalism Review,* with its front cover always an editorial cartoon by Pulitzer prize winner Bill Mauldin, served as an alternative to the news media in that city, although its circulation never did reach a level sufficient to become a valid alternative for mainstream audiences. Like most reviews, it frequently served as a forum for internal complaints; journalists used it as a vehicle to talk to themselves and to pinprick their bosses.

The same could be said about most of the two dozen or so other local reviews that appeared during the late 1960s and 1970s. There may be some question over whether the on-again, off-again journalism review movement is primarily an effort to improve media for the public or to improve media as places of employment. Whatever, it has displayed many of the trappings of the social responsibility theory as envisioned by the Hutchins Commission.

Press Councils

Of all the Hutchins Commission's recommendations for improving the press, the one that seemed most heretical to journalists was the call for an independent agency for evaluating the media. However, even prior to the Hutchins challenge, such efforts were already underway. The first semblance of press councils in America may have been the 1946 advisory councils consisting of community leaders in Redwood City, California, and Littleton, Colorado.

Additional efforts at local newspaper councils and citizens' advisory groups came in 1967, aided in part by a $40,000 grant from the Mellett Fund for a Free and Responsible Press earmarked to "encourage responsible press performance without infringing on First Amendment Freedoms."[23] The four newspaper councils (Redwood City, California; Bend, Oregon; and Sparta and Cairo, Illinois) and broader-based media councils in St. Louis and Seattle met with mixed success.

Over the next several years, similar media–community councils were established in Honolulu, Louisville, and Boston; and America's first statewide newspaper-press council was begun in Minnesota in 1971. The latter uses a grievance hearing panel, which seeks particulars from complainants who previously attempted to seek satisfaction directly through the "offending" newspaper. If the hearing panel decides that the case should be adjudicated, complainants are asked to waive the right to sue the newspaper in a court of law, which serves to protect the newspaper from double jeopardy. In its first half dozen years of existence, the council ruled against the newspapers as often as it ruled for them.[24]

Press councils have no legal authority, and their only real power surfaces if constituent media cooperate by submitting evidence and publicizing the councils' findings. They serve an intermediate function between the routine, informal settlement of a reader–editor conflict and a formal court action. Those in support of the press council argue that the councils aid media by resolving press–audience differences in-house. They are modified forms of self-regulation, seen as far preferable to external control.

National News Council

But not all agree with this premise. When there were calls in the early 1970s for a national news council in America, several major news organizations strongly opposed the proposals. The *New York Times,* for one, maintained that such "voluntary regulation" would diminish press freedom. Nevertheless, there were strong forces in favor of establishing a national council, and those forces, including the American Society of Newspaper Editors, prevailed.

"The cleansing light of publicity" was to be the National News Council's (NNC) only power. If national news media carried stories about the council's actions, the NNC would be far more effective than it could be without such voluntary cooperation. As things have developed, since some of the major media continue to oppose the council, its visibility and therefore its success rate remain relatively low.

In 1975, after a complaint against CBS News for paying former Nixon aide H. R. Haldeman for his interviews by Mike Wallace, the Council proposed a strongly worded guideline regarding the practice of media paying for news, noting that the media should always inform their audiences when such payments are made. In 1976 it expanded its role to take on nationally significant cases whether or not it received any complaints from the public. In so doing it decided to examine news reporting in all media, regardless of whether their initial circulations are national or local.

The problems the NNC has grappled with include the ethical issue of CIA employment of journalists, a practice the NNC opposes. It recommended that media continue coverage of terrorism, with due care, rejecting the proposal that media's reporting of such situations intensifies the terrorism and violence. In 1980 it convinced CBS to make an unprecedented apology, during prime time, for what the NNC called a demeaning and stereotypical portrayal of homosexuals in San Francisco.

The most serious problem facing the NNC and all other press councils may be that the cleansing light is burning on reduced voltage. Numerous commentators, both defenders and detractors of the National News Council, have repeatedly observed that NNC's biggest problem has been the public's lack of awareness that such a council even exists. Even the most optimistic have concluded that it will take a minimum of a decade (ending a few months shy of 1984) before anyone can make a sound evaluation of the council's permanent value. However, critics have not waited the full ten years to point out that the NNC has made mistakes along the way.

Ombudsmen

Ombudsmen are neutral in-house arbitrators, acting on public complaints about the media.

At about the same time a few American communities began experimenting with press councils, another concept of media accountability was initiated: the ombudsman system. *Ombudsmen* are neutral arbitrators usually employed by media to accept and investigate audience complaints and to publish or broadcast corrections and explanations of media policy. It is difficult to tell how many media organizations currently employ the ombudsman system, but a 1973 study indicated that about 9 percent of a random sample of newspapers (the great majority of them with circulations above 100,000) had an in-house arbitrator who could be considered an ombudsman.[25] Three years later, of 105 newspapers surveyed 15 said they had a full-time ombudsman, and 35 others said they used regular staffers for the same purpose.[26] Nationwide, ombudsmen are more likely to be found in newspapers than in other media.

The first ombudsman on an American paper was appointed for the *Louisville Courier-Journal* and *Times* in 1967. He was John Herchenroeder, the assistant to the executive editor, who had been city editor of the *Courier-Journal* for twenty years. At the time of his retirement in 1980, he was receiving and acting upon approximately 4,000 complaints a year dealing with news coverage, advertising, and circulation problems. Corrections were run under the standing headline, "Beg Your Pardon," and regular columns by Herchenroeder explained in some detail how the newspapers operated, so readers could get a greater understanding of the mechanics and thought processes involved in daily production.

Since 1970 at least four staff members of the *Washington Post* have served at different times as ombudsmen. Some of the turmoil over the ombudsman's functions at the *Post* has been echoed elsewhere in the country, as other papers experimented with in-house critics who would also serve as

Janet's World

The Story of a Child Who Never Existed — How and Why It Came to Be Published

By Bill Green
Washington Post Ombudsman
© 1981, Washington Post Co.

"Jimmy" never existed, but his story convulsed the city and humiliated The Washington Post—proud house of Watergate investigations.

The story was a lie and, after all its celebrated achievements, The Post owes its readers an accounting of its spectacular failure.

How did it all happen? Why?

This account was prepared from 47 interviews, primarily with members of The Post's staff. It was written by The Post's ombudsman, who is the fifth person to occupy the position of reader representative since it was created by the newspaper in 1970.

This is essentially a story of the failure of a system that, in another industry, might be called "quality control." On newspapers, it is called editing.

The fabrication of Janet Cooke's story eluded all of The Post's filters that are set up to challenge every detail in every news story the paper publishes. From the time she applied for a job, questions were not asked. Editors abandoned their professional skepticism.

This narrative reconstruction suggests that "Jimmy" moved through the cycle of news reporting and editing like an alien creature, unimpeded by ordinary security devices. This account has available the marvelous tool called hindsight.

It is also the story of a young and talented reporter, flaming with ambition, who showed irresistible promise of achievement. The Post accelerated her success, and may have thereby hastened her failure.

Janet Cooke declined to be interviewed for this report, so her version of events is not represented. Where Cooke is quoted directly, the remarks are usually attributable to those in conversation with her.

For Cooke, it was personal tragedy. For The Post, it was inexcusable.

For instance, none of the editors pressed Cooke for confidential details on the identity of "Jimmy" or his family.

Reporters with doubts about the story discussed their skepticism among themselves rather than taking it up the line to editors who might have taken action.

Some Post staff members, however, did express suspicions to editors who weren't listening.

While some reporters and editors were talking up their doubts, The Post's top news executives, unaware of newsroom anxieties, were nominating "Jimmy's World" for journalism's highest award, the Pulitzer Prize.

At the center of all this was Janet Cooke. Whether diligence in the newsroom would have prevented her hoax no one can say. Nevertheless, The Post didn't work hard enough.

Washington Post ombudsman Bill Green took his own newspaper to task for its handling of the Janet Cooke episode in 1981.
The Washington Post, 19 April 1981

The Ombudsman's Report

- **Warning signals were ignored.**
- **Senior editors were uninformed.**
- **Competition for prizes clouded good judgment.**

public watchdogs. In some cases, staffers seemed resentful of having their newspaper actually pay someone to criticize them, and wondered why it was necessary to hang their dirty laundry out in public. Generally, however, when supported by management, those papers experimenting with ombudsmen have sensed growing public acceptance, manifest in increased credibility.

Toward Professionalism?

Questions are raised over whether journalism *is*, or ever *should be*, a profession. Can an elite group of journalists adequately serve the needs of the public at large?

To hear Max Lerner describe it, journalism was but one of many professional organizations attempting to resolve new issues created by emergent conflicting roles in the 1970s; each of these organizations was caught in something like an identity crisis:

But all of them together share with the larger society something of the anguish of the moral crisis of our time. . . . The social structures that held the professions in balance internally have broken down. They were personal structures, of family, church, small community, face-to-face contracts, training by apprenticeship. They have been replaced by impersonal, massive aggregates, which may be good schools for developing skills but not for developing character.[27]

Given this identity crisis, it can be argued that journalism must transcend bureaucratic tendencies and concentrate on its original ethic—the ethic of fraternity and common values.[28] Codes of ethics could be a start, given their potential for promoting fraternity, and bringing status to the profession, but in another sense such codes can be extremely limiting if they serve to set journalism apart from the very public it serves, insulating journalists from public scrutiny.

In a provocative statement about the place of journalism in society, Association for Education in Journalism President James Carey in 1978 warned journalists of the dangers of professionalism.[29] To appreciate Carey's concerns over professionalism, we should avoid loose rhetorical usage of the term and consider the sociological foundations of the professions. Then we will recall that the professional: (1) works in a closed group and shares certain values and norms with co-workers; (2) works primarily for the satisfaction derived from the work and secondarily for the monetary rewards; (3) unlike the nonprofessional, places high value on prestige, honors, and other types of recognition; (4) places allegiance to the profession rather than to the immediate organization, and (5) wants autonomy in daily work.[30] Additionally, professionals are recognized by adherence to enforceable canons of performance, by high social status, and by extensive and specialized bodies of knowledge capped by examinations leading to entrance into the profession.

Recognizing these standards for professional status, Carey questioned whether it is proper for journalism to attempt to join the elites. He recognized that the rise of journalism education was a response to the need to train professionals, to establish consistent practices, techniques, and standards by which practitioners could be identified, judged, and ultimately controlled. An increase in legitimacy, according to Carey, came to journalism only once it became taught in the universities, yet the industry's motivations for support of journalism education may be suspect. The business itself stood to gain in public acceptance once it allied itself with the universities instead of print-shop apprenticeships for its products, and the business could assert control over its reporters by instituting standards of writing, reporting, and ethical behavior through professional education.

Journalism thus joined engineering, teaching, and even medicine and law in using universities to train new practitioners. As the professions gained an academic toehold during the twentieth century, they assumed new and more important roles in society. Professional people came to be looked upon as being a cut above average, as though they had answers to complex moral, social, and political questions the laypeople couldn't answer.

As professions specialize, they codify their own behavior and frequently reinterpret morality so it fits their peculiar needs. For example, secrecy and privilege among doctors and patients, lawyers and clients, and journalists and news sources may lead to morally defective relationships in which the interests of the patients, clients, and news sources, rather than those of the general public, are served.

Given this relationship, professionals have the tendency to be far more concerned with the way they are viewed by their colleagues than with the way they are viewed by their clients. In journalistic terms, this can be seen time and again when editors and publishers and reporters attend conferences, accepting mutually congratulatory applauses and awards from their peers, frequently not knowing—and perhaps not caring—what their readers or viewers *really* think of them. Such behavior can further isolate professional journalists from their publics. The irony pointed out by Carey is that by publicizing their awards professionals are encouraging the view that their members are people of unusual ability who belong to an elite group and that the public lacks the power to make effective evaluations and criticisms of their work.

"We would, in short, all be better served if professionals, including journalists, were to see themselves less as subject to the demands of their profession and more to the demands of the general moral and intellectual point of view," Carey suggested.[31]

The issue thus returns to the universities, where the general moral and intellectual points of view are supposedly inculcated. The American Council on Education in Journalism and Mass Communication (ACEJMC), which accredits academic journalism programs, has long held to the policy that journalism students should take no more than one-quarter of their courses within the mass media disciplines, and the remaining three-quarters in liberal arts. In its argument that the business of journalism should be peopled with broadly educated citizens empathetic to the needs of the public, ACEJMC has echoed some of Carey's concerns. However, journalism educators have long recognized that the students who get hired into

Professionals codify their morality and gain elite educations. Is that appropriate for journalists? Or are they more concerned about each other than about the public?

the business are frequently the ones who spend most of their collegiate waking hours pursuing immediate journalism interests, working on the student newspapers or other media where it appears they are getting exactly the kind of training needed to enter the pragmatic marketplace. A traditional liberal education appears less attractive to educators than an applied curriculum infused with *relevance*. Since the 1960s, journalism enrollments have grown exponentially—from 10,664 majors in 1958 to nearly 25,000 in 1967 to 77,540 in the fall of 1981.[32] Meanwhile, the voices of Carey and many others are heard crying, "Relevant for what?"

Summary

We have seen that *ethics* and *responsibility* are complex terms that we have frequently used interchangeably. Ethical dilemmas faced by journalists, and research studies on the subject, indicate that there are distinct patterns of performance deemed acceptable by some and unacceptable by others in the business. Junkets and freebies, and payola and plugola, have plagued journalists and broadcasters. For some journalists, such as columnists, opportunities abound to take advantage of the perquisites of the position. Other ethical problems arise when advertisers are given special editorial attention or when public relations firms submit material to newspapers that is printed as news.

Various codes have been created since the 1920s to guide the behavior of media people. These codes are, for the most part, harmless statements of ideal conditions, unenforced and unenforceable, drafted by the accused as blandly as possible as a hopeful stopgap to regulation and control, to gain public credibility, or to encourage internal regulation. We could argue that controls appear inevitable once ethics have deteriorated to the point that codified guidance is demanded. The codes, therefore, of the various media industries can be seen as way stations on the road to controls.

Our discussion of these responsibilities of the mass media revolved around the concerns and pronouncements uttered by the Hutchins Commission on Freedom of the Press. Social responsibility is a protective doctrine labelling humanity as lethargic. As such it has authoritarian overtones, since someone—the government, the media, or organizations of the public—is called upon to see that the lethargic populace is prodded and served.

Gradually, though reluctantly, the media have accepted many of the 1947 Hutchins Commission challenges. Information media have broadened their bases, offering more meaningful news and access for comment and criticism. They now offer a somewhat more representative picture of society, while through interpretative reporting, they clarify social goals and values. Granted, there is much room for improvement if one sees cries for social responsibility to be calls for improvement in media. The public's right to know is increasingly an agenda item, and numerous efforts to improve media through journalism reviews, press councils, and ombudsmen are seen as thrusts in that direction.

Finally we raise a disturbing question about the institutionalization and professionalization of journalism. The thoughtful observations of James Carey cause us to ask what it means to be a professional, and whether it is a goal to be sought by journalists and other media practitioners if the price of such professionalism is alienation from the very publics they should be serving.

Notes

1. From transcript of interview with Phil Donahue on NBC's "Today," 1–2 February, 1982.
2. "Winners of This Year's SDX Distinguished Service Awards," *The Quill,* April 1979, pp. 14–15.
3. Steve Robinson, "Pulitzers: Was the Mirage a Deception?" *Columbia Journalism Review,* July–August 1979, p. 14.
4. David Gordon, "Chicago Journalists and Ethical Principles," *Mass Communication Review,* Fall 1979, pp. 17–20.
5. Keith P. Sanders and Won H. Chang, "Freebies: Achille's Heel of Journalism Ethics?" (Unpublished paper presented to the Association for Education in Journalism, Mass Communication and Society Division, Logan, Utah, 30 March 1979); and "Codes: The Ethical Free-for-All: A Survey of Journalists' Opinions About Freebies," *Freedom of Information Foundation Series, No. 7,* March 1977.
6. Ibid.
7. Harrison B. Summers, Robert E. Summers, and John H. Pennybacker, *Broadcasting and the Public,* 2d ed. (Belmont, Calif.: Wadsworth Publishing Company, 1978), p. 403 n.
8. F. Leslie Smith, *Perspectives on Radio and Television: An Introduction to Broadcasting in the United States* (New York: Harper & Row, 1979), pp. 72, 244.
9. John Hohenberg, *The News Media: A Journalist Looks at His Profession* (New York: Holt, Rinehart & Winston, 1968).
10. Mark Nelson, "Newspaper Ethics Codes and the NLRB," *Freedom of Information Center Report No. 353,* May 1976.
11. Clifford G. Christians, "Mass Media Ethics: An Analysis of the Academic Literature" (Unpublished paper presented to Association for Education in Journalism, College Park, Maryland, August 1976).

12. Edwin Emery and Michael Emery, *The Press and America: An Interpretative History of the Mass Media,* 4th ed. (Englewood Cliffs, N.J.: Prentice-Hall, 1978), p. 511.

13. Upton Sinclair, *The Brass Check: A Study of American Journalism* (Pasadena, Calif.: Published by the author, 1920), p. 436.

14. Charlene Brown, Trevor Brown, and William Rivers, *The Media and the People* (New York: Holt, Rinehart & Winston, 1978), p. 139.

15. Harold L. Nelson and Dwight L. Teeter, Jr., *Law of Mass Communications: Freedom and Control of Print and Broadcast Media,* 4th ed. (Mineola, N.Y.: The Foundation Press, 1982), p. 397.

16. Jack Valenti, "The Movie Rating System," in *Mass Communication: Principles and Practices,* by Mary B. Cassata and Molefi K. Asante (New York: Macmillan Co., 1979), p. 289.

17. Ibid., p. 287.

18. Richard S. Randall, "Censorship: From *The Miracle* to *Deep Throat,*" *The American Film Industry,* ed. Tino Balio (Madison: The University of Wisconsin Press, 1976), p. 447.

19. Warren K. Agee, "The Joining of Journalists," *Quill,* November 1978.

20. Commission on the Freedom of the Press, *A Free and Responsible Press* (Chicago: University of Chicago Press, 1947).

21. Theodore Peterson, "The Social Responsibility Theory of the Press," *Four Theories of the Press* by Fred S. Siebert, Theodore Peterson, and Wilbur Schramm (Urbana, Ill.: University of Illinois Press, 1963), pp. 93–94.

22. John C. Merrill, *The Imperative of Freedom: A Philosophy of Journalistic Autonomy* (New York: Hastings House, 1974), p. 3.

23. William L. Rivers, et al., *Backtalk: Press Councils in America* (San Francisco: Canfield Press, 1972), p. 14.

24. Donald M. Gillmor "Press Councils in America," in *Enduring Issues in Mass Communication* ed. Everette E. Dennis, Arnold H. Ismach, and Donald M. Gillmor (St. Paul, Minn.: West Publishing Co., 1978), p. 342.

25. Keith P. Sanders, "What Are Daily Newspapers Doing To Be Responsive to Readers' Criticisms?, A Survey of U.S. Daily Newspaper Accountability Systems," in *News Research for Better Newspapers,* ed. Galen Rarick (Washington, D.C.: American Newspaper Publishers Association Foundation, 1975).

26. Everette E. Dennis, *The Media Society,* (Dubuque, Iowa: Wm. C. Brown Company Publishers, 1978), p. 123.

27. Max Lerner, "The Shame of the Professions," *Saturday Review,* 1 November 1975, p. 10.

28. Clifford Christians, "Mass Media Ethics."

29. James W. Carey, "A Plea for the University Tradition" (AEJ Presidential Address, Seattle, Washington, August, 1978), *Journalism Quarterly,* Winter 1978, pp. 846–55.

30. Dennis, *The Media Society,* p. 98.

31. Carey, "A Plea for the University Tradition," p. 853.

32. Paul V. Peterson, "Enrollments Reach 77,540, But Growth Curve Levels Off," *Journalism Educator,* January 1982, pp. 3–9.

Glossary

a

AAAA
American Association of Advertising Agencies; national trade organization that has developed extensive standards of good practice to guide agencies in producing ethical advertising

ABC
American Broadcasting Company

account executives
ad agency personnel who maintain a constant liaison with clients, mediating between clients and the rest of the ad agency personnel

A. C. Nielsen Company
the largest commercial ratings service used by broadcasters; makes extensive use of audimeters and diaries; its primary work is with networks

adjacencies
spot announcements before, during, and after network programming

advertising
any paid form of non-personal presentation of ideas, goods, or services by an identified sponsor

affiliate
radio or television station under contract with one of the three commercial broadcast networks (NBC, CBS, ABC); receives but does not have to air programming from its particular network

AM
amplitude modulation

ANPA
American Newspaper Publishers Association

Arbitron Company (ARB)
commercial ratings service used by broadcasters; makes extensive use of diaries and "telephone coincidental surveys"; its primary work is with individual stations

ascertainment
FCC regulations demanding that broadcasters seeking licenses determine the needs, interests, and problems of the communities they hope to reach

ASNE
American Society of Newspaper Editors

Associated Press (AP)
oldest American news service; a cooperative with members

associations
formalized groups of individuals whose activities are regulated by codes; members constitute formal audiences

audiences
large, anonymous, and heterogeneous masses of individuals attending to mass communications

audimeters
tuning meters with recording circuits attached to in-home TV sets to gauge amount and type of TV viewing

audion tube
a vacuum tube that made voice transmission possible; invented by Lee De Forest in 1906

authoritarianism
political system under which communications flows from the top down; centralized control of media is inherent

b

blacklisting
practice in Hollywood in the late 1940s and early 1950s, during "Red Scare" period, by which filmmakers, performers, and others who were accused of left-wing or communistic leanings were ostracized by Hollywood and unable to work in media

black weeks
periods during the year when no ratings are made of TV shows; during these weeks stations and networks tend to air public affairs shows and other programs that do not draw large audiences

blind bidding
film marketing system that demands that exhibitors sign contracts for films before the films are released or, sometimes, prior to production

block booking
film marketing system in which film exhibitors are forced to contract for a number of motion pictures from a studio, including the studio's B-grade films, in order to get the studio's better films for exhibition; the practice has been held to be illegal

brand image
advertisers' attempt to establish a distinction among products on the basis of snob appeal

brand name advertising
one of the earliest advertising techniques, attempting to establish the brand name (Coca-Cola, Kleenex, etc.) as synonymous with the generic product or with quality

budget
wire service's suggested top stories to be transmitted to clients/members during each news cycle

c

Canons of Journalism
code of ethics developed by the American Society of Newspaper Editors in 1923 and revised in 1975, stressing responsibility of journalists

CATV or community antenna television
cable television system by which a town or area wired with coaxial cable receives distant TV signals boosted by a local cable company

CBS
Columbia Broadcasting System

chain ownership
two or more newspapers published in different communities but owned by the same company; term used interchangeably with *group ownership*

channel noise
interference within or external to the medium; physical or mechanical barriers to effective communication

classification
certain kinds of information the government has labeled secret or top secret and withholds from the press and public

classified advertising
sales or merely informational notices, generally non-illustrated, concentrated in one section of a newspaper or magazine

clipping book
collection of articles from newspapers reflecting favorably upon a public relations person's client; used as an unscientific measure of public relations effectiveness

codex
a system by which sheets of papyrus or parchment were tied by cords between wooden boards; invented by the Romans in the fourth century A.D.

cold type
see offset printing

commission system
method used by advertising agencies, who retain about 15 percent of a client's payment to the media in exchange for producing and placing the ads

communication
a stimulus–response process involving a source and human receiver

communications
the means—tools and mechanics— with which the communication process takes place

consent decree
1946 agreement between United States Department of Justice and Hollywood film studios in which studios consented to give up control over film distribution to their own theaters, thereby breaking up studios' production and distribution monopoly

controlled circulation
print media, generally magazines or newsletters, distributed free of charge to preselected groups and underwritten by advertisers or sponsors

copyright
body of law protecting authors, publishers, and other media producers from having their works illegally reproduced

corrective advertising
means by which advertisers found guilty of false or misleading advertising are required by the FTC to use a certain percentage of their future advertising to acknowledge and rectify the earlier misrepresentation

cost per thousand (CPM)
the cost to a mass medium or advertiser of reaching each one thousand members of the audience

CPB
Corporation for Public Broadcasting

CPM
see cost per thousand

d

demographic breakouts
specialized sections or editions of newspapers or magazines intended to appeal to particular geographic, ethnic, or economic parts of each medium's audience

demographics
readily measurable characteristics of audiences such as age, sex, race, income, and level of education

diary
rating system in which audiences keep written records of their TV and radio usage

Direct Broadcast Satellite (DBS)
communications satellites emitting powerful signals that can be received on small and relatively inexpensive roof-top antennas

display advertising
showcase advertisements occupying considerable space and distributed throughout a newspaper or magazine

documentation
FTC requirement that advertisers fully document the claims made in their advertising

dummy
a diagram or mock-up of a print-medium page, indicating where illustrations, advertising, news, and so forth are to be placed

e

electromagnetic waves
electrical impulses used to transmit radio and TV signals

electronic newsroom
contemporary newspaper offices employing video display terminals and computers for reporting, editing, and producing the newspaper

ENG
electronic newsgathering equipment, such as mini-cams and microwave relays

equal time
FCC's Section 315 of the 1934 Communications Act providing that broadcasters provide the same amount of air time on the same terms or at the same cost for all bona fide candidates for political office

f

fairness doctrine
FCC provisions calling for airing of both sides of controversial issues of public importance

family viewing time
provisions of National Association of Broadcasters (NAB) calling for eliminations of violent or sexually oriented programming for the early evening hours when children are most likely to be in the audience

feature syndicates
packagers of entertainment—in verbal and pictorial form—primarily for newspaper clients

Federal Communications Commission (FCC)
broadcast regulatory agency established in 1934 to oversee licensing and operation of all wire and radio communication and to assure stations operated in the "public interest, convenience, and necessity"

Federal Radio Commission (FRC)
broadcast regulatory agency established in 1927, predecessor to FCC

feedback
reactions, either immediate or delayed, of communication receivers; feedback conditions future communication by limiting options of participants

fiber optics
tiny flexible strands of glass capable of carrying beams of light or electromagnetic energy around curves and corners; may revolutionize cable television because of its size, cost, information-carrying capacity, and versatility

First Amendment
Constitutional guarantee of press, speech, and religious freedom; it reads: Congress shall make no law respecting an establishment of religion, or prohibiting the free exercise thereof; or abridging the freedom of speech, or of the press; or the right of the people peaceably to assemble, and to petition the Government for a redress of grievances

FM
frequency modulation; broadcasts over line-of-sight signals

four-walling
film marketing system in which distributors rent theaters directly from theater owners and keep all the box-office receipts for the limited engagements of their films; such films are generally heavily promoted on television and released simultaneously in carefully selected areas

freebies
complimentary tickets, passes, books, records, and so forth offered to journalists by news sources who hope to receive favorable press treatment

free press/fair trial
controversies centering around the media's first amendment rights to gather and report news and the sixth amendment's guarantee of a fair trial unbiased by journalistic coverage

FTC
Federal Trade Commission; national regulatory agency overseeing such trading issues as truth in packaging, lending, and advertising

functions of communication
information, entertainment, persuasion, and transmission of culture

g

gag orders
court-ordered limitations on what attorneys and court officials can say to the news media and, in turn, what the media can publish or broadcast

galley proof
the first printed version of a book or magazine or newspaper article, which is checked for errors before final production

gatekeepers
people who determine what will be printed, broadcast, produced, or consumed in the mass media

group ownership
see chain ownership

groups
collectivities of individuals who share a more specific interest than do publics; membership is voluntary

h

hard news
accounts of "significant" news events, intended to inform and educate audiences about the "real world"

HomeComCen
home communications center, which in its fuller form today might consist of microcomputer, interactive cable television, VCR and videodisc systems, home satellite-receiving dish, telephone interface, and a facsimile printer

hot type
see letterpress

Hutchins Commission
informal but influential 1940s Commission on the Freedom of the Press, headed by Robert M. Hutchins, whose review of journalism enunciated the social responsibility theory of the press

hype
heavy promoting of products or performers, frequently by press agents who are seeking media and public attention

i

iconoscope
camera tube in Zworykin's original television system

instant books
nonfiction paperback books published immediately after major news events

institutional advertising
public relations advertising, in which corporate or governmental agencies attempt to improve their image at the same time they promote their products

International News Service (INS)
news service founded by William Randolph Hearst in 1909, noted for its lively and sensational and international news coverage. INS in 1958 merged with UP to form UPI

invasion of privacy
published or broadcast information that violates an individual's right to be let alone or damages one's peace of mind

inverted pyramid
a style of organizing a news report so that the essential information appears at the outset, with information of decreasing importance following in descending order; sometimes called "journalese"

j

jazz journalism
early twentieth-century newspaper practices aimed at increasing circulation; gawdy pictures, tabloid format, splashy and sensationalistic writing

joint operating agreement
practice by which two newspapers in the same city share printing presses and production equipment in order to reduce costs

journalese
see inverted pyramid

journalism review
formalized media, usually magazines, for self-criticism and public criticism of journalism

junkets
free trips offered to journalists, with the expenses picked up by news sources who hope to receive favorable press treatment

k

kinescope
(1) Zworykin's cathode ray tube television receiver carrying an image consisting of thirty horizontal lines; (2) in the 1950s, a means of taking films of TV programs directly from the TV screen

kinetoscope
Edison's earliest motion picture projector system, invented in the 1880s

l

least objectionable programming (LOP)
a theory that holds that a TV program need not be good or even highly popular to succeed, but that it should be less objectionable—and therefore draw more viewers—than the competition

letterpress
"hot type" typesetting process involving raised and indented lettering and pictures whose images are transferred directly onto paper during the printing run

libel
published or broadcast information that damages an individual's reputation

libertarianism
political system under which communications flows in all directions, without central control of media

licensing
means by which, under authoritarian government, only those media operating in accord with governmental policies will receive permission to publish or broadcast

lowest common denominator or largest common denominator (LCD)
the largest audience likely to consume a given media production; implication is that demographic and psychographic characteristics of such an audience result in the LCD accepting rather bland and inoffensive programming

low power television (LPTV)
ruling recently approved by FCC by which LPTV or "drop-in TV" channels are to serve special interest or geographically limited audiences

m

mass communication
The *process* whereby mass-produced messages are transmitted to large, anonymous, and heterogeneous masses of receivers. Used in the collective singular, the term refers to broad, theoretical considerations, whereas *mass communications* (with an *s*) refers to the mechanics or media involved in achieving the process

mass communications
the *means* whereby mass-produced messages are transmitted to large, anonymous, and heterogeneous masses of receivers; the term is synonymous with *mass media*

mass media
see mass communications

MOR
middle-of-the-road radio music formats, more recently called "adult contemporary"

motivational research (MR)
highly Freudian socio-psychological advertising techniques, based on the idea that people frequently purchase and use products to satiate needs and desires they themselves do not fully understand. The motivations are most frequently sexual in nature

MPAA
Motion Picture Association of America, established in 1945 to replace the MPPDA; its 1968 Code classifies movies into G, PG, R, and X categories

MPPDA
Motion Picture Producers and Distributors of America, a national trade organization begun in the 1930s to assure that Hollywood films were socially acceptable; it drew up the Code of the Motion Picture Industry

muckrakers
journalists, magazine writers, and book authors who uncovered corruption and questionable practices of businesses and government

Multipoint Distribution Service (MDS)
a variety of over-the-air TV that uses a microwave signal to transmit pay programs, generally to a master antenna serving a motel or apartment building or, occasionally, an entire city

n

NAB
National Association of Broadcasters; voluntary trade organization

NBC
National Broadcasting Company

negative option
marketing technique whereby books, records, or tapes are automatically sent to club members unless they specifically decline each offer

neovideo
a generic term to describe new electronic communications technology

news hole
the amount of space remaining in the newspaper after advertising and all the standard feature (non-news) material has been allocated

news management
general term describing the various techniques governments have developed to control access of reporters and the public to news about governmental activities; backgrounders, off-the-record interviews, not-for-attribution statements, and trial balloons are among the techniques utilized

newspaper
a regularly issued, geographically limited print medium, which serves the general interests of a specific community. Printed on unbound newsprint, it commonly contains news, comment, features, photographs, and advertising

nickelodeon
early film-exhibition halls or theaters; admission cost was a nickel

NPR
National Public Radio, network made up of noncommercial stations by the Corporation for Public Broadcasting

o

objectivity
journalistic goal of reporting news without bias or color, staying with the literal, provable truth even if further independent investigation would suggest the reporter should give some interpretation of the news

offset printing
"cold type" reproduction system by which copy is reproduced on a smooth, photographic plate; the printing process occurs when the plate passes over a series of rollers and ink is transferred onto paper indirectly from the plate; it tends to be cleaner printing than the older letterpress or raised-lettering processes

ombudsmen
in-house journalism critics, employed by the newspapers or broadcast stations, who mediate between public and journalists when the press is criticized

op-ed pages
the page opposite the editorial page where guest opinions usually appear

owned-and-operated (O & O)
broadcast outlets owned and operated by the networks; by FCC rules, each network is allowed only seven O & Os, no more than five of which can be the generally more profitable VHF (very high frequency) stations

p

participating spots
isolated commercial messages inserted into broadcast programs by national or local advertisers

pay cable
services such as Home Box Office or sports programs for which cable TV viewers pay an extra fee, usually on a monthly basis

payola
offering of money or other bribes to disc jockeys to encourage them to play a particular recording

pay TV
generic term for pay-cable TV, subscription TV, and Multipoint Distribution Services—all services for which television viewers pay an extra fee

PBS
Public Broadcasting Service

penny press
American newspapers, beginning in the 1830s, that lowered their street sales price to one cent, attracting such large circulations that advertisers were willing to underwrite most of the cost of producing the paper to reach those masses

persistence of vision
psychological principle upon which the motion picture is based, that is, that the eye retains an image fleetingly after it is gone

personalized books
individualized books, with computer-generated personal references to children, family, friends, and locales intended to appeal to a youthful audience

photonovel
paperback of movie script fully illustrated with frames taken directly from the movie

playlists
list of popular songs being played by radio stations

plugola
free boosts or promotional "plugs" made by program writers, hosts, or guests who are frequently paid by manufacturers who wish to gain exposure for their products

positioning
recent advertising techniques of aiming ads, and products, at specific demographic—and psychographic—subgroups within the larger mass audience

press agentry
a form of public relations whose goal is to gain free publicity in the news media for a particular client, often a performer or artist

press councils
external advisory boards that review press performance and serve as a sounding board for public complaints against the press

prior restraint
censorship, through licensing, taxation, or another means, by which media are limited prior to being printed or distributed

PRSA
Public Relations Society of America; professional trade association established to elevate and professionalize the practice of PR

PSA
public-service announcements, print ads, or broadcast commercials for non-profit institutions, usually carried free of charge

pseudoevent
term coined by historian Daniel Boorstin to describe newsworthy events that have been purposively created to be filmed or reported by journalists; such events would not occur if the media weren't there to report them

psychographics
internal characteristics of audiences such as values, needs, beliefs, and interests

public relations
the broad "umbrella" of mass communications including publicity, opinion research, promotion, press agentry, advertising, lobbying, and political campaigning; frequently behind-the-scenes, subtle, ulterior communications

publics
vague, general entities; conglomerates of individuals who generally share a single geographic or demographic trait

Pulitzer prizes
journalistic and literary awards given annually to the nation's most outstanding writers; prizes were established by publisher Joseph Pulitzer

q

QUBE
Warner-Amex's sophisticated two-way cable television system, first introduced in Columbus, Ohio, in 1977

r

ratings
a measure of what percentage of all 81 million TV households happen to be watching a particular show at a given time in comparison with anything else people might choose to be doing

RCA
Radio Corporation of America, parent company to National Broadcasting Company (NBC)

rip 'n' read
practice of radio newscasters who take wire-service news directly from the teletype and read it over the air, without rehearsing or localizing the news

s

scatter plan
advertisers' practice of purchasing time for their commercials to appear during many different programs, at different times, on different networks

sedition
criticism of the state or rulers

selective contract adjustments
system by which theater owners who cooperate with distributors in promoting and running their films are given preferential treatment

semantic noise
interference within the communication process, within the human sources and receivers; psychological or language barriers

share
a measure of what percentage of all the TV sets that are turned on at a given time happen to be tuned to each show; thus, the "share of the audience" at any point in the day

shield laws
laws that protect journalists from having to tell law enforcement agencies the identity of their confidential sources

slogans
catchy capsule summaries of given products or political candidates, used in advertising or political campaigns

social responsibility
twentieth-century political theory holding that instruments of business or communications have responsibilities as well as freedoms

soft news
accounts of "insignificant" events or ideas, frequently intended to amuse or lend generalized insights into the human condition

Soviet totalitarianism
political theory holding that media are branches of the government, aiding the control of information and propaganda

SPJ/SDX
The Society of Professional Journalists, Sigma Delta Chi; largest national organization of working reporters and editors

split run
press run in which half of a given newspaper or magazine edition carries one form of an advertisement, the other half a different form, so relative appeal of the ads can be gauged

star system
Hollywood's method of promoting individual actors and actresses to assure an eager audience for their film, regardless of the quality of a given film

storyboards
static graphic depictions of television commercials, produced by ad agency creative staff

subliminal advertising
advertising intended to motivate consumers' unconscious minds; ad techniques include "embeds," hidden messages in verbal and written ads

subscription TV (STV)
over-the-air pay television, using satellite signals, for which viewers pay an additional fee each time they watch a special program, film, or sports event

subsequent punishment
a form of control over the media, subjecting them to regulations after publication; laws of libel, for instance, are used to remedy damages that media may have caused by publishing and distributing harmful news and commentary

superstation
television station that distributes its signals to a wide area by means of satellites

t

tabloid
technically, the half-sized magazine style newspaper; in common terms, *tabloid* refers to splashy, sensationalistic journalism

talking head
derogatory term to describe dull TV shows, usually on public television, filled with discussion and no action

teletext
information system encoded on an unused space on ordinary TV signal; offers a series of indexed information to viewers who must make selections with a control panel, but does not allow true interactive or consumer-generated information transfer

tie-in
marketing technique by which one medium (book, TV show, film, etc.) is produced and heavily promoted in conjunction with another medium

trade book
books produced for mass or general readership, usually sold through bookstores

u

UHF
Ultrahigh frequency allocations on the TV band; channels 14 through 83

unique selling proposition (USP)
advertising strategy based on the principle that advertising itself must establish in customers' minds whatever difference there is between essentially identical products. Usually the USP is a dramatization or exploitation of some characteristic of the product, even though other products share that characteristic

United Press (UP)
private news service noted for human interest, personalized journalism founded by E. W. Scripps in 1906. In 1958 it merged with Hearst's International News Service to become the UPI

United Press International (UPI)
formed in 1958 from United Press and International News Service; a private news service with clients

USICA
United States International Communication Agency (formerly the USIA); American government's official propaganda and information agency dealing with United States image abroad

v

value-added theory
Martin Mayer's theory that advertising adds a vague dimension to a product, such as raising the consumer's hopes or granting self-fulfillment

VDT
video display terminals; typewriter keyboards and cathode ray tube screens used by reporters and editors; part of the electronic phototypesetting system

VHF
Very high frequency allocations on the TV band; channels 2 through 13

videocassette recorder (VCR)
telecommunications equipment using videotape to record and play back live scenes or programs from television

videodiscs
prerecorded discs that, when played over a videodisc player and shown on a standard television set, allow a variety of viewer controls, such as slow motion, stop action, instant search, and reviewability

videotex
information system providing for consumer control over interactive cable or telephone lines; can be used for information storage and retrieval, in-home banking and shopping, and other interactive communications

w

wireless
system developed by Marconi for transmitting signals over the airwaves, without use of wires; early radios were called "wireless"

y

yellow journalism
sensationalistic journalism in the 1880–1900 period, typified by the circulation-building gimmicks of Hearst and Pulitzer

Bibliography

a

ABC Magazine Trend Report, 1974–78. Chicago: Audit Bureau of Circulations, February 1980.

Abel, Elie, ed. *What's News: The Media in American Society.* San Francisco: Institute for Contemporary Studies, 1981.

A. C. Nielsen Company. "Audience Research." In *TV Guide Almanac,* edited by L. Craig, T. Norback and Peter G. Norback. New York: Ballantine Books, 1980.

Adler, Richard, ed. *Understanding Television: Essays on Television as a Social and Cultural Force.* New York: Praeger, 1980.

Agee, Warren K. "The Joining of Journalists." *Quill,* November 1978.

Agee, Warren K.; Ault, Phillip; and Emery, Edwin, eds. *Perspectives on Mass Communications.* New York: Harper & Row, 1982.

American Newspaper Publishers Association. *Facts About Newspapers, '82.* Washington, D.C.: American Newspaper Publishers Association, April 1982.

American Society of Newspaper Editors and American Newspaper Publishers Association Foundation. *Free Press & Fair Trial.* Washington, D.C.: The Newspaper Center, 1982.

Ames, William E., and Teeter, Dwight L. "Politics, Economics, and the Mass Media." In *Mass Media and the National Experience,* edited by Ronald T. Farrar and John D. Stevens, p. 46. New York: Harper & Row, 1971.

Andrews, Peter. "The Birth of the Talkies." *Saturday Review,* 12 November 1977.

Armstrong, David. *A Trumpet to Arms: The Alternative Press in America.* Los Angeles: Torcher, 1981.

Atwan, Robert; Orton, Barry; and Vesterman, William, eds. *American Mass Media: Industries and Issues.* New York: Random House, 1978.

b

Bagdikian, Ben H. "The Press and Its Crisis of Identity." In *Mass Media in a Free Society,* edited by Warren K. Agee. Lawrence, Kansas: University Press of Kansas, 1969.

Bagdikian, Ben H. *The Information Machines: Their Impact on Men and the Media.* New York: Harper & Row, 1971.

Bagdikian, Ben H. *The Effete Conspiracy and Other Crimes by the Press.* New York: Harper & Row, 1972.

Bagdikian, Ben H. "Newspaper Mergers—The Final Phase," *Columbia Journalism Review,* March/April 1977.

Baird, Kathleen Hunt. "P.M. to A.M.: Is a Trend Building?" *Presstime* (journal of the American Newspaper Publishers Association), December 1979.

Baker, Kent. "Cable TV Reshapes Sports." *The Press,* June 1982.

Barnouw, Erik. *A Tower in Babel: A History of Broadcasting in the United States to 1933.* New York: Oxford University Press, 1966.

Barnouw, Erik. *The Golden Web: A History of Broadcasting in the United States from 1933 to 1953.* New York: Oxford University Press, 1968.

Barnouw, Erik. *The Image Empire: A History of Broadcasting in the United States Since 1953.* New York: Oxford University Press, 1970.

Barnouw, Erik. *Tube of Plenty: The Evolution of American Television.* New York: Oxford University Press, 1975.

Baus, Herbert M., and Ross, William B. *Politics Battle Plan.* New York: Macmillan, 1968.

Bell, D. *The Coming of Post-industrial Society.* New York: Basic Books, 1976.

Bell, D., ed. *Toward the Year 2000: Work in Progress.* Boston: Beacon Press, 1967.

Bergreen, Laurence. "Just Don't Get Booked After the Animal Act." *TV Guide,* 17 March 1979.

Bernays, Edward. *Crystallizing Public Opinion.* New York: Liveright, 1961.

Bernstein, Carl, and Woodward, Bob. *All the President's Men.* New York: Simon & Schuster, 1974.

Bettinghaus, Erwin P. *Persuasive Communication.* New York: Holt, Rinehart & Winston, 1973.

Bittner, John R. *Mass Communication: An Introduction.* 3d ed. Englewood Cliffs, N.J.: Prentice-Hall, 1980.

Bittner, John R. *Professional Broadcasting: An Introduction.* Englewood Cliffs, N.J.: Prentice-Hall, 1981.

Blake, Reed H., and Haroldsen, Edwin O. *A Taxonomy of Concepts in Communication.* New York: Hastings House, 1975.

Blumler, Jay G., and Katz, Elihu, eds. *The Uses of Mass Communications: Current Perspectives on Gratification Research.* Beverly Hills, Calif.: SAGE, 1974.

Boorstin, Daniel J. *The Image: A Guide to Pseudo-Events in America.* New York: Harper & Row, Harper Colophon Books, 1964.

Bower, Robert T. *Television and the Public.* New York: Holt, Rinehart & Winston, 1973.

Boyd-Barrett, Oliver. *The International News Agencies.* Beverly Hills, Calif.: SAGE, 1980.

Brown, Charlene; Brown, Trevor; and Rivers, William. *The Media and the People.* New York: Holt, Rinehart & Winston, 1978.

Brown, J. A. C. *Techniques of Persuasion: From Propaganda to Brainwashing.* Harmondsworth, Middlesex, England: Penguin Books, 1963.

Brown, Les. *Keeping Your Eye on Television.* New York: The Pilgrim Press, 1979.

Burgess, Anthony. "TV Is Debasing Your Lives." *TV Guide,* 18 September 1982.

c

"Cable Advertising in First Quarter: WTBS Gets Half." *Broadcasting,* 10 May 1982.

"Cable Opportunities Beyond the Horizon of Entertainment." *Broadcasting,* 10 May 1982.

"Cable Restraints Dropped." *NAB Radio/TV Highlights,* 28 July 1980.

"Cable Throws a Party in Las Vegas." *Broadcasting,* 10 May 1982.

Cantor, Muriel G. *Prime-Time Television: Content and Control.* Beverly Hills, Calif.: SAGE, 1980.

Carey, James W. "A Plea for the University Tradition." Association for Education in Journalism presidential address, Seattle, August 1978, published in *Journalism Quarterly,* Winter 1978.

Cassata, Mary B., and Asante, Molefi K., eds. *Mass Communication: Principles and Practices.* New York: Macmillan, 1979.

Chiu, Tony. "MSN, MPC and OPT." *Panorama,* March 1980.

Christians, Clifford G. "Mass Media Ethics: An Analysis of the Academic Literature." Unpublished paper presented to Association for Education in Journalism, College Park, Md., August 1976.

Cirino, Robert. *Don't Blame the People: How the News Media Use Bias, Distortion, and Censorship to Manipulate Public Opinion.* Los Angeles: Diversity Press, 1971.

Cole, Barry, ed. *Television Today: A Close-Up View; Readings from TV Guide.* New York: Oxford University Press, 1981.

Commission on the Freedom of the Press. *A Free and Responsible Press.* Chicago: University of Chicago Press, 1947.

Compaine, Benjamin M. *The Book Industry in Transition: An Economic Analysis of Book Distribution and Marketing.* White Plains, N.Y.: Knowledge Industry Publications, 1978.

Compaine, Benjamin M., ed. *Who Owns the Media? Concentration of Ownership in the Mass Communications Industry.* New York: Harmony Books, 1979.

Comstock, George. *Television in America.* Beverly Hills, Calif.: SAGE, 1980.

Comstock, G.; Chaffee, S.; Katzman, N.; McCombs, M.; and Roberts, R. *Television and Human Behavior.* New York: Columbia University Press, 1978.

Cook, Anthony. "The Peculiar Economics of Television." *TV Guide,* 14 June 1980.

"Could the Progressive Help Make Possible a Nuclear Holocaust?" *Quill,* April 1979.

Cowan, Geoffrey. *See No Evil.* New York: Simon & Schuster, 1979.

Crouse, Timothy. *The Boys on the Bus.* New York: Random House, 1973.

Cullen, Maurice R., Jr. *Mass Media and the First Amendment: An Introduction to the Issues, Problems, and Practices.* Dubuque, Iowa: Wm. C. Brown, 1981.

Cutlip, Scott M., and Center, Allen H. *Effective Public Relations.* 5th ed. Englewood Cliffs, N.J.: Prentice-Hall, 1978.

d

Danna, Sammy R. "The Press-Radio War." *Freedom of Information Center Report No. 213.* Columbia, Mo.: University of Missouri School of Journalism, December 1968.

Davis, Dennis K., and Baran, Stanley J. *Mass Communication in Everyday Life.* Belmont, Calif.: Wadsworth, 1980.

Davison, E. Phillips, and Yu, Frederick T. C. *Mass Communication Research: Major Issues and Future Directions.* New York: Praeger, 1974.

DeFleur, Melvin L., and Ball-Rokeach, Sandra. *Theories of Mass Communication.* 4th ed. New York: Longman, 1981.

DeFleur, Melvin L., and Dennis, Everette E. *Understanding Mass Communication.* Boston: Houghton Mifflin, 1981.

De Forest, Lee. *Television: Today and Tomorrow.* New York: Dial Press, 1942.

Denisoff, R. Serge. *Solid Gold: The Popular Record Industry.* New York: Transaction Books, 1975.

Dennis, Everett E. *The Media Society.* Dubuque, Iowa: Wm. C. Brown, 1978.

Dennis, Everette E., and Ismach, Arnold. *Reporting Processes and Practices.* Belmont, Calif.: Wadsworth, 1981.

Dennis, Everette E.; Ismach, Arnold; and Gillmor, Donald, eds. *Enduring Issues in Mass Communication.* St. Paul, Minn.: West, 1978.

Desmond, Robert W. *The Information Process: World News Reporting to the Twentieth Century.* Iowa City: Iowa State University Press, 1978.

Dessauer, John P. *Book Publishing: What It Is, What It Does.* New York: Bowker, 1974.

Dessauer, John P. "The 1977 Census of Book Publishing Reveals Significant Industry Expansion." *Publishers Weekly,* 9 July 1979.

Deutsch, Linda. "Publishers Finance Lavish Book Promotions." *The Salt Lake Tribune,* 28 April 1978.

e

Earley, Steven C. *An Introduction to American Movies.* New York: New American Library, 1979.

Edwards, Kenneth. "Teletext Broadcasting in U.S. Endorsed by FCC." *Editor & Publisher,* 18 November 1978.

Edwards, Kenneth. "Information Without Limit Electronically." In *Readings in Mass Communication,* 4th ed., edited by Michael Emery and Ted Curtis Smythe. Dubuque, Iowa: Wm. C. Brown, 1980.

Efron, Edith. *The News Twisters.* Los Angeles: Nash, 1971.

Ellul, Jacques. *The Technological Society.* New York: Alfred A. Knopf, 1964.

Ellul, Jacques. *Propaganda: The Formation of Men's Attitudes.* New York: Alfred A. Knopf, 1965.

Emery, Edwin, and Emery, Michael. *The Press and America: An Interpretive History of the Mass Media.* 4th ed. Englewood Cliffs, N.J.: Prentice-Hall, 1978.

Emery, Michael, and Smythe, Ted Curtis, eds. *Readings in Mass Communication,* 5th ed. Dubuque, Iowa: Wm. C. Brown, 1983.

Emery, Walter B. *Broadcasting and Government.* East Lansing, Mich.: Michigan State University Press, 1971.

Engel, Jack. *Advertising: The Process and Practice.* New York: McGraw-Hill, 1980.

Epstein, Edward Jay. *News From Nowhere.* New York: Random House, 1973.

Evans, Harold. *Pictures on a Page.* Belmont, Calif.: Wadsworth, 1979.

f

Fadiman, William. *Hollywood Now.* London: Thames and Hudson, 1973.

Fang, Irving E. *Television News, Radio News.* Minneapolis, Minn.: Rada Press, 1980.

Farrar, Ronald T., and Stevens, John D., eds. *Mass Media and the National Experience.* New York: Harper & Row, 1971.

Fascell, Dante B., ed. *International News: Freedom Under Attack.* Beverly Hills, Calif.: SAGE, 1979.

Fischer, Heinz-Dietrich, and Merrill, John C., eds. *International and Intercultural Communication.* New York: Hastings House, 1976.

Fletcher, Alan D. "City Magazines Find a Niche in the Media Marketplace." *Journalism Quarterly.* Winter 1977.

"FM Growth Continues." *Broadcasting,* 16 June 1980.

Foster, Eugene S. *Understanding Broadcasting.* Reading, Mass.: Addison-Wesley, 1978.

Francois, William E. *Mass Media Law and Regulation.* 3d ed. Columbus, Ohio: Grid, 1982.

Franklin, Marc A. *The First Amendment and the Fourth Estate.* Mineola, N.Y.: Foundation Press, 1981.

Friedman, Jack. "Suddenly Cable Is Sexy." *TV Guide,* 19 July 1980.

Friedman, Jack. "Radio, Magazines are Examples for Cable Advertising to Follow, Says Warner's Schneider." *Broadcasting,* 11 August 1980.

Furlong, William Barry. "The Monster Is Lurking Just Over the Hill." *Panorama,* March 1980.

g

Gans, Herbert J. *Deciding What's News: A Study of CBS Evening News, NBC Nightly News, Newsweek and Time.* New York: Pantheon Books, 1979.

Genovese, Margaret. "Transmission by Satellite: Pages Today, Wire News Tomorrow, Ads in the Future." *Presstime,* October 1980.

Gerbner, George, ed. *Mass Media Policies in Changing Cultures.* New York: Wiley, 1977.

Gillmor, Donald M. "Press Councils in America." In *Enduring Issues in Mass Communication,* edited by Everette E. Dennis, Arnold H. Ismach, and Donald M. Gillmor. St. Paul, Minn.: West, 1978.

Ginsburg, Douglas H. *Regulation of Broadcasting: Law and Policy Towards Radio, Television, and Cable Communications.* St. Paul, Minn.: West, 1979.

Goldsen, Rose. "Why Television Advertising Is Deceptive and Unfair." *ETC.,* Winter 1978.

Goldsmith, Alfred N., and Lescarboura, Austin C. *This Thing Called Broadcasting.* New York: Henry Holt, 1930.

Goldstein, Seth. "Cable and Pay-TV." *Panorama,* April 1980.

Gordon, David. "Chicago Journalists and Ethical Principles." *Mass Comm Review,* Fall 1979.

Gramling, Oliver. *AP: The Story of News.* New York: Farrar and Rinehart, 1940.

Greenfield, Jeff. "TV Is Not the World." *Columbia Journalism Review,* May/June 1978.

Grossman, Michael B., and Kumar, Martha J. *Portraying the President.* Baltimore: Johns Hopkins University Press, 1981.

Gumpert, Gary, and Cathcard, Robert, eds. *Inter/Media: Interpersonal Communication in a Media World,* 2d ed. New York: Oxford University Press, 1982.

h

Hafer, W. Keith, and White, Gordon E. *Advertising Writing.* St. Paul, Minn.: West, 1977.

Halberstam, David. *The Powers That Be.* New York: Alfred A. Knopf, 1979.

Harris, Louis. "Public Prefers News to Pablum." *Deseret News.* 1 Jan. 1978.

Head, Sydney W. *Broadcasting in America.* Boston: Houghton Mifflin, 1978.

Hennessy, Bernard. *Public Opinion.* 3d ed. Scituate, Mass.: Duxbury Press, 1975.

Hess, Stephen. *The Washington Reporters.* Washington, D.C.: Brookings Institute, 1981.

Hickey, Neil. "Goodbye '70s, Hello '80s." *TV Guide,* 5 January 1980.

Hickey, Neil. "Read Any Good Television Lately?" *TV Guide,* 16 February 1980.

Hiebert, Ray E., and Spitzer, Carlton, eds. *The Voice of Government.* New York: Wiley, 1968.

Hill, Doug. "Will the Latest in Home Video Empty the Movie Theaters?" *TV Guide,* 20 March 1982.

Hohenberg, John. *The News Media: A Journalist Looks at His Profession.* New York: Holt, Rinehart & Winston, 1968.

Holm, Wilton R. "Management Looks at the Future." In *The Movie Business: American Film Industry Practice,* edited by A. W. Bleum and J. E. Squire. New York: Hastings House, 1972.

Hulteng, John L. *The Messenger's Motives: Ethical Theory in the Mass Media.* Englewood Cliffs, N.J.: Prentice-Hall, 1976.

Hulteng, John L. *The News Media: What Makes Them Tick?* Englewood Cliffs, N.J.: Prentice-Hall, 1979.

Hutchinson, Thomas H. *Here is Television: Your Window to the World.* New York: Dial Press, 1946.

Hynds, Ernest C. *American Newspapers in the 1980s.* New York: Hastings House, 1980.

i

Institute for Propaganda Analysis. "How to Detect Propaganda." *Propaganda Analysis, I.* November 1937.

j

Janowitz, Morris, and Hirsch, Paul, eds. *Reader in Public Opinion and Mass Communication.* 3d ed. New York: Free Press, 1981.

Johnstone, John W. C.; Slawski, E. J.; and Bowman, William W. *The News People: A Sociological Portrait of Journalists and Their Work.* Urbana, Ill.: University of Illinois Press, 1976.

Jory, Tom. "PBS and Corporate Underwriting." *Salt Lake Tribune,* 28 May 1978.

Jowett, Garth. *Film: The Democratic Art.* Boston: Little, Brown, 1976.

Jowett, Garth, and Linton, James M. *Movies as Mass Communication.* Beverly Hills, Calif.: SAGE, 1980.

k

Kahn, Frank J., ed. *Documents of American Broadcasting.* 3d ed. Englewood Cliffs, N.J.: Prentice-Hall, 1978.

Katz, S. N., ed. *A Brief Narrative of the Case and Trial of John Peter Zenger.* Cambridge: Harvard University Press, 1963.

Kilpatrick, James J. "Time to Announce, 'We've Won.'" Syndicated column, *Deseret News,* 9 April 1979.

Kleppner, Otto. *Advertising Procedure.* 7th ed. Englewood Cliffs, N.J.: Prentice-Hall, 1979.

Knight, Arthur. *The Liveliest Art: A Panoramic History of the Movies,* rev. ed. New York: New American Library, 1979.

Kowinski, William. "Talk Back to Television." *Penthouse,* February 1979.

Kraus, Sidney, and Davis, Dennis. *The Effects of Mass Communication on Political Behavior.* University Park, Pa.: Penn State Press, 1976.

Krieghbaum, Hillier. *Pressures on the Press.* New York: Crowell, 1972.

l

La Brie, Henry G., III, ed. *Perspectives on the Black Press.* Kennebunkport, Me.: Mercer House, 1974.

Lachenbruch, David. "The Coming Videodisc Battle." *Panorama,* April 1980.

Lachenbruch, David. "A Buyer's Guide to Videodisc Players." *TV Guide,* 6 March 1982.

Lancaster, Hal. "Mr. McCullough Plans a Little Celebration for a Certain Bridge." *Wall Street Journal,* 5 October 1971.

"Learning to Live with TV." *Time,* 28 May 1979.

Lenhart, Maria. "The Author as Peddler." *Deseret News,* 4 August 1979.

Lerner, Max. "The Shame of the Professions." *Saturday Review,* 1 November 1975.

Lesly, Philip, ed. *Public Relations Handbook.* Englewood Cliffs, N.J.: Prentice-Hall, 1978.

Levy, Leonard. *Legacy of Suppression: Freedom of Speech and Press in Early American History.* Cambridge, Mass.: Harvard University Press, 1960.

Levy, Leonard. *Freedom of the Press from Zenger to Jefferson.* Indianapolis: Bobbs-Merrill, 1966.

Levy, Mark R. "The Audience Experience with Television News." *Journalism Monographs,* no. 55, April 1978.

Levy, Mark R. "Home Video Recorders and TV Program Preference." Paper presented to the Mass Communications and Society Division, Association for Education in Journalism Annual Conference, Boston, Mass., August 1980.

Lichter, S. Robert, and Rothman, Stanley. "The Media Elite." *Public Opinion.* October/November 1981.

Lichty, Lawrence H., and Topping, Malachi C. *American Broadcasting: A Sourcebook on the History of Radio and Television.* New York: Hastings House, 1975.

Liebling, A. J. *The Wayward Pressman.* New York: Doubleday, 1948.

Liebling, A. J. *The Press.* New York: Ballantine, 1964.

Lippmann, Walter. *Public Opinion.* New York: Harcourt, Brace, 1922.

"Low Power Television Pioneers Begin a New Broadcast Era." *Broadcasting.* 17 May 1982.

Lynes, Russell. "The Electronic Express." *TV Guide,* 24 February 1968.

m

Mabry, Drake. "Editors vs. Syndicates." *Presstime,* January 1982.

McCombs, Maxwell E., and Becker, Lee. *Using Mass Communication Theory.* Englewood Cliffs, N.J.: Prentice-Hall, 1979.

MacDonald, J. Fred. *Don't Touch That Dial! Radio Programming in American Life 1920–1960.* Chicago: Nelson Hall, 1979.

MacDougall, A. Kent. "Magazines: Fighting for a Place in the Market." *Los Angeles Times,* 9 April 1978.

McGinniss, Joe. *The Selling of the President.* New York: Trident, 1969.

McKenna, George, ed. *Media Voices: Debating Critical Issues in Mass Media.* Guilford, Conn.: Dushkin Publishing Group, 1982.

McLuhan, Marshall. *Understanding Media: The Extensions of Man.* New York: McGraw-Hill, 1965.

McLuhan, Marshall. *The Gutenberg Galaxy.* Toronto: The University of Toronto Press, 1967.

McQuail, Dennis. *Towards a Sociology of Mass Communication.* London: Collier-Macmillan, 1969.

Madison, Charles A. *Book Publishing in America.* New York: McGraw-Hill, 1966.

Malloy, Michael T. "Newspapers May Some Day Let You Pick News You Want." *National Observer.* 21 February 1976.

Mankekar, D. R. *One Way Free Flow; Neo-colonialism Via News Media.* New Delhi: Clarion Books, 1978.

Mankiewicz, Frank, and Swerdlow, Joel. *Remote Control: Television and the Manipulation of American Life.* New York: Ballantine Books, 1978.

Marzolf, Marion. *Up From the Footnote: A History of Women Journalists.* New York: Hastings House, 1977.

Maslow, Abraham. *Toward a Psychology of Being.* 2d ed. New York: D. Van Nostrand, 1968.

Maslow, Abraham. *Motivation and Personality.* New York: Harper & Row, 1970.

Masmoudi, M. "The New World Information Order." *Journal of Communication,* Spring 1979.

Mast, Gerald. *A Short History of the Movies.* New York: Bobbs-Merrill, 1976.

Mayer, Martin. *Madison Avenue U.S.A.* New York: Harper & Brothers, 1958.

Mayer, Martin. *About Television.* New York: Harper & Row, 1972.

"Media Tie-ins." *Publishers Weekly,* 11 April 1980.

Merrill, John C. *The Imperative of Freedom: A Philosophy of Journalistic Autonomy.* New York: Hastings House, 1974.

Merrill, John C., and Fisher, Harold A. *The World's Great Dailies: Profiles of 50 Newspapers.* New York: Hastings House, 1980.

Merrill, John C., and Lowenstein, Ralph L. *Media, Messages, and Men.* 2d ed. New York: Longman, 1979.

Mogel, Leonard. *The Magazine: Everything You Need to Know to Make It in the Magazine Business.* Englewood Cliffs, N.J.: Prentice-Hall, 1979.

Monaco, James. *How to Read a Film: The Art, Technology, Language, History, and Theory of Film and Media.* 2d ed. New York: Oxford University Press, 1981.

Morris, Joe Alex. *Deadline Every Minute: The Story of the United Press.* New York: Doubleday, 1957.

n

"NCTA Report on Local Cable Programming." *Broadcasting,* 1 September 1980.

Nelson, Harold L. *Freedom of the Press from Hamilton to the Warren Court.* Indianapolis: Bobbs-Merrill, 1966.

Nelson, Harold L., and Teeter, Dwight L. *Law of Mass Communications.* 4th ed. Mineola, N.Y.: Foundation Press, 1982.

Nelson, Mark. "Newspaper Ethics Codes and the NLRB." *Freedom of Information Center Report No. 353.* Columbia, Mo.: University of Missouri School of Journalism, May 1976.

Nelson, Roy Paul, and Hulteng, John. *The Fourth Estate: An Informal Appraisal of the News and Information Media.* New York: Harper & Row, 1971.

Newcomb, Horace, ed. *Television: The Critical View.* New York: Oxford University Press, 1982.

Newsom, Clark. "The Beat Goes on for P.M.s to A.M.s." *Presstime,* December 1980.

Newsom, Doug, and Scott, Alan. *This Is PR: The Realities of Public Relations.* Belmont, Calif.: Wadsworth, 1981.

Newsom, Doug, and Seigfried, Tom. *Writing in Public Relations Practice.* Belmont, Calif.: Wadsworth, 1981.

"Newspapers Are Public's Favorite Ad Medium." *Editor & Publisher,* 29 March 1975.

Nimmo, Dan. *Political Communication and Public Opinion in America.* Santa Monica, Calif.: Goodyear Publishing, 1978.

o

Ogilvy, David. *Confessions of an Advertising Man.* New York: Atheneum, 1963.

p

Packard, Vance. *The Hidden Persuaders.* New York: Pocket Books, 1968.

Panitt, Merrill. "Do the Networks Have a Death Wish?" *TV Guide,* 18 September 1982.

Pearce, Alan. "How the Networks Have Turned News Into Dollars." *TV Guide,* 23 August 1980.

Pember, Don R. *Mass Media in America.* 3d ed. Palo Alto, Calif.: SRA, 1981.

Pember, Don R. *Mass Media Law.* 2d ed. Dubuque, Iowa: Wm. C. Brown, 1981.

Petersen, Clarence. *The Bantam Story: Thirty Years of Paperback Publishing.* 2d ed. New York: Bantam Books, 1975.

Peterson, Theodore. *Magazines in the Twentieth Century.* Urbana, Ill.: University of Illinois Press, 1956.

Peterson, Theodore. "The Social Responsibility of the Press." In *Four Theories of the Press,* by Fred S. Siebert, Theodore Peterson, and Wilbur Schramm. Urbana, Ill.: University of Illinois Press, 1963.

Pope, Leroy. "Pay TV, After a Shaky Infancy, Is Off and Rolling." *Deseret News,* 1 August 1979.

Postman, Neil. *Teaching as a Conserving Activity.* New York: Delacorte Press, 1979.

Powers, Ron. *The Newscasters.* New York: St. Martin's, 1977.

Powers, Ron. "Where Have the News Analysts Gone?" *TV Guide,* 8 Oct. 1980.

"Predictions: Changes to Conjure With." *Publishers Weekly,* 6 August 1979.

Price, Jonathan. *The Best Thing on TV: Commercials.* New York: Penguin Books, 1978.

"Public TV Study Says VCR's Don't Detract from Viewing Levels." *Broadcasting,* 21 July 1980.

"Putting Social Trends to Use in Cable." *Broadcasting,* 10 May 1982.

q

Qualter, Terrence H. *Propaganda and Psychological Warfare.* New York: Random House, 1962.

"Qube Report Card." *Broadcasting,* 31 May 1982.

r

Rambo, C. David. "In the Race for News, Technology Leads at the Wires." *Presstime,* August 1981.

Randall, Richard S. "Censorship: From *The Miracle* to *Deep Throat.*" In *The American Film Industry,* edited by Tino Balio. Madison, Wisc.: The University of Wisconsin Press, 1976.

"Recording Industry a 4-Billion-Dollar Hit." *U.S. News & World Report,* 30 April 1979.

Reston, James. *The Artillery of the Press.* New York: Harper & Row, 1967.

Righter, Rosemary. *Whose News? Politics, the Press, and the Third World.* London: Times Books, 1978.

Rivers, William L.; Blankenburg, William B.; Starck, Kenneth; and Reeves, Earl. *Backtalk: Press Councils in America.* San Francisco: Canfield Press, 1972.

Rivers, William L., and Dennis, Everette E. *Other Voices: The New Journalism in America.* San Francisco: Canfield, 1974.

Rivers, William L., and Nyhan, Michael J., eds. *Aspen Notebook on Government and Media.* New York: Praeger, 1973.

Rivers, William L.; Schramm, Wilbur; and Christians, Clifford G. *Responsibility in Mass Communication.* New York: Harper & Row, 1980.

Robinson, G. O. *Communications for Tomorrow.* New York: Praeger, 1978.

Robinson, Steve. "Pulitzers: Was the Mirage a Deception?" *Columbia Journalism Review,* July–August 1979.

Rodman, George, ed. *Mass Media Issues: Analysis and Debate.* Chicago: SRA, 1982.

Rokeach, Milton. *The Open and Closed Mind.* New York: Basic Books, 1960.

Rokeach, Milton. "Images of the Consumer's Mind On and Off Madison Avenue." *ETC.,* September 1964.

Rokeach, Milton. *Beliefs, Attitudes, and Values.* San Francisco: Jossey-Bass, 1968.

Rokeach, Milton. *The Nature of Human Values.* New York: Free Press, 1973.

Rose, Ernest D. "How the U.S. Heard About Pearl Harbor." *Journal of Broadcasting,* Vol. 5, no. 4, Fall 1961.

Rosenberg, Bernard, and White, David M., eds. *Mass Culture Revisited.* Princeton, N.J.: Van Nostrand Reinhold, 1971.

s

Salisbury, David. "The Third 'Industrial Revolution': Robot Factories and Electronic Offices." *Christian Science Monitor,* 8 October 1980.

Sandage, Charles H.; Fryburger, Vernon; and Rotzoll, Kim. *Advertising Theory and Practice.* Homewood, Ill.: Irwin, 1979.

Sanders, Keith P. "What Are Daily Newspapers Doing to be Responsive to Readers' Criticisms?, A Survey of U.S. Daily Newspaper Accountability Systems." In *News Research for Better Newspapers,* edited by Galen Rarick, American Newspaper Publishers Association Foundation. Washington, D.C., 1975.

Sanders, Keith P., and Chang, Won H. "Codes: The Ethical Free-for-All; A Survey of Journalists' Opinions About Freebies." *Freedom of Information Foundation Series, No. 7,* March 1977.

Sanders, Keith P., and Chang, Won H. "Freebies: Achille's Heel of Journalism Ethics?" Unpublished paper presented to Association for Education in Journalism, Mass Communication and Society Division, Logan, Utah, 30 March 1979.

Sandman, Peter; Rubin, David; and Sachsman, David. *Media: An Introductory Analysis of American Mass Communications.* 3d ed. Englewood Cliffs, N.J.: Prentice-Hall, Inc., 1982.

Seldes, Gilbert. *The New Mass Media: Challenge to a Free Society.* Washington, D.C.: American Association of University Women, 1957.

Schramm, Wilbur, and Lerner, Daniel, eds. *Communication and Change: The Last Ten Years— and the Next.* Honolulu: University of Hawaii Press, 1976.

Schramm, Wilbur; Lyle, J.; and Parker, E. *Television in the Lives of Our Children.* Stanford, Calif.: Stanford University Press, 1961.

Schramm, Wilbur, and Porter, William E. *Men, Women, Messages, and Media: Understanding Human Communication.* 2d ed. New York: Harper & Row, 1982.

Schramm, Wilbur, and Roberts, Donald F., eds. *The Process and Effects of Mass Communication.* Urbana, Ill.: University of Illinois Press, 1971.

Seitel, Fraser P. *The Practice of Public Relations*. New York: Charles E. Merrill, 1980.

Sellers, Leonard, and Rivers, William. *Mass Media Issues*. Englewood Cliffs, N.J.: Prentice-Hall, 1977.

Severin, Werner, and Tankard, James, Jr. *Communication Theories: Origins, Methods, Uses*. New York: Hastings House, 1979.

Shaw, David. "Book Biz Best-sellers—Are They Really? Laziness and Chicanery Play Major Roles." *Los Angeles Times,* 24 October 1976.

Shaw, David. "Newspapers Challenged as Never Before." *Los Angeles Times* 26 November 1976.

Shaw, David. *Journalism Today*. New York: Harper's College Press, 1977.

Shaw, Donald L. "Technology: Freedom for What?" In *Mass Media and the National Experience*. Edited by Ronald T. Farrar and John D. Stevens. New York: Harper & Row, 1971.

Siebert, Fredrick S. *Freedom of the Press in England 1476–1776*. Urbana, Ill.: University of Illinois Press, 1952.

Siebert, Fredrick S.; Peterson, Theodore; and Schramm, Wilbur. *Four Theories of the Press*. Urbana, Ill.: University of Illinois Press, 1963.

Simon, Raymond. *Public Relations: Concepts and Practices*. 2d ed. Columbus, Ohio: Grid Publishing, 1980.

Sinclair, Upton. *The Brass Check: A Study of American Journalism*. Pasadena, Calif.: published by the author, 1920.

Sklar, Robert. *Prime Time America: Life On and Behind the Television Screen*. New York: Oxford University Press, 1981.

Skornia, Harry J. *Television and Society: An Inquest and Agenda for Improvement*. New York: McGraw-Hill, 1965.

Small, William. *To Kill a Messenger*. New York: Hastings House, 1972.

Smith, Anthony. *The Newspaper: An International History*. London: Thames and Hudson, 1979.

Smith, Anthony. *Goodbye Gutenberg: The Newspaper Revolution of the 1980s*. New York: Oxford University Press, 1980.

Smith, Desmond. "What Is America's Secret Weapon in the Energy Crisis? Your Television Set." *Panorama,* April 1980.

Smith, F. Leslie. *Perspectives on Radio and Television: An Introduction to Broadcasting in the United States*. New York: Harper & Row, 1979.

Smith, F. Leslie. "The 'Praise The Lord' Television Network." *BM/E* (Broadcast Management/ Engineering), March 1980.

Smythe, Ted C., and Mastroianni, George A. *Issues in Broadcasting: Radio, Television, and Cable*. Palo Alto, Calif.: Mayfield, 1975.

Stanley, Robert H., and Ramsey, Ruth G. "Television News: Format as a Form of Censorship." *ETC.,* Winter 1978.

Steigerwald, B. "Videodisc: Ultimate Weapon or Video Revolution?" *Los Angeles Times,* 24 March 1981.

Steinberg, Charles. *The Communicative Arts*. New York: Hastings House, 1970.

Steiner, Gary A. *The People Look at Television*. New York: Alfred A. Knopf, 1963.

Stempel, Guido H., and Westley, Bruce H., eds. *Research Methods in Mass Communication*. Englewood Cliffs, N.J.: Prentice-Hall, 1981.

Stephenson, William. *The Play Theory of Mass Communications*. Chicago: University of Chicago Press, 1967.

Sterling, Christopher. "Trends in Daily Newspaper and Broadcast Ownership, 1922–1970," *Journalism Quarterly,* Summer 1975.

Sterling, Christopher H. "Television and Radio Broadcasting." In *Who Owns the Media? Concentration of Ownership in the Mass Communications Industry,* edited by Benjamin M. Compaine. New York: Harmony Books, 1979.

Sterling, Christopher H., and Haight, Timothy R. "Characteristics of Newspaper Readers." Tables in *The Mass Media: Aspen Institute Guide to Communication Industry Trends*. New York: Praeger, 1978.

Sterling, Christopher H., and Kittross, John M. *Stay Tuned: A Concise History of American Broadcasting*. Belmont, Calif.: Wadsworth, 1978.

Sterritt, David. "Movie Ratings—From G to X: Are They Out of Focus?" *Christian Science Monitor*. 16 September 1982.

Stevens, John D. "Freedom of Expression: New Dimensions." In *Mass Media and the National Experience,* edited by Ronald T. Farrar and John D. Stevens. New York: Harper & Row, 1971.

Stevenson, Robert L., and White, Kathryn P. "The Cumulative Audience of Network Television News." *Journalism Quarterly,* Autumn 1980.

Summers, Harrison B.; Summers, Robert E.; and Pennybacker, John H. *Broadcasting and the Public*. 2d ed. Belmont, Calif.: Wadsworth, 1978.

Swain, Bruce. *Reporter's Ethics*. Ames, Iowa: Iowa State University Press, 1978.

t

"Talking Back to the Tube." *Newsweek,* 25 February 1980.

Tannenbaum, Percy H., ed. *The Entertainment Functions of Television*. Hillsdale, N.J: Lawrence Erlbaum Associates, 1981.

Tebbel, John. *Compact History of the American Newspaper*. New York: Hawthorne, 1969.

Tebbel, John. *The American Magazine: A Compact History*. New York: Hawthorne, 1969.

Tebbel, John. *A History of Book Publishing in the United States*. New York: Bowker. Four Volumes: 1972, 1975, 1978, and 1981.

Tebbel, John. *The Media in America.* New York: Crowell, 1975.

Thayer, Lee, ed. *Ethics, Morality and the Media.* New York: Hastings House, 1980.

"The New Face of TV News." *Time,* 25 February 1980.

(The) Roper Organization, Inc. *Public Perceptions of Television and Other Mass Media: A Twenty-year Review, 1959–1978.* New York: Television Information Office, 1979.

Tuchman, Gay. *Making News.* New York: Free Press, 1978.

"Turn on Your Neighbor." *Panorama,* April 1980, p. 21.

U

Udell, Jon G., ed. *The Economics of the American Newspaper.* New York: Hastings House, 1978.

United Press International. "Curl Up With a Good Movie." *Deseret News,* 30 July 1979.

United Press International. "Computers Make Many Functionally Illiterate." *Logan* (Utah) *Herald Journal,* 24 September 1980.

"Up, Up and Away for Radio Networking." *Broadcasting.* 17 March 1980.

"UPI is Sold to Media News Corp." *Logan* (Utah) *Herald Journal,* 3 June 1982.

U.S. Government. *The Global 2000 Report to the President: Entering the Twenty-first Century* (Vol. 1). Washington, D.C.: Government Printing Office, 1980.

V

Valenti, Jack. "The Movie Rating System." In *Mass Communication: Principles and Practices,* edited by Mary B. Cassata and Molefi K. Asante. New York: Macmillan, 1979.

Valenti, Jack. "The Politics of Cable." *Media Digest,* Spring 1980.

"Videodisc." *Media Digest,* Spring 1980.

W

Waters, Harry F. "What TV Does to Kids." *Newsweek,* 21 February 1977.

Weber, Ronald, ed. *The Reporter as Artist.* New York: Hastings House, 1974.

Wells, Alan, ed. *Mass Media and Society.* Palo Alto, Calif.: Mayfield, 1979.

Whetmore, Edward Jay. *Mediamerica: Form, Content, and Consequences of Mass Communication.* 2d ed. Belmont, Calif.: Wadsworth, 1982.

Wicker, Tom. *On Press.* New York: Viking, 1978.

Williams, Frederick. *The Communications Revolution.* Beverly Hills, Calif.: SAGE, 1982.

Williams, Lynne. *Medium or Message?* Woodbury, N.Y: Barron's Educational Series Inc., 24 May 1971.

Williams, Martin. *TV: The Casual Art.* New York: Oxford University Press, 1982.

Wilson, Sloan. *The Man in the Gray Flannel Suit.* New York: Pocket Books, 1967.

Winick, Mariann Pezzella, and Winick, Charles. *The Television Experience: What Children See.* Beverly Hills, Calif.: SAGE, 1979.

Winn, Marie. *The Plug-In Drug.* New York: Bantam Books, 1977.

"Winners of This Year's SDX Distinguished Service Awards." *The Quill,* April 1979.

Withey, Stephen, and Abeles, Ronald P., eds. *Television and Social Behavior.* Hillsdale, N.J.: Lawrence Erlbaum Associates, 1981.

Wolfe, Tom, ed. *The New Journalism.* New York: Harper & Row, 1973.

Wolseley, Roland E. *The Black Press, U.S.A.* Ames, Iowa: Iowa State University Press, 1971.

Wolseley, Roland E. *The Changing Magazine: Trends in Readership and Management.* New York: Hastings House, 1973.

Wolseley, Roland E. *Understanding Magazines.* Ames, Iowa: Iowa State University Press, 1969.

Wood, R. Kent. "The Utah State University Videodisc Innovations Project." *Educational and Industrial Television,* May 1979.

Wright, Charles R. *Mass Communication: A Sociological Perspective.* New York: Random House, 1975.

Wright, Donald K. "Premises for Professionalism: Testing the Contributions of PRSA Accreditation." Paper presented to the Public Relations Division, Association for Education in Journalism Annual Convention, Houston, Texas, August 1979.

Wright, John W., ed. *The Commercial Connection: Advertising and the American Mass Media.* New York: Dell/Delta, 1979.

Index

Hutchins Commission on Freedom of the
Press, 383, 432–36, 438
  access for comment and criticism, 434
  clarifying goals and values, 435
  criticisms of, 436
  meaningful news, 433–44
  people's right to know, 435
  representative pictures of society,
    434–35
  social responsibility theory, 432–33
Hutton, Timothy, 298
Huxley, Aldous, 258
Hypodermic theory, 29

i

IBM, 114, 254, 267
Ice Castles, 133
Iconoscope, 197
Identification, 391
"I Love Lucy," 201
In Cold Blood, 128
"Incredible Machine," 206
Independent Network News (INN), 251–52
Independent network services, 250–53
  all-news TV, 252–53
  special function networks, 250–52
Independent Television Authority (ITA),
  268
Individuals, 24, 29
Inflight, 100
Information, 17–19
Inkjet printing, 73
Instant paperbacks, 131–33
Intel, 267
Inteltext, 268
Interactive TV, 259–60
Intercontinental Press Syndicate, 271
Internal specialization, 74
International News Service (INS), 47,
  144–45, 177
International Telecommunication Satellite
  Consortium (INTELSAT), 254
Intolerance, 284
Intrusion, 393
Invasion of the Body Snatchers, 133
Invasion of privacy, 393–95
Inverted pyramid, 47, 142
Ismach, Arnold, 59

j

J. Walter Thompson Company, 320, 357
"Jack Armstrong," 176
Jackson, Andrew, 353
Jacoby, Jacob, 232
James, Henry, 113
Jankowski, Gene, 274
Jannings, Emil, 286
Japan Victor, 265
Jarriel, Tom, 225
Jarvis, Al, 187
Jascalevich, Mario, 410
Jaws, 132, 292
Jay, John, 43, 80
Jazz, 190

"Jazz Alive," 187
Jazz journalism, 50–51
Jefferson, Thomas, 382–83, 390, 415
Johnson, Lyndon, 204, 388
Johnstone, John, 58
Joint operating agreements, 53
Jolson, Al, 286
Jonathan Livingston Seagull, 127
Journalese, 142
Journalism education, 443–44
Journalism Monograph, 226
Journalism reviews, 436–38
Jowett, Garth, 295, 303, 305
Joyce, James, 122, 396

k

Kaltenborn, H. V., 178
KDKA, 170
Kenaf, 74
Kennedy, John F., 300, 356–57, 388, 401
KFWB, 187
Kilpatrick, James, 342
Kinescope, 197, 201
Kinetoscope, 281–82
King Features Syndicate, 157
Kircher, Athanasius, 280
Kleppner, Otto, 223, 333, 335
KMOX-TV, 269
KMPC, 177
Knight, Arthur, 281
Knight-Ridder, 74, 269–71
Knoll, Erwin, 388–89
KNXT-TV, 269
Koenig, Frederick, 45
"Kraft Television Theater," 201
Kramer vs. Kramer, 249
Krantz, Judith, 119, 127
KSL-TV, 231, 269
Ku Klux Klan, 284

l

Ladies' Home Journal, 81, 82
Landers, Ann, 126
LaserDisc, 265
"Las Vegas Show," 250
"Laverne and Shirley," 202, 312
League of Women Voters, 401
Least objectionable program (lop), 213,
  215, 218
Lee, Ivy, 354
Lerner, Max, 442
Levy, Mark, 262
Lewis, Fulton, Jr., 178
Libel law, 390–93
Libertarianism, 380
Licensing, 40, 380–81
Life, 82, 84–87, 89, 103
Limitations on distribution, 386–87
Limitations on printing, 385–86
Lincoln, Abraham, 361
Lindbergh, Charles, 187, 409
Linotype, 80
Linton, James M., 295, 303, 305
Lippmann, Walter, 60
Literary agents, 123–24

Literary Guild, 128
"Little Orphan Annie," 176
Litton, 114
Lobbying, 352, 364, 374
Local spot TV, 222
Loewy, Raymond, 331
Lombardo, Guy, 175
London Gazette, 38
Long, Huey, 386
Look, 82, 84, 87, 103, 128
Lord Campbell's Act, 381
Los Angeles Times, 61, 73, 125, 151, 297
Los Angeles Times—Washington Post
  syndicate, 154
"Lou Grant Show," 226
Louisville Courier-Journal, 440
Louisville Times, 73, 440
"Love, Sidney," 213
Love Story, 131
Lowenstein, Ralph, 74
Lowest (or largest) common denominator,
  20, 52, 318, 328–29
Low-power television (LPTV), 272
Loy, Myrna, 286
Luce, Henry, 82, 89, 432
Lumber Instant News, 156

m

McBride, Sean, 225
MacBride Commission, 154
McCall's, 81
McCann-Erickson, 320
McCarthy, Charlie, 176
McCarthy, Joseph, 425, 433
McClure, Samuel, 156
McClure's Magazine, 81–82, 96, 156
McClure syndicate, 49
McGovern, George, 30
McGraw-Hill, 115, 126
McGuffey, William Holmes, 112
McHugh and Hoffman, Inc., 230
McKinley, William, 299
McLuhan, Marshall, 109, 273
Macmillan Publishing, 271
MacNeil, Robert, 223
Mademoiselle, 16
Madison, Charles, 114
Madison, James, 43
Madison Avenue, 324, 325, 335
Madison Avenue, U.S.A., 322, 325
Madison Press Connection, 389
Magazines, 77–107
  advertising in, 103–4
  audience composition of city magazines,
    table, 91
  categories of, 88–93
  circulation of top U.S. magazines, table,
    97
  circulation wars, 85
  future of, 105
  golden age of, 80–81
  history of, 78–87
  marketing of, 93–105
  Psychology Today's readers, table, 98
  TV's effects on, 84–85

Van Deerlin, Lionel, 267
Vanderbilt, William Henry, 354
Vann, Robert L., 66
Vanocur, Sander, 233
Variety, 292, 294–95
Variety, Inc., 289
Vaudeville, 282
Verne, Jules, 282
VHD, 265
VHF, 182, 196, 200, 202, 204
Videocassette recorders (VCRs), 239,
   260–62
Videocassettes, 249, 299, 303
Videodiscs, 239, 249, 262–65, 299, 303
Video display terminals (VDTs), 72–74,
   148
Video Jukebox, 263
Videotex, 239, 267–73
Viewdata Corporation of America, 270
Viewtron, 268, 270
Virgil, 352
Vitaphone, 286
Viva, 94
Vogue, 16, 104

W

Wallace, Mike, 439
Wall Street Journal, 36, 87, 244, 255, 335,
   363, 367
Walt Disney Productions, 261
Walters, Barbara, 226
Wambaugh, Joseph, 127
Wang Laboratories, 267
Waring, Fred, 175

Warner-Amex, 244, 249, 251, 257, 259
Warner-Amex Satellite Entertainment, 249
Warner Brothers, 249, 286, 289
Warner Communications, 244, 259
War of nerves, 357
"War of the Worlds," 29
Warren, Robert, 389
Warren, Samuel D., 393–94
Washington, George, 80
Washingtonian, 90
Washington Journalism Review, 437
Washington Post, 388, 410, 415, 417,
   440–42
Watchdog, 90, 367
Watergate Hearings, 132
Wayne, John, 286
W. B. Saunders, 114
WBZ, 170
WEAF, 170–71
Weight Watchers Program Cookbook, 127
Welles, Orson, 29
We Reach the Moon, 132
WESTAR, 254
Western Union, 254
Westinghouse, 98, 167, 169–70, 197, 204,
   244
Westmoreland, General William, 392
WGN, 179
WGY, 198
WHA, 170
Wheeler, Tom, 240
Whitaker and Baxter, 364
White, E. B., 232
Whitney, Eli, 45
Williams, Walter, 425
Wilson, Woodrow, 82, 284, 355
Winchell, Walter, 177
Wire filers, 146
Wire service. *See* News service
Wire service beats, 18, 60, 62, 150–51

WJZ, 171
WNEW, 187
Wolfe, Tom, 69
Wolseley, Roland, 104
Woman's Day, 95, 114
Women in media, 434–35
Women's Home Companion, 81
Women's News Service, 155
Women's Wear Daily, 36
Woodward, Bob, 410
WOR, 179
World Assembly of Public Relations
   Associations, 349
WPIX-TV, 251
Wright, Donald, 373
WTBS-TV, 252
WWJ, 170
Wynn, Ed, 176

X

Xerox, 114, 206

Y

Years of Lightning, Day of Drums, 300
Yellow journalism, 48–50
Young & Rubicam, 240, 320
Your Home, 100

Z

Zamora, Ronny, 409
Zenger, John Peter, 41, 389
Zenith, 199
Zoopraxinoscope, 281
Zworykin, Vladimir, 197

About the Authors

Jay Black, Associate Professor of Communication at Utah State University, has been a reporter and copy editor on four newspapers in Ohio and Missouri, and has taught journalism at Miami University, Bowling Green State University, Lincoln College, and in South Australia. Chairman of the Mass Communication and Society Division of the Association for Education in Journalism and Mass Communication in 1982–83, he has published and delivered some two dozen conference papers on media ethics, propaganda, and international communications. He received his Ph.D. in Journalism from the University of Missouri.

Fred C. Whitney, Emeritus Professor of Journalism at San Diego State University, is a public relations counsel for his own firm. He has worked as a reporter for *Variety*, the *Havana Post*, the *Havana P.M.*, and the Los Angeles *Evening Herald and Express*. He is the founder of the F. C. Whitney Chapter of the Public Relations Student Society of America.